Death Records from Missouri Newspapers: The Civil War Years

Jan. 1861-Dec. 1865

by
Lois Stanley
George F. Wilson
Maryhelen Wilson

Copyright 1990
By: Southern Historical Press, Inc.

All rights reserved. No part of this publication may be reproduced,
stored in a retrieval system, transmitted in any form,
posted on to the web in any form or by any means
without the prior written permission of the publisher.

Please direct all correspondence and orders to:

www.southernhistoricalpress.com
or
SOUTHERN HISTORICAL PRESS, Inc.
PO BOX 1267
375 West Broad Street
Greenville, SC 29601
southernhistoricalpress@gmail.com

ISBN #0-89308-443-3

Printed in the United States of America

Missouri's newspapers were among the casualties of the Civil War. Many an editor who showed the wrong sympathies found his press smashed, his office vandalized, and his situation precarious. (And in that badly divided state it was sometimes impossible to be on the right side.) The newspapers that survived found news aplenty but newsprint scarce. Fortunately for us, enough of them overcame the obstacles to provide death records of more than 6000 Missourians who died in a five-year period and for whom, in most cases, there is no other such record.

As in the past, the majority of these are the standard notices of death: citizens who succumbed to the common scourges -- consumption, typhoid, smallpox, cholera, flux, diphtheria and scarlet fever among the young -- or to the shockingly common accidents -- drowning, burning, steamboat explosions, industrial disasters, the vagaries of horses.

But the Civil War years provided a high proportion of violent deaths -- from the activities of the guerillas or "bushwhackers," from the grudges between neighbors erupting in tragedy, from the numbers of young men who went out to fight for a cause they believed in and died in that faith. (We have included here only the Confederate deaths, since Union records can be obtained from other sources.)

This listing was taken from about 40 primary newspapers, of which copies survive, and represents about the same number of secondary newspapers from which items were quoted, but which have not come down to us. Deaths of children too young to have been in the 1860 census are not included. All of the newspapers are available at the Newspaper Library, State Historical Society of Missouri, in Columbia. The St. Louis papers and a few others are in the library of the Missouri Historical Society, Jefferson Memorial, Forest Park, St. Louis.

Cross-references: surnames of in-laws or other relatives found in some notices, which may provide useful clues, are on pages 191-192.

A small number of items from the Howard County Union and the Ralls County Record, unavailable until the rest of the book had been researched, may be found on page 193.

A list of newspapers, codes, and locations is on the following page.

CODE	NEWSPAPER	GENERAL AREA OF COVERAGE (COUNTY AND LOCATION)
BOBS	Boonville Observer	Cooper: central (Howard, Boone, Saline, Morgan, etc)
BOL	Bolivar Courier	Polk: southwest (St. Clair, Dallas, Cedar, Greene,
BEST	Bethany Star	Harrison: northwest (on Iowa border) /Dade, Hickory)
BOOM	Boonville Monitor	Cooper: central - see BOBS
CAB	Caldwell Banner	Caldwell: northwest (Daviess, DeKalb, Livingston,
CACE) CALM)	California Missourian or Central Missourian	Clinton, Ray, Carroll) Moniteau: central (Cooper, Cole, Morgan, etc)
CANP	Canton Press	Lewis: northeast (Illinois border) (Clark, Knox, Scotland, Shelby, Marion)
CAWN	California Weekly News	Moniteau - see CACE, CALM
CECB	Central City & Brunswicker	Chariton: north central (Linn, Macon, Randolph, Howard, Saline, Carroll, Livingston)
CHAC	Charleston Courier	Mississippi: southeast (on Illinois border) Scott, New Madrid)
COWS	Missouri Statesman, Columbia	Boone: central. Reported from a wide area.
FRED	Fredericktown Conservative	Madison: south central. (Very few issues)
FULT	Fulton Telegraph	Callaway: east central (Audrain, Montgomery, Osage, Cole, Gasconade)
GAL	Northwest Missourian, Gallatin	Daviess: northwest (DeKalb, Grundy, Gentry, Caldwell, Harrison, Livingston)
* GLWT	Glasgow Weekly Times	Howard: central. See BOBS, CECB, COWS)
HOLT	Holt Co. Sentinel, Oregon	Holt: northwest (Kansas-Nebraska border) Atchison, Nodaway, Andrew, Buchanan)
IRON	Ironton Forge	Iron: southeast (few issues)
JCPT JEST	Patriot, Jefferson City State Times, ")	Cole: central. See COWS, FULT, BOBS; also bordered by Osage and Miller)
* HAM	Hannibal Messenger	Marion: northeast (Illinois border) (Lewis, Ralls, Shelby, Monroe)
KCJC	Kansas City Journal of Commerce	Jackson: west central (Kansas border) (Clay, Ray, Lafayette, Johnson, Cass)
LEXUN	Lexington Union	Lafayette: west central. (Jackson, Ray, Carroll, Saline, Pettis, Johnson)
LAJ	Louisiana Journal	Pike: east central (Illinois border) (Ralls, Lincoln, Audrain, Montgomery)
LIT	Liberty Tribune	Clay: west central (Platte, Clinton, Jackson, Ray)
MAG	Macon Gazette	Macon: north central (Sullivan, Adair, Knox, Linn, Shelby, Randolph, Monroe)
MEMP	Memphis Reveille	Scotland: northeast (Iowa border) (Schuyler, Knox, Clark, Lewis, Adair)
MORE	Missouri Republican, St. Louis	St. Louis, but reported from the entire state.
OVAS	Osage Valley Star, Osceola	St. Clair: very few issues. (southwest central)
PALS	Palmyra Spectator	Marion: see HAM
PERU	Perryville Union	Perry: southeast (Illinois border) (Ste. Genevieve, St. Francois, Madison, Bollinger, Cape G.)
RANC	Randolph Citizen (Huntsville)	Randolph: north central (Chariton, Macon, Shelby, Monroe, Audrain, Boone, Howard)
RICON	NW Conservator (Richmond)	Ray: nw central (Clay, Clinton, Caldwell, Lafayette, Jackson)
ROLEX	Rolla Express	Phelps: south central (Maries, Gasconade, Dent, Crawford, Texas, Pulaski)
SJRL SJH	St. Joseph Journal) St. Joseph Herald)	Buchanan: northwest (Kansas border) (Andrew, DeKalb, Clinton, Platte)
SED	Sedalia Advertiser	Pettis: central (Lafayette, Saline, Cooper, Morgan, Benton, Henry, Johnson)
SPRIP	Springfield Patriot	Greene: southwest (Dade, Polk, Dallas, Webster, Christian, Lawrence)
SLMD	Missouri Democrat, St. Louis	St. Louis: see MORE
WARS	Warrensburg Standard	Johnson: west central (Jackson, Lafayette, Saline, Pettis, Henry, Cass)
WEST	Weston Border Times	Platte: west central (Kansas border) (Buchanan, Clinton, Clay, Jackson)

SECONDARY NEWSPAPERS -- source of items quoted by above

Albany News	Cape Girardeau Eagle	Mexico Ledger	Savannah Plain Dealer
Belfast Age	Fayette Advertiser	Missouri Advertiser	St. Joseph News
California News	Grand River News	Moniteau Co. News	St. Joseph Union
Carrollton Democrat	Lebanon Union	Macon Times	St. Joseph Journal
Bethany Union	Louisiana Herald	New Albany Commercial	Springfield Mirror
Boonville Advertiser	Louisiana True Flag	Morgan County Forum	Springfield Journal
Chillicothe Chronicle	Macon Argus	Palmyra Courier	Sp'field Missourian
Chillicothe Constitution	Marshall Democrat	Paris Mercury	Trenton Herald
Central Mo. Advertiser	Mexico Beacon	St. Charles Reveille	Warrenton Nonpariel
Kansas City Press	Wheeling Intelligencer	Warrensburg Missourian	Weston Sentinel

ABBAY, Capt. Jonathan, old and highly respected citizen of Lick Creek,
    Ralls Co., 11 Sep ae (67?). Nashville pc   MORE 23 Nov 1862
ABBOTT, Ephraim 31 Oct ae 48.   SLMD 5 Nov 1861
ABBOTT, James of Gasconade Co. 27 Mar ae 50y 10m. Interred Hermann.   MORE 14 Apr 1865
ABEL, Marcellus shot by Rufus Hayden 4 Jun at Elizabethtown, Monroe Co.
            Verdict: justifiable homicide.   PALS 17 Jun 1864
ABELN, John Henry 4 Jul ae 44. Resided Park near Lafayette.   MORE 5 Jul 1863
ABLE, Anna R. only dau/Capt. Dan and Mollie M., 14 Dec ae 6y 10m. Funeral
    from residence, 7 Papin St. Palmyra pc   MORE 16 Dec 1862
ABLE, Miss Jane in this city 10 Mar ae 42.   HAM 13 Mar 1862
ABLE, John, suicide by laudanum yesterday. Left wife and 2 children.   SJH 1 Jan 1865
ABNEY, W.H. at the Military Hospital Thursday last of epilepsy, member of
    Co. H, Capt. Winter's 7th MO.   MAG 9 Apr 1862
ABRAMS, Mrs. Hannah 15 Dec ae 63. Funeral from home of her son Amos,   MORE 17 Dec 1864
    Chambers betw 12-13. Interred Bellefontaine.
ABSHIRE, John hanged for the murder of William Hayes in Wayne Co. Formerly a
    citizen of Ste. Genevieve, age 21; born Arkansas; had been a
    rebel soldier.   MORE 15 Oct 1864
ABSTEN, Stephen in Independence 16 Jan.   MORE 27 Jan 1861
ACHAFERT, Barbette drowned herself in a cistern at O'Fallon between 23-24.
    Her husband Julius, a carpenter, went to Chattanooga 3 months ago
    leaving his pigeons in her care. According to a neighbor, she
    showed symptoms of insanity at times, was overly conscientious,
    worried. She was about 35, had been married ca 20 years, had been
    in this country ca 15 years, had 2 children who died young.   MORE 6 May 1865
ACHENBACH, Herman, an old citizen, 22 Sep ae 48. Resided 56 Market St.   MORE 23 Sep 1865
ACKLAND, Mrs. Ann 10 Aug ae 69y 7m 10d. Funeral from home of her dau/Mrs.   MORE 11 Aug 1861
    John B. Sheppard, 108 Olive. Baltimore pc
ACKLANDS, James, formerly of Baltimore, in his 77th year. Funeral from home MORE 15 Nov 1863
    of his dau/Mrs. John B. Sheppard, 108 Olive. Baltimore pc
ACOCK, Col. R.E., residing 9 miles south of Bolivar, on 15 Mar.   BOL 16 Mar 1861
ADAMS, David 25 Sep of heart disease ae 27. St. Louis & Cincinnati pc   LIT 3 Oct 1862
ADAMS, Mrs. Deliet 20 Feb ae 60. Resided Main & Mulberry. Chicago pc   MORE 22 Feb 1863
ADAMS, Esther O. wife of W.F. 1 Mar ae 21y 5w. Resided Gratiot betw 5-6.   MORE 3 Mar 1862
ADAMS, Matilda L. wife of Increase 23 Feb in Mexico (MO) ae 39.   COWS 4 Mar 1864
ADAMS, Theodore 27 Jul after a long illness. Old and respected citizen,
    left wife and several children.   LAJ 30 Jul 1864
ADAMS, Thomas Maxwell, late of Jackson Co. MO, 22 Oct of hemorrhage of the
    bowels, ae 53. New York City & Bloomfield NY pc.   MORE 23 Oct 1865
ADDERSON, Dr. A. "old and worthy" on 11 Dec.   CALM 16 Dec 1865
ADEN, ____ shot near Charleston by Aaron W. (Doc) Grigsby; Aden had been with
    Edward Campbell when Campbell killed Moses Grigsby, nephew of Doc,
    but was under arrest when Doc apparently wantonly shot him.
    (Charleston Courier 4 Feb)   MORE 14 Feb 1863
AEHLE, Harry Gordon 16 Sep age 12 and Florence 20 Sep ae 2y 6m, children of
    Charles and E.J., at Boonville.   MORE 26 Sep 1864
AGEE, Rev. Jacob at Monticello 16 Mar ae 25.   CANP 9 Apr 1863
AGNE, Daniel, late of Keokuk, 26 Nov of erysipelas ae 65. Resided 83 Franklin. MORE 27 Nov 1862
    Interred Keokuk.
AGNEW, Mary only dau/Martin Lepere Sr. of Central Twp., 31 Jan ae 29.   MORE 2 Feb 1862
AHALT, Mrs. Eliza of Palmyra 3 Jun in her 68th year.   HAM 13 Jun 1861
    (name shown as Eznia in newspaper of 9 Jun)
AHEARN, Thomas, ae 24, killed in the Camp Jackson affair 10 May. Resided   MORE 11 and
            300 N. 6th.   15 May 1861
AIKEN, Thomas E. of Caldwell's Command, captured in Greene Co. 25 Nov., in
    Gratiot Prison 24 Jan of rubeola.   MORE 27 Jan 1863
AIREY, Josephine "this morning" in 22d year. Interred in Virginia.   MORE 12 Mar 1863

1

AKINS, Mrs. _____, a Miss Jacobs and a Miss Smith all drowned in Livingston Co. near Anderson's Ferry on the East Fork of Grand River Thursday last while bathing. Bodies recovered the next day. — SJH 19 Jul 1864

AKINS, Mrs. Mary Jane at the home of her son-in-law Dr. L. Dunham 25 Jan ae 52. Funeral from Dr. Post's church. Interred Bellefontaine. — MORE 27 Jan 1861

ALABAGH, Rebecca 23 Dec ae 40y 8m "in the family of Rev. J. Jermain Porter." — SLMD 31 Dec 1861

ALBRIGHT, B. A. 6 Jun ae 54. Resided 106 Collins. Cambridge OH pc — MORE 8 Jun 1862

ALBRIGHT, Henry A. of St. Louis at the home of his brother in Ft. Madison IA ae 40. Resident of St. Louis 20 years. /J.W. Albright — MORE 24 Jun 1862

ALBRIGHT, Honoria wife of William 13 Feb ae 27y 2m, of erysipelas. Resided north side of Clark, 3 doors west of 20th. — MORE 14 Feb 1863

ALDER, Mrs. Lydia Ann 22 Nov near Missouri City (Clay Co.) ae 51y 5m 13d. — LIT 9 Dec 1864

ALDRIDGE, Aleck Littell son of A. & America of Howard Co. 25 Jan ae 6m 9d. — GLWT 31 Jan 1861

ALDRIDGE, William H. of Porter's Band, captured in Clark Co, 12 Nov in Gratiot Prison. — MORE 13 & 16 Nov 1862

ALEXANDER, Andrew J., citizen of New Madrid Co., arrested 12 Dec, in Gratiot Prison hospital of inflammation of the lungs. — MORE 2 Feb 1864

ALEXANDER, James of Lawrence Co. in the Prison Hospital in Springfield. — MORE 10 Apr 1863

ALEXANDER, Lucy Fitzhugh, wife of J. B., 15 Jan (suddenly) in her 47th year. — MORE 16 Jan 1864

ALEXANDER, Mary Lillie eldest child of Frank R. and Laura V., 25 Mar ae 5y 3m. — MORE 26 Mar 1862

ALEXANDER, Mary T. dau/James and Lucy, 26 Sep in this city ae 16y 23d. — LAJ 3 Oct 1863

ALEXANDER, Mattie Lou dau/Thomas, formerly of Louisville, 10 Mar in her 23rd year at the home of her brother-in-law, 35 8th St. — MORE 11 Mar 1865

ALEXANDER, Mrs. Virginia in Kansas City 6 May, dau/the late R. C. Thompson. — LIT 10 May 1861

ALEXANDER, William, on the Undertaker's List, 26 Jan of typhoid. — MORE 2 Feb 1863

ALEXANDER, Willis Walker son of Maurice & Clara, 26 Jan ae 15m. — MORE 27 Jan 1861

ALEY, Solomon, citizen of Carter Co., in the prison hospital of erysipelas. Captured 12 Sep. (Undertaker's List) — MORE 16 Oct 1863

ALLDREDGE, Julien Tuesday morning last, 2 Feb. — CAWN 6 Feb 1864

ALLEGA, John, letters of administration in Chariton Co. 17 Aug to Jas. R. Allega. — CECB 4 Sep 1862

ALLEGREE, Miss Sarah F. of Franklin Co., formerly of Fluvanna Co. VA, 13 Mar of consumption at the home of F. M. Wood. — MORE 16 Mar 1863

ALLEN, Judge Charles H. in Palmyra 25 Feb of neuralgia in his 83rd year. Elizabeth his wife 31 March in Palmyra in her 77th year. — MAG 9 Apr 1862

ALLEN, Frank D., a shoemaker living at Spruce between 6th-7th, killed in the Camp Jackson affair. (Later Frank B.) Native of England, ca 55. — MORE 18 & 19 May 1861

ALLEN, Gilbert son of Napoleon B. of Fredericktown, accidentally shot a few days since, died of wound. — PERU 19 Jun 1863

ALLEN, Grace dau of Thomas & Ann of St. Louis in Pittsfield MA 16 Jan of scarlet fever ae 3y 6m 20d. — MORE 26 Jan 1864

ALLEN, Henry C., 3rd MO Reg CSA, at Vicksburg 22 May. — MORE 23 Aug 1863

ALLEN, Henry N. son of Lewis D. & Lucretia Tuesday ae 19. Resided Clark-21st. — MORE 12 Feb 1863

ALLEN, Dr. J. B. 8 Jan ae 22. Native of KY, where his mother lives; survived by young wife and child. Interred Bellefontaine. — MORE 9 & 11 Jan 1865

ALLEN, John son of Marshall of this city 8 Apr in his 18th year. — LAJ 16 Apr 1864

ALLEN, Julia Cornelia eldest dau/Elisha & Julia 30 Sep ae 10y 8m 6d. Resided corner of Pratte & Gamble. — MORE 2 Oct 1862

ALLEN, Kitty T. wife of Grant in Randolph Co. 26 Jul ae 63. — COWS 4 Sep 1863

ALLEN, Mrs. Mollie at Flint Hill, St. Charles Co. 31 Oct. Dau/James A. & Mary Harnett, ae 18y 11m 20d. Married Dr. Albro B. Allen 4 Apr 1865. Native of St. Charles Co.; also survived by a brother. — MORE 5 Nov 1865

ALLEN, Mrs. Pamela 18 Jun at her home near this city, nearly 82. Born in Hampshire Co. VA 8 Sep 1782; to Clark Co. KY with widowed mother in 1792; married Richardson Allen 1795. To MO 1830. Baptist. 16 children. — PALS 24 Jun 1864

ALLEN, Paul Mortimer son of Churchill & Elizabeth T. 4 Dec in Audrain Co. ae 18m. — COWS 20 Dec 1861

ALLEN, Rebecca Ann youngest dau/late Col. G.W., 23 Mar of cerebro-spinal meningitis at the home of W.B. Sappington near Arrow Rock ae 11y 7m 12d. Notice mentions "brothers and sisters." — MORE 1 Apr 1865

ALLEN, W.B. formerly of Price's Army killed near Empire Prairie, Andrew Co. — SJH 12 Jul 1863

ALLEN, Waring Brooks youngest son of William F. & Fannie, 20 Mar of lung fever ae 1y 9m. — HAM 27 Mar 1862

ALLEN, William, killed by guerillas. (Central City & Brunswicker) — MORE 21 Jul 1864

ALLEN, William J. of Porter's Band, captured in Boone Co. 10 Sep, at Gratiot Prison 8 Feb of rubeola. (Undertaker's List says 7 Feb) — MORE 10 & 15 Feb 1863

ALLEN, Judge William S. of Bethany, Harrison Co., burned to death when his home caught fire about midnight 20 Jun; trying to save something from the fire. — RICON 9 Jul 1863

ALLENDORF, Noah, son of a widow, ae 15, drowned in "the lake below town" Wednesday. — SJH 10 Jun 1864

ALLEY, George Dewey son of George & Julia, ae 10m. Resided Bernard near Pratte. — MORE 11 Jun 1861

ALLISON, Isabel wife of Erasmus 20 Oct ae (38?) Resided 265 Carr. Pittsburgh pc — MORE 21 Oct 1861

ALLISON, ___ killed by bushwhackers near Lamar, Barton Co., with ___ Smith and ___ Hightown. (Information from Melville MO.) — MORE 23 Apr 1864

ALLISON, T. W. killed by guerillas in western MO, going from his home in Lawrence Co. to Fort Scott KS with a supply train; formerly of Boonville. Born Wilkes Co. NC 4 Sep 1795, to Boonesborough 1801, to IL 1817, to Cooper Co. MO 1823. "Kind father." — BOOM 11 Jun 1864

ALLMSTEDT, ___ "an old man" abducted and murdered at the time of Porter's Raid into Palmyra; Gen. Merrill shot 10 men in retaliation. — CAWN 1 Nov 1862

ALMSLER, Adolph, ae 3, run over by a wagon. — MORE 4 Feb 1862

ALNUTT, James M. son of James M. & Pamela in Chillicothe 18 Mar ae 18y 3m. — MORE 23 Mar 1863

ALTER, William F. 13 Jan of consumption ae 37. Resided 299 Morgan. Cincinnati pc — MORE 15 Jan 1862

ALTHOFF, William, a suicide -- shot himself in the head, no reason known. Lived at Bremen & 20th; was German, ca 40; worked in a brickyard; left a wife and two small children. — MORE 16 Nov 1865

ALTHOUSE, Christian, son of George, accidentally shot himself while hunting ducks on the Chariton. (Glasgow Times) — RANC 11 Apr 1861

ALTINGER, Henry Edmund son of Charles & Louisa 10 Mar ae 14m. — MORE 12 Mar 1861

ALVORD, James H. 9 Oct of injuries received in an accident on the Hannibal & St. Joseph RR near Bucklin, in his 20th year. (He had jumped from a car when the train parted.) Funeral from home of Wm. B. Alvord, 45 S 5th. — MORE 14 Oct 1862

AMEND, Joseph son of John & Machtilena, 5 Nov ae 14. — MORE 6 Nov 1861

AMCLIN, Timothy 27 Apr ae 22. Funeral, Holy Trinity Church. Chicago pc — MORE 28 Apr 1862

AMONETT, Mrs. Ellen M. consort of John near Caledonia 7 Dec in her 47th year. "Wife, neighbor." — MORE 30 Dec 1863

AMRATY, Julia 23 Dec ae 39. Resided Ham near Hickory. — MORE 23 Dec 1863

ANDERSON, Alex Gordon aboard the Mollie McPike 26 Oct. Funeral from home of his brother-in-law Thomas J. Whitely, 282 Chestnut. Buried Caledonia. — MORE 27 Oct 1864

Alexander M. at Caledonia, Washington Co. 14 Mar of typhoid pneumonia in his 74th year. Born Philadelphia, to Baltimore in 1814; then lived in KY, Wheeling, Pittsburgh, and St. Louis. Veteran War of 1812. — MORE 20 Mar 1864

ANDERSON, Mrs. Ann relict of Thomas Monday ae 64y 3m 8d. Funeral from the Church of the Messiah. — MORE 12 & 13 Jul 1864

ANDERSON, Benjamin B. at Caledonia 13 Jan in his 31st year. — MORE 19 Jan 1864

ANDERSON, Bettie J. 23 Oct ae 14y 7m 17d. Louisville pc — MORE 3 Nov 1862

ANDERSON, Bill, the notorious bushwhacker, reported killed near Richmond, Ray Co. — LEXUN 29 Oct 1864

Bill, another report of his death in Albany, Ray Co., last week. He had $300 in gold, $150 in treasury notes, and some letters from General Sterling Price. — LIT 4 Nov 1864

ANDERSON, Capt. C. J. of flux in the prevailing epidemic. — FULT 19 Aug 1864

ANDERSON, Mrs. Fanny W., wife of Samuel E., 19 Oct ae 24. Baltimore pc — MORE 21 Oct 1863

ANDERSON, Henrietta B. wife of William H. and dau/late John & Rebecca L. Weaver, Thursday after a long painful illness, age 43. Resided 291 Clark. Washington DC & Baltimore pc — MORE 7 Apr 1865

ANDERSON, Capt. James at his home in Camulet Twp. 22 Mar, at an advanced age. COWS 15 Apr 1864

ANDERSON, John, deckhand on the New Iowa, residing near 10th & Broadway, of lung congestion and chill; had been in a fight. MORE 11 Sep 1863

ANDERSON, Rev. John Richard, pastor of 2nd Baptist Church, 20 May. Int Bellefontaine. MORE 22 May 1863

ANDERSON, Joseph - see William Francis Hadley

ANDERSON, Josiah D., letters of administration in Chariton Co. 27 Sep to Jane Anderson. CECB 23 Oct 1862

ANDERSON, Martha Ann dau/Martha & Chesley 8 Jun ae 3y 10m. FULT 20 Jun 1862

ANDERSON, Mary A. relict of Kemp P. at the home of her son-in-law William C. Orr, 6 Sep. Central Presbyterian Church. MORE 7 Sep 1861
(Formerly of Palmyra) HAM 26 Sep 1861

ANDERSON, Samuel K. of typhoid pneumonia ae 28. Interred Spring Grove, Cincinnati. MORE 3 Jun 1865

ANDERSON, Tabitha consort of C., of this city, 15 Sep of fever. SEDA 17 Sep 1864

ANDREW, Aaron; public administrator took over his estate in Chariton Co. (John Dewey) CECB 2 Jul 1863

ANDREWS, Ann relict of Thomas 11 Jul ae 64y 3m 8d. Funeral Church of the Messiah. SLMD 13 Jul 1864

ANDREWS, Edwin James son/Morey T. & Meroe F. at their home in Carondelet 19 Jan ae 6y 9m 3d. MORE 21 Jan 1863

ANDREWS, Isabella wife of C.B. 26 Jan. New Orleans & Baltimore pc MORE 28 Jan 1865

ANDREWS, John, killed by G.W. Sturman ca 6-8 miles from Glasgow. Both from Chariton Co.; trouble over a lawsuit. GLWT 21 Mar 1861

ANDREWS, Sarah D. widow of Joshua of Philadelphia 26 Mar in her 74th year at the home of John C. Evens, 35 S. 16th. Philadelphia pc MORE 27 Mar 1864

ANDREWS, Thomas, 40 years an esteemed citizen of this city, 1 Feb ae 69y 25d. Resided Bernard near Emily. Interred Bellefontaine. Funeral from MORE 2 & the Church of the Messiah. 3 Feb 1863

ANDREWS, Thomas ae 40. Resided 92 N 20th St. MORE 7 May 1865

ANDROS, Mrs. E. W. wife of Capt. Benedict, formerly of Assonet MA, 17 Aug ae 62. SJH 19 Aug 1864
Funeral from the home of W.F. Barrons, corner Sylvanie & 10th.

ANGEL, Dr. J.M. of Boone Co., a bushwhacker, killed Friday by a party of the 3rd Cavalry. He had divided his time between the rebel army and the brush in Boone Co. for 2 or 3 years. COWS 29 Jul 1864

ANNAS, Charles L. 30 Oct in his 47th year. Interred Bellefontaine. Churchville NY pc MORE 31 Oct 1865

ANTHONY, ___ a guerilla killed on Big Perry near McCourtney's Mill in the general area of Waynesville. McCourtney and Stephens also killed. MORE 20 Jan 1865

ANTHONY, Mrs. Sassy in Boone Co. 22 Sep in her 49th year. COWS 29 Sep 1865

APERSCHUFFE, ___ fell from 2nd story window while drinking. Single, ca 35. MORE 19 Jul 1865

APPLEBY, Ann wife of William, residing on Sidney St., 20 Feb. MORE 21 Feb 1861

APPLEGET, Wealthy "fell asleep in Jesus 5 April" in Paris, Monroe Co. RANC 18 Apr 1861

ARGUST, John Owen 27 May ae 19. Resided Collins betw Bates & Columbia. MORE 28 May 1863

ARMOUR, James E.U. of dropsy 10 May in his 45th year; suffered 18 months. Notice signed "Eliza." MORE 11 May 1865

ARMSTRONG, Nancy B. wife of William and youngest dau/S.B. & N.J. Caldwell, 6 Dec. PALS 23 Dec 1864
Survived by husband, 2 small children. Baptist.

ARNETT, William, citizen of Howard Co., of measles 8 Jan. (Undertaker's List) MORE 15 Jan 1865

ARNOLD, P. C., a well-known citizen, suddenly at his home, Sunday night last. FULT 5 Aug 1864

ARNOLD, Sarah J. dau/T.W. & S.J., 4 Jan ae 4y 6m 23d. Lexington MO pc MORE 6 Jan 1864

ARNOLD, Mrs. Thomas (Lucy O.) 13 Apr of inflammatory rheumatism ae 49y 2m 22d. COWS 15 &
(In Boone Co.) 22 Apr 1864

ARNOLD, Susan wife of Dr. E.G. of Lexington in Carroll Co. 10 Jan. MORE 22 Jan 1861

ARNOLD, Thomas of lung disease 28 Feb ae ca 62. LIT 15 Mar 1861

ARNOLD, Wyatt at his home near Carrollton 29 Nov in his (48? 49?)th year. Native of Campbell Co. VA, to MO 1858. Lynchburg VA pc MORE 15 Dec 1862

ARNOUX, Edmund A. 8 Dec of consumption ae 25y 2m 5d. Mother resides Cedar between 3rd & 4th. NY pc MORE 9 Jan 1864

ARRINGTON, Joseph at the home of his father-in-law George Stiles 26 Mar of typhoid. Ae 30y 6m 13d. Funeral St. George's Church. Interred Bellefontaine. MORE 27 Mar 1863

ARTERBURN, John Jr. killed by guerillas in Carroll Co. (Carrollton Democrat)　　　MORE 21 Jul 1864

ASAY, Kate dau/A.B. Tuesday last of consumption.　　　PALS 29 Jul 1864

ASCHE, Henry -- inquest. Ae 18, stabbed by Cyrus Graham.　　　MORE 13 Jul 1864

ASHBROOK, Charles, 7 Mar. Resided Broadway between Palm & Harrison. Interred
　　　　　　　　　　　　　　　　Bellefontaine.　　　MORE 8 Mar 1861

ASHBY, Benjamin, Chariton Co. Petition to sell real estate by James H. Ashby.　　　CECB 9 Jul 1863

ASHBY, Charles H. 5 Apr in St. Louis Co. in his 58th year.　　　MORE 8 Apr 1863

ASHBY, Henry, Chariton Co. Letters of administration 1 Mar to John D. Lock,
　　　　　　　　administrator (with will annexed)　　　CECB 13 Apr 1861

ASHCRAFT, ___ killed by bushwhacker John R. Graves (who was later shot).　　　LEXUN 15 Aug 1863

ASHER, Asenath wife of Julius S. 13 Aug at the home of her brother-in-law
　　　T.A. Newkirk, N 14th betw Madison & N. Market. Louisville pc　　　MORE 15 Aug 1864

ASHOO, John, Chinese, married Sunday, died Wednesday; lived in the alley between
　　　17-18-Wash-Carr; poison suspected at first, but inquest showed　　　SLMD 11 Feb 1861
　　　ulceration and perforation of the stomach. Born Ninpoo, China, ae 35,　　　MORE 14 Feb "
　　　in the US 14 years, in St. Louis 4 or 5 years.

ASHURST, Thomas D. killed Sunday evening last by a squad of men under Sgt. Ecton.　　　LIT 7 Aug 1863

ATCHISON, Capt. George W. at Wellsville, Montgomery Co. (There are two items on　　　MORE 25 May 1864
　　　this man in the same paper; one says in his 75th year, the other in
　　　his 26th year, funeral at the home of C. Bent Carr, 18th & Wash.
　　　Presumably a line of type had been dropped and the second item refers
　　　to someone else.)

ATHERTON, Mary C. youngest dau/George O. & Mary, 8 Aug ae 19y 7m. Home, 236 Biddle.　　　MORE 10 Aug 1863

ATHEY, Mrs. Italia Saturday ae 32; her husband died in the Gasconade disaster.
　　　　　　　　　　　　　　　Interred Calvary.　　　MORE 12 Jan 1862

ATKESON, R. Louisa dau/Capt. William & Louisa 31 Mar near Warrensburg at the
　　　home of her grandfather John Boyles, of consumption, ae 18y 1m 7d.　　　MORE 12 Apr 1861
　　　Formerly of VA.

ATKINS, Robert A., 25 Dec of typhoid pneumonia ae 25.　　　MORE 27 Dec 1863

AUGUSTINE, Amanda only child of A. & M. in Fayette 7 Oct in her 14th year.　　　COWS 27 Oct 1865

A(U)LBACH, Lieut. William shot in St. Louis by an unknown man, Friday evening.
　　　Of the 2nd MO Vols., parents live in Belleville IL.　　　MORE 3 Jan 1864

AULD, Mrs. Julia C. 24 Jan of pneumonia in her 55th year. New Orleans pc　　　MORE 27 Jan 1861

AULL, Mrs. A.J. 20 Aug in her 70th year at the home of her son-in-law
　　　Franklin O. Day, Locust between 6-7.　　　MORE 21 Aug 1864

AULL, Frank Wilson son of Robert & Mary W. 13 Apr ae 5y 4d.　　　MORE 15 Apr 1862

AULT, Sallie P. wife of T.M. at Franklin 30 Sep. Interred St. Louis.　　　MORE 4 Oct 1864

AUSTIN, C.D. son of James L. "old and esteemed" citizen living on Shoal Creek
　　　shot by two invaders looking for arms. (Chilicothe Chronicle)　　　CAWN 5 Jul 1862

AUSTIN, Orlando 20 Nov ca 46.　　　PALS 16 Dec 1864

AUSTIN, Samuel, the oldest man in the county, in Columbia 29 Oct. Born　　　COWS 6 Nov 1863
　　　in Calvert Co. MD 9 Mar 1770 -- thus in his 94th year.

AVERY, Mrs. Lorinda widow of Samuel in Webster Groves at the home of her son
　　　Edward 14 Dec in her 68th year. Funeral from the home of her son-in-law
　　　R.D. Van Nostrand, 30 S. 14th. New Albany IN pc　　　MORE 15 Dec 1862

AVERY, Ponsonby G. at Calhoun, Henry Co. 31 Jan of typhoid in his 43rd year.　　　MORE 13 Feb 1863

AYERS, Arthur in James Bayou Twp. 20 April of pneumonia.　　　CHAC 3 May 1861
　　　Archibald　　　"　　　　　　28 April　　　"　　　.

AYMOND, Nascicante Francis 6 Nov of apoplexy in his 60th year. Resided　　　MORE 8 Nov 1861
　　　on Lesperance between Jackson & Columbus.

AYRES, Josephine 12 Oct ae 10, dau/William H. & the late Eliza M.　　　MORE 13 Oct 1862

AYRES, Willie son of John M. near West Ely, Ralls Co., 29 Oct ae 12.　　　MORE 6 Nov 1863

BABER, Harriet M. wife of Col. Hiram H. in Jefferson City 17 Nov in her 68th year.　　　COWS 29 Nov 1861
　　　Native of Fayette Co. KY, daughter of Judge B. Boone, granddaughter of
　　　Daniel Boone.

BACH, Louis 3 Jan at his home, 10th betw O'Fallon-Cass, ae 53.　　　MORE 4 Jan 1865

BACHMAN, Samuel son/William S. & Ellen 15 Jul ae 6y 8m. Interred Calvary.   SLMD 16 Jul 1864
       Philadelphia pc

BACIGALUPO, Maria, grandmother of V.B., 8 Dec in her 80th year. Memphis pc   MORE 10 Dec 1861

BACON, Charles many years a resident of Pike Co. after a short, severe illness.   LAJ 6 Nov 1862
    Left a large family. (MORE 8 Nov says he died of flux.) Died 2 Nov.

BACON, J. Lee 19 Feb of consumption in his 26th year at the home of George M.   MORE 20 Feb 1864
    Groves, Clark-13th. Funeral from St. John's Church.

BACON, Jerome H. formerly of Warren MA at the home of his brother-in-law M. L. Gray,
    245 Pine, 2 Dec of consumption ae 29.   MORE 24 Dec 1864

BACON, Dr. T.M., many years a citizen of Clay Co., at his home in Santa Fe,   LIT 21 Jul 1865
    Jackson Co., a few weeks ago "nearly 80."

BACON, Willie H. son/William D. & Sarah D. 26 Aug in St. Louis Co. ae 7y 2m.   MORE 3 Sep 1865

BAEHR, Dr. William, a well-known veterinary surgeon, suicide yesterday by
    morphine; domestic trouble. Had married a German actress 2 or 3 years ago,
    she had been previously divorced. She left for CA 6 months ago, had filed   MORE 29 Mar &
    for divorce alleging adultery, he had threatened her, etc.   6 Apr 1865

BAGLEY, Thomas drowned in the quarry pond near the Reservoir between 18-19th sts.
    Son of a poor widow living on 22nd betw Morgan-Franklin; had epilepsy;   MORE 10 Jul 1865
    "a good boy and the support of his mother."

BAILEY, ____ living in Smithville, Clay Co., a Union man, found murdered about   SJH 2 Jul 1864
    7 miles from Liberty, supposedly by bushwhackers.

BAILEY, children of B.F. & M.: Amanda Ann 3 May of scarlet fever ae 11y 1m 8d
        Lillie Branham 15 May ae 4y 7m 9d   FULT 29 May 1863

BAILEY, Bob and Henry, killed by soldiers in lower Cape Girardeau Co.   CHAC 22 Apr 1864

BAILEY, Carter, inquest: hostler at livery stable on 6th & Chestnut found dead in
    bed. Verdict, lung congestion. Ae 20. No known relatives in St. Louis.   MORE 18 Oct 1863

BAILEY, James yesterday of hydrophobia ae ca 14. Bitten by family dog. Resided   MORE 6 Jun 1865
        Collins near Bates.

BAILEY, Jane, a negress, inquest: found dead in "Clabber Alley" 6-7-Wash-Carr.
    Verdict, destitution and want of care.   MORE 1 Jan 1863

BAILEY, John P. in his 47th year. Native of Campbell Co. VA. Lived 6th-Biddle.   MORE 21 Mar 1863

BAILEY, Mary A. wife of George 1 Jan in her 47th year. Lived 126 St. Charles.   MORE 3 Jan 1864
    Interred in the east. San Francisco & Boston pc

BAILEY, Samuel H. 13 Dec in his 43rd year. Lived Olive St. between 8th & 9th.   MORE 14 Dec 1861
        Interred in Connecticut.

BAILEY, John believed to be the mysterious suicide of several days ago -- threw
    himself into the river at night. Lived 10 miles out on Clayton Road.   MORE 17 Nov 1862
    Left wife and child, believed insane.

BAIN, R.E. wife of J.T. in Providence, Boone Co. 29 Jun in her 32d year.   COWS 10 Jul 1863
    Left 3 little boys. Boonville & Mexico MO pc

BAKER, Abraham R. of Oregon Co., arrested 19 Jul, in Gratiot Prison, lung congestion. MORE 27 Oct 1863

BAKER, Charlie Egbert second son/J.F. & M.F. 8 Jul ae 8y 10m. Lived 221 Chestnut.   MORE 9 Jul 1862

BAKER, David J. "one of Poindexter's guerillas" captured in Boone Co. 13 Oct,   MORE 3 Apr 1863
        in Gratiot Prison.

BAKER, Mrs. Elenor P. wife of Alphonso of Boone Co. 6 May ae 29y 12d. Buried in   COWS 23 May 1862
    New Salem churchyard beside her sister Elizabeth Davis, who died more
        than 2 years ago.

BAKER, Mrs. Eliza Gamble, relict of Capt. Samuel, at the home of D.K. Pittman in   MORE 31 Aug 1861
    St. Charles Co. 27 Aug in her 74th year. Late of Culpeper Co. VA.

BAKER, Jackson, prisoner from Dunklin Co., of inflammation of the lungs.   MORE 12 Nov 1863

BAKER, Joseph late clerk to the Provost Marshall, in Detroit ae 43. Funeral from
    his home, Wash betw 24th-25th.   MORE 26 Aug 1863

BAKER, Mrs. Julia D. near Central, St. Louis Co., 20 Mar in her 27th year. Born
    near Front Royal VA, emigrated early to Lewis Co. MO. A Methodist.   MORE 4 Apr 1865
    Leaves 2 little children.

BAKER, Kate wife of Thomas 24 Feb ae 27y 27d. Left husband and children.   FULT 25 Mar 1864

BAKER, Lue Eben eldest son/John F. & M.F. 24 Sep ae 11y 1m 18d. Lived 221 Chestnut.   MORE 25 Sep 1862

BAKER, Robert murdered 5 June last, Thomas Smith now convicted of his murder.   MORE 16 Nov 1862

BAKER, Robert Franklin son/Joseph N. & Lou E. 26 Jun ae 2y 10m 11d at the home of T. R. Dale. — LIT 28 Jun 1861

BAKER, Samuel son/(Bailam?) & Mary, of Cole Co., 20 Jul of pneumonia ae 15. — JEST 4 Aug 1865

BAKER, Sarah Ann wife of John F. in Columbia 25 Jun ae ca 31. — COWS 28 Jun 1861

BAKER, William J. of the 3rd MO, captured in Wright Co. 11 Jan, in Gratiot Prison of pneumonia. — MORE 24 Feb 1863

BAKER, Willie shot at Palmyra by Gen. Merrill in retaliation for the abduction and murder of an old man named Allmstedt during Porter's raid into Palmyra. Baker was from Lewis Co. (Palmyra Courier) — CAWN 1 Nov 1862

BALDWIN, Mary consort of Andrew B. 12 Oct ae 67y 9m 6d. Born in VA Jan 1796, to MO from TN 1816; a Baptist over 40 years. — LIT 30 Oct 1863

    Elder Andrew B. 11 Aug ae 75. — LIT 2 Sep 1864

BALDWIN, C.W. 4 Jun ae 54. Lived on the Olive St. Plank Road. — MORE 5 Jun 1863

BALDWIN, Capt. Hazard L., formerly of St. Louis, in New Orleans 9 Sep. Funeral from the Lindell Hotel. — MORE 26 Nov 1865

BALDWIN, Smith 27 Feb ae 47. Lived on Park Ave. opposite nw corner Lafayette Park. — MORE 28 Feb 1861

BALL, Mary Ann ae 3 killed by a street car on Market betw 21-22; the car was coming down a steep grade from Camp Springs and couldn't stop when the child ran in front. Her parents kept a store nearby on Market St. — MORE 20 Apr 1864

BALL, William H. 10 Apr ae 25. Funeral from home of Mr. Addis on Cook Ave. — MORE 12 Apr 1862

BALLANTINE, David at his home near Boonville 19 May of erysipelas in his 49th year. — COWS 29 May 1863

BALLARD, Elijah at his home near Savannah 28 Apr in his 53rd year. Born in VA, many years a citizen of Andrew Co. — SJH 10 May 1864

BALLARD, Gertrude, only child/R.L. & F.A., 4 Mar ae 6y 17d at the home of James E. Ballard in Ray Co. Kansas pc — RICON 13 Mar 1863

BALLARD, Hugh "a rebel lieutenant" near Cape Girardeau 15 Aug by a scouting party under Maj. Poole. — PALS 21 Aug 1863

BALLARD, Joshua, citizen of Lafayette Co., arrested 8 Aug, died in prison of inflammation of the lungs. (Undertaker's list) — MORE 10 Nov 1863

BALLENGER, Daniel H. from injuries received in the explosion of the City of Madison at Vicksburg (ammunition exploded); aboard the John D. Perry 24 Aug. Funeral from the home of his brother L.S., 318 Pine, Bishop's Row. Interred Bellefontaine. Maysville KY pc — MORE 26 Aug 1863

BALLOU, Columbus, citizen of Grundy Co., 10 Jan of typhoid pneumonia. (Undertaker's list) — MORE 19 Jan 1863

BALLOU or BALLEW James, an old man living 5 miles southwest of Huntsville found dead by his hearth, shot twice in the head. A Union man, presumably killed by bushwhackers. (Randolph Citizen 9 Sep) (MORE 8 Sep refers to him as an old citizen of Randolph Co.) — MORE 12 Sep 1864

BALLOU, DeWitt C., an old citizen of sw MO, at his home in Sedalia 25 Dec. "Lawyer, jurist." Interred in Warsaw. — SEDA 31 Dec 1864

BALLY, Mary E. dau/Joseph & Isabel 30 Nov of diphtheria ae 5y 3m. — MORE 2 Dec 1864

BANES, Margaret, suicide by morphine, "a dissolute character" ae 18; had elder sister in St. Louis, parents in Iowa. — MORE 24 Jun 1864

BANESON, Amanda H. wife of H.A. and dau/Lewis & Disia Davis of typhoid 6 Jan. Born in Crawford Co. MO 6 Mar 1840, married 28 Feb 1862. — MORE 20 Jan 1863

BANISTER, Thomas in Ray Co. 26 May in his 64th year. Native of VA, emigrated first to KY, then MO. Old settler, Justice of the Peace. — RICON 11 Jun 1863

BANKS, Mrs. Jedidah S. mother of B.W., J.W. and W.J. Lewis, in her 73rd year. Interred in family cemetery at Glasgow. (She was first married to a Lewis of that prominent family near Glasgow.) — MORE 29 Apr 1864

BANKS, Dr. Lynn ae ca 40, tribute by Palmyra Lodge No. 18, Masons. Native of Garrard Co. KY, to MO at age 4. Married a Miss Rogers; leaves parents, wife, 3 children. — PALS 7 Apr & 5 May 1865

BANKS, William of Clark's Regiment, captured in Taney Co. 23 Aug, in Gratiot Prison 24 Jan of erysipelas. — MORE 27 Jan 1863

BANNING, Bennet, Chariton Co., letters of administration 27 Sep to G.E.M. Triplett. — CECB 2 Oct 1862

BANNING, Capt. R.B. of the Metropolitan Police, account of his funeral the preceding day. Interred Bellefontaine. — MORE 23 Jan 1865

BANNISTER, John J. of Porter's Band arrested 23 (28?) Oct in Gratiot Prison   MORE 20 Nov 1862
    19 Nov of pleurisy.   "   26 Jan 1863

BANNON, Andrew of St. Louis en route to visit his parents in Ireland, between Cork
    and Dublin, thrown or fell from railroad car; his body was found near
    Rathconnor and taken to the hospital at Thurles.   MORE 29 Aug 1863

BANNON, Henry 27 May ca 45. Funeral from Central House, Chestnut betw 3-4.   MORE 29 May 1863

BANNON, Mary wife of John 29 Apr ca 31. Lived on Morgan St. Interred
    Bellefontaine. Pittsburgh pc   MORE 30 Apr 1862

BANTA, Ric- of Harrison Co., suicide by strychnine. A resident of Eagleville, BEST 25 Feb 1861
    (/paper blurred)   "respectable citizen."

BARBER, Eliza wife of James 1 Nov in Laclede Co.   MORE 11 Nov 1863

BARCLAY, Julia, an inmate of St. Vincent's Asylumm escaped a day or two ago, sold   MORE 28 Mar 1865
    her shoes for 30¢, bought arsenic, swalloed it and died.

BARGETT, Lieut. Joseph of St. Louis, in Gen. Bowen's Brigade, killed at Shiloh. MORE 4 May 1862

BARKELAGE, William, living near Wright City in Warren Co., on Booneslick Road, MORE 21 Sep 1863
        killed in a bushwhacking search. (Warrenton Nonpareil)

BARKLEY, Miss E.M. of Marion Co. 25 Feb at the home of her father ae 21 "and   HAM 13 Mar 1862
        nearly 4 months" of consumption.

BARKER, Newton A. of congestive chills at the home of William M. Cooley near   CHAC 11 Sep 1863
    Charleston. Son of John, former sheriff; resident of Wolf Island Twp,
    in the city on business.

BARNARD, Esther only dau/John H. 12 Nov ae 21. Resided Washington betw 12-13. MORE 13 Nov 1862

BARNARD, Joseph 11 Apr at the home of Jeremy Douglass of disease of the head. LAJ 18 Apr 1863
    Native of Bohemia, ae 14y 10m; left a brother and sister.

BARNARD, Westley Pigman 8 Nov ca 45 at his home near Lucas Bend.   CHAC 15 Nov 1861

BARNARD, William R. of 3rd MO CSA, captured in Saline Co. 13 Oct, in the   MORE 29 Oct 1863
            prison hospital.

BARNES, Elizabeth wife of Rev. James 26 Apr in Randolph Co. of erysipelas and MORE 2 May 1863
    inflammation of the stomach, in her 63rd year. "Calvinistic Baptist."
    Left many children & grandchildren. CA pc

BARNES, George Washington at Benton Barracks 14 May of chronic diarrhoea ae 27y 7m. MORE 1 Jan 1863

BARNES, John Henry only son/Dr. J.H. & A.M. near Carrollton ae 5y 8m 12d.   MORE 27 Jul 1863

BARNES, Margaret wife of Joseph W. at Snow Hill, St. Charles Co., 16 Jun.   MORE 18 Jun 1863
    Funeral from the home of R.S. Platt, 260 Carr St.

BARNES, Moses killed by guerillas in Platte Co. (St. Joseph Herald.)   MORE 16 Jun 1864
            (Son of Lieut. Barnes?)

BARNES, Patrick, inquest: lived alley between 14-15-Biddle-O'Fallon, a laborer, MORE 25 Oct 1863
    ca 37; left wife, 2 children. Lung congestion and intemperance.

BARNES, Samuel of rubeola in Gratiot Prison 2 Nov.   MORE 9 Nov 1862

BARNETT, Hannah Jane wife of Andrew J. and youngest dau/William & Nancy Rogers, MORE 24 Dec 1863
    Platte Co., 10 Dec. Funeral Christ Church. Lexington pc

BARNETT, Robert 26 Jun in his 52d year. Lived on Franklin west of Garrison.   MORE 27 Jun 1865
    Funeral from St. Bridget's Church. Cincinnati & Lancaster OH pc

BARNHURST, Rebecca C. "Sabbath noon." Funeral from home of her brother-in-law MORE 16 Dec 1861
    P.J. Thompson, 4 S. 7th. Interred Philadelphia.

BARNHURST, Washington at Oakhurst, Miller Co., 29 Apr in his 32d year. Former MORE 17 Mat 1862
    pastor of 3rd Baptist Church, St. Louis.

BARNIDGE, John 7 Nov in his 66th year. Native Ireland, in St. Louis 28 years. MORE 9 Nov 1865
    Funeral St. Francis Xavier; interred Calvary.

BARNUM, Mary J., tribute from Western Star Social Temple, mentions parents   LAJ 15 Jan 1863
                 Mr. & Mrs. Barnum.

BARR, Mrs. Dr. E.W. of St. Louis 30 Aug in Dorchester MA ae 25.   Quincy and   MORE 4 Sep 1863
                 Lancaster PA pc

BARR, Capt. William, Comissary of Subsistence, 17 Dec in Denver. Native of   MORE 31 Dec 1864
    Scotland, in US 17 years, leaves widow in St. Louis; they were married
    a few months ago.

BARRET, Andy, inquest: a one-legged man engaged in breaking rock near 4-Mile-House MORE 12 Jul 1863
    on Bellefontaine Road; congestion brain, apoplexy, intemperance "and blows
    on the head inflicted by someone at the house of John Halpin" where the
    inquest was held.

BARRET, Willie D. son/William J. froze to death, ae 16. Had been hunting across   MORE, 5, 6, 10
the Meramec, caught in a storm, died of exposure. Only child. Lived 33 St.Charles   Jan 1864

BARRETT, Aaron of St. Louis drowned in Fraser River near New Westminster,   MORE 8 &
British Columbia ae 32, on 8 July.   10 Aug 1862

BARRETT, Mrs. C. 18 Aug ae 29. Resided 7th near Cass. Funeral St. Patrick's.   MORE 19 Aug 1865

BARRETT, Dr. George R., tribute by the medical profession of Springfield.   SPRIP 21 Sep 1865

BARRETT, James, former Union soldier wounded at Shiloh, shot near 6-Mile-House   MORE 1 Sep 1862
by Ed Ball, a notorious character -- they had had words, Ball followed
him home and shot him.

BARRETT, Miss Martha J. 7 Apr near New Harmony ae 17y 3m 2w   LAJ 23 Apr 1864

BARRETT, Mrs. S.A. wife of Dr. B.A. 29 Nov ae 33; lived on Elm St.   MORE 1 Dec 1865

BARRETT, William 16 Aug near Forest City, of piles, ae ca 50.   HOLS 18 Aug 1865

BARRON, Ann wife of Z. 20 Jan in her 70th year. Funeral from the home of her   MORE 22 Jan 1862
son-in-law Robert Galbraith.

BARRON, children of H.M. & Fannie: Charlsie Vincent ae 6 and Laura Bell ae 1m,   MORE 25 Mar 1862
both on 23 Mar. Lived at #13 13th St.

BARRON, John E. son/William T. & Hannah 30 Apr between Market-Estelle ae 7y 7m 23d.   MORE 1 May 1861
Lived on Mound St. between Market & Estelle.

   William Henry son/William T. & Hannah 25 Feb ae 5y 5m.   SLMD 5 Mar 1861

BARROW, Nathan, a civilian captured 20 Feb in Macon Co., in Gratiot Prison
of inflammation of the lungs.   MORE 28 Apr 1863

BARRY, James a deckhand drowned from the Lake City.   MORE 30 Apr 1862

BARRY, James G. youngest child/James G. & Elizabeth 5 May in his 19th year.   MORE 7 May 1865
Funeral Church of the Annunciation, interred Calvary.

BARRY, Richard, of the police force, funeral notice: St. Patrick's Church to   MORE 22 &
Calvary. Left a sister and brother.   23 Jan 1864

BARRY, Richard shot by Michael Connors 21 Feb at the house of James Kilgore, a   SJH 5 Mar 1864
short distance below town, died of his wounds.

BARTH, Robert youngest child of Robert & Sophy 29 Jun ae 6y 8m. Lived on   MORE 30 Jun 1863
Bellefontaine Road.

BARTHALOW, Laura Theresa wife of Thomas J. of (and in) Glasgow 23 Feb ae 34.   MORE 27 Feb 1862
      Baltimore pc

BARTLETT, Jane wife of William H. at Charleston (MO) 9 Mar. Married on New   CHAC 11 Mar 1864
Year's Eve, shot herself through the heart (ae 21) leaving letters to
her husband and sister, accused husband of moroseness.
(PERU 25 Mar says she was happy in the marriage, he was not, she had
prepared her grave clothes before committing suicide.)

BARTLETT, Sarah A. wife of William H. of Mississippi Co. and dau/B.H. Miles   CHAC 8 Nov 1861
of Cape Girardeau, 4 Nov.

BARTLEY, Sheldon son/George and M., Callaway Co., 8 Nov of brain congestion.   MORE 18 Nov 1863

BARTON, Daniel a resident of Shelby Co. recently arrested and shot by Macon Co.   MORE 13 Jun 1865
militia; he had recently returned from military prison in Chicago. He
was charged with being a bushwhacker. Ae ca 40, left wife and 11
children. (Paris Mercury)

BARTON, Katie only dau/Chauncey & Julia at the home of Mrs. Fields, 7th St.   MORE 3 Jan 1861
ae 3y 1m 8d.

BASHIRE   Elizabeth Sharkey wife of John S. 27 Feb in her 24th year. Funeral from   MORE 28 Feb 1865
(BESHIRE?) home of her brother-in-law, 208 N. 10th.

BASHORE, Elizabeth relict of John 22 Mar in her 61st year, of a long illness.   PALS 31 Mar 1865

BASKET, William, citizen of Howard Co., 13 Feb of erysipelas. (Undertaker's list)   MORE 19 Feb 1865

BASKETT, S. P. in Gratiot Prison of typhoid 5 Dec.   MORE 7 Dec 1862

BASS, Eli E., well-known citizen of Boone Co., 23 Jul ae 59.   COWS 28 Jul 1865

BASS, Enos C. in Dresden, Pettis Co. 10 Jul of consumption ae 24.   WARS 12 Aug 1865

BASS, Mrs. Malvina C. wife of John M. of Nashville TN at the home of Eli E. Bass,   MORE 19 Jul 1863
Forest Hill, Boone Co. 15 Jul while visiting connections in Missouri after
a visit to her husband in Arkansas. Dau/late Felix Grundy, she had lived
in St. Louis the first two years after her marriage.

BASS, Mrs. Permelia J. of Rocheport 28 July of measles ae ca 53.   COWS 1 Aug 1862
    Levi Franklin son/late Permelia of typhoid in Rocheport 11 Aug ae ca 18.   COWS 15 Aug 1862
BASSETT, Aaron -- see BARRETT, Aaron (MORE on 30 Aug 1862 shows Barrett, Bassett 31 Aug)
BASYE, Samuel L. son/John C. & Penninah of Bowling Green in the government   LAJ 31 Oct 1863
    hospital in Paducah 5 Sep. Interred Bowling Green.
BATES, Luther P. of pulmonary disease at New Bloomfield 25 Jan in his 34th year.   COWS 10 Feb 1865
BATES, Mary wife/John 14 Oct ae 51. Funeral from home of her son-in-law Otis   MORE 15 Oct 1861
    Breden (11th betw O'Fallon & Cass). Interred Bellefontaine.
BATES, Reuben S. son/J.P. of St. Louis in New Orleans 4 May, result of wounds   MORE 20 May 1865
    received at Ft. Blakeley, AL, ae 26.
BATTER, Philip a blacksmith run over by a streetcar on the Broadway line Friday,   MORE 15 Aug 1864
    knocked down by a passing wagon. Left wife, 3 children.
BATZ, Richard "an old workman" fell through a hatchway at Stumpf's Beer Cave   MORE 19 Nov 1861
    near Gravois, ae 72.
BAUGHAN, Eddie youngest son/R.A. & Maria R. in Osceola 29 Aug ae 4y 6m.   COWS 11 Sep 1863
BAUGHMAN, John murdered in Florence, Morgan Co.; acting governor Hall offers a   CAWN 15 Aug 1863
    reward for the murderer.
BAUM, Henry, a merchant, 14 Jul in his 65th year. Born at Anspach, Nassau   PALS 17 Jul 1863
    29 Apr 1799; emigrated 1833, in New York 2 years, then to Palmyra.
    Husband, father.   MORE 22 Jul 1863
BAUM, Solomon killed by guerillas in Carroll Co. (Carrollton Democrat)   MORE 21 Jul 1864
BAUMANN, Mary wife of John 2 Oct ae 43. Lived at 119 Collins, near O'Fallon.   MORE 3 Oct 1864
BAUMBAUR, Christof a musician, of apoplexy; addicted to drink; no relatives here.   MORE 13 Oct 1863
BAUMGARTNER, ___, son of John, drowned in the Wyaconda above Ligon's Mill   CANP 28 May 1863
    17 May ae ca 13.
BAUMGARTNER, Francis J. Saturday night near St. Louis ae 46. Funeral from   SLMD 7 Jan 1861
    St. Francis Xavier. Westminster MD pc
BAUMGARTNER, Mark Hamilton son/James & Roxanna 4 Feb ae 1y 7m 27d. Westminster MD pc   MORE 5 Feb 1861
BAUSENKURT, Michael, suicide by strychnine. Disappointed when he didn't receive a   MORE 18 Sep 1861
    small sum due him. Native of Bavaria, ca 34, wife, 5 children.
BAXTER, Mrs. Victoria 9 Apr ae 67. Funeral from home of her son-in-law J. (B?)   MORE 10 Apr 1861
    Mears, 695 Broadway. Cincinnati & Pittsburgh pc
BAYLES, Col. David 18 Dec in St. Louis in his 44th year. Native of Ohio, number   MORE 20 Dec 1862
    of years in St. Louis city and county. Dropsical condition. Left sister,
    3 motherless children. Lived near the Arsenal.   MORE 20 Dec 1862
BAYLEY, Emma Elizabeth, youngest child of Romanzo & Adeline C., in Kirkwood 24 Feb   MORE 25 Feb 1861
    of scarlet fever ae 5y 6m 14d. Interred Bellefontaine.
    Adeline C. wife of R.N. at their home in Kirkwood 11 Jan. Funeral from   MORE 12 Jan 1864
    home of Capt. Rogers, 12 Papin, St. Louis.
BAYNHAM, Charles M. Monday last ae 50.   FULT 25 Mar 1864
BEAHAN, Joseph T. 12 Jan in Carondelet ae 28.   MORE 14 Jan 1864
BEAL, Mrs. ____ living on Wash St., badly burned when her clothes caught fire   MORE 30 Jan 1865
    some 10 days ago, since died.
BEAM, George W. of pneumonia 20 Feb ae (24? 27?) leaving wife, 2 children.   MORE 22 Feb 1863
    Pittsburgh & Erie pc
BEAMER, Ida Emogene dau/W.J. & Emeline 16 Jul ae 10y 2m. Funeral from home of her   MORE 17 Jul 1863
    grandfather S. Woods, 10th & Monroe.
BEANLAND, W. G. at his home near Hopewell, Morgan Co., 15 May ae 20y 2m 7d. Had   MORE 25 May 1861
    been ill about a year.
BEASLEY, John W. 24 May of inflammatory rheumatism ae 33.   COWS 6 Jun 1862
BEATTIE, David 20 Oct ae 39. Resided Clark near 16th.   MORE 22 Oct 1861
BEATTY, Mrs. Martha 7 Oct ae 60. Resided 237 Morgan.   MORE 9 Oct 1864
BEATTY, Zaccheus 12 Sep after a short illnee, ae 35. Resided Spruce between 15-16.   SLMD 13-14
    Cambridge OH pc   Sep 1864
BEATY, David G., citizen of Chariton Co., bronchitis, 22 Feb. (Undertaker's list)   MORE 6 Mar 1865
BEAUVAIS, Francis Augustus son/Francis A. & Sylvania, 12 May ae 13y 7m. Resided   MORE 13 May 1865
    7th betw Lynch-Lancaster. Calvary. St. Joseph pc

BECK, Edward H. second son/Robert B. & Mary H., 5 Apr ae 6y 7m. Philadelphia pc   MORE 6 Apr 1865

BECK, Lucy widow of Rev. Richard at Longwood, Pettis Co. 21 Dec, ae ca 73. Born VA, to Marshall Co. TN ca 1837, to St. Clair Co. MO about 1841. Baptist many years. Her 3 children predeceased her: Mrs. Masey(?) F. Devin, Mrs. Susan D. Gardner, and James W. Beck (former Circuit Clerk, St. Clair Co.)   MORE 8 Jan 1864

BECK, Capt. Mason, a guerilla from Warren Co., killed in a raid at Elmore's Store, Ashley, Pike Co.   MORE 6 Sep 1862

BECKER, Martha wife of Theodore on 10 June.   MORE 11 Jun 1861

BECKER, Mathias 27 Apr in his 6th year of apoplexy, at his home on 18th St. between Biddle & Carr. Interred Bellefontaine.   MORE 28 Apr 1864

BECKET, Elizabeth wife of William, 8 Mar. Lived 37 Ham St. Pekin IL pc   MORE 9 Mar 1865

BECKNOR, Mary, of Clark Co., at the home of E.C. Hyde, Chambers & 13th, 25 Nov in her 22d year.   MORE 26 Nov 1861

BECKWITH, Quiros 3 Sep ae 60 at his home in Wolf Island Twp. Mississippi Co. Emigrated from Va in 1811; a flatboatman, planter, etc. "with one exception by far the richest man in the county."   CHAC 5 Sep 1862

BEEHLER, Maria Catherine wife of Francis 11 Aug ae 44. Lived 5th between Franklin & Wash.   MORE 12 Aug 1864

BEELER, George, Chariton Co.; public administrator took over his estate.   CECB 2 Oct 1862

BEEMAN, Nelson 4 Oct ae 43. Born Westfield VT. Resided 12th & Brooklyn.   MORE 5 Oct 1865

BEER, Henry J. formerly of PA, many years resident of St. Louis, ae 56y 9m 21d. Resided on Chouteau. Interred Bellefontaine.   MORE 1 Jan 1861

BEESON, Mrs. Susan E. 7 Feb of erysipelas ae 42y 8m. Resided at 925 Pine St. Funeral Immaculate Conception Church. Cincinnati, Zanesville, Philadelphia & Brownsville PA pc   MORE 8 Feb 1862

BEHR, Alfred, M.D., 1 Jan after a long illness.   MORE 3 Jan 1862

BEINNET, Charles drowned in a pond when ice broke. Parents live on 12th St. between Buchanan & Angelrodt.   MORE 23 Jan 1862

BEIRNE, Miss Margaret 1 Aug ae 30; cousin of Charles & Patrick McWeeney. Interred Calvary. New Haven CT pc   MORE 2 Aug 1861

BEIRNE, Dr. George W. 4 Jan near Creve Coeur in his 39th year. Formerly of VA. Interred Calvary. VA pc   MORE 6 Jan 1864

BEIRNE, Thomas J. 14 Nov after a protracted illness at the home of John F. Mitchell near Kirkwood. He was an attorney. VA pc   MORE 17 & 18 Nov 1861

BELDEN, Henry H. recently of St. Louis in Nebraska City 5 May, of injuries received when he fell from a wagon.   MORE 23 May 1865

BELL, Mrs. Bettie McDowell wife of Col. T.P., late of Saline Co., in St. Louis 11 Feb of erysipelas in her 33rd year. Born in Rockingham Co. VA on 4 Aug 1832, came to MO quite young; her father died leaving four children, she the oldest. Joined the Presbyterian Church in Independence, married in June 1856 and then joined the Methodist Church as it was her husband's. Left husband and children.   MORE 13 & 25 Feb 1865

BELL, Elizabeth A. wife of Dr. John T. 18 Apr leaving husband, 3 children, aged father, several sisters. Cumberland Presbyterian.   LAJ 25 Apr 1861

BELL, James, citizen of Boone Co., 8 Feb of pneumonia. (Undertaker's list)   MORE 13 Feb 1865

BELL, James 13 Jun ae 66 at the home of his son George W., 194 5th St. Cincinnati pc   MORE 14 Jun 1865

BELL, Lavinia E. wife of Rev. William G. near Boonville 6 Aug in her 51st year. Born Albemarle Co. VA; at the death of her first husband, Alexander Calhoun of Boonville, was left with 2 small children; it was suggested that she return to her father Mr. Harris in Albemarle, but she made her own way, and ran a female boarding school. Married Rev. Bell about 1841; was survived by one son and 3 daughters.   MORE 20 Aug 1864

     Eliza H., step-daughter of Rev. William G. Bell, in Warsaw 3 Sep ae 21.   WARS 9 Sep 1865

BELL, Mrs. Susan at the home of her son-in-law S.K. Davis 13 Mar in her 84th year. Born Prince William Co. VA, to KY 1790. Baptist since ae 40.   PALS 18 Mar 1864

BELLES, John son/Mr. & Mrs. C.T., 25 Feb ae 12.   LEXUN 27 Feb 1864

BELLON, Charles P. 19 Jan ae 59y 7m. Lived on Leffingwell. Peoria & Quincy pc   MORE 20 Jan 1863

BELMAR, Lewis Co. D 3rd MO Cav CSA 21 Dec. (Undertaker's list)   MORE 2 Jsn 1865

BELL, George Thomas 18 Aug ae 6 at his father's home in this city.   WEST 26 Aug 1864

BELT, Laura E. dau/T.H. & M.A. in Knoxville 8 Nov ae 4y 2m 5d.   RICON 21 Nov 1865

BELT, Mary wife of George and daughter of Henry J. Colman near Platte City   SJH 29 Dec 1863
    24 Dec "in the bloom of youth and the prime of life."

BEMAW, William killed by guerillas near Hickman's Mill, Jackson Co.   MORE 12 May 1865

BENEDICT, ____ son/J.W., a boy about 10 drowned from a raft in the Mississippi.   MORE 14 Jun 1864
    Body not recovered. Parents live at 15 Benton.

BENDIGO, see SMITH, Daniel - murdered.   MORE 21 Aug 1862

BENEKE, Alwine wife of Augustus 14 Feb ae 27. Lived on Clark Ave.   MORE 15 Feb 1862

BENJAMIN, Lewis captured in Ripley Co. 25 Dec, at Gratiot Prison of   MORE 2 Feb 1864
    inflammation of the lungs.

BENN, Thomas at his home near Frankford 19 May, one of the county's oldest settlers.   LAJ 8 Jul 1865

BENNETT, Helen second dau/late Dr. at Richmond KY 9 Jul (she had left St. Louis   MORE 17 &
    with her only sister, Mrs. Thomas E. Tutt, to visit relatives there).   22 Jul 1863
    Ae 17y 6m; had attended Mary Institute; was Catholic. Boonville &
    Columbia MO pc

BENNETT, Henry H. of Reeves' outfit, captured in Ripley Co. 25 Dec, in the   MORE 7 Feb 1864
    prison hospital, of measles.

BENNETT, Johanna "keeper of a disreputable house on Green St." suicide by laudanum.   MORE 16 Sep 1862
    Wealthy; real name Wright; had previously attempted suicide.

BENNETT, William, of Russell & Bennett grocery house, yesterday.   SLMD 3 Dec 1861

BENSON, A. J. killed at Portland a few weeks ago; Brashers & Smith now   SEDA 18 Feb 1865
    acquitted. (Fulton Telegraph)

BENSON, Eden, "wealthy" citizen ca 80, near Portland. (Fulton Telegraph)   MORE 20 Apr 1863

BENT, Edwin J. 3 Feb ae 42. Lived 261 Washington. Interred Bellefontaine.   MORE 5 Feb 1862

BENT, Margaret V. widow of John of St. Louis in Philadelphia 1 Jun. Long illness.   MORE 7 Jun 1863

BENTON, Edwin Walter eldest son/Dr. B.L. & Salome 20 Apr ae 8y 2m. (On the
    Carthage Road???)   MORE 23 Apr 1864

BENTROPE, Frederick, laborer on North Market St. near 16th, suicide by arsenic.   MORE 31 Jan 1865
    Had grown children but was on unfriendly terms with them.

BENTZ, Elizabeth, native of Germany, 24 Feb ae 71.   WEST 27 Feb 1864

BEQUETTE, Henry killed by bushwhackers at Flat Creek about 7 miles from Potosi.   MORE 26 Aug 1864
    (letter signed J.W., Jr. dated Potosi 24 Aug)

VERFELD, Pauline, inquest; accidentally drowned in a cistern. Ae 10, lived   MORE 2 Jul 1863
    om 13th between Biddle & Carr.

BERGER, Alice dau/Edmund & Dora 2 Oct ae 11y 22d. Resided Hickory between   SLMD 3 Oct 1864
    Dillon & Park. Interred Bellefontaine.

BERGER, Charles 20 Oct ae 23. Funeral from home of Chas. Deichmann, 4th St.   SJH 21 Oct 1864

BERGER, Mrs. Julia 15 Nov ae 66 after long, painful illness. Funeral from home   MORE 17 Nov 1864
    of J.W. Gunsollis, Olive between 20-21. St Charles pc

BERGER, Paul B., drunk and in the calaboose, beaten by John Doyle of the 49th MO,   MORE 4 Dec 1865
    also in the calaboose, died.

BERGHEFFER, Henry Sunday night last age about 35.   PALS 15 May 1863

BERGMAN, Mena ae 10 drowned yesterday in a cistern. Her family had only been in   MORE 8 Feb 1865
    the city a few weeks, lived 12th St. between Cass & O'Fallon.

BERKLEY, Mrs. Elizabeth 8 Feb ae 49. Lived at 22nd & Chouteau.   MORE 9 Feb 1862

BERNE, Frederick, suicide in Lindell's Pasture near Rock Spring; shot himself in   MORE 8 May 1861
    the head. "Of a pleasant character," owned considerable property; left
    wife and children.

BERNHARD, Christian son/Philip, a gardener living on the south side of Liberty   MORE 13 Feb 1863
    west of Freeman, died possibly of poisoning by "oatmeal soup" made and
    served by servant Mary Steinbrecher, ae 23, who didn't eat it. All
    family members but one little girl (who didn't eat it) were ill:
    Philip, his wife Margaret, Frederick ae 4, Lizzie ae 10, Margaret ae 7,
    and a hired boy Godlief Jaegel ae 10. Inquest to be held.

BERNOUDY, Mary Stella eldest child/Edward A. & Ellen Taylor 3 Sep ae 5y 6m.   MORE 6 Sep 1865

BERRIEN, Joseph W. Saturday in his 46th year. Funeral St. Francis Xavier Church.   MORE 14 Jun 1863

BERRISH, John drowned near the foot of Market St.; drove his team onto the river to cut ice, and broke through. — MORE 18 Jan 1862

BERRY, Alice dau/David & Martha in Boone Co. 6 Dec of diphtheria ae 10. — COWS 18 Dec 1863

BERRY, Franklin Chiles youngest son/Edward & Mary E. in Manchester 10 Aug ae 1y 3m. — MORE 14 Aug 1861

BERRY, William G. in Platte Co. 1 Feb ae 50y 8m 18d. — LIT 13 Feb 1863

BERRYMAN, Maria Emeline wife of Rev. N.G. & dau/Col. William Loving of KY of heart disease 8 Dec. Married 30 years. — PALS 11 Dec 1863

BERTHOLD, Amidie at the home of father in Normandy, St. Louis Co., ae 15y 1m 2d. Funeral from St. Ann's Church. — MORE 8 Sep 1864

BERTHOLF, Henry, ca 45-50, being taken to City Hospital yesterday, died on the way, of consumption. — MORE 11 Mar 1865

BERTHOUD, James R. Washington, only son/Augustus & Catherine A., 11 Nov in 7th year. — MORE 12 Nov 1865

BETTS, Fanny, mother of William B., 1 Apr ae 77. — SLMD 9 Apr 1861

BETTS, William, of injuries received in a fire. Funeral from home of Dr. Smucker, 132 S. 5th. Interred Bellefontaine. — MORE 23 May 1862

BETZ, Sallie wife of Allen in Jefferson City 1 Mar, dau/Mrs. Lynch of St. Charles, formerly of Fulton. — FULT 4 Oct 1861

BETZ, family of John F.: his wife Julia Ann 2 Sep ae 36, dau/Sallie Mary 9 Aug ae 3y 10m, son John Henry, no date, 18m. — FULT 16 Sep 1864

BEUMER, William Jesse, formerly of St. Catherine's, Canada West, 1 Mar ae 35. — MORE 3 Mar 1862

BEVAN, Catherine S. wife of A.C. 30 Mar in Oregon, Holt Co., of inflammation. Born Greenbrier Co. VA 22 Dec 1820, to MO 1840. Husband, 5 children. — HOLS 30 Jun 1865 / SJH 2 Jul 1865

BEVIER, ____ shot in Keytesville. (Brunswicker 18 Jun) — MORE 24 Jun 1864

BEYNON, David at his home in Charleston 24 Jan ae 59. Born in Wales, emigrated to London, was there 16 years; to US in 1846, Charleston 1848. A tailor, mayor of Charleston, left wife and several children. — CHAC 25 Jan 1861

BIBB, John Minor son/L.A. & Elizabeth near Glasgow 20 Aug of diphtheria. Born 20 Feb 1854. — MORE 6 Sep 1861

BIBB, Mrs. Sarah E. at hr home in Franklin Co. of rheumatic heart 20 (29?) Dec ae 62y 4m 29d. Left 2 sons, 2 little grandchildren. — MORE 30 Dec 1864

Mrs. Virginia A. wife of William R. of consumption 20 Oct at the home of Mrs. Sarah E. Bibb, Franklin Co., ae 22y 7m 6d. — MORE 29 Oct 1863

BICHNEL, Willie son/O.P., proprietor of a restaurant at the sw corner of Green & 4th, accidentally shot himself while hunting in Illinois. — MORE 6 Dec 1864

BIGELOW, Allene dau/James 22 Apr at Danville Female Academy. Of St. Charles Co., ae 16. — MORE 27 Apr 1865

BIGELOW, Emma Dickey eldest dau/Jotham & Julia. Lived 142 Chouteau. Interred Bellefontaine. — MORE 23 Jul 1865

BIGELOW, Moses, 21 Jul in 74th year. Born Lebanon Co. PA 6 Aug 1790, to St. Charles Co. MO 1820; married Prethany Bryan 1821. Farmer, husband, parent; left 5 children. PA pc — MORE 6 Aug 1864

BIGGAUNE, Mrs. Anna 8 Sep ae 61. Funeral from home of her son-in-law William H. Brophy, 419 Morgan. St. Bridget's Church. Interred Calvary. Chicago & Decatur pc — MORE 9 Sep 1865

BIGGERSTAFF, ___, small girl, in house fire at Plattsburg 24 Apr. — LIT 1 May 1863

BIGGERSTAFF, G.M. at Plattsburg 29 Nov in his 22nd year. — MORE 13 Dec 1865

BIGGS, Mrs. Ann Eliza wife of William K. of Pike Co. and dau/James Culbertson of Marion Co., 23 Jun. Born 12 Jan 1831, married 27 Apr 1847. Left husband, 6 children, many relatives. — LAJ 2 Jul 1864

BIGGS, James D., city recorder, 31 Aug ae 38. — CANP 4 Sep 1862

BIGGS, Jesse in Gratiot Prison of acute diarrhoea. Mbr 5th MO Cav, committed (BEGGS?) 5 Aug. (Undertaker's list later shows Corp. Jesse Beggs) — MORE 11 & 16 Aug 1863

BILBROUGH, Edward Stanley eldest and only surviving son of Seasome & Elizabeth, 27 Oct of dysentery ae 3y 5m 5d. — MORE 29 Oct 1861

BILLINGSLEA, Dr. Uriah H. in his 25th year after a short illness. Funeral from home of Lafayette Wilson, 100 S. 5th. Baltimore pc — MORE 21 Jul 1861

BILLON, Eulalie Lovely consort of Frederic L., ae 53y 6m. Resided at (134?) Chouteau. Annunciation Church. Interred Calvary. — MORE 5 Feb 1865

13

BINGHAM, John Sr. 27 Nov in his 73d year. Lived on Gravois Road.   MORE 28 Nov 1864
BINTZE, Julius at Pilot Knob 14 Jun ae 18. Funeral from the home of James H.   MORE 16 Jun 1861
       Lucas. Interred Calvary.
BIRD, Mrs. Ingabow wife of John of Bird's Point, Mississippi Co, 17 Apr. Born   CHAC 22 Apr 1864
      30 Nov 1807, dau/Col. Abram Byrd of Cape Girardeau; mother of 12 children,   MORE 2 May "
      5 deceased (other story says she left 7 sons, 2 daughters), most of whom
      live in the same vicinity.
BIRGE, Mrs. (wife of Dr. J.W.) Sunday at the home of A.E. Kroeger, nw corner   MORE 4 Feb 1864
      21st & Estelle. Interred in the east.
BIRKENBINE, Lucille dau/late John suddenly 10 Dec near Manchester ae ca 22.   MORE 12 Dec 1861
           Funeral from Dr. Anderson's Church, 8-Locust, to Bellefontaine.
BIRKS, Nancy A. wife of Thomas 1 Apr ae 29y 10m, of consumption. Int. Wesleyan.   MORE 2 Apr 1862
BISCHOFF, Henry, husband and father, 20 Aug ae 33 at Helena AR, where he was   MORE 24 Aug 1862
         Lieut. Col., 3rd Reg. MO Vols. "Afflicted widow Julia Bischoff."
BISER, Capt. William D. 25 Oct at the battle of Pine Bluffs AR, Adj. 3rd MO Cav   MORE 20 Feb 1864
      CSA, ae 32y 8m 22d. Eldest son/Dr. T. of Burkittsville, MD.
BISHOP, Emalina R. dau/Augustus & Eliza 29 Mar in her 7th year.   LIT 3 Apr 1863
BISSELL, A. M. 27 Feb at Everett House ae 31 (51?). Funeral from Central   MORE 28 Feb 1865
        Presbyterian Church. Hartford CT & Keokuk pc
BISSELL, Lewis son/Capt. Lewis & Mary J. in San Francisco 30 Nov of typhoid ae 22.   MORE 1 Jan 1862
BITTER, Christine, Chariton Co.; Final settlement by Henry F. Grotjan and   CECB 24 Jul 1862
       Henry Buckshard.
BITTICK, Marion in Gratiot Prison 3 Dec of pneumonia.   MORE 7 Dec 1862
BITTICK, William of St. Louis in Gratiot Prison.   MORE 29 Nov 1862
BIXLER, Morgan shot at Palmyra by Gen. Merrill in retaliation for the abduction   CAWN 1 Nov 1862
       and murder of an old man named Allmstedt during Porter's Raid into
       Palmyra. Bixler was from Lewis Co. (Palmyra Courier)
BLACK, C.J. (or J.C.) private in Preston's Command, captured in Stoddard Co.   MORE 1 &
      27 Jan of bronchitis. (Gratiot Prison & Undertaker's list)   3 Mar 1863
BLACK, Maj. John, a well-known citizen of central MO, at Boonville 9 Nov,   LIT 25 Nov 1864
      formerly of Boone Co.
BLACK, John, a shoemaker living in the alley between 2-3-Chestnut-Market, from   MORE 5 Aug 1861
      effects of the heat.
BLACKAMORE, George, a boy from St. Louis in government service, shot 17 Oct at   SJH 15 Nov 1863
           Lexington by Capt. Thomas Townsend of the Alone (mutinous behavior).
BLACKAMORE, William O. at his home 17 July ae 52y 4m. Had held various offices,   LAJ 1 Aug 1863
           was coroner of Pike Co. and sexton of the city.
BLACKFORD, Sarah in Randolph Co. 12 Sep ae 76.   MORE 18 Sep 1864
BLACKMORE, William 14 Mar ae 61. Resided 373 N. 11th. Madison IN & Warsaw KY pc   MORE 15 Mar 1865
BLACKWELL, James, an old citizen 15 May of smallpox, ca 48. Lived on the Savannah   SJH 23 May 1865
          Road 3½ mi NE of St. Joe, left widow and several children.
BLAINE, John L. of St. Louis at Cotton Gin TX on 26 May.   MORE 9 Sep 1865
BLAKE, John William late of England 16 July in his 30th year. Lived on 12th St.   MORE 19 Jul 1862
BLAKE, Louisa Mary dau/Henry in Randolph Co. 3 Aug of typhoid.   MORE 27 Aug 1864
BLAKELEY, Mrs. (no first name or husband), 15 Feb ae 58 at her husband's residence   MORE 16 Feb 1864
         on 164 N. 11th St. Philadelphia pc
BLADEUTOH, Wand, a Bohemian boy employed by a druggist, drowned ae 14.   MORE 31 Jul 1861
BLAISDELL, William 30 Jan of consumption in 31st year. Memphis & Napoleon pc   MORE 1 Feb 1861
BLANCHARD, Lucelle DeVilla dau/DeWitt & Sophia 5 Oct ae 2y 10m.   MORE 6 Oct 1861
BLANCHET, Dr. P.C. in Clinton 23 Sep of typhoid at the home of Prof. S. Mason.   CAWN 3 Oct 1863
         Citizen of Moniteau Co.
BLANDOWSKI, Capt. Constantine 25 May at Camp Jackson.   MORE 31 May 1861
BLANCA, Carlo who kept the Montgomery Hall Saloon on N. Levee, found dead in bed.   MORE 21 Apr 1862
       Lived above the saloon.
BLASSINGER, Joseph, recently ill, started work on the woodboat Faraway, was   MORE 15 Nov 1863
           feeble, was put ashore and died (of intemperance and exposure).
           Ae 36, wife and children on Chopteau Island, IL.

BLATTERMAN, Robert, ca 17, running to catch a horse car on 5th St., fell under it.   MORE 21 May 1862

BLEDSO, Lucy Ann dau/Richard & Susan 12 Sep ae 23.   COWS 17 Oct 1862

BLEDSOE, Mrs. Frances wife of Thomas C. in Lexington MO 1 Apr ae 51.   MORE 3 Apr 1864

BLEDSOE, Dr. Jesse S. at his home near Charleston 14 Aug ae 59. A Mason.   CHAC 22 Aug 1862
    Emigrated from KY in 1838. Lived on a farm 2 miles from town.   MORE 28 Aug "

BLENNERHASSETT, Alice 2nd dau/Theresa M. and the late Richard S., ae 24.   MORE 18 May 1865
    Interred Bellefontaine. New York City pc

BLENNERHASSETT, Edward 20 Apr in Mobile, Sr. 1st Lieut. in Barrett's Battery CSA,   MORE 2 Jun 1863

BLENNERHASSETT, Joseph Lewis 8 Dec in Lincoln Co. MO, ae 51; youngest son of   MORE 17 Dec 1862
    Herman and Margaret of Blennerhassett Island.   ae 25

BLESSING, David 10 May in Canton ae 61y 10m 22d.   CANP 12 May 1864

BLESSING, Margaret wife of Jacob near Canton 18 Jun ae 25y 9m.   CANP 13 Jul 1865

BLOCK, Beckie B., eldest dau/Hyman & Virginia, 18 Dec ae 4y 3m.   MORE 20 Dec 1862

BLOCK, Edward Bates 24 Jan in Troy at the home of his grandfather Francis Parker.   MORE 6 Feb 1863
    Son of Eleazar Block of St. Louis, in his 21st year; had attended Yale but
    left because of ill health. "Son, brother, friend."

    Eleazar 18 Mar of bilious diarrhoea ae 61. Resided 121 Olive. B'nai El.   MORE 19 Mar 1865

BLOCK, Fannie widow of L.F. on 30 Jan. Resided Market between 13th-14th.   MORE 31 Jan 1864

BLODGETT, John 21 Oct at Empire Prairie (MO) ae 70.   SJH 14 Nov 1865

BLOOD, Clarinda wife of Nathaniel 21 Mar at the home of Col. J.H. Blood ae 59.   MORE 22 Mar 1865
    Lowell & Worcester MA pc

BLOOD, Margaretta wife of Henry B. and dau/late William Harshaw. Funeral from   MORE 17 Nov 1863
    St. George's Church.

BLOW, Eliza Augusta Wahlendorf, wife of Taylor, Monday ae 34y 1d, after a   MORE 4 Feb 1862
    lingering illness. Dau/Charles Wahlendorf, granddaughter Joseph & Sarah
    Charless. Left several children. Funeral from St. John's Church.

    Elizabeth Rebecca 17 Oct of diphtheria at the home of her brother,   MORE 20 Oct 1862
    Taylor ae 56y 5m 10d.

BLOW, I. Labeaume son/Peter E. & Sallie N. at Richwoods, Washington Co. ae 12y 9m.   MORE 22 Jul 1863

BLOW, Sarah Charless only dau/William & Julia W. of scarlet fever 6 Oct ae 3y11m17d.
    Funeral and burial at their home on Stringtown Road, South St. Louis.   MORE 8 Oct 1862

    Willie son/William T. & Julia Webster 31 Oct ae 7y 8m 25d.   MORE 3 Nov 1862

BLUE, David, a guerilla, of wounds received at Ashley, Pike Co.; he of Ralls Co.   MORE 6 Sep 1862

BLUE, Mrs. Elizabeth of Audrain Co. "several weeks ago" in her 86th year. Born in   LIT 6 Mar 1863
    NC, "had seen Washington." (Paris Mercury)
    Came to MO from Montgomery Co. TN, to Audrain Co. 1831; born near   MORE 19 Jan 1863
    Fayetteville NC year after the Declaration of Independence; Old Style Presb.

BLUE, John, whose home was in Audrain Co., arrested in IL and killed while trying   CAWN 14 Jan 1865
    to escape. Member of Anderson's gang.

BLUME, Peter, a soldier, crushed between cars of the Iron Mountain RR 1 mile below   MORE 31 Jul 1861
    the Arsenal when the seat broke and he was thrown out. Widow, 3 children.

BLUME, William, living at Blue Ridge near Silver Spring, Cheltenham, killed when   MORE 18 Mar 1862
    he fell under a wagonload of hay.

BLUMEYER, Friedrecke wife of Conrad Jr. ae 22y 5m 17d. Lived 10th & Madison.   MORE 16 Aug 1865

BLUMINGBERG, Charles killed by the fall of a bank on 14th St. north of Pernod.   MORE 18 Mar 1865
    Married, 4 children. Two others killed, all from north St. Louis.

BLUMM, Jacob, former soldier, on the boat from Memphis; of debility, ae 27.   MORE 22 Sep 1863

BLUNDEN, James Sr., long a resident of St. Louis, in Philadelphia 10 Nov ae 70.   MORE 26 Nov 1865

BOARDMAN, Amanda, inquest: lived Broadway between N. Market & Madison, ae 48,   MORE 29 Aug 1863
    husband, daughters age 14y and 2½y. Congestion brain, intemperance.

BOARDMAN, Richard R. son/Carlos & Maria in Linnaeus 10 Jan.   MORE 27 Jan 1861

BOARMAN, E. Gertrude, youngest dau/late Ignatius and Mary of MO, formerly of   SLMD 4 Jan 1861
    Baltimore; in Baltimore 29 Dec 1860 in 29th year, ill 4 years.

BODE, John, a German ae 22, found beaten to death by unknown assailant.   MORE 24 May 1861

BODLEY, James, 26 Nov; born Bedford Co. VA 14 Feb 1760 to Maury Co. TN at about   MORE 6 Dec 1863
    ae 50, to MO 18?9. "Old Grandad Bodley with his hundred bee stands."
    (California News)   /lived in Miller Co. MO

BODSON, Charles, barkeeper at Barnum's Hotel Saloon, killed in the Camp Jackson affair.	MORE 15 May 1861
BOEKHOFF, Johanne Caroline wife of Rudolph. Lived 177 N. 5th.	MORE 4 Sep 1864
Miss Henrika on 7 Oct. Lived at 177 N. 5th.	MORE 8 Oct 1864
BOGGS, Martin, suicide; jumped from the Platte Valley. Unable to find work. Had a brother in St. Louis.	MORE 21 Feb 1861
BOGGS, Owen 6 Apr in Boone Co. of consumption, ae 31.	COWS 22 Apr 1864
BOGGS, Robert killed near Savannah in a Civil War problem.	CAWN 18 Jul 1863
BOGGS, Robert W. at his home in Howard Co. 20 Sep ae 65y 3m 10d. Native of VA, in Howard Co. 24 years. 10 children survive. Washington Co. MO & Cinc. pc	MORE 26 Sep 1862
BOGY, Martin, drowned; walked off the Platte Valley at St. Mary's Landing, ae 25. (BOGGY)(see BOGGS, Martin, above.) Brother in St. Louis. Returning from Cairo.	SLMD 21 Feb 1861
BOHANNON, Mrs. Cynthia mother of Dr. W.C. at Huntsville 26 Jan in her 65th year. Born in Madison Co. VA, to MO 1848.	MAG 4 Feb 1863
BOHANNAN, Lewis "of Laclede Co." at the Military Hospital 3 Dec ae ca 40.	MORE 5 Dec 1861
BOHANNON, Maggie wife of Dr. C.A. 12 Jul in (20th?) year. Resided 50 Pine St.	MORE 14 Jul 1865
BOLARD, Anthony, a tailor living in the alley between Carr-Wash-10th-11th, from effects of heat. Had been married only a week.	MORE 5 Aug 1861
BOLDUC, C.C. 2 Oct ae 28 in Ste. Genevieve. Merchant. "Exemplary character."	MORE 11 Oct 1862
BOLES, Mary S. at the home of her mother Mrs. Sarah Nichols 25 Jun ae 11y 7m 25d.	FULT 15 Jul 1864
BOLIN, John F. a guerilla hung at Cape Girardeau by soldiers and citizens.	MORE 6 Feb 1864
BOLLER, John H. murdered by bushwhackers on the way to town last week, ae ca 60 - a farmer and wine-grower.	BOOM 23 Jul 1864
BOLTON, Dr. William 17 Nov in Jefferson City of apoplexy in his 55th year. Husband, father. "A good man has gone."	MORE 25 Nov 1862
BOLY, Dan killed in Franklin Co., allegedly by his brother John on a spree. John was in jail. (Considerably testimony.)	MORE 3 Dec 1863
BOMPART, Aurore widow of Louis of St. Louis Co. 2 Feb in her 70th year. Funeral from home on Manchester Road to family burial ground.	MORE 4 Feb 1865
BOMPART, Emilie 20 Nov ae 63.	MORE 22 Nov 1862
BOMPART, Louis of bronchitis 28 Dec ae 36.	MORE 30 Dec 1861
BONDS, Creal A.: Chariton Co. Letters of administration to Thomas J. Grace 19 Jan.	CECB 29 Jan 1863
Hugh A. : " Letters of administration to Thomas Abrams 5 May.	" 24 Jul 1862
BONFILS, Eugene H. 2nd son/E.N. & H.B. in Troy 27 Jan ae 4 years.	LAJ 7 Feb 1861
BONGEASER, ___, small daughter of Philip, fell into a kettle of boiling syrup for preserves, fatally burned.	MORE 18 Sep 1863
BONNET, Mrs. Mary 8 Dec ae 37. Lived opposite the MORE office. Interred Calvary. Newport RI, New Orleans, & Charleston pc	MORE 8 Dec 1863
BOONE, Mary C. 18 Mar after a protracted illness, ae 66. Immaculate Conception Ch.	MORE 19 Mar 1862
BOONE, William Wade, resident of Boone Co. for 22 years, formerly of VA, 7 Apr of heart disease ae ca 76. Survived by wife.	COWS 12 Apr 1861
BOOTH, Charles D. oldest son/W.H. & M.E. at Perryville 10 Jan ae 3y 7m 15d.	PERU 15 Jan 1864
BOOTH, Clarissa J. wife of Rev. H.A. & dau/late Ire Barbee, 2 Feb ae (33?)y 9m.	MORE 4 Feb 1865
BOOTHE, Martha A. at the home of her mother in Central Twp. ae (15?)y 11m, on 1 Nov.	MORE 5 Nov 1864
BOOTHE, Mrs. William "a most excellent lady" a few days ago.	FULT 5 Aug 1864
BOOTS, Mrs. Deborah 5 Dec at an advanced age at the home of her son-in-law, William Boswell.	PALS 11 Dec 1863
BORLAND, ___, postmaster in Kansas City, killed in the Platte bridge disaster.	SLMD 10 Sep 1861
BORLAND, J.H. of Barry Co. in the Prison Hospital in Springfield.	MORE 10 Apr 1863
BOSBYSHELL, Charles H. 4 Mar of spotted fever ae 16y 8m 10d.	CAWN 14 Mar 1863
BOSBYSHELL, Mrs. Martha wife of William Sr. 9 Dec at the home of her son Wm. Jr. at 40 St. Charles. Philadelphia pc	MORE 10 & 15 Dec 1862
BOSING, Anna Catherine wife of Francis of Mississippi Co. 25 Jan (?).	CHAC 24 Jul 1863
BOSSERON, Theodore Louis 17 Aug ae 36. Resided 11th & Olive. Interred Calvary.	MORE 19 Aug 1861

BOSSERON, Theodore only son/late T.L. 7 Dec of congestion of the brain ae 15y 11m.   MORE 8 Dec 1864
    Funeral from home of his grandmother, Therese. Interred Calvary.

BOSWORTH, Ebenezer Cole Sr. 5 Aug ae 51y 7m. Lived at 13 S 8th. Baltimore &   MORE 6 &
    Mrs. E. C. 21 Sep in 37th year.   "   Hartford pc   7 Aug 1861
                                                                                           " 22 Sep 1862

BOTTOM, Col. John Monday at St. Joseph ae 68. Born Amelia Co. VA.   LIT 7 Jul 1863

BOTZ, John T. 7 Nov at Gratiot Prison of rubeola.   MORE 9 Nov 1862

BOUGHAN, Eddie 29 Aug at Osceola at the home of his late grandfather Wm. F. Carter,   MORE 13 Sep 1863
    ae 4y 6m. Youngest child/Col. R.S. of CSA & Maria Rosalie.

BOUILA, Elizabeth, inquest: old lady living at Belleview, 9 miles from the city,   MORE 21 Jul 1863
    found dead on Bellefontaine Rd. Verdict, debility.

BOURAW, Joseph 29 May ae 27.   MORE 30 May 1864

BOURK, Bridget wife of John. Lived Cherry between 2nd-3rd.   MORE 6 Oct 1865

BOURLAND, Dr. Reese in Lincoln Co. 9 miles west of Troy, by robbers, 28 Dec.   PALS 6 Jan 1865

BOURN, Clemenza wife of Reuben in Knox Co. 20 Sep of lung hemorrhage, in her 41st y.   PALS 27 Oct 1865

BOURN, Sarah A. wife of Dr. Richard in Mexico(MO) 7 Apr of neuralgia. Born in   MORE 27 Apr 1863
    Georgetown, KY, married there in 1850, to MO the same year. Ae 32y 5d.
    Presbyterian since 1857. Left a 3-year-old daughter.

BOURN, William at Ninevah in Adair Co. 4 May of pleurisy, ill 60 or 70 days.   CECB 11 May 1861
    Said he had a brother in Chariton Co. and family in Texas.

BOURNE, George A. formerly of New York City, 26 Feb.   SLMD 5 Mar 1861

BOURNE, Henry, a blacksmith near Hydesburg in Ralls Co., burned to death; slept in   LAJ 28 Nov 1863
    shop, neighbors saw smoke one morning, found body nearly consumed.
    Believed murdered for money -- some chemical added, fire set.

BOURNE, Robert, pressman on the *Tribune*, recently of Weston, suddenly of   SJH 29 Jan 1864
    diphtheria. Brother of the former publisher of the Platte City paper.

BOUVIER, Joseph Alphonse 2 Nov in his 55th year. Lived on Poplar St. opposite 15th.   MORE 3 Nov 1864

BOW, Margaret relict of Daniel 7 Mar of consumption in her 40th year. 24th-Walnut.   MORE 8 Mar 1861

BOWER, Ann Maria widow of Michael R. in Palmyra 18 May in her 62nd year.   HAM 1 Jun 1861

BOWER, Dr. G.M. at his home in Monroe Co.; formerly in congress.   PALS 23 Dec 1864
    James S., son/Dr. G.M. of Monroe Co., killed by soldiers in Saline Co.   LIT 14 Nov 1862

BOWERS   Lewis, in Merrick's Command, of Carroll Co., arrested 21 Sep, died   MORE 19 &
or BOWEN   of rubeola 17 Nov.   24 Nov 1862

BOWLES, Frances wife of Stephen D. and dau/Alex Judy 16 Feb in her 32d year.   LIT 1 Mar 1861
    A Baptist. Left 4 children.

BOWLING, Robert, a worthy citizen of northwest Randolph Co., suicide by hanging.   RANC 10 Jan 1861
    No known motive. Left wife and 3 children.

BOWMAN, Thomas J., tribute by Liberty Lodge IOOF.   LIT 21 Jul 1865

BOWYER, A.J., Linn Co. guerilla, executed in St. Joseph. Member of Holtzclaw's   SLMD 13 Sep 1864
    gang, Linn and Chariton counties.

BOWYER, Ferdinand, of Madison Co., 4 Dec of pleuritis. (Undertaker's list)   MORE 7 Dec 1862

BOX, William of Barry Co. in the prison hospital in Springfield.   MORE 10 Apr 1863

BOYCE, Mary R. dau/Capt S.H. and granddaughter of Dr. E.S. Fraser 17 Jan ae 7y 4m   MORE 18 Jan 1862
    of burns when her clothes caught fire.

BOYCE, Matthew R. yesterday in his 78th year. Lived on Christy near 23rd St.   MORE 26 Dec 1864
    Funeral from St. Bridget's Church. Interred Calvary.

BOYCE, Capt. Samuel R. of the *Gladiator* suddenly at his home 22 Dec of   MORE 23 &
    congestive chills, ae 40.   25 Dec 1863

BOYCE, Sarah 13 May of consumption ae 49. Lived at 139 Green St.   MORE 14 May 1862

BOYD, Isabel dau/Archibald and Ann, ae 14th. Lived 10th betw Labeaume & Webster.   MORE 28 Jun 1865

BOYD, Robert (I or L) 4 Feb ae ca 50. Lived at 9th & Sylvanie. Suddenly.   SJH 5 Feb 1865

BOYD, Robert William son/John K. & Elizabeth C. 24 Sep in Callaway Co ae 5y10m16d.   COWS 23 Oct 1863

BOYD, Ruth at the home of her son Thomas in St. Charles Co. 11 Sep ae 81y 10m 4d.   MORE 16 Sep 1864
                                                  Louisville pc

BOYDSTON, Samuel, a rebel sympathizer, killed near Union Mills, Platte Co.   LEXUN 21 Jan 1865
    (SJH 10 Jan 1865 calls him "a bitter rebel")

BOYLE, James shot by John Pardee after a political argument died 4 Jul ae 60.   MORE 6 Jul 1862
    A stonemason, survived by wife and children.

BOYLE, Joseph 23 Jun of consumption ae 19. Funeral from the home of his uncle,   MORE 24 Jun 1861
    John Hagen, 195 Broadway. Nashville pc

BOZARTH, John, of Schuyler Co., in Greene's Command, arrested 15 Aug, died of   MORE 17 &
    pneumonia 15 Nov.   24 Nov 1862

BOZARTH, Luther, of Sturgeon, recently in the rebel army, killed trying to escape   COWS 31 Jul 1863
    from prison in Camden Co. 8 Jul. Had been a Captain in Poindexter's
    Command. John G. Hackley also killed.

BRACKENRIDGE, Eve widow of James at the home of her daughter, Mrs. M. Boswell,   MORE 1 Nov 1861
    in St. Louis Co. 31 Oct in her 81st year. Funeral, Fee Fee Church.

BRADERMEES, Jacob, a German gardener, shot by soldiers at his place near the   MORE 16 &
    junction of Grand Ave. and the Pacific RR. He had guns to kill birds,   17 Jul 1864
    but the soldiers thought he was after them. (In the later version it
    was stated that some soldiers had been stealing fruit.) He was about
    35, no children, his wife had died two weeks previously.

BRADFORD, Sgt. ___ of Capt. Davis' Co. 81st EMM found shot to death in DeKalb Co.   MORE 26 May 1864

BRADFORD, Barkley M. only son/Barkley M. & Charlotte, late of Chariton Co., in   MORE 21 Apr 1865
    St. Louis 16 Apr ae 15. Brunswick MO & Nashville pc

BRADFORD, Maj. Charles, late of Portland (ME?) 17 Oct of chronic diarrhoea   MORE 19 Oct 1863
    ae 54. Lived at 110 S. 5th. Boston & Portland pc

BRADFORD, Eliza M. wife of Robert 11 Oct in her 25th year. Married last winter.   CAWN 17 Oct 1863
    (COWS says "of Moniteau Co.)

BRADFORD, George K. only son/George A. at Vicksburg of typhoid pneumonia 26 Dec   MORE 26 Jan 1864
    ae 23y 1m 29d. Born in Belleville, IL, grandson of ex-gov. William
    Kinney of IL; had gone to Vicksburg on business.

BRADFORD, William A. son of the late Thomas H., formerly of Scott Co. KY, in   COWS 13 Feb 1863
    Rocheport 6 Feb ae 26.

BRADLEY, Cornelia Childs dau/Joshua & Sarah of whooping cough, ae 1y 1m 7d.   MORE 5 Jun 1861
    Pittsburgh, New York & IL pc

BRADLEY, Mrs. Elizabeth near Gooch's Mill, Cooper Co., of cancer, ae ca 70.   COWS 15 Mar 1861

BRADLEY, Carrie W. eldest dau/Loring and Eliza, ae 14. Funeral from the   MORE 16 Apr 1861
    Methodist Church at 16th & Walnut.

BRADLEY, Mrs. Hannah Friday last "many years a resident."   PALS 31 Mar 1865

BRADLEY, Terry in Huntsville 17 Apr on his 77th birthday, of "old age and   MAG 23 &
    infirmities." Had been confined to his room for several years past.   30 Apr 1862
    Former county judge, circuit & county court clerk, JP, etc.

BRADY, William J. of Dublin 25 Jan in his 55th year after a long illness.   MORE 29 Jan 1862
    New York & Brooklyn pc

BRADLEY, Mrs. William P. drowned in the launching of the gunboat Chickashaw   MORE 11 &
    near Carondelet when several people became entangled and were pulled   12 Feb 1864
    into the river. Owners not at fault, as seats had been provided but
    people didn't stay in them. Others were rescued. Body not found.

BRADY, Catherine wife of Bryan 13 Aug ae 38. Lived 7th & Carr. Boston pc   MORE 14 Aug 1864

BRADY, James, only son/Mary, 9 Sep ae 16.   MORE 13 Sep 1864

BRADY, John 23 Nov ae 33. Lived on St. Charles Plank Road, south of Benton Barracks.   MORE 26 Nov 1864

BRADY, William 15 Feb in Galway, Ireland father of T.W., architect, of St. Louis,   MORE 9 Mar 1864
    in his 72d year. Interred Augustinian Cemetery, Fort Hill. (He was also
    an architect.)

BRADY, Virginia Hansbrough 2nd dau/Horace D. & Susan H., 4 May ae 11y 1m.   MORE 5 May 1865
    Lived at 174 Pine.

BRAGG, Talbot Jr. at Rock Point Station, Idaho Territory, 28 Nov in his 31st year.   MORE 8 Jan 1864
    Left his home in Troy, Lincoln Co., 11 Nov with his brother, on business;
    destination, Kenyon City. Became ill from the excessive cold. Left
    parents, wife, and 3 children.

BRAHAM, William of lung fever 8 Sep ae 46. Lived at 47 S 4th. Buffalo NY pc   MORE 9 Sep 1862

BRAHE, Eliza wife of Augustus H. of New York and dau/Jacob D. Kurlbaum of St. Louis   MORE 17 &
    in Mannheim, Germany 23 Dec ae 38.   18 Jan 1862

BRAMLEY, John, inquest: arrived Saturday from Chicago, ae 35, English. Debility.   MORE 14 Jul 1863

BRANDEN, wife of Michael, killed in Bowling Green by her husband -- he kicked her in the abdomen.	LAJ 18 Jul 1861
BRANDENBURG, Girard at Fenton ae 66. Funeral from the home of J. Brandenburg, Thomas St. between Eliot & Pratte.	MORE 3 Mar 1863
BRANDENBURG, Horace at Memphis 15 Aug ae 28. Funeral from the home of his brother John, O'Fallon & 19th St.	SLMD 31 Aug 1864
BRANDON, Libbie, shot (supposedly by Jack Smith) in a saloon on Broadway.	MORE 24 Feb 1863
BRANHAM, Charles P., 4th MO Cav, in Gratiot Prison hospital.	MORE 25 Mar 1864
BRANNAN, John 20 Apr at the home of his mother, 9th between Jefferson & Morse, ae 23y 10m 20d. Native of Atheroy, Co. Galway. Interred Calvary.	MORE 21 Apr 1865
BRANNOCK, Michael stabbed by his father; Michael had choked his mother for not having dinner ready, his father interfered, Michael hit him with a chair, his father then stabbed him. They lived near the 3-Mile House on St. Charles Rock Road, in Murphy's Addition. Michael was 28, single.	MORE 24 Jul 1861
BRASHEARS, ___ a discharged soldier from Linn Co. shot and killed at the house of Robert Brashears in Howard Co. "Sunday week."	SJH 17 Jul 1864
BRASHEARS, Levi L. 18 Mar ae 46.	FULT 12 Apr 1861
BRASHEARS, Sidney dau/Morse & Mary Jane, 27 Sep of brain disease ae 3y 3m.	MORE 1 Oct 1861
BRATTON, James M. in Warrensburg 1 Jan.	MORE 17 Jan 1861
BRAWNER, Mrs. Mary in Florissant 10 Feb in her (84th?) year.	MORE 18 Feb 1863
BRAY, Green a member of Capt. Eddlemond's Co. of state militia accidentally shot himself through the head Tuesday, 10 miles beyond Dallas. Resident of this county, "well thought of." Left wife and child.	PERU 13 Sep 1862
BREBAUGH, Simeon 10 Apr ae 36, had been ill 14 days. Lived Collins near Biddle.	MORE 11 Apr 1863
BRECKENRIDGE, George, a wealthy farmer 10 miles north of Savannah, on the Maryeville Road, by unknowns; was a rebel sympathizer.	SJH 7 Jul 1863
BRECKENRIDGE, John, killed in Andrew Co. by John Hart's guerillas.	CAWN 18 Jul 1863
BRECKENRIDGE, Margaret E. dau/late Rev. John of KY and sister of Judge S. M. of St. Louis, at Niagara Falls 27 July at the home of a relative, Miss E. L. Porter.	MORE 2 Aug 1864
BREE, Simon, possibly poisoned by his wife. She was German, ae ca 28, they had been married 9 years, had four children -- 2 boys now living. Resided corner 18th & Davis. His wife's name was Sophia Augusta. Considerable arsenic was found in Simon's body.	MORE 19 Sep & 4 Oct 1865
BREEDEN, Talma, late of KY, in Lexington Thursday.	MORE 27 Jan 1861
BREEN, Mrs. Mary 15 Aug ae 55, native of Tipperary. New York & Boston pc	MORE 21 Aug 1864
BRELL, Sebastian, alias of John Preller -- see Maria Ann Preller.	SLMD 1-3 Jan '61
BREMER, Andrew, a schoolboy, drowned in a pond near the Clay School ae 11y 6m. Parents live on Broadway near the Rolling Mill. He was playing on the ice.	MORE 15 Feb 1865
BREMING, Philomena Catherine, only child/Louis & Catherine, 5 Jun of scarlet fever ae 8y 2m 21d. Interred Calvary.	MORE 6 Jun 1864
BREMNER, George in Salem, Dent Co., 24 Dec 1861 ae 27. Resident of St. Louis.	MORE 7 May 1862
BRENELLA, Lewis, ca 14, accidentally shot while hunting; had gone out from his brother's house on St. Charles Rock Road, his parents lived on 7th between Myrtle & Spruce. Inquest gives name as Piernell, Louis, says his brother-in-law's house in Cheltenham.	MORE 1 Sep 1865
BRENGER, Adolph, inquest: found dead in his room at 243 S. 2nd, of epilepsy and intemperance. Recently discharged from county farm.	MORE 12 Oct 1862
BRENNAN, Cecelia 9 Jun ae 79. Funeral from home of her son-in-law, Charles H. Harrison, 7th betw O'Fallon-Cass. St. Patrick's Church, int. Calvary.	MORE 10 Sep 1864
BRENNAN, Hugh son/Hugh & Margaret Waters ae (4?) of convulsions, 22 March. Interred Calvary.	MORE 23 Mar 1861
BRENNAN, John murdered in Jefferson Co. John Carrigan charged, entered plea of insanity confirmed by jail officials.	MORE 27 Jan 1863
BRENNAN, John a young man shot by H.A. Pryor, clerk at the Fourth Street House, who claimed self-defense. Brennan was head-waiter. Single, ae 27.	MORE 5 & 6 Jul 1864
BRENNAN, John 14 Jul ae 63. Funeral from home of his son-in-law ___ O'Connor, 19th between O'Fallon & Biddle, to St. Bridget's Church.	MORE 16 Jul 1865

BRENNAN, Patrick, 27 Aug ae 28. Lived corner Division & 22nd, betw O'Fallon-Biddle. MORE 28 Aug 1862

BRENNARD, Isaac, accidentally shot himself; drunk and riding with his brother Henry, firing a revolver into the air. SJH 1 Mar 1865

BRESSIE, E.F., late of Dent Co., suit by Martha Rosette, a minor and legatee of the estate, vs various debtors. ROLEX 31 Jul 1865

BRESSLER, Anton a highly esteemed young German suddenly last night of brain congestion. President of St. Louis Saengerbund. MORE 21 Jan 1865

BREVARD, Robert M. captured in Stoddard Co. 27 Jan, of Fielding's Regiment, in Gratiot Prison of pneumonia. MORE 15 Feb 1863

BREVATOR, William son/John & Catherine, ae 3y 10m. Lived at Walnut & Summit. Funeral St. Malachy's Church, interred Calvary. MORE 19 Dec 1863

BREWER, F.M., a prisoner, 27 Jan of typhoid. (Undertaker's list) MORE 2 Feb 1863

BREWER, Felix accidentally killed Saturday morning cutting down a tree, which struck and broke a limb on another tree, which fell and killed him. "Good and honest citizen." Left wife, several children. PERU 24 Feb 1865
MORE 15 Mar "

BREWER, George son/Col. E.M. & Mary, 12 Nov ae 19y 10m 5d. PERU 21 Nov 1864

BREWER, Mary Ellen dau/R.M. & Mary in Perry Co. 18 Mar ae 10y 10m 22d. PERU 25 Mar 1864

BREWER, Raphael, formerly of Franklin's Band, Lewis Co., in Gratiot Prison 12 Nov. MORE 13 Nov 1862

BRICKEY, John at the home of his son-in-law, William S. Howe, in Jefferson Co., 8 July. Born in Botetourt Co. VA 3 June 1782 (of Huguenot descent); to Tennessee as an infant; married Lydia Smith, who was related to Gov. Woolcot of Massachusetts; moved to Potosi in 1812. Was court clerk, judge, etc. (had studied law); a Methodist 40 years; left a large family. He had his tombstone all finished except the date, had written its inscription. Interred Potosi. MORE 9 &
19 Jul 1864

BRICKS, Mrs. Margaret, inquest: fell and hit her head on a stone. (see BROOKS) SLMD 14 Jan 1861

BRIDGEMAN, John shot in Jefferson Co. by James Edmonds (both apparently MORE 27 Aug 1862
BRIDGMAN   bushwhackers). Edmonds brought to St. Louis.
(John was of Tallow Hill, was killed 21 Aug. Edmonds was hanged 3 Mar.) MORE 6 Mar 1863

BRIGGS, David in Carondelet 8 Feb in his 69th year. MORE 9 Feb 1861

BRIGHT, Joseph and Mary, both after short illnesses, at their home in Clay Co. Married in KY 11 Jan 1831 -- she was Mary Caldwell McCoun, ae 19, and he was 27. Joined Presbyterian Church in New Providence KY. He died 10 June (in his 60th year) she 18 June (in 53d year). Left 4 children. LIT 24 Jun 1864

BRIGHT, Mary Ella dau/William F. & Virginia, both deceased, at the home of her grandmother Mrs. Evalina Thompson 7 Jul ae 8y 8m 7d. LIT 11 Jul 1862

BRINKWITH, Harry ae 10 killed when he was run over by a circus wagon; he jumped on the tongue of the wagon, fell off. Accident on Carr betw 7-8. MORE 7 Aug 1864

BRIODY, Lawrence, in St. Louis of typhus contracted in Vicksburg. Native of Maynooth, Ireland. St. Xavier's Church, int. Calvary. Dublin pc MORE 24 Aug 1863

BRISCOE, Louisa dau/Dr. Warren & Jane H. in Warrenton 13 Feb in her 19th year. Formerly of Jefferson Co. VA. MORE 22 Feb 1863

BRISCOE, Winifred S. widow of R.D. of Ralls Co. at Hannibal 23 Mar. Born in Baltimore Co. MD, to MO from KY in 1827. Catholic. MORE 7 Apr 1864

BRIT, Mrs. __ "aged and respectable" citizen of Bowling Green, suddenly Sunday. (Louisiana Herald) HAM 27 Jan 1861

BRITTON, James son/James H. & Almira T. of typhoid remittant fever (?) 28 Jul ae 7y 6m. Interred Troy, Lincoln Co. MORE 29 Jul 1863

BRITTON, Mary consort of John near Troy 18 Jan in her 74th year. MORE 27 Jan 1861

BROADHEAD, Johnny son/James O. 5 May ae 6. Lived on Pine near 14th. MORE 7 May 1863

BROADHURST, Judge John F. of Platte Co., judge of circuit court "for some years." LIT 28 Nov 1862

BROCK, Dr. David S. in St. Louis 18 Aug, late of Uniontown KY, many years a resident of Independence MO. Memphis & Independence pc MORE 26 Aug 1862

BROCKHAGE, Mary Ann Halls 14 Oct after a long illness ae 31. Lived at 205 Morgan. Funeral from Christ Church. MORE 15 &
16 Oct 1864

BROCKMAN, Gustav, killed by explosion of a cannon. Lived at 10th & Maxson. MORE 17 Feb 1861

BROCKMEYER, Elizabeth wife of Henry C. 27 Oct ae 24y 8d, of congestive chills. Lived on Natural Bridge, one block from the junction of Salisbury St. & Natural Bridge Plank Road. MORE 29 Oct 1863

BROHAMMER, Joseph F. 12 Mar ae 76y 6m. Lived at 239 S. 3rd.   MORE 13 Mar 1864

BROKAW, Marian H. wife of Dr. F.V.L. 29 Jun in her 26th year. Lived 244 Chestnut.   MORE 30 Jun 1865

BRONSON, Henry, a soldier, shot at Widow Vernon's in Long Prairie.   CHAC 19 Feb 1864

BROOKS, ___ an engineer killed in an explosion on the railroad 4 miles from Illinoistown. Left wife & 4 children, Brooklyn betw 11-12, St. Louis.   MORE 30 Sep 1862

BROOKS, El___, citizen of Iron Mountain, of pneumonia 17 Jan. (Undertaker's list)   MORE 22 Jan 1865

BROOKS, Ellen found dead in the cellar of her house, had fallen there while intoxicated. (Davis between 23-24). Married, ae 22.   MORE 31 Aug 1864

BROOKS, Frederick W. son/Edward & Virginia C. 15 Jun ae 7y 6m. Lived at 212 Pine.   MORE 16 Jun 1861

BROOKS, Henry, citizen of Chariton Co.; measles, 20 Dec. (Undertaker's list)   MORE 28 Dec 1864

BROOKS, Mrs. Isabella Graham wife of Thomas at her home near Rock Spring, St. Louis Co., in her 40th year. Long illness. Newark pc   MORE 22 Jul 1865

BROOKS, Joseph at his home near Manchester 1 Jan ae 63. Baltimore & Hagerstown pc   MORE 11 Jan 1865

BROOKS, Mrs. Margaret, fell and struck her head on the curb. Lived Centre nr Clark.   MORE 13 Jan 1861

BROOKS, Mary mother of Mrs. J. Fogg of St. Louis, in Rome NY of typhoid pneumonia 8 Sep ae 69.   MORE 3 Oct 1864
     Sperry brother of Mrs. J. Fogg of St. Louis 29 Oct in NY in the St. John disaster.   MORE 13 Nov 1865

BROOKS, Theophilus in the flux epidemic.   FULT 2 Sep 1864

BROOKS, Thomas E.; Chariton Co. Letters of administration to Albert Brooks 4 Aug.   CECB 11 Sep 1862

BROOMFIELD, William W., merchant, 23 Oct ae 49. Funeral from Boatmen's Church. Interred Bellefontaine. (SLMD says Wm. H. , Commercial St.)   MORE 24 Oct 1861

BROOMFIELD, Woodson of Boone Co. recently in military prison in Alton.   COWS 12 Dec 1862

BROSIUS, Johnathan and his family. He -- of Sheets and Brosius -- was shot and killed 21 Dec by P.B. Hunter over an extra charge his firm would not pay for hauling. (Hunter was a teamster). GAL of 1 Dec lists Emma, born 31 Aug 1858, died 4 Oct 1864; Cora died 14 Oct ae 11m 17d; Amanda born 14 Jul 1839 died 16 Nov 1864 "little ones and their mother, neither wife nor child left;" and on 6 Jan gives their names, identifies Johnathan as husband and father.   GAL 22 Dec 1864

BROTHERTON, John Franklin of Carroll Co. son/H.R. & S., 17 Apr ae 21y 3m 9d.   MORE 2 Jun 1864

BROTHERTON, Margaret wife of John 2 Oct ae 36. Lived at 263 Olive. Interred Bellefontaine.   MORE 4 Oct 1863

BROTHERTON, Marshall son/Marshall & Sarah E., 10 Jul ae 16y 21d. Lived on the sw corner of Olive & 13th. Interred Bellefontaine.   MORE 11 Jul 1865

BROWDER, Charles P. son/Joseph A. & Elizabeth 26 Jan ae 2y 1m 15d. Lived on Eugenia west of High. Louisville pc   MORE 28 Jan 1861

BROWN, Mrs. Abigail 12 Feb ae 78. Funeral from the home of her daughter, Mrs. William McDowell, 5th between Cerre & Gratiot.   MORE 14 Feb 1863

BROWN, Anne wife of Jonas ae 23. Lived corner of Adam & Emily.   MORE 17 Apr 1864

BROWN, Annie J. dau/William H. in Ralls Co. ae 9y 22d, after a 6-week illness caused by a fall. Louisville pc.   MORE 24 Apr 1863

BROWN, Bessie Morrison youngest dau/Thomas B. & Bell in High Hill, Montgomery Co. 3 Oct ae 2y 3m. Funeral from home of Alex Leitch, 185 Pine.   MORE 5 Oct 1861

BROWN, C.C. 30 Mar at San Francisco, of Perry Co. MO.   MORE 7 Apr 1865

BROWN, Catherine, inquest: lived 17th between Cass & Columbia. "Over 60." Old age and debility.   MORE 21 Sep 1863

BROWN(E), Maj. Charles F., killed at the battle of Champion Hills, body returned to St. Louis, interred Bellefontaine. Co B, 26th MO.   MORE 6 & 8 Nov 1863

BROWN, D. Perry of Boone Co. at Moore's Mill.   MORE 11 Aug 1862

BROWN, Edward, a bushwhacker, killed south of Springfield.   MORE 31 Jan 1865

BROWN, Dr. Edwin Wallace, oculist & physician, of typhoid 19 Dec. Native of Oneida Co. NY, born 25 May 1816, to MO 1845. Methodist. Left wife and 4 children. Interred in Platte City.   SJH 20 Dec 1863

BROWN, George, inquest: mate on a steamboat, shot 15 Oct in some encounter between police and a group of men; apparently shot by a policeman, but which one not known and the account is not very clear.   MORE 3 Nov 1865

BROWN, Hiram in Cedar Twp, Boone Co. 31 Jul ae 70, a resident of the county 40 years. Son of Phebe Dennison who died in April ae 100.   COWS 25 Aug 1865

BROWN, Dr. J.J. of consumption ae 34y 10m, resident of the county nearly 8 years. Left wife, "orphans."   MAG 27 Aug 1863

BROWN, J. W., 2nd engineer of the Cornelia, shot yesterday by unknown. (May not have died --story says fatal, then implies not dead yet.) Married, had family, lived in the alley behind the jail, between 5th & 6th streets.   MORE 18 Oct 1865

BROWN, James son/Maj. James 14 Feb of typhoid ae ca 16.   COWS 20 Feb 1863

    Major James near Columbia 16 Oct ae ca 58.   COWS 20 Oct 1865

BROWN, Jane A. 7 Mar at the home of her mother-in-law in Perryville, ae (22?)   PERU 17 Mar 1865

BROWN, John, inquest: found dead in basement, Biddle between 7-8. Intemperance and lack of nourishment.   MORE 7 Feb 1865

BROWN, John of this county, a notorious bushwhacker, recently of fever on the Red River.   COWS 3 Jun 1864

BROWN, Laura Virginia consort of Joseph A. and dau/late E.L. Leonard, 4 miles east of St. Joseph, 7 Aug ae 18.   SJH 15 Aug 1865

BROWN, Lydia Ann wife of John G. in Canton 26 Nov ae 38y 6m 19d.   CANP 8 Dec 1864

BROWN, Dr. M.F. "old and esteemed" citizen of the firm of J.B. Brown & Co., of Hannibal, druggists, of consumption.   HAM 13 Jun 1861

BROWN, Margaret consort of James H. in Georgetown MO 27 May in her 28th year.   MORE 31 May 1863

BROWN, Mary, an unmarried school teacher, predicted that she was going to die, and did. Inquest verdict, congestion of the bowels.   MORE 2 Sep 1865

BROWN, Mary wife of Joseph in Boone Co. 11 Apr of typhoid, ca 57.   COWS 19 Apr 1861

BROWN, Mrs. Mary relict of Francis 8 Aug of cancer of the stomach, ae ca 75.   HAM 15 Aug 1861

BROWN, Dr. N.H. of consumption in Cole Camp 10 Mar in his 40th year. Born in western NY, moved to Rock River IL 5 years ago, to Cole Camp last fall. Husband, father, Mason.   CAWN 30 Mar 1861

BROWN, Mrs. N.M. wife of Rev H. of the MO Annual Conference, M.E. South, in Mexico MO 22 Jan. Louisville & Lexington KY pc   MORE 4 Feb 1863
    COWS 6 "

BROWN, Peter, a free negro, murdered in northern Callaway Co. (FULT)   MORE 9 Aug 1864

BROWN, Polk of Shafer's Regiment captured with Reeves gang in Ripley Co. 25 Dec, of inflammation of the lungs in the prison hospital.   MORE 9 Jan 1864

BROWN, Sallie A. dau/John N. & Nancy in Monroe Co. 19 Jul ae 19y 8m.   COWS 31 Jul 1863

BROWN, Dr. Samuel in Canton Twp 17 Jan ae 64.   CANP 21 Jan 1864

BROWN, T.S. of Porters Division, captured in Boone Co. 1 Nov 1862, of typhoid in Gratiot Prison 6 Dec. (Undertaker's list says 7 Dec.)   MORE 10 Dec 1862
    " 15 "

BROWN, Thomas A., taken at Pea Ridge, son/Robert of Cass Co., in Alton Prison in his 20th year. Interred family burying ground.   MORE 26 May 1862

BROWN, Thompson, cripple: inquest. Found dead in bed. Worked on the levee. Verdict congestion of the brain.   MORE 9 Oct 1863

BROWN, Miss Virginia K. dau/Judge 29 Jul ae 22.   HAM 29 Aug 1861

BROWN, William 9 Dec of lung congestion ae 29. Central Presbyterian Church to Bellefontaine.   MORE 10 Dec 1865

BROWNE, Mrs. Mary B. at the home of her son Brig. Gen. Thomas J. Barthalow in Glasgow, Howard Co. 25 March. Born in Howard Co. MD, nee Hood; married Singleton N. Barthalow in 1825, widowed after 11 years and 4 children. Eight years later married Mr. Browne, who died in 1856. She cared for his 3 children; had 3 children near Glasgow; was a Methodist.   MORE 8 Oct 1863

BROWNING, Mrs. Maria in Howard Co. 23 Sep ae 25.   COWS 20 Oct 1865

BROWNLEE, John A. 10 Oct in his 43rd year. Lived at 8th & Pine. A Mason. Funeral from St. George's Church.   MORE 11 &
    14 Oct 1861

BROYLES, Aylette F. in Callaway Co. of consumption in 49th year. Born in Madison Co. KY St. Louis & Richmond VA pc   COWS 6 May 1864

BRUCE, Mrs. Sarah of Renick, Randolph Co. 15 Aug ae 72. Left husband and 3 children. Member of the Christian Church.   MAG 3 Sep 1863
    COWS 28 Aug "

BRUDER, John Jr. son/John, ae 13½, drowned Tuesday in a pond near their home, south side of Benton between 13-14. He was trying to help a fellow skater named Bruckner, who survived.   MORE 29 Dec 1864

BRUNER, Isaac 23 Feb ae 24. Lived at 160 N. 4th St.   MORE 24 Feb 1863

BRUTON, Susan widow of James of Boone Co. 26 Apr ae <u>ca</u> 60.   COWS 1 May 1863

BRYAN, Mrs. Elizabeth 4 Mar at her home in Tennessee Settlement, Ste. Genevieve Co.   COWS 4 Apr 1862
         ae 86.

BRYAN, Ezekiel, well-known citizen of Monroe Co., last week.   PALS 15 Jan 1864

BRYAN, J.S. of Porter's Reg., captured Monroe Co. 22 Nov, of pneumonia Sunday.   MORE 16 &
      (Undertaker's list says died 14 Dec.) See James S. BRYANT /in Miss. St. prison   21 Dec 1862

BRYAN, G.G. of Porter's Reg., captured in Monroe Co. 23 Oct, in Gratiot Prison   MORE 16 Dec 1862
      14 Dec of phthisis.

BRYAN, Samuel of Clark Co. - Wm. Cregar on trial for his murder.   MORE 6 Sep 1865
         also see Samuel BRYANT

BRYAN, William S., a well-known cattle dealer in St. Louis, recently at Sharpe   MORE 6 May 1865
      Landing on the Illinois River; while tying cattle on the <u>City of Pekin</u>
      his foot slipped and he fell overboard.

BRYANT, E.L. at his home in Pike Co. near Ashley 28 Sep ae <u>ca</u> 70, a resident of   LAJ 7 Oct 1865
      the county for more than 40 years.

BRYANT, Eliza wife of David and dau/Judge W.S. Howe 30 Mar near Herculaneum   MORE 4 Apr 1862
         in her 27th year.

BRYANT, James S. of Porter's Band, captured in Monroe Co. 28 Oct, died in   MORE 10 Mar 1863
      Gratiot Prison 14 Dec. (Says not previously reported)

BRYANT, N.J. wife of Thomas in Charleston 12 Jan.   CHAC 18 Jan 1861

BRYANT, Mrs. Sally in Wellington 20 Jan ae 80. Born Loudoun Co. VA, first to KY,   LEXUN 28 Jan 1865
      then to MO where she had lived 25 years.

BRYANT, Samuel - Columbus Shannon being tried by court martial for his murder   MORE 24 Aug 1865
      in Clark Co. 7 Nov 1864.

BRYANT, Maj. Thomas S. of St. Louis in Lexington MO 14 Feb, formerly in the US Army   MORE 19 Feb 1865
      and late Marshal of MO. Philadelphia and Washington pc

BRYSON, William at his home 6 miles from Louisiana on the road to Frankford,   LAJ 7 May &
      5 May of smallpox in his 63rd year, "a good man." Born York District SC   4 Jun 1864
      Dec 1801; his father died 1820, helped care for mother and large family.
      Joined OS Presbyterian Church in 1844, was elder in Grassy Creek which
      his children also joined.

BRYSON, Zadoc "a notorious character," a prisoner being taken to St. Louis by   COWS 29 May 1863
      train, jumped off at Mexico, was shot. Interred at Warrenton.

BUCHANAN, Christian, who with his wife kept a millinery establishment on the nw   MORE 2 Dec 1861
      corner of 5th & Green, became annoyed with some of the shop girls,
      died of a ruptured heart from a violent fit of anger. German, <u>ca</u> 48.

BUCHANAN, Edward son/Robert at the home of his brother H.C. Sunday of consumption   HAM 18 Jun 1861
         ae <u>ca</u> 27. Congregational Church to Methodist Cemetery.

BUCHANAN, John M. son/late George M. at Carondelet of lung congestion 27 Feb   MORE 2 Mar 1865
      in his 38th year. Hannibal & LaGrange MO pc

BUCHANAN, Nancy wife of John 15 Jun ae 32. Lived at 235 Carr. Buffalo &   MORE 16 Jun 1862
                               Newburg pc

BUCK, Isabella wife of John and eldest dau/John McMinn in Maries Co. 29 Dec   ROLEX 10 Jan 1863
      ae 30. (also see Jane WALKER)

BUCKHANNON, George ae 40. Lived at 520 9th St.   MORE 23 Jul 1862

BUCKLEY, Thomas an old and well-known river engineer, 11 Feb in his 39th year.   MORE 3 Mar 1863

BUCKMAN, William Sr. 30 Sep in his 53rd year after a short, painful illness.   MORE 3 Oct 1864
      Bucks Co PA & Wilmington DE pc

BUCKNER, Dr. E.E. at the home of Capt. James Thomson in Sedalia 11 Jan in 74th y.   COWS 27 Jan 1865

BUESEMEYER, Capt. Henry, a policeman, found in a cellar at Fritz & Wainwright's   MORE 21 Nov 1863
        Brewery - had fallen through the hatchway and broke his neck. Lived
        at the corner of 4th & Poplar, was about 55, left wife and large
        family in indigent circumstances. Was formerly captain of the <u>Clermont</u>,
        later an extensive wood merchant; joined the police force 1 Jul 1861.

BUFFINGTON, Lieut. ___ of Carroll Co. at the Battle of Springfield, a Confederate.   LIT 6 Feb 1863

BULL, Dr. John in Chariton Co. 4 Nov ae <u>ca</u> 70. Many years a Methodist preacher;   PALS 20 Nov 1863
      was in congress at one time; ran for governor but was defeated.

BULLENSKI, Christine drowned in a quarry pond at Chippewa near Grand; she had been   MORE 27 Jun 1862
    forbidden to bathe there. "A beautiful girl," only child, ae 14.
BULLOCK, Capt. John W., formerly of St. Louis, near Dumfries VA. 5th VA Cav CSA.   MORE 26 Jan 1863
BULLOCK, Melvina Garland only c/Louis E. & Laura 14 Aug ae 20m 28d. Nashville pc   MORE 17 Aug 1861
    Laura Strong consort of L.E. ae 24. Lived at Gamble & Naomi. Nashville pc   MORE 10 Feb 1864
BULLOCK, Mrs. Maria L., sister of the late Judge Todd & Samuel B. Todd of Columbia,   COWS 22 Nov 1861
    in Lexington KY 1 Oct ae 73.
BULLOCK, Samuel B. of St. Louis 20 Aug at North Branch, Somerset Co. NJ of   MORE 28 Aug 1863
    chronic diarrhoea in his 49th year.
BUNCH, Andrew, of the 10th MO CAV, in the prison hospital.   MORE 2 Feb 1864
BUNCH, James, captured in Dunklin Co. 13 Sep, of the 10th MO CAV CS, in prison   MORE 9 Feb 1864
    hospital of inflammation of the lungs.
BUNCH, Mrs. Jane E. in Richmond 13 Mar in her 55th year.   RICON 26 Mar 1863
BURCH, Jonathan: Chariton Co. Letters of administration to Elizabeth Burch 30 Jun.   CECB 24 Jul 1862
BURCHARD, Mortimer M. eldest son/Mortimer and Jennie G. 16 Mar ae 3. Lived   MORE 17 Mar 1863
    on Clark between 20-21. Int. Bellefontaine.
BURCKHARTT, Capt. N.S. 2 Dec at the home of his uncle, Judge Burckhartt. Born   MAG 10 Dec 1863
    in Randolph Co. 22 Dec 1838, graduate of McGee College; studied law,
    was practicing. Son/Dr. Christopher Frederick & Elizabeth.
BURFORD, Legrand G. near Waverly 18 Jan, formerly of Woodford Co. KY. Baptist.   MORE 28 Feb 1863
    Emigrated several years ago. Left wife, several children.
BURGE, Thomas W. of Randolph Co. 7 Feb, tribute by Roanoke Lodge. "Aged mother."   GLWT 7 Mar 1861
BURGESS, James C. in Richmond 12 Sep ae 24y 2m 15d.   RICON 16 Sep 1865
BURGESS, James M. at Vicksburg.   LIT 31 Jul 1863
BURGESS, Mrs. Mary wife of Thomas of St. Louis Co. near Bethalto IL ae 77.   MORE 17 Jan 1864
BURGESS, Rebecca J. wife of William at Commerce, Scott Co. 9 Sept in her 25th
                                year. Wife, mother.   MORE 20 Sep 1862
    Willie S. only son/William and R.J. at Commerce, MO 20 Nov ae 5y 1m 17d.   "   18 Dec 1863
BURGESS, Thomas at Sisters Hospital of chronic diarrhoea in his 29th year. Funeral   MORE 18 Sep 1864
    from St. Bridget's Church. San Francisco & Sacramento pc
BURGMANN, Henry, ca 30, a single man, drowned in a cistern on Mallinckrodt.   MORE 21 Sep 1865
BURK, Mrs. Mary 20 Dec ae 57. Lived on 14th St. near Clark.   MORE 21 Dec 1863
BURKE, Alexander, inquest: stabbed by James Revels on a ferryboat 14 Feb, later   MORE 27 Feb 1863
    died. Lived 9th between O'Fallon & Biddle, left wife and 3 children.
BURKE, John, inquest: lived 8 miles out on Halls Ferry Road, congestion of the   MORE 16 Mar 1864
    brain. Left 3 children. Ae ca 25.
BURKE, Lawrence 21 Dec ae 66 at the home of his son L.D. St. Patrick's Church   MORE 22 Dec 1863
    to Calvary. New York, Philadelphia, Sacramento pc
BURKE, M.L. a well-known horse and stock dealer of St. Louis killed in Madison Co.   MORE 6 Apr 1865
    IL by the kick of a horse at a farm belonging to Mr. Hardie.
BURKS, Peter, inquest; ae 6 to 8, fell into fire while parents were away.   MORE 9 Feb 1863
    Lived on Papin between 6-7.
BURLEY, Sarah wife of Rufus B. in Kansas City 14 Jul ae 25y 1m, of measles.   MORE 24 Jul 1863
BURLINGAME, George S. only son/J.S. & Emily, at High Hill 28 Feb ae 4y 9m 20d.   MORE 2 Mar 1863
BURMESTER, ___ (poem dedicated to Mrs. Phillipine Burmester as a fair young   MORE 12 Oct 1865
    widow, by Louis Ortenstein)
BURNAM, Argalus M. in Boone Co. 5 Jan ae ca 27.   COWS 16 Jan 1863
BURNAM, Mrs. Ann C. 26 Oct at her husband's home, ae 35y 1m 2d.   COWS 11 Nov 1864
BURNE, Michael, inquest: ae 30, widower, 2 small children in orphan asylum;   MORE 5 Feb 1863
    boarded at 10th & Market. Lung congestion.
BURNES, Harrison killed in Andrew Co. by John Hart's guerillas.   CAWN 18 Jul 1863
BURNES, Mrs. ___, 7th & St. Charles, burned to death.   MORE 12 Jan 1862
BURNETT, Andrew son/Samuel H. of Ste. Genevieve Co. in New Madrid 12 Dec of typhoid. MORE 7 Jan 1862
BURNETT, Catherine wife of John, 6 Feb.   MORE 7 Feb 1864
BURNETT, Wash, body returned from Wheeling where he was killed working on steam-   LAJ 12 Sep 1863
    boat. Wife, several children.   MORE 11 "

BURNS, Alice suddenly of hemorrhage of the lungs; she had supported her crippled husband by washing.   MORE 10 Dec 1864

BURNS, Bridget, inquest: found in an alley between 7-8-Biddle-O'Fallon. Debility and destitution.   MORE 11 Nov 1862

BURNS, Joseph executed as an accessory to the murder of policeman John Gilman. He was born in Limerick, age not known.   MORE 9 May 1863

BURNS, Kate murdered, supposedly by husband Patrick. "A beautiful woman" ae 28, lived on Randolph between 1st & 2nd Carondelet. Cause, whiskey.   MORE 22 Mar 1863

BURNS, Mary Ann wife of Patrick 16 Sep ae (28?) Left husband and children.   LEXUN 1 Oct 1864

BURNS, Patrick, inquest: laborer, single, ae 35. Congestion of the lungs.   MORE 19 Jul 1864

BURNS, Susannah wife of John "Thursday last" at their home 1½ mi n of Savannah.   SJH 8 Oct 1865

BURNS, Thomas Francis eldest son/Henry & Bridget, 18 Jul. Lived at 292 Washington. Interred Calvary.   MORE 19 Jul 1862

BURRIS, James, citizen of Greene Co. captured 21 Feb, in Gratiot Prison of inflammation of the lungs.   MORE 6 Jun 1863

BURROWES, Michael 15 Dec ae 36. Funeral from St. Malachi's Church.   MORE 16 Dec 1864

BURTON, Ellen Lydia dau/William & Elizabeth 18 Dec ae 4.   MORE 19 Dec 1864

BURTON, Mollie youngest dau/Elder William of Howard Co. in Chillicothe 1 Dec of typhoid in her 17th year.   COWS 15 Dec 1865

BURTON, Mrs. Sophia King wife of J. Woodson of St. Louis, formerly of Perryville KY 3 Jan in her 55th year. Lived on Garrison near the Franklin Ave. cars.   MORE 4 Jan 1865

BUSCHMAN, John Heinrich, editor of Wesliche Volksblatt. Born in Bremen 21 Apr 1808, to St. Louis where he was foreman on the Anzeiger, then to St. Joseph about 2½ years ago. Left wife and 6 children.   SJH 15 Sep 1865

BUSH, Miss Lucretia in Platte Co. 23 May in her 17th year.   COWS 10 Jun 1864

BUSH, Robert shot while riding up and down the street in an intoxicated condition during the Boone Fair, died Saturday at the home of Pleasant Bush.   COWS 27 Oct 1865

BUSH, Dr. William Gaston at his home near Warsaw, Benton Co., 30 Dec ae ca 56. Son of Henry Bush, late of Winchester VA.   MORE 10 Jan 1864

BUSH, William of Columbia, a soldier, killed in the late fight at Kirksville. Left widow and several children.   COWS 15 Aug 1862

BUSTARD, Ellen wife of Henry 27 Nov of typhoid pneumonia ae (66?) Interred Calvary. Nashville & Jersey City pc   MORE 28 Nov 1865

BUTCHER, Benjamin suddenly of congestive chills. Lived on Bellefontaine Rd. 7 miles from St. Louis.   MORE 15 Aug 1862

BUTLER, ___ dau/David, living near Butler in Bates Co., 25 Feb ae 5. Burned to death when her clothes caught fire.   BOL 9 Mar 1861

BUTLER, Ann, living near the Reservoir, of intemperance. Left 2 children.   MORE 12 Feb 1862

BUTLER, Edward Sr. in Franklin Co. 23 April of acute bronchitis ae 74. Born in Dublin, lived in Beaufort SC many years, to Franklin Co. in 1854. "Husband, father."   MORE 2 Sep 1862

BUTLER, Eliza dau/late Mann & Martha, very suddenly, 25 Mar.   MORE 27 Mar 1862

BUTLER, Ellen, inquest: fell from chair dead of apoplexy, alley 7-8-Spruce-Myrtle.   MORE 9 Jul 1863

BUTLER, Lysander, Co I, 9th MO, of chronic diarrhoea 21 Oct. (Undertaker's list)   MORE 25 Oct 1863

BUTLER, Mary A. wife of Edward Jr. in Franklin Co. 7 Oct in her (30th? 39th?) year. Left husband and 4 children.   MORE 11 Oct 1865

BUTLER, Thomas, watchman on the Sultana, at Memphis. Funeral from the home of his brother, 2nd between Cherry & Carr.   MORE 1 May 1865

BUTTS, William, a militiaman of Warrenton, killed in Callaway Co.   MORE 20 May 1865

BUZBY, Joseph accidentally shot in Sedalia 8 Jan by his brother. Formerly of the 13th MO Inf.   SEDA 28 Jan 1865

BYARS, Nicholas private in Burbridge's Command, captured in Ripley Co. 28 Feb, in Gratiot Prison of diarrhoea.   MORE 14 Apr 1863

BYLER, Abraham shot by unknown while returning from working in his fields. (Central MO Advertiser 30 Aug)   CAWN 6 Sep 1862

BYRNE, Gregory, eldest son/late Gregory 19 Sep at the home of his brother-in-law Francis McFaul, ae 30y 3m. Funeral St. Francis Xavier.   MORE 20 Sep 1865

BYRNE, James f., son/John Jr. of St. Louis, while swimming in the Rhone in Germany, (at Bannin, Prussia) drowned. Was a student at St. Louis University, lived at 149 S. 5th. Interred Calvary. — MORE 7 Jul & 6 Sep 1864

BYRNE, John H. 26 May. Lived on Clark between 10-11. — MORE 27 May 1863

BYRNE, Nellie dau/Capt. Charles C. & Annie M., 14 Sep ae 12. Lived on Frederick Ave. — SJH 15 Sep 1864

BYRNE, Peter in Cape Girardeau Co. 14 Oct in his 53rd year. — MORE 30 Oct 1864

BYRNE, Peter O'D. 6 Aug in his 43rd year. Funeral from the Cathedral to Calvary, Son-in-law of Edward Fitzpatrick, brother of John Jr. — MORE 7 Aug 1863

BYRNE, Walter Henry in his 35th year. Lived at (303?) Broadway. — MORE 24 Jul 1863

BYRNS, Dr. Robert at Rolla, Phelps Co., 9 Jul ae ca 26. — SLMD 13 Aug 1861

BYWATER, Joseph Porter son/Dr. John C. & Sarah A., 25 Jun ae 16y 8m. — SLMD 2 Jul 1861

CABANNE, John P. son/late John Charles at his mother's home in his 25th year. — MORE 19 Apr 1863

CABLE, Frances Adeline dau/Capt. George W. & Bridget, 11 Sep ae 8y 5m 24d. Funeral from St. Francis Xavier Church. — MORE 12 Sep 1862

CABRILLIAC, August P. 11 Apr ae 10y 4m 17d. — MORE 12 Apr 1863

CAFFRAY, see Louisa A. IVORY

CAFFREY, Mrs. Elizabeth 11 Sep in her (52d?) year, ill one week. A Baptist. — LIT 29 Sep 1865

CAHILL, Sarah dau/Patrick & Mary 18 Apr ae 23. Lived on 12th between O'Fallon-Cass. — MORE 19 Apr 1863

CAIN, Mrs. Rebecca Burden 22 Nov of dropsy ae 28. Funeral from the home of her brother William Burden, Benton between 9-10. — MORE 23 Nov 1864

CAIN, John, a carpenter, killed at the St. Louis Grain Elevator by falling lumber. An honest, hard-working man, living in a basement on the west side of Broadway between Biddle & O'Fallon, left wife and 7 children. Had owned property in southwest MO but lost everything to bushwhackers, even the children's clothes. Moved then to Rolla, to St. Louis a few months ago. — MORE 18 Aug 1865

+ CAIN, Priscilla B. consort of John Jr. and dau/Judge Galyen of Adair Co., in Macon Co. 24 Mar. — MAG 9 Apr 1862

CAIRNS, John 4 Mar in (47th? 49th?) year. Lived on Cherry between Main-2nd. — MORE 6 Mar 1863

CALDWELL, ___ an old citizen ae 68 drowned trying to cross the Platte River on the way to St. Joseph. (see later item from SJH) — WARS 22 Jul 1865

CALDWELL, Mrs. Eleanor at the home of her son Thomas in Callaway Co. 27 Oct in her 77th year. Left 5 sons and a daughter. — MORE 7 Dec 1863

++ CALLOWAY, Annie wife of Stephen and sister of James C. Edwards of St. Louis Co. 16 Apr in her 33rd year, leaving "a number of children." — MORE 21 Apr 1861

+ CAKE, Mrs. Rena M. wife of Amos T. and dau/Judge A.W. Morrison in Howard Co. 21 Sep ae 21. No children mentioned. Louisville & Bridgeton NJ pc — MORE 29 Sep 1862

CALDWELL, ___ old and esteemed farmer of Andrew Co. drowned in the Platte River coming in with a load of produce. Body found, buried yesterday. — SJH 27 Jun 1865

Isabella, consort of the late James who recently drowned at Corby's Mill. Funeral at 6th St. Presbyterian Church. — SJH 2 Aug 1865

CALHOUN, Elizabeth widow of David 21 May ae 45. Lived at Carr & 20th. — MORE 22 May 1865

CALHOUN, Robert in Audrain Co., at Elmwood, 24 Oct in his 59th year. — COWS 25 Nov 1864

CALLAHAN, Daniel drowned in a pond on Carondelet. A boy. Body recovered. — MORE 4 Aug 1863

CALLAHAN, Patrick, a laborer, accidentally drank cyanuret of potassium, mistaking it for water. Lived on 10th St., left wife and 5 children. — MORE 23 Mar 1865

++ CALNEN, Alice dau/Mr. & Mrs., of Richmond, ae 8, when her clothes caught fire. — RICON 21 Jan 1864

CALVERT, Hamlet T. 20 Sep ae 24y 3m 10d. Lived on Pacific St. near Summit. — MORE 21 Sep 1863

CALVERT, Mrs. Rebecca 17 Mar at the home of S.W. Tunnel, 2 miles from Weston, ae 75y 10m 26d. Scott & Owen Co. KY pc — WEST 24 Mar 1865

CALVERT, Sarah wife of Craven in Weston 18 Jan. Long illness. Maysville KY pc — MORE 2 Feb 1862

CALVERT, Susan wife of James L. and dau/John Herndon of Platte City 7 Feb of diphtheria ae 27. Resident of Greene Twp. St Louis pc — WEST 13 Feb 1864

CAMERON, Fanny wife of Capt. Neil and dau/Enoch and Jane Matson of Pike Co. in Saverton, Ralls Co., ae 34y 11m 9d. — MORE 4 & 14 Sep 1861

CAMMEL, ___, young dau/Mr. Cammel of the east part of town, ae 8 or 10, when clothes caught fire. He was returning from a year in Colorado, she was all dressed up to welcome him; mother was at neighbor's. — KCJC 13 Feb 1864

CAMPBELL, James, inquest: ae 9, run over by switch engine of the Pacific RR.   MORE 8 Nov 1863
         Father and 2-year-old brother mentioned.
CAMPBELL, James of Buchanan Co., killed by men sent out by Gen. Craig.   PALS 5 Aug 1864
               (St. Joseph News)
CAMPBELL, James M. son/Samuel W. 28 Jan ae 23.   LIT 30 Jan 1863
CAMPBELL, James B. Born Lexington KY 10 Aug 1791. "Good husband, indulgent father."   PALS 2&10 Oct '65.
CAMPBELL, John S., born Madison Co. KY 17 Nov 1814, to MO about 40 years ago with   LIT 21 Jul 1865
         his father, lived in Clay and Jackson counties. Married Ellen McGee,
         dau/Col. James, in 1843. (Kansas City Journal)
CAMPBELL, Mrs. Mary 16 Aug, dau/Israel Winfrey of Boone Co.   COWS 28 Aug 1863
CAMPBELL, Nancy Ann, youngest (dau? child?) of Marstens in Washington MO   MORE 2 Jul 1861
         23 Jun, of lung disease, in her 22nd year.
CAMPBELL, Peter, Irish, killed trying to help Frederick Kane, who suffocated   MORE 12 Aug 1861
         in a coal pit on Clayton Rd.
CAMPBELL, Robert Jr. son/Robert & Virginia, 9 Jun of diphtheria ae 6y 8m 1d.   MORE 10 Jun 1862
CAMPBELL, William H. 19 Apr in his 27th year at the home of D.M. Barnum of   COWS 24 Apr 1863
         Boone Co.   Richmond KY pc
CANE, William, inquest: an old man, in his 75th year, knocked down and run over by   MORE 14 &
         a street car; had defective sight, intemperate habits. His sister burned to   15 Feb 1865
         death about a year ago, at 6th & O'Fallon. He had been a school teacher.
CANNON, Calvin W. 17 Mar of typhoid, at Rolla, ae 32. Funeral in St. Louis, friends   MORE 19 Mar 1863
         of the O.W. Cannon family invited. Memphis pc
CANNON, Joseph W. 1 Oct of consumption in his 45th year.   MORE 5 Oct 1865
CANNON, Dr. Franklin at his home near Jackson, Cape Girardeau Co. 13 Jun of   MORE 17 Jul 1863
         heart disease, ae ca 68. Born in Cabarras Co. NC, to MO early; married
         Mary Dunklin, dau/late Gov. State senator, lieut. gov., etc. Presbyterian.
CANNON, Samuel R. in Forest City, Holt Co., 12 Oct ae 68. "40 years a Mason."   COWS 30 Oct 1863
                                                                                      MORE 2 Nov "
CANTELL, John and his wife drowned in a flood. (Springfield Mirror)   HAM 25 Jul 1861
CANTHORN (CAUTHORN?), Mary Addie in Waverly, 5 Jun ae 8y 6m 25d.   MORE 18 Jun 1863
CANTLIN, Daniel, inquest: accidentally drowned at the foot of Hazel when he fell   MORE 2 Jul 1863
         from a coal barge near the lower Ferry landing, Monday. Ae 28; wife,
         3 children. Lived on 8th between Biddle-O'Fallon. "Industrious"
CAPLES, Rev. W.G. killed at his home in Glasgow by shellfire from Price's   COWS 4 Nov 1864
                                                         late attack.
         Mrs. E.J. widow Rev. W.G., late of Glasgow, ae 39. Lived at 150 Locust.   MORE 26 Apr 1865
CAPPS, Edward 20 Sep ae 35y 10m 18d, after a long illness. Husband, father.   LIT 29 Sep 1865
CAPPS, John Q. 22 Jan ae ca 32.   LIT 26 Sep 1862
CAPPS, Rebecca 16 Sep ae 67y 7m 13d.   LIT 23 Sep 1864
CAPURRO, Joseph Alexander 10 Nov of consumption in his 27th year.   MORE 11 Nov 1862
CARBY, Edward, ae ca 11, drowned in the Mississippi Sunday at Carondelet,   MORE 6 Jul 1864
         where his parents lived.
CARD, William H. 9 Sep ae 47. Lived on the north side of Labeaume; 22 years a   MORE 10 & 12
         resident of St. Louis. Mason, member IOOF.   Sep 1863
CAREY, John 16 Sep ae 18.   SLMD 24 Sep 1861
CAREY, Thomas 22 Feb ae 62. Lived O-Fallon betw 6-7. Interred Calvary.   MORE 23 Feb 1861
CARGILL, John Jr., in the rebel army, came home to die. Chronic diarrhoea.   SJH 31 Jul 1863
CARICO, Mrs. Harriet in Bethany, Harrison Co., 4 May ae 79.   MORE 14 May 1862
CARKENER, George W. 20 Dec of typhoid and brain congestion. Born 23 Sep 1819.   MORE 21 Dec 1863
         Interred in Michigan. Toledo, Cleveland, & Tecumseh MI pc
CARLE, Karon, living in DeWitt, thrown from a wagon pulled by a runaway team.   MEMP 14 Oct 1865
               (Carrollton Democrat)
CARLIN, Mary S. dau/L.E. & Martha, 13 Jun ae 15y 4d, of consumption. Lived in   MORE 15 Jun 1865
         St. Louis Co. 8 miles north of the city. Canton pc
CARLIN, Sylvan A., of wounds received at Gettysburg 20 July, brought home to be   MORE 30 Aug 1863
         interred in the family burying ground in Carondelet by his father, Delphy,
         of Brooklyn, NY. (Mother's name was Mary.) Ae ca 30.

CARLIN, James F. only remaining son/Delphy (now of Brooklyn NY) at St. Mary's LA   MORE 7 Jan 1865
    of wounds received in a skirmish with Union soldiers. Father from LA,
    mother from VA. (The Carlin graves are in Mount Olive Cemetery, in
    south St. Louis County.)

CARLISLE, Constance at her home in Ste. Genevieve 31 May in her 33rd year.   MORE 3 Jul 1863

CARLOS, Robert son/C.M.D. at his home in Cooper Co. 2 Nov. Member F & A Masons.   CALM 4 Nov 1865

CARMAN, sheriff of Chariton Co., killed by Todd's men. (County history gives   MORE 10 Jan 1865
    his name as Robert, death date as 22 Sep 1864.)

CARPENTER, Abbie (H?) wife of J.M. and dau/A.W. Fagin 24 Apr after a long illness,   MORE 26 Apr 1864
    ae "nearly 28."

CARR, Archibald, old and prominent citizen, first City Recorder, 24 Sep ae 63.   MORE 26 Sep 1865
    Lived at Salisbury & 9th.

CARR, Bridget wife of Patrick 11 Feb ae 32, after a lingering illness.   MORE 12 Feb 1862

CARR, Mrs. Catherine suddenly at 2nd & Cherry Saturday of congestion of the brain   MORE 17 Jul 1864
    due to intemperance. Her 2 little children placed in Sisters Hospital.

CARR, Eliza Todd wife of Charles, Sr. and dau/late Gen. Levi Todd. Born in   MORE 16 Nov 1863
    Lexington KY 1782, married about 1800. Presbyterian. 12 children.

CARR, George Raynor son/G. Wales 5 May ae 19y 9m 5d. Lived at 14 St. Charles.   MORE 7 May 1863

CARR, James from the effect of a blow on the head inflicted by James Nieland   MORE 2 Mar 1863
    10 days ago.

CARR, Margaretta wife of George W. 28 Nov in her 47th year. Lived at 14 St. Charles   MORE 29 Nov 1864
    St. San Francisco pc.

CARR, Walter B. yesterday when he was thrown from his horse. Son of the late   MORE 24 &
    Judge William; left widow, 4 children, mother, brothers, sister. Lived   26 Mar 1865
    at 111 Pine. Ae 33.

CARROLL, E. Llewellyn at his home near Louisiana 20 Oct of typhoid in his 45th   LAJ 6 Nov 1862
    year. Native of Pike Co.

CARROLL, Ellen wife of William 17 Jul of consumption. Lived at 19th & Christy.   MORE 18 Jul 1862

CARROLL, Miss Ellen 28 Aug ae 69. Funeral from St. Francis Xavier Church.   SLMD 29 Aug 1864

CARROLL, John, yesterday, native of (Arthone?), Co. Kilkenny, Ireland, ae 45.   MORE 25 Aug 1863
    Lived on Carr near 8th.

CARROLL, John at his home in Pike C. 21 June in his 78th year. Born in York   LAJ 11 Jul 1861
    District SC, soldier in the War of 1812; moved to IL in 1849, then
    to MO. Married twice, both wives buried in SC. Several children.

CARROLL, Miss Lizzie 2nd/dau Charles C. & the late Ann 31 Dec. Long illness.   MORE 1 Jan 1862

CARROLL, Luman 12 Jan ae 24y 5m. Funeral from the home of W.J. Stratton, 21 S 14th.   MORE 13 Jan 1861

CARROLL, Thomas, caught in a machine at the White Lead Oil Factory, mangled.   MORE 15 Nov 1865

CARROLL, Thomas J. at Sisters Hospital 21 Nov in his 20th year. Funeral from   MORE 22 Nov 1865
    St. Patrick's Church, interred Calvary.

CARROLL, Capt. Thomas M. accidentally drowned off the coal boat *Francis Fisher*   MORE 22 Oct 1865
    Friday night while trying to step from boat to barge. Ae 23, lived Alton.

CARROLL, William, a baker, 19 Jul at Sisters Hospital of typhoid. Baltimore pc   MORE 19 Jul 1863

CARSON, Ann wife of John B., 19 Jan. Lived at Morgan-Garrison. Int Bellefontaine.   MORE 21 Jan 1861

CARSON, Edward D. 20 Apr ae 28y 2(or 7) m 8d. Mason. "Aged parents," wife, and   RICON 28 Apr 1864
    children.

CARSON, Johanna, inquest; alley between Biddle-O'Fallon-7-8, congestion of the   MORE 19 Aug 1863
    lungs; ae 12.

CARSTENS, Hartwig; Chariton Co. Letters of administration 11 Nov 1862 to   CECB 29 Jan 1863
    Lewis Grotjon.

CARTAN, Lawrence, native of Dublin, 23 Mar of apoplexy ae 61. Funeral from the   MORE 24 Mar 1865
    home of his brother David (331?) Morgan to St. John's Church.

CARTER, George, citizen of Holt Co., 16 June of phthisis, in prison.   MORE 19 Jun 1864
    (Undertaker's list)

CARTER, Granville, living on Lick Creek, Ralls Co., murdered by a band of rebels   LAJ 23 Jan 1862
    Wednesday last week. He was a violent Union man.

CARTER, Henry G., of Schuyler Co., rubeola. (Undertaker's list)   MORE 10 Nov 1862

CARTER, Jacob, a Prussian, killed in the Camp Jackson affair.   MORE 18 May 1861

CARTER, Judith A. at the home of her son Steuart, of pneumonia, ae 57. She also left   MORE 3 Mar 1861
   a son John F., a brother D.S. Funeral from St. George's Church.
                                                              Leesburg VA pc
   Steuart 1 Nov of pneumonia in his (39th?) year.   MORE 3 Nov 1862

CARTER, Mildred widow of Jesse near Bridgeton 16 Jan at the home of her son   MORE 24 Jan 1864
   John T. Louisville pc

CARTER, Sarah wife of John 3 Oct in her 60th year. Lived on Ham St.   MORE 5 Oct 1864
                     Interred Bellefontaine.

CARTER, Valentine, "faithful servant of John Darby" 18 Jan.   MORE 19 Jan 1862

CARTER, William "a youth" killed by Jackson's guerillas in Chariton Co. near the GAL 15 Sep 1864
   home of William P. Allega. One of the guerillas was his cousin. (Letter
   dated 25 Aug from Keytesville to the Editor of CECB)

CARTER, William Farley in Osceola 15 Apr ae ca 62.   MORE 4 May 1862

CARTER, William Oliver son/M.J. & C.M. of typhoid ae 13y 26d.   SJH 15 Sep 1863

CARTY, John W., citizen of Reynolds Co., 16 June in prison of phthisis.   MORE 19 Jun 1864
                    (Undertaker's list)

CARVER, Reubin in Pike Co. 17 Feb ae 92y 5m. Born in the lower counties of VA, COWS 1 Mar 1861
   moved from Amherst Co. VA to Pike Co. MO in 1841.

CARY, Ann (nearly 21?) and Mary F. (ae 23?) daus/John & Mary, in Monroe City   PALS 3 Nov 1865
   in October. (Newspaper badly creased.)

CASEY, ____ and his son John shot by soldiers of the MO State Militia in a   SJH 14 &
   dispute over a card game at Hamilton, Caldwell Co. He was one of   15 Jun 1864
   the county's oldest citizens, lived near Gallatin.   LIT 15 Jul 1864

CASEY, Ellen, a young woman, from effects of the heat. Lived at #5 Morgan.   MORE 1 Aug 1861

CASEY, John in his home in Carondelet in his 72d year. Interred in the Catholic MORE 27 May 1863
   Cemetery in Carondelet.

CASEY, Robert, inquest: 2nd between Plum & Cedar. General debility.   MORE 21 Jul 1864

CASEY, Theresa wife of John H. in Potosi 19 Feb of consumption, ae 51y 8m 11d. MORE 25 Feb 1864

CASEY, William in Potosi 7 Feb ae 32.   MORE 12 Feb 1863

CASHMAN, Matthew froze to death 1 Jan in Quincy, on Front St. between Curtis'   PALS 15 Jan 1864
   Distillery and Wells Packing House.

CASSELL, ____ of Jackson Co. killed 6 miles from Fayette on Rocheport Road.   WARS 17 Jun 1865

CASSELL, Isabel Rebecca wife of George B. of Warsaw and eldest dau/George &   MORE 23 Feb 1862
   Elvira Schaffner, 22 Feb ae 21y 4m, at the home of her father.
   Funeral from St. John's Church. Baltimore pc

CASSELL, John, inquest: died in tenement, alley between Biddle-O'Fallon-8-9.   MORE 20 Jan 1863
   Habitual drunk. Left widow and 4 small children.

CASTARPHEN, Oney in Ralls Co. ae 75y 4m. Emigrated from Fayette Co. KY in   HAM 17 Jan 1861
   1819 and settled on the farm where he died.

CASTELLO, Ann, inquest: beaten to death by Kate Hardigan near 21st & Carr.   MORE 8 Sep 1863

CASTELLO, Mrs. Nancy, long a resident of Florissant, 6 Oct ae (76? 78?).   MORE 7 Oct 1863

CASTLE, Otis B. son/Judge E.S. at Benton Barracks, St. Louis. Mbr 5th (51?)   SJH 1 Jul 1865
   Mo. Vols, 3rd son to die in service.

CASWELL, Leon, twin child of Emma & T.A., ae 3y. Lived at 69 N. 5th, near Locust. MORE 30 Aug 1862

CASWELL, Mrs. S.M. 11 Mar ae 52. Lived on Myrtle St. Zanesville OH & New Haven CT pc MORE 12 Mar 1863

CATES, Nancy wife of John C. in Richmond last Thursday ae 37.   RICON 20 Nov 1862

CATES, Owen G. Sr., native of KY where he filled many positions of trust, lived MORE 11 &
   on Pine between 11-12; wife died about a year ago. Interred Frankfort KY.   14 May 1865
   Mary wife of Owen G., 16 Oct. Lived 192 Pine. Interred Frankfort KY.   MORE 17 Oct 1864

CATHCART, William son/Gabriel of Clay Co. 16 Aug at Ft. Laramie, of typhoid, ae 23. LIT 1 Sep 1865

CATLETT, Mary Ellen dau/William & Sarah Laswell in Scotland Co. ae 20y 6m 23d. CANP 2 Mar 1865
                            Methodist.

CATLIN, Clinton youngest son/Daniel & Emily, 27 Sep in his 19th year. Lived on MORE 28 Sep 1865
   Olive betw 20-21.

CATO, W.E.B. in Providence 5 Jul in his 36th year.   COWS 15 Jul 1864

CATRON, Robert in Hannibal 12 Sep ae 57y 11m 12d.   CANP 15 Sep 1864

CAUTHORN, Frankie wife of James A., formerly of Mexico MO, in Sturgeon 9 Jan.   COWS 22 Jan 1864

29

CAVANAGH, John, native of Limerick, 7 Sep of sunstroke ae 25. Funeral from St. Malachy's Church to Calvary. Lived on Emily south of Clark. SLMD 8 Sep 1864
MORE "

CAVANAGH, Michael son/Daniel 28 Nov ae 35. Lived on O'Fallon between 22-23. Interred Rock Spring. MORE 30 Nov 1864

CAVANAUGH, Timothy, citizen of St. Louis, 23 May of dysentery, in prison. MORE 29 May 1864

CAVE, Hudson M. shot near Salisbury by his brother-in-law Jackson Terrill in a family row, Thursday last. (Randolph Citizen) WARS 22 Sep 1865

CAVE, Maj. William, living 1 mile north of town, shot by a scout from Columbia for alleged complicity with bushwhackers. COWS 9 Sep 1864

    James son/Major W.S. & Margaret 24 Jan in Boone Co. ae 6. COWS 25 Jan 1861

CAYTON, Annie W. dau/George J. & Mary E. 9 Apr of whooping cough ae 2y 2m. Lived at 153 Chambers. MORE 11 Apr 1861

CEARY, Mary Ann dau/Martin, 27 Oct. Lived at 48 Biddle. MORE 29 Oct 1861

CEDRY, John, inquest; drowned in the river near Bissell's Point, ae 14. MORE 2 Jul 1863

CELLA, Charles (or Luici?) an Italian fruit dealer at 7th & Pine (or 7th & St. Charles) killed when Col. Kallman's Reg. fire on civilians. MORE 18 Jun 1861
SLMD 25 "

CHADBOURNE, Maggie, youngest dau/Gideon W. & Anna E., ae 5y (3?8?)m, 126 Hickory. MORE 17 Nov 1865

CHADDUCK, L.V.D. (or I.V.D.) 5 Sep in his 29th year. Lived at 191 N 5th. Buffalo NY & Oshkosh WI pc SLMD 6 Sep 1864
MORE "

CHAINEY, Jane 14 May in her 42d year. Left husband, 4 children. SJH 18 May 1864

CHALFANT, Mary Eveline only dau/Louis P. & Maria at Linn Creek 5 Oct ae 5y 9m 5d. MORE 9 Oct 1862

CHALLER, Sarah ae 17 drowned at Carondelet. MORE 2 Mar 1861

CHAMBERLAIN, George in jail, suicide by throwing himself against the wall, also suffered from d.t.s. Ca 27, charged with killing a hack driver 2 years ago. His mother lives in St. Louis. MORE 18 Aug 1863

CHAMBERLAIN, Laura Cornelia wife of G.T. 2 Mar after a long painful illness. Funeral from North Presbyterian Church. Litchfield CT pc MORE 3 Mar 1863

CHAMBERLAIN, Nathaniel 22 Apr ae 63. MORE 23 Apr 1863

CHAMBERS, Capt Benjamin G., CSA, 31 Mar ae 27. Son/late Col. A.B. of St. Louis. MORE 9 Apr 1864

CHAMBERS, Charles 1 Feb of pneumonia ae 80. Funeral from the Cathedral. MORE 2 Feb 1862

CHAMBERS, Mrs. Elizabeth 26 Nov in her (70? 79?) th year, at the home of Dr. A.B. Barbee in Manchester. Widow of Samuel. MORE 28 Nov 1865

CHAMBERS, John M. at his home, Taille de Noyes, Florissant, 5 May in his 39th year. Funeral from St. Francis Xavier Church. MORE 6 &
12 May 1861

CHAMBERS, Sarah A. wife of T.F., 23 Jan. Lived at 56 Market St. MORE 24 Jan 1862

CHAMPION, Rock former resident of St. Louis and well-known river man, killed in battle at Bolivar, TN. A Confederate. MORE 16 Sep 1862

CHAPMAN, Ezekiel at his home between Charleston & Rush's Ridge, 17 Oct ae 48. CHAC 18 Oct 1861

CHAPMAN, John of Clay Co., a bushwhacker, killed by militia at the home of Asa Thompson 6 miles from Fayette near Rocheport Road. COWS 2 Jun 1865

CHAPPELL, William C., Lt Col 1st Reg MO Vols CSA, killed at Prairie Grove AR in Dec, interred at Ft. Smith. Cincinnati & Baltimore pc MORE 19 Jan 1863

CHARDON, Sophia, inquest: jumped from 3rd floor window at Sisters Hospital, ae 21. Thought her husband was leaving her there -- he had brought her because she had typhoid. He didn't return as soon as he had intended. MORE 2 Jul 1863

CHARLES, William Reason, Co B 1st Mo Cav, of pneumonia in the Soldiers' Hospital in his 23rd year. Returned to Gallatin for burial. GAL 26 Jan 1865

CHARLEVILLE, Victoria wid/Joseph at the home of her granddaughter, Mrs. Eliza O'Flaherty, ae 82y 10m. (8th between Chouteau & Gratiot.) "She died a true Christian and was universally beloved." MORE 19 Jan 1863

CHARLTON, George-Ann dau/Mrs. Samuel in Lexington 15 Jan ae 14. MORE 27 Jan 1861

CHARTER, John R. shot by Paul Kingston at Cape Girardeau Saturday evening week before last; Kingston was a private in the 1st MO. PERU 21 Sep 1863

CHASE, Edward Julius, eldest child/Edward & Eliza, drowned 13 June ae 13y 4m. Funeral from Church of the Messiah. MORE 15 &
17 Jun 1861

CHASSAING, Josephine F. dau/late Edward, formerly of Baltimore, 26 Jun ae 19y 7m. St. John's Church, Calvary. /Spruce between 15-16 MORE 28 Jun 1864

CHAUVENET, Mary relict of William M. 20 Aug in her 66th year. Funeral from the home of Chancellor William Chauvenet, 12 Lucas Pl.	SLMD 22 Aug 1864
CHAUVIN, Alexander, eldest son/late L.J. of St. Charles, at Tallahatchie Co MS near Grenada, 19 Jan.	MORE 7 Feb 1863
CHAUVIN, Francis youngest son/Sylvester of St.Louis at Julesburg, NT 7 Jan.	MORE 26 Jul 1865
CHAUVIN, James E. youngest son/late L.J. of St. Charles at Rolla 8 May in his 24th year. Funeral from the home of C.V. Labeau, 16th between Market and Clark. Interred St. Charles.	MORE 11 May 1864
CHAUVIN, Pilagu, widow of Lafrenie, 6 Oct in St. Charles. Funeral from the home of her son-in-law, B. Emmons Jr.	MORE 8 Oct 1861
CHAUVIN, Vilray H., US Volunteers, at Gallatin TN 22 Feb ae 30.	MORE 24 Mar 1865
CHEEK (CHECK?) Absalom of Jeffries Reg., captured in Cape Girardeau Co. 14 Nov, 17 Dec of pneumonia in Gratiot Prison. (Undertaker's list)	MORE 19 & 21 Dec 1862
CHEEK, James, recruit, captured in Bollinger Co. 15 Nov, in Gratiot Prison of typhoid pneumonia.	MORE 1 Apr 1863
CHEEVER, Charlies Lytle only child/Mary A. 25 Dec ae 3y 8m 21d. Mother lived at 206 N. 5th.	MORE 26 Dec 1863
CHENIE, Marie Therese dau/Antoine of the Upper Missouri, at the home of Antoine L., ae 19. Interred Calvary.	MORE 14 Mar 1863
CHESNUT, Samuel of Buchanan Co. killed by men sent out by Gen. Craig. (St. Joseph News) (MORE shows name as Emanuel.)	PALS 5 Aug 1864 MORE 30 Jul "
CHESTER, Thomas C. 14 Oct ae 31 of consumption. Lived on 7th near Sidney.	MORE 15 Oct 1862
CHEVIS, Judge Thomas M. of flux, near Barry in Clay Co., during the past week ae ca 60. Four others also died in this flux epidemic.	SJH 11 Aug 1864
CHEW, Joseph W. in Nevada City CA, late of Kansas City and son/Dr. Joseph of St. Louis, in his 23rd year. Lexington & Louisville KY pc, also Richmond MO & Kansas City	MORE 12 Jul 1864
CHILD, Mary Goodrich wife of Alonzo, many years a resident of St. Louis, at Tarrytown NY 21 Apr.	MORE 26 Apr 1865
CHILDS, Mrs. Ann relict of Nathaniel Sr. of Baltimore Co. MD, at the home of her son Caleb in Lincoln Co. MO in her 80th year. Baltimore, New Orleans & CA pc	MORE 21 Aug 1863
CHILDS, Elizabeth Miller wife of Dominick J. and dau/late Charles and Ann Miller of Baltimore, 15 Sep at the home of John Hardy, Olive near Beaumont. Interred in Baltimore.	MORE 16 Sep 1863
CHILDS, Elizabeth Jane wife of Henry T., 104 Elm, 23 Aug in her 53rd year. Dau/Charles and Elizabeth Carr of Fayette Co. (KY?) Funeral from 2nd Presbyterian Church. Interred Bellefontaine.	MORE 24 & 31 Aug 1862
CHILDS, Letitia wife of Benjamin and dau/Benjamin Dickinson of Lee Co. VA, 26 Sep ae 33. Funeral from the Methodist Church.	SJH 27 Sep 1863
CHILES, Samuel prisoner of war, 5 Feb of variola. (Undertaker's list)	MORE 15 Feb 1863
CHOUTEAU, Edward Augustus 1 Jan ae 49. Lived nw corner Marion & Dexter.	MORE 3 Jan 1864
CHOUTEAU, Mrs. Emilie Gratiot, wife of P. Jr., 24 Aug in her 69th year. Lived on Market St., #172. Funeral from the Cathedral.	MORE 25 Aug 1862
CHOUTEAU, Pierre Jr., ae 77, yesterday at the home of his dau/Mrs. J. Maffitt.	MORE 7 Sep 1865
CHOUTEAU, Sophie consort of the late Auguste P., 5 Sep ae 73y 6n 2d.	MORE 7 Sep 1863
CHRISTEN, Jacob 13 Dec ae 28.	MORE 15 Dec 1862
CHRISTOPHER, Mrs. Elizabeth suddenly 20 Jul ae 91. Funeral from the home of her son John, 123 Chestnut. Rochester & New York City pc	SLMD 21 Jul 1864
John, ae 49, at his home in St. Louis. Interred Rochester NY.	MORE 14 Dec 1864
CISSNEY, Henry T., funeral from the home of his brother John, 10th & Mound. (He CISSNA was killed by his partner in a "substitute" business - providing subs for soldiers.) The partner, Henry Green, was subsequently tried for the murder (MORE 26 May 1865)	MORE 14 Dec 1864 & following
CLAFFY, Mrs. Michael. inquest: lived 14th & Chouteau, fell onto stove while drunk, struck her head, died of brain concussion ae 33. Husband 40. No family.	MORE 27 Jan 1863
CLAGGETT, Mrs. Margaret F. "ceased her sufferings" Wednesday night 4 Oct.	PALS 6 Oct 1865
CLANTON, Samuel Thomas son/William H. & Sarah, ae 4y 1d.	FULT 27 Jun 1862

CLARK, Ellen, suicide by laudanum. Ae ca 22, no motive known. Formerly of IL.	MORE 10 Mar 1861
CLARK, Frank, engineer, killed in the Platte Bridge disaster.	SLMD 10 Sep 1861
CLARK, Henry, Chariton Co.; letters of administration 30 Sep 1862 to Ephraim Clark executor.	CECB 29 Jan 1863
CLARK, Hiram, an old citizen of Moniteau living at Clark's Station, Sun. last.	CAWN 12 Jan 1861
William son/late Hiram Thursday of typhoid, ae 21.	CAWN 19 Jan 1861
CLARK, James Price of Pike Co. in Washington Co. AR 22 Apr after a long illness, effects of measles. Member Co F. 1st Reg Inf, MO Confederate troops. Episcopalian.	MORE 12 Jun 1862
CLARK, Jesse P. formerly of Chillicothe, late of Princeton, shot near Spring Hill. Had been arrested, charged with being a guerilla; had taken the oath and was under bonds. Taken by a party of soldiers to the home of a relative to get clean clothing, but they shot him. (Chillicothe Constitution)	LAJ 11 Sep 1862
CLARK, John A. formerly of Scott Co. IL, brother-in-law of Samuel Spencer, a picture dealer on 5th St., struck by lightning Friday last near Columbia, the horse he was riding was also killed.	MORE 11 Aug 1863
CLARK, Capt. John R. shot by a guard in an affray in which Mary Willis was killed.	MAG 11 Jun 1862
CLARK, Julia wife of Patrick, apparently of injuries he inflicted; she was pregnant. Her dau/Mary Ann ae 18 testified against the father; another sister, little (Bridget) was mentioned by Mary Ann.	MORE 12 Oct 1863
CLARK, Maggie B. 12 Sep in St. Louis, dau/Thomas & Margaret B., formerly of Newport KY, ae 16.	SJh 16 Sep 1865
CLARK, Mrs. Mary at her home in Iron Hill, Franklin Co., 5 Nov of pneumonia ae 76.	MORE 7 Nov 1861
CLARK, Mary relict of Joseph of Baltimore 7 Aug at the home of her brother-in-law Abner Hood, ae 58. Funeral at Immaculate Conception Church.	MORE 9 Aug 1864
CLARK, Mrs., wife of J.B. of Callao (agent for the Hannibal & St. Joseph RR)	MAG 22 Jan 1862
CLARK, Mary wife of Lewis M., Deputy Sheriff of Livingston Co., 8 Jan in Chillicothe ae 51.	MORE 17 Jan 1861
CLARK, Robert, prisoner, 30 Jan of bronchitis and diarrhoea. (Undertaker's list)	MORE 2 Feb 1863
CLARK, Robert, Sunday; body to be interred in Beavey (Bevo?) by friends.	MORE 12 Oct 1865
CLARK, Robert S. of apoplexy ae 19. Lived on 4th near Green.	MORE 1 Mar 1862
CLARK, Seddie L. dau/late George 18 Dec ae 21. Boston & Philadelphia pc	MORE 19 Dec 1864
CLARK, Teresa dau/James decd & Mary, 9 Oct ae 5y 6m 9d.	MORE 10 Oct 1863
CLARK, Dr. William E. at his home near Pevely, Jefferson Co., 23 Jan ae 53.	MORE 24 Jan 1863
CLARKE, James in his 34th year. Lived at 25th & Morgan. Funeral from St. Bridget's Church. Interred Calvary.	MORE 10 Mar 1863
CLARKE, Thomas M., citizen of Texas Co., 16 Feb of pneumonia. (Undertaker's list)	MORE 19 Feb 1865
CLARKE, William Bliss, attorney, formerly of Waltham MA, resident of St. Louis 7 yrs.	MORE 29 Oct 1864
CLARKSON, Mrs. Eliza wife of John 22 May. Funeral from the home of her father, Archibald Gamble, opposite Lafayette Park. Cincinnati pc	MORE 23 May 1864
CLARKSON, Mrs. John near Columbia 2 Jul, of flux.	COWS 7 Jul 1865
CLARKSON, William P. of Boone Co. in TX recently, of consumption.	COWS 10 Jun 1864
CLAYBROOKE, Annie Bell dau/W.P.D. & Ann, 14 Aug ae ca 4.	PALS 19 Aug 1864
CLAYPOLE, Joseph ca 42 in Boone Co. 5 Mar.	COWS 24 Apr 1863
CLEARY, Mrs. ___ wife of Michael 6 Aug ae 26. Funeral from Immaculate Conception Church, interred Calvary.	MORE 8 Aug 1863
Timothy son/Michael & Mary, ae (3? 8?)y 3m 18d. Funeral from the home of Redmond Cleary, 9th between Biddle-O'Fallon. Chicago pc	MORE 31 Aug 1863
CLEAVELAND, William Harvey ae 10 and Emma E. ae 8, children of William H. and Catherine, both died of smallpox on New Year's Day.	SEDA 14 Jan 1865
CLEMENS, Enoch 12 Jan at Sisters Hospital; a pilot, formerly of Cincinnati, ae 40. Funeral from home of James B. Clemens, 115 Locust. Interred Bellefontaine. Cincinnati pc	MORE 16 Jan 1863
CLEMONS, Lucy wife of James, 2 Mar of consumption.	LIT 6 Mar 1863
CLEMONS, Martha wife of William W. in Memphis, Scotland Co., 21 Apr in her 76th y.	MORE 30 Apr 1861
CLEVELAND, Ben Abell Forrest, son/late Capt. William & Jane E. of Randolph Co., a soldier in Price's Army, 21 Nov at Oxford MS ae 19.	COWS 23 Jan 1862

CLEVELAND, Charles W., Asst. Editor of the Merchants Exchange Price Current, in his 46th year. Interred Bellefontaine. MORE 4 Apr 1861

CLIFF, Robert H. in St. Joseph 2 Jan in his 52d year. Born on the banks of the Rhine 13 Jan 1813, married there, to US 18 years ago; resident of St. Joe 10 or 12 years. Left wife, 3 children. SJH 4 Jan 1865

CLIFFORD, Bridget in St. Louis 10 Aug, wife of John C. of St. Joseph, in her 24th y. SJH 13 Aug 1865

CLIFTON, Florence Albertine, only child/D.W. & Sarah, 9 Mar ae 1y 2m 12d. Philad. pc MORE 11 Mar 1861

CLIFTON, Nathan near Marshfield 7 Mar-- his age, 105y 2m 13d! Born in Salisbury District SC 25 Dec 1758. In Col. Turner's Reg. in the Revolution. One son died in TN in Union service. Came to MO 22 years ago. MORE 2 Apr 1864

CLINTON, Franky P. "a bright little fellow" playing in the street, kicked by a mule pulling a street car. Son/Charles & Hattie P. living on 5th near Washington, ae 4y 1m. MORE 23 Oct 1864

CLOSE, Stephen son/Philip & Mary 27 Aug ae 16m. Nashville pc MORE 29 Aug 1861

CLUCUS, James 22 Dec ae 41 of dysentery, native of Cumberland Co. Eng. Lived on 12th between O'Fallon & Cass. MORE 24 Dec 1864

COALTER, Mrs. Mary A. wife of John D. 21 May after a long illness. Lived on 5th St. (#8). Interred Bellefontaine. MORE 22 May 1864

    John D. 19 Oct in his 60th year at #8 5th St. MORE 21 Oct 1864

COATES, Curtis of Pemiscot Co., arrested 16 Sep, of remittent fever in the prison hospital. (shown as Oats on 29 Nov.) MORE 24 Nov 1863

COBB, J.P. found dead on the rr tracks between Herman and Franklin. Name found on exemption from MSM papers which he carried. MORE 20 Oct 1862

COBERTY, John, inquest: wounded by person(s) unknown, attacked at home by 3 men, Mrs. Connerty injured. Robbery probable motive. Lived on 2nd St. between Bates & Columbia. (Name also shown as Connerty) MORE 27 & 30 Jul 1863

COBLE, Peter, prisoner from H. Greers Command, of acute rhinitis. MORE 4 Apr 1864

COCHRAN, Harriet wife of Maj. James of St. Louis at the home of her son-in-law Judge S.M. Hays, Locust Grove, Platte Co. ae 51. Madison IN pc MORE 1 Sep 1861

COCHRAN, Laura Alice 2 May near Hannibal, dau/Joseph & Sarah A., of typhoid ae 19y 11m 24d. Louisville pc MORE 14 Jun 1865

COCKE, Mary J.N.D. consort of Robert P. in St. Clair Co. MO 21 Dec ae 47y 6m. Born in Louisa Co. VA 24 Jun 1813, maiden name Pulliam. Member of the Christian Church. OVAS 17 Jan 1861

CODY, Edward 1 Oct ae 37, native of Ballytobin, Parish of Dunemagin, Co. Kilkenny, resided on Chestnut between 14-15. Interred Calvary. Boston Patriot pc MORE 2 Oct 1865

CODY, William ca 34, injured in the Camp Jackson affair, died 11 May. Funeral from the home of his brother-in-law James Garvin, Walnut St. Int. Calvary. MORE 13 May 1861

COFF, Helen M. wife of James 16 Oct ae 22y 9m 20d. Interred Calvary. MORE 18 Oct 1864

COFFEY, Ambrose son/John & Louise 15 Jul ae 19y 5m. Lily of the Valley Lodge IOGT invited to funeral. MORE 16 Jul 1863

COFFEY, R. L. and wife, both of typhoid, in Knobnoster 25 Dec. MORE 17 Jan 1861

COFFINBERRY, Mrs. Sallie A. 29 Jul ae 58. Funeral from the home of her son Creight, 129 Collins. Interred Wesleyan. SLMD 30 Jul 1864

COFFMAN, Charles 2nd son/John & Jane 18 Dec of typhoid ae 22 in Ste. Genevieve Co. MORE 21 Dec 1864

COGAN, Bridget wife of Dr. J. 19 Oct after a long illness. MORE 20 Oct 1862

COGHILL, Franklin, prisoner, 7 Oct of gastritis. MORE 12 Oct 1862

COGHILL, Jesse of Adair Co., of rubeola. (Undertaker's list) MORE 9 Nov 1862

COHEN, Henriette wife of A. 7 Feb at her home in St. Louis. MORE 9 Feb 1862

COHEN, John Thomas son/late William & Emily, 14 Jun ae 11. Funeral from the home of his grandfather, Thomas, Pratte & Market. MORE 15 Jun 1861

    Thomas ae 85. Funeral from St. George's Church. MORE 27 Feb 1863

COKER, James W., ca 20, accidentally killed near Cottonwood Springs, Neb about a week ago, shot while with his older brother taking a train across the plains. Father, W.P., and 3 sisters live in St. Joseph. SJH 4 Aug 1865

COLBURN, Margaret widow of James at the home of Edward H. Garrigues, ae 76. Cincinnati pc MORE 3 Mar 1865

COLCLAISEAIR, James H. of Clay Co. killed trying to escape from Gratiot Prison.   MORE 19 Jun 1864
COLE, Joe, a notorious bushwhacker of Callaway Co., shot 1 Dec by Wellsville   COWS 25 Dec 1863
    Post soldiers at his home near Portland when he refused to surrender.
COLE, Mary wife of Lawrence 6 Mar at Quincy IL in her 29th year. Funeral from   MORE 10 Mar 1864
    St. Bridget's Church.
COLEMAN, ____ killed in Chariton Co. in retaliation.   MORE 10 Jan 1865
COLEMAN, Henshaw Thursday in his 26th year. Funeral from St. John's Church.   MORE 20 Dec 1861
COLEMAN, John 8 Aug of chronic diarrhoea ae 38. Member 29th MO Vols. Lived at   MORE 9 Aug 1863
    9th-St. Charles. Leeds ENG pc
COLEMAN, John 20 May in his 40th year. Lived on Orchard between 10-11.   MORE 21 May 1861
    Hopkinsville KY pc
COLEMAN, L. Ellen dau/W.H. & Hardenia 21 Aug at Mt. Comfort, St. Louis Co.,   MORE 14 Sep 1865
    ae 22. Richmond VA pc
COLEMAN, Samuel J. in Lincoln Co. (20th?) Mar ae 46. Russellville KY pc   MORE 30 Mar 1864
COLEMAN, Sarah near Pilot Grove 23 Feb, wife of William H. Ae 40 y.   COWS 13 Mar 1863
COLEMAN, Capt. Stephen O., killed in the battle of Wilson's Creek, brought   MORE 13 &
    home for burial in Bellefontaine.   27 Nov 1865
COLEMAN, William L. of St. Louis in Oromosto, NB 24 Aug.   MORE 6 Nov 1862
COLGAN, Ophelia dau/Robert & Caroline 2 Feb ae 9. Interred Calvary.   MORE 4 Feb 1865
COLHOUN, Master William, son/John, suddenly yesterday.   SJH 7 Feb 1865
COLLETT, Ann wife of John and dau/J.C. & H. Mason, at Bloomington 2 Feb.   MAG 18 Feb 1863
COLLIER, George eldest son/late George of St. Louis in Wiesbaden GER 13 Sep ae 29.   MORE 11 Oct 1863
COLLIER, Judith wife of Lewis in Livingston Co. 15 Oct in her 64th year.   COWS 10 Nov 1865
COLLIER, Susan wife of James M. of Randolph Co. burned to death in a buggy en   SJH 18 Oct 1863
    route to visit her father in Howard Co. She was smoking her pipe and
    coals apparently ignited her clothing. (Mexico Ledger)
COLLIGAN, Michael J., funeral from 18th & Orange. Rochester & Toronto pc   MORE 25 Apr 1865
COLLINS, Catherine Monahan wife of Patrick and sister of Patrick Monahan,   MORE 15 &
    14 Oct. Lived 8th-Wash. St. Patrick's Church, interred Calvary.   17 Oct 1864
COLLINS, James, a boot and shoe maker, 13 Aug ae 52. Lived Biddle betw 6-7.   MORE 14 Aug 1864
COLLINS, John S. ae (38?)y 9m 17d 24 Nov of dropsy. Funeral from the home of his   MORE 26 Nov 1865
    brother Monroe R., at Compton & Olive.
COLLINS, Joseph at the home of W. Halliburton in Brunswick 20 Nov in his 76th y.   MORE 25 Nov 1863
    Born in Shelby Co. KY, was in War of 1812, settled in Randolph Co.
    in 1823. (CECB)
COLLINS, Martha W. wife of Morris of St. Louis in Hartford CT ae 33, eldest   MORE 3 Jun 1862
    dau/late John Blatchford of Quincy IL.
COLLINS, Capt. May B. 6 Dec of typhoid ae 47, at Olive St. Hotel. Int Bellefontaine.   MORE 7 Dec 1864
COLLINS, Patrick, a laborer ae 45, of congestion of the brain caused by drinking.   MORE 13 Jun 1862
    Lefta wife and 2 children.
COLLINS, Thomas G. 20 Aug ae 40. Lived at 432 Broadway. Terre Haute & Louisville pc   MORE 21 Aug 1865
COLLINS, William of Grundy Co. in Gratiot Prison of typhoid 3 Dec.   MORE 7 Dec 1862
COLLINS, William 8 Mar ae 18y 7m at the home of Thomas Gogherty, 128 S. 5th.   MORE 9 Mar 1865
    Funeral from Annunciation Church. Iowa pc
COLLINS, William T. son/late R.J. 21 Mar ae 30. Lived at Carondelet & Emmet.   MORE 22 Mar 1865
COLMAN, Clara wife of Norman J. 18 Dec of consumption. Lived on Olive St. Road   MORE 19 Dec 1863
    5 miles west of St. Louis.
COLMAN, Charles killed by bushwhackers in Chariton Co. (RANC 17 Jun)   MORE 19 Jun 1864
COLTON, George A. "well-known citizen of St. Louis" fell overboard the Lake City   MORE 18 &
    and was drowned, 15 Sep. Cincinnati & Boston pc   25 Sep 1861
COLTON, John R. in Carondelet 28 Dec in his 53rd year of (diabetes?)   MORE 30 Dec 1865
    Cincinnati & Indianapolis pc
COLWELL, John, Private in the 5th MO Inf, in the prison hospital.   MORE 17 Sep 1863
COMBS, Leslie son of Warren of MO (apparently Johnson Co.) ae 17, killed in a   WARS 1 Dec 1865
    furnace explosion near Lurey (VA or KY?) where he was visiting
    relatives. (from an unidentified newspaper)

COMBS, Mrs. Sarah consort of John in Palmyra Wednesday last while sitting in her rocking chair, ae ca 50. Had apparently been in good health.	HAM 13 Mar 1862
COMPTON, Sterling of Poindexter's Band, native of Carroll or Chariton Co., in Gratiot Prison 13 Nov.	MORE 14 Nov 1862
COMSTOCK, Charles R. son/Anson at Chattanooga 30 Mar ae 32. Funeral from 1st Presbyterian Church.	MORE 7 Apr 1865
CONAWAY, Charles F. 10 Jul ae 12. Mother lived at 15th-Belmont. Int. Bellefontaine.	MORE 11 Jul 1863
CONDER, Mrs. Maria A. 19 Sep of typhoid ae 28, at the home of her father, O.H. Wade of Warsaw.	WARS 22 Sep 1865
CONDUITT, Napoleon B. son/Dr. C. of Lewis Co. "a young man of promise" shot himself at LaPlata.	RANC 25 Apr 1861
CONKLIN, William R. son/Mr. Conklin of Louisiana MO (city constable) recently at Helena AR, a member of Capt. McKee's Co., raised last summer. Mr. C. had gone to bring him home before news of his death arrived. Tribute from Western Star Social Temple (a Temperance group).	LAJ 12 & 19 Mar & 18 Apr 1863
CONLAN, Bridget, dau/Patrick "not more than 16" after a drunken spree; she had quarreled with her father and brother Thomas, who struck her; at first thought murdered, inquest said no. Lived 24th betw O'Fallon-Cass.	MORE 6 Jan 1862
CONLEY, Thomas J. in Columbia 21 Apr of consumption ae 29.	COWS 24 Apr 1863
CONNELL, James "an inveterate old whiskey sucker" found dead under a tarp by a wine cask on the levee.	MORE 11 Nov 1861
CONNELL, John killed by John Cunningham in a fracas near the Iron Mountain Depot.	MORE 22 May 1861
CONNELLY, James very suddenly of apoplexy. Lived in St. Joseph Alley (Hickory-Rutgers-Carondelet-7th). Left wife and 2 children.	MORE 8 Feb 1862
CONNELLY, James Sanford, formerly of Boone Co., in Shelbina 7 Jan of typhoid ca 24.	COWS 11 Jan 1861
CONNER, Catherine wife of Cornelius at College Farm 14 Sep ae 36. Int. Calvery.	MORE 15 Sep 1863
CONNER, Mrs. E., funeral from the home of Mrs. T.E. Summers, 255 Chestnut. Died 1 Jul. Baltimore pc	MORE 2 Jul 1865
CONNER, John found dead in bed, 2nd St. between Almond & Poplar, of congestion of the brain due to intemperance and laudanum. Had bid his daughter Mrs. Catherine Allin goodbye, telling her he was going on a long journey. Widower, ca 50, left 2 married daughters.	MORE 15 Dec 1863
CONNER, Mary Ann wife of James F. in Cooper Co. 15 Feb in her 37th year.	COWS 27 Feb 1863
CONNER, Capt. S.Y., formerly of Cincinnati, at the home of his daughter Mrs. Abbie W. Hauk, 7 Dec ae 77.	MORE 9 Dec 1865
CONNERTY see COBERTY, John	
CONNERY, Thomas 29 May at Nashville ae 27. Funeral from the home of Thomas O'Brien, on Biddle, to Calvary Cemetery.	MORE 1 Jun 1865
CONNETT, William, an old and wealthy farmer near Sparta, yesterday of apoplexy at his home, White Gates. (Date of death, 30 Dec.) Born Mason Co. KY 3 Jun 1797, in Buchanan Co. nearly 26 years. Had 9 children, 6 survive - 3 sons, 3 daus. Moved early to Hardin Co. KY, served in War of 1812 there, afterwards to Lexington KY, then to MO.	SJH 1 & 10 Jan 1865
CONNOR, Michael "Shanghai" (a fighter) at his boarding house, 12 Morgan, ae 32 of lung disease. (Also shown as ae 28, native of Ireland, int. Holy Trinity.)	MORE 5 & 6 Aug 1863
CONNOR, Thomas at Sisters Hospital 26 Nov in his 22nd year. Native of Maynooth, Ire. Funeral from Mr. Daley's, Carr & 6th. St. Patrick's Church, Calvary Cem.	MORE 27 Nov 1865
CONNORS, Thomas killed yesterday at Franklin Station, Pacific RR - tried to go under the cars but the train started. Ae 45.	MORE 21 Nov 1862
CONRAD, John T. on Sny Island, formerly of Hannibal, 17 Jan ca 40.	HAM 23 Jan 1862
CONRAN, Patrick 14 Oct ae 30. Lived 12th betw Pine-Chestnut. Int. Rock Springs.	MORE 15 Oct 1861
CONRAN, William J. 28 Nov at Memphis ae 34. Funeral from home of his brother-in-law M. Lynch, Grand betw Fairgrounds & Bellefontaine Rd.	MORE 2 & 7 Dec 1865
CONROW, A.H. of Ray Co., former Confederate officer, murdered near Monterey Mex.	MORE 11 Oct 1865
CONROY, Patrick son/John, ca 8, accidentally shot during the holiday celebrations. Lived 2nd St. between Main & Howard.	MORE 2 Jan 1865
CONWAY, Dominick murdered by John Consalles (Gunsollis?) a well-known pilot who was later exonerated. Conway was a carpenter, single, in his woth year.	MORE 17 & 18 Mar 1862

CONWAY, Joseph, inquest: drowned ae 11. Son/Patrick who kept a saloon on the levee. MORE 6 Oct 1862

CONWAY, Mary Ellen wife of Samuel, 29 Dec ae 50. MORE 8 Jan 1864

CONWAY, Thomas, drowned off the Northener 2 weeks ago, body found. Widow lives at Convent-2nd. MORE 2 May 1863

CONZELMAN, Jorgine A. wife of G. 21 Feb ae 39. Lived on Clark between Mercer & Naomi. Interred Bellefontaine. MORE 22 Feb 1861

COOK, Alfred a bushwhacker killed south of Springfield with Edward Brown, Hiram Russell, and 2 Manleys. MORE 31 Jan 1865

COOK, Eli 1 Feb in Columbia of pneumonia ae 39; active service in the Enrolled Militia. Missionary Baptist 16 years. Wife, 1 child. COWS 13 Feb 1863

COOK, J.A.J., citizen of Chariton Co., 10 Jan of pneumonia. (Undertaker's list) MORE 15 Jan 1865

COOK, Henry, old and respected citizen of Boone Co., 24 July. COWS 28 Jul 1865
    John E. son of the late Henry 10 Oct ae 28. " 20 Oct "

COOK, John employed by the Bolivar Courier, 5 Mar. Left parents. BOL 9 Mar 1861

COOK, Dr. M.C. 5 Mar ae 43. Funeral Church of the Messiah. MORE 6 Mar 1861

COOK, Mary Ann wife of David G. of Boone Co. and dau/late James R. Woods, 19 Nov ae ca 35. COWS 22 Nov 1861

COOK, Mrs. Mary P. 6 Feb of lung congestion in her 25th year. Dau/Mrs. Eliza Harker. Funeral from home of her brother-in-law, James D. McGuire, 16th betw Biddle-O'Fallon; St. Paul's Church; int. Bellefontaine. Wheeling pc MORE 8 & 11 Feb 1862

COOK, William, Chariton Co.: public administrator took over his estate. (John Dewey) CECB 24 Jul 1862

COOKSEY, Mary Alice eldest child/Jacob E. & Mellie in Canton 11 Aug ae 3y 11m 6d. CANP 6 Aug 1863

COOKSEY, William P. in Versailles 28 Dec ae 39y 9m 18d; born in Warren Co. TN 10 Mar 1824. Methodist. CAWN 16 Jan 1864

COOLEY, ___, a young man, killed in Macon Co. by Judge Easley. The young man and his mother had been to consult Easley some time before; Cooley took exception to the Judge's advice and shot his horse. The Judge thought he was going to shoot a second time, as he was holding a revolver, so shot him. (Apparently this took place at the Cooley home.) WARS 15 Dec 1865

COOLEY, Edward "one of the oldest and most respected police" at his home on Chestnut betw 14-15, of consumption. MORE 2 Oct 1865

COOLEY, M.C., citizen of Chariton Co., 22 Dec of pneumonia. (Undertaker's list) MORE 28 Dec 1864

COOLIDGE, Edward E. son/Curtis of St. Louis in Worcester MA 29 Jun ae 37. Interred Bellefontaine. SLMD 6 Jul 1864

COONS, Dr. A.J. 21 May at his home, corner 10th & Chestnut. MORE 22 May 1864

COONS, Frederick at his home in St. Louis Co. 25 May ae 39. MORE 26 May 1863

COOPER, Charles killed at Allen's Foundry yesterday, ae 36. Lived in alley between 8th & 9th, on Morgan. Moulder and Vice-pres. International Iron Moulder's Union. Interred Calvary. MORE 11 Oct 1863

COOPER, Edward of St. Louis in Henderson Co. IL 18 Aug ae 33. Interred St. Louis. MORE 23 Aug 1861
    Eliza, mother of Edward of St. Louis, wife of John, at Roney Creek, Henderson Co. IL 28 Feb ae 50y 8m. MORE 7 Mar 1861

COOPER, Mrs. S.J. wife of William B. 11 Nov ae 32. MORE 13 Nov 1864

COOPER, Stephen D. 17 Nov ae 27y 11m 12d. Lived 42 Mound St. Int. Bellefontaine. MORE 19 Nov 1864

COPE, James B. 28 Sep at his home in Montgomery Co. ae ca 67. MORE 18 Oct 1865

COPELAND, Allen 27 Feb of typhoid in Gratiot Prison; of Burbage's Command, captured in Reynolds Co. 1 Feb. MORE 1 & 2 Mar 1863

COPELAND, Nannie consort of John in Buchanan Co. 13 Jan. Funeral at Baptist Church. SJH 14 Jan 1864

COPP, Eliza wife of Josiah at Jonesburg 10 Jun after a short illness. MORE 23 Jun 1861

COPP, Helen M. wife of James 16 Oct ae 22y 9m 28d. MORE 17 Oct 1864

COPP, Henry W. suddenly yesterday, several years an accountant employed by Joseph How of St. Louis, lately employed at John Rogers Counting House. Ae 35. (MORE adds Boston & NY pc) SJH 26 Mar 1865 MORE "

CORBETT, Mrs. Damaris widow of Alexander at her home in Hannibal Sat 29 May in her 46th year, formerly of Delhie, Delaware Co. NY. HAM 27 Jun 1861

CORBETT, Elizabeth wife of John L. and youngest dau/John & Mary Will of Canton 11 Sep ae 18y 11m 12d. CANP 19 Sep 1863

CORBIN, Lovell in Adair Co. 24 Apr of consumption. — MAG 7 May 1862

CORBIN, Mrs. ___ wife of John of this county, 19 Jan. — MAG 22 Jan 1862

CORBIN, Sarah 15 Mar ae ca 17. — LIT 21 Mar 1862

CORBY, Daniel "quite suddenly" at his home, 6th between O'Fallon & Cass. — MORE 17 May 1863

CORBY, William H. 29 June, in a boiler explosion at Rainer & Co. on the levee; he was foreman. An old river engineer, age ca 40, he left a wife and several children at 11th & Brooklyn. Two other men also killed. Pittsburg pc — MORE 30 Jun 1863

CORCORAN, Margaret found dead of intemperance, Lewis above Smith. — MORE 1 Nov 1861

CORCORAN, Mary of burns received some days before when she stepped on some matches on the floor, which ignited her dress. — MORE 13 Sep 1862

CORCORAN, Patrick stabbed and killed by John Thomas at the Orphans' Picnic in Withnell Grove 4 Jul. An old grudge fight, apparently. — MORE 6 Jul 1864

CORCORAN, Dr. Richard of Millwood, Lincoln Co. 10 Mar ae 32. Funeral from the home of his father-in-law Joseph Davis, 14th & Christy; St. Francis Xavier Church; interred Rock Spring. — MORE 11 Mar 1862

CORDALL, C.M. of Marion Co. in the prison hospital in Springfield. — MORE 10 Apr 1863

CORDELL, Presley Bay son/Henry & Caroline J. in Pleasant Hill, Cass Co. 12 Mar ae 12y 6m 18d. — MORE 23 Mar 1862

CORDES, Claus of inflammation of the brain. Lived 16th betw Biddle-O'Fallon. — MORE 21 Jun 1863

COREY, Elizabeth Altha Foote wife of A.W. at Monticello MO 22 Nov ae 45. — SLMD 3 Dec 1861

COREY, Mattie wife of William W. in her 25th year. Funeral from the home of her mother Mrs. Stead, Lacey House, 6th-Washington. Marietta & Cincinnati pc — MORE 30 Apr 1863

CORLEY, Warren C. on the Istan at Vicksburg 4 Jul ae 31. Of St. Louis. NY pc — MORE 20 Sep 1863

CORNEIL, Patrick killed 4 miles out of town on the Pacific RR when he lay down on the track to sleep, train cut off his legs. — JINQ-W 12 Jan 1861 (Weekly)

CORNELIUS, George of Boone Co., of rubeola. (Undertaker's list) — MORE 10 Nov 1862

CORNELIUS, Mrs. Jane, mother of Capt. Joseph S. Nanson, in Roanoke 27 Apr ae 63. Native of England, many years in Howard Co. A widow. Baptist. — COWS 23 May 1862

CORNELIUS, William in Gratiot Prison of rubeola 5 Dec. — MORE 7 Dec 1862

CORNFORTH, Mary Ann wife of Robert H. at Mexico MO 31 Jul ae 37. Born in Washington D.C., to MO in 1844. Left husband and 2 small children; her infant Charles Leavener died 2 Aug ae 6w. Baltimore, CA, OR pc — MORE 5 Aug 1863

CORNWALL, B.F. (?) at Princeton, Mercer Co., Clerk of the Co. Court, 13 Oct /(paper blurred) of typhoid. — SJH 20 Oct 1865

CORNYN, Capt. Florence M. killed at camp in Corinth by Lt. Col. William D. Bowen, both of 10th MO Cav; both of St. Louis; personal difficulty. Funeral from St. Francis Xavier Church to Calvary. — MORE 13 & 17 Aug 1863

CORRILL, Henry, lately from IA, overdose of morphine. Ae ca 47. Lived at Idaho Saloon, 5th betw Green-Morgan. Left 2 sons, one in St. Louis. — MORE 6 May 1865

CORUM, William Henry son/John & Emeline of typhoid in his 25th year. — LIT 16 Dec 1864

CORWIN, John W. 5 Apr of lung congestion in his 25th year. Funeral from the home of his brother William P., 96 11th St. — MORE 6 Apr 1862

COTNER, James B., captured in Cape Girardeau 22 Aug, died in Gratiot Prison 22 Nov. — MORE 25 Nov 1862

COTTER, James at the home of his brother in Jefferson Co. 14 Nov of lung disease ae 48. Native of Ireland. NY NJ & New Orleans pc — MORE 26 Nov 1862

COTTLE, Miss Adelia in Troy, Lincoln Co. 7 Nov in her 35th year, dau/late Sherman. — MORE 11 Nov 1862

COTTON, Rebecca at the home of her son James in Randolph Co. 28 Aug ae 77. Interred at New Paris OH. — SLMD 6 Sep 1864

COURT, Mrs. Susan, formerly of Philadelphia, 25 Dec in her 70th year at the home of her daughter Mrs. Carlisle, 11th betw Olive-Locust. Philadelphia, San Francisco & Worcester MA pc. — MORE 27 Dec 1863

COURTLEY, Edward, run over in train derailment near Pleasant Hill Tuesday. — WARS 6 Oct 1865

COURTNEY, Leander, of Greene's Reg., captured at Hartsville 11 Jan, in Gratiot Prison of chronic diarrhoea. — MORE 13 Feb 1863

COURTNEY, Levinia P. wife of James L. and dau/J.W. Leggett of Pike Co. 30 May ae 31. — PALS 17 Jun 1864

COUSINEAU, John B. 19 Nov in his 57th year. Lived at 163 Biddle. Long illness.   MORE 21 Nov 1864

COUVIONS, Peter 6 Aug ae ca 49, of heat. He lived 1 mile south of the Pacific   MORE 7 &
    Machine Shop, was in the meat business. Interred Calvary.   8 Aug 1861

COUZINS, Tillie F. youngest dau/J.E.D. & Adaline, ae 17y 7m. Funeral from 2nd   MORE 3 Jun 1865
    Baptist Church. NY & Winona MN pc

COWAN, Rev. John F. Sr. Monday ae 61, at his home in Carondelet. Funeral from   MORE 30 Sep 1862
    2nd Presbyterian Church.

COWDEN, George of Poindexter's Command, captured in Boone Co. 4 Apr, in   MORE 5 May 1863
    Gratiot Prison of measles.

COWEN, Mary E. Wells wife of Eustace W. and dau/Joseph & Morgianna R. McEntire   MORE 31 Dec &
    30 Dec of consumption in her 23rd year. Funeral from St. Malachi's   15 Jan 1865
    Church. Interred Calvary. New Orleans & Louisville pc

    Eustace W. 29 Jul in his 27th year. Funeral from his brother's home,   MORE 28 Jul 1865
    9th & Marion.

COWGILL, James in Alexandria, Clark Co. 2 Nov ae ca 37.   CANP 12 Nov 1863

COX, Ann wife of Capt. T.J. in St. Joseph 21 Aug in her 55th year.   SJH 22 Aug 1865

COX, Corp. Bartlett G., Co E 12th MO Vol Cav, in the hospital in Nashville   SJH 8 Feb 1865
    25 Dec of remittant fever.

COX, David B., resident of Pettis Co., 20 Apr ae 30.   MORE 24 Apr 1864

COX, Ellen, mother of Bernard & Philip and mother-in-law of James H. Kelly,   MORE 16 Aug 1864
    15 Aug ae 57 of chills and fever.

COX, Jackson P. son/B.F. & Elizabeth at Chillicothe 1 Jul ae 9y 10m 15d, of   SJH 19 Jul 1865
    scarlet rash. An infant son also died, on 4 Jul.

COX, Louisa C. relict of Caleb at her home near Fredericktown, Madison Co.,   MORE 7 Mar 1863
    in her 65th year. New Orleans and Memphis pc

COX, Margaret wife of Charles C. 6 Mar in her 42nd year. Lived on Grand Ave.   MORE 9 Mar 1864

COX, Sarah A. 4 Sep ae 41y 2m 10d. Left 3 orphan children.   CAB 9 Sep 1864

COYLE, Daniel 9 Nov in his 33rd year. Mother lived on 9th betw Biddle-O'Fallon.   MORE 20 Nov 1864
    Interred Calvary.

COYLE, Grace relict of Patrick, 18 Jan. Funeral from home of D.V. Toy, Smith-Main.   SLMD 19 Jan 1861

COYLE, Margaret wife of Michael at Sisters Hospital 4 May ae (40?49?) Long,   MORE 5 May 1865
    painful illness. Funeral at the Cathedral, interred Calvary.

COYLE, Mary dau/Bernard and Anne 2 Apr ae 5y 1m. Lived 8th betw Cass-Mullanphy.   MORE 4 Apr 1862

COYLE, Michael 13 Jul at Sisters Hospital ae 58. St. Michael's Church, Calvary.   MORE 14 Jul 1865

COYNE, Michael 25 May ae 36. Lived on O'Fallon betw 6th-7th.   MORE 27 May 1864

COZENS, Laetitia wife of William H. and dau/late Thomas O. Duncan, 26 Sep of   MORE 3 Oct 1865
    heart disease ae 39. Funeral, Immaculate Conception Church.

CRABTHER, Jacob 5 Jul ae ca 35.   LIT 17 Jul 1863

CRABTREE, William 14 Apr of typhoid pneumonia at the home of his brother-inlaw   MORE 15 Apr 1863
    David R. Sheppard. Interred Bellefontaine.

CRAFT, Joseph at his home near Herculaneum 14 Aug in his 74th year. Emigrated   MORE 23 Aug 1861
    to Jefferson Co. from Warren Co. OH in 1817.

CRAGHEAD, Mrs. Elizabeth at her home near Fulton 13 Jul, of flux, ae ?-9m-25d.   FULT 28 Jul 1864

CRAIG, Miss Sallie eldest dau/Benjamin F. & Caroline D. near Plattsburg 26 Nov.   MORE 6 Dec 1863

CRAIG, Susan wife of John S. 7 May of liver complaint, ae ca 50.   CECB 11 May 1861

CRAIN, Allen C. in the Federal Hospital in Warrenton 7 Mar ae 32y 3m 21d.   COWS 20 Mar 1863
    Left wife and 7 children.

CRAINE, Daniel 5 Nov. Native of Douglas, Isle of Man; in St. Louis 25 years.   MORE 6 Nov 1862
    Lived in the alley between Market, Walnut, 7th & 8th.

CRAM, Arthur F. son/G.H. and Harriet in Missouri City 10 Mar ae 18m.   LIT 15 Mar 1861

CRAMER, A.P., inquest: congestion of the brain due to intemperance. Ae 55.   MORE 26 Aug 1863
    Lived alone in a room on Soulard betw 12-13.

CRANE, Ben F., resident of St. Louis since 1838, died 30 Nov in his 44th year.   MORE 2 Dec 1861
    Funeral from Methodist Church, Washington-8th. "Prominent jeweler."   SLMD 3 "

CRANE, Frank Eliot accidentally killed at Enterprise Mills near Warsaw IL   MORE 5 Nov 1865
    31 Oct, son/late Col. John of Madison Co. MO, ae 23. New York City &
    Hartford CT pc

CRANE, John A., citizen of Macon Co. arrested 16 Aug, of pneumonia (Undertaker's list) MORE 12 Nov 1862

CRANE, Joseph Olcott son/John and Caroline of Madison Co. killed in retreat at Corinth at Tishomingo. Ae 24y 7m, of Green's Brigade, Maj. General Price's Command. MORE 24 Aug 1862

CRANE, Mary A. wife of William B. of dysentery 9 Feb in Pilot Knob in her 21st year, formerly of Canton. MORE 11 Feb 1862

CRAPSTER, William L., formerly of Baltimore, in St. Louis 23 Jan at the home of George M. Grover on Clark St., ae 60. Baltimore & Carroll Co MD pc MORE 25 Jan 1865

CRAUSMAN, John, a workman engaged in laying gas pipe, of the effects of sunstroke. Had arrived from Ireland 3 weeks ago. Left wife and 6 children. MORE 7 Jun 1865

CRAWFORD, J. of Marion Co. in the prison hospital in Springfield. MORE 10 Apr 1863

CRAWLEY, Elizabeth wife of R.F. of scarlet fever in Keytesville, daughter of W.R. Atterbury of Wheeling VA. MORE 29 Nov 1862

CREEL, Richard, shot and killed near Waverly. A bachelor. LEXUN 7 Apr 1865

CRELEY, Zoe Georgiana dau/Charles & Margaret Elizabeth 5 Jun ae 4y 2m. Lived at Rosatti betw Ann-Arrow. MORE 6 Jun 1862

Julia Melanie dau/Charles & Margaret E. ae 6y 10m 19d. Funeral from home, Rosatti betw Ann & Arrow, to St. Vincent's Church on Decatur. MORE 25 Aug 1862

CRENSHAW, Mary Louis wife of (L?.D.) near Springfield 9 Oct in her 37th year. Born in (Annella?) Co. VA 4 Feb 1828, to MO 1843, married here. SPRIP 12 Oct 1865

CREWS, George shot at Breckenridge by state militia, a bushwhacker. (From the Chilicothe Chronicle.) MORE 5 Oct 1862

CREWS, Gideon, memorial to: died 23 May, refers to absent son and little grandchild. From Revs. Fristoe, Quarles, and Baldwin. MORE 27 May 1865

CREWS, Mrs. Stanley, widow, 25 Jul. COWS 28 Jul 1865

CREWS William, of Poindexter's Command, captured in Howard Co. 17 Sep, in Gratiot Prison of pneumonia. (Also on Undertaker's list) MORE 20 Dec 1862
(CREWES) " 21 "

CRIDDLE, Alexander S. 6 Aug ae 41y 5m. Funeral from home of Mrs. Treadway, 17th betw Biddle-O'Fallon. MORE 7 Aug 1864

CRINNION, Richard 20 Sep of a ruptured blood vessel, ae 69. Funeral from St. Bridget's Church. SLMD 22 Sep 1864

CROCKET, Caswell G. in Boone Co. 10 Oct of flux (or typhoid), member of Little Bonne Femme Baptist Church. Born 6 Jul 1819. COWS 13 & 20 Oct 1865

CROCKETT, Susan in Clay Co. 5 Sep in her 87th year. LIT 19 Sep 1862

CROLE, Charles at the home of his father in Carondelet 13 Jan ae 22y 11m. Funeral from Methodist Church. MORE 17 Jan 1864

CROMWELL, Mrs. Christiana 28 Apr in Lexington ae 75. MORE 17 May 1864

CROMWELL, Stephen A., several years resident of St. Louis, in Richmond ae 29. MORE 31 Aug 1862

CRONAN, Thomas, a boy ae 11 riding on the cowcatcher of a locomotive; engineer pushed him off, he was caught and killed. Mother a widow on Moor St. MORE 19 Jul 1864

CRONK, William 9 Sep, lived at 25 N. 14th. MORE 10 Sep 1863

CROOKS, Emily widow of Ramsay and dau/late Bernard Pratte of St. Louis in New York 20 Sep. Left brother and 2 sisters in St. Louis. MORE 23 Sep 1863

CROSBY, Mrs. Ellen yesterday at her home, 18th near O'Fallon. A widow, bedfast 8 years. MORE 17 Aug 1865

CROSS, James Tuesday last in Moniteau Co. ae ca 65. CAWN 19 Jan 1861

CROSS, John of Howard Co. 10 Mar in his 70th year. Resident of the county 43 years, left aged wife and children. GLWT 21 Mar 1861

CROSSWHITE, Martha wife of F.M. of Boone Co. of consumption in her 25th year. COWS 21 Jun 1861

CROSS, John Saxby son/Joseph & Marie of pneumonia 2 Jul ae 3y 2m 22d. Lived on Christy betw 12-13. MORE 3 Jul 1862

CROSTHWAIT, Mahershalalalhashbaz 17 May in Boone Co. ae ca 25. COWS 30 May 1862

CROTHERS, Mrs. Elizabeth 29 Jun in her 73rd year, formerly of Baltimore. Funeral from the home of her daughter, Mrs. Wash, 13th & Poplar. MORE 30 Jun 1862

CROWELL, Adolphia R. wife of Rev. William of St. Louis at Upper Alton IL 24 Sep ae 48. Boston pc SLMD 1 Oct 1861

CROWLEY, Thomas killed by the fall of a bank at 14th north of Pernod; married left wife and child. Charles Blumebburg & Caspar Dick also killed. MORE 18 May 1865

39

CROWLY, William 19 Nov ae 24. Lived on 2nd betw Mound-Howard.	MORE 21 Nov 1862
CROZIER, Thomas son/Alexander 28 Feb ae 22. Lived sw corner of 14th & Franklin.	MORE 1 Mar 1861
Eliza wife of Alexander 4 Aug. Lived St. Charles-8th St.	MORE 6 Aug 1861
Grace daughter/Alexander 13 Jan ae 19. Lived St. Charles betw 7-8.	MORE 15 Jan 1862
CRUM, James found dead, apparently from a fall from a horse, near Moniteau Creek. "Old and highly respected."	CAWN 19 Mar 1864
CRUNCLETON, William M. at his home in St. Francois Co. 3 Dec.	MORE 22 Dec 1864
CRUTCHER, Charles, well-known citizen of Monroe Co., last week.	PALS 15 Jan 1864
CULL, Edward ae 64. Funeral from his home, 10th betw Franklin-Wash, to St. Lawrence O'Toole Church. Int. Calvary.	MORE 11 Mar 1864
Mrs. Mary ae 63 (68?) Funeral from her home, 10th betw Franklin-Wash, to St. Lawrence O'Toole Church, int. Calvary.	MORE 25 Aug 1865
CULLEN, Patrick accidentally drowned in the ice cellar of Height & O'Brien, 17th-O'Fallon. Sober and industrious, ca 35. There was 12 feet of water in the cellar after a heavy rain.	MORE 18 Sep 1862
CULLEN, Richard, employed by Slicer & Co. Sales Stables, kicked in the head by a mule. Ae ca 14.	MORE 5 Nov 1865
CULLINAN, Tim at his home in Patee Town 31 Dec, baggage master at the Hannibal and St. Joseph RR. Left wife, 3 children. Detroit pc	SJH 1 Jan 1864
CULVER, Dr. John W. at the home of his cousin, Judge G.W., in Plattsburg in his 29th year, "ill many weeks."	LIT 14 Oct 1864
CUMBAST, Wyatt, formerly with Price's army, killed near Empire Prairie in Andrew Co.	SJH 12 Jul 1863
CUMMINGS, widow, missing since last October; body found in river Sunday.	KCJC 2 Feb 1864
CUMMINGS, Green, Chariton Co.; letters of administration to Jas. M. Staples 9/24.	CECB 2 Oct 1862
CUMMINGS, John a bricklayer killed by a wall collapsing, house near 15-Olive.	MORE 3 Aug 1864
CUMMINGS, Mrs. Mary 27 Jun in her 44th year. Lived at 22-Wash. Funeral from St. Bridget's Church, interred Calvary. Louisville pc	MORE 28 Jun 1861
CUMMINS, Dennis, a citizen of Independence, shot by Perry Fenlason, a soldier on a spree.	SJH 17 Oct 1863
CUMMINS, John brother of B.J. (of Paris & Cummins) and eldest son/B. Cummins of Ballygay Ire, ae 41. Funeral from St. John's Church.	MORE 20 Jul 1862
CUNDIFF, Hannah, 25 Sep in St. Joseph. Native of MD, ae 66. "Bereaved children."	MORE 1 Oct 1863
CUNDIFF, William of Boone Co. in Alton Prison in Dec.	COWS 9 Jan 1863
CUNNIFF, Timothy at Sisters Hospital 26 May ae 29. Funeral from home of Mr. Gibbons, Levee betw Green-Morgan.	MORE 27 May 1864
CUNIFFE, Bernard "a middle-aged man" suddenly Tuesday of heart disease. Lived on O'Fallon betw 8-9. Left wife, 4 children.	MORE 17 Jan 1861
CUNIFFE, Michael K., native of Galway and resident of St. Louis 25 years. Funeral from Sisters Hospital to the Cathedral. Interred Calvary.	MORE 2 Sep 1862
CUNNINGHAM, Mrs. Amanda, a young widow employed at the Olive St. Hotel, found dead in bed of heart disease. Originall from VA, in St. Louis some time.	MORE 16 Aug 1865
CUNNINGHAM, Edward: Machine Moulders Union, Trades League, Stove Moulders invited to his funeral. Lived at Biddle & 2nd.	MORE 24 Sep 1865
CUNNINGHAM, Isaac at his home in St. Francois Co. 1 Jul ae 76.	MORE 14 Jul 1861
CUNNINGHAM, Lawrence "an inveterate toper" drank a quart of whiskey, died of pulmonary apoplexy.	MORE 7 Nov 1861
CUNNINGHAM, Lunella May 10 Jan ae 10m 20d, dau/F.M. & Elizabeth E.	SLMD 21 Jan 1861
CUNNINGHAM, Minor son/David of Boone Co., both in Price's Army, killed in a fight at Fort Scott; David died of disease near the same place.	COWS 30 Dec 1864
CUNNINGHAM, Thomas, former steward at Monroe House, 2 Nov ae 52. Lived at 7th & O'Fallon. Interred Calvary.	MORE 3 Nov 1864
CUOLABAN, Mary only dau/J. & L., 3 Oct of scarlet fever. Lived on 16th betw Wash-Franklin.	MORE 4 Oct 1864
CURACH, Ann of debility and intemperance. Left an orphan son ae 12 at 21 Collins.	MORE 21 Nov 1862
CURD, Deborah A. wife of Gen. John B. of Callaway Co., dau/Joseph & Elizabeth Freeland. Ae (39?)y 8m 23d. Left 2 daus "nearly grown," son ae 4wks. Born in KY, married 1842.	MORE 29 Apr 1861

CURD, John of St. Joseph at the home of his brother in Fulton, 13 June in his 48th year. Former treasurer of the TC & T Co. — SJH 18 Jun 1865

CURD, Thomas H. of Fulton, on 28 Apr. — COWS 16 May 1862

CURL, Bennet "a simpleton of Price's army" and his son killed in Andrew Co. by John Hart's guerillas. — CAWN 18 Jul 1863

CURRY, Amos E. in Philadelphia ae 37; funeral from the home of John A. Tackett, 15th & poplar, to St. John's Church. Interred Calvary. — MORE 24 Aug 1865

CURRY, John D. 28 Jul in his 67th year. Born Alexandria D.C. in Nov (year blurred), to Culpepper VA where he married, to MO 1837. Eldest of a large family, looked after orphaned brothers and sisters when their parents died. (COWS 7 Aug says he was proprietor of the Jefferson House, gives his middle initial as B instead of D.) — JEST 1 Aug 1863

CURTIS, Charles, of 73 S. 14th St., 6 Jan ae 49. — MORE 7 Jan 1862

CURTIS, David E., tribute by Concord Lodge AF & A Masons. — FULT 19 Aug 1864

CURTIS, John of Poindexter's Band, captured in Howard Co. 20 Sep, in Gratiot Prison. — MORE 17 Dec 1862

CURTIS, Nannie Jane wife of W.H. and dau/Benedict Whaley of Callaway Co. at Whaley's Hotel, Fulton on 6 Feb. — COWS 13 Feb 1863

CURTIS, Sadie B. oldest dau/Maj. Gen. S.R. and Belinda 26 Mar of typhoid ae 20. Funeral from St. George's Church. — MORE 27 Mar 1862

CURTIS, William Henry, late of Greene Co. IL, 11 Nov ae 19y 10m. — SLMD 19 Nov 1861

CURTRIGHT, Eliza only dau/W.H. and C., 12 Oct ae 9. — COWS 24 Oct 1862

CUSHING, Dr. George at Kingston House 21 Feb, of lung fever, ca 60. An oculist from northern IL, in Louisiana about a year. — LAJ 6 Mar 1862

CUSNA or CUZNA Adelbert died 3 Jan, buried St. Peter & Paul; family suspected poisoning, body exhumed. Stepson of William Kaskar of St. Louis Co., suspect was Barbara Cuzna, his wife. Catherine Versbetz, aunt, testified. Arsenic found in body, but it was questionable if it had been enough to kill. He was 23., from Bohemia 11 years before, lived S 8th St. — MORE 9 Feb & 2 Mar 1865

CUSTIS, John, prisoner, 15 Dec of phthisis. See John CURTIS. — MORE 21 Dec 1862

CUTLER (CUTTER?), S.C., conductor of the train in the disaster at Platte Bridge. Was on his last run, had accepted a job in the east. Left wife, son, daughter. Interred Lewiston ME. — HAM 12 Sep 1861 / SLMD 10 "

DACEY, James at Sisters Hospital 1 Apr ae 35. Formerly of Cork, Ire. Funeral from St. Patrick's Church. Interred Calvary. — MORE 2 Apr 1865

DACHSEL, Sue E. wife of Charles in Columbia 11 Jul. — COWS 14 Jul 1865

DAILY, Caroline wife of P. 26 Jun at the home of her mother, Mrs. L.D. Bates, 106 Elm. Lingering illness. New York & Richmond VA pc — MORE 28 Jun 1865

DAILY, John, inquest: fell from stable loft while intoxicated. Lived corner Spring & Broadway, teamster for Henry Kerr. Left wife, 3 children. (His wife Ellen wrote that he was a sober and upright man, affectionate father, had lived in St. Louis 16 years.) — MORE 29 & 30 Nov 1863

DAILEY, Thomas, a nurse at the military hospital, killed by Solomon King. Left wife and 3 children, one of them a 14-year-old daughter. — MORE 16 Feb 1863

DA-KER-KA-HIER WAR-KA-NAC-KE, inquest: an old Indian found dead in a chicken house on Chouteau near Pratte; from Camp River, tribe not known. Had come to city with squaw some days ago, begging; recognized by French trapper Baptiste Marle and invited to stay with him, which they did for a few days, but left. Very old, age not known, squaw trying to get funds to return to the tribe. Verdict, debility and exposure. — MORE 8 Feb 1863

DAKIN, Mary dau/Mrs. Jennie 12 Apr ae 5. — KCJC 13 Apr 1864

DALE, Campbell son/Alfred, trying to cross Trail Creek, killed when his horse stumbled and fell on him, 13 miles below Bethany. Age about 20. — BEST 14 Feb 1861

DALE, Ellen dau/William and Elizabeth of intermittent fever, ae 3y 11m. Lived on 2nd betw Florida-Mullanphy. (SLMD 6 Mar gives age as 9y 11m) — MORE 6 Mar 1861

DALE, Sarah J. wife of W.J. and dau/W.T. and Frances H. Adams of Randolph Co. in Macon Co. ae 20y 6m 28d. Left husband, 2 children. Baptist. — RANC 4 Apr 1861

DALE, W.W. in Wyandotte KS 23 May in his 43rd year, resident of Parkville for a number of years, a merchant, well known in St. Louis and upper MO. Only child, a daughter, married a month ago; also left wife. — KCJC 29 May 1862

DALE, Weekly 15 Oct in his 63rd year, citizen of Clay Co. nearly 40 years. Ill 2 days.	LIT 21 Oct 1864
DALEY, Kitty ae 11 drowned in a cistern while getting water. Lived Palm betw 9-10.	MORE 23 Aug 1865
DALTON, John, Chariton Co. Public administrator took over his estate.	CECB 24 Jul 1862
DALTON, John at his home in St. Louis Co. 24 Jul, born near (Alsagoon?), Washington Co. VA 29 Sep 1794. In 1803 his father moved to Louisville KY where he died in 1815 leaving 10 children, John the oldest. In 1828 he married Paul (sic) Sugg, dau/Joel D. of Union Co. KY; she survives. To St. Louis 1842, lived on Natural Bridge Plank Road 6 miles from city. Interred Bellefontaine.	MORE 24 & 25 Jul 1865
DALY, John ae 8, son/John, drowned yesterday in a pond on 18th near Mullanphy. Lived on Cass betw 7-8.	MORE 9 Jul 1863
DALLAM, A.P. 30 Dec ae 46, at 112 Pine. Baltimore and San Francisco pc	MORE 31 Dec 1863
DAMERON, Charles T. son/Benjamin and Matilda at the home of his mother in Randolph Co. of typhoid pneumonia, 25 Apr ae 27y 1m 9d.	MAG 19 Mar 1862
DAMERON, J.H., Co A 1st MO Cav, a prisoner, 27 Jan of measles and typhoid. (Undertaker's list)	MORE 2 Feb 1863
DAMERON, Mary E. wife of Logan D. 5 Dec ae 28. Funeral, 1st Methodist Church.	MORE 7 Dec 1862
DAMERON, William, citizen of Randolph Co., 3 Mar of pneumonia. (Undertaker's list)	MORE 6 Mar 1865
DAMERON, William M. in Randolph Co. 21 Dec ae (33?).	MORE 8 Jan 1861
DAMON, George G. killed by guerillas near Huntsville 15 Jul ae 33. Funeral from Everett House. Interred Bellefontaine.	MORE 16 & 17 Jul 1864
DANDRIDGE, Mrs. Charlotte in her 56th year. Lived at Park & St. Ange.	MORE 11 Mar 1861
DANFORTH, James R., many years cashier of the bank, last night. (Springfield "Old and espected." Journal)	SEDA 19 Nov 1864
DANIEL, John, of heart disease 13 Jan.	GAL 26 Jan 1865
DANIEL, Peter V. at the battle of Chickamauga 20 Sep. Born KY, graduate of Yale in 1859, in which year he came to St. Louis.	MORE 27 Oct 1863
DAPRAN, Amable "a very worthy young man of Carondelet" tried to get on a railroad car loaded with hoop poles, fell and was killed, ae 18.	MORE 17 Oct 1861
DARAN, Patrick, an Irishman, killed trying to help Frederick Kane, who suffocated in a coal pit on Clayton Road.	MORE 12 Aug 1861
DARBY, Catherine wife of Hiram and mother of Charles Cady, after a short illness, ae ca 60. Lived on 11th betw Market-Walnut.	MORE 12 & 13 Mar 1863
DARBY, J.W. 19 Oct ae (38?) (Subsequent item asks for verification of this notice.)	MORE 20 Oct 1861
D'ARCAMBEL, Juliette, widow of Felix of Baltimore, 29 Apr ae 62.	MORE 1 May 1864
DARNAL, William and wife of Louisiana MO 9 Mar within a few hours of each other, he ae 75 and she 65.	MORE 23 Mar 1862
DARNALL, Edward after a protracted illness 21 June ae ca 68.	LIT 24 Jun 1864
DARNES, William P., late member of the State Legislature from Scott Co., at his home in Commerce. (Cape Girardeau Eagle)	LAJ 28 Feb 1861
DARRAH, Mrs. Elizabeth ae 77 after a lingering illness. Funeral from the home of her son H.T. Interred Bellefontaine.	MORE 16 Sep 1862
Henry T. 24 Nov ae 59; native of NJ, many years resident of St. Louis. Member County Court. Funeral from 1st Presbyterian Church.	MORE 26 Nov 1864
DARRAH, Patrick killed in a boiler explosion at Rainer & Co. on the levee. A bachelor. Two other men also killed.	MORE 30 Jun 1863
DARROW, Mrs. wife of Rev. J.D., minister of the Christian Church, of Ozark Co., drowned in a flood. (Springfield Mirror)	HAM 25 Jul 1861
DARSE, George A., citizen of Callaway Co., arrested 12 Jul, committed 26 Jul. Acute diarrhoea. (Undertaker's list)	MORE 16 & 18 Aug 1863
DARST, John Alphonse only son/Robert and Julia, 2 May at Memphis ae 16y 10m 12d. Lived at 15th & Poplar.	MORE 7 Jun 1863
DARST, Mary wife of D.H. of St. Charles Co. 16 Jun in her 64th year.	MORE 22 Jun 1864
DARUS, Beverly Allen at Arcadia Seminary, Arcadia, 12 Jan ae 17.	MORE 19 Jan 1864
DAUTEL, Florence only dau/Christian and Mary Ann in Glasgow 2 Dec ae 15y 9m 10d. Typhoid. Cincinnati & Philadelphia pc	MORE 14 Dec 1864
DAUGHERTY, Maj. John 30 Dec in his 70th year; born KY 1791. Indian agent. Left 4 children, one the wife of Maj. Charles Ruff. Long illness. (see next page)	LIT 4 Jan 1861

DAUGHERTY, Maj. John cont. -- once employed by American Fur Company, married in St. Louis, had lately been a farmer. — MORE 6 Jan 1861

DAUGHERTY, William D., a well-known pilot, in New Orleans where he had lately gone for his health. Of St. Louis. Consumption, 19 Jan in 37th year (or 16 Jan) — MORE 16 & 22 Mar 1862

DAVENPORT, Harriet N. dau/H.C. & Mary T. 18 Jan ae 9y 3m. — LAJ 19 Feb 1863

DAVENPORT, Rice son/William and Rachel 11 Apr of scarlet fever ae 4y 1m 26d. — LIT 15 Apr 1864

DAVETT, William M. son/John W. and Wilhamena R. drowned ae 9y 10m. Funeral from the home of William Morse, Benton-10th. — MORE 4 Aug 1861

DAVIDSON, Elizabeth consort of A.S. 24 Sep of consumption. — LIT 26 Sep 1862

DAVIDSON, Pinkney D., 1st MO, captured in Dunklin Co. 12 Mar, in prison hospital 12 Mar of inflammation of the lungs. — MORE 7 Apr 1863

DAVIES, Annie Maria only surviving dau/Col. Benjamin 28 May. Methodist. — PALS 2 Jun 1865

DAVIES, Elizabeth Owen, wife of Thomas, near Caledonia, Washington Co., 8 Oct ae 65y 2m. — MORE 15 Oct 1865

DAVIS, Bruce who lived near the old Sexton place in Columbia killed in Callaway Co. last Nov by a citizen whose house he was engaged in burning. Son of a widow and political cousin of Jeff (Davis)." — COWS 17 Feb 1865

DAVIS, C.E.R. of paralysis of the heart. Kept a boarding house at 6th-St. Charles. Died 9 Jan, left a large family. — MORE 11 Jan 1862

DAVIS, Charlotte "a Creole woman" burned when clothes caught fire. Lived on Chouteau near Pratte. — MORE 8 Mar 1862

DAVIS, Mrs. Elizabeth E. 22 Aug(?) ae 47. Cynthiana & Georgetown KY pc. (prob Oct) — LIT 11 Nov 1864

DAVIS, Mrs. Harriet 30 Dec 1863 at the home of J.W. Taylor. Funeral Methodist Ch. — SJH 1 Jan 1864

DAVIS, James "just turned 16," drowned. Left parents, several brothers. — HAM 8 Aug 1861

DAVIS, James near Williamsburg 7 May ae 34y 7m 2d. — FULT 9 May 1862

DAVIS, James 17 Dec in Boone Co. in his 61st year, of pneumonia. — COWS 12 Feb 1864

Maggie dau/late James and Mary 25 Jul ae 20. Member Salem Baptist Church. — COWS 28 Jul 1865

DAVIS, John W. at Ashburton near Prairieville, Pike Co., 4 Jun ae 64. Formerly of Charlottesville VA. Episcopalian. — MORE 19 Jun 1862

DAVIS, Joseph a civilian capture in Dunklin Co. 5 Mar, in Gratiot Prison of acute pneumonia. — MORE 1 Apr 1863

DAVIS, Mrs. Melinda in Mexico MO 6 Apr in her 76th year. — COWS 12 May 1865

DAVIS, Merrill at the home of E. Davis in St. Louis 19 Apr in his 66th year. Formerly of MA but a resident of MO many years. — SLMD 30 Apr 1861

DAVIS, Oliver of Stewartsville drowned in the Missouri River near Weston when a flatboat collided with the steamboat Majors. — SJH 9 Oct 1863

DAVIS, Mrs. Sarah Ann McCready wife of John in Memphis TN 2 Feb in her 26th year. Born in Wheeling VA, to St. Louis in 1858 to visit her cousin Col. Robert White, met her future husband and married 1 Sep 1859. Member Methodist Ch. South, attended Mound Church in St. Louis. — MORE 10 Feb 1863

DAVIS, Mrs. Vardaman scalded in a mill explosion 5 miles west of Knoxville. (Richmond Conservator) — RANS 24 Jan 1861

DAVITT, Maggie dau/John W. and Wilhelmina, crushed by a tombstone at Bellefontaine, 30 Jun ae 4. Parents had gone there to visit the grave of her brother, ae 9, who drowned the previous year; had also lost another child. Funeral from Simpson Chapel, 9th-North Market. — MORE 1 Jul 1862

DAWSON, John ae ca 39 at Kingston House 30 Mar of lung hemorrhage, formerly of Rockport IL. — LAJ 17 Apr 1862

DAWSON, Mary N. wife of J.W. at Madison, Monroe Co., 8 Aug of flux ae 39. — COWS 2 Sep 1864

DAY, Edward, mortally wounded 15 Dec, died 21 Dec in a hospital in Nashville. Formerly clerk of the West Wind, member 33rd MO Vols. — SJH 29 Dec 1864

DAY, John F. of Lincoln Co., member Co F, 2nd MO Inf CSA, killed either in the battle of Champion Hills, Big Black Bridge, or the Siege of Vicksburg. — MORE 19 Sep 1863

DAYLY, Mrs. Catherine, wife of Morgan, 10 Nov ae 68. Lived Benton betw 12-13. — MORE 11 Nov 1863

DEAN, Capt. A.S., AADC & Chief of Staff to Brig. Gen. Strong, 19 Jul ae 40. Lived on the corner of Locust and Garrison. Brief illness. — MORE 20 Jul 1863

DEAN, Mrs. Ann W. 4 Jun ae 64 and Miss Anna Woods Dean 14 Jul ae 19 in   JEST 14 Jul 1865
        Jefferson City.   MORE 24 "

DEAN, Christopher a cooper living near Pratte, brother-in-law of John Henry,   MORE 14 May 1861
        killed in the Camp Jackson affair.   " 15

DEAN, Elizabeth wife of Henry 26 May in Phelps Co. ae 30.   ROLEX 10 Jun 1861

DEAN, Ephraim of Phelps Co. in Gratiot Prison of pleuritis 2 Dec.   MORE 7 Dec 1862

DEAN, Frank stabbed by his roommate some time ago, died in City Hospital.   MORE 4 Jul 1861

DEAN, George W. in Gratiot Prison 3 Nov of pneumonia.   MORE 9 Nov 1862

DEAN, Minerva Thrush 16 Oct of congestive chills on her 18th birthday.   MEMP 21 Oct 1865

DEAN, Otelia wife of John in Potosi 31 Mar ae 37. "Mother." NY & MA pc   MORE 10 Apr 1862

DEAN, Pilate at Warrensburg 2 May, formerly of Smith Co. TN, ae 58. Louisville   MORE 9 May 1865
        & Nashville pc

DEAN, Samuel, Chariton Co. Public administrator took over his estate.   CECB 28 Aug 1862

DEAN, Thomas A. 1 Feb after a brief illness. Lived on Ashland Hill, St. Louis Co.   MORE 3 &
        (St. Charles Rock Road). Husband, father. Died of pneumonia.   4 Feb 1864

DEAN, William, Chariton Co. Public administrator took over his estate.   CECB 28 Aug 1862

DEANE, Mary Katherine only dau/T.M. and Emily 21 Jan near Boonesboro of   COWS 23 Jan 1863
        scarlet fever, ae 8y 7m 26d.

DEANE, Sarah Skinner wife of John 11 Jan in her 30th year.   LEXUN 21 Jan 1865

DEANE, Sarah W. dau. of E.B. of Cape Girardeay 19 Feb in Chicago ae ca 15.   MORE 2 Mar 1865

DEAVER, Sophia ae 24. Funeral from home of her mother, 182 Olive, to   MORE 25 Dec 1863
        Immaculate Conception Church. Int. Calvary. Baltimore pc

DeCAMP, Lieut. John at the St. Louis Marine Hospital 26 Jul of wounds received   MORE 1 Aug 1864
        at Alexandria LA 28 Apr, ae 24. Son/Capt. Morris and Ann.

DEEGAN, Martin consort of Margaret 16 Apr of bronchitis ae 28. Lived on Biddle   MORE 17 Apr 1865
        betw 6-7. Funeral St. Patrick's Ch., int. Calvary. Nashville & NY pc

DEERING, Jesse S. son/Mortamore and R.J., of meningitis ae 4y 2m 11d.   LIT 18 Apr 1862

DeFRANCA, Emmanuel J. 22 Aug in his 58th year of organic disease of the liver.   MORE 23 Aug 1865
        Nat/Portugal, artist in St. Louis nearly 25 years; first lived, and
        married, in Philadelphia, then to Harrisburg, in St. Louis as early as
        1842. Lived 115 Pine. Interred Bellefontaine.

DeGARRIS, John in Hannibal 15 Jul, buried 16 Jul by Masons, ae 44.   HAM 25 Jul 1861

DEITZEL, Philip accidentally killed at the rolling mill in Bremen Saturday,   MORE 20 Nov 1865
        caught in machinery. Sole support of aged parents.

DEJARNETTE, ae 50, killed near Keytesville in Chariton Co.   MORE 10 Jan 1865

DELAHANTY, Patrick, teamster employed by John Shehan, fell from wagon while   MORE 7 Jul 1861
        intoxicated.

DELANEY, Michael ae 22. Lived at 24th-O'Fallon. New Orleans pc   MORE 31 Mar 1865

DELANY, William run over by a street car on Carondelet near Lynch, ae 14.   MORE 14 Jul 1863

DELAPLAIN, Mrs. Sarah 26 Mar ae 62. "Mother."   MORE 29 Mar 1862

DELASSUS, Leon last Saturday night ae 52, a resident of Perry Co. for a number   PERU 28 Nov 1862
        of years, a merchant the past 10 years, left wife and many children.

DeLAURIER, Miss Mary 8 Dec ae 51. Funeral from the home of her brother-in-law   MORE 9 Dec 1862
        Charles Roderman, 8 miles from the city on Manchester Road.

DELELE, Mrs. Mary 3 Dec ae 80. Funeral from the home of her son-in-law, at   MORE 4 Dec 1864
        Columbus & Anna.

DELFILS, Francis 9 Apr in Carondelet.   MORE 10 Apr 1863

DELGADO, Walter Hanford son/Frederick and Rachel 1 Apr ae 4y 3m. Lived Olive betw   MORE 2 Apr 1862
        22-23. Int. Bellefontaine.
    Rachel wife of Frederick 15 Sep in her 27th year. Funeral from   MORE 16 Sep 1864
        St. George's Church. New Orleans pc

DeLISLE, Henry, Frenchman living in Carondelet shot by Lt. Henry Valker in self-   MORE 31 Aug &
        defense. DeLisle had refused to attend a military meeting.   1 Sep 1862

DELISLE, Mary A. consort of Jules M. and dau/late Stuart Matthews, 3 Jan ae 22.   MORE 4 Jan 1862
        Lived at #9 14th St. Interred Calvary.

DELLINGER, John of the 10th MO Cav, in the prison hospital.   MORE 2 Feb 1864

DEMAREST, Ella Jane eldest child of S.A. and Jane W. 18 Feb ae 4y 1m 5d.	CANP 19 Feb 1863
DEMENT, Charlie son/Dr. William B. and Alzada 17 Dec ae 6; fell from a wagon and was run over.	CANP 22 Dec 1864
DEMETTE, John 23 Jan of consumption ae 37.	MORE 24 Jan 1861
DEMETTE, Louis Francis son/John B. and Rosalie, from a gunshot wound sustained in the Hyde Park riot 4 Jul, ae 15y 7m 7d. St. Joseph MO & Vincennes pc	MORE 6 & 9 Jul 1863
DEMPSEY, Thomas 23 Jun of consumption ae 27. His friends and those of Capt. John Dempsey invited to funeral, 10 Barlow St.	MORE 24 Jun 1864
DEMPSEY, Thomas in Florissant in his 62nd year. Interred Rock Spring.	MORE 22 May 1861
DeMUTH, Christopher Edwin son/C. and Mary of scarlet fever ae 9y 4m. Lived on St. Charles Rock Road 3 doors e. of Prairie House. Int. Bellefontaine.	MORE 3 Jan 1864
DENNIS, David of Gordon's band, taken in Howard Co. 13 Oct, of intermittent fever in the prison hospital.	MORE 7 Feb 1864
DENNISON, Mrs. Phebe in Cedar Hill Twp 10 Apr(?) ae 100.	COWS 25 Aug 1865
DENNY, David R. near Roanoke 25 Jan of pneumonia in his 28th year.	COWS 19 Feb 1864
DENO, Mrs. Rosalie Demette 15 Dec of consumption ae 40y 4m 10d.	MORE 16 Dec 1864
DENUFFE, James R. 7 Feb at his home on Green between 9-10. Interred Calvary. Cairo and Stillwater pc	MORE 9 Feb 1864
DERBY, Charles of St. Louis in Chicago 9 Oct ae 51. Funeral from Trinity Church.	MORE 10 Oct 1863
Harriet C. widow of Charles, in her 58th year. Friends of family and of Elon G. Smith invited. Lived on 7th betw Chouteau-Hickory.	MORE 1 Feb 1864
DERBY, Capt. Charles, USA, funeral. Died in New York, wife lives in Carondelet. St. George's Church, interred Bellefontaine.	MORE 5 Jun 1861
DERIEUX, Mrs. Deborah 4 May in Fulton ae 45 at the home of her son-in-law W.I. Golding.	COWS 12 May 1865
DERN, John native of Austria, in St. Louis about 4 years, suicide ae ca 56. He had been ill, and hanged himself.	MORE 29 May 1862
DERR, John W. son/W.R. 26 Jan ae 21, member of the Varieties Theatre. NY pc	MORE 28 Jan 1865
DESBONNE, Adele Mercier wife of Auguste Sr. Lived on Hickory betw Pearl-Ham. Annunciation Church.	MORE 27 Feb 1861
Augustte Sr. 1 May in his 68th year. Lived Dillon near Chouteau. Annunciation Church.	MORE 2 May 1863
DETERT, John Henry Tuesday in his 38th year after an 8-day illness. Justice of the Peace in the 9th Ward, lived on 15th betw O'Fallon-Cass. Frankfort KY pc	MORE 10 Apr 1862
DeVANNEY, Ann wife of Owen 8 Feb ae 31. Lived on 8th betw O'Fallon-Cass. Funeral from St. Patrick's Church, interred Calvary. Cincinnati pc.	MORE 20 Feb 1864
DEVIN, William tribute from Frankford Lodge F A M, died 22 Jan. Husband, brother.	LAJ 30 Jan 1864
DEVLIN, Lieut. Arthur J., funeral notice. Member IOOF. Methodist. "From this part of the country. . . widow, friends."	SJH 20, 21, 26 Oct 1864
DEVOY, Mary Ann relict of Nicholas 11 Aug ae 48. Lived 3rd betw Convent-Rutger.	MORE 12 Aug 1862
DEWS, Mrs. Mary W. of Portage des Sioux thrown from a wagon 31 Aug, ae 53. Left 5 children. (St. Charles Reveille)	MORE 19 Sep 1863
DEY, J.C., brakeman on the Union Pacific, fell from train, instantly killed.	SJH 4 Dec 1863
DICE, John, riding on a load of wheat with his son, thrown from the wagon and run over, ae ca 55. Interred Palmyra.	PALS 25 Sep 1863
DICK, Caspar killed by the fall of a bank 14th north of Pernod; married, had 2 children. Thos Crowley and Chas. Blumingberg also killed.	MORE 18 Mar 1865
DICK, John D. at Savannah 9 Apr ae 38y 7m 17d.	SJH 12 Apr 1864
DICKINSON, E., merchant in California MO, killed by a shot fired through his window by an unknown assailant.	HAM 15 Mar 1861
DICKINSON, Edmond H., 19 May, only remaining son of Therese, formerly of Manchester Eng., now of St. Louis, in his 18th year. In Capt. Guiber's Company, CSA Mo. Volunteers. Pontiac MI pc	MORE 25 Jul 1863
DICKINSON, S.B. at the home of his brother-in-law W.C. Bagby, St. Aubert, 11 May.	FULT 23 May 1862
DICKS, John, a resident of Cooper Co., killed in the Camp Jackson affair.	MORE 18 May 1861
DICKS, John (E.?) 17 Jan ae 54; lived at 28 S. 8th St. Interred Calvary.	MORE 18 Jan 1865

DICKSON, Alanson of St. Louis in Demarara, Guiana, SA of yellow fever ae 33; was   MORE 19 Mar 1865
   visiting his brother, got yellow fever. Wife, 3 young children. Of
   the late firm of Dickson Orr. Buffalo & NY pc. Died 9 Feb.
DIETRING, Mrs. Sarah, suicide by laudanum. Ca 40, no children, had lived apart   MORE 20 Oct 1865
   from her husband George (also known as "Star Davis") for 2 years.
DIETZLER, H.C. of Poindexter's band, captured in Howard Co. 23 Sep, in Gratiot   MORE 11 Dec 1862
   Prison of pneumonia. (Undertaker's list shows name as DITZLER.)   12 "
DIGGES, Mrs. Sarah D. at Glasgow 31 Dec ae 81.   MORE 10 Jan 1864
DIGMAN, John a discharged soldier found dead of apoplexy; had served in the 3rd   MORE 13 Jan 1865
   MO Inf. Left a child, his wife had died while he was in service.
DILGERT, Ferdinand 15 May ae (53?). Lived on Savannah Road 2 mi. north of the city. SJH 16 May 1865
DILLARD, Dr. F.E. "highly respected" recently in the flux epidemic.   FULT 19 Aug 1864
DILLON, __ killed by __ Strenk at Middletown Saturday week, over a "minor difference." LAJ 8 Aug 1863
DILLON, Arthur J. of consumption 16 Dec ae 22y 8m; mother lived 14th-Papin. Son   MORE 17 Dec 1863
   of late Col. P.M. Funeral Church of the Annunciation.
DILLON, Effie dau/Thomas and Carrie 19 Jan ae 6.   SJH 21 Jan 1864
DILLON, James 25 Dec ae 29. Lived corner of 23rd & Christy.   MORE 26 Dec 1864
DILLON, John, shot by soldiers robbing a house - a teamster, lived at the corner   MORE 31 Aug 1863
   of Gratiot & 10th. Wife mentioned.
DILLON, Judah wife of William 23 Feb ae 35. Lived on Sylvania St.   SJH 24 Feb 1864
DILLON, Michael suddenly of congestion; left a wife.   MORE 16 Aug 1862
DILLON, R.A. wife of William E. at Rockport 14 Jul of a ruptured heart, ae 31y 5m 21d. MORE 25 Jul 1862
DILLON, William 11 Nov ae 40; had been shot in an affray in a saloon a few days
                                                                        earlier.   SJH 12 Nov 1865
DINGS, Elbridge 5 Apr ae 28. Memphis & MN pc   MORE 8 Apr 1863
DINWIDDIE, Loucinda dau/late Samuel 13 Oct in Boone Co. ae 32y 8m 10d.   COWS 20 &
                                                                                       27 Oct 1865
DITTO, Mrs., wife of a wealthy farmer in Cooper Co., living 2 miles below
   Rocheport - a year or two since from KY -- apparently fainted and fell into   COWS 24 Apr 1863
   the fire. Her husband was several miles away.
DITTO, Lewis T. 5 June in his 24th year after a lingering illness. Funeral from   MORE 8 Jun 1863
   the home of Robert Thonrburgh, 276 Carr.
DITZLER, George, ae 6, drowned yesterday in the river.   MORE 21 Jul 1864
DIVERS, __ waylaid and shot in Pike Co., suspected of having recently killed   MORE 2 Oct 1865
   George A. Waters, whose friends are thought to have killed Divers.   MEMP 11 Nov "
DIVINE, Mary, Irish ae ca 55, of brain congestion and intemperance. Left husband   MORE 20 Dec 1861
   "temperate and worthy" and 2 children.
DIX, Henry A. 4 Apr ae 46. Lived at 10th & Wash. Funeral from Fee Fee (Baptist) Ch. MORE 5 Apr 1862
DIX, Jane E. wife of Capt. Edmund F. 18 Mar in her 32nd year after a long and   MORE 19 Mar 1864
   painful illness. Lived at Garrison & Lucas.
DIXON, Jacob of erysipelas and brain injury from attempted suicide - he was a   MAG 9 Apr 1862
   soldier from Athens, Clark Co.
DIXON, Thomas 23 Nov ae 32y 3m. Lived 10th betw Franklin-Wash. NY & Boston pc   MORE 24 Nov 1863
DOAN, Peter with the S.W. Battalion, killed in the Camp Jackson affair.   MORE 14-17 May'61
DOBBINS, John K. at Iron Mountain 21 Jan; of St. Francois Co., ae 27.   MORE 28 Jan 1865
DOBYNS, Jane M. wife of J.R. 15 Nov in her 45th year. Funeral from the home of   MORE 16 Nov 1863
   M.L. Julian, Chestnut betw 13-14.
DOBYNS, children of Dr. R.L.H. and Sallie E., in Boonville of scarlet fever: MORE 15 Mar 1864
   Infant George Henry, Lizzie Stuart ae 2y 4m, and Conrad Hunt 4y 4m --
   "all and only children."
DOBYNS, __ (a man) passenger on the Tipton stage, shot through the head at   SEDA 24 Sep 1864
   Boonville by unknown murderer. (Boonville Advertiser)
DODGE, Christiana wife of ex-Gov. Henry of WI, in Burlington IA in her 81st year. MORE 20 Apr 1865
   Born near Bardstown KY 2 Feb 1785, to St. Louis 1796 with her father, James
   McDonald. Married in Bonhomme settlement Mar 1801. Had 13 children, 9
   attained mature age (7 daus, 2 sons). Left MO 37 years ago.
DODGE, John D. 13 Apr ae 63. Interred Buffalo NY.   MORE 16 Apr 1862

DOHERTY, Mary eldest dau/William and Martha 29 Nov ae 6y 9m.	MORE 2 Dec 1861
DOHRMANN, Johann Diedrich Julian, native of Hanover, 20 Jan of consumption ae 55.	MORE 24 Jan 1861
DOLAN, Miss Lucy E. 6 Oct at the home of her brother ae 26y 3m. Funeral from St. Bridget's Church.	SLMD 7 Oct 1864
DOLE, August, formerly of Franklin Co., captured by Union soldiers in Dent Co., transferred to Rolla, then St. Clair, where he was hanged on a tree near the RR station. "A desperate individual" who had murdered, robbed, and threatened prominent Franklin Co. citizens.	RICON 14 May 1863
DONAHOE, Cornelius 11 Mar ae 66 after a short illness. Lived 2 S. 9th. Memphis & Louisville pc	MORE 13 Mar 1863
DONAHOE, Mary killed by a blow from her husband John - he was drunk. Left 2 small children by first husband, taken to Orphan Asylum. She was ae 35.	MORE 2 & 3 Aug 1864
DONALDSON, Mrs. Amanda, dau/John Berry, 1 Sep of consumption ae ca 35.	LIT 5 Sep 1862
DONALDSON, Isaac P. 11 Aug ae 65. Funeral Union Methodist Ch., int. Wesleyan. (SLMD 13 Aug gives age as 55)	MORE 12 Aug 1864 " 13
DONEGAN, Andrew 21 Aug ae 40. Lived at 23rd & O'Fallon.	MORE 22 Aug 1863
DONELLY, Patrick 5 Apr. Lived at 219 Biddle. Int. Calvary.	MORE 7 Apr 1862
DONNAHUE, Mary a married woman ca 29, of sunstroke; found dead in bed by sister.	MORE 28 Jun 1864
DONNEGAN, James stabbed by Michael J. (Casey?) at St. Paul Station, Pacific RR. Cornelius Moroney also stabbed. All "under the influence."	MORE, 6 Jul & later, 1864
DONNEGAN, Michael, a baggage manager, run over by Pacific RR cars when he tried to jump aboard.	MORE 9 Oct 1861
DONNEGAN, Patrick, stabbed "some time back" by his brother Michael, died at City Hospital. Both river men.	MORE 6 Feb 1865
DONNELLY, Christopher son/Christopher and Mary 2 May of a broken leg, ae 6y 2m. Lived at 253 Chestnut.	MORE 3 May 1863
DONNELLY, Patrick at Corinth MS 24 Jul in his 35th year, of typhoid. Baltimore & Philadelphia pc	MORE 23 Aug 1862
DONOHOE, Catherine ae 38 of debility and lungcongestion. Lived in the alley between 7-8-Elm-Spruce, separated from her husband and 3 children.	MORE 24 Jan 1862
DONOHOE, James R., engineer on the Luminary, 17 Feb ae 38. Lived Carr betw 15-16. Left widowed mother and sister. Funeral home of Mrs. Spalding, 223 Carr.	MORE 22 & 23 Feb 1864
DONOHUE, John at Sisters Hospital 20 Mar ae 37. Cincinnati pc	MORE 22 Mar 1864
DONOVAN, Joseph, suicide by laudanum. A drunkard, lived Cass betw 14-15. Wife mentioned.	MORE 20 Sep 1865
DONWORTH, James 31 Mar of heart disease ae 20y 11m, at the home of his father. A printer. Burlington IA pc.	SLMD 2 Apr 1861
DONWORTH, William ae 15 drowned while playing on a raft.	MORE 20 Aug 1862
DOOLEY, Mrs. Catherine 30 Sep in her 66th year. Lived 147 Collins.	MORE 1 Oct 1863
DOPP, Mary Louisa eldest dau/Col. J. H.(?) and Ann, living on Collins St.	MORE 16 Dec 1863
DOPPMAN, ___ son of John, a saloonkeeper on 8th St. betw Cass & O'Fallon, drowned yesterday in the river ae ca 14.	MORE 8 Jun 1865
DORAN, Bridget wife of John 7 Jun of brain congestion. Sister of Maj. John P. McGrath, US Army. St. Bridget's Church, interred Calvary. Memphis & New Orleans pc	MORE 8 & 11 Jun 1865
DORAN, John, inquest: suffered a blow on the head, from a poker, in Cairo 3 weeks ago; became ill at Rogers Saloon Thursday, died of brain congestion.	MORE 25 Dec 1864
DORAN, John, 24 Sep. Funeral from Farmers' Home, 215 Broadway.	MORE 25 Sep 1862
DORAN, Lucy E. 6 Oct at the home of her brother, ae 26y 2m. Funeral from St. Bridget's Church. New York pc	MORE 7 Oct 1864
DORR, Charles Edward only child/William and Mattie 3 Aug ae 3. Lived on Madison betw 11-12. CA pc	MORE 4 Aug 1861
DORRIS, Francis 10 Apr in his 42nd year. Lived at 328 N. 7th. Pittsburgh pc. (/ later given as ae 38)	MORE 11 Apr 1865
DORSETT, Walter H. of St. Louis Co. 19 Nov at Sisters Hospital in his 67th year. Funeral from his home near Creve Coeur Lake.	MORE 20 Nov 1865
DORSEY, ___ young stranger, drowned 24 Jul in the Nodaway R. Supposedly from IL.	SJH 6 Aug 1865

DORSEY, Andrew B. in the flux epidemic.   FULT 2 Sep 1864

DORSEY, Orlena O. 3 Jul at the home of her father, Elias, near Louisville in her 31st year.   MORE 6 Jul 1863

DORTON, Harriet wife of Willis E. and dau/John Leopard decd of Boone Co. very suddenly in 37th year. Left husband, 7 children. (Date shown as either 31 Jun or 3 Jul, age shown in Fult as 27th year.)   FULT 15 Jul 1864 / COWS 22 Jul 1864
    Children of W.E. and Harriet: Susan Mary 26 Apr ae 5y 7m 17d / Willis 24 Aug ae 1m 24d   FULT 23 Sep 1864

DOTSTE, Gottlieb 2 Apr ae 38, of consumption. Ill 3 months.   MORE 7 Apr 1865

DOTY, Bedford, a farmer at Middletown, Montgomery Co., killed after an argument with a neighbor over a plow. Doty "drunk, worthless,"; the neighbor, Brackwell, of good character. Doty aimed first but his gun missed fire.   HAM 14 Mar 1861

DOTY, John a river man living on O'Fallon betw 7-8, fell overboard at the ferry crossing to IL while drunk. Left a family.   MORE 15 May 1865

DOUBLEBY, Miss Lizzie, stepdaughter of Rev. S.S. Laws, at the home of her grandmother Mrs. William Broadwell in Fulton 13 Aug ae ca 14.   COWS 22 Aug 1862

DOUGHERTY, Bridget wife of James, ae 33. St. Patrick's Church, int. Rock Spring.   MORE 6 Mar 1864

DOUGHERTY, James 10 Dec ae 37. Funeral from home of Martin Carey, 6th betw Biddle-O'Fallon.   MORE 11 Dec 1865

DOUGHERTY, Willie son/Robert and Sarah B. ae 7y 6m. Lived on Olive betw Beaumont amd Leffingwell. Newark pc   MORE 24 Aug 1865

DOUGLASS, Elizabeth wife of Benjamin F. and dau/Eli and Ellen Morton, born in Boone Co. 21 Feb 1841. (COWS 18 Dec gives maiden name as Northcutt.)   MORE 12 Dec 1863

DOUGLASS, Eva Jane 19 Oct of typhoid, in Boone Co., ae 15y 5m 5d.   COWS 28 Oct 1864

DOUGLASS, James A. in Columbia 21 Feb of heart disease ae 42. Formerly of Princeton IL.   COWS 24 Feb 1865

DOWD, John, a steamboatman, very suddenly of congestive chills and erysipelas. Left wife and 3 children.   MORE 23 May 1862

DOWDALL, America consort of P.J. and dau/late William Owen (Over?) of Franklin Co. KY, ae 41.   MORE 8 Feb 1864

DOWDALL, John 27 Oct in his 71st year. Born in VA, raised in KY, private in the War of 1812. Married Miss English, dau/Elisha, long a resident of this city (Carrollton?). Mentions son William T., editorial profession. (from the Carrollton Democrat)   MORE 27 Nov 1865

DOWELL, Samuel "an intemperate man," formerly a government teamster, at Sisters Hosp.   MORE 25 Mar 1862

DOWER, Mrs. Ellen Saturday ae 22. Interred Calvary.   MORE 14 Jan 1861

DOWLING, James 10 Nov at Rolla ae 29y 10m. Funeral from the home of his father, Jackson & Marion.   MORE 12 Nov 1863

DOWLING, John only son/James S. and Anna 5 Nov ae 4y 10m. Lived Morgan & Pratte.   MORE 6 Nov 1863

DOWLING, Mrs. Mary native of Stradballey, Queens Co. Ire., 18 Jan in her 52d year. Lived at 94 S. 14th. Interred Calvary. New Orleans pc   MORE 19 Jan 1862

DOWLING, Mitchell a telegraph repairer killed at Allen by one Combs, living near Milton (all in Randolph Co.) -- stabbed in an argument.   MAG 4 Mar 1863

DOWNEY, Jerome 27 Apr ae 19. Lived at 200 Wash.   MORE 28 Apr 1864

DOWNING, children of Simeon and Anna: Agnes Bell 20 Aug ae 3, youngest daughter / Clara Jane 13 Sep ae 10y 3m 28d, eldest "   MORE 22 Aug 1861 / MORE 15 Sep 1861

DOWNING, Alexander 18 Feb ae 27.   MORE 19 Feb 1863

DOWNING, Alma May dau/J.C. in Jefferson City 18 Jun, of croup, ae 3y 2m 29d.   COWS 26 Jun 1863

DOWNING, Bennie son/Judge James F. in Chillicothe 1 Jul ae 10.   MORE 20 Jul 1865

DOWNING, Margaret wife of James Saturday 17 Sep. Lived 8th betw O'Fallon-Cass.   MORE 18 Sep 1864

DOXEY, Thomas C. ae (30?) in Chariton Co. at the home of Gen. E.W. Price, of typhoid, on 7 Aug. (SLMD says 4 Aug.)   MORE 7 Sep 1864 / SLMD 17 Aug "

DOYLE, J.S., citizen of Macon Co., 26 Dec of measles. (Undertaker's list)   MORE 2 Jan 1865

DOYLE, Dr. James Nash in Cedar Twp., Boone Co., 22 Aug ae 56.   COWS 1 Sep 1865

DOYLE, Malinda wife of William H. 30 Mar in her 50th year. A Baptist.   LAJ 4 Apr 1861

DOYLE, Margaret, a widow ae 30, of apoplexy from intemperance. Lived in the alley betw 7-8-Spruce-Clark. Left 2-year-old son.   MORE 9 Apr 1863

DOYLE, Patrick at Sisters Hospital 10 Nov; native of Tagmon, Co. Wexford; in   MORE 10 Nov 1864
    St. Louis 20 years. Funeral from St. Lawrence O'Toole Church.

DOYLE, Thomas ae 30 after a long illness. Lived on O'Fallon betw 6-7. Int. Calvary.   MORE 15 Aug 1861

DOYLE, William 29 Mar ae 52. Lived 25th & Morgan.   MORE 31 Mar 1864

DOZIER, Louis died 14 Dec, will be buried in Manchester.   MORE 16 Dec 1862

DRAKE, Dr. George ae 47 at his home near the Fairgrounds.   MORE 14 Mar 1863

DRAKE, Ira J. of Jefferson Co. at Sisters Hospital 29 Aug ae 45.   MORE 30 Aug 1864

DRAKE, Mary Maud dau/G.W. & Julia 3 Jul 1860 of whooping cough and her brother   MORE 29 Jan 1861
    David Pipes 21 Jan ae 4m, both at the home of their grandfather.

DRAKE, Mrs. Nancy 12 Jan near Warsaw, Benton Co., wife of Jesse, in her 45th year.   MORE 2 Feb 1864
    Nee Stewart, born in Bullitt Co. KY, to Howard Co. MO with her parents,
    where she married. "Wife and mother." Member Congregation of Disciples.

DRAKE, Judge Theodore H. of hemorrhoids in his 72nd year, late of the St. Louis   MORE 8 Jun 1863
    Transfer Co. Died 7 Jun. Belleville pc

DRAUGHT, John of St. Louis, in Gen. John Bowen's Brigade, killed at Shiloh.   MORE 4 May 1862

DREYER, John Henry of St. Louis at Wenona, IA, trying to help his father, both   MORE 23 Aug 1864
    drowned. Lived on Spruce betw 5-6, kept a store at #5 Main. Left
    wife and 2 children.

DRISCOLL, John (believed to be), body found near Warrenton. Had last been seen   RANC 24 Jan 1861
    intoxicated several weeks ago near there.

DRISCOLL, John J. 15 Jul ae 3y 6m. Lived at Angelica & 14th.   MORE 16 Jul 1862

DRUHAN, Simeon ae 52. Funeral from home of late Dennis Carroll, 7th-O'Fallon.   MORE 24 Apr 1863
    Interred Calvary.

DRUMELLA, Mary L. wife of John B. 10 Oct ae 36.   MORE 19 Oct 1861

DRUMHILLER, Emily Jane wife of Maj. William 1 Dec in St. Joseph ae 20y 3m.   LIT 5 Dec 1862

DRUMMOND, E.? H. 4 Sep near Kidder ae 71y 11m 20d.   SJH 20 Sep 1865

DRUYTS, Very Rev. John B. at St. Louis University 18 Jun.   SLMD 25 Jun 1861

DUBBS, Capt. Martin 28 Apr ae 61. Lived on Orchard betw Burton-Beckwith. Interred MORE 29 Apr 1861
    Bellefontaine. Pittsburgh, Philadelphia, Natchez pc

DUDLEY, Harriet dau/Thomas and Mary 16 Nov in her 20th year. Cincinnati pc   MORE 17 Nov 1864

DUDLEY, Jeptha in Frankfort 1 Apr in his 85th year.   COWS 3 Apr 1863

DUDLEY, Thomas Hart Benton, a guerilla, killed in Callaway Co. by Maj. Miller's   CANP 10 Sep 1863
    1st & 2nd Prov. Regs.

DUDLY, Thomas 18 Nov of typhoid in his 21st year at the home of his father,   COWS 29 Nov 1861
    Capt. A.F., in Audrain Co.

DUERSON, Mrs. Elizabeth 13 Jul in Huntsville in her 87th year.   COWS 28 Jul 1865

DUFF, Joseph, killed near Savannah in some Civil War problem.   CAWN 18 Jul 1863

DUFFIE, Michael stabbed in a scuffle with Michael Dugan, both young, unmarried.   MORE 22 Sep 1865

DUFFIELD, James killed by Stephen Perry, Probate Judge, in self-defense;   BOBS 2 Feb 1861
    Duffield was drunk.

DUFFY, Frank 12 Jun of lung fever ae 22.   MORE 13 Jun 1863

DUFFY, Margaret, inquest: washwoman, ae 28, brain congestion and intemperance.   MORE 12 Jul 1863

DUFFY, Michael at his home, 412 Morgan; citizen of St. Louis 25 years.   MORE 1 Oct 1861

DUFFY, Timothy, a child, drowned; his mother Bridget asks for any information.   MORE 8 Nov 1862
    Lived at Commercial Alley & Green Sr.

DUFFY, Tom, laying stone in a well near St. Joseph, crushed when a stub of stone   SJH 7 Feb 1865
    fell on him. Lef widow and 6 children.

DUFRANE, Charles A. 18 Feb ae 18. Lived at 231 S. 3rd, below Lombard.   MORE 19 Feb 1865

DUGAN, Isaac W. killed by guerillas. (Carrollton Democrat 5 Aug)   MORE 12 Aug 1864

DUGAN, Margaret of lung congestion. Lived 261 Green St.   MORE 29 Jul 1862

DUGGAN, Barney drowned off the Lucy Bertram; was walking with a sack of wool on   MORE 18 &
    his back, slipped. Left wife and children in St. Louis. Body recovered.   20 Jul 1865

DUGGAN, Daniel 27 Feb ae 60, native of Co. Cork. Lived at 9th & Walnut. Funeral   MORE 1 Mar 1864
    at Immaculate Conception Church, interred Calvary.

Entry	Source
DUGHERTY, Mrs. Eliza V. 29 Sep in Macon Co. ae 26y 4m 3d. Left husband and 4 children. Presbyterian.	MAG 15 Oct 1863
DUKE, Mrs. Elizabeth of spotted fever 3 May ae 56.	CAWN 7 May 1864
DUKE, Henry 18 Feb ca 52.	CAWN 23 Feb 1861
DUKE, John 19 Mar ae 70. Funeral from the home of his son-in-law Thomas P. Russell. Interred Calvary.	MORE 20 Mar 1862
DUKES, William 20 Feb ae 56. Lived 14th & Cass. Interred Bellefontaine.	MORE 21 Feb 1864
DULANY, Capt. Joseph S. in Monroe Co. in his 74th year. Moved to MO 1816, one of oldest settlers; spent last 30 years in Monroe Co.	COWS 27 Sep 1861
DULLARD, Bridget wife of Philip (of James Porter & Co.). Lived Chestnut betw 14-15. St. John's Church, interred Calvary.	MORE 3 Dec 1863
DUMAINE, Jules L., youngest son/Lucien, 17 Jan ae 19, after a short illness. Funeral from St. John's Church.	MORE 18 Jan 1862
DUMPHY, John L. in Lincoln Co. 30 Mar ae (48?). Native of Butlerswood, Co. Kilkenny, Ire. CA pc	MORE 24 Apr 1865
DUNBAR, Ann 11 Sep ae 32. Lived on 17th betw Market-Clark.	MORE 12 Sep 1862
DUNBARR, Amanda Jane dau/J.H. & S.J. 4 Feb of pneumonia ae 2y 3m 5d.	OVAS 14 Feb 1861
DUNCAN, David brother of James of St. Louis in Mariposa CA 6 Feb ae 48.	MORE 18 Mar 1863
DUNCAN, George in Fayette 23 Jul ae 69.	COWS 4 Aug 1865
DUNCAN, children of James and Mary F.: Henry H., 3rd son, 1 Aug ae 3y 7m 218 N. 6th St. Thomas, eldest son, 13 Sep ae 12y 10m	MORE 2 Aug 1861 " 13 Sep 1861
DUNCAN, Louisa wife of Samuel in Fayette 25 Nov ae 39.	COWS 4 Dec 1863
DUNHAM, Hugh H. Saturday ae 26. Brother of John S., lived on S 4th St.	MORE 10 Feb 1862
DUNHAM, Mildred Gillian only child of Robert and Alice M., 27 Feb ae 2.	MORE 28 Feb 1862
DUNHAM, Sydney arrested at his home by a scout from Boone Co. (12 MO Vols) shot while being marched near Montgomery Lientz's.	COWS 11 Nov 1864
DUNHAM, Dr. Sylvanus 18 Feb ae 49. Funeral from 2nd Baptist Church. Auburn and Lansingburg NY pc	MORE 19 Feb 1865
DUNHAN, Laura E. wife of Jacob M. and dau/John and Christian Francisco, Sunday ae 21y 21d. Funeral from St. George's Church.	MORE 6 Jun 1864
DUNKLIN, Rachel E. wife of Stephen T. in Potosi 7 Feb ae 50y 1m 13d. Long, painful illness. "Christian, wife, mother."	MORE 13 Feb 1862
DUNLAP, Elizabeth dau/James and Sarah 28 Jul in her 31st year.	FULT 5 Aug 1864
DUNN, Edward G., of Porter's Band, of pneumonia.	MORE 19 Nov 1862
DUNN, Edward L., citizen of Morgan Co., 3 Mar of pneumonia. (Undertaker's list)	MORE 6 Mar 1865
DUNN, George W. Jr., son/Judge G.W., 4 Feb near Richmond in his 16th year.	LIT 12 Feb 1864
DUNN, Johanna wife of Sidney Saturday ae 30.	MORE 7 Apr 1863
DUNN, John, body found; he had drowned in the cellar of an unoccupied house, was missing about 6 weeks.	MORE 22 Apr 1863
DUNN, John Robert 29 Aug in Providence, Boone Co., at the home of Benjamin Crear, ae 18y 5m.	COWS 8 Sep 1865
DUNN, P. C. of Ralls Co., from the kick of a horse. (Hannibal Courier)	SJH 23 Dec 1863
DUNN, Theresa dau/Christ. and Ellen Friday ae 17 at the home of her mother, 112 N. 14th. Interred Calvary.	MORE 8 Aug 1863
DUNNAVANT, James R. 22 Feb ae 27y 5m. Funeral from the home of Samuel Finch on Dixon betw Fillmore-Glasgow.	MORE 28 Feb 1864
DUNNICA, Frank C. only son/John and Sallie, of diphtheria. Lives #9 No. 8th.	MORE 17 Dec 1864
DUNNICA, Parker of St. Louis, in Gen. John Bowen's Brigade, killed at Shiloh.	MORE 4 May 1862
DUNNINGTON, Miss Martha in this county 14 Mar ae ca 16.	MAG 19 Mar 1862
DUNNIVIN, Michael at Rolla House 1 Apr ae 55y 4m 8d. "Companion, father, Christian."	ROLEX 3 Apr 1861
DUPRE, Alphonse H. of St. Louis at Pocahontas AR 1 Jul ae 25.	MORE 16 Oct 1863
DURACK, Ophelia wife of Capt. John 17 Apr ae 49. Long, painful illness. Funeral St. Vincent's Ch., interred Calvary. Capt. John 25 Apr ae (53? 63?). Funeral from St. Vincent's Church.	MORE 18 & 21 Apr 1864 MORE 26 Apr 1865
DURBIN, B.J. "wounded at the affair in Shelbina sometime since," died.	PALS 3 Jun 1864

DURDY, Sallie J. 5 May in her 30th year, after a 10-day illness.   MORE 8 May 1863

DURNIL, Martha A. in Pisgah, Cooper Co. 14 May of typhoid, wife of J.A. Ae 24y 9m 19d.   COWS 23 May 1862

DuROCHE, Mrs. Mary 20 Dec ae 80. Funeral from St. Francis Xavier Church. Interred Calvary. Davenport IA pc   MORE 28 Dec 1864

DUROSS, Catherine wife of James of consumption, ae 21y 11m. Lived at 393 Broadway. Interred Calvary.   MORE 19 Mar 1863

DURRETT, Mary J. wife of William H. in Lewis Co. 18 Nov in her 58th year. Member of the Christian Church.   CANP 23 Nov 1865

DURRETT, Richard, a bushwhacker shot and captured near Arrow Rock, died. (CAWN)   MORE 24 Aug 1864

DUVALL, Mrs. Mary E. of St. Louis at the home of R. McCabe, Hunt's Station OH, 29 Jul in her 52nd year, after a short, painful illness.   SLMD 3 Aug 1864

DUVALL, Silas L. 7 Mar at the home of his son Henry W. in St. Louis Co. ae 81y 11m 7d. Maysville KY pc   MORE 10 Mar 1863

DUVALL, Simeon, one of the oldest citizens of Perry Co., "a few days since" at his home 9 miles west of Perryville, ae between 80-85. Many relatives.   PERU 3 Mar 1865

DWIRE, Margaret, suicide yesterday by laudanum. She had attempted suicide twice before; her husband, a boatman, had been absent from home. Ae 28.   MORE 25 Jul 1863

DWYER, Dennis of congestion of the lungs. Lived at 8th & Cass, left wife and and 2 children.   MORE 9 Jan 1864

DWYER, James 29 Jun ae 30y 6m. Lived at the nw corner of 6th-Poplar.   MORE 30 Jun 1862

DWYER, John killed when thrown from his dray. Left a widow and 3 children living on Gamble near Mercer.   MORE 13 Nov 1862

DYER, Ann of "drunkenness and exhaustion" at Chouteau between 9th-Broadway. Left a 12-year-old boy.   MORE 24 Jun 1862

DYER, Joseph at the home of Henderson Dyer in Phelps Co. ae 84.   ROLEX 8 Jul 1861

DYER, Mrs. Martha Tabb, wife of Samuel Jr., of Fulton, 28 Jul ae 66. Born in Goochland Co. VA 20 Sep 1795, to MO in 1823 with her husband; a resident of Fulton 36 years.   COWS 8 Aug 1862

DYER, Nannie Elliott eldest dau/Thomas B. and Cornelia C. of St. Louis at Fulton 12 Aug ae 12y 4m. Funeral from St. John's Church, 6th-Spruce. Rushville IL & Memphis pc   MORE 15 Aug 1863

DYER, William H. of Jackson Co. in St. Louis 20 Jan in his 74th year. Born in VA, to MO in 1827; lived first in Callaway Co., then in Jackson. Funeral from St. Paul's Church.   MORE 21 Jan 1862

DYER, William H. 7 Apr of apoplexy, ae 30. Lived at 7th & Franklin. Funeral from St. Francis Xavier Church, interred Calvary.   MORE 8 Apr 1861

DYSART, Robert R. son/Nicholas and Eupha 2 Sep near Roanoke (at the home of John Wayland) of typhoid, ae 26.   MORE 18 Sep 1864

EALER, William E. 4 Dec ae 48. Funeral from the home of Christian Scheff, 11-Ann.   MORE 6 Dec 1864

EARICKSON, Perry 29 Sep at the home of his son-in-law L. H. Cason near Glasgow in his 78th year.   COWS 20 Oct 1865 / MORE 1 "

EARLY, Melchisideck, one of the county's first settlers, at his home on Salt River at a "very old age" 18 May.   LAJ 8 Jul 1865

EASTON, William Ward 3 Apr of pneumonia ae 41. Native of New York state.   MORE 5 Apr 1861

EATHERTON, T.J. in Randolph Co. 29 Jul of brain fever, ae ca 22. Son of Benjamin and Mary Ann.   MORE 2 Aug 1861

EATON, Capt. Henry, clerk of the J.H. Dickey which exploded 10 miles above Ste. Genevieve. Son of N.J. Eaton, left wife and 2 small children. Ae 32. Funeral from Church of the Messiah. Interred Bellefontaine.   MORE 8 Nov 1862

EATON, Henry DuPresse 23 Jun ae 20m 8d, only child of H.K. and E.E.   MORE 25 Jun 1861

EATON, Maj. Samuel, formerly an attorney in Perry Co., 7 May -- tribute from some associate.   MORE 2 Sep 1862

EBBERSON, Mrs. Margaret 8 Feb in her 60th year - wife, mother, grandmother.   CAWN 25 Feb 1865

EBERHART, Christian, resident of California MO ae ca 28, in St. Louis while on a business trip.   MORE 8 Aug 1861

EBERT, Maurice, clerk in a drygoods house on Broadway, living on 6th betw Wash and Carr, accidentally shot by member of the Prov. Guard. Left wife and 2 children. German, Hebrew.   MORE 17 & 18 Apr 1865

ECKERT, Martin 17 Aug ae 47. Lived at 161 11th St.   SLMD 19 Aug 1864

EDDS, William P. yesterday ae 27y 2m 5d. Funeral from home of his uncle S.J.   MORE 16 Nov 1863
        Wetherell, 264 Morgan, to St. Xavier Church. Int. Calvary.
      Mary 6 Dec of consumption ae 22y 8m. Funeral from the home of her uncle   MORE 8 Dec 1864
        S.J. Wetherell, Morgan betw 13-14.

EDDY, Clarice Fannie dau/late James 19 Jun ae (10?)y 2m 10 d of typhoid pneumonia.   MORE 21 Jun 1864
                    Interred Bellefontaine.

EDEN, Adolph, picked up at Manchester for not having exemption or enrollment   MORE 22 Oct 1862
      certificate, tried to escape, was shot by Adj. McElhenny, who was acquitted.

EDGAR, Elmira wife of Richard B. 11 Oct in her 32nd year. Lived at 50 Vine St.,   MORE 12 Oct 1863
       betw 3-4. IL, NJ & OH pc

EDGAR, Franky Phillips youngest dau/Lewis H. and Mary 11 Apr of a spasmodic   BOBS 20 Apr 1861
       affection ae 3y 10m 28d.

EDGAR, Jim a noted guerilla captured near Potosi, shot on the way to Pilot Knob.   MORE 4 Jul 1865

EDINGER, Charles, a workman, fatally injured in a shell explosion at the Arsenal.   MORE 17 Sep 1863

EDLAKER, William thrown from a runaway wagon yesterday; lived on Lami Road 3 mi.   MORE 24 Aug 1865
         below Carondelet and had come with a load of peaches for market.
         "Upward of 76," died of a ruptured gall bladder.

EDMONDSON, George of Fielding's Command, captured at Bloomfield in Stoddard Co.   MORE 21 Feb 1863
           27 Jan, of catarrhal fever in Gratiot Prison.

EDMONSON or   Mrs. M.J., wife of Dr. R.T., Sunday. Funeral from her home   MORE 3 &
EDMONDSTONE.   near Bridgeton.   4 Nov 1862

EDMUNDS, James, murderer of John Bridgman of Tallow Hill, Jefferson Co., hanged.   MORE 6 Mar 1863

EDWARDS, George of Lincoln Co. in Co. F, 2nd MO Inf CSA, killed either in the   MORE 19 Sep 1863
         battle of Champion Hills, Big Black Bridge, or siege of Vicksburg.

EDWARDS, Green C. in Boone Co. 12 Feb of consumption ae 37.   COWS 19 Feb 1864

EDWARDS, Harriet in Boone Co. 11 Aug in her 56th year.   COWS 19 Aug 1864

EDWARDS, Mary Jane wife of Richard of St. Louis in Detroit of lung congestion.   MORE 26 May 1862

EDWARDS, R.J. 25 Apr ae 28. Funeral from the Cathedral, interred Calvary.   MORE 27 Apr 1864

EFFNER, John ae 26 crushed by the fall of heavy timber at a shipyard in   MORE 25 Feb 1863
        Carondelet. Had been married 3 weeks.

EGAN, ___ stabbed to death at Fort Henry, Randolph Co. in a fight with   MAG 4 Mar 1863
         William Baker over a young lady.

EGAN, Dr. Augustus 4 Apr at Lindell Hotel, youngest son of Dr. James and   MORE 5 Apr 1864
                       Letitia of New Orleans.

EGAN, James oldest son/Michael and Johanna, of consumption. Funeral from the   MORE 29 May 1862
      home of his mother, 225 12th St. Interred Calvary.

EGAN, Mrs. Mary, eldest dau/late James and Ellen Kreshan. Lived at 18th   MORE 27 Aug 1863
      and O'Fallon. Interred Calvary.

EHLER, Jacob found dead below the window of his home; had been drinking. Native   MORE 13 Jun 1862
       of Germany, single, "an excellent engineer."

EICHTEBERGER, Charles Edgar son/Andrew and Isabella 4 Jan of typhoid ae 4y 6d.   BOBS 12 Jan 1861

EISCHER, ___, a young man (name formerly given as Henry ASCHE) killed by Cyrus   MORE 17 Jul 1864
         Graham a few days ago; Graham arrested.

ELGIN, William a young newsboy of Hannibal assasinated near Caldwell Friday, on   HAM 5 Sep 1861
       a train which was fired upon. Son of Dr. Elgin, ae 15.

ELHORN, ___ an old man living near Louisville MO started home from Louisiana with   LAJ 18 Jun 1864
        a wagonload of lumber last Wednesday, while inebriated, fell in
        front of the wagon and was run over and instantly killed.

ELIOT, Abby Adams (first given as Ada), dau/Dr. Eliot, drowned skating with two   MORE 21 &
       Salisbury teenagers. Ae 17. Daughter of W. & A.A.   22 Feb 1864
     John son/William Greenleaf and Abby 21 Jan ae 2y 12d.   MORE 24 Jan 1862

ELLEARD, Louis run over or tried to jump on a tender train, killed at 18th St.   MORE 7 Oct 1863
         (Pacific RR) Ae 17, student, parents live in Washington Co.

ELLER, David "quiet and peaceable citizen" murdered by unknowns 5 miles from   CAWN 1 Oct 1864
       Lebanon. (Missouri Advertiser)

ELLIG, John, a gunsmith, shot by his tenant Valentine Hanson, a soldier. He   MORE 22 Oct 1863
       lived on 7th betw Geyer-Allen.

ELLIOTT, Mrs. Elizabeth of St. Louis at the home of her son-in-law A. Brown in Carondelet 5 Feb ae 39y 4m 5d.	MORE 6 Feb 1864
ELLIOTT, Eppe in Boone Co. 7 Sep in the 67th year.	COWS 16 Sep 1864
ELLIOTT, Jemma dau/Col. N.J. of Howard Co. in St. Louis 8 Apr of consumption in her 17th year.	COWS 14 Apr 1865 MORE "
ELLIOTT, Mary wife of Morgan of typhoid pneumonia 2 Mar "near 35."	COWS 1 Apr 1864
ELLIOTT, Nannie dau/Col. N.G. at the home of her father in Howard Co., of consumption, ae 22y 2m 3d.	COWS 25 Mar 1864
ELLIOTT, Mrs. Ruth of St. Louis at the home of her son-in-law Thomas Moore in Metropolis City IL ae 65; resident of St. Louis 19 years, native of Northumberland, England. Member Park Ave. Presbyterian Church (Old School). Died on a visit to her daughters.	MORE 9 Dec 1863
ELLIOTT, Sarah Frances dau/Morgan and Mary E. 9 Feb of brain inflammation ae 14y 5m 25d.	COWS 28 Feb 1862
ELLIOTT, William, Chariton Co.: Letters of administration to Elias Elliott 5 Jul. Wilkerson K. "	CECB 24 Jul 1862
ELLIS, Haden G. at Vicksburg 5 Aug of dysentery ae 18y 4m.	MORE 17 Aug 1865
ELLIS, John 15 Nov 1860 of dropsy, in his 85th year.	LIT 8 Feb 1861
ELLIS, only sons of James M. and Martha: John G. 11 Aug ae 8y 1m 11d (of scarlet fever) James M. 29 Jul ae 2y 1m 11d	COWS 14 Aug 1863
ELLIS, John, citizen of Chariton Co., typhoid (15 Jan?) (Undertaker's list)	MORE 22 Jan 1865
ELLIS, Maria C. wife of Pendleton P. at the home of her mother, Mrs. Sarah Hume, in St. Louis Co., 7 Feb ae 27y 3m 10d.	MORE 14 Feb 1861
Sallie in St. Louis Co. 14 Nov of diphtheria, surviving child of Pendleton and late Maria Kate, ae 6y 2m 8d. Another child died previously.	MORE 17 Nov 1865
ELLIS, Mary C. wife of John and dau/James Rogers of Fayette Co. KY 5 Jun in Palmyra in her 58th year. Baptized by Elder Jeremiah Vardeman in 1826; married 1828; to MO 1830. Left husband and one daughter.	PALS 10 Jun 1864
ELLIS, Mary J. wife of E.P. in Boone Co. 12 Jul ae 42; dau/Horace Sheley of this co.	FULT 15 Jul 1864
ELLIS, Reuben, a prisoner, 30 Jan of rubeola. (Undertaker's list)	MORE 2 Feb 1863
ELLISON, James D., 1st MO Cav, captured in Vernon Co. Died in Gratiot Prison of inflammation of the lungs. (1st MO was a Confederate group.)	MORE 25 Mar 1863
ELLITT, H. stabbed by his brother John (temporarily insane) in Gentry Co. Left a large family. Ae ca 40. Both good citizens. (St. Joseph Journal)	HAM 27 Mar 1861
ELLSWORTH, David, citizen of Stoddard Co. captured 14 Aug, died 23 Nov in Gratiot Prison.	MORE 25 Nov 1862
ELMS, Mrs. Charlotte 8 Feb in her 88th year.	MORE 9 Feb 1864
ELSEA, Mary Jane wife of Benjamin F. in Shelby Co. Ill nearly 4 months. Left husband and 5 children.	HAM 3 Apr 1862
ELY, James N., a rebel captain of Ralls Co., killed by soldiers from LaGrange in the north part of Marion Co., ae ca 21.	LAJ 27 Jul 1863
ELY, Martha H. wife of Lewis B. at Carrollton 7 Sep in her 31st year. Louisville & NY pc	MORE 30 Sep 1862
EMANUEL, Jacob, a resolution by the Masons of St. Louis - "over 3 score and 10."	MORE 20 Jan 1865
EMERSON, Edward L. 5 Aug ae 25. MI, VT & MA pc	MORE 13 Aug 1861
EMISON, David 4 Apr near Lexington, formerly of Boone Co. KY.	COWS 5 May 1865
EMMERSON, James near Canton 20 Mar ae 79y 1m 6d.	COWS 23 Mar 1865
EMMETT, Mrs. Evelina consort of William B., ae (54? 64?). Lived on 14th betw Biddle-O'Fallon, left 3 sons and 2 daughters.	MORE 13 Mar 1864
ENDERS, William F., merchant of St. Louis, in Painesville OH 19 Jan in a RR accident. Funeral from St. John's Church. Interred Bellefontaine.	MORE 22 & 25 Jan 1864
ENDRES, Pauline wife of Jacob, living at 506 Morgan, 21 Jun in her 23rd year.	MORE 22 Jun 1865
ENGELS, Christine wife of Charles (former Master Machinist at the St. L. Arsenal) 20 Jun ae 51. Lived on Sydney near 7th.	MORE 21 Jun 1863
ENGELS or Mrs. J. (Margary Scanlan) died after a fit of coughing; lived at 16th ENGLES & Market. Died 7 Dec in her 53rd year.	MORE 9 & 11 Dec 1865
ENGLISH, James ae ca 13 killed in the Camp Jackson affair.	MORE 14 May 1861

ENGLISH, Laura Elizabeth dau/Ezra and Margaret 18 Mar ae 10y 8m 11d.	MORE 19 Mar 1861
ENGLISH, William B. of Richardson & Cook, St. Louis in Pittsburgh 16 Sep ae 59.	MORE 19 Sep 1865
ENNIS, Mrs. Sarah J. widow of William 28 Nov at the home of her son near Des Peres Institute, ae 53y 9m.	MORE 7 Dec 1862
ENRIGHT, Patrick killed in the Camp Jackson affair.	MORE 18 May 1861
ENT, Davis, 3 miles above Amazonia in Andrew Co. Saturday night, a rebel, "quite a wealthy man."	SJH 14 Jul 1863
ENTLER, Josephine wife of George L. 29 Mar in her 25th year.	MORE 31 Mar 1861
ENTOINE, Octavus, a newsboy, killed on the 4th St. RR Saturday when he jumped on the lower step of a car, fell on track. Ca 8, mother a widow.	MORE 29 May 1865
ENWRIGHT, Cornelius, a teamster "young man lately married" thrown from a wood wagon which then ran over him.	MORE 3 Dec 1861
EOFF, John R., tribute by Pacific Lodge AF & AM; mentions widow.	MORE 10 Jan 1864
EPPERLY, William S., citizen of Randolph Co., of laryngitis 1 Mar. (Undertaker's list)	MORE 6 Mar 1865
ESPY, Mortimer Austin son/Milton C. and Mary of St. Louis at Worcester OH 4 Jan. Funeral from 9th betw Morgan-Franklin.	SLMD 16 Jan 1861
ESPY, T.M. proprietor of the Patee House, 7 Aug ae 36y 5m 26d. Had fallen from the 2nd story of the hotel a few days earlier.	SJH 9 Aug 1864
ESSEX, Aurelia M. wife of William T. at Valley Farm, St. Louis Co., 7 Sep. Funeral from Christ Church. Interred Bellefontaine.	MORE 9 Sep 1862
ESSEX, Natta Ann Virginia 1 Nov of consumption ae 21y 5m. Funeral from Rev. James Farrar's Church, 7th betw O'Fallon-Cass.	MORE 3 Nov 1862
ESSEX, Sarah Elizabeth ae 19y 10m, at the home of her father. Funeral from Wesleyan Chapel.	SLMD 27 Aug 1864
ESTES, ___ a young man drowned trying to cross the Platte in a flatboat at Agency Ford; body recovered.	SJH 1 Aug 1865
ESTES, James 3 May in his 80th year at his home in Buffalo Twp.	LAJ 7 May 1864
ESTES, John, many years a citizen of this county, 22 Aug ae ca 50.	LIT 29 Aug 1862
ESTES, Noah of Hayes' Command, captured in Camden Co. 6 Jan, in Gratiot Prison of rubeola.	MORE 20 Feb 1863
ESTILL, Ann Eliza consort of Christopher and dau/Elder William M. Burton at Richland, Howard Co. 8 Mar in her 24th year.	COWS 25 Mar 1864
ESTILL, Tarlton Turner, son of J. Robert, scalded to death when he upset a kettle in the kitchen.	RANC 18 Apr 1861
ETTER, Amanda eldest dau/C.H. and Sarah 20 Dec ae 20y 9m. Lived at 389 Market. Harrisburg & Philadelphia pc	MORE 22 Dec 1862
EVANS, Augustus H. 5 Jun in his 74th year. Funeral from the Methodist Church, Washington-8th St.	MORE 6 Jun 1863
EVANS, Columbus T. of Randolph Co. "a man of excellent character" murdered by a negro.	LIT 22 Dec 1865
EVANS (EVINS), Denton of Clark's Reg., captured in Taney Co. 20 Oct, in Gratiot Prison of pneumonia 25 Jan.	MORE 27 Jan 1863
EVANS, children of George S. and Columbia F. of Arcadia, Iron Co.:	
Virginia ae 9y 2m 10d	MORE 22 Mar 1864
Fannie of congestion of the spinal cord ae 16y 7m 27d. BloomingtonIL pc	" 11 Dec 1863
EVANS, Mrs. Jane 29 Nov in Grundy Co. ae 71y 4m 18d.	MORE 14 Dec 1865
EVANS, John, a little boy, run over by a street car Wednesday last. Ca 12, parents live at 12th & Angelrodt.	MORE 12 Aug 1864
EVENS, Josephine Davis dau/John C. and Elizabeth W. of congestion of the brain, ae 12y 3m 25d. Lived at 16th & Walnut. Philadelphia pc	MORE 26 Apr 1864
EVERETT, Mrs. Julia A. 24 Jan ae 48. Lived at 471 Broadway. Galena & Mt. Carroll IL pc	SLMD 29 Jan '61
EVERHEART, Kate dau/Joseph at Prairie Institute 2 Feb ae (15?y 1m 1d)	FULT 19 Feb 1864
EVERNDEN, Thomas at Gallatin, Daviess Co. 22 Oct, member Western Star Masonic Lodge, ae 39. Tribute.	MORE 9 Dec 1865
EVERSMAN, Lewis Elijah in Saline Co. 18 May ae 15y 8m.	MORE 26 May 1863
EVERSOLE, Felix B. youngest son/Elijah M. and Talitha drowned ae 10y 10m. Lived at 277 Morgan.	MORE 1 Feb 1862

EVERTS, George, a carpenter, of the effects of intemperance ae ca 49. Irish.   MORE 23 Oct 1865
    Left wife and 1 child, lived 7th south of O'Fallon.
EVINS, Henry D. 2 Nov ae 53. Funeral from Bruner House, interred Bellefontaine.   MORE 3 Nov 1863
EYMA, John 5 Dec ae 31 after a long painful illness. Brother-in-law of Francis   MORE 7 Dec 1862
    McDermott and Joseph Leduc. Funeral from mother's home. Stoddard betw
                                    Clay-Elliott.

FALKNER, Miss Mary, native of Ireland, 30 Nov ae 40. Boston pc   MORE 2 Dec 1863
FALLER, William, ae 35, body found; drowned the previous day. Left family.   MORE 21 Jun 1862
FALLSCRAFT, Edward son/George and Mary Jane 27 Jan ae 4y 7m 11d. CA pc   MORE 30 Jan 1861
FANNING, Mary Elma 8 Nov of scarlet fever ae 7, only child/J.A. and E.J.   MORE 24 Nov 1861
FANSEL, Sarah A. wife of John 15 Aug in her 25th year.   MORE 21 Aug 1864
FARISH, Paul Tilghman 10 Mar ae 60. Funeral from the home of his sister Mrs.   MORE 11 Mar 1865
    E.T. McCabe, 163 Olive, to St. Xavier Church. Interred Calvary.
    Richmond VA and Woodsville MS pc
        Frances S. relict of Hazelwood at the home of her daughter Mrs. McCabe   MORE 26 Oct 1861
                        25 Oct ae 78.
FARLEY, Luke 22 Oct ae 47. Lived at (118?) Collins.   MORE 23 Oct 1863
FARLEY, William S., a bushwhacker, member of Jim Jackson's band, shot at Santa Fe,   MORE 26 Jun 1865
    Monroe Co., Monday last; Jackson also shot. (Paris Mercury 23 June)
FARMEHILL, Carolton, Veteran of the War of 1812, 1 Sep ae 74y 9m 9d. Frederick   MORE 23 Sep 1864
    City & Baltimore pc
FARMER, Allen ae 40 shot and killed in Brunswick, Chariton Co.   MORE 10 Jan 1865
FARMER, Edmund B. only son/H.C. and Eugenia 27 Jan ae 16m 28d.   MORE 29 Jan 1861
FARMER, James Alexander son/Thomas and Margaret Ann 7 Dec ae 5y 8m. Lived at   MORE 8 Dec 1861
    11th-Christy.
FARMER, Jane 20 Mar ae 25 at the home of her brother-in-law A.H. Blank on   MORE 22 Mar 1865
    Eugenia west of 21st. Interred Bellefontaine.
FARMER, John killed by guerillas in Moniteau Co. (CAWN 23 Jul)   MORE 24 Jul 1864
FARMER, Robert Elam son/G.E. and grandson of Robert N. Martin drowned in Lucas   MORE 26 Aug 1862
    Pond 24 Aug; had been swimming with the Lucas children and Capt. William
    Corlys of St. Louis. He lived about 10 miles from the city on Natural
    Bridge Plank Road, was 18 (13)y 6?m and 16?d old.
FARMINGTON, Mrs. Mary ae 90y 1m 1d at the home of her son-in-law, Giles F. Filley.   MORE 12 Nov 1863
FARNSWORTH, Margaret A. wife of John C. 31 Mar of consumption ae 33. Lived at   SLMD 9 Apr 1861
        5th and Carr. Interred Boston.
FARR, R. of Franklin's Reg., captured in Lewis Co. 1 Nov, of spinal irritation   MORE 13 Dec 1862
    in Gratiot Prison 11 Dec.
FARRAR, Caroline E. dau/Jackson and C.F. ae 11m 17d. Lived at 96 S. 14th.   MORE 28 Feb 1861
                    Interred Wesleyan.
        Richard H.L. youngest son/Jackson and C.F. accidentally shot 29 Jun while   MORE 30 Jun 1865
        bird-hunting with his two brothers (Jackson ca 15, Charles ca 10) when
        Jackson fired accidentally.
FARRELL, James L. 24 Aug ae 32. Funeral from home of T. Haynes, 4 Centre St.   MORE 25 Aug 1865
FARRIS, Angie Perry only dau/Rev. R.P. and Eliza S. in St. Charles 15 Apr in   MORE 23 Apr 1865
                    her 15th year.
FARRIS, Charlie E. son/John and Mary E. at Fayette 24 Jul ae 2y 5m.   MORE 31 Jul 1861
FARROW, John ae 59; lived at 12th & Christy. Washington DC & New Orleans pc   MORE 1 Jul 1865
FARTHING, Mrs. Amanda at her home on Rollins farm in Boone Co. 16 May ae 44y 2d.   COWS 24 Jun 1864
FARY, Mary Ann wife of Thomas, 5 Apr. Interred Calvary.   MORE 6 Apr 1863
FATE, Rev. Elijah 18 Nov at his home in Holt Co.; of the Methodist Church.   SJH 28 Nov 1865
FAUBION, Addie dau/Mary at Parkville 12 Feb ae 17y 9m 8d of typhoid; refers   WEST 24 Feb 1865
        to two older sisters who had died previously.
FAULCONER, Mattie Bell dau/William and Mollie 27 Nov at the Arthur House in   LIT 4 Dec 1863
        Liberty ae 4y 5m 23d.
FAULKNER, Cornelius 14 May ae 43. Lived 10th betw Wash & Carr. Int. Bellefontaine.   MORE 16 May 1865
FAVOR, Oliver Celsus only child of C.D. and C.A. this morning ae 5y 9m at 4-Olive.   MORE 6 May 1863

FAY, John a shoemaker at 335 Morgan, ae ca 25 years, died as a result of a beating   MORE 30 Aug 1862
     by Michael McGann. Wife, no children.

FEALY, James stabbed Saturday by Thomas Cook, died.   MORE 19 Apr 1864

FEALY, Capt. John 12 Mar ae 54. Unmarried, a city policeman. Funeral from the   MORE 13 &
     home of his brother, 83 9th St.   14 Mar 1863

FEALY, Thomas 27 Mar ae 59. Lived at 90 16th St. Baltimore & Cumberland pc   MORE 28 Mar 1864

FEANY, John a waiter at the Olive St. Hotel fell from a window 21 Jan and died.   MORE 30 Jan 1865

FEEHAN, Mrs. Judith relict of Patrick of Springhill, Co. Tipperary, 25 Jul.   MORE 26 Jul 1864
(or FERHAN)   Funeral from Immaculate Conception Church.

FEES, Elizabeth accidentally drowned in a cistern at the Almshouse. German, deaf   MORE 29 Nov 1862
     mute, part idiot. Ae 16. In State Asylum till Gen. Jackson broke it up.

FELL, Joseph Edward John only child/Edward John and Honora 12 May ae 3y 3m 8d.   MORE 13 May 1863
                              Lived at 275 Carr.

FENIX, Thomas L. a young man shot in Polk Co. by William J. Gordon in a   MORE 30 Aug 1865
     dispute, 12 miles from Bolivar.

FENNELLY, Sister M. David 30 Jan in her (60th?) year, member St. Vincent de Paul.   MORE 1 Feb 1863

FENNERTY, Mrs. James ae 80 after a lingering illness. Lived at 107 N. 6th.   MORE 19 Mar 1862

FENNEY, Jerry tried to board a switch engine but fell and was instantly killed.   SJH 10 Dec 1863
     Left wife and 2 children. (Hannibal Courier)

FENNIGER, Francis 27 Sep of chronic diarrhoea.   SJH 1 Oct 1865

FERGERSON, Mrs. Emma wife of W. 22 Oct. Funeral from the home of   MORE 23 Oct 1863
     Capt. J.B. Holland, 53 Myrtle.

FERGUSON, ___ a young girl ca 14 at the home of her mother, on or near   SJH 25 Oct 1863
     Frederick St.; home alone, her clothing caught fire.

FERGUSON, Emma Jane only dau/John R. and Mary E. 14 Feb ae 3y 4m. Lived on   MORE 15 Feb 1862
                14th betw Franklin-Wash.

FERGUSON, C.D. a Confederate soldier from St. Louis, at Port Gibson.   MORE 28 May 1863

FERGUSON, James youngest son of the late Hugh and Mary, 1 Feb ae 17y 10m 23d.   MORE 4 Feb 1863
     Funeral from home of his brother-in-law I.A. Durow, corner Clark
     & 7th. Interred Bellefontaine.

FERGUSON, John H. at his home on Jamestown Road 21 Nov ae 57. Int. Bellefontaine.   MORE 23 Nov 1863

FERGUSON, Laura L. wife of W.B. at Rock Hill ae 39. Funeral from North   MORE 7 Jun 1862
     Presbyterian Church. Interred Bellefontaine.

FERGUSON, Mary relict of H., 7 Nov.   MORE 9 Nov 1861

FERGUSON, Mrs. Peggy consort of Peter 26 Nov ae 75, after a lingering illness.   MORE 29 Nov 1862
     Peter H. late Judge of the St. Louis Probate Court 12 Jun ae 75y 6m.   " 14 Jun 1863
                   Funeral from St. James Church.

FERHAN, Julia relict of Patrick of Springhill, Co. Tipperary 25 Jul. Funeral   SLMD 26 Jul 1864
(or FEEHAN)   from Immaculate Conception Church.

FERREE, George 28 Nov after a lingering illness.   SLMD 3 Dec 1861

FERRELL, John and Porter, killed in Buchanan Co. by soldiers sent out by Gen.   PALS 5 Aug 1864
     Craig. (St. Joseph News)

FERRIGAN, John drowned yesterday in a quarry pond near 17th St. where it is   MORE 7 Aug 1863
     crossed by the RR. Boarded 10th & Orchard. Ca 19.

FERRIS, Jabez killed in attack on Union troops -- shot through the temple.   SLMD 25 Jun 1861

FERRY, William B., inquest: boy ae 7 killed when a saw log rolled onto him off of   MORE 12 Oct 1865
     a pile; only son of William B. of Franklin Co., was visiting in the
     city with his aunt, Mrs. Booth.

FESSENDEN, A.L. at Gratiot Prison; was to have been released, but died.   MORE 18 Nov 1862

FICHNER, Zachary Taylor son/Adam and Adeline 26 Mar ae 18y 3m 11d. Wheeling pc   MORE 29 Mar 1865

FICKLIN, Richard P. 29 Jun in Louisiana MO ae 30y 8m 18d.   LAJ 23 Jul 1864

FICKLIN, Thomas J. 21 Sep after a long painful illness, ae 37y 5m 17d.   LAJ 24 Sep 1864

FIELD, Eliza W. Owings consort of Col. A.P. in New Orleans 30 Sep. Funeral from   MORE 13 Oct &
     sw corner Pine and 10th. Interred Bellefontaine.   17 Nov 1863

FIELD, Martin, a mail agent, killed in the Platte Bridge disaster.   SLMD 10 Sep 1861

FIELDING, ___, former desperado, shot in Platte Co. (St. Joseph Herald 14 Jun)   MORE 16 Jun 1864

56

FIELDS, Frankie son/William and Mary M. near Canton 15 Jan ae 6y 9m.   CANP 16 Feb 1865
FIELDS, Viola G. dau/Dr. James L. and Emily J. in New Madrid Co. 5 Sep ae 5y 1om.   MORE 17 Sep 1863
    Columbus KY pc

FIFE, John in Lexington 18 Apr ae 63.   MORE 17 May 1864

FINDLEY, Andrew a young man of Lincoln Co. drowned swimming in the Mississippi, body   LAJ 8 Aug 1863
    found the next day. Brother of Col. Findley and "highly esteemed."

FINDLEY, Martha Samuel dau/Milton and Mary S. 5 Apr of scarlet fever ae 5y 3m.   FULT 11 Apr 1862

FINDLEY, Samuel H. native of Pike Co. in Franklin TN, of wounds, 7 Dec 1864 ae 32.   LAJ 8 Jul 1865

FINK, Ernest yesterday of exhaustion; had been sick at the home of his uncle   MORE 13 Aug 1864
    John W. Sibert in Jefferson Co. and was being taken to his home in
    Washington, Franklin Co.; was changing railroads in St. Louis and had
    been attacked on Lemay St.

FINK, Wilhelmina wife of John P. 6 Apr ae 27y 11m.   SJH 8 Apr 1865

FINLEY, Cyrus at his home near Auburn, Lincoln Co. 20 Apr in his 63rd year.   LAJ 1 May 1862
    Native of VA, reared in Shelby Co. KY, married 1828, to MO 1829.

FINLEY, Edwin Bryan son/S.T. and E.B. at Cedar Grove, Marion Co. 14 Sep of   HAM 3 Oct 1861
    diphtheria, ae 6; also his brother Samuel, same date, ae 10.

FINLEY, Elizabeth J. wife of Alexander 17 Aug ae 47. Lived Morgan-18th. Newark pc   MORE 18 Aug 1863

FINNEGAN, Joseph 31 Oct of lung congestion ae 18. St. Patrick's Church, int. Calvary. MORE 1 Nov 1864

FINNELL, Capt. Abner killed in Chariton Co. by state militia, ae ca 55.   MORE 7 Nov 1864

FINNEY, Daniel, tribute by Robert Emmet Club. Died 17 Nov.   LIT 24 Nov 1865

FINNEY, James J. at Memphis, 2nd son/late Bernard, 19 Jan in his 25th year.   MORE 24 &
    Lived at 13th and Clark. Funeral St. Francis Xavier.   26 Jan 1864

FISH, ___ a noted guerilla killed in Lafayette Co. by Capt. Clayton Tiffin's   MORE 3 Feb 1865
    Ray Co. EMM.

FISHBACK, Sallie L. dau/Fant L. and Pamela after a painful, protracted illness   MORE 2 Apr 1863
    14 Mar ae 19y 10m. Louisville & Nashville pc

FISHER, _____ a young man home from college drowned 4 Jul in the river. His   MORE 4 Jul 1865
    parents lived at 3rd & Convent.

FISHER, alias MARTIN, Ann living at 28 S. 10th, clothing caught fire.   MORE 26 Nov 1862

FISHER, Andre, recently of Iowa, intemperance and brain congestion ca 60. Had   MORE 26 Sep 1863
    several married children in Iowa, wife trying to get back there.

FISHER, Appolonie 20 Sep ae 60. Funeral from home of her son-in-law, 221 N. 7th.   MORE 21 Sep 1863
    Frederick MD & Washington DC pc

FISHER, James ae 47 of brain disease. Lived at 96 10th St. (SLMD 16 or 19 Sep 1864, paper had both dates)

FISHER, James H. of Powhatan AR 8 Jul at the home of John A. Hunter near   MORE 17 Jul 1863
    Caledonia MO, had moved early in the war. Left wife, 1 child. Mason.

FISHER, James H.S., president of the Steamboat Mates Benevolent Assn., at his   MORE 4 &
    home on 24th betw Franklin and Wash Monday night of consumption. Native   8 Oct 1865
    of PA. Husband, father. Philadelphia and Reading pc

FISHER, James L. of Lewis Co., in Hendricks Co. IN 24 Nov ae 61y 9m 18d.   CANP 14 Dec 1865
    Interred LaGrange, Mason and IOOF services.

FISHER, John father of Robert of St. Louis in Wheeling VA 16 Aug ae 87.   MORE 22 Aug 1862

FITZGERALD, D.G. killed by bushwhackers near Hickory Grove, Warren Co. (FULT)   MORE 24 Aug 1863

FITZGERALD, Edward, of heat.   MORE 12 Aug 1862

FITZGERALD, Thomas son/Washington and Ann in Franklin Co. 9 Jul ae 12y 3m 6d.   MORE 1 Aug 1863
    Formerly of St. Louis Co. Was leading a mule, halter strap caught
    around his wrist, and he was dragged to death.

FITZGERALD, William 28 Dec at Sisters Hospital. Funeral from the home of   MORE 29 Dec 1863
    William Moore, 7-O'Fallon to St. Patrick's Church. Interred Calvary.

FITZGERALD, William S. of Co. Roscommon, Ire. 20 Jul ae 90.   MORE 22 Jul 1864

FITZGIBBON, Amelia wife of J.H., inquest: had a bad headache, took laudanum and   MORE 16 Dec 1862
    probably overdoses. Died 14 Dec ae 43. Had several children.
    Interred New York. Philadelphia and NY pc

FITZMAURICE, Ellen (later Hellen) wife of John 17 Apr, lived 14th betw Biddle-O'Fallon. MORE 18 Apr'64

FITZPATRICK, John 28 May ae 30y 7m at his mother's home, 280 Morgan.   MORE 29 May 1863

57

FITZPATRICK, William at Bunker Hill IL 30 Aug ae 44. Funeral from the home of his mother, 200 Morgan. MORE 1 Sep 1863

FITZSIMMONS, Peter son/Robert and Mary 16 Jun ae (3? 8?)y 3m 12d. Lived on Lami betw Carondelet-Jackson. MORE 17 Jun 1861

FLANAGAN, Francis J. 20 Feb of lung congestion ae 71y 3m 23d. Funeral from St. Francis Xavier. MORE 22 Feb 1862

FLANDERS, ____, a young man living in Patee Town with his parents, fireman on the Platte Co. RR, run over by train. SJH 12 Sep 1863

FLANDREIN, Francis 24 Mar ae 68, an old resident; born in St. Louis in 1796. Funeral from home of his son-in-law P.J. Gerhart on Randolph, to St. John's Church. Interred Calvary. MORE 26 Mar 1864

FLANIGAN, Mary Ann wife of Capt. P. 10 Mar ae 27. Funeral from the home of her brother-in-law John W. Harris, 58 N 8th. Pittsburgh & Washington pc MORE 11 Mar 1865

FLANNAGAN, Catherine run over by a government wagon, apparently she was drunk. Husband lives in alley betw Carr-Biddle-8-9. MORE 13 Sep 1863

FLANNAGAN, W.W.D. killed near Philadelphia by men said to be Lewis Co. militia. A Mason, left widow and 4 children. PALS 5 Aug 1864

FLANNIGAN, Daniel ae 33, of delirium tremens. Separated from his wife. MORE 31 May 1861

FLEMING, Luke 24 Oct ae 53. Funeral from the home of his son-in-law Peter Hurck, Morgan-Leffingwell. MORE 26 Oct 1861

FLEMING, Thomas T. 1 Sep ae 44. Lived on Broadway betw O'Fallon-Cass. MORE 2 Sep 1865

FLEMING, William, citizen of Shannon Co., 20 Feb of bronchitis. (Undertaker's list) MORE 6 Mar 1865

FLETCHER, Elizabeth M. wife of Mathew Saturday last in her 39th year. Left husband and 6 children. PALS 12 May 1865

FLETCHER, Fannie Mary oldest dau/John B. and Sallie E. in Waverly 24 Apr ae 4y8m28d. MORE 6 May 1863

FLETCHER, children of Benjamin and Elizabeth: Fanny May 3 Feb ae 3y 9m
John M. 28 Jan ae 9y5m3d of meningitis LEXUN 31 Jan & 7 Feb 1863

FLETCHER, Perry B., Mbr Co. B 6th Reg., accidentall shot. Interred DeSoto. MORE 2 Jul 1861

FLOOD, Judge (John J.) ae 60 killed and thrown into the Missouri River in Chariton Co. MORE 10 Jan 1865

FLORE, Ben, a prisoner, 15 Sep of chronic diarrhoea. (Undertaker's list) MORE 21 Sep 1862

FLOURNOY, Dr. William M., an old resident of Lafayette Co., in Lexington last Sun. (MORE 17 May says Dr. M.W., died 3 May) KCJC 21 May 1864

FLUGGER, Mrs. Henrietta 18 Mar of consumption ae 28. Funeral from the home of A. Flugger, Olive west of 17th. MORE 19 Mar 1861

FLUKES, James 8 Sep ae 42. Lived at (148?) N. 8th. MORE 9 Sep 1862

FLYNN, Andrew C. son/Michael and Clarissa of Washington Co. 29 Dec in St. Louis ae 18. Interred in Potosi. Dubuque pc MORE 30 Dec 1863

FLYNN, Emma McNamara consort of William in Mexico MO 19 Apr ae 29. Funeral from the home of John Flynn, 14th-Poplar. MORE 21 Apr 1863

FLYNN, John 16 Jul ae 43. Funeral St. John's Church, interred Calvary. New Orleans and Vicksburg pc MORE 17 Jul 1865

FLYNN, Mrs. Margaret wife of John at Potosi 4 Sep. MORE 10 Sep 1862

FOGARTY (FAGERTY), John fell overboard from the Laclede, ae 24; body found. Wife lives near the Green Tree Brewery bwteen Almond-Poplar. MORE 11 & 16 Oct 1861

FOGLE, Charlotte T. wife of George and dau/late Capt. Elijah Murray 18 Sep ae 44y 22d. Lived at 867 Broadway. Paducah & Steubenville pc MORE 20 & 21 Sep 1862

FOLEY, Mrs. Edward nee Susan McCarthy 7 Mar in her 21st year. Lived #70 18th St. MORE 8 Mar 1863

FOLEY, Michael 20 Mar ae 85 at the home of his son Thomas, corner North & Market. MORE 21 Mar 1865

FOLEY, Thomas, native of Ireland, resident of St. Louis 26 years, on 24 Apr. Lived on Beaumont-Market. Interred Rock Spring. MORE 25 Apr 1863

FONT, Frank H., a Spaniard who came from the south about 2 years ago, a rebel, found dead. Verdict: debility. MORE 27 Dec 1863

FOOTE, Lt. Gerard A. of the 1st MO Rebel Inf. in a hospital in Franklin Co. TN 8 Jan of wounds received 30 Nov. Native of KY, resident of St. Louis at the beginning of the war. MORE 20 Jan 1865

FORBES, Mrs. Elizabeth suddenly of heart disease. Lived at 10th near Chambers, her husband a watchman at Kendall's Bakery. MORE 3 Apr 1862

FORBES, Mrs. Thomas 8 Apr of pneumonia ae 53. Lived Green above 9th. Int. Calvary.   MORE 9 Apr 1864

FORBES, William E., father of Mrs. T.J. Chew of St. Joseph, in New York 5 Oct. His   SJH 16 Oct 1864
    brother John E. died the same day.

FORCEE, Miss Julia of Boone Co. 4 Jul.   COWS 10 Jul 1863

FORD, Mrs. Ellen dau/E.P. and Abby Sophia Ackerman, ae 24. Lived on Cozen St.   MORE 5 Apr 1864
    Interred Wesleyan.

FORD, James M. son/B.F. and Rebecca 15 Dec of membraneous croup ae 5y 1m 21d.   GLWT 31 Jan 1861

FORD, John T. Duncan son/James H. fell through the ice on a pond, ae 11.   LIT 23 Jan 1863

FORD, Martha C. Webb wife of Capt. Rufus of St. Joseph in Van Buren Co. IL   SLMD 16/19 Sep
    5 Sep ae 40. (SLMD for this day carries two dates)   1861

FORMAN, Susan wife of John at Sturgeon, Boone Co. 1 Oct in her 72d year, aunt   HAM 7 Oct 1861
    of Rev. A.F. Forman of Hannibal.   COWS 25 "

FORQUERAN or FARQUERAN, Jane wife of John 3 Sep ae 39.   FULT 6 Sep 1861
    (COWS says FARQUERAN)   COWS 13 "

FORQUERAN, John G. in Knox Co. 22 Apr, formerly of Marion Co., in his 64th year.   PALS 12 May 1865

FORRESTER, St. Clair J. near Nashville TN 27 Mar of pneumonia ae 33.   MORE 4 Apr 1865

FORSMAN, Fillmore Hardin youngest son/W.S. and M.E. in Rolla ae 2y 9m.   ROLEX 11 Feb 1861

FORSYTH, Thomas at his home in Franklin Co. 22 Feb of consumption ae 47.   MORE 26 Feb 1862

FORTMEYER, Bernard killed when earth caved in as he was digging in a brick clay   MORE 13 Feb 1861
    pit. Native of Prussia, ae 35, left wife, 1 child at Madeline & 19th.

FORTNEY, John Sr. 25 Sep in his 70th year, resident of Boone Co. 40 years.   COWS 17 Oct 1862

FOSDICK, Mrs. Clersia 31 Aug ae 65. Lived 8th betw Carr-Biddle. CA pc   MORE 1 Sep 1865

FOSTER, Charles J. Sunday of sunstroke ae 37y 6m. Leading melodramatic actor   MORE 4 &
    in the Varieties Theatre, member Co H 8th EMM. Eastern papers pc   5 Jul 1864

FOSTER, Elizabeth H. wife of R.S. near Independence 14 Feb.   MORE 24 Feb 1865

FOSTER, Mrs. J.J., wife of a Shelbina merchant, died after having given birth to   LAJ 15 May 1862
    triplets, who also died. She previously had twins. (HAM)

FOSTER, Marsh, clerk of the Johnson Co. Court, shot after the polls closed at   MORE 21 Feb 1861
    Warrensburg, reportedly by Col. James McCown, clerk of the Circuit Ct.   CAWN 27 Apr "
    (Later shown as McCowns, with son William H. indicted.)

FOSTER, Peter, funeral from his late home 212 Spruce, betw 12-13.   MORE 31 Aug 1865

FOSTMEYER, see FORTMEYER   SLMD 13 Feb 1861

FOULKS, Catherine widow of Christopher 25 Mar ae 73. Funeral from Centenary   MORE 27 Mar 1864
    Church, interred Bellefontaine. Albany pc

FOUNTAIN, Alexander, an old citizen, killed by 3 men. (LEXUN 15 Mar)   MORE 7 Apr 1865

FOUNTAINE, Mrs. C. relict of Joseph at the home of G.S. Putney 21 Oct.   MORE 22 Oct 1864

FOUPIANO, Dominic, an old Italian who kept the "California Exchange" at 18th &   SLMD 7 Jan and
    Morgan, killed by a gang of young ruffians.   later 1861

FOWLER, Clement, prisoner, 16 Jan of typhoid. (Undertaker's list)   MORE 19 Jan 1863

FOWLER, Elias at his home near Belmont 28 Sep. Mason, member of Wolf Island   CHAC 9 Oct 1863
    Lodge; married a daughter of William Free.

FOWLER, John S. of Poindexter's Band, captured in Howard Co. 11 Oct, in Gratiot   MORE 19 Dec 1862
    Prison 17 Dec of pneumonia.

FOX, family of Anthony: Elizabeth, wife, 18 Jan ae 34. Interred Calvary.   MORE 20 Jan 1861
    /Papin w of 14th   Mary Elizabeth, oldest dau/ 29 Mar ae 8y 6m. Int. Calvary.   .MORE 30 Mar 1861

FOX, Elizabeth wife of William 11 Mar of puerperal fever ae (38?). Lived on 7th   MORE 12 Mar 1863
    betw Morgan-Franklin. Manchester Guardian (England) pc

FOX, John, a brakeman, killed in the Platte Bridge disaster.   SLMD 10 Sep 1861

FOX, Peter shot near Keytesville. (Brunswicker 18 Jun)   MORE 24 Jun 1864

FOY, John C. accidentally killed on the Pacific RR 28 Nov, 140 Market betw 5-6.   MORE 30 Nov 1863
    Philadelphia & Iowa pc (Name also appears as Toy)

FRAKE, Leonora wife of John 6 Jul ae 38. Lived Spruce betw 6-7. Funeral from the   MORE 7 Jul 1863
    Cathedral.

FRAME, Eliza Jane wife of William 15 Apr of consumption in her 22nd year. Lived   MORE 16 Apr 1861
    at 17th-Carr.

FRAME, Thomas 31 Mar of heart disease ae 60. Lived Market betw 15-16.	MORE 3 Apr 1864
FRAME, Thomas F., a clerk in the auditor's office in Jefferson City, 24 Sep. Recently from Daviess Co.	COWS 4 Oct 1861
FRANCISCO, Annie dau/John and Christiana 20 Dec ae 5y. Lived Spruce betw 15-16.	MORE 21 Dec 1862
FRANEY, Edward, stabbed Tuesday by John McGrath, died.	MORE 6 Jun 1863
FRANKLIN, ___, a young man, killed in Chariton Co.	MORE 10 Jan 1865
FRANKLIN, Mrs. Hamilton B. at Tipton 25 Mar ae ca 26, after lingering illness.	CAWN 28 Mar 1863
FRANKLIN, Henry 22 Jan ae 25 at the home of James Duncan, 8th near Chouteau.	MORE 23 Jan 1865
FRANKLIN, N.B. 15 Apr ae 52y 1m. St. Paul & CA pc	MORE 16 Apr 1861
FRAZEG, Mrs. Susannah. mother of one of the proprietors of the Hannibal Messenger, in Chicago 7 Feb. Of Richland MI, and interred there. Funeral from the home of her son-in-law N. Scranton in Chicago.	HAM 20 Feb 1862
FRAZIER, Polk, leader of rebels, killed near Hartsville by a detachment of the 10th IL Cav. (Springfield Journal)	RICON 11 Sep 1862
FRECKENTOCHER, ___, a shoemaker, suicide by hanging. Lived on 11th betw Broadway-O'Fallon. Wife mentioned.	MORE 11 Aug 1863
FREDERICK, John a soldier at the Arsenal, native of France, of injuries received in a fall. A carpenter, left wife and children.	MORE 24 May 1861
FREEMAN, Alton; Chariton Co. Public administrator took over his estate.	CECB 24 Jul 1862
FREEMAN, Jonathan in Columbia 23 Jan ae ca 35.	COWS 25 Jan 1861
FREEMAN, Miss Mary Ann in Columbia 23 May.	COWS 29 May 1863
FREEMAN, Mary wife of Judge ___.R. of the Phelps Co. Court in Mossy Twp 19 Jan ae 34y 13d.	ROLEX 11 Feb 1861
FREEMAN, Thomas W. formerly of MO (Polk Co.) and late of the Confederate Congress, funeral Tuesday. Notorious rebel, born KY, prominent lawyer in sw MO, on his way home to see his parents. Service at Southern Hotel. Husband, father.	MORE 25 Oct 1865 MEMP 11 Nov "
FREEMAN, William citizen of Monroe Co. arrested 10 Oct, of pneumonia. (Undertaker's list)	MORE 12 Nov 1862
FREJER, Antoine, ca 49, unmarried, found dead. Verdict debility.	MORE 28 Jun 1864
FREMON, Celestine Zelina wife of DuBouffay decd, 26 Jun ae 48 at 3rd-Poplar.	MORE 28 Jun 1863
FRENCH, Eliza wife of Simon L. 23 Jun near Hallsville, Boone Co., in her 32nd year.	COWS 3 Jul 1863
FRENCH, Frank E. 5 Jun ae 38y 8m. Funeral from the home of his mother at "Cote Brilliant." New Hampshire & Boston pc	MORE 7 Jun 1865
FRENEY, David, inquest: drowned in a quarry pond on Benton betw 16-17, ae ca 35, had been drunk. Lived near the pond, left wife and 5 children.	MORE 23 Jan 1863
FRETWELL, Milly Jane dau/Joseph and Hannah T. 3 Feb of typhoid pneumonia ae 6y 11m 1d. Paris KY pc	COWS 19 Feb 1864
FREY, Joseph 5 Jan in his 41st year. Lived at Soulard & Menard. Member of DeSoto Lodge #99, IOOF.	MORE 7 Jan 1862
FREY, Mary, inquest: lived in Clabber Alley, Wash-Carr-7-8; ae ca 40. Died of lung congestion due to intemperance.	MORE 21 Aug 1863
FRICKE, Alice, only child of W. and Maggie A., 5 Mar. Lived at 644 Broadway.	MORE 6 Mar 1862
FRIEDLY, James William, a guerilla said to be of St. Charles Co., killed in a fight at Elmore's Store, Ashley, Pike Co., ae 18 or 19.	MORE 6 Sep 1862
FRIES, Peter W. only child of Peter W. and America Elizabeth 8 Jan ae 4y 10m.	MORE 10 Jan 1864
FRIOS, John, member of the city post band, supposedly intoxicated, wandered along the river, got into the mud, and strangled. German, ae 28, no relatives.	MORE 26 Jun 1863
FRITZLEN, Mrs. Elizabeth 5 May ae 71y 4m 28d, a Baptist more than 40 years.	LIT 12 May 1865
FROST, Adaline S. wife of R.C. of Boone Co. 7 May ae 23.	COWS 22 May 1863
FROST, Thomas of McDonald's Command, captured in Cedar Co. 12 Jan, in Gratiot Prison of bronchitis.	MORE 19 Mar 1863
FRY, Benjamin in Clinton Co. 1 Dec "old and respected" - ae 52y 4m 26?d.	LIT 16 Jan 1863 MORE 22 "
FRYER, Emma C. wife of W. de B. 4 Sep in Philadelphia, formerly of Bath Eng., now in the Surgeon General's Office in St. Louis.	MORE 28 Oct 1863
FUCHS, Reinhard, professor of music, 5 Oct ae 50y 6m. Lived at 6th-Market.	MORE 6 Oct 1861

FUGATE, John O.A. killed by his younger brother William near Paris, Monroe Co., after a quarrel a few days ago. — MORE 1 Jul 1861

FUGATE, W.R. of Monroe Co. shot through the window while sitting at the supper table, died in a few hours. — CAWN 28 Jun 1862

FULKERSON, William Henry youngest son/Peter H. and Martha J. at his home in Darst Bottom, St. Charles Co., 21 Feb ae 8m 21d. — MORE 2 Mar 1861

FULL, Rev. George 2 Sep ae 52. Funeral from 1st Methodist Church. — MORE 3 Oct 1861

FULLAGAR, William 9 Aug in his 48th year. Lived corner of Marion-Rosatti. — MORE 10 Aug 1864

FULLER, Mary E. dau/E. and Elizabeth 9 Oct of consumption ae 17. — LAJ 14 Oct 1865

FULLERTON, Mrs. Elizabeth 26 Apr of lung disease in her 81st year. Funeral from the home of her daughter Mrs. Dugan, 24 N. 12th. Philadelphia pc — MORE 28 Apr 1861

FULTON, John at Perry's Mines, St. Francois Co., 14 Oct ae 48. CA pc — MORE 25 Oct 1865

FULTON, Mrs. Mary M. in Weston 10 Mar in her 67th year. — WEST 21 Apr 1865

FUNKHAUSER, Andrew shot himself at his boarding house. Had bought cemetery lot to be buried by Elizabeth Lederer (which see). — MORE 2 & 3 Jul 1865

FUPPIANO, James son/Gaetano 1 Jun ae 20. Funeral from the Cathedral. Boston pc — MORE 2 Jun 1864

FUQUA, ___ murdered in James Bayou Twp., Porter Hunt charged but escaped. — CHAC 17 Jul 1863

FURLONG, Mrs. Catherine found dead in bed at her home on Maiden Lane betw 16th & Reservoir. A widow, her husband drowned at Cairo last year when he fell from a steamboat. Left a daughter ae 13 and a son of 11. — MORE 12 Nov 1863

FURNISH, Samuel B. living near Renick in Randolph Co. hanged himself Tuesday week. Recently returned from CA where he had lived for several years and on 4 July was married to Mrs. E.A. Adams of Randolph Co. — COWS 9 Aug 1861

FYLER, Clarissa widow of Col. James H. 15 Jan of typhoid pneumonia in her 39th year. Funeral from the homestead. Hartford CT pc — MORE 16 Jan 1863

FYLER, Dr. J.D., MD at his home 7 miles out on Old Manchester Road 27 Mar in his 45th year. Hartford CT & Cleveland pc — MORE 28 Mar 1865

FYLER, John F., MD at his home in St. Louis Co. 14 Dec in his 62nd year. Funeral from the homestead. Hartford & New Haven CT & Trenton NJ pc — MORE 15 Dec 1862

GABY, Jonathan 4 Jul ae 54. Lived at 132 Christy. PA, OH & IA pc — MORE 5 Jul 1864

GAINES, Rosa 2 Jun in her 12th year. Funeral from the home of her uncle, A. Beattie. — SJH 23 Jun 1864

GAINES, William of Fielding's Command, captured in Stoddard Co. 27 Jan, in Gratiot Prison of pneumonia. — MORE 10 Mar 1863

GALE, Amos 21 Mar in San Francisco ae 45; family, and brother D.B., in St. Louis. Native of NH. — MORE 22 Apr 1864

GALE, Annie Lena 23 Sep ae 4y 4m and Walter Percy 25 Sep, of diphtheria; twins of William G. and Mary H. NY pc — MORE 26 Sep 1862

GALE, Theodore F. at Gadsden AL in November ae 21; funeral from the home of his father, D.B., Lucas Place-17th. — MORE 23 Nov 1865

GALLAGHER, Catherine wife of Joseph F. 21 Feb ae 25. Lived 802 Broadway. NY pc — MORE 22 Feb 1862

GALLAGHER, Kate of sunstroke ae 21, at 14th & Morgan. — MORE 7 Sep 1864

GALLAGHER, Mary relict of William 26 Nov ae 57. Lived on Bellefontaine Road near the 4-Mile House. Interred Calvary. — MORE 27 Nov 1864

GALLAGHER, Mary Ann at Waltenham, St. Louis Co. 22 Mar, eldest daughter of Esther, formerly of Londonderry, ae (22?). — MORE 23 Mar 1861

GALLAGHER, Richard, an English boy ae 9, drowned in a pond. Parents live near Rock Spring. — MORE 3 Aug 1861

GALLAHN, William of St. Louis, in Gen. John Bowen's Brigade, killed at Shiloh. — MORE 4 May 1862

GALLEHER, Eli at Leesburg VA near the end of Aug, "a poor misguided young man defending the rights of the south." Widowed mother and sister learned no details. (Signed by S.S. Allen from Hannibal) — MORE 14 Nov 1862

GALLION, Robert of Osage Co. arrested 15 Sep, in Gratiot Prison 19 Nov. — MORE 20 Nov 1862

GALLUP, George W. at the home of his father 6 miles north of St. Joseph 30 Apr ae 21y 6m 13d. Son of Thomas & Cynthia, formerly of Oneida Co. NY. Utica pc — SJH 2 May 1865

GAMACHE, Auguste Sr. 11 Apr in his 68th year after a painful lingering illness. Son of early settlers in Carondelet; lived at the corner of Market-4th. Numerous descendants. — MORE 13 Apr 1865

Entry	Source
GAMACHE, E. of Jefferson Co., Co. F 2nd MO Inf CSA, killed either at Champion Hills, Big Black Bridge or the siege of Vicksburg.	MORE 19 Sep 1863
GAMBLE, Gov. Hamilton Rowan 31 Jan in his 66th year. Funeral 2nd Presbyterian Ch. Caroline Coalter widow of Hamilton R. 12 June. Lived 14th & Lucas.	MORE 1 Feb 1864 " 13 Jun "
GAMBLE, Mary Frances wife of William B. Monday ae 25. Lived 353 9th St., betw O'Fallon and Cass.	MORE 15 Jul 1863
GAMMON, Adaline daughter of Noah thrown from a horse, caught her foot in the stirrup, and was dragged to death, ae 18 or 20.	CAWN 30 Aug 1862
GANAG, John a carman found dead in a furniture car on Carondelet Rd., of apoplexy.	MORE 20 Dec 1863
GANNON, John 11 Jul at his home, 227 Washington.	MORE 12 Jul 1863
GANNT, John W. of Buchanan Co. 17 Apr of consumption. Left wife, mother. KY pc	MORE 29 Apr 1865
GARAUCHER, Antoine, inquest: went to the home of John Ockenfriss on Spruce, late at night, and assaulted him; O. fought back, Garaucher later died. Nothing found to incriminate Ockenfriss; verdict, brain congestion from intemperance.	MORE 13 & 15 Dec 1862
GARD, Joseph ae 70 found dead at his home, Papin betw 6-7, of age and debility.	MORE 30 Aug 1864
GARDER, Jacob, a Frenchman, killed in the Camp Jackson affair.	MORE 14 May 1861
GARDNER, Samuel H. 25 Dec, late U.S. Collector of Revenue. Lived at 40 S. 16th, died in his 41st year.	MORE 28 Dec 1864
GARESCHE, J.P. 24 Feb in his 81st year at his home, 8th & Chouteau.	MORE 25 Feb 1861
GARLICHS, Charles Leopold son/Dr. Frederick A.H. and Matilda M. 9 Mar of brain congestion ae 9y 5m 19d. Funeral from the Baptist Church.	SJH 11 Mar 1864
GARNETT, George found dead in bed of apoplexy and intemperance, 191 4th St.	MORE 16 Mar 1864
GARNETT, Ida Mary, only dau/A.M. and M.I., Friday ae 3. Lived at 149 Chambers.	MORE 30 Aug 1862
GARNETT, John 16 Dec in Lewis Co. at the home of his brother Robert, ae 61. KY pc	MORE 25 Dec 1862
GARNETT, Lewis living near Graham in Holt Co. shot by a group who came to his door. He had been in Price's army, was ca 45, left a large family.	SJH 25 Feb 1864
GARRETT, Frances P., Chariton Co.: public administrator took over her estate.	CECB 4 Sep 1862
GARRETT, Mrs. Henry, daughter of John Hile, in Canton 17 Mar.	COWS 23 Mar 1865
GARRITY, Margaret wife of Patrick, 11 Nov. Lived on Summitt Ave.	MORE 12 Nov 1861
GARTH, Lucinda relict of Rodes of KY 18 Nov at the home of her daughter, Mrs. J.B. Ghio, ae 66.	MORE 19 Nov 1864
GARVIN, Jennie J.G. wife of Benjamin D. 11 May in Cuba MO of pneumonia. Late of St. Francois Co., dau/William and Mahala Evans.	MORE 15 May 1865
GARVIN, John (brother of James, keeper of a livery stable at Market-11th) killed on Walnut St. in the Camp Jacksob affair.	MORE 14 May 1861
GARVY, William Henry 23 Feb ae 14 at the home of his parents, 107 S. 14th.	MORE 24 Feb 1862
GASH, Mrs. Eliza at her home near Barry in her 64th year. Ill 3 months. A Presbyterian 47 years.	LIT 14 Jul 1865
GASS, Joseph 30 Aug of consumption ae (30?). Member of the St. Louis Fire Dept. Lived on 11th St. betw Carr-Biddle.	MORE 31 Aug 1863
GASS, Prudence wife of John yesterday at their home on Pine St., ae 55.	SLMD 10 Sep 1861
GASTON, Samuel, an old man, murdered near Greenton. (LEXUN)	MORE 22 Jul 1862
GATCH, Jefferson son/William C. in his 6th year, of a protracted illness, 9 Mar.	LIT 14 Mar 1862
GATES, James R. 13 Jul of bilious fever at his home in St. Louis Co. Ae 60. Telitha 25 Jul of typhoid fever ae 51. Boonville, Bainbridge IN, and Perryville KY pc (all in same item)	MORE 27 Jul 1865
GATES, Mrs. Mabel K. 16 Apr of paralysis in her 73rd year. Funeral from the home of her daughter, Mrs. Washington King.	MORE 17 Apr 1863
GATEWOOD, Mrs. Fanny 25 Sep in her 88th year at the home of her daughter, Mrs. Julia Lincoln. Widow of Col. Peter.	LIT 30 Sep- 7 Oct 1864
GATY, John of Long Prairie, returning from Lane's Landing, killed by a falling tree. Born in MO 1817, a Methodist, lived mostly in Mississippi Co.	CHAC 20 Feb 1863
GAUBATZ, Philip 30 Sep ae 53. Lived at Main-Mullanphy.	MORE 1 Oct 1863
GAUTHIER, a little son of Robert killed by accidental discharge of a gun.	LEXUN 12 Nov 1864

GAY, Mrs. Louisa 3 Jun in her 58th year. Friends of her family and that of Hiram   MORE 4 Jun 1865
   Wolf invited to her funeral. Int. Bellefontaine. New Albany IN, Memphis, New Or. pc

GAYLORD, Edward A. only s/William F. and Sarah A. 1 May at 15th-Poplar ae 3y11m13d.   MORE 2 May 1862

GAYLORD, Sarah Lothrop wife of Erastus 19 Oct of typhoid ae 61y 9m 17d. Lived   MORE 20 Oct 1862
   Chouteau betw 13-14. Pittsburgh, Syracuse NY, Adrian MI pc

GEING, Humphrey, deckhand on the T.L. McGill, fell overboard Saturday, body   MORE 18 Jun 1862
   found yesterday. Left wife and 3 children.

GEMMER, Dr. Albert suddenly yesterday at Mrs. Klans', where he was visiting a   MORE 13 Aug 1864
   patient, of dropsy of the heart.

GENCHER, Jacob, an engineer, in the explosion of a boiler at the Davis & Co. Mill.   MORE 23 Nov 1864
   Lived at Plum-Market, left wife and 2 children.

GENERALLY, Zoe Eglee youngest child of Emile and Rebecca in St. Clair, Franklin Co.   MORE 1 Feb 1862
   28 Jan ae 20m 5d.

GENTRY, Amanda wife of James and dau/Judge William Forman of Ralls Co. near   HAM 17 Jan 1861
   West Ely 13 Jan. Born in MO 10 May 1832, married May 1854; survived
   by 2 children, one pre-deceased her.

GENTRY, Col. Joshua 22 Jan at his home 4 miles west of Hannibal, in his 67th   PALS 5 Feb 1864
   year. Left wife and 11 children including 3 sons in service. Brother of   MORE 4 "
   Rev. Christy Gentry of Ralls Co., who was with him when he died. Former
   senator, a Baptist for 30 years.

GENTRY, Lucie dau/William T. and Hattie, 6 Feb ae 17m 23d at 138 Chestnut.   MORE 7 Feb 1862

GENTRY, Martha wife of Richard at DeSoto KS 4 Dec 1864 ae 61y 4?. Left 10   MORE 12 Jan 1865
   children, numerous grandchildren.
   Richard at his home in DeSoto KS 5 Apr ae ca 71. Born Lexington KY, to   MORE 18 Apr 1865
   Boone Co. MO more than 50 years ago; removed to KS 7 years ago. Left
   10 children, about 40 grandchildren. Wife died 18 Feb last(?!)

GENTRY, Woodson H. in Boone Co. 11 Jan ae ca 50. Lexington KY pc   COWS 23 Jan 1863

GEORGE, Ann Eliza dau/William M. near Fulton 14 Feb of typhoid ae 15.   FULT 1 Mar 1861

GEORGE, Charles, a German, suicide in the near neighborhood of Hudson's Mill   WEST 14 Jul 1865
   of the city. Shot himself. No cause known.

GEORGE, James, late Col. CSA at Vera Cruz of vomito 20 Mar. Native of MD, citizen   MORE 26 Apr 1865
   of MO, converted to Catholicism several years ago.

GEORGE, James of Sullivan Co. en route to Boone Co. for a visit killed near   COWS 2 Oct 1863
   Fayette by federal soldiers.

GEORGE, Susan dau/George W. 24 Apr ae ca 15.   LIT 1 May 1863

GERLACH, Lt. Jacob drowned 24 Mar trying to take a raft of logs to Wilkinson Mills   PERU 8 Apr 1863
   on Apple Creek. "Fine citizen." Left wife, 1 child.

GERSHON, Joseph 2 Apr ae 28 at the home of his brother, M.A. Memphis & NY pc   MORE 3 Apr 1864

GETHIN, Mary Ann wife of Edward of sunstroke 3 Sep ae 35. Husband a soldier.   MORE 5 &
   Lived at Papin-5th.   6 Sep 1864

GETY, Louis pilot of the Dickerson killed in a boiler explosion 8 Oct; body   MORE 23 Oct 1864
   identified. Interred Bellefontaine.

GHEE, Simon Thursday night of hydrophobia; bitten Tuesday. Lived at the corner   MORE 18 Jun 1865
   of 7th-North Market.

GIBBONS, Barney executed (shot) as a double deserter. Left sister and brothers   MORE 13 Aug 1864
   in New York state. Born Madison Co. NY 8 Sep 1836.

GIBBONS, Matilda 14 Apr in her (64? 65?)th year at the home of her son John A.   MORE 15 Apr 1864
   Smithers, 48 S. 15th.

GIBBS, Mrs. E. 13 Mar ae 45.   MORE 16 Mar 1865

GIBBS, William citizen of Ste. Genevieve of typhoid 28 Dec. (Undertaker's list)   MORE 2 Jan 1865

GIBERT, Augusta 23 Jun ae 20 at family home, 15th-Poplar. St. John's Church,   MORE 23 Jun 1865
   interred Calvary.

GIBSON, Clara Marie eldest child of James H. and Margaretta A.R. 29 Jul   MORE 29 Jul 1864
   ae 4y 4m 3d. Lived on Olive betw Garrison-Ewing.

GIBSON, Elizabeth Y. wife of John B., 4 Sep ae 43y 8m. Lived on Grand Ave. MORE & SLMD 5 Sep 1864

GIBSON, Mrs. Elizabeth widow of Philip 22 Nov ae (paper wrinkled) at her late   MORE 24 Nov 1865
   home on Manchester Road west of Grand.

GIBSON, G. W., body recovered; drowned about 3 weeks ago. (Trenton Herald)   BEST 9 May 1861

GIBSON, Philip suicide 28 Oct ae ca 57. (Laudanum) A gardener, had lived on Market   MORE 30 Oct 1865
    Road & Grand Ave. nearly 25 years; took the laudanum while intoxicated,
    near Rock Spring. Leaves a wife, now quite ill.

GIBSON, William, a rebel of Franklin Co., at Douglas Prairie on the Bourbeuse River.   SLMD 10 Sep 1861

GIBSON, William ae 61 at the home of his son-in-law A.C. McCoy, 3 May. Lived in   MORE 4 May 1861
    St. Louis 40 years. Cincinnati, Baltimore, Pittsburgh pc

GIBSON, William, funeral notice: 30 Mar at his home 2 miles se of St. Joseph   SJH 30 Mar 1865
    near the Hannibal & St. Joe RR.

GIDDINGS, Rev. G.P., funeral preached at the Concert Hall in Palmyra.   HAM 18 May 1861

GILBERT, Joshua Thomas 22 May at Little Rock ae 21, member of Merrill's Horse.   MORE 9 Jun 1864

GILBERT, William B. of Ralls Co. killed while trying to save some papers from   PALS 29 May 1863
    the burning home of William H. Brown; Mrs. Brown was his niece.

GILBREATH, Jane wife of Rev. J.N. at Des Peres Institute of paralysis of the   MORE 5 Mar 1863
    lungs 28 Feb ae 41y 6m.

GILES, Thomas M. eldest son/Francis and Ann 17 Sep of consumption ae 22y 10m 17d.   MORE 18 Sep 1865
    Born in St. Louis 16 Oct 1842; family home on S. 5th St.

GILKERSON, Hiram supposedly drowned; assistant engineer on the J.H. Dickey, fell   MORE 25 Aug 1863
    overboard between Hollows Landing and Herculaneum, ae 28. Any
    information to his father, John Gilkerson, at Hambright and Gilkerson, 59 4th St.

GILL, Frances Evans youngest dau/John J. and F.E. 3 Oct ae 1y 9m 24d.   MORE 4 Oct 1861

GILL, Mrs. Sarah A. 26 Jul in her 64th year at the home of her son, George H.,   MORE 29 Jul 1861
    near Kirkwood. Funeral from St. John's Church. Baltimore pc   SLMD 30 "

GILLESPIE, David 17 Jan. Born in NC, to Nashville, to MO 23 years ago; last   MORE 9 Feb 1862
    10 years in Weston. Religious tribute by S.W. Cope, Platte City.

GILLESPIE, Mary Cecelia 1 Jun ae 58. Philadelphia pc   MORE 4 Jun 1865

GILLESPIE, R. B. son/Robert 26 Mar in Boone Co. in his 23rd year.   COWS 5 Apr 1861

GILLESPIE, Sarah wife of John of St. Louis at Lagrange TN 30 Oct. Funeral from   MORE 10 Nov 1863
    the home of William Conway, 343 Broadway.

GILLET, ___ a boy ae ca 12 fell into a vat of sorghum near Poplar Grove.   CALM 18 Nov 1865
    (New Albany Commercial)

GILLIAM, Isham H. of Lewis' men captured in St. Clair Co. 10 Aug, in Gratiot   MORE 2 Apr 1863
    Prison of erysipelas.

GILLIAM, John W., Chariton Co.: public administrator took over his estate.   CECB 23 Oct 1862

GILLICK, Joseph of Co. I, Col. Meyers' Reg., accidentally shot by another member,   MORE 8 Jun 1864
    A. Genther, both about 18 or 20. Gillick survived by his mother.

GILLIGAN, John aboard the Mollie Able 14 Dec ae 15. Cincinnati, Louisville, Chicago pc MORE 22 Dec'64

GILLMAN, Dr. James A. 2 Oct of consumption ae 48.   SLMD 8 Oct 1861

GILMORE, John C., a police officer, shot by a burglar known as Bill Wilson (and   MORE 27-28 Dec
    accomplice Joseph Burns) died of his injuries. Lived on 9th betw   1861 &
    Benton-Broadway. Interred Bellefontaine.   29 Aug 1862

GILMORE, Alex 14 Aug in Monroe Co. in his 74th year.   COWS 2 Sep 1864

GILPIN, Elizabeth dau/Ambrose 13 Apr at the home of James W. Marples in Boone Co.   COWS 17 Apr 1863
    ae 28y 5m 11d.
    Nancy wife of Ambrose near Providence 5 Jun ae ca 58.   COWS 12 Jun 1863

GILPIN, Green in Boone Co. 4 Oct of typhoid ae ca 60.   COWS 13 Oct 1865

GILWILLIAM, Clark B., private Mo Vols, 29th Reg., killed in the explosion of the   MORE 7 Nov 1862
    J. H. Dickey, 10 miles above Ste. Genevieve.

GIPSON, Thomas G., Tribute by the 6-Mile Lodge IOOf. Mentions wife and daughter.   MORE 21 Nov 1861

GIRITY, James native of Ireland of hepatic consumption 14 Feb ae 35.   MORE 16 Feb 1861

GIST, William Jasper at Helena City MT 16 Oct in his 30th year, of typhoid.   CACE 16 Dec 1865
    Native of Moniteau Co. until 2 years ago, wife and infant joined him in
    the spring, now left "in a strange land." Mason. (Montana Post)

GITTINGS, Marshall son of Darius and Phebe 9 Nov ae 3y 2m.   LIT 15 Nov 1861

GIVENS, Capt. ___ living about 3 miles from Kidder accidentally shot Sunday last   MORE 13 Jun 1864
    while hunting an escaped prisoner. (Kingston MO Banner)

GIVENS, Alec "old and esteemed" citizen of Cooper Co. 9 Dec of congestive chills.   COWS 26 Dec 1862

GIVENS, John H. 18 May near Boonville.   MORE 2 Jun 1865

GLANVILLE, William S. in Vicksburg 18 Jan; born St. Louis Co. 1824, his father a   MORE 28 Jan 1864
    Methodist clergyman who emigrated from England. Clerk of the Supreme Ct.
    of MO, appointed 1851. Left state in 1862 to join the Confederates.
    Buried St. Charles beside his wife, who died ca 7 years ago; leaves
    a daughter ae ca 8. His parents both dead many years.

GLASBY, Nandy dau/Alban H. 1 Oct in her 22nd year.   MORE 3 Oct 1864

GLASBY, Mrs. Ruth 7 Aug ae 75. Funeral from the home of her son-in-law
    J.S. McCune. Philadelphia pc   MORE 9 Aug 1861

GLASCOCK, Dr. E.B. of Clark Co. murdered Tuesday betw Williamstown and Fairmont   CANP 18 Jun 1863
    about a mile from home. "Southern sympathizer," wife, several children.

GLASEBROOKS, Susanah at the home of J.J. Dawdy in Adair Co. 24 Mar in her 88th   MORE 12 Apr 1864
    year. Methodist 60 years, cousin of Henry Clay. Funeral at
    Vienna, Macon Co.

GLASGOW, Hiram D., Chariton Co. Public administrator took over estate.   CECB 24 Jul 1862

GLASSCOCK, C.T. of Vernon Co., 2nd MO Inf CSA, list of killed either at the   MORE 19 Sep 1863
    Battle of Champion Hills, Big Black Bridge, or siege of Vicksburg.

GLEASON, Mrs. Ellen 25 Jun ae 47. Lived at Chestnut & 11th.   MORE 26 Jun 1864

GLEASON, Larry, brakeman on the Iron Mountain RR, fell between cars, decapitated.   MORE 5 Jan 1862

GLEIM, Col. C. 23 Sep in his 82d year at the home of his daughter, Mrs. Amos.   MORE 25 Sep 1861

GLENN, Mary E. wife of James 6 Mar at Washington MO ae 30. Funeral from the home   MORE 8 Mar 1863
    of Z.T. Simmons, 118 Olive. Frederick MD pc

GLENN, Sallie, suicide at the home of her aunt (17th betw Christy & Morgan)   MORE 26 Sep 1865
    Sunday; swallowed arsenic. Cause, a love affair.

GLENNY (Elliot?) Marcella E. Elliott, youngest daughter of William W. and Rachel   MORE 13 Dec 1862
    Glenny, 12 Dec ae 21y 17d. Funeral from 8th St. Methodist Ch.
    Lebanon & Cincinnati OH & Nashville pc

GLIME, John 4 May in his 74th year; funeral from the home of his daughter, Mrs.   MORE 6 May 1865
    Alexander, 13th betw Pine & Chestnut. Methodist, int. Bellefontaine.

GLOSSMAN, Mary Ann, a suicide; she was in the habit of getting drunk and   MORE 16 May 1861
    beating her husband, who was blind.

GLOSSOP, Sarah wife of Alfred, formerly Mrs. Waters of Hannibal, in Louisiana MO   HAM 10 Feb 1861
    1 Feb ae 33y 2m.   LAJ 7 "

GLOUNER   Aaron, a citizen of Cedar Co., arrested 31 Aug, of pneumonia in   MORE 5 &
(GLOWMER?)   Gratiot Prison 3 Feb. (Undertaker's list)   8 Feb 1863

GLOVER, Mrs. Ann Smith in Carrollton 23 May of typhoid ae 22.   LIT 6 Jun 1862

GOBATZ, ___ ae 10, son of Frederick of near 3-Mile-House, hit by pole pitched   SLMD 25 Jan 1861
    down from load of hay which his father was having delivered.

GODDARD, John 3 Mar in his 71st year, formerly of MD, late of IL.   MORE 6 Mar 1861

GODFREY, George A. 19 Nov ae 28. Funeral from Union Methodist Church, 11-Locust.   MORE 20 Nov 1864

GODFREY, John C. 12 Jan in his 23rd year, ill 2 years, joined Catholic Church   MORE 19 Jan 1863
    about the time he became ill.

GODFREY, Lawrence, late of the police, funeral yesterday. Lived on 16th near   MORE 24 Aug 1863
    Biddle, was ca 45, left wife and several children.

GODFREY, Moses L. 9 Dec of paralysis ae 70y 4m. Lived at 131 St. Charles St.   MORE 10 Dec 1864

GODLOVE, John, twin son of Emanuel and Louisa, Sunday last ae 8m.   CAWN 2 Feb 1861

GODSEY, Burton in Carroll Co. 24 Apr ae 80, veteran of War of 1812.   MORE 7 May 1862

GOEDEKE, Diedrich, German ae ca 40, suicide due to ill health; was in good   MORE 29 Mar 1862
    circumstances financially. Wife, 5 children, at 296 Biddle.

GOGAN, Mme., a Creole, fell from her balcony at Buel near Menard.   MORE 12 Jun 1862

GOLDING, John, of Carondelet, fell from an Iron Mountain train. No family.   MORE 25 Nov 1862

GOLL, Ida Patton oldest child/Capt. W.A. and Mary E. 24 Aug ae 8y 4m.   MORE 25 Aug 1864
    Interred Bellefontaine.

GOMES, John 1 Apr ae 51y (6m?) 21d. Lived at 16 Cerre St.   MORE 2 Apr 1865

GONNEN, Kate, inquest: lived alley betw Lewis and Bates, west of Main; married,   MORE 26 Apr 1865
    ae ca 28, husband a steamboat man somewhere between St. Louis and New
    Orleans. Found dead in bed of intemperance. Left daughter ae 10.

GONTER, Charlie Francis, only child of Charles G. and Lizzie A.S., 22 Dec of   MORE 23 Dec 1862
    scarlet fever ae 4y 16d. Lancaster PA & Baltimore pc

GOOCH, Sarah Joanna wife of Philip in Farmington 19 Oct in her 26th year, of MORE 9 &
    phthisis pulmonalis. Daughter of Junius M. Roundtree of Springfield.   15 Nov 1861
    Member of the Christian Church, left 3 small children.

GOOD, Edward J. of Franklin Co. at St. Vincent's Hospital in St. Louis 26 May MORE 10 Aug 1863
    ae 52y 9m 7d. Left wife and friends.

GOODFELLOW, Charles K. at the home of Mrs. David F. Goodfellow ae 17y 2m 4d. MORE 21 Nov 1864
    Lived on Eugenia east of 22nd. Interred Bellefontaine.

GOODFELLOW, Jane only daughter of Mrs. Robert Goodfellow, 16 Dec ae 5. SLMD 23 Dec 1861

GOODFELLOW, children of   Mary Ellen, youngest dau, 31 Oct ae 11 MORE 1 Nov 1864
    David and Jane: Robert R., youngest son 25 Nov ae 13y 8m 2d " 26 Nov "
    (Lived on Natural Bridge Plank Road. Interred Bellefontaine.)

GOODIN, Amos, 1st MO, captured in Texas Co. 20 Jan, in Gratiot Prison of bronchitis. MORE 25 Feb 1863

GOODIN, Sarah Leonar dau/Jerome and Theodosea 26 Sep ae 1y 6m 7d. HAM 17 Oct 1861

GOODING, Mrs. Mary Ann wife of A.D. in Macon Co. 27 Jan of fever, ae ca 24. MAG 4 Feb 1863

GOODLETT, Mrs. Charlotte P.C. 20 Sep ae 72. Lived on Walnut betw 15-16. MORE 21 Sep 1862
    Interred Bellefontaine. Nashville pc

GOODLET, Mary A. wife of Col. M.C. 14 Apr at Bridgeton. Nashville & Clarksville pc MORE 16 Apr 1864

GOODLETT, John M. son of Col. M.C. 22 Apr ae 10y 1m 3d, survived his mother only MORE 24 Apr 1864
    one week. Congested stomach and bowels. Nashville & Clarksville (TN) pc

GOODRICH, P., salesman for Harris Goodman Tobacco Co., from Hannibal, SJH 21 May 1865
    of brain congestion.

GOODWIN, Mrs. Amanda M. consort of John C.G. at Vermont MO 15 Mar of bilious MORE 29 Mar 1863
    pleurish ae 40y 8m. Lexington KY pc

GOODWIN, John Nelson killed 1 May on Champion No. 2 at "Grand Encore." MORE 18 Jul 1864
    Ae 27y 7m. Jefferson City pc

GOODWIN, Mrs. Margaret L., an old citizen, 25 Jan. Denver, St. Louis, St. Joseph pc JINQ 26 Jan 1861

GOODWIN, Thomas murdered on the train at Centralia by Anderson (guerilla) on his SJH 2 Oct 1864
    way home from Atlanta; member odd 25th MO Vols, now 1st MO Engineers.

GORDAN, Julia R. wife of John and dau/Sheldon Stanley 23 May ae 23y 7m. Funeral MORE 24 Mar 1864
    from home of Wm. P. Gordan, Dayton e of Garrison. New Britain CT pc

GORDON, Andrew B. 20 Mar of smallpox ae 9y 11m 17d, adopted son of L.D. MAG 25 Mar 1863

GORDON, Isaac suddenly of apoplexy at Frederick House. SJH 5 Aug 1863

GORDON, Lottie dau/William F. and Rebecca 21 Feb ae 3y 9m. LIT 4 Mar 1864

GORDON, Moses G. at Old Mines of consumption of the liver, ae 42y 8m. NH pc MORE 14 Nov 1863

GORDON, Sue F. wife of Boyle and dau/James Watson of Ralls Co. in Boone Co. COWS 28 Oct &
    18 Oct ae ca 22.   11 Nov 1864

GORIN, Gladdie son of Gladdin and Mary E. 30 Mar at 204 Olive ae 2y 6m. MORE 1 Apr 1862

GORIN, Mary Elizabeth wife of H. 23 Sep, dau/Thomas G. Porter, formerly of CHAC 6 Nov 1863
    Louisville KY. Ae 26.

GORMAN, Mack, native of Townland Walleogrange, Co. Kilkenny, ae 30. Funeral MORE 26 Feb 1865
    from home of his brother-in-law Paul Matthews, Main betw Mullanphy
    & Howard, to St. Patrick's Ch. Member Hibernian Benevolent Society.

GORMAN, Capt. Patrick, funeral; St. Francis Xavier, interred Calvary. Murdered MORE 17 Dec 1863
    in the pilot house of the Henry von Phul at Morgan's Bend. (Actually the
    boat was shelled by rebels above Bayou Sara, up from the south.)

GORMAN, Mrs. Teresa 8 Oct ae 82. Funeral from home of Capt. Throckmorton, MORE 9 Oct 1862
    180 Locust, to St. Francis Xavier. Interred Calvary.

GORMLEY, Francis P. 2 Oct at Mobile from injuries received by the breaking MORE 22 Oct 1865
    of a cotton slide on the Alabama River while taking in cotton on the
    Montana. Father, Capt. James Gormley, lives Beckwith n of Chouteau.

GORRELL, John, old and esteemed citizen of Ray Co., suicide at Hardin (cut his RICON 30 Apr 1863)
    throat) 25 Apr. "More or less deranged some time past."

GOSNELL, Mrs. Louisa 20 Apr, consort of George and dau/late Rene Paul, ae MORE 21 Apr 1864
    44y 10m 5d. St. Michael's Church, interred Calvary. Louisville,
    Baltimore, Cincinnati pc.

GOSS, A.E. 26 Mar, tribute from Masons at Marshfield, Webster Co. MORE 24 May 1864

GOUDAY, John, inquest: a laborer, cut his throat Friday at Carondelet, wife MORE 22 Nov 1863
    mentioned. He was "addicted."

GOULEY, Florence Young only child of Frank and Marie ae 3y 11m 10d. DE & Philadelphia pc MORE 8 Dec 1861
GOURLEY, William Walker member MSM shot by Price's men in Franklin Co. LAJ 7 Jan 1865
GRABS, August at Marthasville, Warren Co. 26 Sep ae 60. MORE 4 Oct 1865
GRADY, Patrick drowned 12 May trying to cross the river in a skiff. Family in Memphis. MORE 15 May '65
GRAEVE, Henry 2 Aug ae 37. Lived at 14th & Randolph. MORE 3 Aug 1863
GRAHAM, Archibald, an Irish laborer, in a tenement at Main-O'Fallon after a drunken spree with his wife. MORE 5 Apr 1862
GRAHAM, David W., resident of St. Louis Co., of typhoid pneumonia in his 59th yr. Born in Baltimore 1805; at 33 moved to St. Louis where he was in business with his brother-in-law M. Deaver, now retired. After a disastrous fire several years ago he tried to build up the business but was not successful, and retired to the country, 5 miles from the city. Husband, father. MORE 2 & 6 Feb 1864
GRAHAM, James 17 Apr of consumption ae 31y 3m. Lived at 89 St. Charles St. MORE 18 Apr 1863
GRAHAM, James, Irish "under the influence" shot by James Knowles, town marshall in Independence, while resisting arrest. (Kansas City Press) RICON 17 Jul 1862
GRAHAM, Maj. James, late of St. Louis, at Helena AR. Interred Bellefontaine. MORE 8 Oct 1862
GRAHAM, Margaret native of Co. Tyrone 21 May ae 70. Funeral from the home of her son John, 190 14th St. Interred Bellefontaine. MORE 22 May 1862
GRAHAM, Rosanna, wife of a blacksmith, of apoplexy. Lived in the alley betw 6-7-Carr-Biddle, left 3 small children. MORE 22 Feb 1863
GRAHAM, Sue E. wife of William, 19 May. Fairfield & Chester IL pc. MORE 20 May 1865
GRAMBRA, Elizabeth Hanson dau/Thomas Hudgins of St. Louis 10 Aug ae 20y 10m 28d. MORE 13 Aug 1862
GRANAUGHAN, Thomas of injuries received while he was visiting his cousin, an employee at Wilson's Bakery. Granaughan put his hand on the dough and his arm was pulled through the rollers. MORE 15 Nov 1862
GRANT, Clara Rose second dau/P.B. and Elizabeth in her 18th or 19th year. LIT 30 Jun & 7 Jul 1865
GRANT, Daniel near Columbia 28 Jun, born 25 Mar 1775. "Born in the midst of one revolution and died in the midst of another." COWS 26 Jul 1861
GRANT, Edward, ae 15, stabbed fatally Sunday by a boy named Bush Hart. MORE 20 May 1864
GRANT, Francis William only son of William D. and Margaret 29 Jan. Lived north of 3-Mile-House. MORE 30 Jan 1862
GRANT, Israel B. at Fulton 15 Mar in his 67th year; born in Campbell Co. KY 11 Jun 1797, to MO in 1830. Clerk of court, etc. MORE 22 Mar 1864
GRANT, Robert B. Saturday morning last, of flux, a young man. FULT 19 Aug 1864
GRANT, Sarah T. in Newton Co. 12 Feb, wife of Col. James, ae 77y 3m (2m?) 23d. Formerly of Callaway Co. Lexington KY pc FULT 1 Mar 1861 COWS 15 "
GRANT, Gen. Thomas D. in Canton 28 Jun ae 64y 8m 1d; was in the Florida War, Mormon War, Brig. Gen. Mo. Militia. Mason. Moved to Canton in 1855. CANP 2 Jul 1863
GRANVILLE, John near Tower Grove of effects of the heat. MORE 12 Aug 1862
GRATE, Elias, citizen of Scott Co., laryngitis. (Undertaker's list) MORE 4 Apr 1864
GRAVES, G.M. 1 Dec in Gratiot Prison of pneumonia. MORE 7 Dec 1862
GRAVES, John R. shot near Greenton Valley; a guide for bushwhackers and had previously killed __ Ashcraft. LEXUN 15 Aug 1863
GRAVES, Martin murdered on train at Centralia by Anderson's guerillas, on the way home from Atlanta. Of the old 25th MO Vols, now 1st MO Engineers. SJH 2 Oct 1864
GRAVES, William B. in Livingston Co. 9 Jul, "long and highly respected resident." COWS 31 Jul 1863
GRAY, James 23 Mar ca 28 after a short illness. Montreal pc LIT 24 Mar 1865
GRAY, Mary relict of John 5 Nov in Rolla, of dropsy, in her 68th year. COWS 1 Dec 1865
GRAY, Mary B. wife of S.M. 15 Mar ae 28y 3m 23d. NY pc MORE 19 Mar 1861
GRAY, Sarah Ann wife of Cyrus W. 21 Mar. Lived at 2 S. 15th, interred Wesleyan. MORE 23 Mar 1862
GRAY, Seneca M., 1 May in his 35th year of inflammation of the bowels. Resolution by Old MO Guard. MORE 2 & 3 May 1864
GRAY, William of Daviess Co. murdered near Warrensburg by bushwhackers. GAL 2 Mar 1865
GRAY, William A. 17 Mar of pneumonia ae 25y 8m 2d. Left wife, 3 children. RANC 28 Mar 1861
GRAY, Capt. William T. aboard the McDowell at Bolivar MS 25 Aug ae 52. MORE 5 Sep 1862

GRAYSON, W.S., once editor of the Louisiana Herald, 3 Oct of consumption at the   LAJ 7 &
   home of E.C. Murray. Born Rappahannock Co. VA 10 Aug 1935, son of   14 Oct 1835
                                  George W. & Julia.

GREADY, Patrick 30 Jun ae 36. Funeral from Holy Trinity Church.   MORE 1 Jul 1865

GREASEBACK, ____ son of John, ae 2, living on the riverfront at the old soap   HAM 1 May 1862
   factory above the ferry landing, drowned Friday in the river.

GREEN, Amanda B. relict of Samuel B. of Andrew Co. in St. Joseph 13 Aug   SJH 15 Aug 1865
   ae 41y 5m 22d. St. Louis & Louisville pc   MORE 18 "

GREEN, Annie A. eldest dau/Elder J.S. and Martha 8 Aug of diphtheria ae 7y 4m 25d.   PALS 14 Aug 1863

GREEN, Cyrus Tuesday ae 40y 10m. Funeral from Centenary (Methodist) Church. IOOF.   MORE 11 Jun 1863

GREEN, David at the home of his daughter Mrs. Bartlett 1 May in his (50? 80?)th   MORE 2 May 1865
   year. Pittsfield IL and Troy Times NY pc

GREEN, Edward at Ironton 7 Aug, brother of Thomas and Charles of St. Louis.   MORE 14 Aug 1864

GREEN, Effie Clara dau/J. and S.A. 26 Sep ae 4y 3m 17d, of diphtheria.   MORE 27 Sep 1863

GREEN, George 1 Sep ae 35 at Sisters Hospital. Funeral from the home of John   MORE 3 Sep 1863
   Helpin on Bellefontaine Rd. near 4-Mile-House.

GREEN, Henry S. son/Dr. James B. in Marion City 6 May of congestion of   HAM 18 May 1861
   the brain, ae 22y 9m.

GREEN, J.W., prisoner of war, 3 Feb of variola. (Undertaker's list)   MORE 15 Feb 1863

GREEN, Maria Alberta dau/George R. yesterday of brain fever ae 7y 6m.   HAM 10 Apr 1862

GREEN, Martin "rebel of this state" killed at Vicksburg 27 Jun.   LAJ 18 Jul 1863

GREEN, Thomas, ae 17, an orphan adopted by Edward J. Halliburton, drowned in the   MORE 25 Jul 1861
   river with Halliburton's son George while returning from fishing.

GREEN, W.H.(?) "one of Porter's guerillas" captured in Marion Co.   MORE 3 Apr 1863
   28 Oct, in Gratiot Prison.

GREEN, Yelverton in Centreville, Clay Co. 21 Nov of consumption ae 36.   LIT 24 Nov 1865

GREENE, Charles, citizen of Boone Co., of erysipelas 18 Jan. (Undertaker's list)   MORE 22 Jan 1865

GREENE, Mary Eliza only dau/Isaac T. and Eliza J. 7 Apr ae 17. Boston pc   MORE 9 Apr 1865

GREENE, Minnie only dau/Mosley and Marion 18 Dec ae 2y 9m.   MORE 22 Dec 1862

GREENWOOD, A. Maria wife of E.S., bookkeeper at Rich & Co., 6 Feb ae 31, at 131 Olive. MORE 8 Feb 1865

GREER, Richard of Long Prairie killed in St. Charles Saloon by ____ Mooney,   CHAC 10 May 1861
   bartender, in a knife fight.

GREER, Sarah consort of Samuel T. near Hillsboro, Jefferson Co., 6 Sep   MORE 15 Sep 1865
   ae 54y (11 m?) 9d. Methodist 30 years, wife and mother.

GREER, William killed by soldiers in lower Cape Girardeau Co.   CHAC 22 Apr 1864

GREFENKAMP, Mary E. wife of J.H. 12 Nov ae 46. Interred Calvary.   MORE 13 Nov 1865

GREGAN, Richard ae 44, born in Dunboyne, Co. Meath. Funeral from the home   MORE 15 Apr 1865
   of his brother Nicholas, 7th & Carr.

GREGG, Bill, a Lafayette Co. bushwhacker, recently in Texas.   LIT 12 May 1865

GREGG, Joseph a bushwhacker killed by soldiers near Mt. Pleasant 9 miles   MORE 20 Sep 1863
   from Platte City. (St. Joseph Herald)

GREGG, Sarah wife of Marshall and dau/Jacob P. Hymer 8 Nov ae ca 22.   LIT 17 Nov 1865

GREGG, Timothy ae 30y 3m. Lived at 160 N. 5th.   MORE 11 Apr 1863

GREGORY, Elijah, of Mercer Co., left Chillicothe to go to Spencer Gregory's, near   LIT 19 Sep 1862
   Utica, while intoxicated; lay down on railroad tracks, was run over.

GREGORY, John L. 10 Nov of consumption ae 23y 9m. Funeral from the home of   MORE 12 Nov 1865
   Patrick Gregory, Clark betw 15-16. NY City pc

GREGORY, Martha relict of John in Canton 12 Nov ae 43.   CANP 17 Nov 1864

GREGORY, Mary Alicia dau/Dr. E.H. and J.K., 24 Jul.   MORE 25 Jul 1861

GREGORY, Dr. Otway B. ae 24 at Barnum's Hotel 6 Sep. Funeral from   MORE 7 Sep 1861
   St. Paul's Church. Interred Bellefontaine.

GRETH, Andrew, a painter, killed in a fall from scaffolding "subject to fits."   MORE 17 Apr 1864

GREY, Mrs. Mary relict of John 6 Nov in Rolla, of dropsy, in her 68th y. FULT pc   MORE 16 Nov 1865

GRIER, Rev. John W. 23 Mar at the home of his son M.B. in West Philadelphia in   PALS 6 May 1864
   his 75th year.

GRIFFEN, Ann widow of Timothy 27 Jul. Rochester NY pc. Lived 107 S. Main.   MORE 29 Jul 1864
GRIFFIN, Elizabeth wife of James, Thursday last.   PALS 27 Oct 1865
GRIFFIN, John of cerebral apoplexy. Lived at 162 N. 10th, left a young wife.   MORE 29 Aug 1861
GRIFFIN, P. 23 Mar ae 50. Funeral from the home of his brother, 10 S. Main,   MORE 25 Mar 1863
         to the Cathedral. Interred Calvary. Rochester NY pc
GRIFFIN, Timothy 29 Jun ae 52; lived at Main & Spruce. Cathedral, int. Calvary. MORE 30 Jun 1863
GRIFFITH, John of Reeves' band, captured in Ripley Co. 25 Dec, died in   MORE 4 Feb 1864
                                    the prison hospital.
GRIFFITH, H.A., bushwhacker of Holtzclaw's band, hanged 23 Sep.   SJH 24 Sep 1864
GRIFFITH, Hiram killed by guerillas in Carroll Co. (Carrollton Democrat)   MORE 21 Jul 1864
GRIFFITH, John F. 29 Mar of lung disease ae 17y 3m 5d. Son/B.F. and E.A.   HAM 17 Apr 1862
         (MORE 18 Apr gives mother's initials as E.R., in Ralls Co.)
GRIFFITH, Dr. Joseph in DeSoto, Jefferson Co., 21 Sep of typhoid ae 32.   MORE 30 Sep 1863
GRIFFITH, (Maria G. or Martha Gaiter) 9 Jul of dysentery in her 36th year,   MORE 10 &
         of dysentery. Born Clarksburg, Montgomery Co. MD, came west in   30 Jul 1863
         1846. Left mother, sister, brother. Funeral St. George's Episcopal.
GRIFFITH, Dr. Robert H. of Hannibal suddenly Monday last.   PALS 8 Jan 1864
GRIFFITH, Thompson at his home near Louisiana 17 Jan. Left wife and children.   LAJ 24 Jan 1861
GRIFFITH, Tom killed by soldiers in lower Cape Girardeau Co.   CHAC 22 Apr 1864
GRIFFITH, William B. son/J.A. in Clay Co. 27 Mar of typhoid in his 12th year.   LIT 18 Apr 1862
GRIGGS, John of Callaway Co., formerly of Boone; lived 3 miles east of Fulton;   LAJ 19 Dec 1861
         at advanced age. Veteran 1812, Black Hawk War. (FULT)
GRIGGS, Samuel 20 Sep at his home in Louisiana, of flux, in his 75th year.   LAJ 24 Sep 1864
GRIGSBY, Moses son of John C., ae ca 17, killed by Edward Campbell, a paroled   MORE 14 Feb 1863
         rebel, at Charleston MO. (CHAC 4 Feb)
GRIMM, Chris, a saloonkeeper on Main St. in Carondelet, stabbed Sunday   MORE 1 Aug 1863
         night. George Worley accused.
GRIMSLEY, Martha A. wife of John J. 4 Apr in her 31st year. Centenary (Methodist) MORE 4 Apr 1863
                                     to Bellefontaine cemetery.
         (COWS 24 Apr says she was the dau/John L. Elbert of Lexington KY)
GRIMSLEY, Col. Thornton 21 Dec in his 64th year. Took ill at his store, died   MORE 22 Dec 1861
                         suddenly; funeral St. George's Church.   SLMD 23 "
         Susan Stark wife of Thornton, 7 Sep. Lived 4th betw Elm-Myrtle.
GRISWOLD, Dr. C.G. in Dec ae 73, at Canton Centre CT, father of   SJH 11 Jan 1865
         Capt. Theodore of St. Joseph, his only son.
GRISWOLD, Mrs. Rebecca at her home in Warren Co. 16 May in her 57th year,   MORE 23 May 1863
                                     of lung congestion.
GROAT, Lizzie consort of P.B., General Ticket Agent for the Hannibal & St. Joe RR, SJH 6 Sep 1864
         in Hannibal 2 Sep at the home of the late Col. Crump.
GROJOHN, Henry killed by bushwhackers in Chariton Co. (RANC 17 Jun)   MORE 19 Jun 1864
GROLL, Augustus Franklin in this city ae 4y ?m 23d. St. Louis pc   JEST 14 Feb 1863
GROLL, Mrs. Caroline 5 Oct ae 61.   JEST 6 Oct 1865
GROOM, Eliza H.C. wife of John H. and dau/Joseph Thorp at the home of her   LIT 6 Feb 1863
         father 2 Feb of consumption ae 20y 20d.
GROOMS, ____ in a fight with Harper & Mills at John Fritz's beer saloon on the levee. LAJ 25 Nov 1865
GROOMS, James thrown from a wagon and run over, died later, ae 52.   WARS 6 Oct 1865
         (Livingston Co.? From Grand River News.)
GROTJAN, John F.; Chariton Co. Letters of administration to Henry F. Grotjan 8 Apr. CECB 4 May 1861
GROVE, J.H., inquest: died of intemperance.   MORE 18 Sep 1865
GROVER, Emma Whitcomb youngest dau/George M. and R.J. 26 Apr of scarlet fever   MORE 27 &
         ae 5y 6m. Lived at Clark & 13th.   29 Apr 1862
GROVER, Lizzie E. wife of David at Locust Grove, Lafayette Co. 4 Jun in her   COWS 25 Jul 1862
         33rd year. (MORE shows Lizzie C.)   MORE 15 "
GRUGAN, Patrick R. 5 Oct of chronic diarrhoea in his 26th year. Lived at   MORE 7 Oct 1864
         Soulard & Linn. Funeral St. Vincent's Church, interred Calvary.

GRUMLEY, Emelia A. Wiseman 28 Apr ae 40. Funeral from the home of her son-in-law   MORE 29 Apr 1865
         Thomas Farmer, 14th betw Biddle-O'Fallon.

GRUPE, Sadie Goll youngest dau/George L. and Kate G. 6 Sep ae 4.   MORE 6 Sep 1863

GUDGEL, John T. 11 Jun ae 48 at the home of Spence H. Gregory in Livingston Co.   COWS 30 Jun 1865
         Was the county representative in the state legislature 2 years ago.

GUELBERTH, Isabel relict of Augustus in Central Twp. 19 Mar ae (55?). Funeral   MORE 20 Mar 1865
         from St. John's, 16th-Chestnut. Interred Calvary.

GUERIN, William H. at his home near Bunker Hill, Howard Co., 30 Sep ae 45y 8m.   COWS 27 Oct 1865

GUERIN, William Theodore 2nd son/E.T. and Bettie, Saline Co., 9 Feb of scarlet   MORE 6 Mar 1864
         fever ae 5y 1m; and on 30 Jan their eldest daughter, Minnie Stuard,
         ae 3y 2m 26d.

GUIBERT, Willie Downer son/A.P. & Cordelia M., ae 6y 4m, on 4 Jul. Cincinnati   MORE 6 Jul 1864
                                                       and Newark OH pc

GUIGNON, Eliza dau/Simon A. and Carmelite at Ste. Genevieve, formerly of   MORE 25 Sep 1863
         Fredericktown, 20 Sep in her 20th year. Dubuque pc

GUION, Louis at his home in Carondelet 25 Jan ae (63? 65?)y 1m 18d. Born in   MORE 27 Jan 1865
         Little Prairie, New Madrid Co., resident of Carondelet or environs
         50 years. Son of Amable, said to have been the first male child born there;
         grandson of Marguerite Hebert dit Le Compte. Died suddenly of heart disease.
                                      St. Joe MO & St. Paul MN pc
      Catherine wife of Lewis in Carondelet 22 Feb ae 56.   MORE 3 Mar 1861

GUITAR, Mary H. dau/David and Harriet near Columbia 3 Jul.   COWS 19 Jul 1861

GULACH, Adolphus Gustavus, suicide by laudanum. In service, had met Susan Grig   MORE 13 Dec 1863
         at Rolla, wanted to marry her, father wouldn't permit it.

GUNN, Calvin at his home in Jefferson City 23 Aug. Born Pittsfield MA 1800, to   COWS 6 Sep 1861
         MO 1820; published the Jefferson Republican in St. Charles in 1825, moved   MORE "
         to Jefferson City when the government moved. Paralyzed for several years.

GUNNER, Fred, a German, killed by falling earth on Bellefontaine Road.   MORE 10 Nov 1863

GUNSAULUS, Levi in Jefferson City 3 Jan. IOOF tribute, widow mentioned. JINQ 5 & 11 Jan 1861

GUNSOLLIS, James Ambrose only child/James W. and Julia 7 Oct of diphtheria   MORE 10 Oct 1865
         ae 12y 4m. St. Charles pc

GUNTRAM, Curring killed night before last by a fall from the 3-rd floor window at   MORE 1 Jun 1865
         his home, Jackson near Marion. Plasterer and whitewasher, was drunk.
         German, left wife and child.

GURNEY, ___ formerly merchant in St. Joseph at Northampton MA ae ca 43.   SJH 29 Oct 1865

GUTHRIE, Mary F. wife of J.G. 26 Jun ae 47. Interred Bellefontaine. Canton & Edina pc   SLMD 12 Jul 1864

GUTHRIE, Mrs. Mary 17 Jul in her 77th year. Baltimore pc   MORE 22 Jul 1862

GUY, Mary C. relict of John at Rollas 6 Nov in her (68th?)year. Interred by husband   SPRIP 16 Nov 1865
         at Springfield, he died (1859?).(Paper badly blurred.)

GUYE, Jean Francis native of France, resident of St. Louis 50 years, 3 Oct ae 84.   MORE 4 Oct 1862
         Funeral from home of Ferdinand Gsell in Lowell, North St. Louis, to the
         Catholic Church at Carondelet.

GWINNER, Mrs. Mary Ann at the home of her son F. 12 Jan ae 68. Presbyterian   LIT 18 Jan 1861
         nearly 50 years, "many years much afflicted."

GWINNER, Samuel Tillery youngest son/Frederic and Almerica 29 Dec ae 3y 10m 22d.   LIT 8 Jan 1864

HAAS, Clementine youngest dau/Eugene and Clementine of brain congestion, 6 Nov.   MORE 7 Nov 1861

HABB, Louis S. 10 Dec of chronic dysentery. Lived 10th betw Harrison-Dock.   MORE 11 Dec 1864

HABENDANZ, John killed by a fall from an unfinished building where he was playing,   SLMD 22 Jan 1861
         ae 16. Employed at Post Office Saloon. Father, a widower, has another
         son ae 12 ill at home, Myrtle betw Main-Levee.

HACKERT, John, inquest: found dead in lot near the Arsenal, ca 50. Unmarried.   MORE 13 Dec 1865

HACKLEY, John G. of Sturgeon, recently from the rebel army, killed by a guard   COWS 31 Jul 1863
         while trying to escape from prison in Camden Co.

HADEN, Elder Joel H. in Howard Co. in Feb, in his 80th year. Pioneer of MO,   LIT 4 Apr 1862
         minister in the Christian Church.

HADLEY, Mary Ann wife of James 27 May ae 44y 1m 26d.   MORE 28 May 1864

HADLEY, Willard Francis, a bushwhacker, shot at Warrensburg 20 May, confession.   LIT 17 Jun 1864
         Native of NH, to MO 1860.

HAEFNER, J.W. at Potosi 25 Oct ae 49. Left wife and 6 children.	MORE 27 Oct 1861
HAGAN, James, a stonecutter, 25 Feb ae 63.	MORE 26 Feb 1864
HAGAN, Joseph of Boone Co. in Alton prison in Dec.	COWS 9 Jan 1863
HAGEN, Arthur, prisoner of war, 7 Oct of typhoid. (Undertaker's list)	MORE 12 Oct 1862
HAGENS, George 15 Oct in his 46th year, after a lingering illness. Lived at 373 S. 2nd.	MORE 16 Oct 1861
HAGER, Mollie youngest child/Samuel and Adaline Sunday of diphtheria ae 4y 6m. Lived at Hickory-St. Ange.	MORE 11 Aug 1862
HAGERTY, Michael J. of the firm of John Hagerty & Bro. Funeral from the home of his brother, 30 Collins.	MORE 26 Mar 1865
HAHN, Mrs. Bertha wife of F., native of Hamburg GER, 8 Nov of typhoid ae 29.	MORE 11 Nov 1865
HAIGLER, Cyrus P. son of Jesse of St. Charles in Chariton Co. 22 Nov,; murdered by 10 federal soldiers at his home near Westville. Ae ca 33, member of the Church of God.	MORE 27 Nov 1864
HAINES, Daniel son/late Sidney P. 29 Mar ae 25y 11m.	MORE 2 Apr 1863
HALCOMB, Thomas, a prisoner, 31 Jan of diarrhoea and erysipelas. (Undertaker's list)	MORE 2 Feb 1863
HALDERMAN, William, a teamster, crushed by a falling bale of hay. Lived in Lowell (northern St. Louis) and left a wife and 4 children.	MORE 11 Dec 1864
HALE, Cpl. Frederic B. son/Dr. E. & Harriet 5 Feb ae 16y 8m. Funeral from 1st Presbyterian.	MORE 6 Feb 1863
HALE, John B. of Clark's Command, captured in Dunklin Co. 12 Mar, in Gratiot Prison of erysipelas.	MORE 27 Apr 1863
HALE, Mrs. M.M. wife of Col. F., a merchant, of and at Camden Point 17 Nov. of lung hemorrhage in her 67th year. Harrodsburg & Mt. Sterling KY & Carson City UT pc	MORE 25 Nov 1863
HALE, Mary Frances eldest dau/George W. & Ada H. 25 Nov of lung congestion in her 17th year. Lived at 54 N. 5th. Dover NH pc	MORE 27 Nov 1862
HALE, Mrs. Nancy 31 Jan ae 103. Funeral from Grace Church.	MORE 1 Feb 1864
HALE, Dr. Thomas B., in a group of bushwhackers, killed in a skirmish with Federal troops; he was from Kansas City.	LIT 13 & 20 Feb 1863
HALE, Thomas C., late of Lexington, at Big Sandy en route home from Denver City of "affection of the kidneys" 31 Jan ae 25; recently a Missouri River pilot.	COWS 22 Feb 1861
HALEY, Mary E. wife of Elder Henry H. 26 Sep in St. Louis, at the home of her father John S. Porter, 235 Locust.	MORE 27 Sep 1865
HALEY, Thomas, inquest at Carondelet where his body was found: fireman of the ferry John Trendley, fell off at the foot of Carr St. Left wife, 1 child.	MORE 9 Sep 1863
HALEY, W.B. of typhoid 16 Nov ae 24.	SJH 17 Nov 1865
HALL, Charles Edward son/William and D.F. 10 Nov of flux ae 4y 11m 7d.	LIT 18 Nov 1864
HALL, Elizabeth wife of John, native of Lotherstown, Fermanagh IRE, 18 Jul ae 37. Lived on Magazine betw Webster-Illinois. NY pc	MORE 19 Jul 1862
HALL, Emily shot at Union, Franklin Co. by her brother LeGrand, who was later lynched. LeGrand had been convicted of the murder of Andrew Bullock, then pardoned; he apparently resented the amount of his father's estate left to him as compared to the shares of Emily and a surviving brother.	MORE 22 Jul 1862
HALL, Ephie son/Ephraim L. and Catherine 4 Feb ae 5. Memphis, Helen AR, Vicksburg pc	MORE 6 Feb 1864
HALL, F.P. 19 Mar in Monticello of typhoid, ae ca 40.	CANP 23 Mar 1865
HALL, Flavia C. at Athens AL 14 Jun, wife of Albert E. of St. Louis and daughter of J. Cooper of Fairhaven VT, ae 25. (Her marriage record is in the same paper and gives her maiden name as Capen.)	MORE 24 Jun 1865
HALL, Frank 4 Apr in his 10th year, son of John H. and Mary A., living at the nw corner of Biddle & 17th.	MORE 5 Apr 1862
HALL, George at his home 1 mile north of Bridgeton 30 Oct ae 56y 8m 25d, of pleurisy. Interred Fee Fee Cemetery. Springfield IL & Memphis pc.	MORE 1 Nov 1861
HALL, Col. Henry at Carondelet 31 Jul ae 73y 6m. Funeral at J.C. Hall's home.	MORE 1 Aug 1861
HALL, James, citizen of Howard Co., 24 Feb of pneumonia. (Undertaker's list)	MORE 6 Mar 1865
HALL, Jim, a negro, killed in a stabbing affray at "Fiddler Hall."	MORE 27 Jan 1863
HALL, Capt. John 5 Sep ae 66. Lived at 84 Olive St. Interred Bellefontaine.	MORE 7 Sep 1862

HALL, John Byrd son/Dr. J.B. of Fredericksburg VA and brother of R.P. Hall of   MORE 25 May 1863
    St. Louis 3 May at the Battle of Chancellorsville ae 21.

HALL, John D. 1 Mar ae ca 65.   LIT 3 Mar 1865

HALL, Katie adopted dau/William and Catherine 21 Sep of typhoid ae 20y 9d. Lived   MORE 22 Sep 1863
    on Madison betw 11-12. Bangor ME pc

HALL, Mrs. Louisa A. wife of George D. and dau/Edward Miller 17 Nov in her 25th year.   MORE 18 Nov 1862

HALL, Mary D. at Allenton 14 Jul ae 59. Funeral 9th & Carr. Interred in the east.   MORE 16 Jul 1861

HALL, Mary S. only dau/Willard P. 24 Jun in St. Joseph ae 7.   COWS 10 Jul 1863

HALL, Ralph D. son/Lt. S.K. and Massie D. at their home, 111 N. 8th, ae 5-1/4 y.   MORE 8 Jan 1865

HALL, Susan F. wife of E.H. in Washington DC 3 May after a long illness. Funeral   MORE 7 May 1864
    from the home of her father, Rev. David Anderson, in St. Louis --
    329 Collins. (See also Mrs. V.J. Mitchell.)

HALL, Thomas Edward only son/Lewis and Margaret 7 May ae 2y 10m. Memphis pc   MORE 10 May 1863

HALL, William, of Tipton, shot near Lamine. (Moniteau Co. News)   MORE 24 Aug 1864

HALL, Col. William in Canton 29 Nov ae 71y 9m. Formerly of Syracuse NY. He   CANP 3 Dec 1863
    had been delirious, wandered outside, died of exposure.

HALL, William (of Macon or Monroe Co.) 12 Nov in Gratiot Prison. (13 & 16 Nov)   MORE Nov 1862

HALL, William K. killed in Hardin by Milt Farris in an affray 28 Jul. Farris   RICON 13 Aug 1863
    interfered in a fight between Hall and Love Snowden; cause "mean whiskey."

HALLECK, Capt. L.P. and his son Alonzo, late of Macon City, Confederates, killed   HAM 5 Sep 1861
    at Wilson's Creek. Capt. had formerly lived at Palmyra and was once
    register of US Land Office there.

HALLENBACH, Joseph M., formerly deputy constable of 5th & 6th wards. Funeral from   MORE 28 Sep 1864
    home of John H. Smithers, Chestnut betw 5-6; died at Sisters Hospital.

HALLER, Wash, brother of Bill the noted bushwhacker; body had 14 wounds.   SJH 26 Jan 1863
    (Kansas City Journal)

HALLIBURTON, George son/Edward J., a carpenter, drowned in the river returning   MORE 25 Jul 1861
    from fishing, ae 15. Lived on Biddle near 11th.

HALLIGAN, Charles son/James and Fannie 31 Mar in Union, Franklin Co., in his 3rd y.   MORE 17 Apr 1862

HALLIGHAN, James, inquest; wife hit him with a pitcher in a drunken row last   MORE 6 May 1865
    Monday at their home, 20 Ashley St., but death was ruled as due to
    intemperance after he died suddenly. Also left 2 children.

HALLORAN, Pat, inquest; died of internal injuries ae ca 22, his mother said that   MORE 4 Jan 1864
    Cecelia Hannahan hit him with a hatchet but no marked were found. He
    lived on Collins betw Cherry-Carr.

HALLOWS, Isaac a private in Co C 10th MSM drowned last Sunday in Salt River   LAJ 15 May 1862
    when he was thrown from his horse.

HALOHE, James, deckhand on the Perkins, accidentally ae 29. Wife and 3 children   MORE 23 Jun 1863
    in indigent circumstances at 7th betw Franklin-Wash.

HALPEN, Mary Ann, inquest; took arsenic for her complexion, overdoses ae ca 21.   MORE 13 Oct 1865
    Left 6-year-old son. Sister of the man who had been supporting her took
    charge of the body.

HALPIN, Peter in his 29th year. Interred Calvary. Cleveland pc   MORE 10 Sep 1863

HALSTEAD, Hugh son/Eliza and the late Alexander and grandson of Dr. William   MORE 12 May 1863
    Scott, 16 Apr ae 14y 7m.

HALTER, Charles oldest son/Albert P. and Nancy H. of Jackson Co. at Sisters   KCJC 3 Apr 1864
    Hospital, Leavenworth, 20 Mar ae 19y 1m 28d.

HAM, Jacob, proprietor of Gambrinus Cave, broke his neck in a fall. German ae   MORE 1 Jun 1865
    ca 45, left wife and 3 children.

HAM, Julius eldest son/Peter N. Tuesday in his 27th year. Interred Calvary.   MORE 2 Nov 1865

HAMILL, Samuel Friday of consumption ae 55y 4m; native of Antrim, to US 1831,   MORE 30 Apr &
    in Philadelphia 6 years, then to St. Louis, bringing goods with him on   1 May 1865
    a flatboat. Lived Pontiac near Grand. Interred Bellefontaine.

HAMILTON, Alexander N. 9 Apr ae (48?) at Carondelet of inflammation of the bowels.   MORE 11 Apr 1865
    Lived at 2nd & Pine. Interred Bellefontaine.

HAMILTON, Mrs. F.A. at the home of her son-in-law R.F. Sass 25 Feb after a   MORE 26 Feb &
    lingering illness. (Her name was Eliza.) Ae 48. Funeral from St.   1 Mar 1862
    George's Church, int. Bellefontaine.

HAMILTON, James, an old and respected citizen of St. Joseph, formerly of Baltimore; came to St Joe 14 years ago, had a grocery, then pork packaging plant. Presbyterian, no mention of relatives.	SJH 9 Dec 1865
HAMILTON, James, alias James H. Low, hanged at Macon Friday last. He was a bushwhacker, citizen of Monroe Co.	MORE 7 Mar 1865
HAMILTON, Jennie A. 8 April of brain congestion ae 8y 7m. Lived at Jefferson & Lafeyette. Interred Calvary.	MORE 10 Apr 1863
HAMILTON, Joseph H. murdered 7 Jan at Millwood, Lincoln Co. by Edward W. Rector, over some personal differences. Left wife, 6 children.	MORE 18 Jan 1865
HAMILTON, Mary E. consort of William and dau/Levi Primm of Lewis Co. at the home of her father 6 Jun in her 34th year.	MORE 15 Jun 1862
HAMILTON, Palestine citizen of Boone Co. of pneumonia 16 Jan. (Undertaker's list)	MORE 22 Jan 1865
HAMILTON, Thomas a slave belonging to Amazon Howell of Meramec Twp, shot and killed by Samuel Tyler (apparently white) of the same township.	MORE 21 Aug 1863
HAMILTON, Janet wife of William, living betw O'Fallon & Cass, 29 Jan ae 75. William 13 Jul ae 75, 14th betw O'Fallon & Cass.	MORE 30 Jan 1865 MORE 14 Jul 1865
HAMLIN, Isabella dau/Charles and Maria 28 Jan at the home, 117 N. 5th.	MORE 29 Jan 1863
HAMLIN or HAMLON Jack, a soldier, shot at Palmyra while attempting to pass a picket without orders. Member of Col. Glover's Reg., native of Steubenville OH, resident of Marion Co. 20 years.	HAM 14 & 28 Nov 1861
HAMMER, John, inquest: ae 9, drowned when he fell into the river while gathering wood. Lived at Trudeau and DeKalb.	MORE 17 Aug 1865
HANCOCK, Sarah L. 2nd dau/D.J. and M.E. 1 Aug of scarlet fever and whooping cough ae 4. Interred Bellefontaine.	MORE 2 Aug 1863
HANCOCKER, George of Lewis Co., 3 Dec of brain inflammation. (Undertaker's list)	MORE 7 Dec 1862
HANDY, Rachel R. consort of Judge Noah 8 Oct ae 59, at Matthews Prairie near Charleston, Mississippi Co. Born Somerset Co. MD 26 Feb 1806; married 28 Jan 1827; to MO 1836. Methodist, left husband and dau/Mrs. J.C. Moore. Also had 4 children deceased.	CHAC 20 Oct 1865
HANEY, John Rufus son/E. and Susan 27 Jan ae 2y 6m 16d.	CANP 29 Jan 1863
HANLAN, Miss Mary ae 22 after a long illness. Native of Jefferson City, funeral from home of her brother-in-law E. Sallsman, 5th & Wash.	MORE 4 Dec 1865
HANLEY, Esther Ann wife of Rev. William in LaGrange Saturday last ae ca 60.	PALS 14 Jul 1865
HANLEY, HANLY George son of Bernard and Laura accidentally shot while hunting partridges near Florissant, 26 Apr. Ae nearly 15.	MORE 28 Apr 1861
HANLON, James drowned off the Continental ae 25, left wife and 3 children.	MORE 21 Jun 1863
HANNA, Alexander M. 31 Jan ae 57y 11m 16d.	CAWN 7 Feb 1863
HANNA, Mrs. Caledonia, sister of Edward Wilkerson of St. Louis, 22 Jun of consumption at Lauderdale Springs MS.	MORE 31 Jul 1864
HANNAH, Robert of Kirksville near College Mound mid-December last of consumption.	MAG 15 Jan 1862
HANNAY, Estelle C. dau/James B. and Elizabeth at Versailles, Morgan Co., ae 16y 5d. Memphis, Jackson MS, Ripley MS pc	MORE 20 Feb 1864
HANNEGAN, John ae 9 drowned in a pond on Chestnut betw 18-19; he lived on Gay betw 16-17. S young man (John Maloney) rescued him but could not revive him.	MORE 20 May 1864
HANNIGAN, James E. 28 Mar ae 29. Interred Calvary.	MORE 29 Mar 1865
HANNUM, Joseph W. son/Philip 14 Nov ae (?3?)y 4m.	MORE 15 Nov 1861
HANRATTY, Joseph eldest son/Hugh decd at the home of his mother, 284 Pine, ae 22y 7m. Funeral from St. John's Church. Interred Calvary.	MORE 1 Jun 1862
HANSARD, John "a peaceable, quiet man" stabbed by James Spillers, a neighbor. He had found Spillers drinking at St. Aubert and brought him home behind him on his horse, but when they arrived Spillers killed him. Spillers was reportedly lynched. Both left families. (FULT)	CAWN 30 Aug 1862
HANSEN, Valentine hanged yesterday for the murder of John Ellig.	MORE 16 Apr 1864
HANSON, George Henry 8 Jan in his 32d year of lung congestion. A job printer, left young wife and child. Funeral from St. George's Church.	MORE 9 & 10 Jan 1865
HARBAUGH, Emilie W. wife of Howard S., editor of the Chillicothe Constitution, in that city 14 Aug.	SOWS 26 Aug 1864

HARBINE, Annie oldest dau/Thomas and Kate 18 Jul ae 15. Lived at Farren and 8th in St. Joseph.   SJH 19 Jul 1864

Catherine wife of Col. Thomas 30 Jul. Funeral from the home.   SJH 31 Jul 1864

HARDEN, Mary wife of Maj. H. 7 Nov near Williamsburg, Callaway Co., ae 70.   COWS 1 Dec 1865

HARDEN, Virginia dau/late Joseph and Mary Ann in Washington MO 2 Mar ae 13y 2m.   MORE 7 Mar 1863

HARDESTY, Frank Tuesday ae 57 at his home on St. Charles Plank Road near Benton Barracks. Born in Fayette Co. PA, to St. Louis 1844; int. Bellefontaine.   MORE 14 Dec 1864

HARDESTY, John killed in Jefferson Co. by 47th MO Vols. under Col. Fletcher.   MORE 17 Oct 1864

HARDIN, consort of Dr. T.I. of Audrain Co. in Louisiana 17 Aug ae 30y 8m 18d. Dau/B.F. Hesser of this city (Louisiana). Baptist. (COWS says Dr. T.J.)   LAJ 29 Aug 1861 / COWS 23 "

HARDIN, Hannah relict of Charles at the home of her son-in-law Capt. Andrew Harper in her 69th year. Native of Nelson Co. VA, to MO (near Old Franklin) in 1820, to Columbia 1821; remained there until 1853. Husband died 1830. (MORE says she died 10 May and her son-in-law lived near Florissant.)   COWS 17 May 1861

HARDING, Annie Flowers only child of George M. and Caroline 20 Sep of diphtheria ae 3y 4m.   MORE 21 Sep 1863

HARDING, Mrs. Elizabeth Andrews 31 Dec of typhoid; only dau/Rev. Calvin Lincoln of Hingham MA, sister-in-law of Mrs. R.W. Oliphant of St. Louis (lived 155 Locust). Funeral from Oliphant home, interred in the east.   MORE 1 Jan 1865

HARDING, George E. 28 Mar ae 36. Lived at 259 Washington. Interred Bellefontaine.   MORE 29 Mar 1863

HARDING, Helena M. wife of Joseph 13 Dec in Central Twp, of consumption, in her 73rd year. Baltimore & Carroll Co. MD pc. (Note: she was buried in Des Peres Presbyterian churchyard.)   MORE 17 Dec 1861

HARE, John, ae 8, drowned in the river while picking up wood with his mother; his father was in Vicksburg. Lived at 42 Main.   MORE 9 Sep p863

HAREN or HAVEN, Sophia wife of Edward Sr. 10 Dec in her 58th year. Lived at 253 S. 7th.   MORE 11 & 12 Dec 1863

HARGADINE, Phocion McCreery son/William A. and Acrata yesterday ae 6y 5m.   SLMD 28 May 1861

HARKLERODE, Linneus son/William and Meleina in Carondelet of typhoid 25 Apr ae 15.   MORE 27 Apr 1863

HARLOW, William M., formerly of Albion ME, Sunday ae 40y 11m 17d. Funeral from Dr. Post's Church. Member IOOF.   MORE 8 Mar 1864

HARMAN, Anna wife of Richard, ae 23, at the home of her mother-in-law.   MORE 9 Nov 1863

HARMAN, William, an orphan ae 14, killed in the Camp Jackson affair.   MORE 18 May 1861

HARMANN, Eliza wife of Dr. Thomas K. of Newton Co. in St. Louis 16 Jan ae 49. Dau/Col. John Wood of Scott Co. VA. Methodist 31 years. Wife, mother.   MORE 24 Jan 1865

HARNESS, ___ little son of Peter, living in the upper part of the city, accidentally shot.   SJH 23 Oct 1864

HARON, Thomas A., civilian, a tinner living on the east side of 6th St. betw O'Fallon & Cass, in the Camp Jackson massacre.   SLMD 14 May 1861

HARPER, Capt. Andrew near Florissant 27 Jul in his 64th year.   MORE 28 Jul 1864

HARPER, Miss Annie Jane 9 Dec after a short illness. Funeral from Grace Church, north St. Louis.   MORE 10 Dec 1862

HARPER, Gabriel M., an engineer, accidentally killed on the Pacific RR near Calvey Station about 40 mi. from St. Louis when a bridge gave way after recent rains. Married 8 months. Tribute from Rev. J.S. Phelps of Franklin (town? county?) He was a Mason. Also shown as G.W. & G.N.   MORE 8 & 10 Jul 1863

HARPER, M.S., prisoner 20 Jan of variola confluens. (Undertaker's list)   MORE 26 Jan 1863

HARPER, Mary Smith only dau/Andrew and Arethura(?) near Florissant 4 Jun of scarlet fever ae 8y 10d.   MORE 5 Jun 1864

HARPER, William H., arrested Friday last as a bounty jumper, jumped from train taking him to Chicago, was run over. Wife mentioned.   MORE 20 Feb 1865

HARR, William Henry son/George W. and Eliza in Brunswick 19 Feb in his 18th year.   CECB 26 Feb 1863

HARRELL, James L. 21 Feb in Canton Twp of brain inflammation, ae 39y 2m? 20d.   CANP 26 Feb 1863

HARRINGTON, Dwight F. 31 Jan of consumption at the home of William Betts, ae 28.   MORE 2 Feb 1861

HARRIS, ___, brother of H.H. (Dock) shot by Sgt. Hampton who had come to arrest Dock, 16 Feb.   LIT 19 Feb 1864

HARRIS, children of A.B. & Maggie: Fannie Lee, eldest dau, 24 Jul ae 8y 11m; Mary Price, ygst dau 27 Jul ae 3y 1m 22d; William Andrew, only son, ae 5y 5m 26d. Funerals from home of Mrs. Julia Price, 215 N. 6th. Louisville pc   MORE 26 Jul & 2 Aug 1864

HARRIS, Arthur Edwin youngest son/Oliver and Mary 20 Jan in Ste. Genevieve ae MORE 24 Jan 1861
nearly 8. Parents had lost 2 younger children earlier in the month.

HARRIS, Augustus S. in Richmond VA hospital in July ae 30. Youngest son of Peter, BOOM 2 Apr 1864
of Boonville; in an Alabama regiment; his parents are Union.

HARRIS, Betsy Ann dau/Masten and Rachel 8 Apr at the home of John Ludwig ae 20. FULT 13 May 1864

HARRIS, Elvira wife of James G. 14 May ae 40y 6d. Left husband & 9 children. COWS 20 Jun 1862

HARRIS, Fannie dau/John W. and A.M. of Boone Co. 18 Nov of diphtheria ae 6y 2m. COWS 27 Nov 1863

HARRIS, Frances wife of Daniel Boon and dau/late James Clarkson suddenly 13 Mar. CHAC 15 Mar 1861

HARRIS, Franklin shot and wounded by a concealed bushwhacker while riding along COWS 26 Aug 1864
a road last Wednesday, died Monday.

HARRIS, George Washington 17 Sep ae 44 at the home of his brother near Allenton. MORE 19 Sep 1865

HARRIS, Henry ae 62 in Independence 21 Jul. NY & CA pc MORE 25 Jul 1865

HARRIS, James O. at the home of his uncle J.O. Manion in Howard Co. 10 Aug in his COWS 22 Aug 1862
50th year. Member of the Christian Church. KY pc

HARRIS, John Alfred "4 years lacking 4 days" at the home of his uncle Thomas MORE 8 Jan 1861
Hamilton, 102 Myrtle. Funeral at the Cathedral.

HARRIS, John M. 28 May ae 46. COWS 5 Jun 1863

HARRIS, Margaret Josephine youngest dau/John W. & Margaret 4 Dec of scarlet fever MORE 5 Dec 1861
ae 3y 9m. Lived at 58 N 8th. Pittsburgh pc
Agnes Kate youngest dau/John W. and Margaret 9 Jan of cholera morbus. " 10 Jan 1864
Lived 58 N 8th.

HARRIS, Mary dau/James and Sabra B. 20 Jun of typhoid ae 10y 4m 22d. COWS 27 Jun 1862

HARRIS, Mary Lizzie Duverger at Florissant 23 Dec ae 27y 2m 8d. Memphis pc MORE 9 Feb 1864

HARRIS, Mary S. of Elm Valley, Washington Co. became suddenly ill, lived a few MORE 26 Oct 1864
days, died 18 Sep ae 18y 9m 18d.

HARRIS, Oliver at Ste. Genevieve 19 Aug of chronic diarrhoea ae 53; newspaper man, MORE 23 &
formerly of St. Louis. Had been clerk of court, Justice of the Peace, 24 Aug 1863
etc. Left a large family.

HARRIS, Rev. Rice in Winchester, Clark Co. 19 Apr of erysipelas ae 69y 2d. Methodist. CANP 21 May 1863

HARRIS, Samuel P. in St. Francois Co. 8 Dec ae ca 74. To MO from Madison Co. KY MORE 19 Dec 1863
ca 1820, held various political offices. Richmond KY pc

HARRIS, Sarah Catherine wife of Dr. H.B.C. of Platte Co. 18 Mar in her 30th y. WEST 14 Apr 1865
(Actually says 18th inst; possibly she died early in April.)

HARRIS, children of William of Allenton,   Lewis Clark 1 Jul ae 22y 7d; long illness MORE 10 Jul 1865
St. Louis Co.   Samuel Rice 11 May ae 29, chronic bronchitis " 14 May 1864

HARRIS, William A. of Pike Co. 28 Mar in his 58th year, a prominent Democrat. MORE 5 Apr 1864
Born Fauquier Co. VA 1806; to MO 1854; Baptist, Mason. (Long article)

HARRIS, William J. of Boone Co., a guerilla, hanged yesterday; claimed to be a MORE 25 Mar 1865
regular Confederate soldier. Born Randolph Co. MO, enlisted in Newton Co.
Served 3 years, re-enlisted, deserted. Had wife and child in Audrain Co.
with her father, D.C. Woods. Harris ae 27 or 28.

HARRISON, Bettie at the home of William D. in Audrain Co. 11 Aug in her 21st MORE 18 Aug 1863
year of epilepsy. Methodist.

HARRISON, Carrie Mae only dau/Samuel A. and Hattie 20 Jul ae 2y 4m. RICON 24 Jul 1862

HARRISON, Elizabeth wife of Joseph 9 Oct ae 55. Interred in the family burying WARS 13 Oct 1865
ground at Hazel Hill.

HARRISON, Mrs. Emma E. 18 Dec in her 40th year, at her home, 47 N. 8th. Philad. pc MORE 20 Dec 1862

HARRISON, Col. Hiram murdered near Unionville, Scotland Co. Wednesday last week; MORE 10 Nov 1862
fired on from ambush, apparently by robbers. Had been mule buying and
was returning home, still had considerable money. (CANP)

HARRISON, Jason late clerk of the US District Court, western district of MO, COWS 11 Nov 1864
in Jefferson City 21 Oct.

HARRISON, Rev. Jephtha, DD, at his home in Fulton 30 Oct ae 67. Presbyterian MORE 9 Nov 1863
minister 38 years. Left wife and 4 children.

HARRISON, Mrs. Lizzie M. wife of Charles at Kirkwood 17 Jan of consumption in MORE 19 Jan 1864
her 22nd year.

HARRISON, Rebecca wife of James in Audrain Co. 20 Jul ae 62y 20d. COWS 31 Jul 1863

HARRY, Charles of Ste. Genevieve, pneumonia, 4 Dec. (Undertaker's list) MORE 7 Dec 1862

HARRY, Nathan 14 May in Chillicothe in his 45th year.   COWS 26 May 1865
HARSH, Mrs. Sarah 12 Aug in her 57th year. Funeral from the home of her son,   MORE 14 Aug 1861
       Capt. H., 56 15th St. Cleveland & Nashville pc
HART, Aaron Phillips son/Henry M. and Jane E., formerly of this city, at   MORE 23 Apr 1865
       Enterprise MS 23 Feb of brain congestion ae 18y 3m 25d. Hartford CT pc
HART, Ann T. relict of Samuel L. at the home of her son-in-law Dr. Abbot in   COWS 22 Aug 1862
       Fulton 14 Aug ae 72.
HART, Joe, noted bushwhacker, near Spring hill, 12 miles n of Chillicothe.   SJH 15 Jul 1863
HART, Miss May L. suddenly 9 Mar, sister of Capt. R.C., ACM of St. Louis and   MORE 10 &
       dau/Robert D. of NY (where she was interred). Ae 19y 16d.   11 Mar 1864
HART, Mary E. wife of Oliver A. 13 Feb ae 40y 1m 11d. Lived on Lucas Place.   MORE 16 Feb 1863
HART, Nannie T. dau/Judge R.S. and Susan B., Thursday.   MORE 12 Mar 1865
HART, Mrs. Theresa B. 4 Oct ae 66y 9m, of typhoid. Funeral at Cathedral. New Orleans pc MORE 5 Oct 1865
HARTGROVE, Bennett killed by guerillas in Carroll Co. (Carrollton Democrat)   MORE 21 Jul 1864
HARTLE, Jefferson living on Whitewater killed by robber gang 4 Jul -- the same gang   PERU 8 Jul 1864
       killed Bennett Murray. It included James Collier, Peter Smith, and others.
HARTLE, Jennie wife of Francis at her home in Bollinger Co. 3 Jan ae 21 after a   PERU 23 Jan 1863
       brief illness, of brain inflammation.
HARTMAN, William at the Hickory St. Hospital 19 Jan of pneumonia. Of Adair Co.   MAG 11 Feb 1863
              (/St. Louis)   (Co H 27th MO Inf)
HARTNETT, children of M.J.   Mary 20 Mar ae 5y 4m   MORE 21 Mar 1861
       and Kate   Fanny May 9 Jan of scarlatina ae 3y 7m   " 10 Jan 1864
HARTSHORN, Thomas A. of St. Louis Co. at Rock Island Military Prison, IL, 24 Apr   MORE 12 May 1864
       of pneumonia and erysipelas, ae 20y 3m 3d.
HARTTS, P., an old man living at the Hooss Hotel, Perryville, last Sunday in his   PERU 7 Jul 1865
       69th year "highly respected." Leaves several children.
HARTY, Edward 5 Apr in his 74th year at the home of his son Andrew, Wash betw 24-25.   MORE 7 Apr 1865
HARTZELL, Blooming Marion (male) ae 12 of brain congestion. Funeral from the   SJH 4 Dec 1864
       home of his father, 2nd & Mitchell.
HARVEL, ___, deputy sheriff of Cedar Co., shot in an encounter with ___ Stow.   MORE 11 Oct 1865
       Sheriff John Payntor killed. (Bolivar Sentinel 6 Oct)
HARVEY, Capt. C.C. of State Militia (Co H) 22 Nov of typhoid. Husband, father.   MORE 27 Nov 1862
HARVEY, Charles of St. Louis, in Gen. John Bowen's Brigade, killed at Shiloh.   MORE 4 May 1862
HARVEY, G., prisoner, 10 Dec of pneumonia. (Undertaker's list)   MORE 15 Dec 1862
HARWOOD, Eliza Page dau/late William B. and Martha Ann M., at the home of her   MORE 7 Jun 1864
       mother. Funeral Des Peres Presbyterian Church.
HARWOOD, William B. at his home on Manchester Road 14 miles from St. Louis, of   MORE 19 Jan 1863
       effects of pneumonia, ae 58y 3m. Husband, father.
HASKELL, Col. Truman W. 25 Jul ae 60. Cincinnati & NY pc   MORE 28 Jul 1863
HASKINS, Thomas, of Dallas Co., in the Prison Hospital in Springfield.   MORE 10 Apr 1863
HASSENDEUBEL, Col. Franz, body arrived yesterday. (Killed at Vicksburg?)   MORE 30 Jul 1863
HATCH, Willie son/Samuel A. and Rose 2 Jun ae 10y 11m. Int. Bellefontaine.   MORE 3 Jul 1863
                       Hannibal & Lexington KY pc
HATCHER, Albert M. of Basin Knob, suicide; cut his throat with a razor.   CAWN 27 Apr 1861
                       (Warrensburg Missourian)
HAU, Martin son/Martin and Ernestean 27 Feb of typhoid ae 5y 15d, at 99 15th St.   MORE 1 Mar 1863
HAUCK, ___ little son of Dr. Hauck of Concordia Park, fell from the "carousal,"   MORE 29 May 1864
       and was caught in the machinery.
HAUGH, John, a German ae 35, cut his throat; he was insane.   MORE 12 Jun 1861
HAUK, Capt. William of the Clarabell at Vicksburg 29 May ae 54, late resident of   MORE 5 Jun 1864
       Easton Place south of St. Charles Rock Road.
HAULMUELLERS, Charles, inquest: congestion of brain due to intemperance.   MORE 24 Jul 1863
HAVEN, Laura E. wife of C.H. at Melrose, St. Louis Co., 15 Jul ae 30y 8m 21d.   MORE 22 Jul 1865
HAVERTY, John 6 Jul ae 72. Had come to St. Louis in 1820, held various government   MORE 7 Jul 1865
       positions. Funeral from home of Joseph O'Neil, 14 Orange.

HAWK, Isabella Barclay, only child of Bishop Hawk, 17 Jun ae 13. St. John's Ch.	MORE 19 Jun 1864
HAWKEN, Martha wife of Samuel in her 68th year, at the home of her son-in-law F.M. Colburn, 8th betw Olive & Locust. Resident of St. Louis 42 years. Hagerstown MD, Brownsville PA, & Mercersburg (PA?) pc	MORE 4 Apr 1864
HAWKINS, ____ killed at New London Monday last by __ Williams; a stabbing affray.	LAJ 30 Jan 1864
HAWKINS, Edward son of William of Pike Co., a Confederate soldier, in Corinth MS ca 25. " 27 Nov 1862	
HAWKINS, James, an old citizen of Boone Co., 11 Jan in his 76th year.	COWS 25 Mar 1864
HAWKINS, Josiah H. 30 Sep in his 55th year. Wheeling VA, Louisiana MO, SteubenvilleOH MORE 3 Oct 1864 pc	
HAWKINS, Miss Mary Jane at the home of her father in Callaway Co. 17 Jan of typhoid pneumonia ae 19y 12d.	COWS 29 Jan 1864
HAWKINS, W.W. in Ashland 7 Oct of typhoid, ae ca 35.	COWS 13 Oct 1865
HAWKINS, William 2 Apr at the home of H. Hollyman ae 22y 10m 11d. Brother, son.	PALS 3 Jul 1863
HAWKINS, William G., inquest:run over by Pacific RR locomotive; had been to market and was returning, riding on the step with a basket in one hand an an umbrella in the other; wind caught the umbrella and pulled him off. Unmarried, ca 30, support of mother and 3 younger brothers, 14th & Randolph.	MORE 16 & 17 Jul 1865
HAWTHORNE, Paulina near Providence, Boone Co. in her 20th year.	COWS 15 Mar 1861
HAWTON, Mary Ann dau/Charles and Meriah 8 Feb. Lived 117 N. 5th.	MORE 9 Feb 1863
HAY, John "one of the oldest and most honored citizens of Springfield" ae 91.	COWS 9 Jun 1865
HAYDEL, Anne Cecelia relict of Edward M. and dau/John and Mary Rice, decd, 7 Apr ae 31. Funeral from home of Mrs. P.D. Papin, 4th-Plum, to the Cathedral. Interred Calvary. New Orleans pc	MORE 8 Apr 1864
HAYDEL, Francis Byrne eldest son/Dr. F.L. and M.E.B. and grandson of John Byrne, Jr. 18 Jul ae 7y 4m 4d.	MORE 19 Jul 1864
HAYDEN, Amelia A. wife of Peyton E., 27 Nov.	PALS 9 Dec 1864
HAYDEN, Andrew J. 21 Jun ae 19 at Sisters Hospital, victim of the Camp Jackson affair. Lived on Clark near St. Malachi's Church.	MORE 22 Jun 1861
HAYDEN, J.T. in Gratiot Prison 3 Dec of typhoid.	MORE 7 Dec 1862
HAYDEN, Mrs. James Tuesday last of consumption in her 47th year.	PALS 3 Nov 1865
HAYDEN, William H., killed when he jumped from a runaway wagon and struck his head on the ground. Formery county surveyor; left wife, several children.	PALS 27 Jan 1865
HAYES, Amelia W. wife of Thomas S. and eldest dau/Henry Wilde of Newark NJ, 17 Oct. Funeral at Dr. Post's Church.	MORE 18 Oct 1863
HAYES, James B. 25 Nov in his 32nd year.	MORE 27 Nov 1861
HAYES, W.L. of Audrain Co. suddenly of pneumonia at the home of R.L. Thompson in Mexico MO 16 Nov. At time of death was a prisoner of federal authorities. Left a large and destitute family.	COWS 5 Dec 1862
HAYES, William shot in Jan 1863 at the home of Thomas J. Davidson by John Abshire (subsequently hanged). / in Wayne Co.	MORE 13 Oct 1864
HAYHA, Louis father of George and Charles of St. Louis at his home near Fulton 12 Oct ae nearly (64?) Wheeling VA pc	MORE 15 Oct 1864
HAYMAN, Sallie A. of Monticello MO in St. Louis 31 Jan ae 16, at the home of R.B. Minor. Funeral from Centenary Methodist Church.	MORE 1 Feb 1865
HAYNES, George, of Porter's Band, 24 Nov in Gratiot Prison.	MORE 26 Nov 1862
HAYS, Peter killed by guerillas in Moniteau Co. (CAWN)	MORE 24 Jul 1864
HAYS, William, ae ca 13, playing in a leaky skiff, was swamped by waves from a passing steamboat. Father a street car driver.	MORE 7 Dec 1865
HAYWOOD, Mrs. Phoebe ae ca 50, native of Lincolnshire, Wednesday of "affection of the lungs." In St. Louis 22 years. Funeral from the home of her son John, Clark betw 15-16. Methodist.	MORE 10 Nov 1864
HAYWOOD, Samuel F. in St. Francisville, Clark Co. 27 Mar in his 46th year of typhoid. Methodist.	CANP 31 Mar 1864
HAZZARD, Catherine, youngest dau/William decd and Eliza, 1 Feb of typhoid ae 15y 5m 25d. Philadelphia pc	MORE 10 & 11 Feb 1863
HEAD, Annie M. dau/Jack 21 Jun in Randolph Co. in her (13? 15?) th year.	MORE 14 Jul 1861
HEALY, Daniel assistant pastor of St. Michael's (11-Jefferson) ae 30.	MORE 5 Nov 1861

HEALY, Jeremiah Sr. 13 Jun ae 78 at the home of his dau/Mrs. Margaret Pomroy, 311 6th St. Funeral at Holy Trinity Church.	MORE 14 Jun 1865
HEATH, A.M., Chariton Co.; public administrator took over his estate.	CECB 28 Aug 1862
HEATH, Edmund M. son/Jesse W. of St. Louis and an "angel mother" killed 6 Jun at Columbia AR ae 17y 6m.	MORE 17 Jun 1864
Nancy wife of J.W. 30 Aug ae 41y 2m. Lived at 81 N. 9th.	MORE 31 Aug 1861
HEATH, W.H. in Gratiot Prison 27 Feb of pneumonia. (Undertaker's list)	MORE 1 & 2 Mar 1863
HEATHMAN, Benjamin, one of the oldest settlers in MO in Monroe Co. 9 Jul in his 87th year; resident there 29 years. Old School Baptist "upwards of 60 years."	LIT 9 Aug 1861
HEATON, Daniel, Chariton Co.; public administrator took over his estate.	CECB 24 Jul 1862
HEBBLER, Kate N. wife of Fred S. and sister of Mat Nolan of Corpus Christi TX in St. Louis 18 Aug, left husband and 8-month-old child. New Orleans, Corpus Christi & west TX pc	MORE 21 Aug 1863
HEBERDING, J.M., prisoner, 28 Jan of rubeola. (Undertaker's list)	MORE 2 Feb 1863
HEBRON, William shot Tuesday night by one Magill, cook of the Colorado; Magill also died later.	SJH 16 Jul 1864
HEDENBURG, Charlotte wife of James V. at Jonesburg 29 Sep of bilious fever; formerly of St. Louis. Newark NJ pc	MORE 2 Oct 1862
HEDENBURG, Lucretia J. wife of S.A. in St. Louis 11 Dec on her 30th birthday, of consumption. Funeral at First Trinitarian Congregational Church. (CHAC says she was the dau/late William P. M. Scott, born in Cadiz KY; her mother married Arthur Newman; her brother W.P.M. Scott was a resident of Charleston; she was married in 1853. 25 Dec 1863?)	MORE 12 Dec 1862 (1863?)
HEDENBURG, Stephen 6 Jun of pneumonia ae 38. Lived at 5th-Myrtle. Springfield & Quincy IL pc	MORE 9 Jun 1865
HEDGEPETH, ___ of Ralls Co. drowned trying to cross Salt River in a canoe, by Goodwin's Mill. James Rouse & James Lewellen also drowned.	LIT 2 May 1862
* HEDGEPETH, India Ann wife of Rev. H.H., funeral notice; Methodist Church.	SJH 5 Aug 1863
HEDGES, Mrs. Lucy at her home in Pike Co. 2 Aug ae 21, of consumption. Louisville pc	LAJ 8 Aug 1863
* HEDGPATH, Mrs. India Ann at St. Joseph 4 Aug of consumption, dau/Rev. Samuel and Eunice Keynon. Born in Adams Co. OH, first to KY, then to MO 1839. Married Rev. H.H. Hedgpath 8 Jul 1853.	MORE 17 Aug 1863
HEENAN, Edward of St. Paul MN 22 Dec in St. Louis. Funeral from the home of his cousin Carroll Bergin, sw corner 11th & Morgan.	MORE 23 Dec 1862
HEETHER, Frederick at Allen in Randolph Co. 6 Apr ae 49.	MORE 11 Apr 1864
HEFFERNAN, Ellen wife of Patrick 14 Oct ae 35. Interred Calvary. Boston and Cork IRE pc	MORE 15 Oct 1863
HEFFNER, Daniel 15 Sep ae 44; lived on South Main.	MORE 16 Sep 1862
HEIDMAN, George, inquest: drowned in a cistern at his late residence, 14th & Montrose. Had chronic diarrhoea, apparently fell in during the night. Ae 44, wife, 2 children, "industrious and honorable."	MORE 28 Jun 1863
HEIMBACK, Dr. John 11 Apr of heart disease. Funeral from the home of John Jecko, 225 S. 7th.	MORE 13 Apr 1864
HEINTZ, Charlotte wife of J.N. 3 Aug of subacute dysentery. Interred Holy Ghost.	SLMD 4 Aug 1864
HEISTNER, John, a soldier from Rolla, accidentally shot and killed in St. Louis.	MORE 10 Dec 1862
HEITHAUER, Samuel, inquest: 6th below Market, debility and exposure.	MORE 21 Nov 1862
HELFENSTEIN, Caroline M. of St. Louis 16 Jun in Philadelphia.	MORE 19 Jun 1862
HELFENSTEIN, Laura dau/Charles J. and Helena 19 Apr ae 3y 3m 11d. Lived 22 S. 14th.	MORE 20 Apr 1862
HELGENBERG, Philip Joseph of Snow & Helgenberg 25 Jul in St. Paul of inflammation of the bowels. Funeral in St. Louis.	MORE 31 Jul 1864
HELMERING, Mary found dead in her home, Destrehan-9th, of cerebral apoplexy due to to intemperance. Husband in Cincinnati; 2 children by first husband.	MORE 30 Mar 1861
HELMS, Andrew at the home of his father in Ralls Co. ae 27y 10m 22d. Long illness.	HAM 16 Feb 1861
HELMUTH, John H. 9 Sep in his 58th year. Funeral from the home of Dr. Helmuth at 269 Pine above 12th. Philadelphia & Baltimore pc	MORE 10 Sep 1862
HEMAN, Frederick W. at Elkhorn Prairie IL 21 Oct ae 49. Funeral from his home in St. Louis, 288 N. 13th.	MORE 25 Oct 1863

HEMP, Mary Ellen wife of John 17 Sep in her 18th year. Lived at 217 Washington.   MORE 18 &
    Her infant, also Mary Ellen, died a week later ae 1m. Keokuk pc.   25 Sep 1864

HEMPE, Henry accidentally shot himself in the arm while returning from hunting,   MORE 11 Aug 1864
    and bled to death.

HEMPSTEAD, Elizabeth youngest dau/Stephen, near Cote sans Dessein, 28 Aug ae   MORE 3 Sep 1863
    17y 3m 9d.

HEMSTREET, Minnie Bell only dau/Dr. M. and Lavina at High Point, Moniteau Co.,   MORE 14 Nov 1861
    5 Nov of croup ae 1y 4m 13d.

HENDERSON, A.H., of Portland, in Fulton 1 May ae 59.   MORE 6 May 1863

HENDERSON, Almarinda wife of Ferdinand and dau/Alexander Kinkead at the home of   MORE 22 Oct 1861
    her father in Bonhomme Twp. 16 Oct ae 26y 6m.

HENDERSON, ___ (not named, but a few days later a poem to Jemmie Monroe Henderson   MORE 21 Mar 1864
    appeared) only son/James M. and Kate, of scarlet fever, ae 8y 10m.
    Member 3rd Baptist Sabbath School. Lived Gamble betw Emily-Summit.

    James Monroe at his home on (Gable?) 6 Jun ae 30, an old steamboat   MORE 7 &
    man, ill 6 days. To St. Louis in 1844. Husband, father.   12 Jun 1864

HENDERSON, Johnny H. son/John and Jane 23 Jan ae 2y 3m.   LAJ 24 Jan 1861
    (gives initial as B, mother's name as Ione, father as J.N.)   MORE 27 "

HENDERSON, Minnie Werner Friday morning ae 20y 4m 1d.   FULT 5 Aug 1864
    (gives father's name as James S., death date as 9 Jul.)   MORE 7 "

HENDERSON, Royall eldest son/J.A. and V.L. in Bridgeton 16 Sep ae 4y 3m 24d.   MORE 17 Sep 1864
    Interred Bellefontaine.

HENDERSON, Thomas C., Chariton Co.: letters of administration to John Smith 7 Jul.   CECB 24 Jul 1862

HENDERSHOTT, Mr. J.M. 26 Mar in his 46th year of lung congestion. Cleveland pc   MORE 27 Mar 1863

HENDRICK, Henry Clay eldest son/Moses and Amanda of Pike Co. in Canton MS 20 Feb   LAJ 14 Mar 1861
    of typhoid "5 days before completing his 18th year."

HENDRICK, Judge Littlebury in Springfield, 10 Jan.   LIT 30 Jan 1863

HENDRICK, Milton J. at the home of his father near New Franklin 9 Mar of   GLWT 20 Mar 1861
    consumption in his 20th year.

HENLEY, Frances dau/Samuel and Rebecca in Columbia 28 Aug ae 15.   COWS 1 Sep 1865

HENNES, Mary, inquest: ae 55, perhaps German, husband died a few weeks ago.   MORE 2 Feb 1864
    Intemperance and exposure. Little known of her.

HENNESSEY, James accidentally shot in the street by the dogcatcher. Ae 12, son   MORE 25 Jul 1861
    of a widow, lived on Biddle below Broadway.   /(ca)

HENRICK, Betty, a colored woman, shot and instantly killed by Mrs. Jane Dichoist,   MORE 9 Oct 1865
    also colored. Mrs. D. had been molested by some white men and had shot
    at random, shot going upward through the floor. She was acquitted.

HENRY, ___ son-in-law of Harrison Burnes killed in Andrew Co. by Hart's guerillas.   CAWN 18 Jul 1863

HENRY, James 1 Feb of pneumonia ae 46. Formerly of Boston; NY, Belfast also pc   MORE 4 Feb 1865

HENRY, John killed by guerillas in Carroll Co. (Carrollton Democrat)   MORE 21 Jul 1864

HENRY, Josiah 8 Aug at his home in Louisiana in his 71st year. Born in SC 1794,   LAJ 12 Aug 1865
    to MO 1819. O.S. Presbyterian.

HENRY, Lucy wife of Samuel L. in Boone Co. 17 Feb ae 43. Lexington KY & Paris MO pc   COWS 6 Mar 1863

HENRY, Mrs. Margaret at the home of her son-in-law P.T. McSherry, Benton betw   MORE 26 Apr 1861
    16-17, in her 85th year. Among the earliest residents of KY, where she
    emigrated from VA. Funeral from Christian Church, interred Wesleyan.

HENRY, Marian Stuart oldest dau/Robert and Minnie of brain congestion 24 Mar.   MORE 26 Mar 1863

HENRY, Mary Frances oldest dau/William and Mary Tuesday ae 8y 3m, Green betw 7-8.   MORE 30 Apr 1862

HENRY, Patrick, stabbed by John Hayes in a saloon fight 14 May, now died.   MORE 28 May 1863

HENRY, Samuel W. in Boone Co. 6 Aug in his 22nd year.   COWS 12 Aug 1864

HENRY, Willie eldest son/Capt. R.C. at Parker House in Sedalia 1 Jan ae 13.   MORE 9 Jan 1864
    Philadelphia pc

HENSLEY, John S. son/Morton P. of Howard Co. in Boone Co., of typhoid, 25 Oct ae 19.   COWS 28 Oct 1864

HERBERT, M.J. of consumption 2 Feb (sic) at 82 Maryland? St. Funeral Feb 7,   MORE 7 Mar 1865
    interred Calvary. (February was written out.)

HERBERT, Rudolph son/Alois and Dorothea in South Hannibal ? Feb ae 3y 3m.   HAM 6 Feb 1861

HERCKENRATH, Gertrude C. wife of William 6 Jul in her 29th year.   MORE 8 Jul 1864

HERD, Annie M. 21 Jun at the home of her father, Jack, 2 miles from Roanoke,   COWS 5 Jul 1861
    in her 19th year. Baptist.

HEREFORD, Andrew Jackson only son/John B. and Mary Cozens, ae 10. Charleston SC
                                                                           & Va pc   MORE 20 Jan 1861

HERKENROTH, Rudolph, well-known former Justice of the Peace, yesterday   MORE 22 Oct 1865
  (HERCKENROTH)   at Sisters Hospital of apoplexy.

HERKENRATH, Emma dau/John killed by John Long at the home of her father, William ??   MORE 7 Oct 1864
    in Blumenthal's Row, Carondelet (he then committed suicide). Family
    had come from Lafayette Co. near Lexington. (Father's name not certain.)

HERNANDEZ, Frank "long and favorably known as a pilot on the Missouri River" in   MORE 18 Apr 1863
    his 41st year. Funeral from the home of Mrs. Rice, 39 S 6th.

HERNDEN, Dr. A.P. at the home of his father near Franklin, 16 Nov. Baptist.   MORE 1 Dec 1865
    Apparently member of Mount Pleasant Church.

HEROLD, Pattie only child/William G. and Amire 28 Feb in Wright City ae 4y 4m 7d.   MORE 5 Mar 1863

HERPOOL, ___, resident of Kingston, Caldwell Co., hanged at Cameron; he had   LIT 15 Jul 1864
    been in the rebel army.

HERRICK, Richard 21 Nov ae 27; late of Cork IRE.   MORE 23 Nov 1865

HERRING, Elizabeth dau/James and Sarah 31 Aug in her 13th year, of flux.   FULT 16 Sep 1864

HERRINGTON, Cynthia Jane dau/Jesse and Mary Beeler of Big River, Jefferson Co.,   MORE 6 Jan 1865
                                    30 Dec ae 25.

HERRON, Miss Martha Agnes at Carrollton 1 Oct of typhoid ae 20. Formerly of   MORE 16 Nov 1862
                                    Cleveland OH.

HERSHEY, David, Chariton Co.: public administrator took over his estate.   CECB 24 Jul 1862

HERTLE, ___, son of Charles ae 3 (only child) run over by a runaway horse. His   MORE 9 Jan 1861
    father was a drayman.

HESSE, Bernard, teamster for Ruder and Schroeder, brick burners in Bremen, fell   MORE 3 Sep 1863
    from his wagon when the wheel broke and was run over. Ca 18, parents in WI.

HESSE, Emelee Catherine only dau/Charles and Catherine at Perryville ae 6y 4m 4d.   PERU 7 Apr 1865

HESSEY, Abraham at the home of James Bogg in Boone Co. 2 Apr. St. Louis ps   COWS 15 Apr 1864

HESSIAN, Michael, an Irish laborer living at 24 Myrtle, drowned off the Peoria ae 16.   MORE 30 Jul 1861

HETHFELTER, Mrs. Christiana, inquest: fell to the floor at the grocery store of   MORE 13 Oct 1863
    her son William, 18th-Wash; died of apoplexy ae 70.

HEUERT, Valentine, inquest: died of injuries suffered when a boiler rolled over   MORE 1 Nov 1865
    him at the dry docks in Carondelet. Left wife and child in south city.

HEWITT, Claudia Margaret, native of Cork ae 57, "for the past 10 years cared for   MORE 4 Mar 1862
    the sick at St. Louis Hospital," died 3 Mar.

HEWLETT, Samuel J. of Fielding's Command, captured in Stoddard Co. 27 Jan, in   MORE 10 Mar 1863
    Gratiot Prison of pneumonia.

HEYWOOD, Harrie Houghton son/Charles and Lydia ae 5y 3d. Funeral from the home of   MORE 2 Apr 1863
    Capt. E.W. Paul. Interred Bellefontaine.

HEYWOOD, William E. 10 Mar ae 29 at the home of C.H. Bell, Compton Hill. PortlandME pc MORE 12 Mar'64

HIBBARD, Catherine 1 Dec ae 56 in St. Clair, Franklin Co.   MORE 7 Dec 1863

HIBLER, Andrew J. of this county when his buggy ran off the road into a   MEMP 25 Nov 1865
    wash, broke his neck. (Macon Times)

HICKAM, George L. in Boone Co. 4 May.   COWS 10 May 1861

HICKEY, Henry ae 11 kicked by a mule at a stable 5 miles out on Clayton Road.   MORE 13 Jun 1863

HICKMAN, George 20 Jul in his 72d year, a Methodist 40 years.   CAWN 15 Aug 1863

HICKMAN, Rebecca wife of Capt. Hugh A. near Florida MO 18 Feb of pneumonia in   RANC 7 Mar 1861
                                    her 62nd year.

HICKS, Charles W. 1 Oct ae 40y 1m 10d. Funeral from home of his father-in-law   MORE 2 Oct 1863
                                    Louis Labeaume, Lucas Pl.
    Bertha dau/Naomi and the late Charles in Paris FCE 16 May ae 7y 11m.   MORE 6 Jun 1865

HICKS, Charlie Dolbker youngest child/ Avoline and the late Benjamin H.,   MORE 20 Oct 1863
    at 73 Myrtle, ae 6y 6m.

HICKS, Elizabeth widow of Absolem and mother of Young E., 30 Oct in   COWS 15 Nov 1861
    Boone Co. of cancer of the left hand.

HICKS, Mrs. Isabella at Rocheport 4 Jun in her 64th year.	COWS 17 Jun 1864
HICKS, Robert, member of the Legislature from Ozark and Douglas Counties, 22 Feb in Jefferson City.	LIT 27 Feb 1863
HIGBEE, Martha wife of Asa in Barry, Clay Co., during the past week, of flux; four others also died of the same.	SJH 11 Aug 1864
HIGGINBOTHAM, George murdered in Washington Co. by Hugh Trainer -- testimony before magistrates identifies Trainer.	MORE 22 Jul 1863
HIGGINS, Daniel fell under a street car Saturday night while intoxicated. Left wife and 3 children.	MORE 22 Dec 1862
HIGGINS, Mrs. Sarah late of Co. Mayo IRE Monday ae 70. Funeral from St. Peter and Paul. Lived on Carondelet Ave., son Michael mentioned.	MORE 29 Apr 1862
HIGGINS, Tiff killed by his brother John in a family quarrel in St. Clair. Both married, mother mentioned. (Missouri State Times)	GAL 3 Aug 1865
HIGH, Rosina, inquest: intemperance and exposure.	MORE 28 Nov 1861
HIGHTOWN, ___ killed by bushwhackers near Lamar, Barton Co.; also Messrs. Allison and Smith. (Information from Melville MO)	MORE 23 Apr 1864
HILDEBRAND, James 12 miles southwest of California by "scoundrels." One-time member of Capt. Sappington's militia company.	CAWN 15 Apr 1865
HILDEBRAND, Sam, a notorious bushwhacker, wounded in a skirmish with the 1st MO Cav. several weeks ago, died 7 miles from Bloomfield.	MORE 10 Jan 1864
HILDRETH, Mrs. Margaret 6 Aug; funeral from home of son Hugh, 42 Brooklyn St.	MORE 7 Aug 1864
HILE, Cornelius B. 21 Mar of consumption ae 29, in Canton.	CANP 24 Mar 1864
HILE, Mrs. Maria at the home of her son in Monticello 21 Jun ae 64.	CANP 29 Jun 1865
HILL, Mrs. Charlotte, inquest: lived at Dry Hill on Clayton Rd; lung congestion.	MORE 15 Oct 1863
HILL, David W. 28 Oct ae 35. Brother of Britton A., unmarried. Fell through skylight in interior well of a building. Funeral Centenary Church.	MORE 30 Oct 1865
HILL, Mrs. E.B. at the home of Dr. Albert Koch near Yager's Garden 1 Apr ae 66y 9m. Friends of James McCord also invited. Interred Bellefontaine.	MORE 3 Apr 1862
HILL, Elihu of consumption at Vicksburg. Funeral from the home of his mother-in-law Mrs. C. Full, 16th betw Christy-Morgan.	MORE 25 Feb 1865
HILL, Ida Frances dau/Samuel G. and Mary A. 27 May ae 1y 9m 5d. Wheeling pc	MORE 29 May 1862
HILL, J.P., citizen of Pike Co., 6 Dec of pneumonia. (Undertaker's list)	MORE 7 Dec 1862
HILL, J---inn, 14th KS Cav. Funeral notice. Friends of A.M. Henderson invited.	MORE 12 May 1865
HILL, Mary Rebecca dau/Isaac N. and Jennie 2 Oct ae 22m. Funeral from the home of James C. Essex, Natural Bridge Plank Road.	MORE 3 Oct 1861
HILL, Richard of northwest Monroe Co. shot himself 24 Mar because of charges derogatory to his character. Left wife, several children. (Paris Mercury)	RANC 4 Apr 1861
HILL, Robert A. of McKee & Hill, living on 10th near Spring, 16 Aug ae 42.	MORE 17 Aug 1864
HILL, Sallie Johnson dau/R.M. and Nancy 21 May ae 11y 9m. Lived at 214 N. 6th. Wheeling pc	MORE 22 May 1861
HILL, Mrs. Susannah at Sparta 26 Oct ae 47.	SJH 28 Oct 1863
HILL, William, citizen of Callaway Co., 4 Feb of chronic diarrhoea. (Undertaker's list)	MORE 7 Feb'64
HILL, William, 33rd MO captured 21 Feb, died in Myrtle Street Prison.	MORE 24 Feb 1863
HILL, William 18 Apr at the home of Samuel Ashlock ae 58. Lexington KY pc	COWS 22 Apr 1864
HILLGAERTNER, Dr. George, former editor of Neue Zeit and more recently of Missouri Radical, yesterday at 14th & Spruce in his 44th year, of typhoid. Left wife and 3 children. Resident of St. Louis 20 years.	MORE 24 Oct 1865
HILLIARD, William, inquest: mate of the War Eagle, struck in the temple by a loaded derrick at Hill's Landing, lived 2 days. Lived at 129 N. 14th, was ca 30, left wife and one child. (Death notice says ae 31)	MORE 19 Oct 1865
HINDE, Dr. Thomas H. at his home in Marion Co. 16 Dec "old and respected."	PALS 30 Dec 1864
HINDMAN, David of Jackson Co., of typhoid "one of our most valuable citizens." Died Thursday at Mr. Camp's home on Main. Funeral Methodist Church.	KCJC 2 May 1862
HINES, Doc, Bill, and Caleb, a noted bushwhacker, killed near Sturgeon by Harvey Rucker.	MORE 6 May 1865
HINKEY, ___ killed near Lexington on Salt Pond Road 15 Mar by bushwhackers. Recently from Springfield, MO. (LEXUN 18 Mar)	MORE 7 Apr 1865

HINMAN, Mollie (Mary Susan) dau/Holly and Lizzie at her grandmother's home 8 Dec of croup ae 3y 5m. (also shown as Hindman)	LIT 18 Dec 1862
HINTON, Mrs. Sarah widow of Rev. J.T. 10 Jan ae 63. Funeral from 2nd Baptist Church. New Orleans & San Francisco pc	MORE 11 Jan 1865
HIRSCH, Samuel 29 Apr ae 58, at 24 South St. Interred B'nai El.	MORE 30 Apr 1863
HIRT, Ludwig, only son/John and Mary 20 Nov at 796 Broadway, ae 6.	MORE 22 Nov 1865
HIST, Andrew killed in a fall from the upper porch of his home, 210 Columbia. Left wife and 4 children.	MORE 24 Jul 1865
HITCHCOCK, Artemus of Rocheport IL, father of Mrs. Louise McDowell of Carondelet. He had come to visit her, hearing she was ill; walked to her home from the station, sat on a bench in the yard, and died.	MORE 14 Oct 1865
HITCHCOCK, Elmira consort of Abner 4 Oct of cerebral apoplexy. Hartford CT & Catskill NY pc	MORE 5 Oct 1861
HITE, Rev. A.T. murdered in Chariton Co. 3 weeks ago, the murderer, Briggs, now captured in Sullivan Co. (RANC) SEE BELOW	PALS 15 Apr 1864
HITE, J.T. murdered and robbed near Glasgow, his wife Eliza J. offers a reward for the killers.	CAWN 9 Apr 1864
HITT, William Y., an aged citizen, near Sturgeon 8 Jul.	COWS 15 Jul 1864
HIX, Willis Ann consort of E.D. of Saline Co., 11 Oct.	MORE 6 Nov 1863
HOAGLAND, Walter B., funeral from the home of J.M. Jarboe to the Catholic cemetery. Died of erysipelas ae 23y 2m 16d, left mother, sister, brother. Baptist.(?)	KCJC 2 & 3 Feb 1864
HOBBS, Thomas 16 Apr of epilepsy in Sedalia. Funeral from the home of his brother-in-law William R. Hopkins, 19th betw Wash-Carr. Baltimore & Frederick MD pc	MORE 18 Apr 1864
HOBEN, Mathias, from exposure; had lain out in a field overnight and frosted his feet and legs.	MORE 15 Nov 1861
HOBIN, John son of the proprietor of the Douglas House killed by Peter Curtin, watchman on the Skylark. Hobin had been aboard and in some trouble.	MORE 13 & 14 Nov 1861
HOBLIN, Casper, a wagonmaker ae 37, fell downstairs while drunk. Unmarried.	MORE 10 Sep 1861
HOCKADAY, Irvine O. near Fulton 22 Jan in his 67th year. Came to MO from Clark Co. KY 1821; clerk of Callaway Co. court many years. Presbyterian.	MORE 30 Jan & 9 Feb 1864
HOCKADAY, Richard Weightman youngest son/Philip and Marie at Middleton MO 9 May of scarlet fever ae 14y 5m 3d.	MORE 15 May 1863
HODGE, Isaac W., 6th MO Cav., in Gratiot Prison of dysentery.	MORE 12 Apr 1863
HODGE, Samuel J., 5th MO CSA, taken at Vicksburg 4 Jul, in Gratiot Prison of typhoid.	MORE 20 Aug 1863
HODGEN, Frank P. youngest son/Dr. G.T. and D. 3 Nov, at 4th and Walnut.	MORE 4 Nov 1863
HODGES, John F. of Benton Co. (possibly AR) in Gratiot Prison 9 Apr of pneumonia. Arrested in Little Rock 10 Sep.	MORE 12 Apr 1864
HODNETT (HEDNETT), Margaret Jane wife of E. at Moselle, Franklin Co., 28 Feb of typhoid ae 20y 6m 6d. San Francisco pc	MORE 1 Mar 1865
HOFFMAN, Augusta ae 9 drowned while picking up driftwood.	MORE 3? Jul 1861
HOFFMAN, Fred W., Chariton Co.: public administrator took over his estate.	CECB 24 Jul 1862
HOGAN, Alice eldest dau/Edmond 12 Jul ae 20, at Austin betw 15-16. Interred Rock Spg.	MORE 13 Jul 1864
HOGAN, Ellen ca 9 and James ca 10, drowned; had made a little boat out of planks. Father, a widower, had lost another child, drowned, a year ago.	MORE 20 Aug 1865
HOGAN, Maggie Brown dau/John M. and Elizabeth 8 Jul ae 8y 10m.	LIT 18 Jul 1862
HOGAN, John C. eldest son/P.G. and B.A. Wed of neuralgia of the brain, ae 17y 2m 10d. Lived at 141 S. 7th. Wilmington DE and San Francisco pc	MORE 30 Jun 1864
HOLBROOK, John 28 Dec of typhoid ae (23? 25?). Formerly of Worcester MA.	MORE 30 Dec 1864
HOLDAN, James shot while stealing wood. Left wife and 2 children.	MORE 26 Jan 1862
HOLEMAN, Mrs. ___, mother-in-law of Amos Stillwell, yesterday of intermittent fever.	HAM 13 Jun 1861
HOLLAND, August 2 Jun ae 39. Funeral from the home of Louden Berry, Randolph-13-14.	MORE 3 Jun 1863
HOLLAND, John C. 30 Apr ae 28.	MORE 1 May 1864
HOLLAND, Lydia Helena only dau/W. Henry and Kate 4 Nov ae 6y 10m 20d. Milwaukee & Meadville PA pc	MORE 6 Nov 1865
HOLLAND, Martha A. 9 Jan ae 26. Funeral from the home of R.F. Holland on 11th St.	MORE 11 Jan 1865

HOLLIDAY, John fell from a boat 16 Sep; body recovered at Ft. Lesperance.	MORE 22 Sep 1863
HOLLIN, Morris, driver for James Maloy the hackman, thrown from a sleigh and injured, died of the cold.	MORE 3 Jan 1864
HOLLINGHAST, William, a German cabinetmaker and member of the Home Guards, killed in the Camp Jackson affair.	MORE 14 & 17 May 1861
HOLLIS, Jessie dau/Elder J.A. in Columbia 9 Dec of scarlet fever ae ca 6.	COWS 11 Dec 1863
HOLLWEG, John "our husband and father" 15 Feb ae 76. Signed by Catherine and children, living at Montgomery & 9th. CA pc	MORE 17 Feb 1865
HOLMAN, Solomon W. 6 Mar ae 73y 5m 16d. Funeral from the home of his daughter on N. 9th. Dubuque & Jeffersonville IN pc	MORE 8 Mar 1863
HOLMES, Arthur 19 Nov in his 26th year at the home of his brother-in-law R.H. Ross, Myrtle betw 5-6.	MORE 21 Nov 1863
HOLMES, Charles N. son/L.D. and Margarette 30 Mar of typhoid ae 3y 8m 15d.	MORE 31 Mar 1862
HOLMES, L.D. merchant of St. Louis in Nashville Wednesday of pneumonia.	MORE 14 Mar 1864
HOLMES, Robert suddenly yesterday at 30 S. 5th, member of the Co. Court. In his 48th year. Funeral 2nd Presbyterian Church.	MORE 17 Jul 1863
HOLTON, Melissa Belle wife of Charles A. 1 May in her 27th year. Lived in Lorenz's Addition.	MORE 2 May 1863
HOLTZCLAW, Mrs. Elizabeth wife of R. at Paris MO 15 Nov.	LAJ 20 Nov 1862
HONN, David, Co. C (or E) 3rd MO Vols, killed at Glasgow.	GAL 17 Nov 1864
HOOD, Susie J. Hull wife of George J. 14 Jul in her 23rd y. Funeral from Immaculate Conception Church.	MORE 16 Jul 1865
HOOK, James William son/Zadok and Mary E. in Callaway Co. 8 Oct ae 11y 3m 22d.	MORE 19 Oct 1863
HOOK, Miss Zerelda C. 22 Feb of consumption at her mother's home, ae 39. Paris KYpc	FULT 15 Mar 1861
HOOPER, Caroline Archer wife of Henry R. of Ray Co. at the home of her grandmother Nancy Reeves in Ray Co. 17 May ae 19y 8m.	RICON 31 May 1861
HOOTEN, Jesse of Boone Co. in Alton Prison in Dec.	COWS 9 Jan 1863
HOOTON, Mrs. Mary Beeson(?) 18 May of rheumatism of the heart ae 25y 8m. Funeral from St. John's Church.	MORE 19 May 1865
HOOVEN, Henry in Beaver Meadow PA, father of Mrs. E.C. Barrett of Canton, 20 Dec ae 73.	CANP 31 Dec 1863
HOOVER, Isaac near Platte City 13 Apr of consumption ae 48.	COWS 6 May 1864
HOPE, Prosper citizen of Clinton Co., in the prison hospital.	MORE 8 Sep 1863
HOPKINS, Mrs. Mary B. wife of Ashley C. in Ste. Genevieve, of consumption, ae 28. Funeral from P.A. Berthold home, St. Louis. Interred Calvary.	MORE 29 & 30 Mar 1864
HOPKINS, William Granville son/John H. and Harriet Rowen 25 Mar ae 6y 6m. Lived NE corner 14th & Olive, St. Louis. Frankfort KY pc	HAM 27 Mar 1861 MORE 26 "
HOPKINS, William R. 14 Nov of consumption ae 49. Lived 19th betw Wash-Carr.	MORE 15 Nov 1864
HOPMAYER, see Fanny WILSON	
HOPPER, F.W. wife of John Sr. 5 Aug in her 77th year.	COWS 11 Sep 1863
HOPPER, Robert, late of Canton (family still there) in the asylum at Columbus OH 11 Aug ae 32.	COWS 17 Aug 1865
HOPPERS, Franklin, 6th MO Cav, taken in Stoddard Co. 27 Jan, in Gratiot Prison of fever.	MORE 14 Feb 1863
HORAN, Anthony, late of Swineford, Co. Mayo, at Sisters Hospital 23 Sep ae 54. Funeral from the Cathedral.	MORE 24 Sep 1864
HORAN, Richard 11 Jun ae 54. Lived on Orchard St. Interred Rock Spring.	MORE 12 Jun 1862
HORAN, Rpbert 26 Sep ae 44, resident of St. Louis 25 years. Interred Rock Spring. New York & Sacramento pc	MORE 27 Sep 1861
HORDENBROOK, George, a guerilla, in Johnson Co.	SJH 24 Dec 1863
HORN, Louisa wife of Charles W. 31 Jan ae 49y 7m, after a lingering illness. Lived 228 Wash, near 16th. Interred Bellefontaine. (Shown as HAM on 2/1)	MORE 1 & 2 Feb 1864
HORNBERGER, Nicholas, a fireman, killed in a boiler explosion ar Boos & Bonsocks steamboat lumber planing mill, where employed, yesterday. (31 S. Levee)	MORE 2 Dec 1865
HORREL, John Sr. of Cape Girardeau 19 Mar, "2 days short of 51."	MORE 2 May 1864

HORTIZ, Mary Maria wife of John B. 14 Apr ae 67y 6m, on her 50th wedding anniversary.   MORE 15 Apr 1865

HORTON, John N., 6th MO, captured in Stoddard Co. 27 Jan, in Gratiot Prison of   MORE 17 Mar 1863
    erysipelas.

HORWITZ, Mrs. Victoria wife of Harry of St. Louis in Petersburg IL 11 Oct ae 25.   MORE 17 Oct 1863

HOUCK, William R., oldest son/Isaac N. and Susan M. in Howard Co. 22 Oct of   MORE 17 Dec 1862
    diphtheria ae 4y 2m 15d.
    Sallie A., twin daughter of above, at the home of her grandmother Mrs. Jane
      C. Robinson in Howard Co. ae 1y 6m 21d
    Isaac N., Jr., twin son, 29 Nov at home of grandmother 1y 7m 7d
      Hannibal and Columbia pc

HOUDYSHELL, Mrs. Sarah wife of the late John 30 Jan in her 71st year. Funeral   MORE 1 Feb 1865
    from home of Thomas Houdyshell, west of Pratt, to Fee Fee Church.

HOUGHAN, Dr. Thomas Wednesday in his 69th year. Funeral from Christ Church.   MORE 15 Aug 1862
    Interred Bellefontaine.

HOUGHTON, Dr. E.B. 19 Mar. Funeral from 2nd Baptist Church.   MORE 30 Mar 1862

HOUSE, ____ captured 1 mile from Carrollton killed by militia under Capt. Hoover.   RICON 1 Jul 1865
    Had 2 sons in the rebel army, one killed at Wilson's Creek. The
    militia was looking for forage.

HOW, St. Louis son/John and M.T. 11 Aug at the home of Mrs. Bryan in   MORE 13 &
    Geneseo, NY. Funeral from his parents' home on Lucas Pl.   14 Aug 1864

HOWARD, Agnes at the home of her sister Mrs. Haynes, 5th near Myrtle, 17 Apr   MORE 18 Apr 1862
    in her 16th year. Funeral from St. John's Church.

HOWARD, Cassius 28 Feb (sic) ae 7y 6m 5d. Lived Geyer & 2nd Carondelet.   MORE 5 &
    Interred Rock Hill Presbyterian Churchyard.   9 Mar 1861

HOWARD, Catherine wife of W.P. 8 Apr. Interred in Savannah.   MORE 9 Apr 1862

HOWARD, Christian C. 29 Jun of inflammation of the brain, ae 15. Third son of   MORE 24 Jul 1865
    James and Rebecca S., born in Giles Co. TN 18 Jul 1849.

HOWARD, Eliza S. Keesacker, wife of R.J., 29 Apr. Funeral from First Presbyterian   MORE 1 &
    Church. Philadelphia pc   3 May 1864

HOWARD, John ca 9, whose parents live at 21st near O'Fallon, drowned in a pond.   MORE 11 Jul 1865

HOWARD, Col. J.B., funeral today from 6th Presbyterian Church.   SJH 23 Feb 1865
    "For many years a citizen of Columbia, in St. Joseph 22 Feb."   COWS 3 Mar "

HOWARD, Maria D. consort of William B. of Jackson Co. near Hodgenville KY 16 Feb.   MORE 22 Feb 1865

HOWARD, P.H.   Nov in Gratiot Prison of rubeola.   MORE 5 Nov 1862

HOWARD, Thomas, inquest: ae 12, drowned about a week ago, body just recovered.   MORE 29 Aug 1865
    Parents live on 13th betw O'Fallon-Cass.

HOWE, Alex C. son/John W. and Sarah F. 4 Mar ae 14m 15d.   FULT 14 Mar 1862

HOWE, Cecelia V. wife of A.W., of St. Louis, in Jerseyville 19 Sep.   MORE 24 Sep 1861

HOWES, Capt. Abner, late of Buffalo NY, in St. Louis 7 Oct. Funeral from the home   MORE 9 Oct 1865
    of his brother-in-law William Simpson, 215 Olive. Buffalo & Boston pc

HOYLE, Hannah relict of Lawrence 2 Dec, suddenly, in her 73rd year.   SLMD 10 Dec 1861

HOYT, ___, Chancellor of Washington University, services Friday.   MORE 29? 1862

HOYT, Jane "of spotless reputation" living with her stepmother on Carondelet near   MORE 6 Dec 1865
    Arsenal, drowned herself in the river after a disagreement with her step-
    mother who accused her of "bad doings." Left a younger sister.

HUBBARD, George Conger son/H.S. and Martha near New Bloomfield 29 Aug ae 5y 5m 2d.   COWS 13 Sep 1861

HUBBARD, Harrison a citizen killed in Lincoln Co. "some time back." (by soldiers?)   MORE 30 Jan 1865

HUBBARD, Nanna dau/R.W. and M.F. in Rocheport 16 Jul of cholera infantum, ae 1y9m17d.   MORE 19 Jul 1865

HUBBARD, Rees/Enos (?) , citizen of Carroll Co. (Undertaker's list)   MORE 9 Jan 1865

HUBER, Pauline wife of Martin, of Glasgow, 9 Jun.   GLWT 13 Jun 1861

HUBER, William an old resident of St. Louis killed in a rr accident near Cincinnati   MORE 3 Oct 1865
    30 Sep; going from one car to another, thrown under train. Kept a store
    on Broadway; returned to St. Louis for burial.

HUDGINS, Nancy wife of Judge William in Richmond 10 Jan ae 69.   MORE 27 Jan 1861

HUDSON, Herbert shot at Palmyra by Gen. Merrill in retaliation for the murder of   CAWN 1 Nov 1862
    an old man named Allmstedt at the time of Porter's Raid into Palmyra.
    Hudson was from Ralls Co. (Others were also executed.)(Palmyra *Courier*)

HUDSON, James B. son/Judge H.H. 23 Feb ae 14y 1m 15d.   CAWN 7 Mar 1863

HUDSON, James F., tribute by Farmers' Bank, Lexington.   LEXUN 10 Jan 1863

HUDSON, Sela, postmaster at Westport, formerly of Lexington, 15 Jul ae 54.   SLMD 21 Jul 1864

HUFF, C.H. "old and respected" clerk of county and circuit courts suddenly Saturday. Left a large family. (Morgan Co. Forum)   CAWN 8 Jun 1861

HUFFAKER, Horace, only son/Rev. S.J. and Kate M., 19 Nov in his 8th year.   GAL 24 Nov 1864

HUFFARD, _____, living near Greenton, murdered by ___ Turner. Turner had married Huffard's niece; it was a family feud.   LEXUN 15 Aug 1863 / MORE 19 "

HUFFINGTON, Annie G. youngest dau/G.M. and A.P. 29 Nov of bronchial croup ae 7y 1m 5d. Interred Rock Spring.   MORE 30 Nov 1863

HUFFMAN, William, a young unmarried man, run over by the Iron Mountain train.   MORE 21 Sep 1865

HUGGINS, Sallie 3 Dec in her 68th year at the home of George W. Harlow near Paris.   COWS 26 Dec 1862

HUGHES, Mrs. Charlotte 14 Aug in Chillicothe at the home of her son Thomas C. ae 77. Native of MD, in MO 25 years; a Baptist.   PALS 28 Aug 1863

HUGHES, Mrs. Elizabeth A. in Carondelet 25 Nov ae 68y 8m. San Francisco & Kansas City pc   MORE 26 Nov 1863

HUGHES, James tribute by Liberty Lodge #31 AF & A Masons.   LIT 15 Mar 1861

HUGHES, James Madison of St. Louis at Jefferson City Tuesday; had been president of the Bank of MO. Funeral from home of Thos. Marshall, Chestnut-12th.   MORE 28 Feb 1861 / SLMD 5 Mar "

HUGHES, Lizzie oldest dau/Joseph S. and Ann L. at the home of her father in Ray Co. 4 Oct in her 16th year.   RICON 7 Oct 1865

HUGHES, Michael killed in a boiler explosion at Rainer & Co. on the Levee. Left family in Carondelet. (2 other men also killed.)   MORE 30 Jun 1863

HUGHS, Edward 18 Apr in his 43rd year. Funeral from the home of his mother-in-law Mrs. Brady, 41 Christy.   MORE 20 Apr 1863

HUILLIER, Clarissa, a Frencwoman, died as a result of beating by her husband, Henry, a locksmith, at a house on the levee between Myrtle-Spruce. (But charges against him were dropped for lack of evidence.)   MORE 13 Aug 1864

HULETT, Ezra 29 Nov of pneumonia in Columbia, ae ca 50.   COWS 4 Dec 1863

HULL, John son/James 5 Sep ae 4y 8m, at 144 Morgan.   MORE 6 Sep 1864

HULL, William at the home of John Snider in Andrew Co., ca 20y 6m.   MORE 9 Jan 1861

HUME, George Sr. in Boone Co. 14 Mar ae 62.   COWS 20 Mar 1863

HUME, Mrs. Lucy wife of George after a long, painful illness. Lived in St. Louis Co. Ae 68y 2m. Funeral from Fee Fee Church.   MORE 9 Feb 1863

HUMPHREY, Mary dau/Samuel and Elizabeth in Callao 17 Jun of congestion of the stomach and bowels, ae 1ly 3m 4d.   MAG 25 Jun 1863

HUMPHREY, Peter, found floating; fell overboard from the New York last Friday. Left wife and children on Franklin betw 5-6.   MORE 31 May 1865

HUMPHREYS, Albert T. at Madora, Osage Co. 4 Sep ae 34. Left wife, 3 children.   FULT 16 Sep 1864

HUMPHREYS, Helen A. widow of Thomas Keyes, formerly of Charleston, Jefferson Co. VA at Oakland, near Belmont, St. Louis Co. 3 Dec of typhoid. Fulton pc   MORE 10 Dec 1865

HUMPHREYS, Ann wife of James in her 67th year. Funeral from home of Mrs. Walter Ransom, her daughter, Bernard west of Pratte. Int. Bellefontaine. James 5 Jan in St. Charles Co. ae 66. Funeral from home of dau/Mrs. Ransom. "   MORE 24 Apr 1863 / 9 Jan 1864

HUMPHREYS, Mary Ann only dau/James and Anna in St. Charles Co. 9 Sep in her 10th year. Funeral from home of Mrs. Walter Ransom, Bernard-Pratte.   MORE 11 Sep 1864

HUMPHREYS, John W. 21 Aug in Callaway Co. ca 48.   FULT 6 Sep 1861

HUMPHREYS, Mary Ann dau/Robert H. and Sarah Jane 6 May ae 3y 8m. Lived at Missouri & Park.   MORE 7 May 1863

HUMPHREYS, William 28 Jun of liver complaint in his 63rd year. Lived on Park Ave.   MORE 29 Jun 1862

HUMSTON, Thomas, of Lewis Co., shot by Gen. Merrill at Palmyra in retaliation for murder of an old man named Allmstedt at the time of Porter's raid into Palmyra. (Others also executed.) PALCO   CAWN 1 Nov 1862

HUNER, Harry 6 Jun near Canton of heart disease, ae 58; for 32 years a resident of Canton Twp.   CANP 8 Jun 1865

HUNT, Andrew J. 20 Jan in Randolph Co. ae ca 47.   COWS 29 Jan 1864

HUNT, Edward Hale son/Sanford M. and Fanny R. 12 Nov of typh ae 11. Youngest child.   MORE 14 Nov 1865

HUNT, Ellen wife of Timothy 3 Oct in her 53rd year. Interred Calvary. MORE 4 Oct 1861

HUNT, John of Osage Co. in Gratiot Prison of diphtheria 5 Nov. MORE 9 Nov 1862

HUNT, Capt. John P., formerly of Charleston, Mississippi Co., suddenly 27 Dec CHAC 4 Jan 1861
    at Cape Girardeau.

HUNT, Mrs. Sarah L. wife of the late A.J. in Randolph Co. 11 Mar. MORE 21 Mar 1864

HUNT, William 14 Apr ae 20y 3m 28d after a short illness of meningitis. LIT 18 Apr 1862

HUNTER, Mrs. Acenite at her home near Kansas City 24 Apr ae 56y 11m 25d. KCJC 27 Apr 1864

HUNTER, Robert W. in Portland, Callaway Co. 13 Sep ae 48y 3m 19d. MORE 17 Sep 1864

HUNTLEY, Seth at Vicksburg. LIT 31 Jul 1863

HUNTSMAN, Isaac, of Randolph Co., of rubeola. (Undertaker's list) MORE 10 Nov 1862

HUNZINGER, Jacob, native of Switzerland, killed by the explosion of a 12-inch shell MORE 20 Aug 1865
    while employed in removing powder from shells. Left 4 young children
    and one grown daughter, 5th north of Arsenal.

HURLBURT, Henry, 2nd MO, taken in Wright Co. 11 Jan, 14 Feb of pneumonia in MORE 17 &
    Gratiot Prison. (also undertaker's list) 22 Feb 1863

HURSH, Jacob, tribute by the Crestomathean Society. SPRIP 9 Nov 1865

HURT, Moses, cousin of Judge Hurt, killed by federal officers in Chariton Co. MORE 7 &
    and thrown into the Missouri River. Ae 60. 10 Jan 1865

HURTESTON, ____, noted guerilla, killed in Lafayette Co. by Capt. Clayton Tiffin's MORE 3 Feb 1865
                                                                        EMM.

HUSBANDS, Daniel J. son/James A. and Petronel 23 Oct ae 19y 7m. MORE 30 Oct 1863

HUSEMAN, Philip 22 Nov in his 18th year. Funeral from his mother's home, 16-Wash-Carr. "   23 Nov 1861

HUSSEY, Charles E. eldest son/Authur and Mary M., 2 May. SLMD 7 May 1861

HUSSEY, Thomas, boarding betw Washington & Green on 8th St., asphyxia. MORE 19 Jan 1863

HUSTON, Mrs. C.U. in Warrenton of lung congestion, ae 46, at the home of L.J. Dryden. MORE 25 Mar '63

HUSTON, Maj. George Webster 12 Apr at his home in Troy, ae 52; prominent politician, MORE 19 Apr 1862
    born Shenandoah Co. VA, to MO 1836. Long, painful illness.

HUTCHESON, Charles Thomas, only child of David and Lizzie, ae 4y 5m 29d. New York MORE 26 Jun 1863
    & Patterson NJ pc

HUTCHINS, Isabelle Sewell dau/Thomas and Jane 17 Nov ae 13, at Missouri betw MORE 18 Nov 1861
    Lafayette-Geyer. (SLMD 26 Nov says ae 3)

HUTCHINSON, Carey youngest son/Rev. Dr. Edward C. and Lucy at Vicksburg 10 Jul of MORE 28 Jul 1863
    brain congestion ae 19y 9m 10d. Member 1st Reg MO Vols CSA.

HUTCHINSON, Eliza Israell wife of Capt. B.F. in Philadelphia 3 Aug. MORE 10 Aug 1864

HUTCHINSON, John, Chariton Co.: Final Settlement by Cyrus Hutchinson. CECB 26 Mar 1863

HYDE, James, 2 Feb on 24th St. betw Carr and Biddle. MORE 2 Feb 1865

HYMER, Sarah P. consort of Jacob 22 Jul ae 66y 22d. Born Madison Co. KY, to LIT 31 Jul 1863
    Clay Co. MO 1836. Baptist.

HYNES, James at his home near Albany, Gentry Co., 14 Dec, when thrown from and WARS 29 Dec 1865
    dragged by his horse.

HYNSON, Gussy only son/Augustus R. and Nannie 10 Apr of lung fever ae 4. Lived MORE 12 Apr 1862
    at 312 N. 6th. Memphis & Baltimore pc

ICENHOWER, Andrew 5 Sep ae (58?). MORE 7 Sep 1862

IDLER, Catherine wife of John 20 Aug ae 25y 8m 3d, at 15 N. 3rd St. MORE 22 Aug 1865

IFINGER, Lizzie wife of John 14 Apr in her 20th year. Funeral from the home of MORE 15 Apr 1862
    Thomas Morrison, 125 Olive St.

IFRIEL (FRIEL?), Peter at Sisters Hospital ae 31, native of Rathmullen, Co. Donegal. MORE 11 Sep 1865
    Member Young Mens' Sociality.

IHMSEN, Charles H. 19 Sep ae 34 at the home of his father, Henry. Int. Calvary. MORE 21 Sep 1864

INGE, Mary at the home of Emile Generally in St. Clair, Franklin Co. 11 Jun in MORE 15 Jun 1862
    her 68th year. Formerly of Pittsylvania Co. VA.

INGE, Rosalie drowned in the Bourbeuse River near Union. (Children of C.S. & A.V.) MORE 14 &
    Fillmore (her brother) ".   Rosalie was 16y 10m, Fillmore was 12y 11m. 16 Jul 1864
    They had gone fishing with another sister, the little boy went in after minnows,
    beyond his depth; Rosalie went after him, and both drowned.

INGRAM, Milton J. 10 Dec of pneumonia ae 25y 2m. Funeral from the home of his parents, sw corner 10th-Chestnut.	MORE 12 Dec 1863
Mrs. Eliza 16 Dec ae 45y 6m, at 10th & Chestnut.	MORE 17 Dec 1863
INGRAM, James A. 21 Aug in his 53rd year, at the home of his son-in-law, M.P. Owen, Warren betw 15-16. Cincinnati, Pittsburgh, Wheeling pc	MORE 22 Aug 1864
INGRAM, John C., Chariton Co.: Public administrator took over his estate.	CECB 24 Jul 1862
Sale of real estate by Dewey Moxley (petition for).	" 7 May 1864
INKS, Maj. William C. at his home near Allenton 24 Sep of consumption in 51st year.	MORE 25 Sep 1864
INMAN, James H. pvt 1st MO CSA, arrested in Howell Co., in the prison hospital of inflammation of the lungs.	MORE 10 Nov 1863
INMAN, Mrs. Susan wife of Maj. Hiram 10 Apr of smallpox.	MORE 11 Apr 1863
IRWIN, Mrs. Sally 3 Apr in Independence, at her home, ae 77y 4m 16d.	MORE 17 Apr 1863
ISAACS, Henry 2 May ae 58 at 177 Olive. New York pc	MORE 3 May 1864
ISH, Miss Leonora H. 16 Oct at Lexington "in the bloom of youth."	MORE 18 Nov 1863
IVER, Charles of consumption Friday at the home of Capt. Jackson Ivers, 1 mile west of Farr's Grocery on Natural Bridge Plank Road. Funeral from the home of his uncle, not given. Ae 28y 4m.	MORE 20 Jul 1861
IVERS, Jackson M. son/Jackson and Susan of consumption ae 19y 19d. Lived on Spring betw 9-10. Interred Bellefontaine.	MORE 9 May 1863
IVORY, Louisa A. wife of Christopher J. Caffray(?) 19 Jun in her 24th year. St. John's Church, interred Calvary. (Surname is questionable.)	MORE 20 Jun 1864
JACCARD, Miss Lilly Amanda B. at St. Paul 12 Nov, of consumption, ae 26. Funeral from home of Eugene Jaccard, Grand-Washington. Int. Bellefontaine.	MORE 22 Nov 1865
JACCARD, Maria 2nd dau/D. Constant and Emiline of St. Louis at Belleview, Madison Co. IL 11 Jul ae 6y 6m 10d.	MORE 17 Jul 1864
JACKMAN, Porter 10 Aug in Howard Co. ae 73. Came to MO in 1816; member of the Christian Church.	COWS 18 Aug 1865
Polly wife of Porter in Howard Co. 9 Oct.	COWS 27 Oct 1865
JACKSON, ____ lately killed by bushwhackers at his home in Chariton Co.	MORE 10 Jan 1865
JACKSON, Andrew killed when he tried to jump on a flatcar of the Iron Mtn RR at Ivory Station. Resident of Linn, Osage Co., ae ca 40.	MORE 23 May 1865
JACKSON, Carrie wife of John P. of Audrain Co. and dau/Benedict and Harriet Whaley of Callaway Co. in Audrain Co. 22 Sep ae 25y 5m.	COWS 4 Oct 1861 MORE 6 "
JACKSON, Claiborne Fox, late Governor of MO, in the vicinity of Little Rock 6 Dec 1862, of stomach cancer. Born in Fleming Co. KY 4 Apr 1807, to MO at age 18. Long eulogy. (Little Rock True Democrat)	CANP 15 Jan 1863
Mrs. Claiborne Fox, widow of the late Governor, in Texas.	LIT 2 Sep 1864
John B., son of the late Governor, in the asylum at Fulton. Int. Arrow Rock.	" 27 Oct 1865
JACKSON, Eliza Jane relict of Dr. Samuel D. of Canton in St. Louis 29 Oct ae 44y 6m.	CANP 2 Nov 1865
JACKSON, James E. son/Daniel and Alvernon, late of Rappahannock Co. VA 16 Apr of gastro-enteritis, ae 6y 1m 2d, at the home of Dr. H.H. Cropp	GLWT 25 Apr 1861
JACKSON, Jane at the home of her son-in-law J.M. McCormick in Canton 15 May in her 56th year. Baptist; interred Mt. Moriah Methodist cemetery.	CANP 4 Jun 1863
JACKSON, John Duke, native of Lynn Regis ENG, nephew of M.C. of St. Louis, Tuesday.	MORE 29 May 1862
JACKSON, Joshua "Dr." a free man of color, highly regarded among the blacks for his medical knowledge, 27 Jan of typhoid.	HAM 31 Jan 1861
JACKSON, Caroline M. wife of Linus 25 Mar ae 33. Lived at 14th-Dodier.	MORE 26 Mar 1862
Linus 12 Feb in his 51st year; lived at Collins-O'Fallon. Boston pc	" 13 Feb 1864
JACKSON, Moses, living at 9th-Franklin, of intemperance ae ca 45.	MORE 12 Feb 1862
JACKSON, Thomas, inquest: accidentally shot himself on St. Charles Road when his pistol discharged. Had relatives at Cap au Gris, Lincoln Co.	SLMD 14 Jan 1861
JACKSON, Thomas "many years a resident" 23 May ae 55. Funeral from Christ Church. New York, Boston, Newburyport pc	MORE 25 May 1864
JACKSON, William R., one of Porter's men arrested 13 Nov, died Sunday; father will take body to Mexico MO for burial. (11/24 says he was of Price's Army, died of typhoid pneumonia.	MORE 18, 19, & 24 Nov 1862
JACOBS, Miss ___ drowned near Anderson's Ferry, east fork of Grand R., Livingston Co. while bathing. Body recovered. Mrs. Akins and Miss Smith also drowned.	SJH 19 Jul 1864

JACOBS, Miss Lucy 8 Jan in Monroe Co. in her 65th year. Cumberland Presbyterian.	COWS 5 Feb 1864
JACOBS, Thomas W. at his home near Wellington; born Madison Co. KY 4 Aug 1809.	RICON 12 Jul 1861
JACOBSON, Capt. Thorwald 3 Jan at Larkinsville, AL, funeral from Church of the Messiah, St. Louis. Brother of Lt. Col. Jacobson.	MORE 22 Jan 1864
JACQUET, Joseph, a jeweler living in Carondelet, run over by Iron Mtn RR train. Left wife, 1 child. Ae 49.	MORE 27 Oct 1863
JAMES, Eddie Rees oldest son/T. and Fannie, Monday at 16th-Hickory ae 4y 9m.	MORE 1 Oct 1862
JAMES, John in St. Charles Co. in his 24th year.	MORE 15 Apr 1864
JAMES, Mrs. Sabray, inquest; found dead in bed in her husband's home, 3 miles out on Clayton Road. Verdict, congestion of the heart.	MORE 27 Jan 1863
JAMESON, Alex R. 6 Sep ae 68, native of Lancaster PA. In Cincinnati 30 years, to St. Louis ca 20 years ago. Funeral from home of Amos Cutting. Interred Bellefontaine.	MORE 7 & 8 Sep 1861
Elizabeth relict of Alexander R. Sunday ae 65; funeral from home of her son-in-law Amos Cotting, 8th-Chestnut. Born in Lancaster Co. PA, to Warren Co. OH 60 years ago, married 1820; in St. Louis 25 years.	MORE 10 & 16 Apr 1865
JAMESON, Mrs. Rebecca, native of Green Co. PA, ae 20; had been consumptive. Lived in Hickory Co. but had left there because of "disturbing conditions." Married about a year.	MORE 26 Nov 1861
JAMESON, Robert D., tribute by Masons of Marshfield, Webster Co. Died 30 Nov 1863.	MORE 24 May 1864
JAMISON, Sallie T. dau/late John near Fulton 11 Nov ae 21.	COWS 4 Dec 1863
JANIS, Antoine, old and highly estemmed resident of Ste. Genevieve, 16 Jul.	MORE 24 Jul 1861
JANNEY, Sarah widow of N.E. of St. Louis in Pittsburgh 20 Nov.	MORE 26 Nov 1863
JAQUITH, Maria wife of P.H. 23 Feb in Pilot Knobb ae 31y 2m. Ill 4 months.	MORE 24 Feb 1862
JARAND, Felix, a diver, drowned trying to examine the sunken Moderator; wore diving suit, possibly too much weight attached. Wife ("and we believe some children") on O'Fallon.	MORE 11 Feb 1864
JARRET, James 20 Aug at Carondelet ae 58y 3m 20d. Native of Scotland.	MORE 22 Aug 1865
JARRETT, Charles J., captured in Wright Co. 1 Feb, in Prison Hospital of measles.	MORE 12 May 1863
JARRETT, J., citizen of Wright Co., 7 Feb of (bronchitis?) (Undertaker's list)	MORE 15 Feb 1863
JARVIS, Calvin of Porter's Division in Gratiot Prison; captured in Schuyler Co. 18 Oct. (MORE 15 Dec shows Undertaker's list, cause of death typhoid)	MORE 10 Dec 1862
JASPAR, Marie Elizabeth Lydie relict of F.J., nee Desbonne, native of Guadeloupe, W.I., 19 Apr in her 57th year. Funeral, Church of the Annunciation.	MORE 20 Oct 1862
JEFFERSON, Dudley, citizen, 2 Apr of a gunshot wound. (Undertaker's list)	MORE 17 Apr 1865
JEFFERSON, Robert R., Masonic tribute; mentions children and relatives.	JEST 18 Aug 1865
JEFFREYS, Mary Ann widow of Col. Peter at Blithedale Farm, Jackson Co., formerly of Nevis W.I., 30 Aug ae 60.	MORE 18 Sep 1861
JENKINS, James L., "old and highly respected" in LaGrange Mon. last of cramp colic.	HAM 19 Feb 1861
JENNINGS, ___, son-in-law of Peter Fox, both shot near Keytesville. (Brunswicker)	MORE 24 Jun 1864
JENNINGS, Bridget, inquest: murdered by her husband Pat, a steamboat man; beaten 3 weeks ago and died of effects. Testimony by her son William Riley.	MORE 28 Apr 1864
JENNINGS, Jane wife of C. Sunday on Chambers St. ae 43y 7m.	MORE 4 Feb 1862
JENNINGS, Dr. John C. 23 May at the home of his mother, Jennings Station, North MO RR, in his 37th year. Interred Bellefontaine.	MORE 25 May 1863
JENNINGS, Thomas Arthur son/William H. and Hannah W. 14 Aug ae 3y 8m, at 113 Pine.	MORE 15 Aug 1861
JENSIN, Charles, killed in Chariton Co. "in retaliation."	MORE 10 Jan 1865
JERDY, Jack, a Frenchman, killed in the Camp Jackson affair.	MORE 18 May 1861
JETER, Dr. Andrew F. at his home in LaGrange 3 Feb in his 37th year, born VA; representative for Marion Co. in the state legislature.	HAM 27 Feb 1862 MORE 25 "
JETER, Zachary Taylor, eldest son/Mary and Loyd, 5 Jul of bilious dysentery ae 17y 10m 5d. Funeral from home of W.P. Mullen, 212 N. 6th. Palmyra pc	MORE 6 Jul 1865
JETT, ___ shot by squad of 7th KS, formerly a rebel but had lived quietly at home last year or more.	LAJ 4 Jun 1864
JEWELL, Dr. William B. 25 May of consumption at the home of his grandmother Mrs. Lenoir in his 21st year. Left wife and baby. His parents had died when he was an infant	MORE 16 Jun 1865 COWS 2 "

JEWETT, Jackson formerly of Howard Co. 12 Sep in Carroll Co. ca 48.   COWS 30 Dec 1864

JOCKERS, Joseph, a soldier, murdered at Cape Girardeau by the bugler of 2nd MO Cav.   PERU 15 Jan 1864

JOHANN, George Matthew 17 Dec ae 62, living at Jackson above Miller. Formerly of   MORE 19 Dec 1863
    Philadelphia.

JOHLE, John 17 Jul ae 46 at his home on Natural Bridge Plank Road. Funeral from   MORE 18 Jul 1864
    Holy Trinity.

JOHNS, Joseph 6 Sep at the home of his father-in-law J.C. Harris in his 26th year.   WEST 23 Sep 1864
    (apparently of consumption) Left a wife.

JOHNS, Prof. William C. 11 Oct ae 23, of a fall from a horse which he kept at   MORE 12 &
    Huntingdon's Livery Stable. Music teacher, unmarried, ca 25.   13 Oct 1865

JOHNSMEIER, Diederick, a gardener, found stabbed to death on St. Charles Rock Rd.   MORE 25 Sep 1863
    4 miles from the city near the Tollgate. Had a large garden in
    partnership with ___ Hagar, with whom he boarded and whose sister he
    was soon to marry. Ae ca 28.

JOHNSON, Aleck, a negro, shot in a saloon Tuesday, now died.   SJH 10 Dec 1864

JOHNSON, Ann consort of William 3 Dec ae 62, at 8th betw Morgan-Franklin.   MORE 4 Dec 1864

JOHNSON, Ann wife of Robert 18 Mar in her 23rd year, at 432 Broadway.   MORE 19 Mar 1863

JOHNSON, Ashton son/Ashton P. of St. Louis, aide-de-camp to Gen. Wm. B. Quarles,   MORE 11 Sep 1864
    CSA 27 Jul at Atlanta in his 19th year.

JOHNSON, Charles H. 27 Jul ae 30 of a lingering illness at his mother's home,   MORE 28 Jul 1865
    237 Locust. Interred Bellefontaine.

JOHNSON, David of Co. A, 9th MO, a prisoner, 28 Dec of chronic dysentery.   MORE 3 Jan 1864
    (Undertaker's list)

JOHNSON, David, Chariton Co.: petition to sell real estate by John A. Crawley, exr.   CECB 13 Apr 1861

JOHNSON, Eleazar murdered near Warrensburg by Daviess Co. bushwhackers. Wm. Gray   GAL 2 Mar 1865
    also murdered. (Letter from Wm. C. Gillehan, 1st Cav MSM, Warrensburg)

JOHNSON, Elijah E. in Audrain Co. 10 May ae 25, son of Elijah of Boone Co. where   COWS 16 &
    he lived until 2 years ago. Married Eliza Davis.   23 May 1862

JOHNSON, Emma wife of Jack 30 Jul ae 28, at 61 Green St.   MORE 1 Aug 1861

JOHNSON, Harriet S. wife of James I. 7 Jan ae 37 of a protracted illness. Interred   MORE 8 &
    Bellefontaine. Baltimore, Boonville MO & Jacksonville IL pc   9 Jan 1864

JOHNSON, Hayden shot by Benjamin Keene in a dispute over a card game.   LIT 27 Nov 1863

JOHNSON, Mrs. Hettie 24 Aug ae 84. Funeral from the home of her son-in-law Morris   MORE 27 Aug 1863
    Pawley, Grand betw Lafayette-Park. Newark pc (see Moses Johnson)

JOHNSON, James 3 Dec in Gasconade Co. in his 57th year. Born in Alexandria VA,   MORE 4 Apr 1865
    to St. Louis about 1835. Baptist. Left wife and several children.

JOHNSON, James C. 13 Mar of consumption ae 36. Funeral from 1st Methodist Church.   MORE 14 Mar 1863
    CA & Louisville pc

JOHNSON, Capt. James H., late of the Die Vernon, at his home in Louisiana MO of   LAJ 4 Apr 1861
    typhoid. Born in KY 1 May 1818, to MO at age 5. Mbr IOOF. Husband,   HAM 2 "
    father. Interred Louisiana cemetery.

JOHNSON, James M. 15 Oct. Funeral from the home of Mr. Jennings, Madison-13-14.   MORE 16 Oct 1863
    Members of St. George's Society invited.

JOHNSON, Jane dau/A. of Maries Co. 14 Feb of measles ae 17y 6m 7d.   ROLEX 24 Feb 1862

JOHNSON, John W., 4th MO, captured in Howard Co. 24 Sep, in Gratiot Prison.   MORE 15 Mar 1863

JOHNSON, Mrs. Lyde 29 May in Boone Co. of consumption ae 29.   COWS 2 Jun 1865

JOHNSON, M.R. of Jefferson Co., Co. F 2nd MO Inf CSA killed either in the battle   MORE 19 Sep 1863
    of Champion Hills, Big Black Bridge, or siege of Vicksburg.

JOHNSON, Maggie F. 22 Oct in Boonville ae 11y 7m 19d, dau/William and Gabriella.   COWS 10 Nov 1865

JOHNSON, Mariam wife of Moseby in Tywapitty Bottom, Scott Co., 30 Jul.   CHAC 31 Jul 1863
    Moseby in Tywapitty Bottom 27 Aug ae 37; born in Hardin Co. KY,   "   4 Sep 1863
    emigrated about 9 years ago.

JOHNSON, Capt. Mason 6 Dec of consumption ae 39, son of the late Sallie Mason and   MORE 7 Dec 1862
    Thomas B. Johnson, son-in-law of J.V. & M.H. Machette. Baltimore &
    Washington DC pc

JOHNSON, Minerva F. wife of Rev. J.T.M. at Ashland 18 Mar ae 34y 8d.   COWS 29 Mar 1861

JOHNSON, Moses 21 Jan ae (90?) years. Funeral from the home of his son-in-law MORE 22 Jan 1863
Morris Pawley on Grand Ave. Newark pc (also see Mrs. Hettie Johnson)

JOHNSON, Novazembla of New York in Chillicothe 30 Nov ae 48. Funeral from the MORE 6 Dec 1864
home of his brother, A., Washington-Garrison. Died of congestive chills.

JOHNSON, Robert W. in Lincoln Co. 21 Sep ae 21, after a 2-year illness. MORE 6 Oct 1864

JOHNSON, Miss Rosa (later shown as Dora) 24 Aug of typhoid ae 28, at the home of MORE 25 &
her brother-in-law John W. Harris (later Horres) 58 N. 5th St. Int. Calvary. 26 Aug 1864

JOHNSON, Samuel W. and wife of eastern Monroe Co. recently of a virulent fever MORE 2 Oct 1865
which lately appeared in that locality.

JOHNSON, Rev. Thomas murdered by bushwhackers at his home near Westport. MORE 10 Jan 1865
(Killed 2 Jan at his home near Westport.) LEXUN 21 "

JOHNSON, William killed by the explosion of a boiler 1 Jun at O'Fallon Lead Works, MORE 9 Jun 1863
exhumation and inquest. Verdict: he was negligent, not enough water was
in the boiler. Interred Bellefontaine.

JOHNSON, Rev. William C. and his family; he died 29 Apr ca 43. R.H. died 3 May MORE 28 May 1861
ae 17. Lucy Ann died 12 May ae 18. (Newton Co.)

JOHNSTON, Mrs. Anna Eliza 29 May at the home of her mother, Mary Davis; also COWS 28 Jul 1865
dau/late James. Ae 25, member Salem Baptist Church.

JOHNSTON, Elijah 11 Aug in Boone Co. of stomach inflammation, in his 71st year. COWS 29 Aug &
Born Harrison Co. KY; in War of 1812; to Boone Co. in 1830. 3 Sep 1862

JOHNSTON, Dr. Greenberry C. at the home of his father-in-law Creed Carter in COWS 6 Mar 1863
Callaway Co. 17 Feb in his 39th year.

JOHNSTON, James H. in Hudson MO 16 May ae 2y 2m 7d. RANC 23 May 1861

JOHNSTON, Peter W. "long a Justice of the Peace in the 5th Ward" 31 Jan ae 71. MORE 1 Feb 1862
Lived at Montgomery-Broadway.

JOHNSTON, Robert, formerly of Philadelphia, 28 May ae 56. MORE 30 May 1862

JOHNSTON, Stephen at his home near Platte City 25 Apr in his 51st year. "Merchant, WEST 12 May 1865
husband, family."

JOHNSTON, William J. 5 May at his home near Potosi. Born Fluvanna Co. VA 7 Sep 1832, MORE 17 May 1865
married 30 Oct 1855, to Washington Co. MO 1858. Had a sawmill and
lumber business. Left wife, 4 daughters, mother. Richmond VA pc

JOHNSTON, Dr. Zachariah G. 9 Jun in Monroe Co. ae 26y 4m 15d. MORE 30 Jun 1863

JOICE, Festus, section boss on the RR, killed on a street in Chillicothe by SJH 11 Aug 1863
Jefferson Garr.

JOLLY, George S. in Audrain Co. 13 Mar ae 42. FULT 22 Mar 1861

JONES, Adam 22 Apr ae 43 at his home on St. Charles Plank Road, 10 miles from the MORE 24 Apr 1865
city. Interred Central burying ground. Boston pc

JONES, Amanda wife of Richard near Ashley, Pike Co., 12 (14) Jun in her 42nd year. COWS 14 Jul 1865
(Shown as wife of R.T., with second date.) LAJ 24 Jun "

JONES, Andrew P. 25 May of phthisis pulmonalis, ae 29y 3d. Funeral from home of his MORE 26 May 1865
brother-in-law (not named) sw corner 14th-Market. Rock Island & Henry Co. IL pc

JONES, Mrs. Anna of Arrow Rock in Boonville 15 Aug in her 79th year. COWS 9 Sep 1864

JONES, Anne E. wife of Capt. Isaac H. 28 Feb in her 39th year, dau/late Matthew MORE 1 Mar 1864
Irwin and Anne E. Walker of Fayette Co. PA. Louisville & Pittsburgh pc

JONES, Asa E. 21 Nov in his 35th year. Funeral from the home of his father-in-law, MORE 22 Nov 1863
Robert Forsythe. Eastharam & Benson VT pc

JONES, Charles of Howard Co., captured in Saline Co. 31 Oct, in Gratiot Prison MORE 17 Mar 1863
of typhoid pneumonia.

JONES, David at Williamsburg Sunday last ae 86. FULT 9 May 1862

JONES, Doniphan son/Elder A.E. and Kate in Platte City 13 Aug ae ca 2. LIT 15 Aug 1862

JONES, Edward/lost in the Sultana disaster; funeral from his home, 10th betw MORE 4 Jun 1865
Warren-Montgomery.

JONES, Elizabeth R. wife of Andrew P. 22 Feb ae 15y 11m 22d, at 39 S. 6th. MORE 25 Feb 1864

JONES, G.W. of Hamilton's Battalion, 8 Feb of pneumonia. (Undertaker's list) MORE 15 Feb 1863

JONES, G.W., prisoner, 28 Jan of variola confluens. (Undertaker's list) MORE 2 Feb 1863

JONES, George James son/James and Sarah, ae 8y 9m, at 76 S. 4th St. MORE 4 Nov 1862

JONES, Gideon of Boone Co. shot from brush near the Fairgrounds a week ago, by his own friends, believed mistaken for a Union man. "An avowed Secessionist." COWS 11 Jul 1862

JONES, Gordon, ae ca 50, at Sisters Hospital. An educated man, had been a tutor in several institutions, connected with the press in NY, St. Louis, Chicago. MORE 5 Oct 1862

JONES, Hardin G., pvt in Capt. Snell's 1st Prov. Reg., in the military hosp., Fultom. MORE 7 Dec 1863

JONES, Harriet consort of Harrison 21 May ae 31 after a long illness. (COWS 5 Jun says Harrison B., died 28 May) CANP 4 Jun 1863
    Morton C. son/Harrison B. of Boone Co., injured in a train collision near Laclede, 10 Nov, leg amputated, died the next day. Interred Macon. COWS 16 Dec 1864
    Manlius T., another son of Harrison, in the rebel army under Price, was killed in a fight near Fort Scott. "

JONES, Heath shot at Frankford by a Home Guard picket. LAJ 25 Jul 1861

JONES, Hetty Coons dau/Maj. C. and Mary A. 21 Jan of convulsions ae 3y. Funeral from home of V.B. Bacigalupo, Rosatti betw Soulard-Carroll. MORE 22 Jan 1863

JONES, James native of Wexford 20 Apr ae 23. Funeral from the home of his brother on St. Charles Plank Road. MORE 21 Apr 1863

JONES, James, a river cook on the Die Vernon, fell dead on the street of heart disease; had recently been in bad health. Lived at the corner of 13-Wash, was in his 30th year; left "family." MORE 12 & 13 May 1864

JONES, Jeff F. in Randolph Co. 22 Dec of brain congestion, in his 32d year. Fredericksburg VA pc MORE 22 Jan 1863

JONES, Jeremiah B. son/Charles C. and Margaret 12 Nov of typhoid at the Pacific House, S. Hannibal, ae (6? 8?)y 6m 3d. Buffalo pc HAM 21 Nov 1861

JONES, John in Arrow Rock 26 Mar in his 77th year. COWS 10 Apr 1863

JONES, John M. at the home of his brother, E.D., 9th near Mallinkrodt, Monday. Funeral from the Baptist Church, 12th-Benton. MORE 12 Oct 1864

JONES, John P. 24 Aug ae 56 at his home, 201 Morgan. MORE 25 Aug 1861

JONES, Lewis Cass only son/Dr. W.W. 19 Jul ae ca 5. MORE 20 Jul 1864

JONES, M.A., war prisoner, 22 Jan of variola confluens. (Undertaker's list) MORE 26 Jan 1863

JONES, Margaret T. wife of J.B. in Rocheport 28 Nov ae 51y 5m 26d. COWS 11 Jan 1861

JONES, Michael Henry eldest son/A.R. and Margaret C. 5 Dec ae 17y 6m. MORE 6 Dec 1863

JONES, Peter W. 6 Oct near Mound City ae 31, of jaundice and chronic diarrhoea. Tribute by Quitman Masonic Lodge. SJH 15 Oct 1865 " 24 "

JONES, Samuel, hit on head by unknown. Intemperate. Unmarried. MORE 4 Nov 1863

JONES, Shadrick W., prisoner, 25 Sep of phthisis pulmonalis. (Undertaker's list) MORE 29 Sep 1862

JONES, Susie dau/Richard 29 Oct in her 16th year. LAJ 7 Nov 1863

JONES, Teresa wife of Capt. J. Riley, #8 Meyers Row, ae 32y 4m 20d. MORE 10 Mar 1865

JONES, W.T. in Gratiot Prison of meningitis 4 Dec. MORE 7 Dec 1862

JONES, William B. ae 18 at the home of his brother, E.D., 17th betw Morgan-Christy, 19 Mar. Joined the Baptist Church in Pittsburgh in 1857. MORE 20 & 21 Mar 1862

JONES, William C., late of Washington Co. PA, killed at Warsaw; had emigrated to western MO, left wife, 1 child, and father who had accompanied them. MORE 4 Oct 1865

JONES, William T. at the home of C.W. Jones, of typhoid, in his 27th year. CALM 30 Sep 1865

JORDAN, Clara, niece of W.H. Whitehill, ae 21. Interred Bellefontaine. MORE 3 Oct 1864

JORDAN, Eliza native of Ireland, in a house in the alley betw 3-4-Convent-Rutgers, of uterine hemorrhage. MORE 12 Feb 1861

JORDAN, Thomas, Irish, ca (20?), a widower with 3 children in destitute condition, of lung congestion and intemperance. MORE 14 May 1862

JORDAN, Virginia dau/H. 2 Feb ae ca 17. HAM 3 Feb 1861

JOUETT, Nannie wife of William R. and dau/late Charles Schaumberg, 7 Apr. Interred Bellefontaine. NY, Philadelphia, New Orleans, Louisville pc MORE 8 Apr 1865

JOYAILE, Anthony 16 Oct at his home, 107 S. 4th, ae 33. MORE 17 Oct 1864

JOYCE, Mary ae 11 accidentally shot at the home of her uncle, Mr. Lightburne, on Clark betw 16-Moore, playing with a loaded revolver. MORE 24 Aug 1865

JOYCE, Patrick H. found drowned at the foot of Chestnut St.; father on 8th St. MORE 8 Oct 1862

JUDD, Willis, 2nd MO Cav CS, captured Benton Co. 8 Oct, of measles in Gratiot Prison. MORE 19 Feb 1864

Entry	Source
JUDGE, Catherine, inquest: fell dead, verdict congestion of the brain. Irish, lived at Morgan & main; husband a fifer with 7th MO. Left 2 children.	MORE 2 Oct 1862
JUDLIN, Isabel only dau/J.W. and Fanny, ae 3y 11m. Baltimore pc	MORE 25 Nov 1863
JUDY, Daniel at the home of his father 5 Sep of dyspepsia and consumption; ill 2 yrs. Had lost his wife and 2 infants in 13 months.	LIT 7 Oct 1864
JUDY, Lavinia wife of David J., formerly of Clark Co. KY, 1 Jan in Callaway Co. ae ca 43.	FULT 4 Jan 1861 HAM 10 "
JUDY, Susan wife of Alexander and dau/John Bradly of Bourbon Co. KY 3 Apr of "beetle fever" ae (55?)y 9m 10d. Baptist.	LIT 15 Apr 1864
JULIAN, Lovenia dau/Armine and Elizabeth 6 May ae 4y 7m; and a younger daughter, Mattie Armine, 11 May ae 1y 5m.	MORE 8 & 12 May 1864
JULIEN, John 8 Nov at the home of his uncle, John Butler. Native of Queens Co. IRE, resident of this country 15 years; in his 28th year.	MORE 9 May 1865
JUNGLE, Henry, a gardener living at Grand-Market, killed in the Camp Jackson affair.	MORE 18 May 1861
JURGENS, Theodore son/Henry and Mary, ae 20y 4m, Sunday.	MORE 3 Jun 1861
KALLEHER, Dennis, ae 15, shot in the Camp Jackson affair, died at Sisters Hosp.	MORE 20 Jun 1861
KAMPKIN, Mollie dau/Dr. J.W. and Marianne Thursday ae ca 4.	PALS 22 Jan 1864
KANE, ___ dau/John and Mary, ae 2½, of "neglect and want of medical attendance."	MORE 29 May 1862
KANE, Frederick, a young English collier, suffocated in a coal pit on Clayton Rd. Two Englishmen trying to help him also died.	MORE 12 Aug 1861
KANE, Isabella, ae (68?). Funeral from the home of her son John, 16th near Cass.	MORE 18 Jun 1864
KANN, Rebecca Stooman wife of Gustavus Adolphus, at 85 St. Charles, ae 29.	MORE 2 Feb 1863
KANSCHEN, Henry, suicide by pistol near 15th-Carr. Had lent money to his brother in Kansas, who repaid with worthless currency, and was disconsolate.	MORE 30 Jan 1862
KARNS, John N. in Buchanan Co. 18 Mar ae ca 45. COWS 28 Mar 1862	MORE 1 Apr 1862
KARST, Joseph Alvis 1 Dec in his 73rd year, on 12th St. betw Market-Clark.	MORE 2-3 Dec'65
KARST, Mina Tourney wife of Emile 23 Aug ae 27y 11m, at #8 Targee. Funeral from St. Xavier.	MORE 24 Aug 1861
KASTEN, J.H.G., cashier of the Citizens' RR Co., 29 Aug ae 68. 21st-Morgan-Franklin.	MORE 30 Aug 1863
KATING, Mary of lung congestion, ae 6, on 3rd betw Spruce-Almond.	MORE 12 Jun 1863
KAY, J.L. at the home of H. Lamme in Boone Co. 5 Mar in his 38th y. Lexington KY pc	COWS 22 Mar 1861
KAY, Mrs. Mary ae (33?), late of Cincinnati, at the home of E. Morgan, Gratiot betw 8-9. (SLMD gives ae as 33)	MORE 28 Aug 1861 SLMD 3 Sep "
KAYDEL, Edward M., late of St. Louis, at mother's home, St. Jame's Parish, LA.	SLMD 9 Apr 1861
KAYS, Carrie, only dau/Amos and Ellen, 17 Jun of scarlet fever ae 4y 9m. Lived on Randolph betw 18-19.	MORE 19 Jun 1863
KAYSER, Alexander 17 Oct after a short illness, ae 49y 8m, 15th betw Market-Clark.	MORE 19 Oct 1864
KEACH, Fannie M.G. wife of John R. and dau/G.M. Grover (Clark & 13th) ae 23. St. Xavier's Church. Baltimore & Frederick MD pc	MORE 15 Mar 1864
KEADY, Bertie, eldest child of John G. and Julia, 4 Feb ae 4y 2m, at 153 Chestnut.	MORE 5 Feb 1864
Mrs. Isabella 26 Sep ae 64. Funeral from home of her son, John G., at 8th & St. Charles.	MORE 27 Sep 1861
KEAN, John, a levee hand, killed when a bale of cotton fell on him; he was passing a warehouse where men pushing bales out of the second floor failed to see him. (James Kennedy and Richard Harrigan arrested.) Lived at 2nd & Ashley, left wife and 5 children.	MORE 15 Jun 1865
KEANE, Michael, native of Co. Limerick, at the home of his son William, sw corner 16th & Carr, 20 Oct. Interred Calvary.	MORE 21 Oct 1865
KEARNEY, Gregory at Sisters Hospital Sunday ae 61.	MORE 12 Jan 1864
KEARNS, Michael, to be hanged today for the murder of Robert Baker. (Thomas Smith also to be hanged.)	MORE 23 Jan 1863
KEARY, John 16 Sep ae 18; funeral from the home of his brother Martin, Biddle betw 6-7. Survived by parents and brothers.	MORE 18 Sep 1861
KEATING, ___, a boy ae 7 drowned in a pond between 19-20-Olive-Pine. Only son of widowed mother, a poor washwoman, living on 21st St. in the vicinity.	MORE 25 Jun 1864
KEDDIE, William ae (53?) 21 Jan. Lived Elm betw 5-6, interred Wesleyan.	MORE 22 Jan 1861

KEEFE, Miss Margaret 23 Sep at the home of Samuel Maisanvugh, 105 N. 8th, ae 17. MORE 1 Oct 1862

KEEGAN, Mrs. Roxanna wife of the late Patrick, ae 60, at Cass betw 19-20. MORE 23 Nov 1862

KEELER, George W.R. 11 Aug in Platte Co. of flux, ae 52. LIT 19 Aug 1864
    Mary W. ae 42 and her infant daughter, 9 Aug.

KEEMLE, Charles 27 Sep ae 68, living on Compton Hill, interred Bellefontaine. Born MORE 29 Sep 1865
    in Philadelphia of Dutch descent, orphaned young; public official,
    printer, etc. Left widow and 3 children. (Long account.)

KEENAN, Peter J. 19 Oct of consumption, ae 18y 5m 19d, at the family home on Cerre. MORE 21 Oct 1865

KEENEY, John B., 3rd MO Cav captured in Hartville KY 11 Jan, in Gratiot Prison; typhoid. " 14 Mar 1863

KEEVES, Eliza J. wife of James A. 9 Nov at Oregon MO, of typhoid/ae HOLS 10 Nov & SJH 12 Nov 1865
                                                        /17

KEIR, J.M. of Greene Co. in the prison hospital in Springfield. MORE 10 Apr 1863

KEISTER, William hanged himself in Chillicothe, "one of our oldest and most CANP 22 Oct 1863
    respectable citizens;" deranged. Had previously tried to drown two
    of his sons. (Chillicothe Chronicle)

KEITH, John Sr. of Boone Co. 22 Dec in his 98th year. COWS 26 Dec 1862

KEITH, Lt. W.B. of St. Louis Co., under Marmaduke, Price's Command, killed at Elkin's MORE 21 Aug 1864
    Ford, 4 Apr. Born Fauquier Co. VA 3 Nov 1832, to MO 1855. 2nd MO CSA. Left
    wife and 2 children. Baltimore, Wheeling, Clarksburg & Richmond VA pc

KEITHLEY, ___ died of injuries received in a boiler explosion at Clarksville. LAJ 19 Sep 1863

KEITHLY, Monroe, ae ca 14, drowned; body recovered 6 Jun. Mother a widow, father MORE 6 &
    killed in army. Lived 181 5th St., betw Wash-Carr. 8 Jun 1865

KELL, Peter, suicide Thursday; cut his throat. Lived Plum near 3rd; a tinner, had MORE 16 Jun 1862
    been sick, was deranged. Ca 35, left wife and family.

KELLAM, James ae 6 and Sarah Eliza ae 2, children of William, late of near Corinth MS WEST 20 Feb 1864
    /12 Feb   / (later?)   in Weston. " 27 "

KELLEHER, Timothy native of Ireland 8 Jun ae 25; funeral from the home of his MORE 9 Jun 1865
    brother-in-law Henry English, Plum betw 2-3. Boston pc

KELLER, Abraham 6 Mar at the home of F.M. Hutchinson in his 28th year; ill 36 hrs. LIT 14 Mar 1862

KELLER, Hattie dau/John and Harriet 7 Nov in her 7th year; brief, painful illness. MORE 10 Nov 1864

KELLER, Jennie dau/S.P. and Kate W. 29 May ae 6y 11m 28d. MORE 1 Jun 1864

KELLEY, I.M., war prisoner, 28 Feb of pneumonia. (Undertaker's list) MORE 15 Feb 1863

KELLY, ___, a returned rebel, hanged "summarily" a few days ago at Bergen, MO; GAL 14 Sep 1865
    had attacked a lieutenant of militia.

KELLY, ___, of St. Louis, a bushwhacker, killed 6 miles from Fayette on RocheportRd. WARS 17 Jun 1865

KELLY, Daniel, ae 33, at corner of Angelrodt-Bellefontaine. Interred Rock Spring. MORE 2 Apr 1865

KELLY, Elizabeth, inquest: lived 9th betw Biddle-O'Fallon, had cooked dinner for MORE 17 Dec 1862
    her husband, apparently in good health, but was dead when he returned.
    Husband Michael, a "very respectable looking man" works at a pork house.
    Left 4 small children, youngest only 3 months old. Apoplexy.

KELLY, Elizabeth "this morning" ae 50, at 490 Morgan. Interred Calvary. MORE 12 Apr 1862

KELLY, George W. 16 Aug ae 50. Funeral from the home of his son-in-law J.A. MORE 17 Aug 1864
    Browder, corner 6th-Bremen.

KELLY, Hugh "an industrious laborer" suddenly "of a fit" ae 37. Wife, 1 child. MORE 1 Mar 1863

KELLY, James, a printer, 5 Feb ae 34y 4m. Funeral from the home of his brother-in- MORE 7 Feb 1864
    law L.H. Drake, Carondelet betw Miami-Chippewa, to Center Church.

KELLY, Lt. James Arthur at Memphis of wounds received in the battle of Helena. MORE 19 Jul 1863
    In his 22nd year, graduate of St. Louis U. 1858, later studied law.

KELLY, John, native of Co. Kerry IRE at 193 Green St. in his 25th year. Funeral MORE 6 May 1864
    from St. Francis Abbey.

KELLY, Kate dau/Michael and Alice 9 Oct of diphtheria ae 6. MORE 10 Oct 1861

KELLY, Miss Mary Ann 28 Mar ae 21. Funeral from home of uncle, William Wood, MORE 29 Mar 1864
    on Lucas betw 16-17.

KELLY, Peter 1 Feb in his 19th year. Funeral from the home of his brother James H., MORE 2 Feb 1861
    151 Walnut. Interred Calvary.

KELLY, Robert of Columbia 8 Sep of typhoid ae 31. COWS 13 Sep 1861

KELLY, Mrs. Sarah 8 Apr in her 61st year. Funeral from the home of B.F. McPherson, HAM 9 Apr 1861
    Centre-3rd. Int. Methodist Cemetery.

KELLY, Thomas ae 25, remains arrived from Cairo; funeral from his former home, 22nd-O'Fallon.	MORE 1 Sep 1865
KELLY, Tommy, a little boy, run over by an express wagon Monday night.	MORE 16 Mar 1865
KELSO, Alexander, ae 15, drowned yesterday when he fell off the Die Vernon; son of Mr. Kelso of Weil & Bros., employed by B.F. Sass. Body not found.	MORE 7 Jul 1864
KELTY, Dennis, inquest: suicide, disappeared 28 May, body found in well. Had said he was hiding from snakes and devils. Unmarried, ca 30, a carpenter.	MORE 5 Jun 1865
KEMP, Sarah wife of Alexander in St. Joseph 18 Aug. Funeral from Reformed Church.	SJH 19 Aug 1864
KEMP, William P. 7 Jan ae ca 25 at his father's home.	FULT 11 Jan 1861
KEMPER, A. Theodore, buried yesterday; body brought here by aged parents, Simeon and Jane. Born St. Joseph 31 Jul 1841, died Montgomery Co. KY 26 May. One of 10 children, now only one survives.	SJH 4 Jun 1865
KEMPER, Richard Henry son of (not clear, possibly Simeon) and Jane, 7 Nov. Age not given but referred to as Mr. Methodist.	SJH 9 Nov 1864
KEMPER, Charles killed near Spanish Lake Saturday last; Wm. Lahae and Tim O'Connor arrested. His brother Henry testified at the inquest; there appeared to be 8 or 9 men in a group, Charles was cut in the abdomen, died.	MORE 5 Feb 1864
KEMPER, Lillie dau/Thomas J. and Rachel B. 11 Apr of congested bowels ae 3y 5m.	KCJC 18 Apr 1862
KEMPFF(MUELLENKEMPFF?) Herman Muellen, inquest: died 3 miles below Carondelet on Morgan's Road, of congestion of the brain and intemperance. Left 3 children now in charge of his relatives.	MORE 11 Dec 1862
KENDALL, Edwin L. son/Charles M. and Cinderella 10 May of lung congestion ae 11y 1m 2d. Kansas City & Cincinnati pc	MORE 11 May 1864
KENDALL, Robert V., St. Louis and New Orleans pilot, 22 Apr in his 30th year, Jackson betw Marion-Carroll. Pittsburgh pc	MORE 23 Apr 1864
Joseph, Saturday in his 6th year. "	MORE 29 May 1864
KENEY, James M. Sgt Co. A 4th MO Cav, in Alton prison of gunshot wounds.	MORE 28 Jul 1864
KENNA, Miss Anastacia ae (29?) at the home of her brother-in-law, Christy-Beaumont.	MORE 19 Jul 1864
KENNEDY, ___ youngest son of James of near Fredericktown, fell into scalding water.	PERU 21 Nov 1862
KENNEDY, Alice "in a state of helpless intoxication" drowned in a pond near Summit and Clark. Left husband, several children.	MORE 8 Jan 1862
KENNEDY, Barney killed in Cole Co. 11 May last; Wm. Stephens, a soldier, sentenced to 25 years hard labor.	MORE 28 Jul 1863
KENNEDY, George, one of the oldest citizens of Louisiana, at the home of William Alexander 18 May, of apoplexy, in his 80th year.	HAM 24 May 1861 LAJ 23 "
KENNEDY, Martin, a carpenter ca 45, fell overboard the Edward Walsh.	MORE 21 Feb 1862
KENNEDY, wife of Michael, murdered by her husband and Bridget Fallon, who also claimed to be his wife. Mrs. Kennedy had a sum of money she had deposited with the Bishop, which the murderers wanted. Weapon, arsenic. She had recently had a child, who also died.	MORE 17 Mar 1861
KENNEDY, Capt. W.K., murder suspected; left 2 months ago for Quincy, family has not heard from him since.	MORE 2 Nov 1865
KENNEL, Jacob 26 Jul ae 50 at No. 6 14th St., betw Market-Chestnut.	MORE 27 Jul 1863
KENNEL, Nicholas 1 Jul ae 57.	MORE 2 Jul 1863
KENNETT, Col. Ferdinand, many years a prominent citizen of MO, Sunday last at Selma, his home in Jefferson Co.	CAWN 25 May 1861
KENNETT, Orlando S. son/W.C. of Callaway Co. 4 Jul ae 12y 1m 8d. St. Louis pc	JEST 7 Jul 1865
KENNON, Florence dau/F.A. and Harriet L. in Carondelet Tuesday of croup, ae 8y 6m. Frankfort pc	MORE 24 Dec 1863
KENNY, Thomas 8 Dec ae 58; lived north side of Biddle betw 23-24.	MORE 9 Dec 1862
KENNY, William son of Michael, ae 10, of injuries received when he was run over by a cart on the levee. Lived on 7th betw Biddle-Carr.	MORE 11 & 12 Nov 1861
KENRICK, Archbishop, of Baltimore - calls for memorial Mass.	MORE 14 Jul 1863
KENT, Maj. John A., Co A 1st Reg 1st Brigade Mo Conf troops at Corinth MS 3 Oct. Born Pike Co. MO, to VA at early age, admitted to Bar, returned to Louisiana MO. Ae ca 25.	MORE 13 Dec 1862 LAJ 27 Nov "
KENTON (or KEYTON), Colvin, citizen of Chariton Co., 24 Dec of rheumatism. (Undertaker's list)	MORE 28 Dec 1864

KENYAN, Albert 25 Sep in Fredericktown ae 37. Toledo pc	MORE 12 Oct 1861
KERBY, Sgt. John, Co K 9th MO Cav MSM, 4 Jul ae 22; wound received while scouting in Clay Co. Interred Liberty Cemetery. Left wife, small child, father, mother, 3 brothers, 2 sisters. Louisville & Frankfort KY pc	MORE 18 Aug 1864
KERNAN, Charles, ae 45, at 7th & Lancaster.	MORE 12 Feb 1864
KERNE, Margaret, fatally burned; lived with her brother, O'Fallon betw 5-6.	MORE 27 Jan 1864
KERNES, Mrs. Mary, in the vicinity of Platte Bridge, Buchanan Co., of typhoid ae 84.	SJH 7 Dec 1863
KERNESIA, George, German citizen and union man, shot by unknown Saturday night; had left home to hunt. Left aged mother, other relatives.	FRED 21 Jun 1862
KERNS, John, native of Louisburg, Co. Mayo IRE, 7 Nov ae 31. Interred Calvary.	MORE 8 Nov 1865
KERONE, Mrs. Sarah 22 Sep ae 66. Funeral from the home of her son, west side of Carondelet south of the Arsenal.	MORE 24 Sep 1864
KERR, Augusta consort of A.L., 13 Nov ae 29, at 267 Olive.	MORE 15 Nov 1864
KERR, Augustus ae 64, on 11 Feb. Funeral from Planters House, int. Bellefontaine.	MORE 12 Feb 1861
KERR, James B., Orderly Sgt. in Gen. John Bowen's Brigade, killed at Shiloh.	MORE 4 May 1862
KERR, Dr. John D. son/Prof. W.D. at the Deaf and Dumb Asylum 1 May in his 26th yr.	FULT 13 May 1864
KERRIGAN, Patrick found drowned. Laborer, left family on Cherry betw Main-2nd.	MORE 7 Sep 1862
KERRIGAN, William, funeral notice. Lived at 81 Spruce.	MORE 16 Oct 1864
KERWIN, Dennis killed hunting near Meramec Station. From New York City, left wife and child. Interred in the east.	MORE 17 Oct 1865
KESSLER, John H., an old policeman, 8 Nov at his home on Menard near 18th. Left family. Eight years on the force, "efficient yet humane."	MORE 8 & 9 Nov 1862
KETCHUM, Frank Bowman youngest child of Ewing C. and Louisa 25 Nov of scarlet fever ae 7y 2m 102. Lived at 8th & Locust.	MORE 26 Nov 1861
KETCHUM, Isaac F., hospital chaplain at Benton Barracks, 13 May ae 67. Born in Poughkeepsie, entered the ministry of the Dutch Reformed Church in 1818; minister, then Indian agent; farmed several years. (long obituary)	MORE 16 Jun 1863
KETCHUM, James in Howard Co. 17 Sep of brain congestion ae 15.	COWS 29 Sep 1865
KETERSTEIN, Olga Anna dau/F.W. and Mary, ae 3y 11m. Interred Bellefontaine.	MORE 22 Dec 1863
KETTERER, John H. 29 Jan near the Arsenal, 2 days short of his 21st year. Funeral from St. Louis University; Assumption Church; interred Calvary.	MORE 31 Jan & 5 Feb 1865
KEY, Louisa A. wife of Jefferson and dau/Richmond Pearson in Audrain Co. 8 Jun of consumption, ae 31.	MORE 19 Jun 1864
KEYES, Robert, pilot of the *Lafayette*, at Baton Rouge of typhoid, ae 60.	MORE 16 Aug 1863
KEYS, Mrs. Nancy P. wife of Robert 22 Jul ae 51y 6m. Funeral from Centenary Methodist Church. Interred Bellefontaine.	MORE 25 Jul 1861
KIBBEE, Miss Harriet at Ninevah, Lincoln Co. 13 Jun of congestive fever in 18th y.	MORE 31 Jul 1863
KIDD, James, prisoner; of Boone's Reg., captured in Jefferson City 10 Nov; died 10 Dec of erysipelas. (Undertaker's list)	MORE 12 & 15 Dec 1862
KIDWELL, Washington R. in Portland 21 Apr in his 53rd year; tribute by Williamsburg Lodge AF & AM.	FULT 29 Apr 1864
KIELY, John; Timothy F. Slattery on trial for his murder.	MORE 24 Jul 1863
KIESECKY, Christian, a Pole, drowned Thursday when he rode one of his teams into a quarry pond betw Carondelet-Barry-Victor despite warnings that it sloped abruptly. Fell off, drowned, horses swam to shore. Lived on Columbus near Benton, left wife and 2 children.	MORE 25 Jul 1863
KIGER, Robert L. 2 Nov of consumption in his 29th year.	MORE 4 Nov 1864
KILBURN, Sarah Maria wife of Artemus 15 Jun of chronic diarrhoea ae 36y 8m 19d. Burlington & Northfield VT, Keene NH & Boston pc	MORE 17 Jun 1865
KILLIAN, Mary Jane wife of B. Doran 25 Jan of consumption ae 26y 8m 13d. Funeral from Assumption Church, interred Calvary. Lived at Russell-Gravois.	MORE 26 Jan 1864
Sue, sister of B. Doran, 17 Sep of typhoid ae 19, at Russell-Gravois. Funeral from the "Catholic Church on Sydney St." to Calvary Cem.	MORE 18 Sep 1864
KILLORAN, Patrick 14 Nov ae 28; native of Co. Sligo, IRE. Funeral from the home of his brother-in-law Lawrence Gannon, 42 Carr.	MORE 15 Nov 1865
KILLORAN, Thomas 15 Jan of inflammation of the lungs, ae 50, at 161 14th St.	MORE 17 Jan 1862

KILPATRICK, Dr. T.J. 6 Aug in his 54th year, ill several months; funeral from the   MORE 7 Aug 1864
     home of his brother-in-law John S. Smithers, 48 S. 5th.

KIMBALL, Rev. James 16 Mar of heart disease at the home of his son-in-law S.B. Kellogg.
     Ae 58, formerly of Oakham MA. Funeral from 1st Presbyterian Church.   SLMD 18 Mar 1861
     Springfield and Boston MA pc.

KINCAID, Peter at St. Albans, Franklin Co., 12 Oct, approximately in his 76th yr.   SLMD 29 Oct 1861
     Native of Edinburgh SCO, citizen of MO 44 years, left large family.

KING, Capt. B.B., killed in Pittsburgh battle, body returned to Marion Co. for burial.   LAJ 1 May 1862

KING, Mrs. Emma Chiles wife of Thomas B. and dau/Mrs. E.A. Chiles and the late   COWS 23 May 1862
     Walter B., at her mother's home in Jefferson City ae 20y 8m 11d.

KING, George Sr. at his home near Manchester 16 Apr ae 80. Born VA, married   MORE 22 Apr 1863
     Miss Caldwell, to MO 1808. Wife died 2 years ago.

KING, James killed by soldiers in lower Cape Girardeau Co.   CHAC 22 Apr 1864

KING, Jimmy B., youngest son/J.C. and E.W., 31 Dec in Lincoln Co. ae 6y 2m 3d.   MORE 22 Jan 1864

KING, Jinnie L. wife of Hon. Robert A. and only dau/James Bibb decd. in Union   MORE 27 Jan 1861
     11 Jan, of typhoid pneumonia, ae 21y 11m 11d. Richmond VA pc

KING, John, inquest: levee laborer, died of congestive chills; left wife and   MORE 21 Mar 1864
     one child on Carr St.

KING, Martin "old and respected citizen," native of Prussia, born 6 Jan 1796.   JEST 23 Jun 1865
     Came to US ca 30 years ago; soldier in Mexican War. Husband, father.

KING, Mary Susan near New Bloomfield 3 Jan ae 6y 2m 18d, dau/William & Sarah Ann.   FULT 11 Jan 1861

KING, Miss Serena Ann ae (22?) at the home of William P. McDonald in Newport,   MORE 16 Apr 1865
     Franklin Co., 10 Apr.

KING, Washington, living at 311 Morgan, 27 Aug of apoplexy. (During a heat wave.)   MORE 31 Aug 1861

KINGDON, Mrs. Mary A. 5 Dec in her 70th year. Funeral from the home of her son,   MORE 7 Dec 1864
     William A. Chouteau, west of 7th St. Baltimore & Washington pc

KINGSBURY, Jerre (Jere) at his home in Howard Co. 5 Apr ae 78y 4m. Born in MA,   COWS 17 Apr 1863
     reared in NJ, married in NC, emigrated to MO in 1818 and settled on
     the farm where he died. Twice married, second wife (1854) was Polly
     Cornelius of Randolph Co. Had 11 children of whom 6 daus and 2 sons
     survive. A Union man.

KINGSTON, William shot by men he had recognized as horse thieves and was trying   LAJ 24 Dec 1864
     to stop; they were said to be brothers John and James Lindsey of near
     Paris, Monroe Co. Kingston left wife and children. (CAWN 14 Jan 1865
     refers to Lindseys as "the mule thieves.")

KINKEAD, Capt. Samuel at his home in St/ Francois Co. 20 Sep in his 75th year,   MORE 5 Oct 1862
     one of MO's earliest settlers.

KINKEAD, Sarah dau/Alexander, Sr. 2 June in St. Louis Co. ae 23. (The same   MORE 6 Jun 1865
     paper reported deaths of 2 young children of Alexander, Jr., on
     10 and 25 May.)

KINKLE, Emily Catherine dau/Dr. J.C. and Loveday 29 Mar ae 6y 2m. Baltimore   MORE 2 &
                                                                  & Hagerstown pc   4 Apr 1862
     James Clinton, 5th and only (sic) son of Dr. J.C. and L.G. 11 Sep at   MORE 18 Sep 1863
     Perry Springs, of pericarditis, in his 11th year.

KINNEY, James, native of Ireland, at his home on the Salt River 17 May at a very   LAJ 8 Jul 1865
     old age. One of the county's first settlers.

KINSEY, Thomas J. at Knob View 23 Jul ae 41. Cincinnati & Pittsburgh pc   MORE 25 Jul 1865
     Masonic resolution from St. James, mentions widow and child.   " 12 Oct "

KINSEY, Capt. Zebulon, well-known commander and owner of the Independence, fell   MORE 2 May 1865
     downstairs at his boarding house, fractured skull. Resident of Dubuque
     where his daughter lives, invalid wife now in OH.

KIRBY, Franklin youngest son/Capt. F.F. and Kate 3 Mar of typhoid ae 10y 8m.   COWS 13 Mar 1863

KIRBY, Dr. J.H., an old citizen, suddenly Wednesday last; took strychnine or some   PALS 1 Jan 1864
     other poison; was suffering from a painful disease. Wife, several children.

KIRBY, Mrs. Mary, dau/Jacob and Eliza Shaffner, 2 Nov ae 40 after a long, painful   MORE 3 Nov 1864
     illness. Funeral from the home of S.C. McCormick, 10 betw Warren-Montgomery.

KIRBY, Zillah dau/John and Ann 25 Mar ae 4y 8m 19d, at 281 S. 2nd.   MORE 27 Mar 1863

KIRCHNER, Clara wife of Jacob 4 Sep ae 27y 6m, at 6th betw Edmond-Charles.   SJH 4 Sep 1865

KIRK, Mrs. Helen M. wife of Abel D. and dau/Mrs. Mary A. Donovan of Sparta MO 11 Sep. Left a young child.	MORE 25 Sep 1863
KIRK, "Brigadier Gen. Joe," a bushwhacker, killed by a German citizen of Lafayette Co. (Chillicothe Chronicle)	LIT 7 Nov 1862
KIRK, Thomas ae (26? 28?) 10 Jul at Sisters Hospital; a policeman, stabbed while arresting Charles Zuckschwerdt. Mother 2 sisters dependent on him.	MORE 11 Jul 1861
KIRKBRIDE, Jonathan son/Jonathan and Mary W. of Columbia in Morrisville, Bucks Co. PA 6 Sep in his 5th year.	COWS 20 Sep 1861
KIRKER, John killed by guerillas. (Carrollton Democrat 5 Aug)	MORE 12 Aug 1864
KIRKPATRICK, Hardeman killed by soldiers in lower Cape Girardeau Co.	CHAC 22 Apr 1864
KIRKPATRICK, John in Lexington 11 Apr ae 42.	MORE 17 May 1864
KLAUSMANN, Charles ae 6y 4m drowned at the foot of Vine St. while trying to get a drink. Mother lives (in? on?) Carondelet.	MORE 10 Jul 1861
KLEIN, Mrs. Caroline, mother of Jacob and Lena, 27 Jan at her home, east side of Decatur betw Geyer-Allen. Ill 8 months. Ae (53? 58?)y 9m 18d.	MORE 29 Jan 1864
KLEIN, Hannah, servant at Patterson's Boarding House, 11-Biddle, killed by the accidental discharge of a pistol.	MORE 2 Nov 1864
KLEINMANN, Gottfried, 27 Jun ae 52y 5m at 7th-Spruce.	MORE 29 Jun 1863
KLIECKER, Charles, ca 16, drowned in a pond near the City Hospital Tuesday.	MORE 8 Jun 1865
KLINE, Louis, lately a policeman, suicide by poison. Recently dismissed from the force for tippling in a saloon while on duty. Had been on force only about 2 months. Left family in destitute circumstances.	MORE 13 Nov 1862
KLOSTERMAN, Henry 9 Jul ae 34 at Cass & Pratte.	MORE 10 Jul 1864
KLOTZ, Victor, native of Alsace living at 19th-St. Charles, 23 Mar ae 31.	MORE 25 Mar 1864
KNAPP, Albert Leo son/E.J. and Emily 8 Sep ae 4y 1m 7d.	SJH 9 Sep 1864
KNAPPER, Frederick, a tobacco roller ae 21, stabbed by Clemence Kramer. Lived on High St. betw Biddle-O'Fallon, left wife, 2 sisters, a brother on the police force. (Also shown as KNIPPER; Kramer also CREAMER)	MORE 23 Feb 1865
KNEEDLER, James E. of Louisiana MO 5 Jan in St. Louis of typhoid ae 31y 7m. Left wife, mother, sister "only son and brother." (A confusing item; he became ill in St. Louis but may have died in Louisiana.)	LAJ 15 Jan 1863
KNEISLEY, Ann wife of James at the home of her brother, William McLeod, in McDonough Co. IL Sunday last. Interred Palmyra.	PALS 30 Sep 1864
KNEEVES, William H. ae (43?) at #6 Market St. Interred Bellefontaine.	MORE 12 Aug 1861
KNIGHT, Mrs. Anna, wife of Godfrey and mother of James K. of St. Louis, 7 Mar of apoplexy in Kalamazoo Co. MI, in her 68th year.	MORE 18 Mar 1863
KNOBLOCH, Nicholas (family in Pittsburgh) killed in the Camp Jackson affair.	SLMD 21 May 1861
KNOWLES, Harry T. only child of Henry and Eliza 12 Sep ae 1y 7m.	MORE 15 Sep 1861
KNOX, Lizzie Gertrude, youngest dau/Timothy H. decd and R.S.C., 21 Aug of typhoid ae 6y 7m 2d, at the nw corner of 18th & Christy, her mother's home.	MORE 22 Aug 1864
KOERPER, John, a barber, killed in the Camp Jackson affair.	MORE 18 May 1861
KOHLMEYER, Amelia wife of Christian 14 Dec ae 22.	LIT 15 Jan 1864
KONIG, Urban, a street inspector in the 3rd & 4th wards, fell downstairs at the home of Fritz Heldecker, 4th near Hazel, during a dancing party. He was 30, left a wife and 2 children.	MORE 12 May 1863
KOONTZ, Joseph and Charles, shot near Syracuse 29 Aug, considered Southern sympathizers. (Central MO Advertiser)	CAWN 12 Sep 1863
KORFF, Charles, Chariton Co.: Public Administrator took over his estate.	CECB 24 Jul 1862
KOWER, Frederick, 4 Mar ae 41 at Hickory near Stoddard.	MORE 5 Mar 1863
KRAEMER, George at Hermann, former teller of the Franklin Savings Institution of St. Louis, 29 Oct ae 33 after a long, painful illness.	MORE 2 Nov 1864
KRAETTLE, Peter 23 Dec -- Masonic tribute from Hermann lodge. Left wife and several children.	MORE 13 Feb 1864
KRAMER, Henry, a butcher ae ca 25, rode his horse into a pond on Easton betw Clay and Pratte, was thrown and drowned.	MORE 12 Apr 1861
KRAMER, Mrs. Margaret M. 1 Jul in Hannibal, ae 24. Dau/Rev. M.M. Barron.	HAM 4 Jul 1861

KRAPP, Dominick killed by the fall of earth near Sidney, betw 9-10. Left wife and 5 children.	MORE 8 Nov 1863
KRAUSSE, Herman 1 May ae 33, on 13th betw Chouteau-Hickory. Interred Bellefontaine.	MORE 2 May 1864
KRETSCHMAR, Frederick in his 59th year. (Long article; native of Westphalia, born at Hagen 11 Aug 1806, to US 1830, married in Philadelphia 1832, to Cape Girardeau 1836, St. Louis 1838. Lived 13th-Chouteau. Left widow and large family.	MORE 2 May 1865
Fred M., inquest: lived 13th & Chouteau, died 19 Aug in his 31st year, apparently of an overdose of laudanum. Unmarried.	MORE 20 Aug 1865
KRETSCHMAR, Mollie E. wife of Lou T. at Arkadelphia AR 14 Nov ae 18y 1m 5d.	MORE 30 Nov 1865
KRIBBEN, Christian 14 June, born in Cologne 5 May 1821, to St. Louis June 1835, a year later to St. Charles, back to St. Louis 1846. On Doniphan's Expedition. Leaves 2 children.	MORE 16 Jun 1865
Edith, wife of Christian and dau/John and Edith Delafield, of a lingering illness, ae 28. Funeral Grace Church, interred Bellefontaine. Memphis, Cincinnati, New York, Liverpool pc	MORE 29 Mar 1864
KRIEG, J., a tinner, suddenly Friday night. Member of the Turners and German dragoons. Buried Picott's German Protestant cemetery.	SLMD 21 Jan 1861
KRIEGER, Charles, inquest: run over by Iron Mtn RR flat cars. Left 2 children.	MORE 13 Nov 1865
KRITSER, Theodore W. at the home of his father in Jackson Co. 5 Jul ae 28y 10d.	SLMD 13 Aug 1861
KROFT, Throngott returned from New Orleans, died of heart disease at the tea table.	MORE 25 Sep 1865
KROUSE, Edward drowned in a pond near Grand, ca 22, married, native of Switzerland. A carpenter, also has a brother here.	MORE 5 Sep 1865
KROUSE, Jacob, inquest: a stranger taken in by Jacob Schreiner at Dry Hill, died of debility. Papers indicated he had been picked up, passed, by military.	MORE 15 Feb 1863
KROY, John, 15 Mar ae 38, ill 6 months. Lived on Adams near the Wedge House.	MORE 17 Mar 1865
KRUEER (sic), August, former editor of German papers and current Justice of the Peace 2nd Ward, at his home on Carondelet Ave.	MORE 22 Dec 1863
KRUF, ____, son of Frank, drowned; body recovered by his father.	MORE 16 Jun 1864
KRUST, Christian, ae 8, drowned in a pond at Carondelet, only child of a "respectable German mechanic." Charles Schearloh also drowned.	MORE 21 Apr 1865
KRUTCH, ____ youngest son of Mr. Krutch living in Franklin, run over on the Pacific RR a mile from there Monday, jumping between cars.	MORE 5 Nov 1862
KUHN, Gottlieb Thursday in his 33rd year, on Market betw 17-18.	MORE 7 Feb 1862
KUHN, Jacob, murdered with an ax on the way home from town; Green Willis and Charlie Clark accused (also of murder of John Lohr). Willis subsequently confessed to both murders.	SJH 22 & 23 Dec 1865
KUMP, Christian at the home of his son F.H. 16 Mar ae 64, a resident ca 5 years. Interred Catholic cemetery.	KCJC 17 Mar 1864
KUPFERLE, John 11 Apr of apoplexy ae 53. A brass founder on Broadway, living on Broadway betw Chambers-Madison.	MORE 12 Apr 1863
KURLBAUM, Charles L. son/Jacob D. of St. Louis in Allen KS 20 Jun, ae 29, while en route to New Mexico.	MORE 1 Jul 1862
KURTZEDORN, Jacob W. 20 Oct of heart disease.	MORE 21 Oct 1864
LABARGE, Peter, inquest: hit by a runaway horse when getting off the cars. Foreman at W.C. Turner's millwright shop, leaves wife and 2 daughters, also a brother at Walnut west of 20th, where he was taken after the accident.	MORE 16 Nov 1865
LaBEAU, Chauvin V. 13 Sep in his 52nd year. Native of St. Louis. Funeral St. John's.	MORE 14 Sep 1861
LABEAUME, Louis T. near New London, Ralls Co., 21 Feb ae ca 50.	MORE 26 Feb 1864
LACHANCE, Mary Louise wife of J.D. and dau/Michael and Virginia Schaller 28 Dec ae 26y 1ld, of congestive chills. Funeral from her mother's home, corner Rosatti & Marion.	MORE 29 Dec 1864
LACKAY, Adam drowned in a pond near Leffingwell and Morgan.	MORE 8 Apr 1864
LACKEY, Robert J., obituary (mostly unreadable); born Northumberland Co. VA 1828. Tribute by Masons. Husband, father.	JEST 8 & 15 Apr 1865
LACKLAND, Anna dau/John in Columbia 2 Nov ae 10.	COWS 8 Nov 1861
LACKLAND, Dennis 31 Mar ae 82. Lived in Central Twp. Funeral at Fee Fee Church.	MORE 1 Apr 1864

LACKLAND, Eliot (?), youngest son of Rufus J. and Mary S., ae 9y 6m. Lived on Lucas Place betw 16-17. Interred Bellefontaine.	MORE 4 Jan 1864
LACKLAND, Mary D. wife of James R., in her 30th year. Nee Southern, born in Danville KY 10 Aug 1834, married 23 Oct 1856; lived on 8th betw Chouteau & Gratiot; left husband and child. Louisville, True Presbyterian pc	MORE 13 Feb 1864
LACKLAND, Mary D. wife of Norman of Mexico MO at the home of her mother, Mary G. Otey, in St. Charles 4 Feb. Richmond & Lynchburg VA pc	MORE 9 Feb 1861
LACKNER, Mathias, employe at Christian Reineke's dairy, Manchester-Chouteau, asphyxiated in a cistern of malt. Reineke died trying to help him.	MORE 2 Mar 1861
LACROIX, Lucille widow of Lucien, 9 Jun. Funeral from the home of Joseph Widen, Leffingwell betw Green-Morgan.	MORE 11 Jun 1863
LACY, Julia Lee youngest dau/Minerva A. and the late Lewis F., 23 Oct ae 9y 3m 9d.	MORE 25 Oct 1865
LACY, William H. son of R.D. 18 Mar of consumption ae ca 20. Methodist.	HAM 19 Mar 1861
LADEW, Charles of St. Louis accidentally killed in a fall downstairs at his hotel in Kansas City, 4 Jun.	MORE 5 & 10 Jun 1862
LADY, Leonora wife of John 7 May in her 51st year, at 145 Chestnut. Funeral from Immaculate Conception Church, interred Calvary.	MORE 8 May 1862
LAFLIN, Anna Belle 2nd dau/Sylvestre H. and Anna, 3 Mar ae 4y 4m at 206 Olive.	MORE 5 Mar 1861
LaFORCE, W.W. of Columbia "away from home;" had gone to Omaha intending to go into business, died 21 May. (Omaha Nebraskian)	COWS 2 Jun 1865
LaFRANCE, Charles, native of St. Louis, 17 Feb of consumption. Funeral from father's home, 94 Brooklyn. In 32nd year. Interred Bellefontaine.	MORE 18 Feb 1861 SLMD "
LAIR, Marion of Ralls Co. shot by Gen. Merrill at Palmyra in retaliation for the murder of an old man named Allmstedt at the time of Porter's Raid into Palmyra. (Palmyra Courier)	CAWN 1 Nov 1862
LAKE, Eleazer, of Scotland Co., shot by Gen. Merrill at Palmyra. (see above item)	CAWN 1 Nov 1862
LAKIN, Eliza Ann wife of Jordan at her home 3 miles north of Carrollton 30 May in her 41st year.	MORE 5 Jun 1861
LAMAR, William H. of Poindexter's Band, resident of Randolph Co., arrested in Chariton Co. 8 Aug, in Gratiot Prison of pneumonia.	MORE 20 & 22 Nov 1862
LAMBERSON, David B. 6 Mar in his 47th year. Funeral from the home of his son-in-law, Fred Brasher, 12th near Hickory. Jamaica LI pc	MORE 8 Mar 1862
LAMBERT, Mary wife of Charles 28 Oct ae 32, on Warren betw 14-15.	MORE 29 Oct 1863
LAMPKIN, Hiram, 15 Mar at 107 N. 3rd. Canada pv	MORE 17 Mar 1865
LAMPTON, Joshua D. "Cap" in Boone Co. 20 Jan.	COWS 3 Feb 1865
LAMPTON, Lucinda wife of Beverly in Platte Co. ae (42?).	LIT 15 Sep 1865
LAMPTON, Martha Sue consort of Elder E.J. 6 Apr in Randolph Co. ae 20y 3m 11d. Left husband, mother, friends.	MAG 15 Apr 1863
LANCASTER, James 31 Jul at Cadet MO in his 55th year; native of Orange Co. VA. Spent the last 30 years as a citizen of Washington Co.	MORE 3 Aug 1864
LANCASTER, Jeremiah 20 Jun ae 82 at the home of J.H.C. Phillips. Born St. Mary's Co. MD, emigrated to Washington Co. KY, then MO. Presbyterian.	PALS 26 Jun 1863
LANCE, Melinda 4 Apr ae ca 15.	LIT 8 Apr 1864
LANDON, Dr. G.W.H. 4 Nov ae 58y 4m 10d. Once a member of the OH legislature. Interred Wyandot City KS	SJH 5 & 6 Nov 1863
LANE, Henry T. 27 Apr ae 23.	MORE 30 Apr 1865
LANE, James, of Macon Co., thrown from a horse at Macon City Saturday week.	MORE 2 Oct 1865
LANE, Jesse Hardiman at Lane's Landing 9 Sep ae 36. Married Monica E. Glasscock. A Mason.	CHAC 11 Sep 1863
LANE, John, a guerilla, killed in Linn Co.	MORE 14 Jan 1865
LANE, Mrs. Margaret B., relict of James S. and dau/late Gov. Ninian Edwards of IL, 3 Sep ae 56. St. Michael's Church, interred Calvary.	MORE 5 Sep 1863
LANE, Mary Ewing wife of the late Dr. William Carr, 3 Nov ae 71.	MORE 4 Nov 1865
LANE, Mary N. relict of Washington at her home in Lewis Co. 24 Jan.	CANP 29 Jan 1863
LANGDEAN, Lillie dau/Lawrence and Laura 5 Oct of diphtheria ae 11y 2m 3d.	MORE 7 Oct 1861
LANGEMANN, Henry 21 Feb at the home of Joseph Drepe, ae 30.	FULT 26 Feb 1864

LANGLEY, Archibald, taken in Callaway Co. 10 Nov, in Gratiot Prison of rubeola   MORE 17 &
            14 Feb. (also on undertaker's list)   22 Feb 1863
LANGLY, Payton and wife in Callaway Co., suicide pact, result of jealousy; he   LIT 11 Aug 1865
            shot her, then himself. (FULT)
LANHAM, Joseph B., oldest son/Philip and Sarah L., in St. Louis Co. 28 Mar ae 11y 4d. MORE 30 Mar 1864
LANIER, James of Andrew Co. sentenced to be shot at Savannah 10 June for "giving aid LIT 27 May 1864
            to the rebellion" etc.
    SJH 11 June, reporting the execution, gives his name as Joseph.
LANSING, Charles Robert, eldest son/Charles F. and Adelaide V., at Warsaw MO   MORE 18 Sep 1865
            12 Sep ae 5y 11m 10d.
LANSING, Susan, ae 8, burned when her clothing caught fire. Mother, a   MORE 27 Aug 1865
            "respectable widow" lives at Cass & 20th.
LAPPE, Conrad, agent of a singing society, killed on Walnut St. in the Camp
                                                                Jackson affair. MORE 14 May 1861
LARIMORE, Harriet wife of Wilson in St. Louis Co. 10 Aug in her 54th year.   MORE 21 Aug 1864
            KY & Cincinnati pc
LARIMORE, Susie wife of N.G. and youngest dau/Levi Ashbrook 27 Jul ae 25y 6m 8d. MORE 29 Jul 1862
            Covington & Winchester pc
LARKIN, Joseph 17 Sep in his 58th year, at 97 Mulberry. New York & San Franc. pc MORE 18 Sep 1864
LaROSE, Paul, citizen of Ste. Genevieve, 20 Jan of pneumonia. (Undertaker's list) MORE 22 Jan 1865
LARSH, Abraham at his home in Lafayette Co. 2 Dec ae 85; native of Baltimore.   LEXUN 21 Jan 1865
LASWELL, Hester, nee Sheckel, consort of Charles, 13 Apr. Born in Nelson Co. KY CANP 12 May 1864
            in 1807; Methodist since 1823. (Letter from David Shackelford, Colony MO)
LATHAM, Miss Martha at Novelty, Knox Co. in July in her 21st year. Baptist.   PALS 18 Sep 1863
LATIMER, Eveline E. dau/John, near Florissant, 16 Sep ae 29y 8m 26d.   MORE 27 Sep 1865
            John, at his home near Florissant, 9 Nov ae 55y 8m 1d. Native of VA. MORE 14 Nov "
LATOUR, Armand, a Belgian carpenter, killed in the Camp Jackson affair. Lived   MORE 14 &
            on O'Fallon near 24th.   18 May 1861
LATOURETTE, Henry drowned from the Robert Campbell Jr. at Sioux City 18 Apr in   MORE 3 May 1863
            his 43rd year. "Kind and affectionate husband and father."
LATTIN, Mrs. Ellen at the home of her brother-in-law Laselle McCoy, of   MORE 13 Jan 1864
            pneumonia, ae 53. Natchez & New Orleans pc
LAUCK, Alice youngest dau/Lewis M. and Emily J. 19 Jun ae 3y 8m, at 218 Chestnut. MORE 20 Jun 1863
LAUGHTON, Jack, inquest: ae 64, found dead in bed, Webster betw Broadway-9th.   MORE 28 Apr 1864
            Heart disease.
LAVEILLE, Thomas at Sisters Hospital 5 Sep ae 28.   MORE 6 Sep 1865
LAWLESS, H.H.(?), citizen of Cooper Co. (Undertaker's list)   MORE 9 Jan 1865
LAWRENCE, Emma wife of Solomon, at 6th betw O'Fallon-Cass. Quincy & Keokuk pc   MORE 31 May 1865
LAWRENSEN, Thomas J. 22 Sep in Potosi at the home of Maj. John Deane, ae 25. He MORE 24 Sep 1864
            was a lawyer, born in Ireland.
LAWSON, Lizzie Clay only dau/William R.B. and P.C. in Boonville 6 Jan in her 19th y. COWS 22 Jan 1864
LAWSON, Mason 7 May at the home of his brother-in-law Philip Baker, after a   PALS 15 May 1863
            long illness.
LAWSON, MRS. Sue of consumption (11 Apr?) ae 24.   MORE 21 Apr 1863
LAWSON, William D. at the post hospital in Lebanon 11 Dec ae 20.   MORE 23 Dec 1863
LAWSON, William P. 1 Feb ae 89.   MORE 3 Feb 1865
LAX, Hattie youngest child of E.C. and H.A. 18 Aug of dysentery ae 18m 9d.   MORE 23 Aug 1861
LAYPOLE, Nelson (paper folded, name not clear), Irish, found dead in woods. Thought LAJ 12 Dec 1863
            to have frozen while "under the influence."
LEA, Albert son of John and Jane 21 Apr ae 10m. Cincinnati & Newport KY pc   MORE 23 Apr 1861
            Jane wife of John 27 Feb ae 29. Cincinnati & Trenton NJ pc   MORE 1 Mar 1863
LEAHY, Michael, native of Limerick (which pc) at Sisters Hospital of typhoid ae 22. MORE 5 Nov 1865
LEAR, Johnson son/Thomas and Julia Ann of Marion Co. 26 Aug in Virginia City,   PALS 21 Oct 1864
            Nevada Terr.
LEARNED, Daniel D.P. son/Henry 24 Apr ae 21y 5m 13d, at 16 Gay St. CA & Boston pc MORE 25 Apr 1863
LEARY, Arthur A. 15 Aug of consumption ae 26. Memphis pc   MORE 10 Sep 1865

LEARY, Dennis Sunday while riding a fractious horse, which threw him and then fell on him. Lived at 231 O'Fallon, left a family.	MORE 15 Jul 1862
LEAVENWORTH, Ralph B. 18 Jun ae 43. Interred Bellefontaine.	MORE 19 Jun 1865
LEAVER, Mrs. Margaret 27 Mar in her 68th year. Funeral from the home of her brother Joseph Goodfellow, St. Louis Co., to Centenary Methodist Church.	MORE 29 Mar 1864
LEAVITT, Obediah killed some time last winter in Oregon Co. -- Thomas J. Thorpe sentenced to be hanged for the murder.	MORE 12 Aug 1864
LeBEAU, children of John B. and Ophelia: Amanda Sylvanie burned when playing hide-and-seek; had gone into a room alone. 19 Jan ae 4y 5m. Lived at Ohio & Rosatti, interred Calvary.	MORE 21 & 21 Jan 1861
Edward Augustus ae 11y 8m9d oc brain congestion. Funeral from home, Ohio-Rosatti, to Assumption Church, interred Calvary.	MORE 22 Jan 1865
LeBEAUE, Oliver, a young man, drowned at the foot of Carr St. Friday while painting the hull of a steamboat; the platform was submerged by waves from a passing ferry.	MORE 4 Jul 1865
LEBENDOFF, ___, an old German found dead in bed at his home, 5th betw Carr-Biddle; "want of attention and exposure."	MORE 28 Dec 1864
LEDERER, Elizabeth, drowned herself in the river from the Illinois side, apparently disappointed in matrimony by Antone Funkhauser. (see his name also)	MORE 7 Jun 1865
LEDFORD, Mrs. Nancy at her home in Ralls Co. 3 Feb ae 78y 4m 15d. Dau/Nathaniel W. Ralls, born VA, emigrated young to KY; married Capt. James Ledford in Bath Co. ca 1798, came to MO 1831. Baptist.	HAM 12 Feb 1861
LEDUC, Amaranthe wife of Louis Sr. 22 Nov after a brief painful illness, at the home, 27 N. 7th. Ae 66y 9m 12d. Interred Calvary.	MORE 23 Nov 1864
LEDUC, Mary Josephine dau/Joseph and Margaret 26 Feb ae 1y 14d, on 7th St. betw Franklin-Wash.	MORE 28 Feb 1861
LEE, Adkison H. 5 Apr in Howard Co., of typhoid, in his 56th year; a citizen of Boone Co. 33 years. Buried by Freemasons, of which he was a member.	COWS 17 Apr 1863
LEE, Miss Aura J. 28 Feb of consumption at the home of William P. Swank in Matthews Prairie, ae 22y 5m 2d. Born Hardin Co. KY, to Mississippi Co. MO in 1856 to live with Mrs. Swank, her sister. Since then, a brother and sister have died.	CHAC 4 Mar 1864
LEE, David of Ripley Co. in the Myrtle Street Prison hospital.	MORE 3 Sep 1863
LEE, Douglas 3 Oct at Atlanta IL ae 20y 9m; funeral from the home of his brother Alfred, 311 Pine St.	MORE 6 Oct 1865
LEE, Mrs. E.H.B. in Dover, widow of Edward and dau/James and Phebe Warren, 26 Feb.	MORE 20 Mar 1863
LEE, George Thayer son/Alfred and Sarah G. 4 Jul ae 6.	MORE 8 Jul 1862
LEE, Henry 30 Mar ae 83 at the home of his son James in Charleston. Born in MD, in 1781; to Bullitt Co. KY, to Cape Girardeau 1848. Wife died 1854. Catholic.	CHAC 8 Apr 1864
LEE, Joseph ae 10 killed while playing in Hide & Patterson's Warehouse at Main & Green when an employee pushing a hand truck knocked down some bundles of iron, which fell on Joseph. His father, a tailor, worked on Main St.	MORE 4 May 1865
LEE, Martha A. wife of Josiah and dau/Thomas Warren of Livingston Co. in Carroll Co. 2 Jan ae ca 37.	MORE 17 Jan 1861
LEE, Poliche wife of the late Maj. Gen. Elliott 30 Sep ae 60, at Main-Poplar. (SLMD 8 Oct gives name as Polegia.)	MORE 1 Oct 1861
LEE, Robert, a child, inquest: lit matches and burned himself to death. Parents live on 9th betw O'Fallon-Cass.	MORE 14 Nov 1862
LEE, Col. Stephen at his home on Centre St. 20 Sep in his 74th year. Formerly of Maysville KY, veteran of the War of 1812; was at Ft. Meigs and others with Gen. Harrison, later Gen. Scott. Episcopal Church to Baptist Cemetery.	HAM 26 Sep & 3 Oct 1861
LEE, Thomas in St. Charles Co. 8 Nov. Funeral from the home of Hampton Woodruff, 28 S. 16th.	MORE 11 Nov 1864
LEE, Thomas Sr. 16 Sep of dropsy ae 57, at Webster betw 10-11. Buffalo pc	MORE 17 Sep 1864
LEE, Woodruff H. Tuesday ae ca 35; left wife and 4 or 5 small children.	PALS 1 Sep 1865
LeFAIVRE, Charles at Portage des Sioux 11 Mar of typhoid ae ca 47. CA pc	MORE 16 Mar 1863
LEFFINGWELL, Loura Grace only dau/Hiram and Susan M. in Kirkwood 7 Aug of whooping cough ae 1y 2m 17d.	SLMD 13 Aug 1861
LEFTRIDGE, William in workhouse cell of cerebral congestion; ca 46, native of OH. Former steamboat engineer.	MORE 4 Jan 1861

LEGET, Mary at the home of her father in Marion Co. 17 Sep ae ca 24.	HAM 17 Oct 1861
LEGG, Colmore Lovelace at the home of his father in Lewis Co. 20 Aug ae 20y 8m.	SLMD 29 Aug 1864
LEGGETT, Joseph B. at Gravois Coal Mines 4 Jan ae 31, formerly of Guelph, Can. West.	MORE 12 Jan 1861
LEGUERRIER, Charles Sr. at the home of his daughter Mrs. Vien, 17 Feb ae 54.	MORE 19 Feb 1863
LEIGHTON, Joseph Sr. 4 Dec at a very advanced age at the home of his son-in-law, Orlando Austin 4 Dec after a short illness.	PALS 11 Dec 1863
LEISTER, Philip, killed in the Camp Jackson affair; son of Elizabeth, ae 18, a brick moulder, born Philadelphia, sole support of 5 little brothers & sisters.	MORE 14 & 15 May 1861
LEITENSDORFER, Euphrosine widow of Col. Eugene 27 Jul ae (70?). Interred at their home in Carondelet.	MORE 29 Jul 1864
LeMETRE, Louis, inquest: lived on Louis near Levee, left wife, 1 child. Apoplexy.	MORE 3 Sep 1863
LEMMON, Mrs. Susan 14 Apr ae 63. Pittsburgh pc	MORE 15 Apr 1861
LEMP, Adam 22 Aug after a short illness; funeral from his late home, Lemp's Cave.	MORE 24 Aug 1862
LENOIR, Fannie C. wife of Dr. W.T. 13 Apr in Boone Co. ae 29.	COWS 15 Apr 1864
LENOX, John, heirs of, named in a suit in Dent Co.: W.J., D.W., John T., Mary E., Martha J., Frances M.; suit by John Arthur to collect on mortgage given him by John Lenox decd & wife Elizabeth 13 Nov 1860.	ROLEX 31 Jul 1865
LEONARD, Judge Abiel in Howard Co. 28 Mar in his 66th year. Born Windsor VT 16 Mar 1797, to MO 1818, etc. (a long obituary)	MORE 5 Apr 1863
LEONARD, Benjamin G., oldest son/Nathaniel and Margaret of Cooper Co., 3 Sep ae 32.	MORE 8 Sep 1865
LEONARD, Mrs. Georgianna, inquest: wife of Johnson, an actor at the St. Louis Theatre, living at 102 S. 4th; had a habit of drinking liquor mixed with laudanum and was (understandably) found dead in bed.	MORE 2 Oct 1862
LEONARD, Oscar J., printer, recently employed by SJH, murdered by Indians a few days ago in an attack on emigrant train. Mother said to live in Louisiana, Pike Co.; father on way to Idaho.	SJH 18 Aug 1864
LEONARD, Richard G. formerly of Columbia in St. Louis 30 Jan of pneumonia.	COWS 3 Feb 1865
LEOPARD, John A. of Boone Co. shot and instantly killed by Alfred Wells near Boydsville, Callaway Co. Tuesday night; they had been friends. (LAJ 21 Aug gives killer's name as Alfred Benjamin.)	COWS 8 Aug 1862
LEOPARD, Nancy Jane wife of Arner B. and dau/C. Clatterbuck of Callaway Co. at her home in Boone Co. 23 Dec of pneumonia ae 20y 4m 14d.	COWS 15 Jan 1864
LEOPOLD, Mrs. Rosanna 23 May of fever following variola, at 108 Green St. in 28th y.	MORE 25 May 1863
LePAGE, Louis 8 Jul at Portage des Sioux ae 62y 3m.	MORE 13 Jul 1865
LEPERE, Martin Sr. of Central Twp. 30 Jan ae 68.	MORE 31 Jan 1862
LESSLEY, John 31 Dec ae 54.	BOL 5 Jan 1861
LESSLEY, Joseph, war prisoner, 2 Feb of variola. (Undertaker's list)	MORE 15 Feb 1863
LETCHER, Isaac A. 1 May in his 42d year. Interred Bellefontaine.	MORE 3 May 1865
LETCHWORTH, James M., formerly of Clay Co., killed by soldiers at St. Joseph; was beaten, shot. Had been a Secessionist but lately said to have supported the Union. (RICON al May gives name as J.H.)	LIT 15 & 22 May 1863
LEVERING, Euphemia A.B. wife of Septimus of St. Louis 21 Oct at the home of Mrs. J. Haslam, Dorris Row, Olive St., ae 39. Interred Bellefontaine.	MORE 22 Oct 1861
LEVERING, Charles W. 21 Mar ae 51 at the home of Mr. Simmons, 118 Olive.	MORE 22 Mar 1864
LEVIN, Heyman after a long painful illness, ae(63?65?) Lived on 7th betw Chouteau-Papin. Interred Bellefontaine.	MORE 29 Nov 1862
LEVINDROW, Peter, a German ae ca 65, of apoplexy.	MORE 22 Mar 1863
LEVY, Patrick, a government teamster recently returned from Little Rock; had a brain injury but was incapable of stating the cause. Abscess developed.	MORE 25 Feb 1865
LEWELLEN, Green, inquest: intemperance and exposure. "Kindly," had led a "harmless, fruitless life." Brother of Richard and late James R.	MORE 17 Feb 1863
LeWELLEN, Sarah wife of Thomas in Monroe Co. 18 Nov ae 27.	COWS 29 Nov 1861
LEWELLEN, James of Ralls Co. drowned trying to cross Salt River in a canoe, at Goodwin's Mill. James Rouse and ___ Hedgepath also drowned.	LIT 2 May 1862
LEWELLIN, James H., inquest: prop. of Douglas House Hotel, stabbed by Geo. Foster in an affray when L. tried to break up a disturbance. Int. Wesleyan.	MORE 17 & 18 Dec 1862

LEWIS, Aaron J. 9 Mar, 5 miles west of Canton. He was born in Christian Co. KY 2 Feb 1799, emigrated to St. Charles Co. MO 1818, to Lewis Co. 24 years ago.	CANP 26 Mar 1863
LEWIS, Asahel Hooker, principal editor of the Mo. Democrat, ae 50. Long illness.	MORE 26 Sep 1862
LEWIS, Basil W., arrested in Taney Co. 11 Nov, 5 Feb in Gratiot Prison of rubeola. (Undertaker's list)	MORE 7 & 8 Feb 1863
LEWIS, Charles L. shot at his home near Cote sans Dessein, about noon; murderer hid behind the stable. He had given information to the federal government. Ca 60, left a "helpless family." (FULT)	CAWN 5 Jul 1862
LEWIS, James, inquest: Irish, lived at O'Fallon & Main; married, no children. Intemperance.	MORE 20 Apr 1864
LEWIS, James stabbed by Patrick White ? Nov at 3rd near Cedar; no known reason.	MORE 14 Nov 1864
LEWIS, James B. fell from verandah while drunk. Married, no children.	MORE 20 Aug 1862
LEWIS, John L. of Lewis & Groshan, 30 Sep ae 35. Funeral from the home of John Christopher, 123 Chestnut.	MORE 1 Oct 1862
LEWIS, Martrom at his home opposite Glencoe, a resident of St. Louis Co. 67 years. Born 19 Oct 1795 on the south branch of the Potomac; married Elizabeth Darby in 1822. Methodist 40 years. Interred family burying ground.	MORE 9 & 12 Apr 1863
LEWIS, N.B. of Platte Co. and Coon Thornton's band "of cutthroats" hanged at Macon "Friday last" ca 38. (Macon Argus)	GAL 20 Apr 1865 SJH 12 Apr "
LEWIS, Thomas M. at his home in Lincoln Co. 4 miles north of Auburn in his 68th y. Born Albemarle Co. VA, to MO 1836. Left widow and numerous offspring.	MORE 19 Apr 1865
LEWIS, Dr. Waldo suddenly at his home in Huntsville in his 38th year.	MORE 24 Sep 1864
LEWIS, William, of Pennick's Reg., suicide by laudanum; despondent over the death of his wife "several weeks ago." (LIT)	RICON 4 Sep 1862
LEWIS, William, Co D43 MO Vols killed at Glasgow.	GAL 17 Nov 1864
LEWNEY, Mary Ann wife of Thomas, 5 Mar. Liverpool and Isle of Man pc.	MORE 12 Mar 1865
LEWRIGHT, Dr. John S. in Washington, MO of consumption in his 66th year, formerly of Union Co. KY. KY pc	MORE 27 Apr 1865
Mrs. Mary in Washington MO 12 Jul of consumption in her 50th year, formerly of Union Co. KY. KY pc	MORE 24 Jul 1865
Bettie A., only dau/Dr. John S., at New Haven, Franklin Co. 8 Aug of consumption.	MORE 12 Aug 1863
LEYLAND, Thomas 2 Mar on Gravois Road, ae ca 38.	MORE 4 Mar 1862
LIDDY, Michael, inquest: run over by street car on Broadway opposite Bates, lived on Wright near 9th; a carpenter, married, no children.	MORE 2 Jan 1865
LIENTZ, Mary C. wife of Montgomery P. in Boone Co. 31 Oct.	COWS 13 Nov 1863
LIGHTFOOT, Benjamin F., river mate, 1 Oct of inflammation of the bowels ae 47. Pittsburgh pc	MORE 3 Oct 1864
LIGHTNER, Lt. Isaac CSA of wounds received at Lost Mountain, LaGrage GA, 23 Jun in his 26th year.	MORE 13 Aug 1864
LIGHTNER, James S. killed at Lexington by a Federal guard who said that Lightner (a violent secessionist, influential and popular citizen), being held, tried to attack him with a chair. Lightner was Director of the Farmers' Bank, a large land owner and trader.	SLMD 6 Aug 1861
LILLARD, Jerry V. tribute by Monticello Lodge #58; died 22 Apr ae 55.	CANP 7 May 1863
LINCOLN, Mrs. America, widow of David, 20 Aug at the home of her son-in-law Wm. W. Estes of a paralytic affliction, ae 65.	LIT 25 Aug & 15 Sep 1865
LINCOLN, David 4 May ae 52.	LIT 9 May 1862
LINCOLN, Mortie wife of George 28 Feb ae ca 20.	LIT 15 Mar 1861
LINDELL, Peter 26 Oct in his 86th year, at Bates & Collins.	MORE 27 Oct 1861
LINDELL, Peter J., nephew of the late Peter, 18 Apr in his 40th year at 87 St. Charles. Left widow, 3 sons. Funeral 1st Methodist Church South.	MORE 20 Apr 1862
LINDELL, William ae 36 at the home of Capt. James J. Davis in DeSoto. Funeral from 8th St. Methodist Church.	MORE 19 Jul 1864
LINDERY, Mrs. Alcey W. 6 Oct ae 62. Funeral from the Christian Church at 8th & Mound. Chester IL, Georgetown & Louisville KY pc	SLMD 8 Oct 1864
LINDLEY, Samuel Glover youngest son/James J. and Josephine at LaGrange ae 10?5m. Davenport & San Fr. pc	MORE 5 May 1864

LINDO, Mary Ann wife of a soldier in the 3rd MO of intemperance ae 43. Lived at 10-   MORE 2 Apr 1863
    O'Fallon-Cass, left daughter ae 23 in indigent circumstances.

LINDSAY, John and James, who recently murdered William Kingston, shot near   LAJ 21 Jan 1865
    Mexico MO Saturday while trying to escape from their guard.

LINDSAY, Mary wife of William 4 Dec at 5th & Cerre, after a long illness. Funeral   MORE 4 Dec 1864
    from Church of the Annunciation, interred Calvary. NY & Washington pc

LINDSEY, Mrs. Alcey W. 6 Oct ae 62. Funeral from the Christian Church, 8th-Mound.   MORE 8 Oct 1864

LINDSLEY, Frank, printer at the Democrat, fell overboard the Warsaw while on an   MORE 6 Jul &
    excursion party, ae 17. Parents live at 143 13th St.   27 Aug 1865

LINDSLEY, Rose youngest dau/Malcolm and Sarah, on 6 Feb.   MORE 7 Feb 1862

LINEN, John "a good fellow with few faults and many friends" done in by liquor.   MORE 11 Jul 1862
    Lived alley betw 9-10-Market-Walnut.

LINGECLOTH, Mrs.(wife of Moritz), Monday; interred St. Charles where she has   MORE 23 Oct 1862
    relatives. He was with the editorial department of Neve Zeit.

LINGO, Lucy, an old VA negro, found dead on Pacific St. east of Summit; heart dis.   MORE 5 Feb 1865

LINKEMEYER, Agatha relict of Henry 25 Mar ae 59y 6m, at 300 S. 3rd.   MORE 26 Mar 1863

LINMAN, James, citizen of Chariton Co., 15 Mar. Chronic diarrhoea. (Undertaker's list)   " 19 Mar 1865

LINN, Edward M., tribute by Paulingville Masons.   MORE 15 Mar 1865

LINN, Julia A. wife of Dr. J.S. and daughter of Francis and Eleanor Watts, in   LAJ 21 Mar 1861
    New Hope, Lincoln Co., 23 Oct 1860.

LINN, "Mrs. Senator" of MO at the home of her son-in-law Dr. P.F. Browne in   MORE 17 Sep 1861
    Accomac Co. VA 3 Sep. Temporarily interred in Judge Bayly's vault, later
    to be moved to Ste. Genevieve.

LINN, Mollie J. wife of Rev. A.P. and daughter of Herod and Edith Glasscock at   CANP 6 Aug 1863
    Paynesville MO 10 Jul; born 9 Nov 1840, married 8 Sep 1856. M.E. Church South.   MORE 19 Jul "

LINN, Capt. Thomas M., a Missouri River pilot, fell from a window in the City   MORE 31 Aug 1862
    Hospital, where he was recovering, 30 Aug ae 56. Marysville CA, Pittsburgh,
    and St. Joseph MO pc

LINN, William L. in Wright City, Warren Co., 24 Sep ae 26y 5d.   MORE 6 Nov 1862

LINNENFELSER, Frederick 28 Oct ae 46.   MORE 30 Oct 1865

LINT, Frederick ae 17, drowned 3 Jun, body found. Father at Columbus-Lesperance.   MORE 11 Jun 1861

LINVILLE, William executed for the murder of Thomas Henry; his mother lived   SJH 7 Nov 1863
    4 miles from Chillicothe.

LIONBERGER, Isaac 16 Feb near Boonville in his 57th year, "one of Cooper County's   COWS 4 Apr 1862
    best citizens."

LIPSCOMB, Mrs. Lucy M.W., daughter of Thomas and Rebecca Wood, at the home of her   PALS 26 May 1865
    son Col. H.S. 24 May. Born 20 Aug 1794 in Madison Co. Va; she married
    Stapletone C. Lipscomb of Fredericksburg VA 9 Sep (1811? 1814?).
    Widowed 10 Jan 1822, came to MO with her brother-in-law William Wright
    in 1824, to Palmyra in 1834.

LIPSMEYER, Bernard, suicide (cut his throat). A teamster, living near Angelrodt-11,   MORE 13 Nov 1863
    had previously been thrown from wagon, possibly had a brain injury
    causing aberrations. Left "feeble" wife and 2-year-old child.

LISLE, Sue daughter of the late R.M. at her mother's home in Jefferson City   SJH 25 May 1864
    20 May of brain congestion in her 20th year.

LITTELL, William T. 11 Nov ae 43; formerly of Newark, 15 years a resident of   MORE 12 &
    St. Louis. Left wife and 1 child. Funeral from home of late Mayor King.   15 Nov 1865

LITTLE, Ida Helen youngest daughter of Samuel H. and Ann, 23 Nov of typhoid   SLMD 3 Dec 1861
    ae 9y 6m 16d. Hagerstown & Williamsport pc

LIVERMORE, Elizabeth Ella, daughter of Emory and C. Mary F. of St. Louis,   MORE 25 Feb 1864
    at St. Paul 21 Feb ae 5.

LIVERMORE, Miss Eliza, living near the cemetery, 1 May of palsy.   SJH 2 May 1865

LIVINGSTON, Francis H., son/Henry and Rachel A., late of Claverick, Columbia Co. NY,   MORE 13 Nov 1861
    11 Nov at Planter's House ae 7y 7d.

LIVINGSTON, John, student at Washington University, 5 Jul ae 23, Funeral from the   MORE 6 Jul 1864
    home of D.B. Gale, 17th-Lucas Place. Albany pc

LIVINGSTON, James I. at home of M.H. Goode near Fenton, late of Cruger IL but for   MORE 24 Nov 1865
    (cont.)

(LIVINGSTON, James, cont.) many years preceding the war a merchant in Versailles,   MORE 24 Nov 1865
    Morgan Co. MO. Moved to IL in 1863. Left widow, sons, daughters.
    Presbyterian. (Tribute by Milton Adkisson, Manchester MO)

LIVINGSTON, James Jr., son/James Sr. and Jane E., at Versailles of spinal meningitis. MORE 21 Jan 1863

LIVINGSTON, William Jackson hanged yesterday as a spy. Born in Shelby Co. KY 1817,   MORE 20 Aug 1864
    to Marion Co. MO (1858?); joined the rebels, was captured inside
    federal lines, imprisoned, escaped. Has wife and sister in Kansas.

LOCK, B.(?) S., prisoner, Co H 5th MO, 17 Nov of chronic diarrhoea. (Undertaker's list) MORE 22 Nov'63

LOCK, John, prisoner, 2 Feb of pneumonia. (Undertaker's list)   MORE 8 Feb 1863

LOCKE, Gennevie E., only daughter of Joseph H. and Cassandra E., ae 19y 6m 6d. MORE 27 Aug&3 Sep 1865

LOCKE, Jesse, member 14th Cav., shot by Michael Gallagher at Banjo Saloon. A quarrel. MORE 4 Nov 1865

LOCKER, William, an old man upwards of (60? 80?) returning home from Gentryville   GAL 26 Jan 1865
    last week, intoxicated, fell off the wagon and was killed. Had considerable
    money with him. "Peculiar. . . dissipated" (Grand River News, no date)

LOCKETT, John Sargeant son/John and Sarah Ann 1 Jul ae 2y 5m 13d.   MORE 2 Jul 1862

LOCKWOOD, _____ an old man living in the vicinity of New Castle, Gentry Co.,   SJH 21 Oct 1864
    "a notorious rebel," recently shot.

LOCUST, Aaron, inquest: lived 7 miles out on Gravois Road. Apoplexy, due to   MORE 7 Jul 1863
    exposure to hot sun.

LOFTS, Martin son/James and Bridget Tuesday, ae 7. Interred Rock Spring.   MORE 14 Jul 1864

LOGAN, Emma D. daughter of John and Drucilla Friday, of measles, ae ca 10.   PALS 22 Apr 1864

LOGAN, Mary Frances wife of Dr. H.B. and daughter of Pines H. Shelton of Hill Co. TX   MORE 29 Jun 1865
    at Wentzville 13 Jun of a protracted illness.

LOGAN, Olive Thomas daughter of Capt. Floyd and Augusta 16 Apr in her 7th year, on   MORE 17 &
    Pine between Leffingwell-Ewing. Cincinnati & Washington DC pc   18 Apr 1863

LOGAN, Hon. Robert A. of DeKalb Monday last, member of the state legislature, ae   SJH 5 Oct 1865
    ca 50. (MORE says Robert W.)   MORE 9 "

LOHFINK, George at Little Rock 16 Jun of typhoid ae 46.   MORE 3 Jul 1864

LOHMAN, William, a Union soldier arrested for desertion (3rd MO Vols.) shot by   MORE 24 &
    guard; had his head out of window, may not have heard guard tell him not   25 Dec 1862
    to. Charge against him was unfounded; he was to have been discharged. The
    guard acted recklessly. Wife found Lohman dead when she came to visit.

LOHR, John, a citizen of Marion Twp., murdered some time ago; Green Willis and   SJH 22 &
    Charlie Clark now being tried for the murder of Jacob Kuhn, Willis   23 Dec 1865
    confessed to that murder as well as that of Lohr.

LOKER, Annie A. only daughter of W.H. and Annie, ae 11y 4m.   MORE 18 Mar 1863
    Mrs. Annie A., wife of W.H. of St. Louis, at St. Mary's Co. MD 9 Aug   " 19 Aug "
    ae 36. Funeral from home of G.H. Loker to St. George's Church.
    Interred Bellefontaine.

LONDREGAN, Edward or Ned: killed in a fracas with fellow police officers, or by   MORE 24-25 Oct &
    two policemen trying to arrest him. Various stories.   1 Nov 1861

LONERGAN, Dr. Thomas L. ae 33. Funeral from St. John's Church, interred Calvary.   MORE 13 Dec 1865

LONG, Col. Alton 7 Feb in his 54th year.   MORE 8 Feb 1865

LONG, Mrs., wife of Dr. Benjamin F., of flux near Barry, Clay Co., during the   SJH 11 Aug 1864
    past week. Ae ca 35. Four others also died.

LONG, Elizmond B. 13 Sep in 13th year, on returning from Texas.   LIT 13 Oct 1865

LONG, Herman N. yesterday of chronic diarrhoea, ae 47, at 24 St. Charles St.   MORE 6 Jan 1865

LONG, I.D. killed by bushwhackers in north Chariton. (Bruns. Central City 7/23)   MORE 29 Jul 1864

LONG, John 18 Oct at his home, 25th & Market, ae 80.   MORE 19 Oct 1865

LONG, John committed suicide after killing Emma Herkenrath. Motive, jealousy. He   MORE 7 Oct 1864
    was in the Enrolled Militia.

LONG, Lewis 8 Nov in St. Joseph ae 44. Baltimore and Leavenworth pc   SJH 9 Nov 1865

LONG, Patrick 7 Jul of continued fever in his 36th year. Funeral from the home   MORE 9 Jul 1865
    of Andrew Smith, 339 7th (betw Cass-O'Fallon).

LONG, Philip G. at his home near Farmington 15 Feb, of dropsy, ae 59.   MORE 5 Mar 1864

LONG, William S. of Poindexter's band in Gratiot Prison 11 Dec, of pneumonia;   MORE 13 &
    captured Boone Co. 18 Oct. (Undertaker's list)   15 Dec 1862

LONGTAIN, Paul at Fort Randall of apoplexy 29 Jul; born St. Louis 26 Oct 1826,   MORE 17 Aug 1863
    a lifetime in the fur trade. Buried with military honors under charge   " 14 & 15 Jul '65
    of Charles Chouteau, leaves son and 2 sisters; will be reinterred in
    St. Louis. (Later) funeral from the home of his brother-in-law William
    Bayes (Boyes?), 44 Cedar; remains being brought from Ft. Randall.

LONGWELL, William 7 Apr in his 61st year. Funeral from the home of his son-in-law   MORE 19 Apr 1861
    B.F. Dix, 14th-Franklin. Interred Bellefontaine.

LOOMIS, Anson 5 Nov in his 49th year. Interred Cleveland.   MORE 6 Nov 1863

LOUDON, Philip, editor of the Sunday Neue Zeit, yesterday; in St. Louis ca 6 months.   MORE 31 Dec 1863
    Novelist, ae 31, native of Prussia.

LOUGHRIDGE, Samuel 1 Dec ae 37. Funeral from the home of his mother, 21 S. 14th.   MORE 4 Dec 1861
    Interred Bellefontaine.

LOVE, Calvin, reportedly shot by Robert W. Swinney near Middle Grove, Monroe Co.   HAM 1 Aug 1861
    Monday last. Political differences.

LOVE, Mary, eldest daughter of James, 25 May ae 25 at 456 Morgan; int. Bellefontaine.   MORE 27 May 1862

LOVELACE, Newton killed near Crow's Cross Roads by soldiers or bushwhackers   LAJ 28 Jan 1865
    passing as soldiers.   PALS 10 Feb "

LOVELADY, Eliza daughter of A.J. suddenly 10 Feb, ae 17.   WEST 27 Feb 1864

LOVING, ___, a young man formerly with Price, in Lincoln Co. last week. (Killed.)   LAJ 27 Mar 1862

LOW, James H. - see James HAMILTON.

LOWE, an old man and his son, lately killed at home by bushwhackers, Chariton Co.   MORE 10 Jan 1865

LOWE, Lamont eldest son/William and the late Mary B., ae (13? 18?)y 6m, at   MORE 8 Jan 1865
    their home, 28 S. 14th, of a lingering illness.

LOWREY, John G., formerly of Bellefonte PA, 21 Jul ae 86.   SLMD 23 Jul 1861

LOWRY, Mrs. Rachel E. 24 Jun in her 70th year. Funeral from the home of her son   MORE 25 Jun 1864
    John H. Lightner, Washington-16th. Interred Bellefontaine. Philadelphia
    & Lancaster pc

LOWRY, Samuel Henry at the home of Mrs. Clapp Sunday ae 40. Funeral St. Xavier's.   MORE 18 Feb 1862

LUCAS, Mrs. Keturah of St. Louis, formerly of Independence; removed to KY by   MORE 5 Feb 1864
    husband and brother to be interred by parents in Laurenceburg.

LUCAS, Thomas killed Sunday night in a groggery. Martin Hill was arrested (but   SJH 19 May 1865
    acquitted, paper of 21 May).

LUCE, Homer J., only son of William and Minerva, in Louisiana MO 12 Jan of   MORE 19 Jan 1863
    consumption ae 25y 10m 24d. Left a young wife, aged parents, 3 little
    children. Leavenworth KS & Warrick IN pc

LUCK, Mrs. Elizabeth 25 Sep in Louisiana MO after a short illness, ae 63.   LAJ 10 Oct 1863
    Hannibal & St. Louis pc

LUDINGTON, Mary yesterday of pneumonia ae 52. Funeral from City Workhouse.   MORE 26 Nov 1865
    (Doesn't sound like an inmate - mentions carriages waiting, etc.)

LUDWIG, Thomas, eldest son of Mathias and Theresa, 17 Oct ae 11, at 25th-Biddle.   MORE 18 Oct 1863

LUHAN, Ellen wife of Coleman 15 Apr ae 30. Funeral from St. Laurence O'Toole   MORE 16 Apr 1861
    Church, interred Calvary. Limerick, Cork, NY pc

LUKE, Eliza L. daughter of John and Elizabeth in Clarksville 19 Apr of congestive   MORE 20 Apr 1863
    chills, at the home of James W. Booth, ae 18.

LULY, John, native of Ireland, 6 Sep ae 72; resident of St. Louis 24 years.   SLMD 7 Sep 1864
    Lived at 119 S. 6th. Milwaukee pc

LUNN, William 9 May ae 54, at 87 Collins.   MORE 12 May 1865

LUNSTROTH, Mrs. ___ and infant. She had a sudden attack of congestion of the lungs   MORE 17 Dec 1861
    and paralysis; the infant suffocated.

LUTHERCORD, F.H. 2 Mar ae 32y 8m after a 10-day illness, at Morgan betw 21-22.   MORE 4 Mar 1862

LYDA, Mary E. wife of Charles 8 Feb ae 26, at 8th betw O'Fallon-Cass. Wash. DC pc   MORE 9 Feb 1865

LYLE, Phaona G., only daughter of John A., at their home in Carondelet ae 5y 5m.   MORE 23 Dec 1864
    Funeral from the home of A.L. Lyle. Interred Bellefontaine.

LYLE, Eva Della 14 Dec in Carondelet of scarlet fever, ae 8y 4m; youngest daughter   MORE 14 &
    of Alex and Caroline. Interred Bellefontaine.   15 Dec 1864

LYNCH, Charles David, youngest son of William A. and the late Catherine, 28 Sep at   MORE 1 &
    Milliken's Bend, MS on the ill-fated Robert Campbell. Ae 28y 5m 24d.   2 Nov 1863
    Funeral from the Cathedral to Calvary Cem.

LYNCH, David: Texas Co. Letters of administration to John T. Lynch, 12 July. ROLEX 31 Jul 1865
LYNCH, David Jr. son of David D. 20 Jul ae 1y 5m. MORE 22 Jul 1861
LYNCH, Mrs. Ellen, native of Killarney, Co. Kerry, 19 Apr in her 71st year. Funeral MORE 20 Apr 1862
    from the home of her son-in-law Francis Buckley, 522 Morgan. Int. Rock Spring.
LYNCH, George W. 17 Dec in his 43rd year. Funeral from Assumption Church to Calvary MORE 19 Dec 1863
    Cemetery. Cincinnati & Pittsburgh pc
LYNCH, John, rebel prisoner (Co B 3rd MO) of diarrhoea 20 Nov. (Undertaker's list) MORE 22 Nov 1863
LYNCH, Louisa V. widow of John H. in Columbia 9 Jan. COWS 16 Jan 1863
LYNCH, Mrs. Mary of cerebral palsy "after a drinking bout." MORE 24 Nov 1861
LYNCH, Oliver son of Mrs. W. 21 Feb ae 2. MORE 22 Feb 1862
LYNCH, Washington, a tinner ae 44, fell while working on the cornice of a 5-story MORE 20 Jan 1861
    building and died, 19 Jan. Left wife, 3 children. (SLMD says 5 children) SLMD 21"
LYNCH, William of St. Ferdinand Twp. murdered by Edward R. Kangley because of his MORE 5 Jun 1863
    "undue intimacy" with Kangley's wife.
LYNES, Alice daughter of James M. in Boone Co. 21 Nov, of whooping cough, ae 4. COWS 29 Nov 1861
LYNES, Mary wife of Perry of Boone Co. 21 Apr ae 36. COWS 1 May 1863
LYNN, John Taylor at Ft. Galpin of galloping consumption. Pittsburgh & Wheeling pc MORE 27 Nov 1863
LYON, James H. ae 36 and his daughter Missouri Alabama, ae 12, refugees from AR. MORE 7 Aug 1864
    Mother Nancy Caroline and 2 children ae 10y and 20m survive.
LYON, Mary Margaret daughter of William W. and Poline of Boone Co. 2 Mar ae 4y3m21d. COWS 15 Mar 1861
LYONS, Cyrus killed by guerillas in Carroll Co. (Carrollton Democrat) MORE 21 Jul 1864
LYONS, Mary A., consort of Jesse P.; tribute by Plattsburg Lodge IOOF. LIT 18 Mar 1864
LYSTER, Margaret 25 Jul ae 56 at her home, 16-N. Lucas. NY & Chicago pc MORE 26 Jul 1865
    William, a stonecutter, 21 Oct of bronchitis at his home, 16th-N. Lucas. " 22 Oct 1865
            Iowa pc

McAFEE, Jane Rochester wife of Rev. R.L. of Boone Presbyterian Church, in her COWS 4 Sep 1863
    57th year. Danville KY pc
McALLISTER, Jane 6 Mar ae 56, at 13th & Cass. MORE 7 Mar 1865
McALLISTER, William W., Chariton Co.; letters of administration to J.A. McAllister CECB 2 Oct 1862
    27 September.
McANESPY, Mrs. Belle, wife of John, at the home of her brother Isaiah P. Smithers, MORE 7 Jun 1864
    113 Chestnut, 6 Jun after a short illness. Lexington KY pc
    John, at the home of his brother-in-law I.P. Smithers, 30 Nov in his MORE 5 Dec 1865
        (40th?) year. Lexington KY pc
McASHAN, ___ (John T. per co. history) killed and thrown into the Missouri River MORE 10 Jan 1865
    in Chariton Co.
McATEE, James son of Thomas H. in Sisters Hospital 25 May. MORE 26 May 1865
McAULIFF, Mrs. Rebecca Ann, wife of J.D., a victim of the Camp Jackson affair; MORE 14 &
    she was ae 16, pregnant. 15 May 1861
McAULIFFE, Florence Dennis, father of Dennis and Daniel of St. Louis, 10 Jul ae 63. MORE 11 Jul 1864
    Funeral from Dennis' home, Biddle betw 6-7. Cork IRE pc SLMD "
McBAIN, James son of J.T. and R.E. in Providence 18 Jan of brain congestion, COWS 30 Jan 1863
    in his 7th year.
McBANE, V.J. in Buffalo, Dallas Co., 24 Apr. COWS 17 May 1861
* McBRIDE, Charles Mace son of James and Emilie Choron 15 Feb at 278 Olive, ae 4y4m17d. MORE 17 Feb 1861
McBRIDE, Ellen wife of Bernard 11 Jul ae 26, at Main & Bates. MORE 12 Jul 1864
* McBRIDE, Emily Choron daughter of James J. and Elisabeth Choron 6 Jun ae 9y 7m. MORE 8 Jun 1864
McBRIDE, Jackson, citizen of Chariton Co., 3 Mar of erysipelas. (Undertaker's list) MORE 19 Mar 1865
McBRIDE, James R. son of John L. and Fanny 27 June ae 2y 1m 15d, at 15th-Clark. MORE 29 Jun 1862
McBRIDE, John M., railroad mail agent reported to have died of wounds at Springfield, HAM 31 Oct 1861
    actually died of illness; was never in the army but was a nephew of COWS 18 Oct "
    rebel Gen. McBride and had been to see him on private business. (COWS
    says he was a son of Judge P.H., of Boone Co., died 2 Oct ae 27.)
    Mary Ann 2nd daughter of Judge P.H. in Boone Co. 27 Feb at the home of COWS 4 &
        her father, in her 34th year. 18 Mar 1864

McBRIDE, Mrs. Peggy of Boone Co. in April ae ca 70.   COWS 1 May 1863
McBRIDE, Stephen, Chariton Co. Public administrator took over his estate.   CECB 24 Jul 1862

McCABE, James, ca 14, run over by a street car Sunday. He worked for Dr. Boisliniere.   MORE 29 Nov 1865

McCABE, John, a hackman, fell from his hack while intoxicated; left wife and four   MORE 11 Nov 1863
    children, alley betw 10-11-Market0Walnut. "Quiet, unassuming, more an enemy
    to himself than anyone else."

McCABE, Patrick, inquest: sunstroke, ae 27, only relative a brother-in-law.   MORE 3 Jul 1864

McCAIG, Mrs. A. 26 Sep ae 64. Funeral from the home of her son-in-law John   MORE 27 Sep 1865
    Nicholson, S. 7th near Arsenal.

McCALL, John killed when the boiler blew at Union Foundry. Ae 26, lived on Ann   MORE 12 &
                       betw 7th-Decatur.   14 May 1863

McCAMANT, Woodford W., eldest son of James and Sarah S., 21 Aug ae 35, after an   MORE 22 Aug 1863
    illness of 6 months. Interred Bellefontaine. Louisville and Shelbyville KY
                         Keokuk IA, Clarion PA pc

McCANDLESS, William 16 Feb ae 74. Pittsburgh and Allegheny pc   MORE 18 Feb 1864

McCARDIE, James, yesterday in Charles Meyer's saloon of brain congestion, ae 46.   MORE 12 May 1864
    His wife Nancy committed suicide 9 Dec 1862(see below). Left several
    children, two of them young ladies living with relatives near this city.

McCARDLE, Nancy wife of James, in her 39th year; drowned herself in a cistern   MORE 10 Dec 1862
    during temporary aberration. Member 2nd Baptist Church, left 3 daughters.

McCARRON, John 23 Jan ae 22y 10m, on 11th betw Carr-Biddle.   MORE 24 Jan 1857

McCARTAN, Patrick, native of Co. Leitrim IRE, 25 years a resident of St. Louis,   MORE 1 Nov 1863
    31 Oct ae 52.

McCARTHY, Catherine wife of Timothy 29 Jan, ae 54, at the home, 22nd-Carr.   MORE 29 Jan 1862

McCARTHY, Daniel, 12 Dec ae 26. Funeral from 83 Levee St.   MORE 13 Dec 1863

McCARTHY, Henry O'Clarence of St. Louis at St. Paul MN 24 Aug ae 29. Deputy head   MORE 28, 29,
    of Centre Fenian Brotherhead, native of NJ. Funeral, St. Patrick's.   30 Aug 1865
    (Parents lived in St. Louis.)

McCARTHY, James P. 24 Feb in Clay Co. ae 44y 4m 12d.   MORE 9 Mar 1875

McCARTHY, Mrs. Michael 5 Oct ae 55. Funeral from St. Malachy's to Calvary Cemetery.   MORE 7 Oct 1864
    (SLMD, same date, doesn't say "Mrs." Michael.)

McCARTNEY, M.D. 11 Mar in Rocheport ae ca 75.   MORE 28 Mar 1862

McCARTY, Isabella wife of John 14 Mar, ae 39, at #7 Russell. Philad. & New Orl. pc   MORE 15 Mar 1862

McCARTY, James 24 Feb ae 44y 4m 12d. Left "mother and other relatives."   LIT 3 Mar 1865

McCARTY, Mary J. wife of William G. of Jefferson City in St. Louis 3 Dec of typhoid   MORE 4 Dec 1864
    ae 27y 23d. Left husband, 2 helpless children. Interred Jefferson City.   " 1 Jan 1865
    Daughter of James R. and Maria L. (or Martha) Boyce. KY, Denver, Salt Lake pc

McCARTY, Sue E. wife of John in Audrain Co. at the home of her father, in her 22d y.   CANP 22 Oct 1863
    (COWS 23 Oct says she died 30 Sep in her 32d year.)

McCARTY, daughters of   Mary, 15 Feb of whooping cough & scarlet fever, 4y 6d   LIT 19 Feb 1864
    William and Alla: Lucy 16 Feb ae 2y 2m 8d

McCARTY, Capt. William A. Monday last of heart disease ae ca 39.   LIT 3 Feb 1865

McCAUSLAND, Mark 24 May in his 58th year at 208 Christy.   MORE 25 May 1862

McCAW, James of St. Louis, son of Leonard of Ballycross, Co. Down IRE, 25 Jan.   MORE 26 Jan 1861
    Funeral from the home of his brother William, 541 Broadway.

McCHESNEY, Alexander 21 Dec of typhoid; interred in the east. Troy & NY City NY pc   MORE 25 Dec 1864

McCLANAHAN, Mrs. Robert at the home of her mother, Mrs. Miller, Sunday night last   FULT 19 Aug &
    of flux, in Fulton.   2 Sep 1864

McCLEARY, ___ killed near Pilot Grove; J. Hiltebridal tried and dismissed, self-   BOOM 19 Mar 1864
    defense on his own premises.

McCLEARY, Andrew 9 Dec in his 37th year at 65 Brooklyn. Interred Bellefontaine.   MORE 11 Dec 1864

McCLELLAN, widow of R.A., in the flux epidemic.   FULT 2 Sep 1864

McCLELLAN, Thomas, a bushwhacker, killed near Millersburg.   FULT 30 Sep 1864

McCLUNEY, Rev. John P. near Oak Grove Church, Johnson Co., 3 Sep ae 50y 7m 7d,   WARS 9 Sep 1865
    effects of a wound received at the Battle of Lexington. St. Louis,
    Wellsburg VA, Washington & Pittsburgh pc

McCLURE, David, Chariton Co.: Final Settlement by William West.	CECB 12 Feb 1863
McCLURE, Elizabeth G. wife of William 1 Apr of lung congestion in her 45th year. Native of Garrard Co. KY, daughter of William Slaven; to MO when quite young, settled in Boone Co. in the area now known as Bonne Femme.	COWS 10 Apr 1863
McCLURE, family of Robert: Kate Bell dau/Robert and Susan 12 Apr ae 3y 9m 5d. Lived Clark-Emily. Bloomington IL pc	MORE 13 Apr 1863
Frankie F. son/Robert and Sue 21 May ae 6y 6m. Lived Clark-Emily.	MORE 22 May 1863
George W. 6 Feb in 37th year, funeral from the home of his brother Robert, Clark-Emily. Int. Bellefontaine. Bloomfield IL & Princeton IN pc	MORE 8 Feb 1864
McCLURE, Thomas, prisoner of war from Boone Co. in the hospital in St. Louis 15 Jan ae 18. Interred Boone Co.	COWS 20 Jan 1865
McCLURE, William, found dead in bed at the boarding house of Jacob Smith near Bissell Point, of lung congestion. Laborer, left wife and child but their whereabouts were not known.	MORE 10 Jan 1864
McCLURG, Mary C. wife of Col. J.W. of Linn Creek in Jefferson City 17 Dec.	SLMD 23 Dec 1861
McCOLGEN, John only son of John and Mary Esther 5 Nov ae 21y 1m, of inflammation of the brain. Cape Girardeau & Baltimore pc	MORE 6 Nov 1865
McCOLLIN, John ae 27. Funeral from St. John's Church.	MORE 21 Jan 1864
McCOMBS, John L. 1 Jun ae 53, formerly of Denton MD. Funeral from the home of Peter Lindell, Bates-Collins.	MORE 2 Jun 1861
McCONNELL, W.J. (originally given as McCullom); John Bryan, bartender at the Gen. Taylor House, charged with his murder; later testimony indicated that McC. stumbled and fell leaving the barroom, hit his head.	MORE 31 Oct & 1 Nov 1865
McCORD, Arthur S. 26 Mar ae 33. Brother of R.C.C.W. (sic) and J.H. Pittsburgh pc	MORE 27 Mar 1864
McCORMACK, Elizabeth murdered by her brother Edward; lived in the alley between Biddle-O'Fallon-10-11; he beat her, had also beaten and killed a man named Butler last year near the Reservoir.	MORE 30 Aug 1862
McCORMACK, Sarah "poor, degraded" found dead (drowned) in a pond at Spruce-Poplar-10-11. Ae 30.	MORE 3 Dec 1864
McCORMACK, William, a drayman ae 35, kicked by a mule. Unmarried.	MORE 25 Apr 1863
McCORMICK, ____, wife of Thomas, near Columbia 20 Feb.	COWS 22 Feb 1861
McCORMICK, Edward, at Sisters Hospital; a chisel had dropped on his head at the powder magazine, where he was employed. Unmarried.	MORE 29 Nov 1865
McCORMICK, Fannie wife of Milton P. at Paris, Canada West, 21 Mar after a short illness. Daughter of W. Alderson of St. Louis.	MORE 23 Mar 1865
McCORMICK, Michael 30 Jan ae 35 at his home, 11th betw Cass-Mullan. Member of Hibernian Benevolent Society. Interred Rock Spring.	MORE 31 Jan 1864
McCORMICK, Mrs. Nancy 31 May in her 60th year at her home on Gravois Road.	MORE 2 Jun 1861
McCOUN, Mrs. Mary in Clay Co. 23 March.	MORE 26 May 1864
McCOURTNEY, ____, a guerilla, killed on the Big Perry (or Piney?) near McCourtney's Mill, area of Waynesville. __ Anthony & __ Stephens also killed.	MORE 20 Jan 1865
McCOY, Arthur William son of Arthur C. and Louisa 7 Feb ae 5y 7m. Funeral from home of Mrs. Gibson, Green betw 9-10. Ste Genevieve pc	MORE 8 Feb 1864
McCOY, George W., Chariton Co.: letters of administration to Margaret McCoy 15 Oct.	CECB 23 Oct 1862
McCOY, Joanna T. wife of Dr. Milton and daughter of John Craig, in Tipton 5 Jul. Born and raised near Buffalo, Putnam Co. VA; married there 1852; to MO 1853. Ae 27y 9m. Baptist.	CAWN 29 Nov 1862
McCOY, Spencer, a Confederate soldier of Clay Co., killed at the Battle of Springfield.	LIT 6 Feb 1863
McCRACKEN, Capt. W. M., ACS, at Cape Girardeau ae (53?) formerly of Lexington KY.	MORE 19 Aug 1864
McCRAITH, Hannah wife of Jeremiah, 10 March. Funeral St. Malachy's Church.	MORE 12 Mar 1864
McCREANOR, Patrick 6 Sep. Funeral from home of his nephew Patrick Bradley, Walnut below Summit, to St. Malachy's. Interred Calvary. Philadelphia pc	MORE 8 Sep 1864
McCREARY, Gardner and George, Co H 3rd MO Vols, killed at Glasgow.	GAL 17 Nov 1864
McCREE, John Cameron son of John and Jane 24 Jan ae 2y 8m. Jane, wife of John, 8 Feb of lung fever in her 42nd year. Cumberland Presbyterian since age 14. Left husband, 6 children.	LAJ 31 Jan 1861 " 28 Feb "

McCREERY, Isabella wife of A.J. of St. Louis in Hardinsburg KY 14 Feb in her 30th y.	MORE 20 Feb 1861
McCREERY, Jesse, of disease in the military hospital in Glasgow.	GAL 17 Nov 1864
McCREERY, Phocion R. 30 Nov ae 44. Lived Olive-10th. Interred Bellefontaine.	MORE 1 Dec 1861
McCUE, ___ a bushwhacker killed by scouts under Cols. McFerran and Neill.	LEXUN 15 Aug 1863
McCUE, James, porter on the Wyaconda, drowned when the boat caught fire and burned; he gave the alarm and was the only life lost as he jumped overboard before they grounded the boat. Wife and family in St. Louis.	MORE 15 Jul 1865
McCUEN, Rebecca widow of John at the home of her son Jo. in her 74th year. Cumberland Presbyterian 30 years.	LAJ 10 Oct 1861
McCULLOCH, H.G., formerly of Louisville, in Brookfield.	MORE 24 Apr 1863
McCULLOCH, Jeannette wife of Daniel 18 Jun, on Morgan betw 18-19.	MORE 19 Jun 1862
McCULLOCH, John G., texas keeper on the Jennie Deans, suddenly ae 20; had complained of a headache. Left 2 sisters in St. Louis.	MORE 10 May 1862
McCULLOUGH, Emma daughter of the late David 1 Dec of consumption in her 17th year. Funeral from 2nd Presbyterian.	MORE 3 Dec 1861
McCULLOUGH, Maj. John, state senator from Livingston Co. and member of the 23rd MO Vols., "the other day."	SJH 15 Oct 1863
McCULLOUGH, Thomas, ae 7, fell while at play: verdict dropsy of the heart. Father a soldier, mother very poor, 2 other children on 5th St. betw Green-Morgan.	MORE 8 Jan 1864
McCUNE, Abraham, Chariton Co.: public administrator took over his estate.	CECB 2 Jul 1863
McDANIEL, Ambrose, a rebel sympathizer of Buchanan Co., living near Agency Ford, found dead in a field.	SJH 31 Jul 1864
McDANIEL, Mary S. wife of John near Whitesville, Andrew Co. 29 Dec.	MORE 9 Jan 1861
McDANIEL, William, citizen of Nodaway Co., of inflammation of the lungs. (Undertaker's list)	MORE 19 Jan 1864
McDANIELS, J., prisoner, of variola. (Undertaker's list)	MORE 15 Feb 1863
McDERMOTT, Francis 17 Sep ae 53, on Stoddard betw Elliott-Clay. St. Bridget's Church, interred Calvary.	MORE 18 Sep 1865
McDERMOTT, James, formerly of Frederick MD, at 53 Elm in his 34th year. Int. Calvary.	MORE 1 Mar 1861
McDONALD, Col. Charles of St. Louis in Memphis 12 Dec ae (23?) WI pc	MORE 21 Dec 1864
McDONALD, Emmet Brig. Gen CSA killed at Hartsville, Wright Co. 11 Jan 1863; funeral from home of his sister Mrs. Dean, New St. Charles Rock Road. (Permission had been given to return his body and that of John Wimer to St. Louis for burial, McDonald in Bellefontaine. But the bodies were given to the regular undertaker in charge of military burials, and were interred in the reserve section of Wesleyan, apparently for fear of trouble at the funeral. A notice had been served on their relatives and friends to bury them in a quiet and private manner.)	MORE 7 & 8 Feb 1863
McDONALD, Frank oldest son of James R. of Howard Co. 26 Feb in his 18th year.	MORE 7 Mar 1863
McDONALD, James, ae 16, killed in the Camp Jackson affair. Lived Olive betw 7-8.	MORE 18 May 1861
McDONALD, Capt. James of DeKalb murdered 19 May by two men named Robinson. (rebels?) (Savannah Plain Dealer)	MORE 1 Jun 1864
McDONALD, Mary wife of C.A., 12 Jul. Lived on Lynch St.	MORE 13 Jul 1862
McDONALD, Michael ae 23 of lung congestion caused by intemperance.	MORE 5 Mar 1863
McDONALD, Owen "connected with the Pacific RR for 7 years" of sunstroke. Lived on Barlow near Chouteau.	MORE 10 Aug 1861
McDONALD, Patrick, consort of Mary, 13 Apr of dropsy ae 50. Native of Co. Mayo, lived at 5th & Biddle. New Orleans pc.	MORE 14 Apr 1865
McDONALD, Samuel, 28 Jun ae 43 on O'Fallon betw 6-7. Member of Western and Southern Engineers Benevolent Association.	MORE 29 Jun 1865
McDONALD, Sarah wife of James 29 Jun at the home, Bellefontaine Road. Chicago, Vicksburg, Albany NY pc	MORE 30 Jun 1865
McDONALD, Asst. Engineer, William I., son of Philip and the late Bridget of St. Louis, at Natchez 7 Apr; scalded on the Alf Cutting. Washington DC pc	MORE 8 May 1864
McDONELL, John G. son of James of Toronto, Can. Westm at the home of Basil T. Elder, 23 Dec in his (28th?) year. Interred in Toronto.	MORE 25 Dec 1864

McDONNELL, John son of Patrick and Mary 5 Mar of consumption ae 24y 4m, at 5th and Biddle. New Orleans pc — MORE 11 Mar 1865

McDONOUGH, John, native of Ireland, 4 Jul of typhoid ae 33. Funeral from the home of John Burns, 96 N. Levee. — MORE 6 Jul 1862

McDONOUGH, Mary Jane wife of Capt. James 5 Nov in her 33rd year, at 214 Pine. — MORE 6 Nov 1861

McDOUGAL, Miss Mary 9 Aug at advanced age. Funeral from the home of her brother-in-law, John Brady Smith, 102 S. 4th. Interred Bellefontaine. — MORE 11 Aug 1863

McDOWELL, John L. of Capt. Dusold's Command, ae 17, killed at Glasgow. Co A 43rd MO — GAL 17 Nov 1864

McDOWELL, Mary T. youngest daughter of Mrs. Arghange (sic) 8 Dec of consumption ae 19y 8m 10d. Keokuk, Altun, Dubuque pc — MORE 9 Dec 1862

McDOWELL, Col. W. Wallace in Boone Co. 13 Jan ae (80? 50?) formerly of Danville KY. — COWS 14 Feb 1862

McDOWELL, Walter killed in the Camp Jackson affair; lived on Elizabeth St. — MORE 14 May 1861

McDOWELL, Willie son of Mrs. ___, S 5th below Cerre, 10 Nov ae 8y 9d. — MORE 12 Nov 1862

McELDERRY, Mary Isabella daughter of Joseph Harding in Central Twp. 25 Jan in her 42nd year. Carroll Co. MD pc — MORE 29 Jan 1862

McENNIS, Elizabeth relict of John, Dodier betw 14-15, 18 Sep ae 66. — MORE 20 Sep 1861

McEVOY, Ann wife of Lawrence, inquest: alley betw 8-9-Market-Walnut. Heart disease. — MORE 11 Sep 1863

McEVOY, John 10 Aug at the home of Frank Murphy, 119 Collins, ae 38. NY pc — MORE 11 Aug 1864

McEVOY, Patrick, only son of Lawrence and Jane, Christy betw 16-17, ae 9y 2m 13d. Indiana & Maine pc — MORE 26 Mar 1862

McFADDEN, Henry 30 Jul in his 49th year after a brief illness. Phil pc — MORE & SLMD 6 Aug 1861

McFADDEN, Lysander, prisoner, 18 Jan of typhoid pneumonia. (Undertaker's list) — MORE 26 Jan 1863

McFARLAND, Stilwell, killed by soldiers in lower Cape Girardeau Co. — CHAC 22 Apr 1864

McFAUL, Ambrose son/Eneas and Mary A., Green betw 10-11, in his 23rd year. Lingering illness. Baltimore pc — MORE 5 & 6 Jan 1864

McGARRAH, Gates, a pilot, stabbed by George Rosch at the 6-Mile-House on St. Charles Rock Road, 1 Mar in his 31st year. Left wife and 4 children. — MORE 2 & 3 Mar 1863

McGARY, John 28 Feb at 10th & Howard in his 26th year. Cincinnati pc — MORE 1 Mar 1863

McGEARY, Mary wife of Lawrence, 19 Sep, at 161 S. Main. — MORE 20 Sep 1862

McGEE, A.H. of Dade Co. in the prison hospital in Springfield. — MORE 10 Apr 1863

McGEE, John 20 Apr of epilepsy at his parents' home, O'Fallon betw 22-23, in his 31st year. — MORE 21 Apr 1863

McGEE, John 5 Jun in his 50th year. Lived at O'Fallon betw 23-24; interred Holy Trinity. Macon MO pc — MORE 6 Jun 1865

McGEE, Samuel W. son of John S. 24 Mar in Monroe Co. ae 27y 1m 1d. — COWS 7 Apr 1865

McGEE, W.L. of Lafayette Co., arrested 1 Oct, in Gratiot Prison 19 Nov. — MORE 20 Nov 1862

McGEORGE, T.C. 4 Dec on Morgan near 21st, ae 38. — MORE 6 Dec 1863

McGHEE, W.L., of Porter's Command, of pneumonia. (Gratiot Prison?) — MORE 18 Nov 1862

McGILL, Benjamin, prisoner, 12 Dec of pneumonia. (Undertaker's list) — MORE 15 Dec 1862

McGILL, Theodore L., formerly of Von Phul & McGill of St. Louis, at Chatawa, Pike Co., 19 Feb ae 64. — MORE 21 Mar 1863

McGINNIS, John 19 June at Warrensburg ae 29. — WARS 24 Jun 1865

McGINNISS, Emarine wife of J.M. 5 Sep of consumption. Born in Clay Co. MO 13 Sep 1830, a Baptist, left husband and 2 daughters. — LIT 16 Sep 1864

McGIVNEY, children of Peter, 190 N. 5th NY & New Orleans ps — Edward Franklin of mucus tissue 13 Aug ae 14m 7d. (shown as Peter and Mary Ann) — MORE 14 Aug 1861

Isaac 9 Aug, inflammation of bowels, ae 24. — ??

Julia 15 Apr ae 22y 8m — MORE 16 Apr 1863

McGOVERN, James, a soldier killed "some days ago" on the No. MO RR about 2 mi from St. Charles. Trying to take some corn, opposed by farmer. — MORE 18 Dec 1862

McGOVERN, John, native of Ireland, 3 Oct at Pleasant Hill, MO. Funeral from St. Patrick's to Holy Trinity cemetery. Rochester NY pc (WARS 6 Oct says he belonged to the US Telegraph Corps, erecting a line along the railroad, was drunk on the track, run over.) — MORE 5 Oct 1865

McGRATH, Ellen, 7 Apr ae 51. Funeral from St. Malachy's Church. — MORE 9 Apr 1862

McGRATH, Mary daughter /Philip and Catherine 3 Apr ae 6, at the home, one block west of the Wedge House.	MORE 4 Apr 1864
McGRATH, Patrick, Co F 5th Mo Vols, at Corinth ae 26.	MORE 16 Nov 1862
McGRATH, Thomas "a fine little boy" ca 3, drowned in a cistern. Parents lived on Magazine near Webster.	MORE 10 May 1861
McGRATH, Thomas at Sisters Hospital ca 40. Funeral at Cathedral, int. Calvary.	MORE 19 Mar 1864
McGRATH, William 28 Jun of consumption ae 26. Funeral from the home of his brother, 8th betw O'Fallon-Cass. Interred Calvary.	MORE 29 Jun 1862
McGREADY, Lucy wife of Israel at Potosi 13 Jun in her 58th year, ill 5 months. Daughter of the late Col. John McIlvaine. Edward Perryman, infant son of the late Fermin, at the same time. Carlinville IL, Louisville, Lone Star TX pc	MORE 19 Jun 1865
McGUIRE, John H., Co F 4th MO, captured in Cape Girardeau 17 Sep, at the Prison Hospital of lung congestion. (Undertaker's list MORE 18 Oct)	MORE 15 Oct 1863
McGUIRE, William P. at Fort Garland, KT returning home to St. Louis from New Mexico, 30 Apr in his 23rd year.	MORE 3 Jun 1862
McGUNNEGLE, Elizabeth wife of George K. 27 Oct in her 55th year, at 218 Locust. Long, painful illness. Interred Bellefontaine.	MORE 28 & 29 Oct 1864
McGUNNEGLE, Wilson, Lieut. Com. US Navy, at Annapolis 2 Apr in his 34th year.	MORE 3 Apr 1863
McHENRY, John, native of Cork IRE, 21 Aug ae 35. Funeral from the home of John Wheeler, 7th betw Franklin-Wash.	MORE 23 Aug 1863
McHENRY, Oliver P. in Boone Co. 29 Oct of congestive chills, ae ca 51.	COWS 1 Dec 1865
McILVAIN, Rebecca consort of Benjamin 19 Jan near Potosi, ae 52y 5m 20d.	MORE 22 Jan 1865
McINTIRE, Thomas near Fulton 23 May ae ca 39. COWS 29 May &	MORE 1 Jun 1863
McINTOSH, Miss Katie V. at the home of Capt. James Gormly (former home of Hon. Edward Bates) 4 miles west of the courthouse on Clayton Road, in her 27th year. Interred Bellefontaine.	MORE 25 Sep 1863
McINTYRE, Patrick, found dead of a broken neck with cuts on his head, alley betw 7-8-Biddle-O'Fallon, wife Margaret drunk, suspected. (Daughter also Margaret works out, testified.) Later story says wife in jail, had 4 sons with her.	MORE 3 & 6 Jan 1864
McJILTON, James F. 19 Mar in his 47th year. Baltimore pc	MORE 24 Mar 1864
McKEE, Amanda consort of Judge R.A. in Clark Co. in her 54th year.	MORE 24 Apr 1863
McKEE, Ferdinand, formerly of Hagerstown MD, at Pierce's Hotel of apoplexy.	SLMD 9 Apr 1861
McKEE, James of 125 N. 5th at Skipworth Landing MS 14 Sep; body brought home by his brother Alexander of the St. Louis Metro Police Dept.	MORE 4 Oct 1865
McKEE, Mrs. Jane in her 76th year at the home of her daughter Mrs. Eliza Rogers, 21 N. Market.	MORE 10 Oct 1862
McKELLOPS, Genevieve, youngest child of Dr. H.J. and Anna, 30 Jun.	MORE 1 Jul 1863
McKENNA, Mary Ellen youngest daughter of Robert and Ann 28 Apr ae 2y 7m 20d. Interred Rock Spring.	MORE 29 Apr 1862
McKENNA, Patrick of heart disease 25 Jun of heart disease ae 28. Int. Calvary.	MORE 26 Jun 1861
McKENZIE, May, ae 8, niece of Mrs. Corkins (west side of 20th betw Morgan-Franklin) burned to death. Her aunt was in the country; two girls employed as mantua makers were in the house, also May's sister Belle and two boys, Alex and Archie McKenzie, possibly brothers. May was shown as orphan.	MORE 30 Nov 1863
McKEON, Mrs. Margaret 12 Aug ae 58; funeral from home of her son Edward, 208 N 10th.	MORE 13 Aug 1864
McKIM, Ann Margaret daughter of Isaac and Isabella 31 Aug ae 1y 29d, 125 11th St.	MORE 1 Sep 1861
McKIM, Eben Stawood son of William A. and Sarah C. in Canton 24 Oct ae 6y 8m, of diphtheria. Boston & Augusta ME pc	MORE 27 Oct 1861
McKIM, Julia wife of Robert of Callaway Co. 24 Aug ae 29y 8m.	COWS 2 Sep 1864
McKIM, Mary wife of J.W. 20 Feb ae 29. FULT 1 Mar &	COWS 15 Mar 1861
McKINNEY, William, a colored man, ar Sisters Hospital; shot by unknown on 25 Oct.	MORE 10 Nov 1865
McKINSTRY, George 9 Nov ae 27.	MORE 11 Nov 1861
McKITRICK, Norman son of Hugh and Mary W. 2 Nov ae 4.	MORE 4 Nov 1863
McKNIGHT, Mrs. Elizabeth, found dead in bed at 88 Mound St., of intemperance. Her husband left her 6 months ago taking their 2 daughters.	MORE 17 Mar 1865

McKOWN, Capt. Thomas Brison 7 Feb ae 71, of palsy and paralysis; suffered a long illness. Came to St. Louis at an early day as a mechanic and manufacturer; raised a large family of sons and daughters, all married and settled. Was in the War of 1812; captain of Washington Blues in Baltimore 1816, captain of Carroll Blues in Pittsburgh. In 1840 raised a company of Native American Rangers in St. Louis. Presbyterian, born in Pittsburgh, married and lived in Baltimore; lived in IL and MO. MORE 8 Feb 1863

McLAGEN, Alexander a boss stonecutter fell from the 3rd floor of the New Polytech Building, where he was working, yesterday; injuries resulted in his death. Lived at the corner of Washington-Grand. MORE 5 Nov 1865

McLAIN, Hannah C. wife of George E., formerly of Pittsburgh, 4 Jul. Brief illness. MORE 7 Jul 1862

McLAUGHLIN, Elizabeth, found dead; was drinking, had been vomiting blood; some mystery. " 17 Sep 1861

McLAUGHLIN, Patrick 20 Mar ae 55; funeral from Central House, E. St. Louis. MORE 21 Mar 1864

McLEAN, A.L., formerly of Lafayette Co., adj. to Gen. Sterling Price, killed in Washington TX by Col. Robert Wood, son of Milton of Saline Co., over refusal of a furlough. MORE 25 Jul 1865

McLEAN, Richard 5 Jun ae 20y 6m, at 203 N. 8th. San Francisco & Memphis pc MORE 6 Jun 1864

McLELLAN, Dr. John J., husband of Mary E., 6 May in Versailles ae 50, and his infant son John S. 12 Feb ae 4m. CAWN 25 Jul 1863

McLURE, Ruth wife of C.C. 9 Apr ae (54?). Funeral from Central Presbyterian to Bellefontaine. Philadelphia pc MORE 10 Apr 1865

McMAHAN, Jane consort of Jefferson and daughter of Thomas and Elizabeth Brooks, 18 Jun. Born 3 Sep 1838. Left 3 children. FULT 4 Jul 1862

McMAHON, Margaret, inquest: Bates betw Main-2nd. Intemperance and exposure. MORE 8 Dec 1862

McMANUS, Sarah daughter/John and Sarah 18 Oct, ae 6, at 292 N. 7th. MORE 19 Oct 1864

McMAREY, Thomas at Clover Hill (13 miles out on St. Charles Road) of "strong mental excitement" -- actually heart disease. "An old man" ae 48(!) Dairy farmer, left wife, 4 children. MORE 3 Apr 1863

McMASTER, Samuel K. at his home 1 miles west of town, 10 Jun, ae ca 51. Left (/later H.) wife and several children. HAM 11 & 13 Jun 1861

McMECHAN, Mrs. ___ 17 Mar ae 40 at 11th-Brooklyn. Interred Bellefontaine. MORE 18 Mar 1863

McMENAMY, James, oldest son of B., 21 Apr at their home in Bridgeton. MORE 12 May 1863
James, near Bridgeton, 2 Oct ae 76. " 3 Oct 1862

McMILLAN, James at his home in Etlah, MO ae 24, ill 25 days; left a wife. Masonic tribute from Hermann, also one from New Haven (not a member there, but a friend). MORE 16 May 1864

McMINNIS (McMEENS, Samuel of Co. C 10th MO, captured Mississippi Co. AR 12 Sep, MORE 11 &
McMENNUS) in the prison hospital 10 Oct of lung inflammation. 13 Oct 1863

McMURRAY, Abigail wife of Gen. G. in Wolf Island Twp. 21 Jan. CHAC 30 Jan 1863

McMURTRY, Mrs. Sarah 28 Apr in her 63rd year, 72 S. 6th. Philadelphia pc MORE 30 Apr 1865

McNAIR, Marguerite S. relict of Alexander, 1st Governor of MO, at the home of her son-in-law Jule Cabanne ae 75y 4m. Funeral from the Cathedral to Calvary. (Long obituary on 19 Jun.) MORE 18 Jun 1863

McNAIR, Mary E.C. daughter/A.R. and Cornelia J. 26 Jun ae 18y 11m 5d. Funeral from Immaculate Conception Church. Philadelphia & Pittsburgh pc MORE 27 Jun 1865

McNAMARA, Daniel 3 Oct of chronic diarrhoea, 8th betw O'Fallon-Cass. Brooklyn NY pc SLMD 14 Oct 1864

McNAMEE, Margaret wife of William 10 Jul ae 50, at 10th-Gratiot. Philadelphia & MORE 12 Jul 1865
Memphis pc
William 23 Jul in his 58th year, 10 th-Gratiot, "old and respected." " 24 Jul "

McNEIL, Gordon 20 Nov ae 57 on 14th betw Carr-Biddle. Interred Bellefontaine. MORE 22 Nov 1865

McNEILY, McNEELY, Alphus E., private 5th MO, captured at Vicksburg, in Gratiot Prison of typhus. MORE 16 Aug 1863

McNERNY, John, a boy, killed in the explosion of a powder magazine, used for storage by merchants. Son of Peter. John Morrison also killed. SJH 14 May 1864
MORE 18 "

McNEW, Edward Weston son/Allen and Elizabeth B., 6th betw Robidoux-Farnon, ae8y 2m. SJH 19 Aug 1863

McNIFF, Mrs. Eleanor 5 Oct in her 45th year. MORE 9 Oct 1862

McNUTT, Eliza Swink 9 Oct ae 3y 5m 21d and James ae 5y 5m 21d, children of George and Sarah of Jefferson Co. MORE 19 Oct 1861

McPHEETERS, Mrs. Cynthia W. in Lewis Co. 25 Jul ae 61y 4m.　　　　　　　　　CANP 3 Aug 1865
　　　　　　　Hettie wife of Charles 27 Jul ae ca 25 and her daughter Lena May,
　　　　　　　ae 1y, also in July.

McPHEETERS, sons of Dr. Wm. M.　George Buchanan 21 Apr ae 12y 9m. Short illness.　MORE 23 Apr 1863
　　　　　and Sallie　　William, youngest son, ae 6y 9m.　　　　　　　　　　　　　MORE 30 Jan 1862

McPHEETERS, James son/Joseph H. of Palmyra 14 miles south of Rock Port AR at the　PALS 27 Nov 1863
　　　　　　　home of Mr. Green, of flux, ae 25. Ill 5 days.

McPHEETERS, John Y. of Lewis Co. shot by Gen. Merrill at Palmyra in retaliation　CAWN 1 Nov 1862
　　　　　　　for the death of an old man named Allmstedt at the time of Porter's
　　　　　　　Raid into Palmyra. Several others also executed. (PALCO)

McPHERSON, Mary Mills only daughter of E.B. Jr. and Mary, ae 3y 1m. 15 Larned's Row.　MORE 17 Feb 1862

McPIKE, sons of　　Zachariah Taylor born 4 Jul 1848; though not quite 15 he　　PALS 8 May 1863
　　　　James B.　　weighed 180 pounds.
　　　　　　　　　　Charles 8 Nov of consumption in his 26th year. Mbr Bethel Church. "　1 Jan 1864

McQUEEN, Dudley, a bushwhacker, killed near Long's Mill.　　　　　　　　　　　　LAJ 16 May 1863

McQUEEN, Margaret wife of Edward in Boone Co. 11 Oct ae 66y 1m 6d.　　　　　COWS 27 Oct 1865

McQUIE, Mrs. Elizabeth Mosely 14 Jun at Macon ae 64y 9m "wife and mother."　MORE 28 Jun 1865
　　　　　Louisiana MO & Keokuk pc

McREYNOLDS, ___ of Saline Co. shot at his home last Saturday ae 58, left wife and　MORE 7 Jan 1865
　　　　　　　7 children. Killers identified themselves as militia, but may
　　　　　　　not have been. (LEXUN)

McSHERRY, Patrick T. 1 Aug ae 52. Lived on Benton. Brief illness. Pittsburgh pc.　MORE 2-4 Aug'61

McSORLEY, Sarah wife of William 22 Jul ae 27, 16th betw Biddle-O'Fallon. NY pc　MORE 23 Jul 1864

McSORLEY, William Wednesday of consumption ae 34. Interred Calvary.　　　　MORE 10 Jul 1862

McSWEENEY or　　Edward, native of Ireland, in St. Louis Co. 3 Oct ae 27.　MORE 5 &
　McSHEENY　　　　　　　　　　　　　　　　　　　　　　　　　　　　　　　　　　　6 Oct 1865

McVEIGH, Hiram in Hannibal 26 Nov in his 67th year. Alexandria VA, Baltimore,　MORE 10 Dec 1865
　　　　　　　　　　　　　　　　　　　　　　　　NY, Little Rock pc　　　　　　　PALS 22 "

McVEIGH, son of Hiram　Jesse in Hannibal 15 Nov in his 15th year.　　　　　MORE 14 Jan 1864
　& Mary E.　　　　　Jesse. . . shot and killed in Hannibal by a negro, not　" 21 Nov 1863
　　　　　　　　　　　clear if accidental. (Hannibal Courier)

McVICKER, Thomas H. eldest son of Thomas H. and Elizabeth 30 Sep at Chattanooga　MORE 26 Nov 1864
　　　　　　　ae 18. Funeral from the home, Beckwith St. Interred Bellefontaine.

McWILLIAMS, Mrs. John killed in Livingston Co. accidentally, a few days ago, by　RICON 4 Jun 1863
　　　　　　　her husband, when she stepped between him and John Sneed (her
　　　　　　　brother?). McWilliams claimed Sneed had attacked him.

MABEE, David Wendell only son of S. and J.E. at Bird's Point 6 Feb ae 3y 11m.　MORE 17 Feb 1861

MACK, Magdalene wife of Peter 16 Nov ae 37, after a short illness.　　　　　MORE 17 Nov 1864

MACKAY, George A. 29 Sep at Sisters Hospital ae 51y 2m 11d.　　　　　　　　MORE 30 Sep 1862

MACKAY, Isabella wife of James at the home of Louis Guion in Carondelet 25 Feb　MORE 3 Mar 1861
　　　　　ae 77.

MACKAY, Mrs. Maria 7 Oct ae 56 at her home on Gravois Road.　　　　　　　　MORE 8 Oct 1864

MACKENZIE, Kenneth, born in Scotland, many years a resident of St. Louis, 26 Apr.　MORE 27 Apr 1861
　　　　　　Mary 2nd daughter of late Kenneth and Mary Marshall 25 Mar of　　" 26 Mar 1863
　　　　　　brain congestion ae 4y 4m. Lived on Pine betw 16-17.

MACKEY, Susannah wife of John A. and daughter of James S. McLeod at her home near　LAJ 1 Jul 1865
　　　　　Clarksville 21 Jun of consumption ae 30y 7m 22d. Left 1 son, 3 brothers.

MACKEY, William 2nd son of Dr. A.P. 18 May of consumption ae 19.　　　　　SJH 16 May 1865

MACON, Emily youngest daughter of Francis and Louise, 6th betw Cerre-Gratiot,　MORE 27 Aug 1864
　　　　26 Aug ae 10y 10m.

MACRAE, Mrs. Gwenthelean, wife of Maj. N.C., at Jefferson Barracks 8 Jul of　MORE 9 Jul 1861
　　　　　hydrophobia ae 48y 6m. Cincinnati & the National Intelligencer pc

MADDOX, Dial murdered 1 Dec at Knob Noster by George Kirkpatrick and P. McQuerter;　WARS 8 Dec 1865
　　　　　John D. Mulkey also killed. All had been drinking.

MADDOX, J.W. 9 Jan in Pike Co. of pneumonia in his 19th year. Mbr Infantry, Co D.　LAJ 9 Jan 1862

MADDOX, Jerome of a shoulder wound in Portland, MO at the home of W.M. Alkire,　MORE 18 Nov 1863
　　　　　26 Oct.

MADDOX, __ Johanna, negro slave of Mr., drowned in a cistern; inquest, suicide.	MORE 6 Jul 1863
MADDOX, John W., 8th MO Inf CSA, in Gratiot Prison of consumption.	MORE 19 Jan 1864
MADDOX, Larken of Jackson Co. tried to board a moving train at Pleasant Hill on Thursday last, was run over, died in a few hours ae ca 65-70.	LAJ 9 Sep 1865
MADDOX, Stephen of Callaway Co. 28 Aug ae 80.	MORE 14 Sep 1863
MADISON, Mrs. Sarah M. in Ste. Genevieve Co. at the home of her father, George Taylor, 10 Jan ae (54?).	MORE 3 Feb 1865
MADISON, Dr. T.C., formerly of the Federal army, late of Confederate service, 7 Nov in his 49th year, suddenly. Wife, child. Petersburg & Richmond VA pc	MORE 25 Nov 1865
MADSON, John in Palmyra 14 Jan of diphtheria ae 27.	HAM 23 Jan 1862
MAFFITT, Dr. William at Olive-6th in his 53rd year. Funeral from the Cathedral.	MORE 29 Oct 1864
MAGCHAN, Mrs. Maria mother of Charles Klunk and relict of James M. Magchan. Funeral from home of Wm. F. Gaylord, Polar foot of 15th. Ae 64y 5m.	MORE 1 May 1865
MAGEE, Elizabeth wife of John in Gentry Co. 27 Apr of palsy, in her 61st year. Formerly of Madison Co. KY.	COWS 31 May 1861
MAGEE, William L., son of Madison J. of Harrison Co., a prisoner of war, in Sisters Hospital ae 25.	MORE 18 Feb 1863
MAGEHAN, Joseph M., 125 S. 13th, 29 Apr ae 56. Elmsburg & Harrisburg pc	MORE 30 Apr 1863
MAGINN, John A. of St. Louis in St. Paul 13 Jun. Lived on 10th betw Franklin-Wash.	MORE 18 Jun 1863
MAGINNIS, Elizabeth relict of J.P. and sister of Rt. Rev. John Timon of Buffalo, 31 Mar ae 56. Funeral from Annunciation Church.	MORE 1 Apr 1865
MAGNAR, Edmund, ae 25, on 15 May; had been stabbed a few nights previously by Miller Allen, mate of the Southwestern. John Magnar mentioned.	MORE 16 May 1862
MAGNER, Catherine daughter of John, 79 N. Levee, 2 Jun ae 2y 10m.	MORE 3 Jun 1863
MAGUIRE, James, a bartender, 29 Jan. in his 20th year. Took arsenic (by mistake for salts).	MORE 30 Jan 1861
MAGUIRE, John, inquest: effects of heat. Irish, single, bus driver, ca 45.	MORE 5 Sep 1865
MAGUIRE, Mary A. wife of Constantine of St. Louis at the home of her father, Dr. John Polin, in Springfield KY on 29 Aug.	MORE 3 Sep 1862
MAGUIRE, Sarah Ann relict of James 22 Apr ae 72. Immaculate Conception Church.	MORE 23 Apr 1862
MAHAFFEY, Samuel of 166 N. 7th, 11 Jul ae (36?).	MORE 12 Jul 1865
MAHAN, William Andrew son of G.A.H. and C.J. in Warren Twp 30 Mar of croup ae 4y6m.	PALS 15 Apr 1864
MAHER, Catherine found smothered in a mudhole, may have been pushed in while drunk. Husband Daniel left her 2 months ago; suspected, but exonerated.	MORE 10 Nov 1863
MAHER, Mrs. Catherine found dead in a room at the corner of Main-Howard, widow of (MAHN) Richard, killed by Mooney, on whom inquest was held last Sunday; cause not given. (Mooney discharge MORE 28 Jul shows name as MAHN.)	MORE 21 Jul 1864
MAHER, Patrick run over and killed -- thrown from the wheel of a watermelon wagon. (He was standing on the wheel looking at the melons when the wagon started.) Lived alley, 6-7-Cass-O'Fallon; mother has 3 other children ae 6m, 3y, 8y. Father in prison for assault with intent to kill on Dennis Doyle.	MORE 11 Aug 1864
MAHERN, John, laborer on the Pacific RR, killed at Franklin; was drunk, lay down on tracks, run over. Left wife, 2 children.	MORE 5 May 1863
MAHONE, William C. 26 Aug in his 23rd year. Funeral from the home of Frederick Mathews, 14th-Franklin.	MORE 27 Aug 1864
MAHONY, Simon, 2nd betw Spruce-Almond, 4 Mar in his 35th year.	MORE 6 Mar 1862
MAHONY, Thomas 14 Feb in his (31st?) year. Funeral from the home of P. Rogers, Christy-corner 20th. Alton & Halifax NS pc	MORE 15 Feb 1865
MAJOR, James at his home on Benton Wednesday night ae 91y 2m 4d.	MORE 25 Dec 1862
MAJOR, John son of Stephen S. 19 Jan in his 8th year.	LIT 21 Feb 1862
MAJOR, William L. "an old citizen of Pettis Co." shot by enrolled militiamen, in his own yard, 2 May. Brother-in-law of George Knapp, of MORE.	MORE 4 May 1863
MALEY, family of Michael Andrew, only son of Michael and Bridget, 23 May of Michael scarlatina.	MORE 24 May 1862
Bridget, wife of Michael, 27 May at 118 Christy, long illness.	MORE 28 May 1862
MALLETT, Lamartine, inquest: run over by train at Carondelet. Age not given.	MORE 26 Jan 1863
MALLET, Capt. Francis in St. Joseph 11 Apr at advanced age, "many years' resident."	SJH 15 Apr 1863

MALLEY, Michael at Sisters Hospital ae 50. Funeral from the home of Mr. Malley, stable-keeper, 7th betw O'Fallon-Cass.	MORE 15 Feb 1865
MALLICOAT, Mora, arrested in Taney Co. 11 Nov, in Gratiot Prison of typhoid 24 Jan.	MORE 27 Jan 1863
MALLICOT, John C., captured in Taney Co. 1 Nov, in Gratiot Prison of consumption. (of the 5th MO)	MORE 9 Jun 1863
MALLORY, Clement son/Edward H., near Macon City; a brakeman, fell from a Hannibal and St. Joseph RR car.	PALS 2 Sep 1864
MALLORY, James formerly of Palmyra killed near Philadelphia (MO) by men said to be Lewis Co. militia. Left wife and 10 or 12 children.	PALS 5 Aug 1864
MALLORY, William T. in Fayette in his 66th year. Born Hanover Co. VA, to MO 1840. First Baptist, then joined Christian Church. Postmaster. Left wife and 4 daughters. (Death date shown as 2 Oct in SJH 18 Oct & COWS 16 Oct.) (MORE 8 Oct says ae 65y 3m 20d.) (Also in MAG 15 Oct.)	MORE 19 Oct & 5 Nov 1863
MALTBY, Gilford H. only son/Mrs. Frances F. 5 Jul ae 18y 8m. Int. Bellefontaine. Utica NY pc	MORE 6 Jul 1862
MAMM? ___ killed in Chariton Co. "in retaliation."	MORE 10 Jan 1865
MANDER, Thomas, shot himself. Native of Manchester, ENG; a mechanic, ae 32. Left wife and 3 little children.	MORE 27 Aug 1861
MANGE, Christian, inquest: butcher at South Market, found dead in bed. Verdict, apoplexy. Left wife and several children.	MORE 8 Dec 1862
MANLY, ___ 2 bushwhackers by this name killed south of Springfield along with Alfred Cook, Edward Brown and Hiram Russell.	MORE 31 Jan 1865
MANN, George Louis at Ottaway Center 22 Mar ae 5y 1m 11d, eldest and only surviving son of George and Aline.	MORE 2 Apr 1862
MANNING, Ben killed by bushwhackers in Carroll Co. (CECB)	MORE 21 Jul 1864
MANNING, Mrs. Jane stabbed by her husband Wednesday, died at City Hospital. Lived at 3rd and Convent. Inquest and other reports.	MORE 7 May and later, 1864
MANNING, John W., unmarried man ae 27, jumped or fell from a flat roof adjoining his room. Nephew of George W. Manning, 4 S. 16th. Member of police several years. Had throat infection, was treating it with whiskey.	MORE 21 Feb 1865
MANSUR, Ellen B. wife of Stephen of St. Louis in Lowell MA 20 Feb.	MORE 22 Feb 1862
MANTER, Col. Francis H., died at Little Rock 13 Jun when a horse fell on him; tribute by St. Louis Bar Assn.	MORE 26 Jun 1864
MANWARING, Capt. C.C. shot by guerillas 22 May ae 32, left wife and child. Tribute by Hermann Masonic Lodge.	MORE 3 Jun 1864
MAPES, ___ and ___, two men, killed in a mill explosion 5 miles west of Knoxville. (RICON)	RANC 24 Jan 1861
MARKERS, Jeff, citizen of Shannon Co., 12 Dec of pneumonia. (Undertaker's list)	MORE 19 Feb 1865
MARKS, Anna Mary daughter of Conrad R. and Rebecca in Canton 12 Oct ae 15y 23d.	CANP 19 Oct 1865
MARKS, Elizabeth, mother of David, 6 Apr of paralysis at the home of her son in her 81st year. Methodist.	LIT 15 Apr 1864
MARKS, Mrs. Mary 6 Jul in her 78th year. Funeral from the home of her son-in-law Matthew Rippey, 15th-Poplar.	MORE 7 Jul 1865
MARKSBERRY, Gabriel youngest son of William 16 Aug ae 17y 10m 8d. Short illness.	PALS 19 Aug 1864
MARLACK, "Capt." James, bushwhacker, captured by Capt. Clark, tried to escape while en route to Macon and was killed.	LIT 5 May 1865
MARLEY, Margaret Susan eldest daughter of Michael and Mary 15 Nov, ae 16y 9m 4d, on Gamble betw Pratte-Emily.	MORE 18 Nov 1862
MARMADUKE, Mrs. Darwin 2 Nov at the home of her mother in Saline Co., daughter of the late E.D. Sappington, granddaughter Dr. John Sappington and of Gov. Breathitt of KY. Native of Saline Co., married Sep 1860.	MORE 13 Nov 1865
MARMADUKE, Gov. M.M. of Saline Co. 26 Mar ae 73 of bowel disease. Native of VA, to MO 1828, brother-in-law of Claiborne Fox Jackson and father of Gen. John S. of the Confederate army and Henry of the Rebel Army, and Vincent, member of the State Convention. Gov. M.M. was a Union man.	MORE 8 Apr 1864 MORE 8 Apr 1864
MARNEY, William last Saturday at Allen, son of William D. of Boone Co.; a bushwhacker, new recruit of Anderson's band.	COWS 29 Jul 1864
MARR, Adaline relict of William T. in Florida MO 4 Apr.	RANC 18 Apr 1861

MARRELL, Mrs. Isabella at the home of James M. Torrants near Cheltenham MORE 2 Sep 1865
  1 Sep in her 73rd year. Lexington KY pc

MARSH, Darius 28 Sep of dysentery in his 69th year, at 318 N. 7th. MORE 29 Sep 1864

MARSH, Waldo of the Belle of Peoria 6 Apr ae 42. Winchester IL pc MORE 7 Apr 1864

MARSHALL, James C. at his home on Manchester Road 9 miles from the city; many years MORE 4 &
  a resident. Ae 60y 5d. 5 Feb 1864

MARSHALL, Joseph Alford son of William D. and Caroline, at the home, Chambers MORE 2 Feb 1865
  betw 11-12, ae 5y 2m 3d. Interred Bellefontaine.

MARSHALL, Samuel S. in Platte City 9 Nov of consumption in his 22nd year. MORE 18 Nov 1863

MARSHALL, Willie son of Marcus and Lucinda 11 Apr of consumption ae 15m. Funeral MORE 13 Apr 1861
  from the home of William Marshall, Morgan St., to Bellefontaine Cem.

MARTIAL, Salvador ae 10 and Francis ae 14, drowned 4 Jun while picking up wood; MORE 9 &
  widowed mother lives in Carondelet. Bodies found. 11 Jun 1861

MARTAIN, Eveline wife of Charles E. 9 Mar ae 24y 8m near Osage, Crawford Co.
  Ill 5 months. MORE 18 Mar 1863

MARTIEN, Harriet L. 12 Jan at the home of her parents, Dr. J.M. and N.M., in MORE 8 Mar 1865
  Callaway Co. of inflammatory rheumatism ae 18y 3m 12d. Buffalo & Philad.pc

MARTIN, ___ a carpenter, formerly of Sedalia, killed by a fall; had been sick WARS 10 Nov 1865
  several days and was insane at the time.

MARTIN, Andrew, Sgt. in Reeves Com., taken in Ripley Co., died in Gratiot Prison MORE 15 Jan 1864
  (taken 25 Dec or died that day) /of bowel inflammation.

MARTIN, Annie Ranlett eldest daughter of Charles G. and Sophia, Clark betw 11-12, MORE 13 May 1861
  ae 12y 10m. NY & Baltimore pc

MARTIN, Arsinoe at Dr. Seeley's Water Cure, Cleveland, 20 Aug in her 60th year. MORE 25, 27,
  Relict of Rev. Corby, lived past several years with her only daughter, 28 Aug 1864
  Mrs. Wesley Fallon, St. Louis. Funeral from home of Joseph A. Jamison.
  Interred Bellefontaine.

MARTIN, Miss Augusta of New Madrid at Memphis 29 Jan ae 19. MORE 9 Feb 1865

MARTIN, Daniel P at his home on Belmont betw 15-Targee, Sunday; police officer MORE 16 Dec 1862
  about 2 years.

MARTIN, Edgar E. son/George M., formerly of Baltimore, killed in the battle of MORE 14 Jul 1854
  Moore's Bottom, AR 29 Apr ae (23?). Baltimore pc

MARTIN, Elizabeth F. wife of A.J. of Howard Co. in Memphis 19 Jul at the home of MORE 9 Aug 1862
  A.J. Donnelson. Ill 8 weeks.

MARTIN, Mrs. Elizabeth wife of John 21 Sep at the home, 12th-Morgan, in her MORE 22 Sep 1863
  66th year. Interred Rock Spring.

MARTIN, George, an old nurse at the City Hospital, of heat "a very worthwhile MORE 8 Aug 1861
  member of society, now in reduced circumstances." Lived St. Ange-Carondelet.
  Mrs. Isabella at the home, St. Ange below Park, of pulmonary apoplexy; MORE 10 Aug 1861
  "her husband died of the same cause that morning." Left 3 children.
    (Original item referred to George as "English.")

MARTIN, George Warren, a printer, 29 Mar ae 47y 3m, of paralysis. Lived at the MORE 30 Mar 1861
  se corner of 7th-St. Charles. Fredericktown MD, Louisville, Delaware, OH pc SLMD "

MARTIN, Dr. Honore, native of Rockville, Montgomery Co. MD, 20 Apr in his PALS 1 May 1863
  56th year. To MO in 1838.

MARTIN, James of Boone Co. in Alton Prison in Dec. COWS 9 Jan 1863

MARTIN, James of Pulaski Co. in Gratiot Prison 22 Nov. MORE 26 Nov 1862

MARTIN, Leila daughter of J.W. and A.F. in Independence 6 Jan ae 2y 10m. MORE 27 Jan 1861

MARTIN, Louis at 7th & Russell 26 May ae 63. MORE 27 May 1865

MARTIN, Lieut. P. of Capt. Hardin's Military Co., by accidantal discharge of a LAJ 3 Oct 1861
  gun. Son of J.M. Martin, Circuit Clerk. Interred Bowling Green.

MARTIN, Sarah M. wife of William B. and daughter of Joseph Gooding at College Mound MORE 22 Jan 1865
  (Macon Co.) 16 Jan in her 37th year.

MARTIN, Smith "old, idiotic, blind" killed near Ashley; no known reason. (LAJ) MORE 9 Aug 1864

MARTIN, Willis F. at his home in Jefferson Co. 28 May ae 57. MORE 14 Jun 1864

MARTINDALE, Wallace W. 19 Dec ae 27. Funeral from home of C.D. Faver, Locust-8th. MORE 20 Dec 1861

MASE, Adam, an old settler, at his home in Frankford. Once represented the LAJ 8 Jul 1865
  county in the legislature.

MASLIN, Phil T. of Baltimore in St. Louis 20 Jul ae 60y 9m 17d.	MORE 21 Jul 1864
MASON, George W., MD, at his home in Tipton 10 Apr ae 41.	CAWN 15 Apr 1865
MASON, Capt. James C. in the <u>Sultana</u> disaster; body not recovered. Tribute by Knights Templar and Masons.	MORE 21 & 23 Jun 1865
MASON, Jesse killed by bushwhackers in northern Chariton Co. (CECB)	MORE 29 Jul 1864
MASON, Mrs. Melinda M., relict of Joseph of Dixon IL, at the home of her son, E.R., in Webster Groves 17 Feb ae 73. Interred in Dixon.	MORE 19 Feb 1865
Lucinda M. wife of E.R. 29 Oct in Webster Groves. Funeral 1st Congregational.	" 30 Oct 1865
MASSEY, John "a fast young man" killed by Ulysses Harrison 18 Nov 1860 in a fracas at Kate Gallagher's house. Harrison found guilty of 2nd degree murder.	MORE 26 Mar 1861
MASSEY, Mrs. Maria wife of B.F., formerly secretary of state, and daughter of Mrs. Col. Pierce, Boonville, 23 Jul in her 43rd year.	MORE 2 Aug 1864
MASSEY, Sarah Jane wife of H.A. and daughter of William D. and Frances Murphy at Jefferson City 19 Mar of phthisis pulmonalis.	MORE 28 Mar 1865
MASSIE, Mrs. Lucretia G. 25 Apr at the home, Spruce betw 15-16. Louisville, Maysville, Richmond pc	MORE 26 Apr 1862
MASTERSON, Hannah, inquest: debility from intemperance. Lived at 23-O'Fallon, left 3 daughters, 2 in Sisters Hospital; the third, ae 2, taken there.	MORE 16 Mar 1864
MASTERSON, John Thomas only child of Peter and Maria, 25 Aug at 17th & Wash., ae 12y 20d. Interred Calvary.	MORE 26 Aug 1864
MASTERSON, Mrs. R.A., relict of James, in Decatur 19 Apr ae 46. Funeral from the home of P. McCarren, 265 Pine, to St. John's Church; int. Calvary.	MORE 21 Apr 1865
MASURE, Augustus A, 23 Nov of heart disease ae 27y 3m 10d. Funeral from the home of his mother, 147 S. 4th, to the Cathedral. Interred Calvary.	MORE 24 Nov 1864
MATH, John, a grass cutter, on the Erskine farm 8 miles out Lami Ferry Road. Cause unknown.	MORE 15 Jun 1863
MATHER, Mary E. wife of B.T. at Spring Fork Post Office 16 Oct ae 32. St. Louis & Cincinnati pc	SEDA 10 Dec 1864
MATHEWS, Alexander 27 Sep in his 68th year. Funeral from the home of his son-in-law William Smith, 117 N. 14th. Pittsburgh & Philadelphia pc	MORE 28 Sep 1865
MATHEWS, Edwin killed by guerillas in Carroll Co. (Carrollton <u>Democrat</u>)	MORE 21 Jul 1864
MATHEWS, James T., a bushwhacker, shot at DeSoto in transfer to St. Louis.	MORE 14 Aug 1864
MATHEWS, Samuel W. 1 Mar in his 34th year. CA pc	MORE 2 Mar 1865
MATHIAS, Christian, a carpenter ae 19, drowned from a skiff at the foot of Chambers St.; left mother, 3 sisters on Webster near Broadway.	MORE 13 Apr 1862
MATLACK, Harry 2nd son of Earl and Sabrina in Dakotah Terr. 2 Jun ae 7y 11m.	MORE 16 Jun 1865
MATSON, Abraham S. Jr. son of Abraham and Phebe Ann 9 Apr in Missouriton of brain inflammation ae 2y 3m. Hannibal pc	MORE 11 Apr 1861
MATSON, Athalia G. wife of A.M. at their home in Pike Co., of consumption.	MORE 29 Mar 1862
MATSON, Enoch at his home in Pike Co. 12 Jul after a 16-day illness. Born in Bourbon Co. KY 9 Jan 1787; married Miss Shobe there 10 Oct 1810. To MO 1816, settled here 1821. Paris & Hickman KY & Columbia MO pc	MORE 17 Jul 1863
MATTHEWS, Mrs. Ellen, wife of George (of Cook & Matthews) Wednesday.	SLMD 19 Mar 1861
MATTHEWS, Eliza in Columbia 23 Apr, mother of J. Lawrence and Milton S. Born in Philadelphia 1785, to Richmond Co. VA as infant. Moved to Columbia with sons about 1837 after husband's death.	COWS 3 May 1861
Julia E. daughter of Milton S. and E.L. 2 May, <u>ca</u> 11.	COWS 3 May 1861
MATTHEWS, Emma 3rd daughter of Elijah B. and Sarah of Washington Co. 7 Sep. CA pc	MORE 21 Sep 1865
MATTHEWS, James B. son of J.L. of Columbia, 30 Mar ae 21.	COWS 3 Apr 1863
MATTHEWS, Capt. John W., Co A 8th MO Cav at Duval's Bluff AR 12 Dec, wounded by guerilas.	MORE 12 Jan 1864
MATTHEWS, Lawrence 30 Sep in his 51st year. Funeral from the home of J.E. Ashbrook, 9th & Spring. Interred Bellefontaine.	MORE 2 Oct 1865
MATTOX, Thomas W. 29 Oct ae 44; lived opposite Henry Shaw's Tower Grove.	MORE 30 Oct 1865
MAUGHAS, Dr. M.M. 18 Jun in Callaway Co. Born Fleming Co. KY 6 Jun 1799, to MO 182? (4?). Lived St. Charles, then Montgomery Co., last 20 years in Callaway Co. Member House of Reps, State Senate. (FULT 2 Sep says Maugha<u>m</u>)	MORE 29 Jun 1864

MAUPIN, Cornelius in Boone Co. 13 Nov of pneumonia ae ca 40. COWS 17 Nov 1865

MAUPIN, Margaret C. wife of Dr. D.G. of Millersburg 21 Aug; born Trumbull Co. OH COWS 4 Sep 1863
22 Aug 1826. Left 7 small children. Methodist.

MAUPIN, W.W. of Callaway Co., son of Waller W. of Boone Co., a bushwhacker, killed COWS 2 Jun 1865
by militia at the house of Asa Thompson 6 miles from Fayette near LIT 9 "
Rocheport Road. WARS 17 "

MAURER, Elizabeth wife of Michael, a respectable lady at 49 S. 7th, suicide by MORE 31 Oct 1865
(MOWER) arsenic. Her husband, a butcher, had bought a farm and she said she would
not live there. Had previously attempted suicide.

MAURO, Charlotte E. wife of Charles G. of St. Louis and daughter of George M. Davis MORE 28 Jan 1864
of Washington DC, 26 Jan ae 27. Funeral St. John's Episcopal.

MAUS, Mrs. Frederick instantly killed near Lookout Station, Pacific RR, when their JCPT 15 Nov 1865
wagon was struck by a train; husband not expected to live. (The ? Times)
(CACE 18 Nov says her husband was Christopher -- perhaps she was Fredericka?--
and that he died a little later. She was about 80.)

MAXEY, Elisha A. 25 Apr of bowel inflammation, in this county, ae 50y 2m 2d. MAG 18 Jun 1862
Joel H. 12 May of the same disease, ae 51y 9m 5d.

MAXSAINE, Peter, inquest: German carpenter ae 53, suddenly of heart disease; left SLMD 1 Jan 1861
an orphan child.

MAXWELL, Amanda C. daughter of John near Rocheport 6 Aug ae 23. COWS 15 Aug 1862

MAXWELL, John T., one of Porter's men, arrested 15 Aug, died Monday, of rubeola. MORE 19-24 Nov 1862

MAY, Alice S. daughter of Robert and Martha 30 Nov of typhoid ae 15y. MORE 3 Dec 1861

MAY, Josephine, drowned a few days ago at foot of Anna St., body found. MORE 23 Jun 1861

MAY, Nancy widow of Henry 19 Feb ae 87. FULT 8 May 1861

MAYBERRY, S. 9 Feb in his 41st year at the home of S. Meyer. MORE 10 Feb 1862

MAYER, Francis J. yesterday ae 23y 3m. Native of New Orleans, which pc. MORE 27 Sep 1865

MAYERS, Caroline M. wife of Edward 10 Nov in her 52nd year, at their home, MORE 11 Nov 1864
81 N. 7th. Boston & Nashville pc

MAYFIELD, Fannie eldest daughter of Jacob and Jettie, 2 Mar ae 4y 5m 12d. FULT 8 Mar 1861

MAYO, Jane in Columbia 8 May ae 17. COWS 12 May 1865
Rebecca, of typhoid, 29 Oct ae 20y 6m. "   3 Nov 1865

MAYO, William murdered in Cooper Co. by militiamen. (Killed at the post office.) MORE 8 &
Large landowner, merchant. (BOOM 11 Jun says killed by bushwhackers near 9 Jun 1864
Pilot Grove.)

MAYS, Joseph son of John C.(and Mary)at their home, 14 Aug 1862 in 25th y. Baptist. PALS 7 Aug 1863
Corbin " 27 Jul ae 20m 10d. (Mother not shown for Joseph)

Kate at the home of her father, John, 30 Aug in her 18th year. Member PALS 18 Sep 1863
of Bethel Church since 1860.

MAYS, Sarah at the home of her brother Latham 20 Aug in her 47th year. Member of PALS 18 Sep 1863
Bethel Church for many years.

MEAD, Jennie Davis Thursday ae 22. Funeral from her mother's home, 136 Locust. MORE 24 Nov 1865

MEAD, John A. son of Peter 28 Jan of consumption in his 29th year, at 207 Morgan. MORE 29 Jan 1861

MEAD, Lucien H. son of Lucien and Mattie at their home near Jennings Station, MORE 9 Mar 1863
ae 3y 6m 7d. Interred Bellefontaine.

MEAD, Mary wife of John, 15 Aug in her 39th year. Funeral from the home of her MORE 17 Aug 1864
brother, Lawrence Harrigan, 153 Biddle.

MEAD, Theodore W. 27 Aug ae 47y 4m 10d. NY pc MORE 28 Aug 1864

MEADOWS, ____ killed near Agency Ford trying to escape from militia after arrest. SJH 1 Aug 1864

MEADOWS, J.B., citizen of Callaway Co., 8 Jan of measles. (Undertaker's list) MORE 15 Jan 1865

MEDDLING, Gottlieb, an old man, inmate of the poorhouse, of sunstroke. He had been MORE 8 Aug 1864
there since 26 Jul, had left to get his shoemaker tools, died on the trip.

MEEK, Charles, a bartender, burned on the Cherokee. MORE 17 Jul 1864

MEEK, Mary Ann wife of James, 177 S. 5th, 4 Nov ae 46. MORE 5 Nov 1865

MEEK, Jane, wife of William, 12 Mar ae 38, at 265 Carr. MORE 14 Mar 1863

MEIER, George, citizen, 28 Feb of chronic diarrhoea. (Undertaker's list) MORE 13 Feb 1865

MEIER, Henry, well-known saddler and harness-maker on E. side 14th betw Poplar and   MORE 28 Apr 1865
    Chambers killed at the 7th St. Depot yesterday while trying to board the
    train; his foot slipped. Ca 40, German, 4 or 5 children.
MELHOLLEN, Thomas B., citizen of Boone Co., of pneumonia 21 Jan. (Undertaker's list) MORE 22 Jan 1865
MELLINGER, August at the home of his stepfather John Boeringer 10 May ae 25y 6m.   MORE 13 May 1861
    Interred Bellefontaine.
        Edward eldest son of the late August and Pauline Krieger at the home of   " 21 Sep 1864
        John Boeringer, ae 9, of heart disease.
MELTON, Adam, 10 miles sw of Independence ae 40. Left widow and 6 children.   MORE 27 Jan 1861
MENANES, Mrs. Wilh. 21 Jan. in her 40th year, at 172 4th St.   MORE 22 Jun 1864
MENARD, Joseph Cyprian, oldest son of L.C. and Augustine of Ste. Genevieve, at   MORE 31 Mar 1864
    St. Mary's College, Perryville, 26 Mar in his 17th year.
MENDENHALL, Richard 11 Mar at Friend's Mission ae 46.   KCJC 12 Mar 1864
MENEFEE, Ferdinand N. at Quincy, formerly of Macon Co. MO, 16 May ae 26y 4m.   MORE 28 May 1865
MENGE, Fanny Eliza only child of J.H. and Fanny Dodd, 15th St. south of Morgan,   MORE 15 Apr 1861
    14 Apr ae 1y 8d.
MENIFEE, Lafayette S. 2 Dec 1864 at his home in Richmond MO, of typhoid, in his   MORE 12 Jan 1865
    42nd year. Born Culpeper VA, to MO 1844, married Mary H. Colgan in
    Jefferson City; leaves wife, 4 children. Methodist South.   & 6
+ MENKENS, Anthony H. 2 Aug at the corner of 13th & Wash, 2 Aug, of a lingering   MORE 3/Aug 1864
    illness. Left widow and children.   SLMD "
MENOWN, Maggie Isabella only daughter of Andrew and Essey 21 Oct ae 8y 11m. 150 Collins. MORE 22 Oct'65
++ MEREDITH, C. Ed in Jefferson City 23 Jan of consumption; left wife, 2 children.   JEST 24 Jan 1863
+ MENKENS, Bernard 28 May at the home of A.H. Menkens.   MORE 29 May 1863
MERCER, Mary Elizabeth wife of Dr. Charles F. and daughter of Dr. C.C. and Lucy Ann   MORE 4 Mar 1862
    Campbell 17 Feb in Knob Noster ae 23y 24d, of brain congestion. Left
    4 small children. Cooperstown OH pc
MERCHANT, Mrs. William 7 Nov, corner 9th-Chambers. Springfield MO pc   MORE 9 Nov 1863
++ MEREDITH, John W. at his home in Boone Co. 15 Mar ae 76y 6m 26d. Member of the   COWS 10 Apr 1863
                                                    Christian Church.
        Jane wife of John decd in Callaway Co. 22 Nov ae 79.   JCPT 13 Dec 1865
MERIGOLD, Charles Ingersole at his father's home, 345 7th St., 11 May of consumption MORE 13 May 1862
    ae 22y 9m. Canada pc
MERIWETHER, Dr. Fontain at Springfield, Lincoln Co., 30 Apr in 65th year. Born VA.   MORE 11 May 1861
MERRELL, Alfred, Texas Co.: letters of administration to Margaret Merrell 21 Jun.   ROLEX 31 Jul 1865
MERRIFIELD, Jerry, actor at the Melodeon, of intemperance.   MORE 10 Aug 1862
MERRILL, Thomas 16 Dec at LaGrange ae ca 55, father of Mrs. Leonard Bradford, QuincyIL. " 20 Dec 1861
MERSER, Henry, elderly German at 10th near Davis, of heat.   MORE 14 Aug 1861
METHVIN, Maj. John W. of McBride's Brigade, captured in Marion Co. 16 Oct, in   MORE 10 Dec 1862
                                                    Gratiot Prison.
MEYER, Charles, inquest: German, hanged self at his boarding house. Unmarried.   MORE 28 Jan 1864
MEYER, Francis "respectable and industrious German citizen on 10th near Biddle,   MORE 2 Apr 1865
    suddenly Friday of heart disease ae ca 60. Emigrated 23 years ago, to
    St. Louis 20 years ago. Left wife and 5 children.
MEYER, Henry P., of Tamm & Meyer, 6 Feb in his 30th year.   MORE 9 Feb 1864
MEYERS, Edmond, 8 Jul in his 71st year. Funeral from the home of his son John E.,   MORE 9 Jul 1863
    #6 Convent St. San Francisco & Sacramento pc
MEYERS, Samuel, son of E.S. and Margaret, at 90 Market St. ae 5.   MORE 27 Sep 1863
MICHAEL, D.C. 12 Mar of pleuro-pneumonia ae 48. Funeral from Central Presbyterian,   MORE 14 Mar 1861
    interred Bellefontaine. Cincinnati pc
MICHEL, William Amede 4 Jun of bowel inflammation. Born Harrisburg PA 1832, of   MORE 5 Jun 1864
    French extraction; grandfather fled France during the Revolution. Family
    to Dayton in 1841, widowed mother still there. Funeral from home of his
    brother J.C., 262 S. 7th. Harrisburg, Cincinnati, Dayton pc
MIDER, Bernard, member 10th Ward Home Guard, killed in the Camp Jackson affair.   MORE 18 May 1861
MIELKE, August, only son of Michael and Anna Dorothea, 4 Sep ae 5y 6m 10d.   MORE 6 Sep 1863
MIELER(MILLER), Increase at Sisters Hospital of paralysis ae 52. Int. Bellefontaine. MORE 13 Feb 1863

MIGHELS, Mrs. M.J. 10 Sep at Clark and Monroe. Interred Bellefontaine.   MORE 11 Sep 1863

MILBURN, J. Vanderburgh, youngest son of the late Gen. William, at St. Louis U. ae (15?)y 6m. Funeral Trinity Church, 11th-Washington.   MORE 4 Dec 1864

MILBURN, Lillie daughter of Harry and Elizabeth 13 Dec ae 6.   MORE 17 Dec 1864

MILES, J.M. citizen of Randolph Co. 21 Jan of smallpox. (Undertaker's list)   MORE 22 Jan 1865

MILES, Mrs. R.M. wife of R.E. at the home of her mother, Mrs. Sheriff, in Fulton 25 Jul ae 30.   COWS 8 Aug 1862

MILLAN, Clara Cook youngest daughter of Alex G. and Adaline 6 Aug ae ca 6.   PALS 14 Aug 1863

MILLAN, James at 88 Olive St. 11 Jan in his 53rd year. Palmyra & Alexandria VA pc   MORE 12 Jan 1861

MILLAN, Thomas, Friday last. A Mason.   PALS 1 Dec 1865

MILLER, Adam, funeral to be preached next Sunday in Fulton by Elder T.M. Allen.   COWS 17 Apr 1863

MILLER, Andrew, a hairdresser living at #12 Centre St., ae 3? y.   MORE 12 Nov 1861

MILLER, Annie M. wife of Rev. E.K. 26 Apr ae 25. Left 3-week-old infant. Interred Methodist cemetery.   HAM 28 Apr 1861

MILLER, Mrs. Caroline M. at the home of her son-in-law Gabriel Alexander in Milton MO in her 79th year.   MORE 21 Apr 1862

MILLER, Mrs. Daniel: husband arraigned for her murder, convicted of manslaughter in the 4th degree.   MORE 19 Jul 1863

MILLER, Eddie Turner eldest son of Adelle and the late Joseph J. 9 Mar of laryngitis ae 7y 7m. Funeral from home of Dr. Wm. Barker, 10th-Monroe.   MORE 14 Mar 1863

MILLER, Elizabeth (see Mrs. Daniel, above) stabbed by her husband Daniel while he was drinking. Notice mentions son.   MORE 18 Apr 1863

MILLER, Evans, prisoner, 31 Jan of erysipelas. (Undertaker's list)   MORE 2 Feb 1863

MILLER, Fayette M., MD at his home in Jackson Co. 1 May in his 39th year. Son of Dr. A. and Elizabeth of Madison Co. KY.   COWS 30 May 1862

MILLER, Frank (or Francis L.) of New Market: trial of Samuel Hill, charged with his murder.   WEST 2 Jun 1865

MILLER, George W. 27 Apr ae 70, resident of Marion Co. 40 years. A Methodist.   PALS 6 May 1864

MILLER, George W. 6 Mar of typhoid pneumonia in his 25th year, at 483 Morgan.   MORE 8 Mar 1863

MILLER, Mrs. ____ wife of the late George W. 30 Jul in her 24th y. Int. Fee Fee. (8 Aug says granddaughter of Judge Olly Williams, St. Louis Co; Martha A.)   MORE 1 & 8 Aug 1863

MILLER, Gideon 27 Apr ae 70.   COWS 13 May 1864

MILLER, Hugh, who lived near Pilot Grove and disappeared last August; body found near McGee's Grove, believed killed by bushwhackers.   BOON 12 Mar 1864

MILLER, Jennette E. wife of Francis M. in Carroll Co. 28 Sep ae 29y 7m 2d.   COWS 16 Oct 1863

MILLER, Jessie E. daughter of Edward and sister of Mrs. George D. Hall of St. Louis in Blythedale, Jackson Co. 8 Mar in her 21st year,   MORE 15 Mar 1862

MILLER, John in Callaway Co. 17 Aug ae 29y 11m. Left wife, 2 children.   FULT 26 Aug 1864

MILLER, John C. 14 May in his 25th year.   MORE 15 May 1861

MILLER, Joseph Gilman 12 Feb in his 38th year.   MORE 19 Feb 1863

MILLER, Dr. John B. of Ste. Genevieve 24 Mar in St. Louis in his 31st year. Interred Ste. Genevieve.   MORE 26 Mar 1863

MILLER, Lydia Ann wife of Rev. G.W. and daughter of John and Malinda Graves in Chillicothe 13 Mar ae 27.   MORE 23 Mar & 4 Apr 1863

MILLER, Mrs. Margaret at her home in Monroe Co. 1 Nov in her 86th year, a Methodist 60 years.   MORE 14 Nov 1865

MILLER, Margaret J. consort of S.K. and youngest daughter of Maj. Alfred Basye (late of Jefferson City) at Manchester 17 Aug in her 34th year.   MORE 23 Aug 1864

MILLER, Mary of Hannibal, obituary from the Mexico Ledger, no facts.   HAM 23 Jan 1861

MILLER, Mrs. Mary N., mother of John of St. Louis, ae 71.   MORE 3 May 1864

MILLER, Mary Philomene Lafon, wife of Frederick, ae 24y 7m. Funeral from the home of her aunt, Mrs. Mary R. Provost, 2nd-Lombard. Cincinnati & Boston pc   MORE 26 Dec 1863

MILLER, Nannie Peters daughter of William and Eliza O. 12 Dec ae 6y 11m, at 9th-Walnut. Cincinnati pc   MORE 13 Dec 1864

MILLER, Richard W. of St. Louis near Smithville AR 18 Oct 1862 ae 22y 2m.   MORE 17 Mar 1863

MILLER, Sarah Bell wife of L.C., of Fulton, at the home of her mother Mrs. Shanks   FULT 4 Jan 1861
       in Jackson Co. 22 Dec.
MILLER, Thomas, a returned Federal soldier, killed at High Hill 25 Aug by Wm. Wilson. PALS 22 Sep 1865
MILLER, Thomas E. of Randolph Co. at Camp Morton IN 28 Jan ae 24.   MORE 13 Mar 1864
MILLER, William ae ca 8 drowned in 3 feet of water in a pond near Marion and   MORE 24 Jun 1864
       Carondelet.
MILLER, W.B., a militia of Warrenton, killed in Callaway Co.   MORE 20 May 1865
MILLER, Mrs. ___, mother of W.W., in a flux epidemic.   FULT 2 Sep 1864
MILLS, Harry son of Mrs. Mary, 103 Pine, 22 Feb ae 13y 7m 20d. Cincinnati pc   MORE 23 Feb 1864
MILLS, John L. at Sisters Hospital yesterday ae 64. Interred Bellefontaine.   MORE 15 Oct 1865
       Lancaster OH pc
MILLS, Lucy 25 Jul at the home of her daughter. Born in VA, later went to KY;   FULT 28 Jul 1864
       married John Mills; came to MO in her old age.
MILLS, Mrs. Nancy 10 May in her 57th year.   GLWT 23 May 1861
MILLSPAUGH, Clara daughter of Jerre and Rosetta 20 Jun at their home on St. Charles   MORE 21 Jun 1864
       Rock Road, ae 4y 5m. Interred Bellefontaine.
MILMAN, Henry, a cook employed at Hambright Johnson's restaurant, believed drowned.   MORE 9 Jul 1861
       Clothes found on river bank. Ae 21, "much liked" by his employers.
MILTENBERGER, Charles L. eldest son/Eugene and Mary at Stringtown near Carondelet   MORE 16 Mar 1862
       14 Mar ae 10y 7m 28d. Funeral at St. Francis Xavier Church.
MINARD, Mrs. Mary D. wife of Rev. P.R., 14 Nov ae 55. Funeral Christ Church Chapel.   MORE 16 Nov 1864
MINOR, John A., Chariton Co.: letters of administration to Josephine Minor 2 Dec.   CECB 29 Jan 1863
MINOR, Nannie Drench daughter of the late William G. at the home of her uncle,   JEST 3 Sep 1864
       Gen. James L., near this city, 1 Sep ae 18. Grandmother mentioned.
MINOR, Sarah and Joseph: Chariton Co. Final settlements by Daniel B. White.   CECB 24 Jul 1862
MINOR, Thomas G. son/John and Camille in Fayette 22 Aug, of throat disease, ae 4y8m. COWS 30 Aug 1861
MINORCE, James, prisoner of war, 22 Jan of typhoid pneumonia. (Undertaker's list)   MORE 26 Jan 1863
* MINTER (family of   Harriet, wife of John 16 Mar in her 64th year. Born Shelby Co. KY,
  Clay Co.)   in MO more than 20 years. Baptist since age 14.   LIT   8 Apr 1864
                     Martha Jane wife of Robert 16 Mar; also born in Shelby Co. KY;
                     "sisters, mother- and daughter-in-law."
MINTER, Mary Elizabeth 17 Sep, daughter of Thomas and Mary E., "a little over 3."   LIT 23 Oct 1863
MINTER, Ann Eliza wife of Thomas 16 Apr of consumption in her 25th year.   LIT 24 Apr 1863
* MINTUR, Mrs. Robert, 10 miles north of Liberty, "day before yesterday" when her   KCJC 18 Mar 1864
       clothing caught fire.
MITCHEL, Mildred Medora youngest daughter of S.J. and Mildred, ae 9y 9m, at   MORE 2 Jul 1865
       21st and Wash. Interred Bellefontaine.
MITCHELL, Alexander suddenly 5 Dec at the home of his father in Randolph Co.,   MORE 19 Dec 1861
       ae 8y 2m 15d.
MITCHELL, Dr. Alexander W. 18 Jan 1874. Funeral from the home of his son-in-law   MORE 20 Jan 1862
       Col. B.G. Farrar. Philadelphia pc
MITCHELL, Andrew, brother-in-law of J.R. Finley of St. Louis, at St. George's,   MORE 5 Apr 1865
       Bermuda, where he had gone for a change of climate, 3 Mar.
MITCHELL, Charlies Eddie youngest son of Thomas and Mary 2 Nov ae (3?8?)y 2m 17d.   MORE 5 Nov 1862
MITCHELL, Col. D.D., native of VA, 23 May in his 55th year. Funeral from the home   MORE 25 May 1861
       of Dr. E. Bathurst Smith. Interred Calvary.
MITCHELL, Eleanor M. wife of the late Robert S. at Maysville KY 10 Feb. Funeral   MORE 21 Feb 1865
       from the home of William Matthews, 202 Chouteau.
MITCHELL, Elizabeth Jane daughter/Alexander and Louisa of West Ely 3 Feb ae ca 20.   PALS 10 Feb 1864
MITCHELL, Henry S., a mulatto boy, killed by a poison orange supposedly given to him MORE 14 Feb 1863
       by a mulatto girl, Caroline Baltimore, who had a grudge against his
       mother. Inquest showed no evidence of poison; apparently not corrosive.
MITCHELL, Martha Adaline of Bates Co. in Clay Co. 16 Feb at the home of   LIT 28 Feb 1862
       M. Mitchell, ae 59.
MITCHELL, Mary Brent wife of A.S. of St. Louis in Danville KY at the home of her   MORE 25 May 1861
       father, A. Gallatin Talbott, 21 May. Ill 3 weeks.

MITCHELL, Michael, a laborer at Jefferson Barracks, found dead of brain congestion   MORE 14 Oct 1863
          caused by intemperance. Wife and little girl lived at 7th-Papin.

MITCHELL, Slack son of N.Y. and K.W. 6 Oct of diphtheria ae 10y 7m 13d.   COWS 15 Nov 1861

MITCHELL, Lieut. Thomas, 1st MO Artillery, killed in ammunition explosion on the   MORE 27 Aug 1863
          Madison near Vicksburg; funeral St. Louis, interred Calvary.

MITCHELL, Mrs. V.J. wife of Gen G.D., CSA, in Nolasulga AL 14 Jan. Sister of Mrs.   MORE 7 May 1864
          Susan F. Hall, daughter of Rev. David Anderson; sisters separated since
          the war. Chicago, Lexington MO, Carrollton MO pc

MITCHELL, William Fleming 30 Jan in his 24th year. Funeral at the Baptist Church.   SJH 31 Jan 1864

MOBERLY, ___ a bushwhacker killed by scouts under Cols. McFerran and Neill.   LEXUN 15 Aug 1863

MOFFAT, Marian relict of James 7 Apr of consumption in her 40th year. Funeral   MORE 9 Apr 1862
          from 1st Presbyterian.

MOFFET, Miss Robena M. 27 Sep, daughter of P.M.A. and Elizabeth. Born in   MORE 4 Oct 1862
          Scotland, age 11y 10m.

MOFFETT, George W. son of the late Joseph F. and Esther 25 Aug of typhoid pneumonia MORE 27 Aug 1862
          ae 11y 3m. Formerly of Washington DC, which pc

MOLDER, Judge Haley W., an old man, murdered by bushwhackers on James Bayou 3 Mar.   CHAC 4 Mar 1864

MOLINEAUX, Thomas G. of valvular heart disease 24 Feb. Native of England, resident   MORE 5 Mar 1861
          of St. Louis 6 years, ae 49. Philadelphia pc. (SLMD 28 Feb says ae 42)

MOLLOY, Capt. John aboard the Empress 10 Aug in his 42nd year. (It had been bombar- MORE 16 &
          ded by guerillas.) Funeral from the home of Mrs. Patterson, Lucas Place-18th   21 Aug 1864
          to St. John's Church; interred Calvary. Came to St. Louis with his parents
          as an infant, worked at the grocery house of Sproule & Buchanan, started on
          the river ca 1850. Was 2nd mate on the Amaranth, StL-NO, 2 years; later
          clerk on the Aleck Scott, Shenandoah and J.C. Swon. Commanded Orleans and
          John Walsh (of which he supervised the building, in Cincinnati). Also
          commanded the Illinois, Planet, Mollie Able and Empress.

MOLONEY, Johanna youngest daughter of Patrick and Mary ae 14y 8m. Long illness.   MORE 23 Sep 1863

MOLOY, James D. in Macon 22 Mar of measles, member of Capt. Loring's Co. 7th MO Reg, MAG 2 Apr 1862
          ae 19y 2m 28d. From near Bynumville, son/James C. of the same company.

MONNIER, Edward at Rock Hill 19 Feb in his 32nd year.   MORE 21 Feb 1864

MONROE, Ethel (Hubbie, Hettie, or Hattie) Lee, daughter of J.R., 18 Mar in   COWS 3 Jun & 1 Jul 1864
          Callaway Co. ae 5y6m16d. (MORE says Hattie, ae 5y 6m 26d)   MORE 4 Jul "

MONROE, Mrs. S.S. wife of R.S. of Buchanan Co. 10 Jul.   SJH 11 Jul 1865

MONTAGUE, sons of Robert V.   Mickelborough Lawrence, eldest, in Vicksburg of   MORE 26 Jul 1863
          and Emily G.   measles 18 Jul ae 31. Glasgow MO pc
                                Henry Clay, youngest, 4 Aug ae 17y 64 27d. Funeral MORE 5 Aug 1863
                                  from home of Mrs. Ann B. Jennings, Halls Ferry.
                                  Interred Bellefontaine. Glasgow MO pc

MONTGOMERY, Georgia youngest daughter of Dr. Thomas in Georgetown MO 8 Mar in her   MORE 12 Mar 1863
          21st year.

MOODY, William "many years a citizen" 8 Jun in Boone Co., formerly of Madison Co. KY. COWS 27 Jun 1862

MOONE, Mrs. Adeline L. 11 Dec in her 59th year. Funeral from the home of her son,   MORE 12 Dec 1865
          H.D., North 9th betw Benton-Warren.

MOONEY, Elizabeth Cecelia and Hannah, daughters of John, killed by the falling of   MORE 14 Jun 1864
          the commissary store in Memphis, interred in Calvary Cemetery.

MOONEY, Francis only son of the late Francis A. at the home of his mother, Mrs.   MORE 1 Sep 1865
          Joseph Murphy, 31 Aug, in Carondelet. Funeral St. Mary's, Carondelet.

MOORE, Alexander 27 Dec in his 67th year. Native of Lancaster Co. PA.   SLMD 31 Dec 1861

MOORE, Anne daughter of Levi N. and Caroline at Bridgeton 14 Aug ae 16y 2m.   SLMD 17 Aug 1864

MOORE, Dr. Benjamin James at Charleston MO 5 Jun, representative from Mississippi Co. MORE 24 Jun 1864

MOORE, Dr. Benjamin W.D., formerly of KY, number of years a practicing physician in MORE 21 Dec 1862
          Kansas City, died in Franklin Co. 19 Dec.

MOORE, Carrie Atwood daughter of Henry C., Gen. Supt. St. Louis, Alton & Terre Haute MORE 26 Aug 1864
          RR, 23 Aug at Newberry VT ae 7y 11m.

MOORE, Charley, a foreman, killed in the Platte Bridge disaster.   SLMD 10 Sep 1861

MOORE, Elizabeth wife of Davis 19 Feb ae 50, at 117 N. 6th. Interred Bellefontaine. MORE 20 Feb 1861
          Davis, 1 Sep ae 50. (shown as 177 N. 6th)   " 2 Sep 1864

123

MOORE, Franky eldest son of Eli and Mahala 30 Aug ae 9y 9m 3d. SJH 1 Sep 1865

MOORE, George at Cincinnati 3 Apr ae 40, after a lingering illness. MORE 9 Apr 1864

MOORE, Mrs. George 7 Mar at 307 Franklin in her 34th year. Richmond VA & New Orl. pc MORE 8 Mar 1861

MOORE, George M. at Bridgeton 16 Nov in his 60th year; resident of this county 36 years. To be interred at Central Church (? St. Martin's?) on Old Bonhomme Road. State representative. MORE 18 Nov 1863

MOORE, George W. 25 Apr of bowel stricture in Palestine Twp., Cooper Co., in 61st y. COWS 17 May 1861

MOORE, Henry C. Jr. son of Col. Henry C. and Amanda 28 Sep ae 5y 1d. Lived on St. Ange near Hickory. MORE 29 Sep 1863

MOORE, James at the home of his son L.S. in Pike Co. 22 Sep in his 85th year. Served in War of 1812, to MO in 1819. LAJ 8 Oct 1864

MOORE, John G. shot "last Saturday" at his home 1 mile south of Keytesville. (CECB) LIT 22 Jan 1864

MOORE, Mrs. Kate, nee Cassady, in St. Louis 7 Mar; her brother William H., native of Richmond VA, 16 Mar in New Orleans at the home of another brother, John L. (of consumption) ae 37. SLMD 26 Mar 1861

MOORE, Ketia 2nd daughter of John and Ann, 19 N. 4th, 27 Mar ae 6y 7m 8d. MORE 28 Mar 1862

MOORE, Lewis in Oregon, Holt Co. 26 Nov of typhoid ae 30. "From Ireland," formerly of Lucas, Moore in Leavenworth. Left wife and infant. MORE 30 Nov 1861

MOORE, Linea wife of William 4 Feb at Farmville Mills, Ray Co. in her 55th year. A Methodist; had 10 children; one daughter preceded her in death. RICON 19 Feb 1863

MOORE, Matilda C. daughter of William N. and Malinda 9 Nov ae 3y 11m 13d. (MORE 3 Dec says "in Monroe Co.") COWS 29 Nov 1861

MOORE, Michael ae 7 drowned in McDonald's Quarry. Parents at Main near Howard. MORE 3 Aug 1861

MOORE, Pres killed by soldiers in lower Cape Girardeau Co. CHAC 22 Apr 1864

MOORE, Rebecca A. wife of James M. 9 Jan of pneumonia ae 22y 2m 11d. BOBS 19 Jan 1861

MOORE, Richard E. in Kansas City 1 Aug ae 24, after a protracted illness. LIT 9 Aug 1861

MOORE, Sarah wife of G.W. and daughter of Perry Balay, 28 Mar. CAWN 25 Apr 1863

MOORE, Simeon son of Benjamin recently in Jackson Co. ae 13. KY pc MORE 23 Oct 1863

MOORE, Strother, Chariton Co.: letters of administration to Mary C. Moore, exr, 4 Apr. (See "Death Records from Missouri Newspapers 1854-1860") CECB 20 Apr 1861

MOORE, William, hanged as a guerilla ae 22; parents in Texas Co. MO. MORE 10 Sep 1864

MOORE, William J., employed by the OH & MS RR Transfer Co., fell from the train; died 25 May ae 19y 1m 15d. Lived 7th below O-Fallon-Cass. Interred Calvary. Cincinnati pc. MORE 26 May 1864

MOORMAN, Thomas J., Chariton Co.: letters of administration to Mary E. Moorman 30 May. CECB 1 Jun '61

MORAN, Ellen consort of Thomas 23 Jun. Funeral from the home of Michael Malay, 7th betw Cass-O'Fallon. MORE 24 Jun 1864

MORAN, Katy ae 5 murdered by Kate McCoy. (Subsequent stories say Mrs. McCoy had a grudge against the child's father.) MORE 21 Apr 1863

MORAN, Mary 21 Nov at the home of her parents, 126 Collins, in her 22d year. NY pc MORE 22 Nov 1864

MOREHEAD, Turner in his (80? 89?)th year at the home of his son Garrett W. near Glasgow, Howard Co., 16 Jan. Served in War of 1812; born Fauquier Co VA 8 May 1784, to Baltimore at ae 19. Father was a colonel in the Revolution; he often saw Washington as a child in VA. Baltimore & Philadelphia pc MORE 7 Feb 1864

MOREHISER, Mary Magdeline consort of Philip 18 Jul. Formerly of Baltimore, late of Dubuque; mother-in-law of John Rosecan, 16th-Biddle. Ae 74. MORE 19 Jul 1862

MORELAND, Mrs. Mary L. widow of Hanson B. 20 Mar in her 65th year. Funeral from Centenary Church. Interred Bellefontaine. Philadelphia, Washington, Staunton & Wheeling pc MORE 21 Mar 1864

MORELOCK, Mrs. Ann Elizabeth wife of David and daughter of James A. Adkins in Adair Co. 25 Mar in her 22nd year. MAG 9 Apr 1862

MORGAN, Edward eldest son of E. 26 Mar of scarlet fever ae 6y 10m 21d, at Gratiot east of 9th. MORE 27 Mar 1862

MORGAN, Edward ae 38. Funeral from Christ Church. Cincinnati pc. MORE 12 Apr 1865

MORGAN, Henry O. 7 Oct ae 27. Funeral from the home of his father, 114 S. 5th. Interred Bellefontaine. Pittsburgh pc MORE 9 Oct 1865

MORGAN, J.D. Sr. at his home 5 miles east of Salem 28 Aug in his 61st year.	MORE 7 Sep 1862
MORGAN, J.W. 15 Nov in his 51st year. Native of Lynchburgh VA, left wife and several children. Interred Hannibal.	LAJ 5 Dec 1861
MORGAN, Maranda (male), an old citizen killed instantly at the Warrenton Steam Sawmill when he fell on the saw, 7 Aug.	CANP 20 Aug 1863
MORGAN, Margaret, inquest: intemperance and debility. Lived in an alley near DeKalb and Sidney; left husband and 2 children.	MORE 20 Sep 1862
MORGAN, Solomon formerly of Hannibal but last 4 years in Louisiana MO, died there Thursday; interred Methodist Cemetery in Hannibal. (See J.W. Morgan?)	HAM 21 Nov 1861
MORIN, William, a Canadian, many years a resident of St. Joseph, recently of St. Louis, ae 66. Formerly of Buffalo, NY. Funeral from the home of J.H. Fisse, 91 Market.	MORE 8 Aug 1861
MORITZ, Joseph Francis 16 Nov ae 60, at Main south of Mulberry. Citizen 27 years.	MORE 17 Nov 1864
MORITZ, Mildred S. wife of William Monday last age 25.	FULT 12 Apr 1861
MORLEY, Mrs. Elizabeth, lately from Lancashire ENG, at her home, Carr-10th, of heart disease.	MORE 3 Dec 1861
MOREL(L), Alden, inquest: formerly cook at Antoine Curate's Restaurant, ill for a few days, found dead in bed at his boarding house. Congestive chills.	MORE 8 Feb 1863
MORONEY, Cornelius stabbed by Michael J. Casey at St. Paul Station, Pacific RR; James Donnegon also stabbed. All "under the influence."	MORE 6 Jul 1864
MORRIS, Charles R. 21 Sep near Louisville ae 62y 5m 23d.	LAJ 30 Sep 1865
MORRIS, Ida youngest daughter of D. and Emily Tuesday at 205 Carr ae 5y 20d. Pittsb pc	MORE 3 Jun '63
MORRIS, James 17 Jun at the home of James M. Morris in his 82d year. Born in Essex Co. NJ in 1779, to Mason Co. KY, to Clay Co. 13 years ago. Husband, father.	LIT 5 Jul 1861
MORRIS, Leanna, only daughter of T.M. of St. Louis Co., ae 5y 3m 14d.	MORE 8 May 1864
MORRIS, Mrs. Roann at Jefferson City ae 22 at the home of her brother, Allen P. Richardson, 12 Sep. Long painful illness.	RICON 2 Nov 1862
MORRISON, ____, murderer of Peter Taylor in Tuscumbia, killed by militia.	CAWN 29 Apr 1865
MORRISON, son of Henry ae 5 accidentally killed by pistol shot. Family had moved to the country a few days before.	MORE 17 May 1861
MORRISON, Archibald, resident of Saline Co., 28 May ae 53. Born Woodford Co. KY 4 May 1811.	MORE 15 Jun 1864
MORRISON, George citizen of Monroe Co. of pneumonia 24 Feb. (Undertaker's list)	MORE 6 Mar 1865
MORRISON, John 17 Dec ae 46, on 12th betw Christy-Morgan.	MORE 18 Dec 1861
MORRISON, John, a boy (son of a widow) killed in the explosion of a powder magazine used by merchants in St. Joseph. James McNerny also killed.	SJH 14 May 1864
MORRISON, Leon son of Henry and Cassandra 12 Mar ae 1y 9m.	MORE 14 Mar 1861
MORRISON, Kate wife of William and daughter of William D. Swinney of Howard Co. in Glasgow 8 Jun.	MORE 10 Jun 1861
MORRISON, Mary mother of Henry of St. Louis in Jefferson Co. KY 2 Jul ae 65.	MORE 9 Jul 1864
MORRISON, Melina C. wife of Capt. Mott, Chouteau betw 7-8, on 13 Jul.	MORE 14 Jul 1862
MORRISON, William M. 22 Jul in his 51st year, funeral from the home of R.J. Lockwood, 135 Locust. Born in St. Charles, in business first with his brother-in-law Wm. Pettus, later with George Collier. Methodist.	MORE 23 Jul 1865
MORRITT, Gertrude Hallett youngest daughter of Henry B. and Maria L. 19 Apr of typhoid, ae 3y 2d, at 47 S 16th. Interred Bellefontaine.	MORE 21 Apr 1862
MORROW, Capt. Christopher, formerly of Clark Co. KY, 4 May at the home of his son-in-law Thomas F. Birch near Glasgow, ae 74.	MORE 7 May 1865
MORROW, George Earnest oldest son of Edward and Julia 25 Sep at 13th near Hickory, ae 8y 9m.	MORE 26 Sep 1862
MORROW, George W. in Gratiot Prison; arrested in Butler Co. 14 Apr. (Was of that county.) Chronic diarrhoea	MORE 22 & 28 Sep 1863
MORSE, Col. Brastus of 22nd MO of wounds received near Renick. Native of NY, many years resident of Hannibal. (HAM)	LAJ 9 Jan 1862
MORTAN, Samuel 7 Jan ae 80y 6d, native of KY, in MO about 36 years.	PALS 15 Jan 1864

MORTIMER, Elizabeth daughter of Edward and Sidney Ann 15 Aug of gangrenopsis, ae 10y 3m, at the home, Thomas betw Clay-Glasgow. — MORE 16 Aug 1862

MORTIMER, Mary Ann wife of James and only daughter of Thomas and Ann Shirgas, of consumption, 19 Apr ae 22. — MORE 22 Apr 1863

MORTLAND, Ann wife of Thomas 17 Jun of consumption. — SLMD 25 Jun 1861

MORTON, George, native of Scotland, 9 Jan of pneumonia ae 74. Resident of St. Louis 47 years; of the firm of Morton & Laveille. — MORE 10 & 11 Jan 1865

MORTON, John A., tribute by Springfield United Lodge #5. Mentions wife, children. — SPRIP 27 Jul 1865

MORTON, children of Joseph & Jane in Cloverdale, Clay Co. Ida Theresa, ae 4y 18d, on 15 Aug William ae 11m " — LIT 19 Aug 1864

MORTON, Margaret Elizabeth 6 Apr of puerperal fever ae 25y 1m 7d. Wife of Henry. Milwaukee pc — MORE 14 Apr 1861

MORTON, Nathaniel 13 Nov ae 44 at Olive-8th. Covington KY & Portsmouth OH pc — MORE 14 Nov 1863

MORTON, Mrs. Peter of dropsy 22 Aug ae 76. Funeral from the home of George Morton, (69?) Spruce. — MORE 24 Aug 1862

MORTON, Sarah A. wife of Elder Richard C. 28 Jan ae 27; in declining health for two years. Member Christian Church 10 or 12 years. Left husband, 3 children. — LIT 1 Feb 1861

MORTON, Thomas M. son of Mrs. A.T. of Clay Co. in Buchanan Co. 4 Sep ae 14y 8m 3d. — LIT 13 Sep 1861

MOSELEY, George W., Chief Clerk in the Auditor's Office of MO, 5 Oct in Jefferson City. Husband of Ann M., father of 5 children; youngest child of the late Thomas, late of Owensboro KY; born Hartford Co. KY Dec 1812, youngest of 18 children. Louisville KY & Fairfield IA pc — MORE 9 Oct 1862

MOSELY, John P. at St. Vincent's Asylum in St. Louis 7 Dec ae 28. — COWS 19 Dec 1862

MOSELY, William Jr. son of Jacob in Boone Co. 20 Sep of lung congestion ae 24. — COWS 25 Sep 1863

MOSES, A.P. of Sedalia killed when disbanded soldiers of the 4th MO Volunteers went on a spree. — SPRIP 9 Nov 1865

MOSIER, Jane wife of Jonah and daughter of the late Lee Rollins of Clay Co. in Warren Co. OR 28 Aug in her 42d year. Born in Bourbon Co. KY. — LIT 24 Nov 1865

MOSS, Annie wife of Robert W. 27 Sep in her 23rd year. — MORE 28 Sep 1864

MOSS, Crittenden son of James H. and Susan Thursday at the home of his uncle, A.P. Moss, ae 23m. — LIT 18 Jul 1862

MOSS, Mason F. 11 May ae 45; funeral from home of Mrs. B.I. Boyd. — SJH 12 May 1865

MOSS, Preston T. in St. Joseph 1 Jun ae 40. — COWS 28 Jun 1861

MOSS, Mrs. Susan wife of Carter in St. Louis Co. 27 Apr ae 58y 9m 25d. Funeral from Fee Fee (Baptist) Church. — MORE 28 Apr 1864

MOSSE, Albert "who formerly kept the Union Hall Saloon on 2nd betw Mulberry & Lombard," stabbed to death by John O'Neil. — MORE 24 Mar 1863

MOTHERSHEAD, Nathaniel 30 Jan ae 62. Born Anderson Co. KY, to MO 25 years ago. — LIT 7 Feb 1862

MOTONGER, Henry, coming from Stark Co. OH with his family to locate in Gentry Co., died suddenly in St. Joseph ae 59, having sent his family on to Gentry. (Albany MO News 10 Oct) — HOLS 20 Oct 1865

MOTT, Nathan, citizen of Wright Co. captured 10 Jan, in Gratiot Prison. — MORE 1 May 1863

MOULDER, W.H., an old man living near the mouth of James Bayou in Mississippi Co., killed by guerillas at his home 3 Mar ae ca 65. His wife and son were absent at the time. — MORE 11 Mar 1864

MOUNT, Samuel at the home of his nephew William Mount in St. Louis Co. 21 Dec in his 76th year. Born in NJ Mar 1788, to St. Louis 1816. Funeral from William's home (Mrs. Barker's) on Clayton Road. — MORE 23 Dec 1863

Mrs. Mary relict of Samuel 13 Jul of cancer in her 70th year. Funeral from the home of her nephew Martin F. Walsh, Clark betw 21-22. — MORE 14 Jul 1864

MOUNTJOY, Capt. Charles 31 Dec at his home near Paynesville in his 67th year. Born KY, to MO as a territory; soldier in the War of 1812. — LAJ 2 Jan 1862

MOUSER, Michael, prisoner, 3 Feb of measles. (Co I? 18? MO?) (Undertaker's list) — MORE 7 Feb 1864

MOWETT, Abbie Letitia only daughter of Charles and Clara E. 6 Jul ae 5y 1l, 11d. Funeral from the home of Mrs. M.H. Carroll, North Market betw 12-13. — MORE 7 Jul 1864

MOXLEY, John H., Chariton Co.; Letters of administration to Nancy Moxley 7 Aug. Henry, ": petition to sell real estate by Dewey Moxley. (also see John C. Ingram) — CECB 11 Sep 1862 / " 7 May 1864

MOZER, Mrs. Ann in Clarksville, Pike Co., 7 Mar ae 46. She had united with the   LAJ 19 Mar 1864
     Presbyterian Church in OH in early youth, but was a Methodist more than 20
     years. Left 2 daughters. (Notice signed J.C. Van Deventer)

MUDD, Susan Maria eldest daughter of Maj. Alexis and Carrie at Olive-18th, ae   MORE 21 Jan 1862
     13y 11m 12d. Interred Bellefontaine.
     Alexis 22 Feb ae 38 at his home, 4th-Walnut.   MORE 23 Feb 1863

MUELLENKEMPF -- see KUEMPF

MUENCH, John kicked by a mule he had been whipping (last Wednesday), now died.   PERU 15 Apr 1864
     Employed by Adam Fath.

MUER, Mrs. Angelina ca 40 found dead in her rooms, Vine betw 2-3; possibly dead   MORE 20 May 1864
     since Jan when her landlady last saw her. Room in neat condition, no sign of
     foul play, cuase of death indeterminable. Had been a chambermaid on boats
     and a nurse, had a son in the Army.

MULCH, Lizzie daughter of Louis, living 6 miles south of Kirksville, 14 Apr of   MAG 30 Apr 1862
     diphthera at the home of B.G. Barrow, in her 20th year.

MULDROW, George F. at the home of his son-in-law Judge John P. Clark, in Mexico MO, COWS 19 May 1865
     3 May in his 72nd year.

MULDROW, William E. ae 17, son of John G., accidentally shot himself Monday last.   SPRIP 17 Aug 1865
     (Mexico Beacon)

MULHALL, Mary Nenett only daughter of George and Mary Ann, living at Easton and   MORE 9 Apr 1865
     Glasgow, ae 5y 6m. Vicksburg pc

MULHAREN, Henry fell through a hatchway at the State Tobacco Warehouse, ae 24.   MORE 26 Mar 1863
     Lived 7th betw Carr-Biddle, left wife and baby. "Highest terms of
     praise by all who knew him."

MULLIGAN, Edward, fireman on the R.B. Converse, drowned at the foot of Green St.   MORE 31 May &
     Lived on Gay betw 23-24, left wife, 2 children. Body later recovered.   19 Apr 1863

MULHOLLAND, Jane Agnes daughter of James and Jane, ae 14m. Funeral from the home   MORE 15 Sep 1861
     of John Mulholland, 15th-Poplar.

MULHOLLAND, Willy only son of Jabe and Ellen 12 May of intermittent fever, ae 2y9m. MORE 13 May 1862

MULKEY, John D. murdered at Knob Noster 1 Dec by George Kirkpatrick and P. McQuerter. WARS 8 Dec 1865
     (Dial Maddox also killed.) All had been drinking.

MULLALY, Elly E. only daughter of Patrick and Rosy 27 May of scarlatina, at   MORE 28 May 1862
     15th-Market, ae 2y 2m 10d.

MULLEN, Laura Maria only daughter of William P. and Ellenora 20 Aug of   MORE 21 Aug 1861
     peritonitis at 340 N. 7th, ae 3y 2m 3d.

MULLEN, Lizzie Jane eldest daughter of J.T. and Maggie 23 Dec at 5th-Rutgers, of   MORE 24 Dec 1861
     scarlet fever, ae 3y 10m 4d. Maysville KY & Massilion OH pc

MULLER, George B. only son of George C. and Rosina at 16th-Papin, ae 18y 11m 15d.   MORE 19 Oct 1864
     Interred Bellefontaine.

MULLIGAN, Col James A.: notice to those who wish to participate in obsequies.   MORE 2 Aug 1864

MULLINS, Paddy, a noted bushwhacker, shot in Tipton 23 Apr by order of Gen. Brown. BOOM 30 Apr 1864

MULLOWNEY, James, a suicide "despondent over the recent order in relation to the   MORE 26 Jul 1862
     enrollment of militia." Left wife, 1 child, Decatur betw Ann-Russell.

MUNDAY, Joseph at his home in Pike Co. 20 Jan of lung fever in his 59th year, a   LAJ 28 Jan 1865
     resident more than 20 years. St. Louis & Pike Co. IL pc

MUNDAY, Mrs. Stephen died of grief after her husband had been sentenced to 2 years MORE 20 Nov 1861
     for perjury, leaving 4 small children. He had been respectable and honest
     but had misrepresented his finances and an "unfortunate situation" resulted.

MUNDAY, Wade H. near Canton 16 Feb of dyspepsia. Born in KY, to MO in early days.   CANP 9 Mar 1865
     Interred Baptist Church Cemetery, Wyaconda. Mason. St. Louis & Louisville pc

MUNRO, George in Livingston Co. 16 Mar in his 58th year. Born in Warren (now   MORE 18 Jun 1862
     Allen) Co. KY, to MO 1810; married Mary Morin 14 Apr 1829. Lived in
     St. Charles (now Howard) Co., then to Cooper Co., to Livingston 20 years
     ago. Member of the State Legislature.

MUNTWILER, John, inquest: native of Canton d'Argove, Switz.; died in a destitute   MORE 11 Apr 1864
     shanty on 10th near Lafayette, ae 68, of apoplexy.

MURPHY, Mrs. ____ 15 Jan ae 70. Funeral from home of her son-in-law William Conway MORE 16 Jan 1865
     at (343?) Broadway, interred Calvary.

MURPHY, Mrs. Ann 24 Sep at the home of E.W. Peay, Grand Ave. in (63rd? 83rd?) year. MORE 25 Sep 1863
     Funeral, St. Bridget's Church.

MURPHY, Annie wife of Dennis B. and daughter of the late Edmund Harnett of Listowen,   MORE 1 May 1865
Co. Kerry IRE, at the home, 40 Collins. Funeral from St. Patrick's Church,
interred Calvary. NY, Baltimore, Chicago, Cork & Kerry pc

MURPHY, Bartley, Irish fell overboard while clinging to the hull of the Prairie State.   MORE 20 &
His brother was near him. Body later recovered in Carondelet.   26 Aug '65

MURPHY, Edward eldest son of Dennis B. of debility resulting from sunstroke, ae   MORE 1 &
(23? 25?)y 4m 23d. Lived at 40 Collins. Interred Calvary.   2 Jul 1864

MURPHY, Mrs. Ellen ae 56; lived on Pine betw 15-16. Funeral St. John's Church.   MORE 12 Mar 1864

MURPHY, Ellen F. wife of David and daughter of Zachariah and Amelia G. Foss, at   MORE 10 Nov 1863
Washington, Franklin Co. 6 Nov ae 23y; also her infant son.

MURPHY, Frank "clever but intemperate" froze to death near his home, near   HAM 15 Jan 1861
Rockbridge Mills, Thursday.

MURPHY, John, a sawyer living at 314 Broadway, yesterday. Left wife in Ireland.   MORE 7 Dec 1865

MURPHY, John P. son of Mary and the late James 12 Jul of dysentery ae 15y 8m.   MORE 14 Jul 1865

MURPHY, Lizzie G. wife of Thomas A. and daughter of Lawrence Fallon, 5 Dec in her   MORE 6 Dec 1865
23rd year. Funeral from the home of her brother-in-law, Peter Farley, on
Summit Ave. Interred Calvary.

MURPHY, Michael, a merchant of Rolla and native of Co. Clare, IRE, ae 39. Funeral   MORE 5 Sep 1864
from his late residence, 73 St. Charles St., St. Louis.

MURPHY, Michael, native of Co. Mayo, 18 Aug ae 65 at 39 Orange St.   MORE 19 Aug 1862

MURPHY, Patrick 23 Sep ae 48 at Jefferson & Lafayette.   MORE 24 Sep 1865

MURPHY, Peter J. 30 Oct at Mineral Point of consumption in his 21st year.   MORE 8 Nov 1864

MURPHY, Mrs. Thomas from the effects of a blow on the head (with a bottle) by her   MORE 16 Jul 1861
husband, who "keeps a groggery on 3rd & Almond." She lived 5 weeks. The
article mentions "family."

MURPHY, Thomas C. at Old Mines, Washington Co. 29 Aug of typhoid ae 57y 3m.   MORE 4 Sep 1861

MURPHY, Walter "an old and efficient member of the police force" at his home,   MORE 1 &
221 12th St., if typhoid. Interred Calvary. Ae 28.   2 Aug 1861

MURPHY, Capt. William D. of Linn Creek 5 Sep. Interred Jefferson City.   MORE 6 Sep 1864

MURRAY, Maj. ____, a rebel who drowned a few days ago, body found; had two   LAJ 29 Aug 1863
revolvers strapped to his body.

MURRAY, Bennett murdered Sunday 3 Jul near the home of Joseph P. Eddleman on   PERU 8 Jul 1864
Greenville Rd. by a robber gang. "One of our best citizens." (also see
HARTLE, Jefferson)

MURRAY, Edward P. of St. Louis (in Gen. John Bowen's Brigade) killed at Shiloh.   MORE 4 May 1862

MURRAY, John, inquest: shot in back of head at boarding house of Mrs. Elizabeth   MORE 13 &
Nixon, 8th-Biddle. She and Adam Purcell suspected. Verdict: unknowns.   14 Jun 1865

MURRAY, Nannie McGary second daughter of Ben F. and Celia Phillips 2 Oct ae 10y1m13d.   MORE 15 Oct 1863
Bowling Green KY & Austin TX pc

MURRAY, Patrick died of intemperance because his wife deserted him some time ago.   MORE 23 Aug 1864

MURRAY, Samuel, a farmer, in Audrain Co. 20 Sep in his 66th year.   COWS 4 Oct 1861

MURRAY, Sarah daughter of Oliver and Louisa Friday morning ae ca 7.   PALS 16 Dec 1864

MURRAY, Maj. Thomas, Chief Clerk of the late House of Representatives (MO), a   LEXUN 10 Jan 1863
printer, editor of Warsaw paper, killed in the battle of Prairie Grove.

MURRIN, James 4 Jan ae 50 at the home, 7th-Wash.   MORE 4 Jan 1862

MURRY, Hugh, a barkeeper on the Von Phul, killed there (with Patrick Gorman).   MORE 17 Dec 1863
Lived Monroe betw 16-17. Funeral St. Michael's Church. int. Calvary.

MUSICK, Nancy relict of Eli in Franklin Co. 30 Jul in her 76th year.   MORE 9 Aug 1862

MUSSER, Jacob, inquest: fell down embankment at Quarry Saturday. Unmarried, ca 23.   MORE 23 Oct 1865

MUSSER, Richard in Clinton Co., only son of Adolphus and Mattie, 19 Apr ae 5y 11m.   MORE 20 May 1862

MUSSI, Giovanni "this day," native of Italy, old resident of St. Louis. Lived in   MORE 3 Feb 1863
alley betw Market-Walnut-3-4. Ae 53y 6m. Interred Rock Spring.

MUTZ, John, ae 26, Sunday.   SLMD 14 Aug 1864

MYERS, Charles Edwin son of Samuel and Jemima at their home in Pike Co. 19 Nov   LAJ 21 Nov 1861
ae 2y 7m.

MYERS, Jacob at the home of his son Edward in Bonhomme Twp. 8 Mar ae 93y 24d.   MORE 15 Mar 1863
       Native of Baltimore, a Presbyterian 50 years.

MYERS, Col. William at Benton, Scott Co. 3 Jan in his 76th year. A pioneer, to MO   CHAC 25 Jan 1861
       ca 1808-9. Had 6 or 7 children, all dead except Mrs. Thomas Hunter of this co.

MYNAGHAN, John shot yesterday in an affray at Central House Saloon, Chestnut-3-4.   MORE 11 Aug 1863
       Supposedly by James Franey. Both tailors.

NABER, Harman B. 24 Apr at City Hospital of apoplexy ae 32. Germantown & IA pc.   MORE 12 May 1864

NABOR, Elizabeth wife of H.B. 7 Jan.   MORE 8 Jan 1862

NAGEL, George 17 Dec ae 43y 7m. (Notice by Elizabeth.) Lived at 19 Myrtle.   MORE 18 Dec 1864

NALLAGAN, ___ daughter of Simon, ae 5, at Allenton; burned to death playing   MORE 25 Apr 1863
       with matches.

NAMPAIGNE, Joseph of the 1st KS Vols, 9 Feb ae 22. Funeral from father's home,   MORE 10 Feb 1865
       229 Green.

NANCE, John of typhoid pneumonia 25 Mar in his 50th year, at 12th-Benton.   MORE 26 Mar 1861
       Boston & Galena pc

NAPIER, Mrs. Catherine, wife of the fireman on the Dickerson (boiler exploded   MORE 23 Oct 1864
       8 Oct); body identified.

NAPTON, Malinda wife of Hon. W.R. and daughter of the late Thomas Williams of   COWS 16 Jan 1863
       Knoxville TN in Saline Co. 31 Dec.

NAUFANS, Augustus near Camp Granville of heat.   MORE 12 Aug 1862

NAUGHTON, Eliza Mary Ann Agnes Blond wife of Joseph L. 18 Jun in her 37th year.   MORE 21 Jun 1863
       Funeral Church of the Annunciation, interred Calvary. Manchester ENG
                                                                    & Dublin pc

NAVALLIS, Mary at her home, Lombard betw Main-2, 19 Jan ae 63. St. Joseph MO pc   MORE 20 Jan 1865

NAYLOR, Margaret 29 Sep in Howard Co. ae 20y 9m 3d.   COWS 20 Oct 1865

NAYLOR, Rosanna only daughter of Silas H. and Mary M. 19 May of scrofula ae 15y 26d. MORE 30 May 1864

NEAD, Matthew 20 Jul ae 49 at his home, sw corner of Morgan and 9th.   MORE 22 Jul 1865

NEAF, Charles Joseph of dropsy ae 72y 9m 5d. (Father of Mrs. Coules?)   MORE 8 May 1864
       Funeral from 225 N. 6th St.

NEAGLE, James, a sheet iron worker ae 29, apoplexy caused by intemperance.   MORE 20 Apr 1863

NEAL, James son of Sydney of Perch Twp., a bushwhacker, killed by Thomas Adams   CAWN 13 May 1865
       at Millersburg, Callaway Co.

NEBER, Dederick, a German boy, drowned Friday; body found Tuesday. Ae 12.   SJH 18 Aug 1863

NECKER, Ernest, stabbed himself with a pocket knife; had been ill with smallpox.   MORE 7 Mar 1863
       Ca 30, lived Mulberry betw 3-4, left wife and one small child.

NEFF, Mrs. Eliza, tribute: member Christian Church 20 years, ae 48.   LIT 24 Mar 1865

NEILL, Joseph at Cheltenham 20 Mar in his 67th year after a lingering illness.   MORE 23 Mar 1865
       Benton OH & CA pc

NEISER, John ae 9 fell from a car of the Iron Mountain RR while hitching a ride.   MORE 20 Sep 1861
       Parents lived on Lesperance.

NEITERS, Henry, an orphan living with his uncle, a jeweler on Franklin Ave.   MORE 6 Jul 1863
       betw 5-6, killed in a riot at Hyde Park 4 Jul.

NELSON, A.R., Saturday last; resident of this city a number of years.   CAWN 12 Jan 1861

NELSON, Abraham, obituary: born Campbell Co. TN 30 Dec 1829, joined Methodist Church SJH 2 Apr 1865
       South 1851, married Louisa Stout 9 Jan 1853; to MO (Nodaway Co.) 1856.
       Enlisted 23 Jul 1863, died in Little Rock hospital 13 Jun 1864.

NELSON, Addie daughter of Capt. E.R. and Adeline 30 Oct in Carondelet ae 9y 3m.   MORE 1 Nov 1865

NELSON, Addie R. 13 Dec ae 20y 9m 4d, daughter of James and Mary E.; born in   CAWN 24 Jan 1863
       Cooper Co. 9 Mar 1842. Methodist. Ill 10 days.

NELSON, Cora Eugenia only daughter of Capt. William S. and Diana B. 15 Mar ae 3y 4m. MORE 16 Mar 1861
       Funeral from Church of the Messiah. Interred Bellefontaine.

NELSON, James in Tully, Lewis Co. 14 Nov ae 70. Veteran War of 1812. Methodist, Mason. CANP 20 Nov '62

NELSON, James O. Sr. 15 Dec 1861 ae 59y 7m 10d. Emigrated from Fauquier Co. VA   CAWN 8 Mar 1862
       in 1836, a Baptist since 1855.

NELSON, John N. stabbed Friday in a fight with Charles Newlee.   LIT 23 Aug 1861

NELSON, ___ wife of N., 22 Jan 1865.   PALS 17 Feb 1865

NELSON, Noah M. at Selma, Jefferson Co. 11 Jan of smallpox; of Co K 14th AL CSA. MORE 20 Jan 1863
(Put off steamboat, said he was from Bexar, Marion Co. AL, son of Moses.)

NELSON, Mrs. Sarah W. 24 Feb in her 34th year, at Washington-Garrison. Late of TN. MORE 25 Feb 1865

NESBITT, John at his home in Fulton Tuesday last. FULT 28 Jul 1864

NETHERTON, William B., of 23rd MO, in Kansas City 8 Jan of typhoid; interred here. GAL 26 Jan 1865

NETTLETON, William G. 11 Nov of consumption in his 39th year. Funeral from the MORE 13 Nov 1864
home of Joseph Bruen, 9 Orange. Interred Bellefontaine.

NEUGENT, Joseph killed at Warsaw by John and Duff Towns, brothers, former rebels. MORE 22 Oct 1865
Neugent "quiet, elderly, simple-minded." (letter from Warsaw 17 Oct)

NEUN, Lieut. H., killed in Dallas GA 29 May 1864, funeral 26 Nov from the home of MORE 26 Nov 1865
his parents. Interred St. Mark's.

NEVENS, J., citizen of Callaway Co., 9 Jan of typhoid. (Undertaker's list) MORE 15 Jan 1865

NEWBERRY, Capt. John of U.S. Police at Prov. Marshall's office from the effects MORE 29 Aug 1863
of a beating by several U.S. soldiers. Left wife, 16-year-old daughter.

NEWELL, Clara wife of Charles, Bellefontaine Rd. near Bissell's Lane, ae 29. MORE 22 Mar 1863

NEWELL, Louis 9 Oct in his 49th year. Funeral from the home of John Young, corner MORE 10 &
of Gamble-High. Resolutions by Engineers Association. 11 Oct 1865

NEWELL, Capt. William N. of St. Louis at the home of his brother in Maysville KY MORE 14 May 1864
12 May in his 47th year.

NEWGENT, William only son of James and Mary 22 Apr ae 3y 1m, at Franklin-22nd. MORE 23 Apr 1862

NEWHOUSE, Mrs. Jane 20 Nov at the home of her son, 548 Monroe, ae 70. MORE 22 Nov 1864

NEWKIRK, Mrs. C.--(?) (Drake? Burke?)(Paper badly spotted.) CAWN 9 Feb 1861

NEWKIRK, Sarah consort of William 6 Nov at the home of her son, N. 14th betw MORE 8 Nov 1864
N. Market-Monroe, ae 69y 9m 11d. Louisville & New Albany pc

NEWLIN, Charles L. 6 Oct in his 27th year. Funeral from home of his friend, MORE 7 Oct 1865
John B. Hughes, 124 Walnut. NY pc

NEWMAN, Mrs. Elizabeth wife of David at High Ridge, Jefferson Co. 30 Sep MORE 5 Oct 1862
ae 18y 6m 9d. Birmingham ENG pc

NEWMAN, Isaac J.W. of Jeffries' Band, captured in Howell Co. 28 Jan, in MORE 18 Feb 1863
Gratiot Prison of pneumonia.

NEWMAN, Margaret Ann wife of Arthur R. in Charleston MO 1 Jun. Born 8 Aug 1817 in CHAC 3 Jun 1864
Henderson Co. KY; married W.P.M. Scott, settled in Cadiz KY. Left a widow
in a few years, moved with father and brothers to MO in 1840, married Mr.
Newman in 1847; moved to New Madrid, then St. Louis, then to Charleston.
Methodist. Left husband, 2 sons, 2 daughters.

NEWPORT, John B. of Ralls Co. stabbed 1 Apr by ___ Haddock, who lives at the LAJ 11 Apr 1863
edge of Pike Co.

NEWSHAM, Eliza Corless at the home of her brother-in-law Charles Speck, near MORE 13 Mar 1862
Carondelet, 12 Mar ae 18y 2m 25d. Funeral from the home of Samuel
Stelle, Dillon-Hickory.

NICHOL, John B. "long a watchman at Underwriter Engine House," a young man. Funeral
from the home of his father on Carondelet opposite the Arsenal. MORE 26 May 1864

NICHOLS, Henry, a boy, drowned at the foot of Jefferson yesterday while bathing. MORE 1 Jul 1863

NICHOLS, Iselina youngest child of Perry and Jane 23 Mar of scarlet fever ae 5y8m11d. CANP 26 Mar 1863

NICHOLS, John W. in Callaway Co. last Sunday ae 30. COWS 31 Jul 1863

NICHOLS, John, a bushwhacker, executed in Jefferson City. Born in Mercer Co. KY CAWN 7 &
23 Aug 1841; his parents moved to Pettis Co. MO the same year. 21 Nov 1863

NICHOLS, Robert on 28 Sep ae ca 42. COWS 15 Nov 1861

NICHOLS, William H. ae 6 accidentally shot himself. His stepfather (W.H. Irwin) MORE 14 Nov 1864
was working on an old pistol; the child grabbed it and it fired. Lived
on Wright betw 5-6. The stepfather was prostrate.

NICHOLSON, Virginia 3 Sep at her father's home in her 24th year. FULT 16 Sep 1864

NICOL, John at the home of his parents, Carondelet & Gate, 14 May of consumption ae 23. MORE 25 May'64

NIDDY, John, a tailor, "in a fit of suffocation." Lived O'Fallon-9th, ae ca 38, MORE 5 May 1861
left wife, one child. Died 4 May.

NIDELET, Pratte 28 Jun of consumption in his 33rd year. Son of Celeste and the MORE 30 Jun &
late Stephen A. Funeral from mother's home, 142 S. 5th. NY, Philadelphia, 1 Jul 1864
Richmond pc

NIEDEN, William John son of Rose Ann, 7 May ae 3y 4m. Lived Moore betw 16-17-   MORE 8 May 1863
    Market-Clark (?).

NIEDERHEUTER, J.L., a wine dealer on Walnut betw 4-5, killed on Walnut St. in the   MORE 14 &
    Camp Jackson affair. (Later shown as Jacob Lawrence.)   18 May 1861

NIEMANN, Lizzie, ae ca 8, killed near Bissell's Point when a pile of planks fell.   MORE 7 Oct 1864

NIESLANG, Frederick 19 Apr ae 39 at 12th-Carr. Interred Calvary.   MORE 20 Apr 1861

NIXON, John, native of England, 1 Jan of dropsy in his (38th?) year.   MORE 3 Jan 1861

NIXON, William, son of Richard of Nixon & Ellison, 27 May at 74 Wash St.   MORE 28 May 1864

NIXON, William 15 Dec ae 36 at 261 N. 7th. Funeral from St. Patrick's. Interred   MORE 16 Dec 1863
    Calvary. Philadelphia pc

NOBLE, Elijah 20 Aug in his 75th year at the home of Thomas H. Noble in Rock Spring   MORE 21 Aug 1861
    Addition, Clayton Road. Formerly of KY. Louisville pc

NOBLE, Frankie ae 6 run over by a street car "Sunday week," died Sun. at Olive-9th.   MORE 26 Apr 1864

NOEL, Rev. E.P. at Troy, Lincoln Co. 22 Mar in his 60th year. Presbyterian pastor.   COWS 15 Apr 1864

NOELL, Hon. John W. of Perryville in Washington DC Saturday last, ill 2 weeks; state   PERU 20 &
    representative, senator. Born Bedford Co. VA 22 Feb 1816, to MO 1831.   27 Mar 1863
    Married Mary Moreland 1836, commenced law practice in 1845. Union man,
    Catholic, left wife and family.

NOERR, Solomon "a respectable young man" found beaten to death. Employed as a   MORE 22 Aug 1865
    clerk, found near Kerzinger Cave. Mother lives on Wash betw 14-15.

NOLAN, Michael in Sisters Hospital 3 Jun of typhoid. Of Nolan & Caffrey. Funeral   MORE 4 Jun 1864
    St. Xavier, interred Calvary. Cincinnati & Montreal pc

NOLAN, Richard ae 70 run over by No. MO RR train while walking on a trestle.   MORE 8 May 1862

NOLLY, M. wife of Maj. Daniel in Fulton 16 Mar.   COWS 25 Mar 1864

NOLP, Emma Sophie only daughter of Herman and Johanna 22 Jul ae 1y 26d.   SLMD 30 Jul 1861

NOLTE, Charles 2 Aug ae 52 on Market betw 8-9.   SLMD 3 Aug 1864

NOONAN, Daniel "of an old and highly respected family" shot yesterday bu John Wagner.   MORE 21 Aug 1865
    Ae ca 22. Reason not known. Brother James E. Noonan mentioned.

NOONAN, Harmon ae 11y 11m 17d drowned while bathing in the river, 11 Aug; body   MORE 15 &
    found at Carondelet. Funeral from St. Xavier's. Interred Calvary.   16 Aug 1863

NORCOM, Eugene 19 Aug in his 28th year. Funeral from Immaculate Conception Church.   MORE 21 Aug 1864

NORDIKE, Mrs. Martha wife of Thomas 22 Aug ae (63? 68?) at 131 Wash. Memphis,   MORE 23 Aug 1863
    Vicksburg and New Orleans pc

NORMAN, Alfred shot by one of his negro boys, 4 miles south of California MO.   CAWN 18 Jul 1863

NORMAN, Mary burned when her clothing caught fire, on Gay betw 15-16.   MORE 9 Mar 1862

NORRIS, Robert A. son of Julius and Priscilla 1 Apr ae 6y 7m 22d. New Orleans &   MORE 3 Apr 1865
    Baltimore pc

NORRIS, Samuel "who claimed Louisiana MO as his residence but spent most of his   LAJ 17 Sep 1864
    time on a flatboat on the Illinois side, keeping a whiskey shop and
    resort for gamblers" shot last Saturday by Ben Thompson of Louisiana.

NORTH, Mary at the home of her son William near Grays Summit, Franklin Co., 2 Jan   MORE 8 Jan 1862
    in her 87th year. Born in Campbell Co. VA, many years resident of MO.

NORTHCUTT, Mrs. Eleanor 24 Feb at the home of her son-in-law, James McClintock,   COWS 17 Mar 1865
    in Boone Co. in her 66th year.

NORTHRUP, Mrs. Lucy Minerva wife of Ashley K. and daughter of the late Thomas S.   MORE 2 Jun 1861
    Hereford, Tuscumbia, AL, 1 Jun ae 27. Interred Bellefontaine.

NORTON, E.W. of intermittent fever, 7 Oct. Detroit and Buffalo pc   MORE 10 Oct 1863

NOURSE, Samuel 8 Oct of pneumonia ae 62, funeral from Rev. Post's church.   MORE 9 Oct 1863

NUCKOLS, Lizzie G. daughter of A.W. and M.A. 17 Apr ae 7 at the home of her grand-   RICON 21 Apr 1864
    father A.H. Ringo. "She had been by sea to California and British Col."

NUGENT, Thomas "lately dissipated" shot himself 18 Jul in St. Louis Twp., ae 41.   MORE 20 Jul 1861
    Former prop. of the 8th Ward House on Franklin Ave., then partner in a
    mercantile firm. Lived New St. Charles Rd. near Clay. Wife mentioned.

NUGENT, Thomas suddenly in the workhouse of brain congestion due to intemperance.   MORE 12 Jun 1863
    Left wife and several children in extreme indigence.

NUTT, Mrs. Mildred A. 7 Dec ae 60y 7m. Born Frederick Co. VA, in St. Louis Co.   MORE 8 Dec 1863
    (cont)

NUTT, Mrs. Mildred, cont. -- 25 years. Funeral from the home of her son-in-law MORE 8 Dec 1863
    James N. Barnett on St. Charles Rock Rd. east of Prairie House. Richmond pc

OAKES, George, Pvt Co B 40th MO Vols, 1 Apr of wounds received at Spanish Point AL. MORE 18 Apr 1865
    Late of St. Louis. Detroit pc

OATS, Curtis C., prisoner from Pemiscot Co., 22 Nov of remittent fever. (COATES?) MORE 29 Nov 1863

OBEAR, Daniel 16 Apr in Boone Co. in his 87th year. COWS 6 May 1864
    Allen B. 27 Apr of pneumonia ae 58.

OBEAR, Mary Alice 25 May ae 2y 9m 9d, daughter of E.G. and Sarah, on 12th betw MORE 26 May 1863
    Christy-Morgan.

O'BRIEN, Daniel 16 Oct ae 31, at 31 16th St. St. Michael's Ch., int. Calvary. MORE 17 Oct 1861

O'BRIEN, Daniel Sr. 23 Jan in his 80th year. Funeral from St. Michael's Church. MORE 24 Jan 1865
    NY & Boston pc

O'BRIEN, John of Millwood, Lincoln Co. 17 Dec at the home of his brother-in-law MORE 18 &
    Matthew R. Boyce. Funeral from the home of his brother Andrew, 488 Morgan.   20 Dec 1864
    St. Michael's Church, interred Calvary. Brief illness.

O'BRIEN, Julia Teresa wife of Timothy and 4th daughter of Bryan McSweeney, Tom MORE 19 Aug 1863
    Moore House, Killarney, on 15 Aug. Cork & Tralee pc

O'BRIEN, Mary of New Ross, Co. Wexford, 30 Apr in her 69th y. Clark betw 10-11. MORE 2 May 1865

O'BRIEN, Mary Agnes daughter of John and Ellen, 1 Aug ae 15m 17d. SLMD 6 Aug 1861

O'BRIEN, Michael, living in alley betw 10-11-Biddle-O'Fallon, fell from 5th story MORE 26 Sep 1862
    of the Southern Hotel; was wheeling a barrow along a plank. Wife, no children.

O'BRIEN, Patrick, section boss on the SW Branch RR, died of debility; brought to MORE 21 Jan 1864
    St. Louis for burial, interred Holy Trinity.

O'BRIEN, Patrick run over by horse cars, leg crushed, subsequently died. MORE 5 Oct 1861

O'BRIEN, Capt. Thomas AQM at Rolla 24 Oct of inflammation of the liver, ae 37. MORE 26 &
    "Masonic service, funeral from the Cathedral." Philadelphia pc   27 Oct 1863

OCHS, Bernard, a Frenchman, in a small tenement on Pratte betw Maynard-Rosati, of MORE 18 Jan 1861
    "mania a potu." (SLMD same date mentions wife and children.)

O'CONNELL, Hanora wife of John 18 Mar ae 28y 2m, at 84 Locust. Funeral from the MORE 20 Mar 1864
    Cathedral. Interred Rock Spring.

O'CONNELL, Joseph, ae 18, driver of a sprinkling cart, run over and killed 5 Sep. MORE 6 &
    Son of James, living on Spruce betw Main-2nd.   7 Sep 1864

O'CONNELL, Richard, only son of John, 22 Mar ae 7 at 84 Locust. MORE 23 Mar 1863

O'CONNELL, Vincent son of J., 2 Aug ae 17m 10d. SLMD 6 Aug 1861

O'CONNER, Mary, of intemperance. Lived on 7th St., left 3 little boys being cared MORE 20 Mar 1863
    for by Mr. & Mrs. Powers, who had a grocery on Papin St.

O'CONNER, Michael of apoplexy 12 Nov. Lived at Grand and St. Charles Road. MORE 13 Nov 1861

O'CONNOR, Patrick 21 Feb at 355 Broadway. Interred Calvary. MORE 22 Feb 1864

O'CONNOR, Peter, a prisoner, of pneumonia. MORE 18 Nov 1862

O'CONNOR, Thomas 10 Feb ae 24. Funeral from the home of John O'Neil, Lombard MORE 11 Feb 1863
    betw Main-2nd. Interred Calvary.

O'CONNOR, Thomas, cook at the Virginia Hotel, of heat. Lived on Ham St. near MORE 6 Aug 1861
    Chestnut, left wife and 2 children.

O'DEMPSEY, Francis, tribute by Georgetown Sons of Temperance. Died 2 Mar. GLWT 11 Apr 1861

ODEN, Hezekiah in Ashley 21 Feb in his 87th year. Born in MD, moved with his parents LAJ 28 Feb 1861
    to Londen (prob Loudoun) Co. VA. At ae 37 emigrated to Bourbon Co. KY, then
    to Pike Co. MO in 1828. Member of the Christian Church, left 4 children.

ODEN or   William, living on Horse Shoe Lake, killed yesterday at a grocery store SJH 7, 8, &
ODOM,   below town by one Millen, later arrested and discharged. Oden was an   10 Dec 1864
    innocent bystander when Millen's store was invaded by rowdy drunks.

ODENWELDER, Albert E. son of Albert and Lucy, Hickory betw 8-9, 5 Mar ae 2y 6m. MORE 6 Mar 1862

O'DONNELL, Ann daughter of Hugh and Mary of Danndeowin, Parish of Kilmacrenan, MORE 6 Aug 1864
    4 Aug ae 28 of typhoid. Philadelphia pc

O'DONNELL, William 28 Jan ae 79, resident of St. Louis 24 years. Patterson NJ pc MORE 29 Jan 1861

OFFATT, Oshias, citizen of Johnson Co., 2 Mar oc chronic dysentery. (Undertaker's list) " 6 Mar 1865

OFFER or OFFUTT, Lewis killed near Savannah MO by a bushwhacker. (Sav. Plain Dealer) MORE 16 Sep 1863
    / which see   (/ OR he was one)

OFFICER, A.J. a southern sympathizer killed in Andrew Co.	CAWN 18 Jul 1863
OFFUTT, Mr. ___ killed at North Prairie, Andrew Co. Friday night by men representing themselves as soldiers. (St. Joseph News) See Lewis OFFER	RICON 17 Sep 1863
OFFUT, Eli in Callaway Co. 3 Feb in his 77th year.	MORE 23 Mar 1863
O'FLAHERTY, George in Little Rock 17 Feb of typhoid in his 23rd year. Had been secretary to Gen. Hindman of the Confederate army.	MORE 15 Mar 1863
OGLE, Benjamin at his home 2½ mi. east of St. Louis 4 Sep ae 46.	SLMD 24 Sep 1861
O'HARA, James 18 Mar at the home of his son-in-law Samuel B. Cecil, St. Charles Road near Abbey. Interred Calvary. NY & Philadelphia pc	MORE 19 Mar 1865
O'HARA, John B. 24 Aug ae 28y 4m of brain congestion, at 278 N. 6th. Funeral from St. Patrick's. Left wife, 2 children. Ill health since serving in Co. F, National Guard last June. Former deputy clerk, Recorder's office.	MORE 25 & 26 Aug 1864
O'HEA, Mrs. Hannah 29 May ae 49. Funeral from the home of her sister, Mrs. D.H. Donovan, (413?) Morgan. St. John's Church, interred Calvary.	MORE 30 May 1864
O'HEIM, Charles of injuries received when he fell through a hatch at Eckerle's Brewery, where he worked.	MORE 24 Sep 1865
OHLMAN, Anthony son of Lawrence and Susan yesterday at 58 Brooklyn, ae 7y 7m.	MORE 29 Jul 1862
O'KEEFE, Dr. P.E. 20 Jun of congestive fever, 9th betw Clark-Walnut. Chicago, NY & Canada pc	MORE 21 Jun 1865
O'KEEFFE, Julia daughter of James 10 Aug in St. Joseph ae 9.	SJH 11 Aug 1864
O'LAUGHLIN, Margaret eldest daughter of Michael and Mary, 15 Aug ae 3y 10m 14d. (LO?) Interred Calvary.	MORE 16 Aug 1862
"OLD RATS," an ancient Negro for 12 years frequented the thoroughfares of the city carrying a rag on a long pole, faintly printed "Rats" -- he sold ratbane. Died of smallpox.	MORE 3 Feb 1863
OLDHAM, Jarvis G., Chariton Co.: letters of adm. 17 Jul to Harrison G. Oldham.	CECB 24 Jul 1862
OLDHAM, Martin E. of Boone Co. taken from his home by 3 men in Federal uniforms in Sep., and hanged; 3 members of the Cavalry Regiment, MO State Militia, now being held for trial.	SJH 23 Dec 1863
OLDHAM, Samuel at the home of Mrs. Talbot 13 Jan in his 88th year.	LIT 21 Feb 1862
OLDS, George of Schuyler Co. found dead about a mile west of Lancaster on 26 Dec, murdered by unknown.	MEMP 30 Dec 1865
OLIVER, Arena daughter of Samuel 2 Sep in her 19th year.	LIT 6 Sep 1861
OLIVER, George very suddenly 12 May ae 33y 7m.	FULT 27 May 1864
O'MALLY, Margaret 4th daughter of Michael, 52 Second St., 20 Jan of cholera morbus ae 15y 7m. Galena pc	MORE 25 Jan 1864
O'MARA, John, a stonecutter, of internal hemorrhage ae 48. Left wife and children, 20th betw Morgan-Franklin.	MORE 15 Feb 1861
O'NEIL, Charles, a performer at the Bowery Theatre, drowned himself Tuesday, from grief at the recent death of his mother.	MORE 23 Jul 1863
O'NEIL, Eliza wife of Joseph 21 Mar ae 32, on Orange betw 12-13.	MORE 22 Mar 1861
O'NEIL, James, inquest: jumped from window at Sisters Hospital. Unmarried, ca 30.	MORE 25 Sep 1865
O'NEIL, James L., cashier at the Western Bank, yesterday of pneumonia. (item from the St. Joseph Union, no date)	MORE 22 Feb 1865
O'NEIL, John, member of the Fire Dept., ae 34. Lived at Centre-Market. New Orl. pc	MORE 12 Nov 1863
O'NEIL, Patrick ae ca 14 drowned in a quarry pond on 17th near the Pacific RR. Parents live in alley betw 7-8-Olive-Locust.	MORE 10 Jul 1862
OPPENLANDER, Mary M. wife of Christian 25 Mar in her 33rd year. Funeral from Simpson Chapel, 10th-N. Market. Cincinnati & Pittsburgh pc	MORE 27 Mar 1862
OREAR, Mary wife of Jeremiah in Columbia 12 Dec.	COWS 16 Dec 1864
O'REILEY, Christopher 22 Jan ae 55, Olive betw 12-13. Interred Calvary.	MORE 23 Jan 1865
O'REILLY, Mary Anne only daughter of Edmund and B. 23 Jul ae 4y9m. Int. Calvary.	MORE 24 Jul 1862
O'REILLY, Patrick 22 Apr in his 48th year at 4th-Morgan. Int. Calvary. New Orl. pc	MORE 23 Apr 1864
O'RILEY, James son of Catherine and the late Owen 15 Apr ae 3y 3m 10d. Funeral from the home of his uncle Patrick O'Riley, 175 N. 4th.	MORE 16 Apr 1863
O'RILEY, Mrs. Patrick 30 Oct ae 21 at 125 Morgan.	MORE 31 Oct 1865

ORNDORFF, Edward only son of Joseph and Jane, 686 Broadway, 18 Jul.	MORE 19 Jul 1865
ORR, A. Perry late of Ashley MO, brother of William of St. Louis, aboard the Roanoke near Ft. Sally, Dakotah Territory. Ae 37. Buried at the mouth of the Cheyanne River.	MORE 30 Jun 1865
ORTEN, J.M. near Big River Mills, ae 24. A Mason.	MORE 22 Feb 1865
OSBORN, children of John OSBORNE and Lydia Jane, Callaway Co. (all of scarlet fever) Lavina Jane 11 Apr ae 1y 1m 11d Kitty Ann 14 Apr ae 5y 7m 11d George William 14 Apr ae 2y 1m 14d John Simpson 16 Apr ae 3y 8m 6d (or Sampson)	FULT 22 Apr 1864 MORE 26 "
OSBORN, John at his home in Victoria, Daviess Co., of typhoid pneumonia in his 60th year. Left wife and 7 children.	MORE 7 Feb 1864
OSBORN, John (B? G?) of Osborn & Tolle, St. Louis, 13 Jul in Davenport IA of consumption ae 47. NY, Boston, Lynchburgh pc	MORE 19 Jul 1863
OSBORNE, George F. 27 Sep of dysentery ae 41y 1m, at 15 S. 15th. Binghamton NY pc	SLMD 28 Sep 1864
O'SHA, Mike, an Irishman "inebriated and threatening" fell into Noix Creek and drowned. From Bowling Green, body recovered at mouth of Buffalo Creek.	LAJ 14 Apr 1861
O'SHEA, Michael little son of Michael J. drowned yesterday while swimming in the river. Reward for recovery of body. (SJH 8 Jul, body found)	SJH 6 Jul 1865
OSTERHAUSE, Mathilda consort of Gen. P.J. at their home on Gratiot betw 5-6. Int. Bellefontaine.	MORE 6 Nov 1863
OTTO, William of Audrain Co. in Gratiot Prison of chronic diarrhoea.	MORE 18 Mar 1863
OVERSTOLZ, Catherine H. Becker wife of Ferdinand 10 Feb in her 35th year, at 5 N. 5th St. Long, painful illness.	MORE 11 Feb 1861
OVERSTOLTZ, Mrs. Therese 9 Jan in her 72nd year after a short illness. Lived at Broadway & North Market. Interred Calvary.	MORE 10 Jan 1862
OVERSTREET, William, Chariton Co.: Public Administrator took over his estate.	CECB 24 Jul 1862
OVERTON, ___ killed by guerillas in Platte Co. (SJH 14 Jun)	MORE 16 Jun 1864
OVERTON, Dr. Dudley H. of Fulton mortally shot 14 Feb, died 16 Feb. Born in Callaway Co. 27 Jan 1828. Louisville pc. (LAJ 6 Mar says he was killed in a duel with ___ Williams.)	COWS 6 Mar 1862
OWEN, John of St. Louis 18 May in New Orleans of wounds received on the Red River. Notice by AF & AM.	MORE 27 May 1864
OWEN, Sarah wife of Col. Thomas J., formerly of Howard Co., 5 Feb of erysipelas near Brunswick. (CECB) Also GLWT 21 Feb and COWS 22 Feb.	RANC 14 Feb 1861
OWENS, Berry, Chariton Co.: Public administrator took over his estate.	CECB 24 Jul 1862
OWENS, Catherine, inquest: a widow ae 63, dropped dead in Shieder's store. Mentions sister Jane McGrath.	MORE 23 Mar 1865
OWENS, George a carpenter found dead in bed of heart disease at 102 Carondelet.	MORE 27 Dec 1861
OWENS, James son of Richard and Mary 4 May ae 15y 4m 10d. Interred Calvary.	MORE 5 May 1864
OWENS, W.W. of Elliotts' Battery, CSA, 27 Apr of chronic diarrhoea. (Undertaker's list)	" 1 May 1865
OWINGS, Robert F., in Nebraska City NT 19 Jun in his 43rd year. Born Scott Co. KY 13 Feb 1823. Wife mentioned.	GAL 20 Jul 1865
OWINGS, Ensign Samuel J. of the Louisville, USN 7 Oct of brain inflammation ae 46. Born Emmetsburg MD, lived on Gratiot betw 15-16. Baltimore pc	MORE 8 Oct 1863
OXLEY, Jonathan, old and highly respected citizen of Porch's Prairie near Brunswick of pneumonia. (Letters of administration to Rebecca Oxley 1 Mar - CECB 4 May 1861)	MORE 15 Feb 1861
PACK, Erie F. of Musser's Command, captured in Maries Co. 1 Sep, in Gratiot Prison of lung inflammation.	MORE 14 Oct 1863
PAGE, Deborah N. wife of Daniel D. 19 Jan of paralysis and apoplexy in her 74th y. Funeral 1st Presbyterian, interred Bellefontaine. NY, Boston, San Fransc. pc	MORE 21 Jan 1864
PAGE, Eliza Wash eldest child of John Y. and Elizabeth C.W. 15 Apr ae 18m 9d, on Pine betw 16-17 in "Bishop's Row."	MORE 16 Apr 1861
PAGE, Mrs. Jane (E?) 24 Jul at the home of her son-in-law Dr. C.A. Williams in Chillicothe.	SJH 1 Aug 1865
PAGE, John G., Chariton Co.: Final Settlement by W.V. Hall.	CECB 13 Apr 1861
PAGE, Mrs. Mary daughter of Gen. B.M. Prentiss jumped into a cistern at Quincy 12 Dec. "Mental aberration."	PALS 22 Dec 1865

PALM, Wilhelmina wife of William 18 Apr ae 49, on 3rd betw Plum-Cedar.   MORE 19 Apr 1865

PALMER, Bartley D. 10 Apr near Danville in his (20? 28?)th year.   MORE 28 Apr 1863

PALMER, James Alexis son of W.M. and S. (B?) at Lost Creek, Lincoln Co. of brain   LAJ 13 Mar 1862
    congestion ae 7y 4m 6d.

PALMER, John J. 15 Feb in his 57th year. Funeral from the home of his son-in-law,   MORE 16 &
    William Edgar, 7th & Sidney.   17 Feb 1865

PALMER, Joseph G., 1st MO, captured in Texas Co. 20 Jan, in Gratiot Prison of rubeola.   MORE 25 Feb 1863

PALMER, Lutitia wife of Thomas in Columbia 21 Apr.   COWS 6 May 1864

PALMER, Robert 26 Feb at the home of James Palmer of Boone Co. ae 32y 1m 14d.   COWS 20 Mar 1863

PALMER, Mrs. Samuel 20 Aug at her home, 12th betw O'Fallon-Cass, ae 38. Funeral   MORE 22 Aug 1865
    from 2nd Baptist. Newark pc

PANDERBURGT   Mrs. Ellen, widow of John A., suddenly in her 64th year. Native of   MORE 21 Sep 1863
 (VANDERBURG?) Holland, to US 1849 with 7 daughters and 2 sons, her husband having
    preceded her here the year before. He died in 1856 leaving her 5
    daughters and 1 son to raise. All her girls are married, her son has
    completed his apprenticeship. Funeral St. Xavier, interred Calvary.

PAPIN, Julia W. wife of Theophile and daughter of William and Marie (Henrie?) of   MORE 24 Feb 1861
    Prairie du Rocher 23 Feb ae 25y 8m.

PAPIN, Mary eldest daughter of Henry and Harriet 22 Jun near Webster Station, ae 4.   MORE 23 Jun 1864

PAPIN, Annie M. daughter of Dr. Timothy and Margaret G. 26 Nov of scarlet fever   MORE 27 Nov 1861
    ae 3y 3½m, at 9th & Locust.
    Pierre M. youngest child of " 4 Aug ae 16m 10d.   " 5 Aug 1861
    Sylvestre Vilray son of Dr. T.L. Sunday ae 12y 3m.   " 7 Nov 1864

PARATY, Antheny, inquest: deckhand or fireman on Alton packet B.M. Runyan, missed   MORE 16 Dec 1862
    4 days ago. Drowned in river, body recovered by son and friends. No
    evidence of foul play.

PARCELS, Eliza Jane wife of William H. in Kirksville 10 May.   COWS 6 Jun 1862

PARDENHEIMER, killed in retaliation in Chariton Co. (Parkenheimer in co. history.)   MORE 10 Jan 1865

PARKE, Rosaline A. daughter of the late N.B. Franklin in Jefferson Co. 28 Dec.   MORE 4 Jan 1865
    ae 33. CA pc

PARKER, ___ only daughter of William, ae ca 5, ? Apr of diphtheria at the home   ROLEX 3 Apr 1861
    of William Fallowell in Maries Co. (Paper creased.)

PARKER, Mrs. Elizabeth wife of Col. W. at Troy, Lincoln Co. 6 Jul in (30?39?)th year.   MORE 13 Jul 1864

PARKER, George of Providence RI at the home of his uncle H.S. Parker ae 26.   MORE 7 Feb 1864

PARKER, Lucy wife of Thomas C. in Boone Co. 11 Apr, ae ca 35, and Thomas C. on   COWS 17 Apr 1863
    14 Apr ae ca 37, both suddenly.

PARKER, Oliver A. of Columbia 17 Sep ae 27. Funeral from Presbyterian Church.   COWS 27 Sep 1861

PARKER, Mrs. Robert T. at the home of her father William Smith in Franklin Co.   MORE 17 Jul 1861
    8 Jul in her 27th year, after a 3-month illness.

PARKER, Samuel Martin of Independence in Sep ae 26 (28?), shot on the plains by an   MORE 31 Dec 1864
    employee while conducting a train near Purgatoire Creek. Married only a
    few weeks before.

PARKER, William C. and daughter, 6 miles south of Tipton, killed when lightning   CAWN 30 Mar &
    struck their house Tuesday last. Mrs. Parker was injured. He was a   20 Apr 1861
    Good Templar.

PARKS, Levi, old and well-known citizen of Boone Co., at his home near Centralia.   COWS 26 Jun 1863

PARKS, Peterson B., Chariton Co.:   Final settlement by Peterson Jr.   CECB 16 Oct 1862

PARKS, Price R. in Boone Co. 14 Jan of typhoid erysipelas, ae ca 58. Georgetown KY pc   COWS 22 Jan 1864

PARLE, Patrick 1 Aug of consumption ae 38. Funeral -- alley above O'Fallon betw 7-8.   MORE 2 Aug 1864

PARMALEE, Henry A. of St. Charles Co. 19 Oct at Yellville AR ae 29.   MORE 15 Nov 1862

PARROTT, William, "a rebel sympathizer," killed near Union Mills on the Platte-   LEXUN 21 Jan 1865
    Buchanan Co. line.   SJH 10 "

PARSONS, M.M. in Old Mexico, a Missourian native of VA, ca 44. Married daughter of   MEMP 7 Oct 1865
    R.W. Weeks in Jefferson City, supported the rebel cause, was in Price's
    Army. Had been attorney general; father in Jefferson City. (JEST 29 Sep
    gives name as Monroe M., once rep. Cole, Camden, Miller, Maries counties;
    was a general in Price's army.

PARSONS, Sylvester L., formerly of Greenville MA, 27 Nov ae 24.	SJH 29 Nov 1865
PARTEET or PURTEET, L., arrested in Reynolds Co. 7 Oct, in Gratiot Prison of pneumonia 14 Dec.	MORE 16 Dec 1862
PASAQUA, Clarissa ae ca 85 at the home of George R. Taylor, 3rd-Elm. She was raised in the family of Augustue Chouteau, remained with his widow and then with other family members; she had been with the Taylors 15 years.	MORE 24 Feb 1861
PASQUIER, Paul 19 Apr ae 32 at Carr betw 5-6. Left wife, mother, brothers, sister.	MORE 20 Apr 1862
PATRICK, Lydia daughter of R.M. and M.C. near Fayette 20 Mar ae 3y 1m.	MORE 29 Mar 1863
PATTEN, Thomas a farmer living near the Platte River killed by ___ Keeney at (PATTON) Corby's Mill. Patten was drunk and quarrelsome.	MEMP 30 Sep 1865 WARS 22 "
PATTERSON, Alexander in St. Francois Co. 9 Dec.	MORE 22 Dec 1864
PATTERSON, Elijah S., thrown from a buggy on 30 Nov, developed gangrene and died Saturday ae 52. From KY to MO in 1838.	CANP 10 Dec 1863
PATTERSON, Mrs. Elizabeth near Potosi 24 Sep in her 80th year.	MORE 3 Oct 1862
PATTERSON, Mrs. Hannah 11 Nov ae 75. Funeral from the home of her son-in-law George K. Budd, 172 Pine. Interred Cincinnati.	MORE 12 Nov 1862
PATTERSON, Harriet Johnson wife of Samuel W. of St. Louis in New Bedford MA 4 Aug in her 28th year.	MORE 22 Aug 1865
PATTERSON, Lucy Randolph daughter of Henry L. and Theodosia yesterday ae 12.	SLMD 3 Dec 1861
PATTERSON, Mary, inquest: found dead in a hovel betw Morgan-Franklin, utterly destitute. Husband said to be a soldier in 19th IL. She was "addicted," died of lung congestion and intemperance.	MORE 13 Oct 1863
PATTERSON, Mary A. of consumption 23 Jul ae 40y 6m, at 379 N. 11th.	MORE 24 Jul 1865
PATTERSON, Sanford M. of Boone Co. in Alton Prison, brought home for burial.	COWS 17 Jul 1863
PATTON, Dominic, a farmer near Bridgeton, murdered by soldiers ot eh 21st MO Inf. Abram Purbis and Eph Richardson charged.	MORE 20 Nov 1864
PATTON, Emily daughter of Thomas, on 5 Aug.	FULT 5 Aug 1864
PATTON, John W. son of Joseph and E. in Macon 16 Apr in his 26th year. Long illness.	MAG 6 May 1863
PATTON, Leanah 21 May in Howard Co. ae (15?). Granddaughter of Mrs. H.B. Hern.	MORE 1 Jun 1863
PATTON, Mary W. in Callaway Co. 14 Apr ae 68.	COWS 28 Apr 1865
PAUL, Mary S. wife of Adolphe 9 Jan in her 26th year. Lived on Chouteau Ave.	MORE 10 Jan 1862
PAYNE, Elder A.H.H. (or A.H.F.) of Clinton Co. recently killed by Federal soldiers. Squad went to his home, forced him to accompany them; body found in the woods 2 weeks later. "He was a rebel and attempted to run away, and was shot." (St. Joseph Herald) LIT says he organized the Christian Church in Liberty more than 30 years ago.	COWS 19 Jun 1863 LIT 12 "
PAYNE, Ann M. wife of Benjamin F. in St. Charles Co. 27 Mar ae (31?).	MORE 8 Apr 1861
PAYNE, Mattie daughter of Dr. J. and Mary M. 1 Mar ae 15. Interred OH.	MORE 3 Mar 1865
PAYNE, Rebecca, Chariton Co.: public administrator took over her estate.	CECB 24 Jul 1862
PAYNE, William C. at his home in Shelby Co. 5 Apr of pneumonia ae 76y 3m 5d.	PALS 7 Apr 1865
PAYNTOR, Sheriff John of Cedar Co. killed while trying to arrest ___ Stow. Deputy Harvel also killed. (Bolivar Sentinel 6 Oct)	MORE 11 Oct 1865
PEABODY, Mrs. Mary Virginia, wife of Dr. J.H. of Washington DC, 26 Jul in St. Louis ae 31. Funeral from 240 Chouteau. Louisville pc	MORE 27 Jul 1865
PEACHER, Peter, citizen of Howard Co., 2 Mar of pneumonia. (Undertaker's list)	MORE 6 Mar 1865
PEARCE, Nannie Artus daughter of Albert and Julia 21 Mar ae 3y 11m 15d, at 16th & Olive.	MORE 22 Mar 1862
PEARSON, Martha A. wife of John V. in Audrain Co. 18 Mar ae 23.	COWS 7 Apr 1865
PEARSON, William Henry (of Lockwood, Pearson & Co.) 17 Apr in his 32nd year, at 78 Myrtle. Interred Calvary.	MORE 18 Apr 1861
PEASE, Henry L., long a resident of CA, presently of St. Louis, 10 Feb ae 51. Funeral from home of his brother S.S., 159 Pine. Interment Christ Church Cemetery. Hudson NY, San Francisco & Sacramento pc	MORE 12 Feb 1865
PECK, Mary Jane wife of John W. and daughter of Andrew and Mary Ramsey of Philadelphia, at Olive-Leffingwell. Interred Bellefontaine.	MORE 10 Jul 1862

PEERS, Gen. Edward J. at his home in Lincoln Co. in his 67th year, a resident of MO since 1822. Attended West Point. Three children survive.   MORE 15 Sep 1862

PEERY, Thomas shot at Breckinridge by state militia - a bushwhacker. (County history says he was from Daviess Co.) (Chillicothe Chronicle)   MORE 5 Oct 1862

PEETE, Paul F. son of G.W. and Rosa McD. 16 Jul. Norfolk & Petersburgh pc (COWS says PEET, son of Dr. G.W. of Huntsville.)   MORE 19 Jul 1865 / COWS 28 "

PELL, Precilla wife of Capt. Charles, formerly of Paducah KY, 17 Jul ae 57. Funeral from the home of Capt. Frank Clayton on Thomas St., betw Clay and Glasgow. Louisville & Chicago pc   MORE 18 Jul 1864

PELLOT, Franz Carl, a Swiss, of heat ae ca 60. Lived 7th-Rutgers, a single man.   MORE 8 Aug 1861

PELTIER, Eliza (Elizabeth) wife of Germain, Cedar betw 2-3, ae 54. Short illness. (Inquest: found dead in bed, apoplexy. Mentions son and daughter.)   MORE 8 & 9 Jul 1863

PEMBERTON, Matilda C. 1 Dec in Monticello of consumption. Lived with her widowed mother and brother-in-law W.G. Watson. The youngest child.   CANP 10 Dec 1863

PEMBERTON, William killed by Capt. W.W. Lair, or some of his men, in a dispute /(of Marion Co.) over a horse.   PALS 19 Aug 1864

PENCE, Edward, formerly of Clay Co., in Platte Co. 1 Feb.   LIT 8 Feb 1861

PENDER, Louis Edward only son of Martin and the late Mary, ae 9y 2m 20d. Funeral from 720 Broadway, interred Calvary.   MORE 13 Aug 1864

PENDLETON, James B., 17 Jul. A Mason, lived at 5th & Sylvanie, left wife and children.   SJH 19 Jul 1865

PENDLETON, William, a citizen, killed at Linnaeus by bushwhackers.   SJH 23 Jan 1865

PENN, Ludlow C. youngest son of Dr. George and (J.B.?) on 17 Apr in St. Louis Co., at the family home, ae 15.   MORE 19 Apr 1865

PENNINGTON, William, an Englishman ae ca 30, crushed when an embankment fell on him. Lived Broadway betw Angelica-Penrose with wife and children.   MORE 22 Mar 1861

PENNOCK, Lieut. Joseph N., Adj. 7th Cav. MSM, in St. Louis 14 Apr ae 34. Funeral from the home of his brother-in-law Charles Mehaffy, 73 N. 18th.   MORE 15 Apr 1865

PENNY, Mary G. wife of John H. and daughter of the late William G. Sears of Spotsylvania Co. VA in Randolph Co. 11 Feb in her 47th year. (Mary Gay)   GLWT 21 Feb 1861 / MORE 24 "

PENNY, William killed at Jacksonville by W.R. Brown in a quarrel. (RANC 14 Feb)   MORE 22 Feb 1865

PENSCHBACKER, little daughter of Frederick, fatally burned. 8th betw Morgan-Franklin.   SLMD 29 Jan 1861

PEPPER, Samuel killed in Jefferson Co. by 47th MO Vols. under Col. Fletcher; he was shot through the arms and head, nose shot off, ears cut off.   MORE 17 Oct 1864

PEPPER, Sarah widow of E.F., formerly of Mason Co. KY, 12 Apr in her 53rd year.   PALS 21 Apr 1865

PERDUE, Thornton Grimsley oldest son of Thomas Franklin and Cornelia 12 Jun of lung congestion ae 4y 9m 5d. Funeral from the home of his grandmother, Mrs. Spalding, 223 Carr.   MORE 14 Jun 1863

PERKINS, John "an inoffensive old man" living near Rush Tower, shot. (letter from DeSoto MO)   SLMD 1 Oct 1861

PERKINS, Philetus in Quincy 4 Jan ae 80y 4m 8d.   HAM 9 Jan 1861

PERKINS, Thomas M., Chariton Co.: public administrator took over his estate.   CECB 24 Jul 1862

PERRET, Martha Jane wife of A.L. in her 31st year. Funeral from the home of J.V.D. Skillman, 115 Chestnut.   MORE 25 Nov 1861

PERRIN, Aubert son of C.A. and A. at Callao 18 Feb ae 5y 6m.   MAG 26 Feb 1862

PERRY, Dr. Lilburn F. 21 Jun in his 53rd year. Funeral from Trinity Church.   MORE 23 Jun 1862

PERSINGER, Martin killed by Federal troops while running (to escape from them) from Joseph Persinger's house, 6 miles se of Columbia.   COWS 5 Sep 1862

PETERS, Emilie wife of Louis 17 Nov at 61 5th St., of apoplexy, ae 39y 9m.   MORE 19 Nov 1861

PETTIJOHN, Andrew, a southern sympathizer, killed in Andrew Co.; left wife and 11 children.   CAWN 18 Jul 1863

PETTIS, Mary Dwight eldest daughter of Mary D. and Henry, 14 Jan ae 21.   MORE 16 Jan 1863

PETTY, William of 10th MO, captured in Murfreesboro, of chronic diarrhoea in Gratiot Prison.   MORE 21 Feb 1863

PEW, Sgt. James of 10th MO Vols. killed at Corinth. Brother of William B. and R.C., both of Louisiana MO.   LAJ 12 Jun 1862

PEYTON, Elizabeth wife of Valentine S. 6 Aug ae 74 y and about 10m.   LIT 7 Aug 1863

PEYTON, R.L.Y. "bogus Senator from MO in the Confederate Congress" 3 Sep at Bladen Springs AL.	MORE 19 Dec 1863
PFEIFFER, Francis A. "an old resident" 3 miles north of Kirkwood, formerly a road overseer, 9 Oct.	MORE 11 Oct 1861
PFOHN, Joshua of paralysis in Gratiot Prison.	MORE 21 Jan 1863
PHARR, George W. at his father's home in Audrain Co. 14 Aug ae 25. 9th MO MSM Co C.	MORE 20 Aug 1863
PHELAN, Thomas Ignatius son of Wm. & Bridget, Washington betw Ewing-Leffingwell, 4 Feb of diphtheria ae 4y 10m.	MORE 5 Feb 1861
Edward youngest son of " 21 Mar ae 2y 4m. Washington-Ewing.	MORE 22 May 1862
PHELPS, 2 children of Phillip in Polk Co. crushed when a log fell on them at Laramond's Mill.	LIT 1 Mar 1861
PHILLEBAUM, Sarah J. youngest daughter of J.H. and Mary E. at Bethany 21 Aug ae 1y28d.	MORE 27 Aug '61
PHILLIPS, ___ a Union man attacked by a bushwhacker and killed his assailant but was himself killed, in Chariton Co.	MORE 10 Jan 1865
PHILLIPS, Adele T. consort of Shapley R. decd at the home of Samuel Davis in New Madrid 19 Jan.	MORE 8 Feb 1865
PHILLIPS, Benjamin, prisoner of war, 30 Sep of stomach congestion. (Undertaker's list)	MORE 5 Oct 1862
PHILLIPS, Elder C.M.W. killed by bushwhackers 26 May. (CECB 26 May)	MORE 1 Jun 1864
PHILLIPS, Elizabeth Mary wife of Edward at Price's Branch, Montgomery Co., 18 Oct ae 45. Formerly of Manchester ENG.	MORE 23 Oct 1863
PHILLIPS, Franklin W. son of (Warn?) in Boone Co. 16 Mar of congestive chulls ae 28y 7m.	COWS 5 Apr 1861
PHILLIPS, Gabriel, tribute by Frankford Lodge 192 F & A Masons; died 6 Dec near Frankford after a long illness.	LAJ 23 Dec 1865
PHILLIPS, John, gardener at Bellefontaine Cemetery, 8 Nov.	MORE 9 Nov 1864
PHILLIPS, Mary Ella oldest daughter of Richard and Mary A. 22 Aug ae 8y 7m 25d.	COWS 28 Aug 1863
PHILLIPS, Richard R. of Pemiscot Co. at his father's home in New Madrid Co. 25 Oct of pneumonia ae 31y 8m 24d.	MORE 3 Nov 1865
PHILLIPS, William H. at Rocheport (the 1st settler there) 22 Jul ae 58.	COWS 15 Aug 1862
PHILPOT, Horatio, father-in-law of Judge Hurt, killed in Chariton Co. by militia.	MORE 7 Nov 1864
PHIPPS, Mrs. Rosina "a very respectable lady" suddenly of heart disease. Native of Westmoreland Co. PA.	MORE 8 Sep 1861
PICKETT, Capt. J.A., US Detective, killed in Blackfoot country, Boone Co. MO, by bushwhackers. (Letter from Fayette signed John Wilcox dated 21 Feb.)	SJH 26 Feb 1865
PICKETT, Thomas 19 Jul in his 54th year, at Felix betw 7-8.	SJH 19 Jul 1863
PICKLES, Ann widow of William at her home near Valle Forge, St. Francois Co., 20 Nov.	MORE 25 Nov 1861
PIERCE, John at Sisters Hospital 4 Oct ae 22. Interred Potosi.	MORE 5 Nov 1865
PIERCE, Mary wife of Joseph of Shipman IL and daughter of Thomas Pratt (Convent betw 2-Main) 14 Mar at her father's home ae 32y 3m.	MORE 15 Mar 1865
PIERNELL, Louis - see BRENELLA, Louis	
PIGG, Henry of Boone Co. at Moore's Mill.	MORE 11 Aug 1862
PIGG, John A. of Boone Co., a released prisoner aboard the Spread Eagle between St. Louis and Providence. Body returned for burial Wednesday.	COWS 17 Apr 1863
PIKE, Charles, inquest: fell from a boat 2 or 3 days ago. Employee of Keokuk Packet.	MORE 17 Sep 1863
PIKE, Minnie last surviving child of H.S. and M.A. 25 Oct ae 5y 6m 1d. Funeral from home of her grandfather David Anderson, Collins St. Baltimore and Lexington MO pc	MORE 27 Oct 1863
PILCHER, Anna Maria wife of Thomas E. 21 Aug ae 18y 7m. Funeral from the home of her mother, 234 Biddle.	MORE 22 Aug 1861
PILCHER, Daniel F. in Mexico MO 14 Oct ae 45. Richmond VA pc.	MORE 22 Oct 1862
PILLSBURY, Mary killed by lightning in her bed. (Clara Goodwin also killed.) (Wheeling Intelligencer)	MAG 25 Jun 1862
PIM, Johnny son of Capt. John S. and Julia E. 12 Jul ae 11y 2m 10d, at their home on Wash near 17th.	MORE 13 Jul 1865
PIM, Thomas at the home of his son-in-law D.C. Fornsby 3 Feb ae 74. Resident of Farmington many years. Philad., Wilmington, Cinc. pc	MORE 7 Feb 1864

PINN, George of measles Sunday last ae ca 20. Of near Huntsville, in Capt. Bredett's MAG 2 Apr 1862
    Co., 7th MO.
PIPES, James in Randolph Co. 25 Dec of inflammation of the liver, ae ca 62. COWS 29 Jan 1864
    Pleasant in Randolph Co. 19 Jun ae ca 90. "   1 Jul 1864
PIRTLE, Harvey, prisoner from Stoddard Co., of pneumonia. (Undertaker's list) MORE 8 Nov 1862
PITZER, Dugeld shot near Morris Mills, Jefferson Co., Tuesday last. Six member of MORE 26 Aug 1864
    the (6th? 8th?) MO Cav. arrested.
PIXLEY, ____ ae 55 killed in Chariton Co. MORE 10 Jan 1865
PLATT, Miss Sarah Mills at Roscoe IL, late Asst. in St. Louis Normal School, ae 20y8m. " 28 Jul 1863
PLEMMONS, Basil W. of the 3rd MO CS, captured in Carter Co. 5 Sep, in the prison
    hospital. MORE 4 Nov 1863
POCOCKE, Leander Rodney son of the late W.H. of St. Louis at Helena, Montana Ter., MORE 4 May 1865
    7 Mar ae 25.
POE, Wilson in his 53rd year. Born in Franklin Co. KY, to IN with his parents; GAL 9 Feb 1865
    married there; to MO 1853 (ca). Large family, 4 sons now serving the Union.
POGUE, Samuel 19 Nov in his 68th year. LIT 25 Nov 1864
POHLMAN, Francis, unmarried carpenter ca 29, fell from a building. Has married MORE 15 Nov 1865
    sister and uncle in St. Louis.
POINTER, Mrs. Mary in Jefferson City at the home of her son-in-law Gen. J.B. Read MORE 26 Mar 1862
    ae (84?)y 1m 1d. Born VA, many years resident of St. Louis. Methodist.
POLITE, Stephen 22 Oct of consumption in his 54th year, at 8th & Cass. MORE 23 Oct 1863
POLLARD, Cary oldest son of Dr. W.H. and Addie in Prairieville, Pike Co., 20 Jan MORE 11 Feb 1864
    ae 4y 3m 7d.
POLLARD, Emma E. wife of Seymour E. and daughter of John W. and Sarah Bemis 5 Jan
    in Sedalia ae 28. SEDA 7 Jan 1865
POLLARD, George L., late of NY and VA, at Montrose, St. Louis Co., at the home of MORE 25 Jun 1864
    Mrs. John Graham, in his 44th year. Funeral from Trinity Church.
POLLARD, Mrs. Susan M. in St. Louis Co. 26 Apr ae 25. MORE 27 Apr 1861
POLLARD, Thomas in Independence 21 Jan in his 85th year. MORE 4 Feb 1861
POLLOCK, James 4 Jul in his 85th year at the home of his son David near Oregon. HOLS 14 Jul 1865
    Born near Philadelphia, married at ae 21, to OH 1822, to IN 1850, to
    Holt Co. MO 1863. Presbyterian.
POLLOCK, L.O., a soldier from Clark Co., of pneumonia. MAG 9 Apr 1862
POLLOCK, Lottie Teese, eldest daughter of Henry W. and Lida P., 16 May on 16th MORE 17 May 1864
    south of Morgan, of diphtheria, ae 5y 3m 9d.
POLLOCK, James 6 Jul æ 47. Resolution by Caledonian Society refers to relatives MORE 8 Jul 1863
    here and in the "old world," spells last name Pollok.
POMEROY, Robert E., a hatter of St. Joseph, 24 Mar of consumption. Nephew of Judge FULT 1 Apr 1864
    James H. Birch of Clinton Co. Harrison KY pc. Ae 31 SJH 25 Mar
PONDER, Louis Edward only son of Martin and the late Mary 12 Aug ae 9y 7m 28d. SLMD 13 Aug 1864
    (PENDER?) Lived at 729 Broadway. Interred Calvary.
POPE, Henry L.Y. in Boonville; born Westmoreland Co. VA 11 Nov 1796, to MO 1837, MORE 16 Aug 1862
    died 9 Aug.
POPP, Mrs. "an old lady" thrown from wagon pulled by runaway horse, broke her neck. PERU 7 Jul 1865
PORTER, Mrs. Angeline at the home of her brother-in-law K. McKenzie, 39 Randolph, MORE 17 Oct 1864
    in her 27th year.
PORTER, Mrs. Amelia M. wife of Dr. R.H. yesterday of heart disease, ae 37. Lived MORE 8 Jul 1864
    at 117 Chestnut. Formerly of Independence MO. Louisville & Paducah pc
PORTER, Mahala A. wife of Judge James 6 May in Howard Co. ca 60, formerly of COWS 17 Jun 1864
    Independence.
PORTER, Mary Ida daughter of John P. and Margaret C. in Lewis Co. 10 Jul ae 8y 5m 13d. CANP 17 Aug '65
PORTER, Newton of 3rd MO, arrested in St. Louis 7 Jul, died in prison hospital. MORE 10 Nov 1863
PORTER, Stanfield in Boone Co. 11 Feb ae 69. COWS 22 Mar 1861
POSTAL, Frank Carter son of William C. and Cecelia 14 Feb at 19 14th St. ae 2y 17d. MORE 15 Feb 1861
POSTON, Deborah J. 26 Dec at the State Lunatic Asylum, Fulton, ae 45. MORE 15 Jan 1865
POSTON, Richard C. 6 Apr in St. Francois Co., ca 69. Born in Caswell Co. NC. MORE 17 May 1862

POSTON, Dr. William J. at Wilmington MO 16 May of consumption ae 25y 11m 5d.   MORE 28 May 1865

POTTER, George M. 23 Oct ae 32 after a long illness.   LIT 31 Oct 1862

POTTS, James drowned in backwater from Beaver Dam Creek about 1/2 miles east of Mexico MO, "bright and promising boy." (Mexico Beacon)   SPRIP 17 Aug 1865

POTTS, James W. of Boone Co. in Alton Prison in Dec.   COWS 9 Jan 1863

POTTS, John in Audrain Co. 17 Oct in his 59th year, leaving wife and large family. Born in Wythe Co. VA, to E. TN at early age, then MO; resident of Audrain 25-30 years. Member of the Christian Church.   COWS 21 Oct 1862

POTTS, Mattie J. wife of Dr. J.S. and eldest daughter of John S. Henderson, in Concord MO 2 Jan.   MORE 25 Jan 1865
   COWS 27 "

POTTS, Miss Nannie E. in Audrain Co. at the home of her mother 22 Oct, of epilepsy, ae 20y 8m 6d.   COWS 18 Nov 1864

POURCELLI, Jean in Carondelet 9 Apr ae 81. "Christian, father, Creole." Funeral from St. Mary's Church.   MORE 10 Apr 1864

POURCELLIS, Antoine in Carondelet 2 Oct of typhoid pneumonia, ae 43y 8m.   MORE 4 Oct 1861

POWDERLY, Patrick, private watchman at the Western Foundry, suicide; drowned self in a pond while "under the influence." Blamed on wife's dissipation. Leaves wife and little daughter.   MORE 14 Oct 1865

POWELL, John H. in Marion Co. 6 Aug of consumption in his 32nd year.   HAM 8 Aug 1861

POWELL, Col. L.E. 8 Apr in his 59th year; to St. Charles County MO from Loudon Co. about 40 years ago. Held a number of political offices.   MORE 15 Apr 1864

POWELL, N.A. of Adair Co., of rubeola. (Undertaker's list)   MORE 18 Nov 1862

POWELL, S. Virginia wife of M.T. at the home of her father, James Jones, in Saline Co. 20 Jan of consumption ae 25.   GLWT 31 Jan 1861

POWER, Annie Joseph wife of Philip A. 10 Dec ae 22. Born in Pittsburgh, educated at Florissant and Visitation Academy, married 1y 10m, leaves a daughter. Funeral from Fr. Ryan's Church, interred Calvary.   MORE 20 Dec 1863
   " 12 "

POWER, Michael killed by Thomas Garrity (subsequently acquitted).   HAM 24 & 26 May 1861

POWERS, ___, little daughter of Sylvester living near Cheltenham, died when her clothing caught fire. Ae 8, two younger children in the family.   MORE 26 Nov 1865

POWERS, Honore wife of Thomas suddenly due to "whiskey," Orange St. betw 16-17.   MORE 8 Apr 1862

POWERS, Capt. J.F., member of the Legislature from Lincoln Co., in Jefferson City 20 Feb.   PALS 17 Mar 1865

POWERS, Mary daughter of Peter 6 Mar ae 20 at 141 Orange. Interred Calvary.   MORE 7 Mar 1865

POWERS, Patrick inhaled poison gas (accidentally) at St. Louis Coal Oil works. Unmarried, support of mother, Cozzins St. east of Pratt.   MORE 2 Feb 1865

PRAIRIE, Henry 11 May of typhoid pneumonia ae 16y 1m 17d. Funeral from the home of B. Bompart, 9 miles from the city.   MORE 12 May 1864

PRATT, Edward son of a widow living at the Missouri Hotel, drowned from a skiff.   MORE 29 May 1865

PRATT, Elijah C. 14 Sep in his 45th year. Funeral from St. Xavier. Cincinnati pc   MORE 15 Sep 1861

PRATT, Nehemiah M. killed in the Recorder's Court in the Col. Kallman's Regiment
PRATTE affair. Policeman, living on 11th St. betw Cass & O'Fallon, ae 28. Left wife, 2 children. Interred Bellefontaine. (SLMD says he had been a witness at court, was standing on the balcony overlooking the parade.)   MORE 18-19 June 1861

PRATT, E. living near Williamstown, Lewis Co., murdered by a party of men headed by ___ Baker.   LAJ 14 Aug 1862

PRATT, Ezekiel of Bunker Hill, Lewis Co., killed by rebels. Son-in-law of Justice Hequemburg of St. Louis. (Same as previous item?) See Ezekiel PRATTE.   MORE 11 Jul 1862

PRATTE, Charles, arrested last week and lodged in the Perry Co. jail, taken from the jail for a trip to Bollinger Co. by Capt. Minor's Co., shot the same night.   PERU 9 Jun 1865

PRATTE, Ezekiel shot near Williamstown "last year" by Willis Baker over Civil War differences. (Palmyra Courier)   CAWN 1 Nov 1862

PREISINGER, ___ living on 9th betw Biddle-O'Fallon fell down the steps of his house and broke his neck.   MORE 19 Nov 1861

PRELLER, Maria Ann: her husband John held for her murder, she swore out a complaint against him before dying. He is shown as alias Sebastian Brell.   SLMD 1 & 3 Jan 1861

PREMUTTA, Mrs. Mary E. 23 Oct ae 46, nw corner of 2nd & Cedar.   MORE 24 Oct 1865

PRENATT, Isadore Monday morning last ae ca 47, many years a resident. Left wife and several children.	PALS 10 Mar 1865
PRESBURY, G.G. Sr. at the home of his son-in-law Thomas Love, at Loveton MD near Baltimore, 8 Aug at advanced age. "Long a resident of St. Louis."	MORE 20 Aug 1863
PRESTON, John B. (of H.A. Homeyer & Co.) drowned at Lockport IL 13 Apr. Lived at 449 Pine.	MORE 17 Apr 1865
PREUITT, Arabella at the home of her brother in St. Louis Co. ae 19. Louisville pc	MORE 13 Mar 1861
PREWITT, Mary W. wife of Dr. T.F. in Utica, Livingston Co. 4 Jan in her 30th year.	COWS 16 Jan 1863
PRICE, Almira wife of Enoch at the home of her son-in-law F.A. Lane, ae 57. Funeral from St. George's Church.	MORE 24 May 1864
PRICE, Harriet L. wife of James S. 19 Aug in her 32d year. Funeral from the home, 9th & Washington. Lynchburgh VA pc	MORE 21 & 30 Aug 1862
PRICE, Josiah, Chariton Co.: Final Settlement by J.A.J. Cook.	CECB 5 Mar 1863
PRICE, Milton citizen of Stoddard Co. captured 6 Oct, in Gratiot Prison 23 Nov.	MORE 25 Nov 1862
PRICE, Minerva, Chariton Co.: public administrator took over her estate, her former executor non-resident.	CECB 26 Mar 1863
PRICE, Robert 19 Oct at Price's Landing ae 44. Born in southern IL, to MO with his brother Archie; married daughter of Maj. Sayers in 1855. Died of brain fever. A Mason.	CHAC 25 Oct 1861
Archibald, formerly of Price's Landing, at his home in TN 18 Feb.	CHAC 6 Mar 1862
PRICE, Susan wife of Dr. Edwin decd in Brunswick 6 May. Born 2 Mar 1794 in Spotsylvania Co. VA. Member of the Christian Church.	COWS 9 & 16 May 1862
PRICE, Dr. William of Saline Co. 30 Sep 1865, born 10 Dec 1811 in Baltimore. Graduate of Washington Medical College 1832, moved to Arrow Rock 1833, married Mary Ellen Sappington, dau/Dr. John. Int. Sappington cemetery.	MORE 13 Dec 1865
PRIDDY, John, living 3 miles west of Bolivar, ae 76y 2d.	BOL 16 Mar 1861
PRIEST, Robert, prisoner of war from Madison Co., of brain congestion.	MORE 18 Nov 1862
PRIETTO, Antonetta daughter of Anton and Levinia 7 Nov ae 1y 7m.	MORE 10 Nov 1861
PRIMM, Frederick Kretchmar son of Wilson 28 Sep ae 14.	MORE 29 Sep 1861
PRIMM, Mary Eliza wife of Hubert and only daughter of William A. and the late Catherine Lynch, 27 Jan ae 24y 7m. Funeral, Cathedral to Calvary cemetery.	MORE 28 Jan 1864
PRIOR, Mrs. David Ella wife of (Prior E.?) in Columbia 24 Jul ae 35. Louisville, Lexington, & Frankfort KY pc	COWS 28 Jul 1865
PRIOR, Henry ca 13 drowned in a pond near the City Hospital. Parents live on 13th betw Spruce and Poplar.	MORE 28 Jun 1864
PRIOR, Leslie citizen of Monroe Co. 13 Jan of peritonitis. (Undertaker's list)	MORE 15 Jan 1865
PRITCHARD, Nicholas William son of John N. and Amelia, 13th-LaSalle, of diphtheria ae 4y 7m. NY and Baltimore pc	MORE 21 Apr 1861
PRITCHETT, Abraham, citizen arrested in New Madrid 25 May, in Gratiot Prison of pneumonia 25 Jan.	MORE 27 Jan 1863
PRITCHETT, Abram of Pike Co., 9th Reg MSM, 27 Aug of typhoid in Macon. (MORE 14 Sep says ae 20y 5m.)	LAJ 12 Sep 1863
PROCTOR, Columbus S. at his home in Union Twp. Tuesday last, in ill health several years. Born in Jessamine Co. KY 4 Feb 1810, a Baptist.	PALS 7 & 14 Jul 1865
PROUD, Laura R. daughter of John and Sarah near Oregon 26 Jul ae 16y 16d.	HOLS 18 Aug 1865
PROUT, Hiram A. M.D. 21 Apr at Locust-6th, ae ca 54. Interred Bellefontaine.	MORE 22 Apr 1862
Mary Kearney only daughter of the late Dr. H.A. and Lizzie 28 Apr. 38 N 6th.	" 29 Apr 1863
PRUDOFF, Michael, inquest: "old German in a miserable garret" on Franklin betw Beaumont-Leffingwell. Debility and exposure, ae 60.	MORE 11 Apr 1864
PRUETT, Lave killed in Jefferson Co. by members of the 47th MO Vols. (Col. Fletcher) / ae 67	MORE 17 Oct 1864
PRYOR, Mrs. Margaretta B. wife of Hiram A. ae 29. Funeral from the home of her father, John S. Thompson, nw corner 9-Locust. Pittsburgh pc	MORE 4 Oct 1863
PUGH, Annie daughter of Andrew and Ardelia, 27 Jun. (MORE 14 Jul says Abbie daughter of Andrew and Amelia.)	GLWT 4 Jul 1861
PUGH, Virginia of Callaway Co. at the home of her brother in DeKalb Co. 15 Mar ae 24y 17d.	FULT 25 Mar & 1 Apr 1864

PULS, Conrad 9 Jan of smallpox ae (35?) at 71 Carr.   MORE 10 Jan 1865

PURCELL, John in Boone Co. 27 Dec in his 52nd year. Athens TN pc   COWS 11 Jan 1861

PURMORT, Nettie "an estimable young lady" at her mother's home 7 Nov. Brief illness.   MEMP 11 Nov 1865

PURTEET (PARTEET), I., citizen of Reynolds Co. 14 Dec, pneumonia. (Undertaker's list)   MORE 21 Dec 1862

PURVIS, Abraham ae 16, native of Scotland Co., hanged for the murder of Dominick Patton 17 Oct near 6-Mile House. Ephraim Richardson also executed. Both were soldiers.   MORE 14 Jan 1865

PUTNAM, Harriet R. wife of J.G. 31 Mar in her 51st year at 18 Papin.   MORE 1 Apr 1864

PYPER, William M., tribute by the Caledonian Society. He died in Kearney City Neb. 17 Dec. Mentions family.   MORE 9 Jan 1865

QUARG, Samuel, an old whitewasher at Broadway-Hempstead, debility and intemperance.   MORE 23 Jan 1861

QUARLES, Margaret A. 28 Jan at the home of her father, J.A., in Louisiana, of consumption.   LAJ 31 Jan 1861

QUARLES, William Mills 26 May ae 5y 11d at 39 6th St. Boonville & Glasgow pc   MORE 27 May 1865

QUIGLEY, Thomas "well-known member of the city police" Thursday of erysipelas ae 32. Left wife and 2 children.   MORE 6 Jun 1863

QUINETTE, Sophie L. wife of Francis A. suddenly 11 Mar of lung hemorrhage. New Orleans & Meadville PA pc   MORE 13 Mar 1865

QUINN, Ella wife of Robert near Roanoke 13 Apr ae ca 18.   COWS 22 Apr 1864

QUINN, Mrs. Margaret 9 Oct, at her home on Chestnut betw 21-22.   MORE 11 Oct 1863

QUINN, James an old man living on Lick Creek in Ralls Co. shot twice and killed by his son-in-law last week, reason not known.   LAJ 18 Feb 1865

QUINN, Lieut. Richard 4 Jan in Roanoke, Randolph Co., of pneumonia ae ca 25.   COWS 13 Jan 1865

QUINN, Sarah ae 10 drowned in a cistern on Pratt near Benton.   MORE 28 Oct 1863

RACINE, George "late cook of the Everett House" in his 34th year. Recently member of the IOOF in Philadelphia.   MORE 5 Aug 1861

RAGAN, M.J. who moved from MO to Nevada Terr. in 1862 murdered by Indians; his wife died 6 weeks ago. Left 2 little boys. Couple originally from PA. Left property in MO, NV, and NB.   MORE 30 Jun 1865

RAGSDALE, John W. in Monroe Co. in his 53rd year. "Worthy citizen."   MAG 15 Oct 1863
    Mrs. Sophia at the home of her son J.W. 8 Dec in Monroe Co. in 86th y.   COWS 26 Dec 1862

RAHE, Mrs. W. 4 Dec ae 59. Funeral from 17th & Wash.   MORE 5 Dec 1865

RAISBACH, John died in the county jail. He had been committed on 3 Dec. for altering Treasury notes.   MORE 18 Mar 1864

RALLI, George W. 31 May ae 21 at 97 Walnut.   MORE 1 Jun 1862

RALLS, Elizabeth, funeral from the home of her father John G. Hayden. (see below?)   KCJC 3 Mar 1864

RALLS, Elizabeth P. wife of Samuel 26 Feb ae 27 and her infant daughter ae 3w on 14 Mar, at Richmond & Wash.   MORE 17 Mar 1864

RAMSEY, Frank, noted bushwhacker, reported killed in Callaway Co.   MORE 2 Aug 1864

RAMSEY, T.J. of Burbridge's Command, captured in Stoddard Co. 1 Mar, in Gratiot Prison of lung inflammation.   MORE 29 Apr 1863

RANDALL, Thomas I. on 14 Apr in his 77th year. Funeral from the home of his daughter Mrs. S. Monroe, 21 N. 6th. Baltimore pc   MORE 16 Apr 1864

RANK, Elizabeth wife of Theodore 11 Sep ae 25y 6m, on the corner of South and Autumn. Short illness.   MORE 14 Sep 1865

RANKIN, Hannah wife of Newton 9 Apr ae 33 at 10th & Cass.   MORE 10 Apr 1862

RANNELS, Charles son of Charles and Mary Warden, of a gunshot wound, 4 Apr in 11th y.   MORE 5 Apr 1863

RANNING, Lucinda T. wife of Ralph P. 19 Nov of consumption ae 46. Interred Bellefontaine. Jackson MI & Buffalo NY pc   MORE 21 Nov 1863

RANSDELL, Mrs. Lucy 10 Apr in Allen of typhoid ae ca 60.   COWS 15 Apr 1864

RANSOM, Walter 6 May in his 42nd year on Barnard near Pratte. Rochester, Philadelphia & New Orleans pc   MORE 11 May 1861

RAPHAEL, Robert A. 12 Dec of erysipelas ae 44. Presbyterian, int. Bellefontaine. /Pine St. Church   MORE 13 Dec 1863
     " 14

RARITAN, James "an old man" killed at Laclede. A rebel, he had been involved   SLMD 29 Oct 1861
    in a fight in Carroll Xo. a few days before.

RASBACH, Christian died while cleaning a privy at 11th-Carroll, 28 May; ae 45,   MORE 30 May 1863
    left wife and 2 children. (John Michael Roth also died.)

RAWLINS, Judge Owen 27 Aug near New Franklin in his 67th year, of heart disease.   MORE 12 Sep 1864
    Emigrated from KY more than 45 years ago. Member of the Christian Church.

RAY, James H., 5th MO Cav, captured in Benton Co. AR 17 Oct, in prison hospital.   MORE 10 Feb 1864

RAY, Johanna "a poor woman" found dead of intemperance, alley betw 10-11-Wash-Carr.   MORE 23 Jan 1861

RAY, Joseph shot by his brother Harvey in Fishing River bottom, upper edge of this   RICON 26 Mar 1863
    county; "on opposing sides in this conflict." Joseph called Harvey an
    Abolitionist, with disastrous results.

RAYMOND, John M. 24 Aug ae ca 60.   LIT 28 Aug 1863

RAYMOND, Thompson S. 22 Oct at 51 Gay St., ae 31. Winona MN & Rome NY pc   MORE 23 Oct 1865

REA, Margaret V. wife of John G. 31 Aug ae (36?). Boston pc   MORE 2 Sep 1863

READING, W.R. ae 65 killed in Chariton Co.   MORE 10 Jan 1865

READY, Ellen L. at the home of Maj. Alvan Lightbourne 16 May ae 13; ill 2 mos. +.   LIT 19 May 1865

REARDIN, Denny A. son of John and Elizabeth 13 Feb ae ca 5.   LIT 19 Feb 1864

REAVIS, Mary Ann ae 39. Funeral from the "homestead."   MORE 26 Feb 1864

RECTOR, Robert H., citizen of Pettis Co., 25 Dec of pneumonia. (Undertaker's list)   MORE 2 Jan 1865

REDD, L.B., citizen of Randolph Co., 12 Feb of measles. (Undertaker's list)   MORE 19 Feb 1865

++ REDFORD, Mrs. Cizziah B. 3 Dec of bilious fever ae 48y 2m 22d.   CAWN 12 Dec 1863

REDMOND, Mrs. Jane M. yesterday ae 69. Funeral from the home of Andrew O'Brien,   MORE 1 Nov 1863
    488 Morgan. Interred Calvary.

REED, George C. 25 May. Funeral from the home of Mrs. J.A. Brownlee, 18-Franklin.   MORE 28 May 1862

REED, Jane "a married lady who came from TX a few days ago" found dead in bed of   MORE 28 Jun 1864
    lung congestion.

REED, Samuel G. 2 Jan ae 37 at 515 Pine. Interred Bellefontaine.   MORE 3 Jan 1862

REEDER, Capt. Ambrose 15 Nov in his 49th year at 189 Olive. Interred Bellefontaine.   MORE 16 Nov 1864

REEDER, Salena wife of Elmer and daughter of P.V. and S.A. Bassett 18 May in her   MORE 19 May 1863
    20th year of phthisis pulmonalis. Cincinnati pc

REES, Mary J. wife of Thomas O. and daughter of Edward and Gabriella White,   CANP 21 Jan 1864
    15 Jan in Canton ae 40y 3m 8d.
    Emma, youngest daughter of Thomas O., 31 May in Canton ae 10.   CANP 2 Jun 1864

REES, Sarah W. daughter of Michael and Sarah 19 Apr in Randolph Co., of measles,   MAG 23 Apr 1862
    ae 1y 21d.

REESE, Mrs. Elizabeth 26 Aug at Pleasant Hill, of dysentery, ae 58. MORE 18 Sep &   WARS 2 Sep 1865

REESE, Ellen M. wife of Dr. A.W. 27 Nov in her 36th year. Funeral preached by   WARS 1 Dec 1865
    her brother-in-law Rev. G.K. Dunlap of Kirkwood, at the Episcopal   MORE 3 "
    Church.(Ae 26 according to MORE, died of typhoid.)

REESE, James W. of Marshall Twp. caught in the machinery while oiling a   LIT 14 Aug 1863
    threshing machine. (Weston Sentinel)

REESE, Margaret consort of A. in Canton 16 Feb.   CANP 19 Feb 1863

REEVER, George ae 4 run over near Lowell by a government wagon. Son of David, an   MORE 29 Jul 1864
    employee at Bellefontaine cemetery.

REEVES, Benjamin G. at his father's home in Howard Co. 17 Sep from the effects   MORE 1 Oct 1865
    of a gunshot wound in his arm.   COWS 29 Sep "

++ REDFURN (originally REDFORD), John, stabbed by John Maley (later James Malloy)   MORE 30 &
    proprietor of a number of hacks; a quarrel, not specified. Redfurn was   31 Jul 1864
    a native of Mohill, Co. Leitrim IRE, in US 15 years, St. Louis 5 years;
    was 35, left wife and 2 children, on Spruce betw 5-6.

REGAN, James "many years a resident of St. Louis," native of Co. Down IRE, at   MORE 5 Apr 1862
    151 N. 5th 4 Apr of pneumonia.

REGAN, John "many years a resident of St. Louis," native of Co. Down IRE, 10 Dec.   MORE 11 Dec 1862
    Funeral from the home of his brother-in-law James Gresham, 16 Wash.
                                       Pittsburgh pc

REGAN, Matthew A. son of Michael, 3 Jun ae 25y 8m. Interred Calvary.   MORE 5 Jun 1865

REGAN, Thomas J. 10 May of consumption in his 23rd year.   MORE 13 May 1865
REID, Albro eldest son of Alex J. and Annie A. of rheumatic heart ae 8y 8m. LAJ 12 Feb 1863
      (also COWS 20 Feb & MORE 22 Feb)
REID, George A. youngest son of James of Lincoln Co. shot at a Democratic   LAJ 24 Sep 1864
      Conservative meeting at Troy; apparently a wanton killing by a faction
      trying to break up the meeting.
REID, Capt. James B. "most popular pilot on the Missouri, lower Mississippi and MORE 18 Oct 1865
      all tributaries of the Father of Waters," 16 Oct ae 40.
REILLY, Maggie Bell eldest child of James and M. Josephine 22 May ae 6y 4m at MORE 23 May 1863
                              233 Chestnut.
                                                                              MORE 22 Jan 1863
REILLY, Owen at his home, 19 S. Levee, ae 38.
REILY, James L. at his home on west Walnut 5 May in his 55th year. Funeral from MORE 6 May 1865
      St. Malachi's, interred Calvary. Pneumonia. Gettysburg & Baltimore pc
REILY, Capt. Robert of St. Louis Sunday in Cairo. Funeral from the home of   MORE 26 Mar 1862
                              George P. Doan.
REINEKE, Christian, proprietor of a dairy on Manchester & Chouteau, asphyxiated MORE 2 Mar 1861
      in a cistern full of malt while trying to help his employee Mathias
      Lackner (also killed). Left wife, 3 children.
RELF, Hermine C. 14 Jan at the home of Bishop Payne in Cavalla, Africa in her MORE 12 Mar 1861
      29th year. An Episcopal missionary, late of Missouri.
RELFE, Dr. James H. at the home of his son in Caledonia 14 Sep in his 72d year. MORE 18 Oct 1863
      Long a resident of se MO, state Marshal, in congress, etc. Wheeling pc
REMINGTON, Stephen J., longtime baggage master for the Hannibal & St. Joseph RR, SJH 26 Nov 1864
      in St. Joseph 23 Nov ae 32y 4m 21d. "Remains taken east by his sisters."
REMINGTON, William C., late of Platte City, in Nebraska City 20 Dec of pneumonia. SJH 22 Dec 1864
REMINGTON, William H. 4 Sep at his home, west of Grand, north of St. Charles Rock MORE 5 Sep 1865
      Rock Road. IOOF. Interred Bellefontaine.
RENFREW, John at 342 N. 7th Wednesday ae 55. Pittsburgh pc   MORE 31 Jan 1862
RENFREW, Samuel, 10th MO, in Gratiot Prison of lung inflammation.   MORE 27 Dec 1863
RENFRO, A.A. 25 Dec in Boone Co. in his 39th year. Baptist.   COWS 4 Jan 1861
RENICK, Isabel Hamilton eldest daughter of Col. Robert M. and Anna R. (living on MORE 10 Aug 1864
      Chouteau) in Sault Ste. Marie MI 3 Aug in her 23rd year. Funeral from SLMD "
      parents' home. Baltimore, Philadelphia, Lexington MO pc
RENKUS, John, an aged German, suicide by hanging. Ae 95, left wife "young daughter." MORE 7 Apr 1861
      Gravedigger in Germany, professional beggar 10 years. "He ate 1/2 bushel
      of potatoes daily." Had tried to kill his wife with a hatchet.
RENNICKS, Mrs. Joyce Monday last at the home of her son-in-law Fielding Fleming, PALS 31 Jul 1863
      of cancer, in her 66th year. Daughter of Joseph Falkland of
      Fayette Co. KY. Baptist.
RENSHAW, William Sr. at the home of his son in Fulton 14 Mar ae 72. Resident of MORE 17 Mar 1864
      St. Louis 45 years. Funeral from 2nd Presbyterian.
RENTER, William member of the police, from a fall down some steps. Lived on MORE 19 Jan 1863
      Julia betw 7-8. Left wife and 4 small children.
REUTER, Fred, a boy, killed in a boiler explosion at the shop of Wm. Eagleson MORE 10 Aug 1864
      near 14-Papin; he lived in Cheltenham.
REX, Virginia Hooper eldest daughter of John and Mary, Pine betw 16-17, ae 8y 7m. MORE 25 Jun 1862
      Baltimore & Philadelphia pc
REYNOLDS, ____, son of Dr. Reynolds of Clarksville, ca 9, accidentally shot by LAJ 8 Apr 1865
                              another boy.
REYNOLDS, Andrew (1st Co Mtd Rifles, SW Batt.) ae 19. Father's home, 11-Franklin-Wash. MORE 7 Jun '61
REYNOLDS, family of Willis, Lincoln Co. Camilla J., wife, 12 Sep ae 41y 8m 7d LAJ 23 Sep 1865
      (2 mi n of Auburn)   Elizabeth Ann eldest dau/12 Sep ae 31y 6m 3d MORE 25 "
                            St. Louis pc   (MORE gives Elizabeth as 21)
REYNOLDS, Catherine ae 61 at the home of her son-in-law Charles Cordanau, betw MORE 15 Nov 1863
      Green & Morgan, of heart disease.
REYNOLDS, Charless 8 Feb in his 45th year of a lingering illness, at his home on MORE 9 Feb 1862
      Morgan St. NY pc
REYNOLDS, Edward P. ae 20, died 27 Mar (sic). Funeral from home of James Reynolds, MORE 1 May 1864
                              16-O'Fallon.

REYNOLDS, Horace very suddenly at his father's home, 8th betw Cass-O'Fallon, ae 7.   MORE 26 Jan 1862

REYNOLDS, James in Cape Girardeau 14 Sep in his 61st year, former resident of St.   MORE 23 Sep 1865
   Louis -- "one of the best millwrights in the West."

REYNOLDS, Sarah wife of W.B. in Lewis Co. 8 Apr. Daughter of J.M. Atchinson,   CANP 20 Apr 1865
   born 28 May 1829, married 27 Feb 1849; member Church of Christ.

REYNOLDS, W.T. shot by an unknown soldier at his business house 3 weeks ago, died   LIT 21 Apr 1865
   20 Apr. Left wife and 2 young children.

RHODES, William, Chariton Co.; notice to unknown heirs to clear title, Wm B. Parker.   CECB 28 Aug 1862

RICE, Bernard M. son of the late John and Mary at Eau d'Enghien near Paris, 11 Aug   MORE 29 Aug &
   ae 23. To be interred in St. Louis. Member St. Louis Bar.   5 Oct 1865

RICE, Dr. C. in St. Charles 1 Jan of lung congestion.   (see RICH)   COWS 13 Jan 1865

RICE, Eliza Jane wife of James M. in Boone Co. 15 May in her 26th year.   COWS 22 May 1863
   Edgar son of James M. 18 May ae 3y.   "

RICE, Jameson W., late of Helena AR, 14 Aug. Funeral from his late residence on   MORE 15 Aug 1863
                                                      Clark betw 20-21.

RICE, John son of Capt. Joel 15 Dec of chronic diarrhoea contracted while   LAJ 23 Dec 1865
   serving in Co D 33rd Reg.

RICE, Jonothan W., old citizen of St. Charles Co., suicide by hanging 23 Jun.   WARS 15 Jul 1865

RICE, Mr. Rachel 1 Mar in Boone Co. ae 62y 2m 24d. (MORE 17 Mar says Mrs.)   COWS 15 Mar 1861

RICE, Stephen at Sisters Hospital 11 Aug ae 53, paralyzed nearly a year. Clerk   MORE 12 &
   of the Circuit Court.   14 Aug 1864

RICH, Albert Smith youngest son of Shebnah and Delia, Park Ave. opposite Lafayette   MORE 24 May 1862
   Park, very suddenly 23 May ae 3y 13d.

RICH, Dr. C. at St. Charles 1 Jan of lung congestion. Born in Rhode Island, moved   MORE 8 Jan 1865
   with parents to OH until 1832, to St. Louis 1840, then to St. Charles.
   Left wife and 8 children. (See RICE)

RICH, Hiram son of the late Col. Hiram of Ft. Leavenworth 10 Feb of consumption,   MORE 12 Feb 1865
   at the home of his brother-in-law Maj. O.D. Green, ae 21y 9m. Funeral
   from St. John's Episcopal, interred Bellefontaine.

RICH, William G. 12 Jun ae (39?). Philadelphia pc   MORE 13 Jun 1865

RICHARDS, Angeline eldest daughter of William and Mary 24 Nov ae 13y 3m. Memphis,   MORE 25 Nov 1862
   Corinth and Holly Springs MS pc

RICHARDS, David R. at 3rd & Green in his 26th year. Cincinnati & Crawfordsville IN pc MORE 17 Dec 1863

RICHARDSON, David, a Confederate soldier of Platte Co., at the battle of Springfield. LIT 6 Feb 1863

RICHARDSON, Ephraim, native of Scotland Co. ae 18, hanged for the murder of Dominick   MORE 14 Jan 1865
   Patton near 6-Mile-House 17 Oct. Abraham Purvis also hanged. (soldiers)

RICHARDSON, James in Boone Co. 23 Feb ae ca 60.   COWS 4 Mar 1864

RICHARDSON, John captured in Polk Co. 21 May in Springfield Prison of phthisis   MORE 10 Jun 1863
   pulmonalis.

RICHARDSON, John alias "Louis Napoleon" convicted of counterfeiting Confederate   LIT 5 Sep 1862
   money, hanged near Liberty 4 Sep.

RICHARDSON, Julia Ada daughter of West and Elizabeth, on Summit betw Clark and   MORE 11 Apr 1863
   Manchester, 10 Apr ae 2y 9m 28d.

RICHARDSON, Judge Thomas S. "a rebel" shot near his home in Scotland Co. He   SLMD 26 Nov 1861
   was Judge of the 5th Judicial District.

RICHART, Virginia wife of A.L. near Canton 30 Jan in her 34th year. Born in   CANP 2 &
   Danville KY, to Lewis Co. in 1858.   9 Feb 1865

RICHMOND, Henry M. at his father's home in Randolph Co. 15 Feb of consumption, ca 26. MORE 13 Mar 1864

RICHMOND, Mary A. wife of Rollin suddenly 14 Jun, of heart disease -- dropped   MORE 15 &
   dead during a conversation with her pastor about charities.   16 Jun 1864

RICKETTS, Robert Luther son of Judge Benjamin and Rebecca 4 Aug ae 23.   LIT 9 Aug 1861

RICKETTS, Theresa Ora youngest daughter of Francis in Mexico MO 17 Feb of lung   MORE 21 Feb 1862
   congestion, ae 5y 5m.

RICKEY, Joseph in Boone Co. 5 Oct of bilious fever, ae ca 60.   COWS 13 Oct 1865

RICKMAN, Mrs. Mary Sunday in her 60th year. Interred Bellefontaine.   SLMD 12 Feb 1861

RICORDS, James, an undertaker, 1 Feb in his 53rd year after a short illness.   MORE 2 Feb 1863
                     Cincinnati & Bridgeton NJ pc

Entry	Source
RIDER, David A. 13 Feb ae 25. Baltimore & Washington pc	MORE 14 Feb 1864
RIDER, Thomas L. in Macon 10 Mar of typhoid ae 28; left young wife and child.	MORE 25 Mar 1865
RIDGWAY, Jefferson B., citizen of Boone Co., shot by Federal pickets in Columbia.	MORE 14 Oct 1864
RIDGWAY, Thomas in Boone Co. 9 Jan ae ca 60.	COWS 11 Jan 1861
RIELLY, Christopher only son of Christopher 18 Sep ae 23 Olive, ae 5y 6m 13d. McKee IA & Perry Co. IL pc	MORE 19 Sep 1862
RIGGS, Jesse killed in a mill explosion 5 miles west of Knoxville. (RICON)	RANC 24 Jan 1861
RIGHTER, Ann Eliza wife of William H. of St. Louis at the home of her father in Wright City 14 Feb. Daughter of Dr. H.C. and F.M. Wright. Her infant daughter also died.	MORE 10 & 14 Feb 1864
RIGHTMIRE, Mary, wife of a soldier, drowned in a cistern at 208 N. 12th. Body discovered by her stepdaughter.	MORE 23 Mar 1862
RILEE, Amilia Hughes wife of H.D., native of Liverpool, 18 Nov ae 38.	MORE 28 Nov 1864
RILEY, Col. A.C. of wounds received near New Hope Church 30 May. 1st MO Inf, ae 27. Interred Atlanta.	MORE 17 Jun 1864
RILEY, Eliza Ann consort of John 21 Feb ae 39. "Wife, mother, sister." Cumberland Presbyterian.	RANC 28 Feb 1861
RILEY, Eunice wife of William H. suddenly, apparently poisoned; no suspects. Left 2 small children.	PALS 11 Dec 1863
RILEY, John, inquest: died at the workhouse of brain congestion, ae 30.	MORE 8 Oct 1862
RILEY, John Sr. at his home on St. Charles St. betw 23-24, native of Lismore, Co. Waterford IRE. Died 29 April.	MORE 30 Apr & 1 May 1865
RILEY, Lucy daughter of Maj. Alfred M. of Clay Co. at the home of her aunt, Mrs. Arnold, near Nicholsville, Jessamine Co. KY 20 Jun ae ca 20. COWS 4 Aug &	LIT 21 Jul 1865 SJH 6 Aug "
RILEY, Mary relict of John P. 20 Mar ae 61. Funeral from the home of Joseph Foster, 170 S. 4th. Interred Calvary.	MORE 22 Mar 1862
RIMMER, Samuel 17 Mar ae 63. Funeral from the home of his son-in-law S. ?. Bilbrough, 16th-Papin.	MORE 18 Mar 1862
RING, Martin of brain inflammation Monday in his 40th year. Funeral from the home of James Gresham, Wash betw 5-6. St. Patrick's Church, int. Calvary.	MORE 7 Jul 1863
RINGER, Abraham "an old man" living 6 miles east of Potosi, shot.	SLMD 13 Aug 1861
RINGO, Martin late of Clay Co. and recently of Gallatin, en route west between Salt Lake and Fort Laramie, killed by the accidental discharge of a gun. His family went on to CA.	LIT 9 Sep 1864
RIPLEY, Dr. Joseph D. 9 Mar ae 50y 1m 24d, at 29 Benton. Interred Bellefontaine. New Orleans & Cincinnati pc	MORE 10 Mar 1861
RISBEY, Mrs. Hannah, native of Bristol ENG, 10 Dec at the home of her daughter, ae 71. Many years a resident of St. Louis.	MORE 12 Dec 1862
RISK, Sarah suddenly last Sunday at the home of William Sites, ca 18. Methodist.	PALS 14 Aug 1863
RITTENHOUSE, Cora Bell eldest child of J.M. and Susan 5 Mar ae 6y7m. Cincinnati pc	MORE 7 Mar 1865
RITCHIE, A.W. 18 Mar in his 67th year, at 11th & Olive.	SJH 19 Mar 1865
RITTENHOUSE, Erastus T. youngest child of Louise and the late Erastus T., 26 Dec. E.T., ae 29y 10m, on 17 Dec. Keokuk and Cincinnati pc	MORE 28 Dec 1863 " 19 Dec "
RITTERSKAMP, Henry at the home of his son, ae 69.	MORE 1 Aug 1861
RIVENS, Louis 25 Mar ae 74 at his home in Carondelet.	MORE 26 Mar 1864
RIVES, Lucy only daughter of the late Robert at the home of Mrs. Watkins, near Richmond, 30 Aug ae ca 17.	RICON 9 Sep 1865
RIVES, Naomi Burd only daughter of Dr. T.L. and G.S. 4 May at St. Charles of scarlet fever ae 5y 3m.	MORE 12 May 1865
ROACH, James, suicide ae 22 (shot himself); no known reason. Had enlisted twice, mother procured discharge first time. Employed Colman's turning shop.	MORE 11 Apr 1864
ROACH, Thomas, native of Mayo IRE, 1 Apr at 72 Chestnut ae 37. Funeral from the Cathedral, interred Calvary.	MORE 2 Apr 1864
ROBERT, Sanderson in Cincinnati 5 Jan in his 61st year.	MORE 15 Jan 1864
ROBERTS, Charles Pearce son of Col. Sidney R. and Martha A.W. drowned in Linn Creek 24 Jun ae 8y 4m 20d.	MORE 13 Jul 1861

ROBERTS, Mrs. Elizabeth 19 Jan ae 62. Funeral from the home of her son,   MORE 20 Jan 1863
   J.F. Fraser, sw corner Barry-Fulton. Interred Calvary.

ROBERTS, George Albert only child of George P. and Annie M., 40 S. 14th, Sunday   MORE 14 Apr 1863
   last of consumption in his 17th year.

ROBERTS, Isabella youngest daughter of Capt. William H. and Henrietta 9 May in   MORE 10 May 1861
   her 11th year.

ROBERTS, James, of Texas Co., captured 6 Oct, died in Gratiot Prison 11 Dec.   MORE 13 &
   (Possibly a civilian.) Undertaker's list shows pneumonia.   15 Dec 1862

ROBERTS, James W. at the Planters' House 26 Sep.   MORE 27 Sep 1864

ROBERTS, Dr. Jerome E., formerly of this city, in Springfield MA 19 Feb.   LAJ 18 Mar 1865
   Assistant surgeon in the Army at the time of his death.

ROBERTS, William on his farm near Allen in Randolph Co. 5 Apr, "old citizen."   MAG 9 Apr 1862

ROBERTSON, James at his mother's home on Biddle west of 15th, 2 Nov ae 27y 6m.   MORE 5 Nov 1865

ROBERTSON, Milus McCorkle son of the late Dr. Hugh, formerly of Nashville, 27 May   MORE 28 May 1865
   ae 26. Nashville pc

ROBERTSON, Sarah H. consort of Junius and daughter of the late Israel B. Grant,   MORE 5 Apr 1865
   of Callaway Co., 21 Mar ae 33. Left husband and one child.

ROBESON, Mrs. Amie D. 11 May in her 66th year. Funeral from the home of her   MORE 12 May 1865
   son-in-law, Henry C. Bernard. Protracted illness.

ROBINETT, Mrs. Margaret at the home of her son-in-law T.B. Nesbitt in Fulton   FULT 28 Jul 1864
   Tuesday last.

ROBINS, Job, a refugee from Douglas Co. ae ca 45, in the military hospital   ROLEX 29 Nov 1862
   in Rolla 5 Nov.

ROBINSON, Rev. ___, southern Methodist, lately killed in Chariton Co.   MORE 10 Jan 1865

ROBINSON, Anna A. (or Anna), wife of Jeremiah R. in Ste. Genevieve 6 Aug of cholera   MORE 10 Aug 1863
   morbus ae 56y 1m 3d. Daughter of Jesse and Elizabeth Bryan, born in
   Clark Co. KY 3 Jul 1807; to Ste. Genevieve 1822. Wife, mother. Columbia MO,
   Louisville KY, Marysville & Sacramento CA pc

ROBINSON, Elizabeth consort of William near Canton 5 Dec ae 42.   CANP 18 Dec 1862

ROBINSON, Henry, a young unmarried man whose parents lived in Gasconade Co., killed   MORE 29 Mar 1865
   Monday at the 14th St. Depot while coupling freight cars.

ROBINSON, Hillman 17 Aug "near 58." Interred Wesleyan.   MORE 18 Aug 1861

ROBINSON, J. C. of Arrow Rock 29 Sep at Sisters Hospital of consumption, ae 37.   MORE 30 Sep 1862
   Formerly of VA. Interred Bellefontaine.

ROBINSON, James R., late of St. Louis, shot by a guerilla at Cypress Bend MS   MORE 30 Jun 1863
   22 Jun ae 27y 6m.

ROBINSON, John A. " an estimable, quiet and orderly citizen" in Callaway Co. killed   CAWN 6 May 1865
   by ruffians led by Warren Martin, ae ca 75-80.

ROBINSON, Lucy wife of Roger of, and in, Randolph Co. 6 Aug of bloody flux,   COWS 12 Aug 1864
   ae 62y 3m. Native of Clark Co. KY, mother of Elder J.M. Robinson of Columbia.

ROBINSON, Mary A. wife of Dr. Alex 15 Aug in Boone Co.   COWS 19 Aug 1864

ROBINSON, Mary Jane wife of Radford and only daughter of Otho Barnes 11 Sep in   COWS 27 Sep 1861
   Boone Co. of typhoid, in her 36th year. Native of Montgomery Co. KY
   where she lived until 10 years ago, then came to Boone Co.

ROBINSON, Patrick, inquest: fell from the Levator, drowned. Left family in St. Louis.   MORE 10 Jun 1864

ROBINSON, Robert M. 22 Oct ae 37.   MORE 29 Oct 1861

ROBINSON, Mrs. Tabitha in Bellevue Twp. Washington Co. 13 Jul in her 60th year.   MORE 19 Jul 1861
   Mother of Thomas Claiborne of St. Louis. Married twice; Presbyterian;   SLMD 23 "
   interred family burying ground, Potosi. (SLMD shows Thos. Chadbourne)

ROBINSON, William knocked down in the Arcade saloon by an acquaintance, Theodore   MORE 4 May 1865
   Hart, died of skull fracture. Ae 28, wife and 2 children at 8th-Cass.

ROBNETT, Mrs. Margaret at the home of her son-in-law Thomas B. Nesbit near Fulton,   COWS 12 Aug 1864
   28 Jul. Native of KY, born 1797, to MO with her husband David and settled
   on 2-Mile Prairie in Boone Co. when it was new and uninhabited. Her
   husband died of cholera in Oct 1832.

RODEHAVER, Eliza Ann wife of E.H. and daughter of C. Woolverton 18 Feb in her 42d   MORE 7 Mar 1863
   year, in St. Louis Co. Uniontown PA & Morganton VA pc

RODEHEFFER, Eleazer H., shot some two weeks ago in St. Louis Co. by a young man   MORE 20 &
    Walker Henley; had been buried, exhumed for inquest (died Saturday).   22 Apr 1864
    Henley had quarreled with Rodeheffer's son, ae 15, whipped him, may
    have thought R. was after him. Henley went to Idaho after the shooting,
    apparently a wanton act.

RODGERS, Samuel "many years a resident of St. Louis" 1 Jan ae 47. Mason.   MORE 3 Jan 1861
                       Interred Bellefontaine.

ROE, Mrs. Elizabeth formerly of Louisville in her (23rd?) year. Funeral from the   MORE 28 Dec 1863
    home of her brother-in-law, John J. Roe, Compton Hill.

ROEVER, Louis of "convulsions caused by great mental anguish." Had been charged   MORE 25 Apr 1862
    with raping a young woman on an omnibus (the driver was outside and there
    were no other passengers.) Wife, 3 children "in comfortable circumstances."

ROGAN, Elizabeth consort of Martin yesterday of consumption, on 8th betw O'Fallon-Cass. MORE 15 Oct '62

ROGERS, Judge James A., formerly of St. Louis, in Jefferson City 25 Jan. MORE 28 Jan & COWS 3 Feb 1865

ROGERS, Joel M. 21 Jan in his 30th year. Funeral from his mother's home (313?)   MORE 22 Jan 1863
                             Franklin.

ROGERS, Mrs. Mary Angeline wife of J.M. 2 Aug of brain congestion ae 18y 10m.   MORE 13 Aug 1861
    Newark & Mount Vernon OH pc

ROGERS, Nancy widow of Peter at the home of her brother Thomas Gardner 23 Jan ae 84.   LIT 5 Feb 1864

ROGERS, Rodney A., living on Clark's Row, Olive St., ae 52. Rochester NY pc   MORE 20 Nov 1864

ROGERS, William burned to death while "under the influence." A carpenter, had   MORE 23 Feb 1861
    locked himself in a building, sparks from his pipe ignited some shavings.

ROGERS, William 18 Jan ae 73. Interred Calvary. Baltimore & Louisville pc   MORE 20 Jan 1861

ROHE, Johanna, inquest: lived on O'Fallon betw 8-9 in a "disgusting wretched house." MORE 11 Apr 1864
    Brain congestion, intemperance, exposure. Had 5 children, oldest "no more
    than 10." Husband had left 2 days before; evidence indicated she had
    quarreled with someone, possibly him, but foul play not suspected.

ROHRER, Amanda wife of Judge Upton near Fillmore, Andrew Co. 20 Mar ae <u>ca</u> 48.   MORE 3 Apr 1863
    Born in Knox Co. OH, daughter of John Kerr; to MO 1837. Died of pulmonary
    disease, left 2 sons and 3 daughters.

ROLAND, Jacob killed near Agency Ford trying to escape from militia after arrest.   SJH 1 Aug 1864

ROLAND, W.J. of Poindexter's Band, of pneumonia. (Gratiot Prison?)   MORE 19 Nov 1862

ROLK, Louis, inquest: German died suddenly at his home near 7th-O'Fallon of   MORE 3 Jul 1863
    brain inflammation, ae 40. Left family.

ROLLINS, Mrs. Nannie L. at her husband's home, Collins Park, Boone Co., 16 Jul.   COWS 25 Jul 1862
    Only daughter of Richard Stowers of Pendleton Co. KY.

ROLLINS, Robert Rhodes, ae <u>ca</u> 46, at the home of J.S. Bellins near Columbia 2 Mar.   COWS 11 Mar 1864

ROMANS, Catherine J. consort of John 21 Jun ae 54y 14d, of gastroenteritis.   MORE 4 Jul 1865

ROOSE, Anton, inquest: carriage maker, worked at the Arsenal, lived on Victor betw   MORE 17 Nov 1863
    Carondelet-Eastern. Lung congestion, ae <u>ca</u> 40. Left "four orphan children
    in very destitute circumstances."

ROOTES, Thomas Reed son of Dr. L.J. and J.A. 17 Sep ae 10y 5m 11d.   FULT 23 Sep 1864

ROSE, Fritze, a German shoemaker, shot himself 5 Jul; had a disorder of the nervous   MORE 6 Jul 1865
    system. Left wife and 2 children.

ROSE, James son of Rev. William of Louisiana MO 7 Dec at the home of Dr. Adams, of   HAM 19 Dec 1861
    diphtheria, ae 5y 5m.

ROSE, John, 22 Mar at 24th-Wash, ae 57y 11m 16d. Cincinnati, Allegheny, NY pc   MORE 26 Mar 1864

ROSE, Margaret wife of Edward, nee McHose, Saturday. Funeral from Louis Ottenard's   MORE 24 Mar 1861
                                            home.

ROSE, Mathias D. only son of E.H., of Audrain Co., 17 Oct at Hudson House in CA   MORE 21 Nov 1861
    of bowel inflammation, in his 25th year.

ROSE, Michael, of Fremont's Body Guard, killed at Springfield 25 Oct in 30th year.   MORE 19 Nov 1861

ROSE, Peter, inquest: died in City Hospital ae 40, injuries inflicted by Theodore   MORE 21 Aug &
    Schedde (Schuder) 27 Jun. Rose was drunk, was struck with a spade.   later, 1863

ROSE, William Albert 25 Sep of diphtheria, ae 11.   MORE 29 Sep 1861

ROSENFELD, William J. oldest son of Isaac and Eliza E. 13 <u>Jun</u> (sic) on Olive   MORE 15 Jul 1863
    near Leffingwell, ae 8y 16d.

ROSENTHAL, Samson S., Spruce betw 15-16, on 30 Jun.   MORE 1 Jul 1862

ROSENTHAL, Z.A. of 11th-Chestnut at Columbus KY 17 Oct ae 47. Philadelphia pc — MORE 20 Oct 1863

ROSKILLY, Mrs. Nancy 14 Jul in her 42d year. Funeral from home of Thomas Allen on McClure Ave. — MORE 15 Jul 1865

ROSS, Mrs. Eliza M. near New Haven, Franklin Co. 18 Sep ae 65. — MORE 24 Sep 1865

ROSS, James son of Rev. William in Pike Co. 7 Dec ae 5y 5m. — LAJ 12 Dec 1861

ROSS, Lucus son of Mrs. Lear and the late James in Howard Co. 19 Jun ae 17. — COWS 22 Jul 1864

ROSS, Robert in Spencer Twp, Pike Co. 18 Dec ae ca 52. — MORE 17 Jan 1861

ROSSITER, Dr. Charles H. shot by his brother-in-law John Nelson (son of the late Capt. James) of Tully in an argument over division of corn crop. (CANP) — CAWN 29 Nov 1862

ROTH, John Michael 28 May ae 21 while cleaning a privy. Unmarried. — MORE 30 May 1863

ROTH, V.W. 1 Jun ae 50y 5m 15d. Funeral from the home of Mrs. George W. Sparhawk, 12th N of Clark. NY & New Orleans pc — MORE 2 Jun 1864

ROTHROCK, George T., funeral preached at Camden 5 Oct by Rev. Joseph Devlin. — RICON 23 Sep 1865

ROTTCHER, Frederick, suicide by drowning ae ca 53; "mental aberration." — MORE 5 Jun 1862

ROUSE, James of Ralls Co. drowned trying to cross Salt River in a canoe at Goodwin's Mill. James Lewellen & ___ Hedgepeth also drowned. — LIT 2 May 1862

ROUTT, Emma daughter of Judge Henry L. and Kate 4 Oct in her 10th year. — LIT 7 Oct 1864

ROWDEN, "the notorious Jim" killed in Vienna in Maries Co. by William Breedon. "A terror" for 3 or 4 years. — JCPT 18 Oct 1865

ROWLAND, Col. David of Richmond KY at the home of his son D.P. in St. Louis, 1 Aug in his 62d year. Louisville, Lexington, Cincinnati pc. Int. Richmond KY. — MORE 2 Aug 1864

ROWLAND, J. of Polk Co. in the Prison Hospital in Springfield. — MORE 10 Apr 1863

ROWLAND, Mattie Shackleford wife of D.P. and daughter of W.H. Shackelford, 175 Chestnut, 8 Sep ae 24y 7m 25d. Left an infant. Interred Bellefontaine. Louisville, Paris & Danville KY pc — MORE 9 & 14 Sep 1864

ROZIER, Ferdinand Sr. 1 Jan at Ste. Genevieve ae 86. Louisville, Philadelphia, & New Orleans pc — MORE 10 Jan 1864

ROZIER, Julius, eldest son of Judge Francis, obituary. — MORE 23 Sep 1864

RUBEY, Letha A. daughter of Thomas P. and E.C., 45 S. 16th, (16? Aug) ae 21. — MORE 17 Aug 1864

RUBEY, John H. at the home of his father, U.E. near Allen in Randolph Co. 30 Dec of apoplexy, in his 30th year. — COWS 15 Jan 1864
U.E. in Macon City 8 Jul ae 58. MORE 17 Jul & COWS 22 Jul 1864

RUBY, Mrs. Mary J. wife of C.W., of Lebanon MO, 12 Mar of chronic dysentery ae 26. Funeral from the home of L.W.H. Wright, 9th-Salisbury. — MORE 13 Mar 1863

RUBY, Virginia Woods wife of John B. 30 Dec ae 24. — MORE 8 Jan 1864

RUCKER, Dr. A.A. at Forest City 23 Jul ae 45. Had accidentally cut himself with a penknife 2 months before, died of complications. — HOLS 28 Jul 1865

RUCKER, Judge Ephraim 30 May in Brunswick in his 45th year, a county judge. (Public administrator took over his estate, CECB 28 Aug 1862) — LAJ 26 Jun 1862

RUCKER, "Captain" and his brother, bushwhackers captured by Capt. Clark, tried to escape while en route to Macon and were killed. (MORE 6 May gives name as Harvey Rucker, place of death near Sturgeon.) — LIT 5 May 1865

RUCKER, Thomas P. son of the late L.F. and E. at the home of George W. Rucker, cor. Washington-Garrison, 14 Feb ae 21y 4m. Interred Bellefontaine. Louisville & Kansas City pc — MORE 15 & 16 Feb 1863

RUFFNER, Madeleine S. eldest child of Lewis and Virginia at the home of her grandfather T.H. West 9 Apr, of pneumonia, ae 3y 7d. Cincinnati & Lexington MO pc — MORE 10 Apr 1862

RUGGLES, Charles L. eldest son of Capt. Levi and Catherine M. 2 Jun in his 16th y. — LAJ 24 Jun 1865

RUGGLES, John S. 1 Jan of typhoid at Planter's Hotel, formerly of MA. Employed by Keokuk Packet Co. Interred Baptist Cemetery. — HAM 9 Jan 1862

RUGGLES, Margaret Jane daughter of Moses W. and Mary E. 20 Mar ae 8y 7m 20d. — SLMD 21 Mar 1861

RUHR, Charles died when his mother accidentally gave him oxalic acid instead of salts. Lived on Benton betw 13-14. — MORE 22 Aug 1864

RUMBOLD, Emma S.M. wife of Dr. T.F. and daughter of Dr. M. Meeker (of Meeker's Grove WI) of bowel inflammation ae 26y 8m 28d. Funeral from Jefferson Barracks to Bellefontaine Cem. Davenport & Galena pc — MORE 7 Nov 1863

RUMBOLD, Lilla Josephine daughter of William and Hannah 28 Nov of diphtheria ae 4y 2m 21d.	MORE 29 Nov 1862
RUMMELL, Catherine, inquest: lived on (Pwicok?) betw Picot-Lesperance, left husband and 4 children, oldest 10, youngest 15m. Died of epilepsy.	MORE 3 Jul 1864
RUNNELLS, Jane E. wife of John L. (now pvt with 19th IA Vols near Vicksburg) in Carondelet 1 Jul ae 23. "Wife, mother, neighbor, Christian, friend."	MORE 3 Jul 1863
RUNRECHT, Elizabeth, a German girl, of apoplexy ae 16 at 342 S. 3rd.	MORE 22 Apr 1862
RUNYAN, Adam E., citizen of Dunklin Co. captured 25 Aug, in Gratiot Prison of diarrhoea.	MORE 14 Mar 1863
RUPPERT, Jacob, a barber, found dead on the street, head bloody; ruptured aneurism.	MORE 16 Nov 1865
RUSHER, Frank, walked out a 2nd-story door and was killed. Unmarried.	MORE 15 Aug 1864
RUSSELL, Bette E. daughter of David and Amelia and granddaughter of Elijah Johnston, near Ashland 30 Jul ae 9y 8m 24d.	COWS 12 Aug 1864
RUSSELL, David in Cedar Twp. 16 Aug ae 74y 9m.	COWS 1 Sep 1865
RUSSELL, Frederick Pitkin son of T.P. and Emily G. near Ironton 5 Jan ae 4y 2m.	SLMD 14 Jan 1861
RUSSELL, Hiram, a bushwhacker, killed south of Springfield (along with Alf Cook, Edward Brown, and 2 Manlys).	MORE 31 Jan 1865
RUSSELL, Isabella on Franklin betw 18-19, of diphtheria, 14 Dec ae 7y 3m.	MORE 16 Dec 1862
RUSSELL, James Gustine son of Trumbull J. and Julia A. at 295 Olive, 4 Sep, ae 8y 11m 9d. Washington DC pc	MORE 5 Sep 1863
RUSSELL, Mary, a servant girl, burned to death when a lamp overturned.	MORE 20 Sep 1865
RUSSELL, Mrs. Mary, former resident of Ray Co., in Salt Lake City 21 May ae 53y 15d.	RICON 26 May 1864
RUSSELL, Mary Edward daughter of David D. and Amelia C. at the home of Thomas H. Roberts in Boone Co. 25 Jul ae 8y 11m 2d.	COWS 2 Aug 1861
RUSSELL, William thrown from a horse while watering it in the river, and drowned. Ae ca 12, employed by Mr. Roberts, 10th betw Howard-Mound.	MORE 3 Oct 1865
RUST, Adolphus, living on 3rd betw Walnut-Elm, died 11 Dec.	MORE 12 Dec 1864
RUST, John Patrick, suicide by hanging. Unmarried Carpenter, ae 54.	MORE 10 Jul 1864
RUTER, Augustus Tilford 17 Sep of bowel ulcer, in 21st y. Pittsburgh pc	MORE 24 Sep 1865
RUTH, Charles R. son of Charles F. and Almira 7 Apr at 36 Centre St., ae 4. Interred Bellefontaine.	MORE 8 Apr 1863
RUTH, Mrs. Isaac M., 168 N. 5th, on 9 Dec. Interred in Jackson MI.	MORE 10 Dec 1865
RUTH, Mrs. Mary B. 19 May ae 52, on Beaumont betw Washington-Christy. Friends of her brother Charles G. Ramsey invited. NY City & Trenton NJ pc	MORE 21 May 1865
RUTHERFORD, Ann C. wife of Archie near Huntsville 2 Jun ae 52.	COWS 30 Jun 1865
RUTHERFORD, George S. 27 Oct in his 61st year, on State St. betw Sydney-Lynch. Funeral from St. John's Church.	MORE 28 Oct 1864
RUTHERFORD, Tillman H. formerly of St. Louis Co. in CA 2 Jul 1862 ae 40.	MORE 11 Apr 1863
RUTHERFURD, J. Miller son of Archie S. and Cornelia W. in Carondelet 10 Jan, ae 11. Funeral from the Presbyterian Church in Carondelet.	MORE 13 Jan 1865
RUTTER, Richard P. formerly of Palmyra at the home of Thomas Cobb in Warren Twp, Marion Co. Wed last ae ca 28. Funeral from Methodist Church.	PALS 10 Jul 1863
RYAN, Mrs. ___ at the home of her son-in-law James Moonan on Market St. Road near Wesleyan Cemetery, 3 Dec in her 66th year. Int. Calvary. Pittsburgh pc	MORE 4 Dec 1865
RYAN, Mrs. ___ ae 78 at her son's home in Catawissa. Funeral from Immaculate Conception Church, interred Rock Spring.	MORE 11 Oct 1865
RYAN, Anney Jane, youngest daughter of Michael and Ellen, on Spring betw Mercer-Naomi.	MORE 9 Jul 1863
RYAN, Dennis (believed to be), body found floating at Carondelet. Carrying Provost Marshall's pass to go to Memphis to join company, from Young's Point. Also carrying note re grocery, St. Louis House, betw O'Fallon-Cass. Had been in water 2 or 3 days, was 5'6", close shaven, short black hair.	MORE 29 Jun 1863
RYAN, Honora relict of William 14 Sep ae 53y 5m. Funeral from her daughter's home, 9th St. four doors north of O'Fallon. Newark pc	MORE 15 Sep 1863
RYAN, James, a young boy, from drinking too much whiskey; he and two other boys had got a jug belonging to the father of one of them. Son of Patrick.	PALS 25 Sep 1863
RYAN, Mrs. James W. (Nancy) 10 Apr of consumption in Boone Co.	COWS 15 Apr and 10 Jun 1864

RYAN, Michael watchman at the 7th St. Pacific RR Depot run over by a freight train. Left wife, 1 child, on Randolph betw 17-18.   MORE 17 Nov 1864

RYAN, Mrs. P. in Catawissa ae 43. Funeral from the 14th St. Depot, Pacific RR. Immaculate Conception Church, interred Rock Spring.   MORE 27 Aug 1863

RYAN, Thomas 27 Nov in his 19th year. Funeral from his brother's home, Gamble St.   MORE 28 Nov 1861

RYAN, William 17 Feb of consumption in his 34th year. Funeral from the home of his brother-in-law Andrew Smith, 339 7th St.   MORE 18 Feb 1865

RYDER, Mrs. Kizzie Moore wife of William B. in her 28th year. Interred in Wilmington DE. Philadelphia & DE pc   MORE 7 Apr 1865

RYLER, Arch son of the late Dr. A.A. last Sunday near Fulton.   FULT 28 Jul 1864
     Emma daughter of the late Dr. A. at the home of her uncle in Columbia 4 Nov. " 10 Nov '65

ST. CYR, Maria M. wife of P.H. and daughter of the late John B. Taylor at her home, Twin Mound Farm, Bellefontaine Rd., 9 Jun. Baltimore pc   MORE 10 Jun 1862

ST. GEMME, Auguste Sr. in Ste. Genevieve (23?28?) Mar in his 71st year. Nashville pc   MORE 30 Mar 1862

ST. GEMME, Augustus 21 Dec in Ste. Genevieve in his 32d year; recently a clerk on western river boats, lately on the Memphis Packet Co. Left wife, child.   MORE 30 Dec 1864

ST. John, Mrs. ___ of injuries received when she was kicked by a cow, at 9-Walnut.   MORE 3 Jul 1862

SALISBURY, Lord W. in Kansas City 14 Mar at the home of his brother Robert, of dropsy, in his 36th year. Formerly of NY, went first to Montgomery Co. MO, then Kansas City in Oct. A lawyer, left wife and 2 children.   MORE 22 Mar 1861

SALISBURY, children of the secretary of Home Mutual Insurance Co., drowned in a skating accident near their home on Papin. (Parents Thomas L. and Eliza, Cote Brilliant.) Mary ae 18y 8m 13d, Thomas ae 14y 4m 21d. (Abby Adams Eliot, dau/Dr. Eliot, also drowned.)   MORE 21 & 22 Feb 1864

SALLEE, John H. 15 Apr of apoplexy and paralysis, ae 72. Veteran War of 1812. From Palmyra to Mexico MO about 1858. (Mexico Ledger)   MORE 25 Apr 1864

SALOMAN, William of Marmaduke's Command, captured in Springfield 1 Feb, in Gratiot Prison of bronchitis.   MORE 14 Mar 1863

SALTMARSH, Capt. William E. 31 Jan of dysenteria maligna, ae 49y 6m. Lived at (104?) N. 9th. Cincinnati & Syracuse pc   MORE 2 Feb 1863

SAMMER, Mary, ae ca 10 or 11, drowned in the river while gathering wood; parents live at 258 Carondelet, have a stand in the French market.   MORE 15 Jul 1865

SAMPSON, Richard at his home in Boone Co. 31 Oct in his 84th year. Baltimore, Richmond KY & St. Louis pc   COWS 6 Nov 1863

SAMSTAG, Nicholas 14 Mar od consumption ae ca 45. Tribute, LaGrange IOOF.   CANP 17 Mar 1864

SAMUEL, Amanda wife of James 4 Jun near Providence ae 27y 3m 28d.   COWS 5 Jun 1863

SAMUEL, Rebecca wife of G.W. in Columbia 27 Jul.   COWS 29 Jul 1864

SANDERS, Daniel W. in Gratiot Prison 7 Nov of rubeola.   MORE 9 Nov 1862

SANDERS, Edward, inquest: a "contraband" lately from Memphis. Smallpox.   MORE 12 Feb 1863

SANDERS, J.M. 7 Jan, born in Crawford Co. 7 Apr 1838. Baptist, Mason, member of the Lebanon Lodge, Steelville, left wife and infant.   MORE 4 Feb 1862

SANDERSON, Dr. George B. stabbed by Judge Aylett Buckner in the Broad Gauge Saloon 31 May, died ae 56. Lived on Yeatman's Row, native of Yorkshire. Cause, political argument.   MORE 2 & 3 Jun 1861

SANDFELDER, Benne son of Sigmund and Eliza of St. Louis in Sedalia 7 Mar of brain fever. Lived at 102 Myrtle.   MORE 9 Mar 1864

SANDFORD, Maj. Albert in Jefferson City 2 Feb in his 77th year, formerly of KY, to MO many years ago.   MORE 17 Feb 1863

SANDLIN, John of Co. B 30th Reg Mo Vols at Perryville of flux, last Wednesday.   PERU 5 Dec 1862

SAPP, Nancy Jane wife of Elijah and daughter of Elder B. Wren at her home 14 Jun of typhoid.   COWS 21 Jun 1861

SAPPINGTON, Mrs. Elizabeth in St. Louis Co. 9 Apr ae 74y 3m.   MORE 11 Apr 1861

SAPPINGTON, John of Gravois, in St. Louis Co. with his family since 1804, a farmer all his life, of pneumonia in his 74th year.   MORE 18 Mar 1864

SAPPINGTON, children of James and Anne near Saverton, Ralls Co.: John Hammond 9 Oct ae 10m; Anna Maria 16 Oct in her 5th year   PALS 27 Oct 1865

SAPPINGTON, Robert, Chariton Co.: Public administrator took over his estate.   CECB 24 Jul 1862

SARPY, Col. Peter A., pioneer of the upper Missouri valley, at Plattsmouth 4 Jan "in the prime of life." Descendant of a St. Louis family.	SJH 25 Jan 1865
SARTAIN, David, citizen of Howard Co., 13 Mar of apoplexy. (Undertaker's list)	MORE 19 Mar 1865
SASS, Edward V. 19 Jun after a short illness. Funeral from the home of his brother, B.F. Sass. Interred Bellefontaine. (see below)	MORE 20 Jun 1863
SASS, Victoria eldest child and only daughter of R.F. and Victoria A., 15 Jun of diphtheria ae 5y 9m 13d. Interred Bellefontaine. Chicago, Cleveland, Pittsb pc	MORE 17 Jun 1864
SAUNDERS, Eliza wife of John Sr. 19 Feb in St. Joseph ae 55y 9m 26d.	SJH 23 Feb 1865
SAUNDERS, James 4 Jul in his 47th year. Funeral: 5 Jul says St. Vincent's, 6 Jul says St. John's Episcopal.	MORE 5 & 6 Jul 1863
SAVAGE, N.W. suddenly at Wood's Hotel, formerly employed at a house on Main St., of aneurism of the aorta. Formerly of Keytesville, a Mason, ae ca 38. Interred Bellefontaine.	MORE 9 & 11 Sep 1861
SAVIER, Col. William C., formerly of Versailles (Morgan Co.), a lawyer, killed in New Orleans; had been beaten by a man suspecting him of larceny, 12 Sep.	MORE 27 Sep 1865 JEST 6 Oct "
SAWYER, Nellie Dora only child of Ezra and Mary R. 14 Aug ae 1y 3m. Formerly of Medford MA. Boston pc	SLMD 20 Aug 1861
SAYERS, Catherine wife of William B. 23 Mar at 19th-Orange ae 23y 2m 24d. Peoria & Boston pc	MORE 25 Mar 1864
SAYLE, Catherine wife of E.O. at Ridgely 22 Jul of consumption, in her 29th year.	LIT 1 Aug 1862
SBARBARO, Vincent 10 May ae 28. Funeral from the home of his brother, 11-Christy. Memphis pc	MORE 11 May 1865
SCALES, Harriet only surviving daughter of Mrs. C., 10th betw Pine-Chestnut, 6 Jul ae 22 after lingering illness.	MORE 7 Jul 1862
SCALES, Thomas Gray youngest son of Thomas and Euphemia, Dodier near 16th, ae 6y5m9d.	MORE 2 Sep
SCAMELL, George at Pewarkee, Waukesha Co. WI, at the home of his son-in-law William Haskins, 21 Jan ae 85. Father of Isaac Scamell of St. Louis. Native of ENG, last 18 years resident of WI; an old English marine who fought at Trafalgar aboard the Victory, had a British pension.	MORE 7 Feb 1864

SCAMELL, children of Isaac   Isaac Thomas 1 Mar of diphtheria ae 6y 10m 8d
         and Mary Ann   Frances Maria 19 Feb of diphtheria ae 4y 26d
(MORE 24 Jan 1865 notes death of an infant, says this family had lost
                     5 children in 2 years.)
	MORE 3 Mar 1863
	" 21 Feb "

SCANLAN, Mrs. Mary 16 Aug ae 51.	SLMD 27 Aug 1861
SCANNELL, John Thomas son of P.B. and Catherine 10 Nov ae 3y 3m 1d, int. Calvary.	MORE 11 Nov 1862
SCANNELL, Patrick, corner Lynch and Carondelet, on 4 Mar.	MORE 6 Mar 1864
SCHABEL, George Thomas son of James F. and Mary E. 21 Nov ae 8y6m23d. Memphis pc	MORE 24 Nov 1864
SCHABERG, Henry, a carpenter, fell from roof. Married 6 months, left father ae ca 73 and wife.	MORE 20 Nov 1864
SCHAEFFER, Henry drowned in the Mississippi ae ca 25; lived in upper St. Louis, was fishing across the river at Cahokia Creek.	MORE 3 Jul 1865
SCHALLER, Michael, formerly Justice of the Peace, 4 Mar ae 49y2m3d. St. Mary's IN pc	MORE 6 Mar 1864
SCHARBAUM, Mary Elizabeth, servant girl at the Green St. Exchange, accidentally killed while cleaning a pistol.	MORE 2 Sep 1865
SCHARFFER, George Andrew 31 May, 23rd betw Morgan-Franklin, ae 54y 11d.	MORE 1 Jun 1863
SCHARWITZ, Mrs. Franciska 24 Jan at the home of her son-in-law John T. Tisemann, in her 68th year. Interred Bellefontaine.	MORE 26 Jan 1865
SCHEARLOH, Charles "industrious and respectable German mechanic's" son, ae 10, drowned in Carondelet Pond; grandmother mentioned. Christian Krust also drowned.	MORE 21 Apr 1865
SCHECHT, ____, boy ca 14, son of a sailor, drowned at the foot of Miller St.	MORE 15 Jun 1864
SCHEITZ, George, inquest: accidentally killed by John Santcraft while hunting.	MORE 1 Apr 1862
SCHIELE, ____ a German ragpicker ca 60 who lived in the body of an omnibus placed up on logs, found dead 2nd-Mulberry. Heat and debility. No relatives.	MORE 27 Aug 1862
SCHLACHT, C., with the Army of the TN, died suddenly, body returned, no information.	LAJ 12 Sep 1863
SCHLAGTER, Adam, 4th near Myrtle, fell from the ferry. Left wife, 5 or 6 children.	MORE 13-14 Nov '64

SCHMIDT, John Adam, native of Wurttemberg, of cerebral apoplexy. An "honest, hard-working laborer." Left wife, 1 child.   MORE 6 Feb 1861

SCHMIDT, Robert, inquest: lay down on Iron Mountain RR track where hay had been spilled, run over. Ae 60, German, no relatives in this country.   MORE 26 Jun 1863

SCHNEEBERGER, Mary adopted daughter of Ferdinand and Caroline Stoewener, 27 Dec of consumption ae 22. Lived on Julia betw 7-8.   MORE 28 Dec 1864

SCHOELTEN, Delilah F. wife of Henry and eldest daughter of William and Margaret Moore, formerly of New Hope, Lincoln Co., 27 Feb of lockjaw at Pleasant Hill, Pike Co. IL ae 28. Wife and mother.   MORE 6 Mar 1865

SCHOEMAN, Christopher drowned trying to cross from one boat to another. Parents live at Victor-Carondelet.   MORE 21 Mar 1862

SCHOENTHALER, Maj. Godfrey at his home on Carondelet Ave. 14 Sep ae 55y 4½m.   MORE 15 Sep 1861

SCHOFIELD, Nancy A. wife of Ellis and daughter of Henry F. Foster in Ralls Co. 5 Jun ae 21 9m 3d. (HAM 27 Jun says Nancy G. and Ellis H.)   MORE 22 Jun 1861

SCHOLTEN, see SCHOELTEN

SCHRAMM, Lydia at Mt. Pleasant IA 30 Jun, wife of Oscar of St. Joseph. Consumption.   SJH 8 Jul 1864

SCHREITER, William, a woodcutter in the American Bottom, of apoplexy. Left wife and child in indigent circumstances.   MORE 19 Mar 1863

SCHRICK, Ernest 26 Sep ae 25y 4m, at 18 N. 6th St.   MORE 28 Sep 1861

SCHROEDER, children of Barnard T.,   Henry ae 3y 4m. Interred Trinity Cemetery.   MORE 18 Jul 1861
    10th-O'Fallon   Mary ygst dau 30 Jul ae 11m 5d. "   " 31 "

SCHROEDER, Herman, Justice of the Peace in the 2nd Ward. Short illness.   MORE 9 Aug 1861

SCHULER, John G., a lawyer, Wednesday night after an illness of 5 or 6 weeks.   MORE 7 Feb 1862

SCHULMEYER, John killed at a charivari in Carondelet - objects thrown at the house of a Mrs. Stange, she shot, no damage; group went on, 2 more shots fired by unknown. Schulmeyer shot in leg, died 12 hours later. No relatives.   MORE 20 Nov 1862

SCHULTIES, Mrs. Margaret wife of Peter at Litchfield IL 8 Oct ae 32y 8m 9d. Funeral home of sister Miss Rover, 9th betw Montgomery-Spring, St. Louis.   MORE 10 Oct 1865

SCHULTZE, ____, 3-year-old son of George (CarOndelet south of Hickory) kicked by a horse while playing in the street.   MORE 19 Apr 1862

SCHUMAKER, Louisa drowned herself in a pond near Lesperance and the Iron Mtn. RR. Recently had tried to kill her infant. Had beautiful auburn hair.   MORE 11 Oct 1863

SCHWABE, Nicholas, Chariton Co.: sale of personal property by public administrator.   CECB 24 Jul 1862

SCHWARZKOPF, Louis at 153 N. 5th, 18 Dec ae 41.   MORE 19 Dec 1863

SCHWARTZTRAUBER, Frank 3 Jun. Lived on High St., ill several weeks.   JEST 4 Jun 1864

SCHWEIGERT, ____ (15th betw Wash-Carr) died of injuries received in the Camp Jackson affair. Left wife, 2 children.   MORE 25 Jul 1861

SCHWIMMER, Annie youngest daughter of James and Jane 4 Feb ae 2.   LAJ 7 Feb 1861

SCOTT, Mrs. and infant, drowned in a flood. (Springfield Mirror)   HAM 25 Jul 1861

SCOTT, ____ shot near Fillmore by militia. Brother of Silas, belonged to one of Paw Paw Militia Cos. (also in MORE 21 Aug)   SJH 14 Aug 1864

SCOTT, Andrew J. son of William A. and Mary E. 24 Mar ae 15m.   HAM 27 Mar 1861

SCOTT, Eliza A. wife of Robert H., 52 Collins St., ae 24y 20d.   MORE 11 Oct 1865

SCOTT, Fanny Louise wife of James, at 452 Morgan, 22 Apr ae 27. Interred NY.   MORE 23 Apr 1864

SCOTT, Franklin Clay son of S.C. and Annie E., 315 Franklin, ae 4y 10m 20d.   MORE 21 Aug 1863

SCOTT, James M. "an old citizen."   FULT 1 Apr 1864

SCOTT, Jasper, pvt 3rd Rebel MO, captured Polk Co. 14 Jan, in Gratiot Prison.   MORE 4 Mar 1863

SCOTT, Col. John yesterday at his home in St. Joseph, "long a resident." Many prominent positions in city government. Ae "over 50."   SJH 2 Mar 1865
    Fannie daughter of the late Col. John 5 Oct ae 13y 3m. Funeral from the home of Mrs. Scott.   " 6 Oct 1865

SCOTT, John A. formerly of Porter's Band, from either Macon or Marion Co., in Gratiot Prison 12 Nov.   MORE 13 & 16 Nov 1862

SCOTT, Dr. John W. in Millersburg of consumption 18 Feb ae ca 34.   COWS 15 Mar 1861

SCOTT, Maggie and Lizza, daughters of Mrs. Allen, in the flux epidemic.   FULT 2 Sep 1864

SCOTT, Margaret "a poor abandoned creature," ae 39, of intemperance and exposure. Lived in alley betw Green-Morgan-10-11.	MORE 28 Oct 1863
SCOTT, Martha Jane daughter of Joseph 6 Mar in her 17th year. Also left mother, brothers and sister.	LAJ 12 Mar 1864
SCOTT, Mary P. wife of William A. at Mattawan MI 16 Jan ae 28. Funeral from home of A.L. Scott, S. 13th betw Hickory-Chouteau, to Fr. Ryan's church.	MORE 21 Jan 1865
SCOTT, Samuel B. in Pettis Co. 11 Jan of dropsy in his 44th year.	MORE 27 Jan 1861
SCOTT, Mrs. Sarah J. 9 Dec in her 58th year. Funeral from the home of her son, Dr. James M., 296 Pine.	MORE 10 Dec 1864
SCOTT, Thomas 26 Jan ae 39y 3m, on 21st north of Clark. Int. Bellefontaine.	MORE 28 Jan 1861
SCOTT, Walter son of Col. John of St. Joseph killed while recruiting for rebel services on the White River in Ar. (also see Col. John)	LIT 3 Jun 1864
SCOTT, William in Gratiot Prison of erysipelas 2 Dec.	MORE 7 Dec 1862
SCOTT, Hon. William late President Judge of the Supreme Court of MO at his home in Cole Co. 15 May. Had been sick more than a year.	CAWN 24 May 1862
SCOTTEN, John B. citizen of Howard Co. 13 Feb of pneumonia. (Undertaker's list)	MORE 19 Feb 1865
SCRIBNER, H.C. brother of Mrs. J.O. Sawyer of St. Louis, of enlarged liver, in Youngsport LA 23 Mar ae 19.	MORE 10 Apr 1863
SEAMAN, Mrs. Mary S. 20 Nov ae 35. Funeral from the home of her sister Mrs. Rozier, 20 S. 6th. NY & Cincinnati pc	MORE 21 Nov 1862
SEARCY, George N. of Boone Co. recently in Fulton ae 35.	COWS 1 Dec 1865
SEARCY, Lemuel B. in Boone Co. 17 Nov of typhoid pneumonia ae 68. Lexington KY & Liberty MO pc	COWS 28 Nov 1862
SEARL, David, Maries Co.: letters of adm. 25 Oct to Robert Rowden.	SLMD 5 Nov 1861
SEARS, Llewellen in the prison hospital, came up on boat from the south, said to have come up from the south. (Gratiot Prison list says he was from Randolph Co., news item says he was from St. Louis.)	MORE 13 Oct 1863
SEDASKEY, Joseph found dead Saturday morning on Market St.	MORE 10 Sep 1865
SEIVAER, William, clerk in the Quartermaster's Depot, heat and exhaustion.	MORE 12 Aug 1862
SELBY, Cephas, respected citizen of Callaway Co., suicide by hanging 4 Jan. No known cause.	GLWT 24 Jan 1861
SELBY, Julia A. consort of William J., 6 Oct ae 54. FULT 11 Oct &	COWS 25 Oct 1861
SELBY, Mary S. widow of Samuel 7 Nov in her 20th year. Funeral from the home of her father-in-law W.T. Selby, 222 Chestnut. Interred Wheeling VA.	MORE 8 Nov 1864
SELBY, Thomas C. in Columbia 23 Oct ae 26y 3m 5d.	COWS 27 Oct 1865
SELF, Thomas P. son of P.J. and Martha 18 Aug ae (21?)y 4m 3d.	COWS 28 Aug 1863
SELIMON, William in St. Joseph 27 Feb of bilious fever; family in Gasconade Co.	MORE 3 Mar 1861
SELINGER, Edward J. of St. Louis in Denver 17 Aug of consumption ae 18.	MORE 13 Sep 1863
SELLECK, Sands E. formerly of St. Louis at his mother's home, Fairfield CT, 21 Aug.	MORE 2 Sep 1865
SELLERS, Capt. Isaiah at Memphis 6 Mar ae 61, senior of the lower Mississippi pilots. Funeral from home of his nephew Isaiah W. Hood, Carr betw 6-7.	MORE 10 & 17 Mar 1864
SELLERS, Laird at his home in Moniteau Co. 5 Dec ae 91.	MORE 23 Dec 1862
SEMPLE, Charles, ae (49? 19?) (paper wrinkled). Funeral from home of L.E. Clarke, Locust betw 11-12.	MORE 9 Oct 1862
SESEY, Sarah Ella eldest daughter of Jacob, late of the Palmyra Whig, of membranous croup, ae ca 4.	HAM 8 Jan 1861
SESSINGHOUSE, Charles, recently elected councilman of the 10th ward, at Northampton MA where his wife had gone for her health some time ago. His train caught fire, he walked some distance in the cold. Brother mentioned. (/ in Northampton)	MORE 29 Dec 1863
SESSINGHOUSE, Fred W., 9th and N. Market, 15 Jun ae 67.	MORE 16 Jun 1864
SESSON, Augustus 21 Feb ae 27.	LEXUN 27 Feb 1864
SETTLE, Mary Virginia daughter of Thomas G. 30 Sep in St. Ferdinand Twp ae 3. Interred Bellefontaine.	MORE 1 Oct 1861
SETTLE, William L. in Boonville 29 Mar of consumption in his 44th year. Native of KY, formerly of Bates Co. Widow, 3 children. A Mason.	BOOM 2 Apr 1864

SETGER, Edward W. at Cottleville, St. Charles Co., 29 Feb ae 51. At one time resident MORE 17 Mar 1864
of St. Louis. Left wife and 5 children. Harrisburg & Philadelphia pc.

SETTOON, E.J., engineer on the Pacific RR, in an accident near Jefferson City. MORE 11 Aug 1861
Resident of St. Louis, family in the city.

SEVAN, Tom a prize fighter working on the Bostona No. 2 (?) dived and hit his head, MORE 9 Jul 1864
below Louisiana MO. Rescued but died. Interred Quincy.

SEWILL, Miss Martha 20 Oct. Chicago pc MORE 23 Oct 1863

SEXTON, George Harlan formerly of Boone Co., last 2 or 3 years in Kansas City, COWS 2 May 1862
15 Apr of a "phthisic affliction" he had had for 20 years. Methodist.
(KCJC 18 Ap says ae 51.)

SEXTON, Mary Ann only child of T.J. and Phebe 9 Jun ae 9. (Mother deceased.) MORE 10 Jun 1864
Funeral from home of Dr. Hupple, 9th-Spring.

SEXTON, Phebe wife of John Sr. of apoplexy in her (69th?) year, 18 May. Funeral MORE 20 May 1863
from the home of her son H.C., Howard-8th.

SEYMOUR, Catherine V. wife of M. 12 May ae 59y 11m 29d. Formerly of VA. MORE 18 May 1862

SHACKELFORD, Alley wife of Ryland 10 Apr ae 51. Ill many months. Presbyterian. LIT 27 Oct 1865

SHACKELFORD, Jane S. relict of John at the home of her son-in-law Gen. Ranney 16 Nov MORE 17 Nov 1864
in her 79th year. In St. Louis nearly 50 years. Presbyterian.

SHACKLEFORD, Mary Alice daughter of R.L. and Mary in Callao 23 Mar ae 9y 7m 23d, MAG 9 Apr 1862
suddenly of unknown cause.

SHACKELFORD, Sallie 19 Sep at her father's home after a brief illness, ae ca 17. LIT 2 Sep 1865

SHAFFNER, William, inquest: cabinet-maker, ae 35, no family. Brain congestion. MORE 2 Apr 1864

SHAFFNER, Stephen, inquest: brain congestion. Ae ca 40, left wife and 2 children. MORE 28 Aug 1865

SHANDS, Joseph, living on Franklin east of Garrison, Wednesday ae 51. MORE 10 Nov 1864

SHANKBEER, John, member 10th Ward Home Guard, killed in the Camp Jackson affair. MORE 18 May 1861

SHANNON, Austina Piggott, wife of Joseph R., in New Orleans 21 Jan. Born in MO in MORE 2 Feb 1865
1836, to be interred in Louisville.

SHANNON, Catherine 2 Sep at her mother's home (328 N 6th) ae 7y 8m. SLMD 3 Sep 1864

SHANNON, James 11 Nov ae 46. Lived on Broadway betw O'Fallon-Cass. Funeral from MORE 12 Nov 1861
St. Patrick's Church. Interred Rock Spring.

SHANNON, John on 9 Apr, ae 65. MORE 10 Apr 1861

SHANNON, Mary Eugenia daughter of the late Pres. James 9 Jul ae 19, in Columbia. COWS 14 Jul 1865

SHAPLEIGH, Mrs. Dorothy 13 Feb ae 85. Funeral from the home of her son, A.F., MORE 14 Feb 1863
275 Washington.

SHARKEY, Christopher, deckhand on the Robert Campbell, killed by the mate, John MORE 8 Aug 1863
Miller. Last of 3 brothers who died on the river: one drowned, one
was scalded in a boiler explosion.

SHARKEY, William A. Saturday of brain congestion in his 30th year. Brother-in-law MORE 16 Feb 1863
of Edward S. McKeon.

SHARP, Frank, found murdered beside the river near Kansas City. LIT 15 Jul 1864

SHARP, Weedin H., living on Georgetown Road near Tabo Church, killed by robbers. MORE 16 Feb 1865
An old citizen. (LEXUN 11 Feb)

SHARP, William of Winston's Command, captured in Clay Co., in Gratiot Prison MORE 6 Feb 1863
5 Jan of rubeola.

SHARPE, Janet at Glasgow SCOT 25 Sep 1860, sister of Dr. H. B. Thomson of MORE 14 Feb 1861
Saline Co. and John Thomson (which see).

SHAW, Barbara wife of Robert 15 Nov near Savannah ae 35y 6m 22d. SJH 19 Nov 1863

SHAW, Bettie J. wife of Charles H., 30 Oct. Funeral from Central Presbyterian. MORE 31 Oct 1863
Columbus OH pc

SHAW, Charles William son of James and Mary E. 5 Nov of pneumonia ae 2y 8m. MORE 9 Nov 1862

SHAW, Christopher R. at his home in Richmond 14 Nov, of typhoid. RICON 25 Nov 1865

SHAW, James R. only son of Joel K. and Ann M., 10 Jun ae 7. LAJ 26 Jun 1862

SHAW, Morris stepson of Dennis Gunn, living on N. Market, drowned in a quarry pond MORE 27 Jun 1865
at 18th & Warren Sunday ae 15 or 16. Dived, struck his head on a rock.

SHAW, Sarah 18 Nov in Rochester NY, mother of Henry and Mrs. Morisse of St. Louis. MORE 26 Nov 1861

SHEA, James 5 Oct ae 38. Lived on 6th betw O'Fallon-Cass. Interred Calvary. MORE 6 Oct 1862

SHEEHAN, Eliza daughter of Edward and Fanny 29 Apr ae 12y 2m 7d. SJH 30 Apr 1864

SHEEHAN, John, a teamster, drowned when his team became frightened and plunged into the river. Left a wife. Body found later. MORE 7 & 24 Apr 1861

SHEFFIELD, William, a stonecutter from Michigan living on O'Fallon betw 7-8, killed in the Camp Jackson affair. MORE 18 May 1861

SHELBY, Cephas, suicide by hanging; lived 3 miles north of Millersburg. Brother Parker had committed suicide a few years ago. No motive. (see SELBY) CAWN 19 Jan 1861

SHELBY, James B. in Carroll Co. 20 Nov 1861, ae 54y 6m 24d. MORE 19 Feb 1862

SHELBY, children of Evan and Nancy, Carroll Co.   Anna Maria 5 Feb of diphtheria ae 6y 4m 21d   Henry C. 26 Jan ae 3y 8m 13d MORE 19 Feb 1862 " 5 "

SHELDON, Wesley E., formerly of Cincinnati, 19 June ae 36y 3d. Funeral from the home of his mother. MORE 20 Jun 1863

SHELEY, Ben Franklin son of George, 24 Feb ae 21, of consumption. Only son. WEST 27 Feb 1864

SHELEY, Patsy wife of Ben in New Bloomfield 6 Dec ae 76y 9d. COWS 22 Dec 1865

SHELEY, Singleton at the home of his son-in-law J.M. Duncan 3 Mar ae 70. In Col. Johnston's KY Reg., War of 1812. FULT 15 Mar 1861

SHELL, Margaret, said to have been an actress in the east, hanged herself in the calaboose; had been picked up drunk. MORE 18 Nov 1863

SHELTON, John, formerly of Wyola, Monroe Co. in Neosho 4 Jun. Property to be administrated. SPRIP 13 Jul 1865

SHELTON, John in Carroll Co. while trying to make a returning rebel soldier named Pate give up a pistol. CALM 30 Sep 1865 WARS 22 "

SHELTON, Dr. O.P. of St. Louis at the home of his aunt, Mrs. J.S. Simonds, in New Orleans 22 May of consumption, ae 25. MORE 10 Jun 1862

SHELTON, Elizabeth wife of William beaten to death with a stick of wood by her husband, 7th near O'Fallon. Daughter mentioned. (He was exonerated at the inquest, death caused by previous injuries and dissipation.) MORE 20 Jul 1861

SHENEHAN, Thomas stabbed by Mat Ryan in a drunken fight at Mary Grady's house. MORE 17 May 1864

SHEPARD, J.S. of Marion Co. in the Prison Hospital in Springfield. MORE 10 Apr 1863

SHEPARD, Martha Ramsey wife of A.C. of Warsaw MO in Bethel CT 23 Jul ae 32. (COWS 1 Aug spells the name Shepherd.) MORE 29 Jul 1862

SHEPARD, Mary Thomas wife of Elihu H. 6 Jun at the home of her son-in-law Robert Barclay in her 67th year. "A remarkable woman" born in Wytheville VA 10 Mar 1798, married Aug 1823. A teacher. Left a daughter. MORE 8 & 9 Jun 1864

SHEPARD, Stella A. only child of George and Stella A., 3 May of scarlet fever ae 6. Funeral Annunciation Church. MORE 4 May 1865

SHEPHERD, William K., funeral preached by Rev. James W. Campbell at Concord Church the 2nd Sunday in Dec. LAJ 25 Nov 1865

SHEPHERD, John H. son of Humphrey 18 Dec in Alton Prison ae 20. (MORE 17 Jan "of Pettis Co." poem to "brother signed "Annie.") SEDA 14 Jan 1865

SHEPHERDSON, Arthur Renick son of J.K. and Margaret in Chariton Co. 20 Sep ae 7y5m15d. MORE 27 Sep '65

SHEPHERDSON, John Thompson 21 Dec at 324 Morgan ae 2y 4m 3d. Int. Bellefontaine. MORE 22 Dec 1861

SHEPLEY, Charles "an intelligent boy of 13" drowned in the river. MORE 10 Aug 1861

SHEPPERD, Ann E. wife of D.W. and daughter of Eugene and Louisiana Garaghty in Cape Girardeau 22 Oct in her (25th?) year. MORE 26 Oct 1861

SHERIDAN, Bernard, in jail; had been beaten when he tried to burglarize a house Abbey, died in convulsions. "Congestion of brain and intemperance." MORE 10 Jul 1863

SHERIDAN, Capt John, many years a resident of St. Louis, native of Ireland. Had been interred temporarily, moved to Calvary. MORE 12 & 23 Sep 1862

SHERMAN, Dr. E.W. 11 Jan of lung fever. Funeral from the home of J.B. Ricord. NY pc MORE 12 Jan 1862

SHERMAN, Rhoda Adele consort of Capt. Harry, 12th MO Cav, 27 Feb of smallpox ae 27y6m. " 3 Mar 1864

SHERMAN, Samuel B. of St. Louis at his mother's home in Fairdale, PA 17 Feb of consumption ae 31. A Mason. In the freight business. MORE 6 Mar 1864

SHERMAN, Mrs. Sylvia 14 May ae ca 74 at the home of her son-in-law N.D. Marvin in Pike Co. St. Louis pc LAJ 20 May 1865

SHIELDS, Cecelia wife of the late William 3 Sep at Fox Creek, St. Louis Co., ae 74.   MORE 17 Sep 1865
    Alton & Montreal pc

SHIELDS, E.Y. former editor of the St. Joseph *West*, a rebel, killed in Mississippi.   CAB 18 Nov 1864

SHIELDS, Eliza wife of William (living 8 mi. from Columbia) 10 Feb in her 68th year.   COWS 13 Feb 1863
    Born in E. TN, daughter of Judge Conway, to MO with her husband in 1820.

SHIELDS, Elizabeth relict of James (Broadway betw O'Fallon-Cass) 4 Aug ae 70 of   MORE 5 Aug 1861
    congestion and general debility. Mobile & CA pc

SHIELDS, Ellen, *ca* 30, debility and exposure caused by intemperance.   MORE 8 May 1862

SHIELDS, Felix, 7th betw Biddle-O'Fallon, in his 48th year after a long illness.   MORE 14 May 1864

SHIELDS, Thomas eldest son of Thomas and Mary 13 Aug, ae 13y 1m, of a fall from a   MORE 14 Aug 1862
    horse. Lived on Olive betw 23-24, interred Bellefontaine.

SHIELDS, Prof. William C. 3 Jul in Columbia of consumption ae *ca* 40.   COWS 7 Jul 1865

SHIPP, Zilphy wife of B.H. and daughter of Hiram and Dorcas Ballew 14 Jan ae   GLWT 24 Jan 1861
    51y (6?)m 5d.

SHIRLEY, Charlotte wife of Ephraim, 22 17th St., 17 Nov ae 46. Long illness.   MORE 18 Nov 1864

SHOEMAKER, Bright ae *ca* 22 at the home of Dr. William Fort in Randolph Co. of   COWS 28 Jul 1865
    chronic diarrhoea.

SHOEMAKER, Russell, Chariton Co.: Final settlement by J.A.J. Cook.   CECB 7 May 1864

SHOOKMAN, Michael recently in Boeuf Twp, Franklin Co. Born in Loudon Co. VA 1759,   MORE 16 Oct 1863
    to TN, then to MO about 1830. Had 22 children, 82 grandchildren, 30
    great-grandchildren. Oldest child is 80, youngest is 3.

SHOOP, Miss Jennie (Virginia M.) at her father's home near Richmond 9 May in   RICON 13 &
    her 18th year. (later, 17y 7m)   20 May 1865

SHORES, Barilla daughter of L.W. near LaPlata 12 Mar.   MAG 19 Mar 1862

SHORT, Mrs. Jane, living on 10th betw Market-Walnut. Clothing caught fire.   MORE 21 Sep 1863

SHORTRIDGE, George A. 6 Oct in Macon Co. in his 46th year.   COWS 20 Oct 1865

SHOTT, Alley consort of Jonah of Adair Co. 23 Apr of consumption.   MAG 7 May 1862

SHOUSE, John, resident of Clay Co. 36 years, in June ae *ca* 60.   LIT 5 Jul 1862

SHRADER, Eliza wife of Col. Stephen and daughter of J.T.V. Thompson in her 35th y.   LIT 20 Nov 1863
    Left children. Presbyterian.

SHREVE, Eliza J. wife of L.M., 6th-St. Charles, 4 Oct.   MORE 5 Oct 1864

SHRIVER, ___, deputy sheriff in Daviess Co. (formerly 1st MSM Cav) shot in a saloon   MORE 8 Jan 1864
    by P.E. Hammond of Co. I, 5th Prov Reg EMM. (LEXUN)

SHROPSHIRE, Andrew J. 23 Nov of congestive chills in his 50th year.   PALS 9 Dec 1864

SHROPSHIRE, Jeremiah Monday morning last in his 70th year, a few miles east of   PALS 12 Feb 1864
    Palmyra. On the same farm 36 years, member "Old Baptist Church."

SHRYOCK, Adelaide M. wife of Samuel W. and daughter of John McKeagn at Sturgeon MO   MORE 5 Nov 1863
    30 Oct. Clarksville TN pc

SHUCKEY, ___ ae 65, killed in Chariton Co.   MORE 10 Jan 1865

SHULL, Jonathan ae (41 or 44?). Funeral from the Methodist Church, 11-Locust,   MORE 16 Jan 1864
    Philadelphia pc.

SHULMAN, Elleck 15 Jul in his 26th year. Funeral from the home of his brother-   MORE 16 Jul 1864
    in-law S. Schiele, 194 Locust.

SHULTZ, Leon, citizen of St. Louis, 18 Jun in prison of a gunshot wound.   MORE 19 Jun 1864

SHURLDS, Edward F. 30 Jan ae 28.   MORE 1 Feb 1865

SIBLEY, Elcott B., chief clerk in the general freight office of the St. Louis,   MORE 29 Oct 1864
    Alton & Terre Haure RR, 28 Oct of typhoid ae 35. Int. Bellefontaine.

SIBLEY, Maj. George Champlin at Elma, his country home in St. Charles Co., 31 Jan   MORE 13 Mar 1863
    ae nearly 81. (a very long obituary)

SIDENER, Polly at the home of her son James in Livingston Co., in her 73rd year.   MORE 7 Mar 1861
    Wife of Jacob Sr. of Fayette Co. KY

SIDNER, Capt. Thomas A. of Monroe Co. shot by Gen. Merrill at Palmyra in retaliation
    for the murder of an old man named Allmstedt at the time of Porter's Raid   CAWN 1 Nov 1862
    into Palmyra. (Palmyra *Courier*)

SIEBERT, ___, small child of Henry, run over by a railroad omnibus.   MORE 12 Apr 1861

SILL, Mrs. Ann Caroline, 261 S. 7th, 21 Mar ae 52y 4m.   MORE 22 Mar 1861

SILL, John F. at DeSoto 8 Jan ae 44, late conductor of the St. Louis & Iron Mtn. RR. MORE 9 Jan 1865
    Interred Carondelet.

SILCOTT, William, of Gratiot St. betw 5-6, Saturday ae 63. Formerly of VA.   MORE 16 May 1864

SILVEY, Belle only child of Capt. D.H. at the home of Rev. J.W. Lewis, St. Louis Co.,
    ae 4y 8m. Baltimore & Wilmington DE pc   MORE 11 Jul 1862

SIMMONS, Edward Allen son of Samuel D. and Keturah in Barry, MO 15 Jul ae 8y 5m 22d; LIT 29 Jul 1864
    and his infant sister Lula on 17 Jul.

SIMMONS, Henry, inquest: young man attendant at Sisters Hospital, killed when   MORE 6 Aug 1863
    struck by runaway horse. Concussion. Brother mentioned.

SIMMONS, Julia wife of Cyrenius C. on Saturday of consumption, ae 29y 8m. Funeral   MORE 18 Aug 1862
    from St. John's Episcopal, interred Bellefontaine.

SIMMONS, Mrs. Katherine 5 Jan ae 77.   CAWN 16 Jan 1864

SIMMONS, Lacy N. murdered in Clinton, Henry Co. by a negro soldier named Harrison   WARS 17 Nov 1865
    Fleming. Simmons was helping a deputy sheriff arrest Fleming.

SIMMONS, Samuel C. in St. Louis 3 Aug "in his country's service." IOOF tribute.   WEST 25 Aug 1865

SIMMS, ___ a little girl ae 7 or 8, living near Hardwick's Mill in Carroll Co.,   RICON 7 Oct 1865
    accidentally shot by her brother, ca 12. (Carrollton Democrat)

SIMONDS, John eldest son of Elizabeth and the late William, at his mother's home in   MORE 18 Mar 1861
    Clarksville, 13 Mar of consumption ae 22y and nearly 7 months.
    Mrs. Elizabeth H. of Clarksville, relict of William, 3 Apr while visiting   MORE 10 Apr 1863
    friend in Carlyle, IL. Ae 56y 7m 27d.

SIMPSON, ___ killed in Jefferson Co. by 47th MO Vols under Col. Fletcher.   MORE 17 Oct 1864

SIMPSON, Elizabeth Ellen wife of J.P., of Greene Co., 29 Jun of typhoid.   SPRIP 6 Jul 1865

SIMPSON, Greenbury 17 Oct at the home of his son, L.L., in Lewis Co. ae 78.   CANP 26 Oct 1865

SIMPSON, Miss Jane, late of Howard Co. MD, 5 Nov in her 17th year. Interred   MORE 6 Nov 1865
    Bellefontaine.

SIMPSON, Mary wife of J.B. near Osage, Crawford Co. 11 Feb ae 32y 1m 11d. Daughter   MORE 21 Feb 1861
    of Judge James Sanders. Left 5 small children.

SINCLAIR, Mrs. Ann Eliza wife of Daniel and daughter of Charles Clay, in Monroe Co., MORE 22 Mar 1864
    11 Mar ae 27.

SINGLETON, Henry in Kirkwood 24 Dec in his 72nd year, formerly of Norfolk VA.   MORE 27 Dec 1863
    Funeral from Kirkwood Presbyterian Church. Norfolk pc

SINKLEAR, Walter W. of typhoid 2 May ae 28y 10m 20d.   LAJ 7 May 1864

SINNOTT, Nicholas Cullen 22 Oct in his 52nd year, fifth and youngest son of the   MORE 23 Oct 1862
    late Pierre of Curraclos, Barony of Shermeiar, Wexford.

SISK, Mrs. Benjamin F. at High Hill 5 Sep ae 56y 1m 27d. Maiden name, Biddie   MORE 25 Sep 1864
    Yowell. Born in Madison Co. VA, to MO 1837.

SITES, Elizabeth wife of Elijah in Ralls Co. 18 Dec, 1860.   HAM 16 Jan 1861

SKAGGS, Alexander killed by guerillas in Carroll Co. (Carrollton Democrat)   MORE 21 Jul 1864

SKALLIN, James 10 Nov in his 34th year. Native of Wexford. Funeral from   MORE 11 Nov 1862
    St. Francis Xavier, interred Calvary.

SKEEL, Delia T. wife of William of Carondelet 11 Mar ae 35, at the home of   MORE 12 Mar 1864
    Sarah H. Skeel of Jefferson Co.

SKEWES, Miss Louisa daughter of William and Eliza near Ste. Genevieve 20 Nov ae 23.   MORE 27 Nov 1862

SKINKER, Jane wife of Thomas of St. Louis Co., 4 Aug ae 50. Interred family cemetery. SLMD 5 Aug 1864

SKRAINKA, Joseph 17 Nov ae 45. Lived on 16th betw Market-Walnut. Memphis pc   MORE 18 Nov 1864

SLACK, Maj. John in Boonville 21 Oct in his 74?th year.   COWS 18 Nov 1864

SLATER, Benjamin (of Slater & Virden) 29 Mar in his 54th year. Funeral from the   MORE 30 Mar 1864
    Baptist Church at 6th-Lucas. Boston, Worcester, Philadelphia, & ME pc

SLAUGHTER, Annette M. daughter of Martin in Lafayette Co. 28 Nov of typhoid   COWS 19 Dec 1862
    ae 19y 10m 28d.

SLAUGHTER, Hessie Henry youngest daughter of Thomas J. and Mary J., 181 Chestnut,   MORE 18 Mar 1862
    17 Mar of whooping cough ae 2y 9d.

SLAYMAKER, Adam shot himself 9 Jul "disappointed in love." Native of PA, many years   MORE 10 Jul 1865
    in the west. Ae ca 32. Mother in Lancaster PA.

SLEATER, William James, late U.S. Express Messenger, of consumption ae 19y 6m at the   MORE 18 May 1864
    home of his brother-in-law A.F. McCleery, 56 Brooklyn.

SLEETH, Harriett M. wife of William, ae 36y 5m 22d. Funeral from the home of   MORE 17 Jul 1865
    L.M. Sleeth, 236 Morgan. Cincinnati pc

SLEVIN, Lizzie wife of James M. in Niagara Falls 18 Sep in her 23rd year. Funeral   MORE 21 &
    from her mother's home on Lucas Place to St. John's Church.   22 Sep 1864
            Cincinnati, Louisville, Philadelphia & NY pc

SLEVIN, Mary Louisa daughter of Bernard and Catherine 23 Dec ae 3y3m20d. Int. Calvary.   MORE 24 Dec '61

SLICER, William G., of 208 N. 6th, 27 Jul ae 55.   MORE 28 Jul 1864

SLOCUM, Miss Hattie of 141 Morgan, 31 Mar.   MORE 2 Apr 1862

SLOHEY (SLOWEY), John, a contractor, suffocated when a bank of earth fell on him,   MORE 18 &
    while blasting. Died 17 Aug ae 48. Left wife, Chouteau-Pratte.   20 Aug 1865

SLOSS, Mrs. E.S. wife of William L. 8 Jul ae 57, at 162 Market (betw 6-7).   MORE 9 Jul 1863
    William L., 160 Market, 28 Feb ae 61y 2m 7d.   " 29 Feb 1864

SLYE, Veva Theresa only child of D. Webster and Ste. Genevieve 15 Jan of   MORE 16 Jan 1861
    diphtheria in her 3rd year. Washington & Baltimore pc

SMALL, Eleanor relict of David, many years a resident of St. Louis, 8 Apr in her   MORE 9 Apr 1862
    74th year. Funeral from home of her son-in-law N.J. Calhoun, 7th-Chestnut.

SMALL, James F. at 174 Locust 20 Oct in his 45th year.   MORE 21 Oct 1865

SMALLWOOD, Amelia daughter of Walter Sr. 25 Oct after a (3-week?) illness.   LEXUN 12 Nov 1864

SMART, ___ ex-judge of the Circuit Court, Saline Co., killed by Capt. Love's men;   LIT 1 Aug 1862
    had been hiding in the brush, ordered to halt, didn't, was killed.

SMART, Newton son of Stephen in Carroll Co. 28 Apr of brain inflammation, ca 10.   MORE 7 May 1862

SMITH, ___ killed by bushwhackers near Lamar, Barton Co.; Allison and Hightown   MORE 23 Apr 1864
    also killed. (Information from Melville MO.)

SMITH, Miss ___ drowned near Anderson's Ferry, East Fork of Grand River, 3 miles   SJH 19 Jul 1864
    from Chillicothe, while bathing Thursday last. Two others also drowned.

SMITH, Alfred 24 Sep at his home near Oakfield P.O., Franklin Co., ae 45.   MORE 30 Sep 1863
    Husband, father.

SMITH, Alfred son of James, of Matthews Prairie, Sunday 8 Sep.   CHAC 13 Sep 1861

SMITH, Amanda daughter of William J. and Olevia, Boone Co., 26 Sep ae 3.   COWS 4 Oct 1861

SMITH, B.F. in Boone Co. 7 Sep ae 57y 5m 5d. Mt. Sterling & Paris KY pc   COWS 16 Sep 1864

SMITH, Benjamin F. 15 Apr ae 29. Left wife, 5 ch, mother, 4 sisters. (also see   MORE 1 May 1863
    William and Levin J.)

SMITH, Caroline L. eldest daughter of Julius H. 19 Dec of consumption ae 23.   MORE 21 Dec 1861
    Cincinnati, Memphis & Little Rock pc

SMITH, Charles B. son of Capt. Henry W. and Susan F., Clark betw 16-17, 17 Dec   MORE 18 Dec 1861
                ae 10y 2m.

SMITH, Charles Edward murdered Christmas Eve near Turners Hall. (LEXUN)   SEDA 7 Jan 1865

SMITH, Charles T., late steward on the Thomas E. Tutt, 26 May in Vicksburg ae 29,   MORE 6 Jun 1864
    of brain congestion. Interred Bellefontaine.

SMITH, Daniel (alias Bendigo) stabbed, Christopher Kaiser charged with murder.   MORE 21 Aug 1862

SMITH, Mrs. Daniel G. at her home in Frankford, of consumption, in her 32d year.   LAJ 8 Jul 1865

SMITH, Rev. David Reed in Oct at the home of his father, Edward, in his 21st y.   GAL 24 Nov 1864
    Methodist Church, MO Conference, recently appointed to Gentry Co. circuit.

SMITH, Mrs. Drusilla 9 Nov in Trenton, of consumption, ae 39. Wife of Elder B.H.,   MORE 18 Nov 1864
    pastor of the Christian Church at 17th-Olive, St. Louis.

SMITH, Elizabeth wife of John and daughter of S.B. Sappington, 5 Dec ae 20.   COWS 18 Dec 1863

SMITH, Elizabeth wife of Irwin Z. and daughter of the late Matthew Kerr, 14 Dec.   MORE 15 Dec 1863
    Funeral from the Congregational Church at 10th & Locust.

SMITH, Frank, suicide. "Formerly held a good position in society; a man of   MORE 2 Aug 1861
                considerable talent."

SMITH, Dr. George A. at his home, "The Woodlands," Big River, Jefferson Co. on   MORE 27 Dec 1863
    (13? 18?) Dec. Emigrated from England 20 years ago. Wife, 1 child.

SMITH, Dr. Hamilton, "one of the oldest and most influential citizens of   SJH 1 Aug 1865
    Andrew Co." in Savannah Saturday last.

SMITH, Hampton 28 Sep of consumption in Charleston, ae 21.   CHAC 2 Oct 1863

SMITH, Hiram of Knox Co. shot at Palmyra by Gen. Merrill in retaliation for the   CAWN 1 Nov 1862
death of an old man named Allmstedt at the time of Porter's Raid into
Palmyra. Several others also shot. (Palmyra Courier)

SMITH, Mrs. Isabella 14 Jan ae 43. Funeral from the home of Mr. Speck (State betw   MORE 15 Jan 1865
Arrow-Ohio). Assumption Church, interred Calvary.

SMITH, Judge Jacob, citizen of Linn Co., killed by guerillas at Linnaeus. SJH 23 Jan, MORE 14 Jan 1865

SMITH, Jake, fireman on the John Warner, died from drinking ice water while heated.   MORE 11 Aug 1863

SMITH, J. Lockart "esteemed by his friends for his generous and courteous nature"   MORE 16 Oct 1864
died Friday night.

SMITH, James at the Abbey on Rock Road 13 Jul ae 66. "Scotchman, gardener, friend,   MORE 15 Jul 1864
much esteemed." Funeral from the Abbey.

SMITH, Rev. James G., young Baptist minister, at Fulton "a few days since."   LIT 24 Jul 1863

SMITH, James R., son of the late sheriff, at Vicksburg.   LIT 31 Jul 1863

SMITH, James Weathers 28 Mar at his home in St. Francois Co. in his 72nd year. Born   MORE 23 Apr 1862
in Loudon Co. VA 1790; to KY; to MO 1812. A teacher, married Lucinda,
daughter of William Smith of Fayette Co. KY. Became a farmer. Preceded in
death by wife, 2 sons, 1 daughter. Survived by a daughter Mrs. John Coffman
of Ste. Genevieve Co.

SMITH, Jerry, a well-known resident and rebel sympathizer 4 miles from St. Joseph,   SJH 31 Jul &
fired upon and died, Saturday.   1 Aug 1864

SMITH, John Andrew 5 Jun at Rough and Ready, Nevada Co. CA in his 38th year; thrown   MORE 30 Jul 1863
from horse. Born in Moray, Fairfax Co. VA; to Callaway Co. MO 1839, CA 1849.

SMITH, John Brady 16 Mar in his 64th year. Came with his father to St. Louis at   MORE 17 &
early age, last of 4 or 5 sons. First Pres. Bank of MO. Int. Bellefontaine.   18 Mar 1864

SMITH, Capt. John 11 Mar of consumption ae ca 50. Funeral from the home of his   MORE 12 Mar 1861
daughter Mrs. George Townsend, 79 N. 7th.

SMITH, Mrs. John J. who lives with her husband near the headwaters of Buffalo Creek   LAJ 2 Apr 1863
about 10 miles south of town killed when an old tree blew down on the family
wagon. They had started to town (7 people) when heavy wind blew the tree
down. No one else injured. (MORE 25 Apr quoting the Louisiana True Flag says
Mrs. John T. of near Crow's Cross Roads.)

SMITH, John N., a nurse at Benton Barracks, killed in the Hyde Park riot; lived   MORE 8 Jul 1863
20 minutes after being shot, wanted his property to go to a niece in
Nodaway Co.; had relatives in KY.

SMITH, 3 children of Joseph near Greensburg, Knox Co. ate poisoned roots in a field   HAM 26 Mar 1861
where he was plowing. One lived 60 hours, the others less time.

SMITH, Josy adopted daughter of Irwin and Elizabeth K., 167 Olive, 19 Apr of   MORE 20 Apr 1862
putrid sore throat ae 5y 4m 7d.

SMITH, Miss Julia Adeline daughter of the late Capt. John 20 Feb ae 34 in St. Chas. Co. " 2 Mar 1864

SMITH, Laura wife of John Burgess Smith and daughter of Samuel L. Wells of St. Louis FULT 11 Jan 1861
Co. 29 Dec in her 28th year.

SMITH, Laura Ann daughter of Thomas G. and Nancy 6 Apr at 5th-Felix, ae 8y 7m 13d.   SJH 7 Apr 1864

SMITH, Levin J. in Alton Prison 9 Mar; left mother, 4 sisters. (also see
Benjamin F. and William)   MORE 1 May 1863

SMITH, Lizzie daughter of Elkennah of Fulton 4 Sep ae 25. (FULT 16 Sep says 26)   COWS 30 Sep 1864

SMITH, Lizzie B., tribute by alumni of Gilead School; died 4 Dec.   LIT 16 Dec 1864

SMITH, Maggie A. in Canton 27 Sep; born Taylor Co. KY, April 1840. Only daughter of   CANP 5 Oct 1865
James M. Hubbard. Baptist.

SMITH, Maria wife of Ephraim in Monroe Co. ae 61.   COWS 6 May 1864

SMITH, Miss Mary daughter of Capt. C.F. and Elizabeth 8 Nov of typhoid.   SJH 10 Nov 1864

SMITH, Mary wife of Silas in Long Prairie 5 Jan.   CHAC 11 Jan 1861

SMITH, Mary wife of William H. near Readsville, Callaway Co. 6 Sep in her 53rd y.   COWS 20 Sep 1861

SMITH, Matilda I. wife of Macklin J. of Texas, daughter of the late Adam L. Mills   MORE 1 Jan 1865
of St. Louis, at Monterey MEX 10 Aug 1864.

SMITH, Michael ae 40 of sunstroke. Left wife, 2 children, Garrison betw Franklin-
Morgan.   MORE 18 Aug 1863

SMITH, Missouri Ann eldest daughter of Conrad and Isabella in Louisiana MO 24 Oct of typhoid ae 17y 5m.	LAJ 31 Oct 1863
SMITH, Nancy wife of William H. near Readsville 5 Sep in his 53rd year.	FULT 13 Sep 1861
SMITH, Mrs. Nancy E., 201 Christy, on 3 Mar.	MORE 5 Mar 1865
SMITH, Col. Peter, resident of Potosi 25 years, of St. Louis the previous 20 years, 18 Feb of pneumonia. Interred Potosi.	MORE 19 Feb 1863
SMITH, R.S., resolution by AF & AM. Died 11 Feb, ae not given. Husband, father.	LAJ 18 Feb 1865
SMITH, Ransom brother of Capt. Henry W. of St. Louis at Metropolis IL 27 Sep.	MORE 29 Sep 1865
SMITH, Robert H. of St. Joseph, in the Confederate Army, at the Battle of Helena.	SJH 15 Jul 1863
SMITH, Robert H. 7 Mar ae 65.	KCJC 8 Mar 1864
SMITH, Robert S. eldest son of Gen. A.J. and Ann M. yesterday ae 10. Funeral from the home of his grandfather Dr. Simpson, 3rd-Elm. Int. Bellefontaine.	MORE 29 Aug 1862
SMITH, Sallie only daughter of R.D.C. and J.E. in Portland 1 May ae 10. (MORE 17 May says she died 24 Apr.)	FULT 13 May 1864
SMITH, Samuel J., body found in the Mississippi, supposed accidental drowning. Left family on Green St.	MORE 16 Jul 1862
SMITH, Miss Sarah J. on the farm of her father, Johnathon -- where she was born, lived, died -- 26 Jan of typhoid ae 23y 2m. Baptist.	GAL 9 Feb 1865
SMITH, Sarah M. wife of Thomas in Rocheport 22 Feb of consumption ae 28y 2m 7d.	COWS 1 Mar 1861
SMITH, Stephen R. hanged as a guerilla. Born in TN, lived in Oregon Co., was 37, an elder in the Campbellite Church. Left wife and 2 children.	MORE 10 Sep 1864
SMITH, Tartan "a well-known citizen" yesterday at his home.	FULT 8 Jul 1864
SMITH, Thomas only son of Mrs. Anna M. 26 Nov at Potosi of acute meningitis, 5y 2m.	MORE 1 Dec 1865
SMITH, Thomas to be hanged today for the murder of Robert Baker. Michael Kearns also sentenced.	MORE 23 Jan 1863
SMITH, Thomas of 14th-Papin, 28 Feb in his 62d year. Church of the Annunciation.	MORE 2 Mar 1863
SMITH, Thomas Sr. at the home of Braxton Smith 27 Sep ae 82.	MEMP 14 Oct 1865
SMITH, W.L. stabbed and killed by George Starr; both produce dealers on Broadway. Ae 40, lived at 27 S 8th, unmarried.	MORE 28 & 29 Jan 1865
SMITH, William of gunshot wounds in Cole Co. 23 May, 1862. Left mother and 4 sisters. Ae 32. (also see Benj. F. and Levin, apparently brothers.)	MORE 1 May 1863
SMITH, William, well-known river pilot, found dead in bed at Everett House of visceral inflammation. Left wife and 2 children at Newport KY. Int. Cincinnati.	MORE 12 & 13 Jan 1865
SMITH, William J. in Boone Co. ae 59y 4m. Native of KY, to MO 1819. Baptist. New Albany & St. Louis pc	COWS 19 Sep 1862
SMITH, Dr. William in California MO 16 Jan. Born Fauquier Co. VA 22 Jun 1824, son of John P. and Mary; resident of MO about 12 years.	CAWN 24 Jan 1863
SMITH, William W., sheriff of Clay Co., 14 Jan of typhoid ae 44y 3m 8d.	LIT 16 Jan 1863
SMITH, Willie 7 Nov ae 18, injured in the J.H. Dickey explosion 10 miles above Ste. Genevieve. Funeral from home of his mother, Mrs. Hineman, 54 S. 4th.	MORE 8 Nov 1862
SMIZER, Mrs. Josephine Grace wife of Brig. Gen John W., CSA, and daughter of William H. Merritt of St. Louis, near Little Rock 2 Sep.	MORE 19 Sep 1863
SMOOT, Eleven H. 8 Sep 1862 of a protracted illness (10 years) ae 51y 5m 22d.	CAWN 24 Jan 1863
SMUCKER, Willie Loomis son of Fannie L. and D.R. 4 May ae 6y 7m. Int. Bellefontaine.	MORE 6 May 1864
SMYTH, Lizzie Brown only daughter of Isaac S. and Annie, 241 Pine, 16 Mar ae 4y 8m.	MORE 17 Mar 1863
SNAIL, __ "a brigand" killed by Capt. Davis' men in Platte Co. "a few days since."	SJH 6 Nov 1864
SNEED, John killed in Livingston Co. a few days ago by his brother-in-law John McWilliams (also see McWilliams).	RICON 4 Jun 1863
SNELL, Robert 17 Nov in his 88th year. Born in Scott Co. KY, leaves several mature children and "four of tender years," also a wife. LIT & MORE pc	WEST 9 Dec 1864
SNELL, Maj. Willis W. in Fulton 6 Feb in his 71st year. Formerly of KY, veteran of War of 1812, in Callaway Co. 40 years.	MORE 13 Feb 1862
SNELLING, ____ "notorious bushwhacker" executed at Clinton.	LEXUN 15 Aug 1863
SNELSON, Mary J. wife of Dr. William R. and mother of Dr. J.B., 27 Jul ae 57. Presbyterian. Richmond VA pc	SJH 28 Jul 1865

SNOW, R.B. of St. Louis 3 Oct in New York.   MORE 4 Oct 1865

SNYDER, Andrew, a guerilla, executed (shot) at Macon. (MAG)   FULT 13 May 1864

SNYDER, George 24 Dec ae 50. Funeral from Christian Church, 17th-Olive.   MORE 25 Dec 1863
        Interred Bellefontaine.

SNYDER, Capt. Henry of Chariton Co., an old resident, killed by bushwhackers.   MORE 21 Jul 1864
        Left young wife and large family of small children. (CECB)

SNYDER, children of John and   Johnny Clinton 15 Jun ae 3y 6m 9d   MORE 16 Jun 1862
        Marcena, 227 Pine   Eddie Lay youngest son 18 Jun ae 2y 4m 14d   "   19   "
        Springfield IL & Pittsburgh pc

SNYDER, Henry C. 28 Feb of brain fever ae 30, at 13th-Poplar. Cincinnati &
                                                                    Newport KY pc MORE 1 Mar 1862

SOBOLISKI, Mrs. Isabella (formerly Garneau) 21 Oct. Funeral from the home of   MORE 22 Oct 1863
        Samuel Bowen, 15th-O'Fallon.

SOEHMAN, George, a farmer, living near Wild Hunters Tavern on Carondelet Road,   MORE 7 Jan 1862
        fell under a wagon. His skull was crushed.

SOLP, August, soldier in Col. Blair's Reg., drowned Thursday.   MORE 17 Jun 1861

SOMMERS, Emily daughter of Harrison, Carr 17th, 10 May ae 14, victim of the   MORE 11 &
        Camp Jackson affair.   15 May 1861

SOPER, J.W.P. 3 Jul ae 26. Tribute by Liberty Lodge, Masons   LIT 8 & 15 Jul 1864

SORRELS, Rube "notorious bushwhacker" reported killed in Gasconade Co. 27 Sep.   MORE 2 Oct 1863

SOSEY, John Augustus son of the proprietor of the Palmyra Spectator Sunday night   PALS 22 Jan 1864
        last in his 23rd year; ill many months.

SOUTH, Gen. John of Lincoln Co. in St. Louis 19 Mar in his 65th year. Interred in   MORE 20 Mar 1865
        the family burying ground, Pike Co.

SOUTH, Col. Samuel D. 25 Aug. Born in KY, to Clark Co. MO 1835; married Sarah   PALS 1 Sep 1865
        Easton, daughter of Rufus, 1839. Wife, 7 surviving children. (Long obit.)

SPALDING, Agnes P. wife of Josiah, also "mother." Int. Bellefontaine.   MORE 20 & 21 Feb 1865
        Lieut. Edward son of the late Josiah and Agnes 27 May ae 22.   MORE 28 May 1862

SPALDING, Reese 7 Feb in his 47th year; lingering illness. Zanesville pc   MORE 11 Feb 1863

SPALDING, Sarah E. wife of Charles W., 3 Jul. Funeral from the home of her brother-   MORE 5 Jul 1864
        in-law Ely Metcalf on Easton Pl. north of St. Charles Rock Road.
        Maysville KY & Bloomington IL pc

SPANN, Eliza Ann consort of S.W. 4 Dec at Sacramento CA, daughter of John F.   KCJC 19 Jan 1864
        Crutchfield of Westport MO. Born KY 9 Oct 1830, moved with father to
        Independence, then Westport; married 1858, then to CA. Methodist.

SPANN, Dr. J.W.B. at Sisters Hospital of diarrhoea 23 Nov, formerly of Mt. Vernon MO. MORE 25 Nov '62

SPARHAWK, George Sr. 20 Nov, Clark N. of 12th, ae 64. New Orleans & Cincinnati pc.   MORE 21 Nov 1863
        George W. Jr. 16 May at the home of Mrs. G.W. Sparhawk, 12th betw   "   17 May 1865
        Market-Clark, 16 May ae 48(?).

SPARKS, George M. of Porter's Band, arrested 18 Jul, in Gratiot Prison 19 Nov,   MORE 19 &
        of lung inflammation.   20 Nov 1862

SPAULDING, James H. living near Florida, Monroe Co., taken from home by a band of   COWS 19 Aug 1864
        rebels, shot, between Elizabethtown and Monroe Station.

SPEAR, Mrs. ___, daughter of Isaac Brown, a war widow, suicide by hanging.   SJH 12 Dec 1863
        (Bethany Union)

SPECHT, William, body found in river and buried last week, resident of Waterloo MO.   MORE 23 Sep 1862

SPEED, Sallie at the home of her brother-in-law Willis Hood, St. Louis Co.,   MORE 25 Oct 1864
        ae 21y 7m. CA pc

SPENCE, Andrew 3 miles north of Columbia 10 Jan ae ca 75.   COWS 23 Jan 1863

SPENCE, Henry 3 Oct in his 68th year. Member 1st Methodist Church. NY, Providence,   MORE 4 Oct 1863
        Texas and KY pc.

SPENCE, Mary Jane wife of W. Riley and sister of Col. Odon Guitar near   COWS 28 Mar 1862
        Columbia 24 Mar ae ca 32.

SPENCER, John, a steamboat waiter, of chills. Lived betw 14-15-Franklin-Wash.   MORE 15 Nov 1863

SPENCER, Perry in Boone Co. 29 Apr in his 66th year.   COWS 13 Jun 1862

SPENCER, Martha Elizabeth wife of Rev. William G. (Rector of St. John's) and   MORE 26 Feb 1864
        daughter of George Cannon, latterly of Logansport IN, ae 25y 8m.

SPENCER, Sarah L. in Buchanan Co. 20 Apr in her 75th year. Born in KY, to NC,   WEST 30 Apr 1864
    then MO, a widow 15 years. Has buried 4 grown sons, 2 of them murdered.
    Obituary by Julia Burgess, her granddaughter.
SPILLMAN, James M. of St. Louis in Marshall Co. VA 30 Aug of consumption, in 21st y. MORE 13 Sep 1863
    John W. of St. Louis in Marshall Co. VA 7 Oct of consumption in 21st y.   "   14 Oct 1864
SPIRES, ___, an old man, taken from his home by rebels, body found Monday last near HAM 1 May 1862
    Jacksonville in Randolph Co. (MAG)
SPLAWN, J.W. of Ralls Co. at Moore's Mill.   MORE 11 Aug 1862
SPOORE, Daniel ae 73; lived on Second Carondelet.   MORE 1 Aug 1863
SPORER, Edward 30 Jun in his (45th?) year.   MORE 3 Jul 1862
SPRAGUE, Capt. J. Keness of Gen. John Bowen's Brigade, a Confederate from St. Louis, MORE 4 May 1862
    killed at Shiloh.
SPRECHT, Henry, bookkeeper for the Westliche Post, drowned while sailing with a   MORE 30 Jun 1862
    friend. He was 27, black curly hair, 5'9" tall.
SPRING, James, inquest: a "contraband" ae 27, died of debility.   MORE 14 Jan 1864
SPRINGER, Samuel D. 17 Oct ae 26. Funeral from the home of N. Springer, 233? Pine. MORE 19 Oct 1865
SPRINKLE, C.W., a merchant in Shelbina, 8 Jul.   PALS 21 Jul 1865
SPRINKLE, Harry Johnson son of William B. and Mary J. in Canton 29 Sep ae 7y 1m 24d. CANP 5 Oct 1865
SPROULE, Florinda J. wife of Andrew, Olive above 22nd, on 28 Jun ae 35.   MORE 29 Jun 1865
SQUIRE, John 16 Oct in his 43rd year. Interred Marion Co. Geneva NY pc   MORE 17 Oct 1863
STACK, Thomas C. at 118 N. 12th on 16 Jul, ae 42.   MORE 17 & 18 Jul 1864
STACKHOUSE, William 23 Jan of consumption ae 32. Pittsburgh & Johnstown PA pc MORE 26 Jan 1863
STADDEN, Charles H. son of William H. and Mary of Springfield MO 4 Dec ae 2y 6m. SLMD 10 Dec 1861
STAGG, Edward at his home on Chestnut St. 12 May ae 45, after a short illness. MORE 13 May 1863
    Funeral St. George's Church, interred Bellefontaine.
STAGG, Warren (of Stagg & Bro., St. Louis) drowned in Helena AR when a river bank MORE 10 &
    caved in as he was watering his horse. Lived NE cor Olive-17. Int. Bellefontaine. 23 Sep 1862
STAMPER, Zachary Taylor son of Hiram 1 Apr of pneumonia and inflammation of the RANC 11 Apr 1861
    head, ae 13y 10d.
STANDISH, Austin M., former Confederate officer, murdered near Monterey.   MORE 11 Oct 1865
STANSBURY, Emerson Larkin son of Emerson and Catherine M. 5 Aug at 53 S. 5th, MORE 6 Aug 1864
    ae 12. Baltimore pc
STANSBERY, Ezra 25 Jun at 171 St. Charles St. ae 42.   MORE 26 Jun 1864
STAPLETON, George of Howard Co. shot on his way home from Rocheport 4 Feb by ___ BOOM 13 Feb 1864
    Jennings, who claimed Stapleton stopped at his house and was
    intoxicated and abusive.
STAPLETON, John son of William H. and Evalina 16 Jan in Fayette ae 7y 11m 26d. MORE 27 Jan 1861
STARK, ___ ("James" per county history) hanged in Chariton Co. by Trueman,   MORE 10 Jan 1865
    serving under Rosecrans.
STARK, James H. 20 Jan ae 41; lived on Penrose betw Broadway and 10th.   MORE 22 Jan 1863
STARK, Jasper of Hickory, St. Clair Co. in Gratiot Prison of chronic diarrhoea 5 Nov.   "   9 Nov 1862
STARK, Vestine consort of J.K. of Independence and daughter of Judge James Porter. MORE 1 Feb 1865
    Interred Bellefontaine Cemetery, St. Louis.
STARKE, Dr. Edwin A. at the home of his late father, Newman B., at Oakland,   MORE 16 May 1861
    Boone Co. 1 May of consumption ae (ca 27 COWS, 29 MORE)   COWS 3 "
STARKEY, John captured in Barry Co. 28 May of pulmonalis phthisis 28 May in   MORE 10 Jun 1863
    the Prison Hospital, Springfield.
STARKS, ___ hanged near Keytesville. (BRUNS 18 Jun)   MORE 24 Jun 1864
STARN, John H., 10 Jan. Tribute by Farmington Masons. Left "widow and orphans." MORE 27 Feb 1864
STARNES or STEARNES, James M., M.D., asst. surgeon 11th Cav MO Vols, at Benton MORE 23 Jan 1864
    Barracks ae 31. St. Joseph pc
STATZER, John "old and esteemed" at his home a few miles southwest of town.   CAB 7 Apr 1865
STAUTERMAN, William, a boy, tried on jump on a government wagon, fell under. Son MORE 1 Nov 1864
    of poor Germans around 11th-O'Fallon.

STEBER, Louis, native of Metz FRA, ae 78. Funeral from the home of his son Nicholas, MORE 2 Nov 1863
   3rd near Lombard (#215 S.). Interred Calvary.
   Margarette wife of Nicholas 4 Dec ae 38y 10m, 215 S. 3rd. Interred Calvary.   MORE 5 Dec 1863
   Nicholas 30 Apr ae 53 y 3m 20d. 215 S. 3rd. Interred Calvary.   "   1 May 1865

STEEL, Samuel B. at his home near Fulton 23 Apr ae 63y 11m.   MORE 29 Apr 1861

STEELE, Esther wife of Thomas J. 30 Jun, at Carr-Biddle. Dublin, Baltimore, NY pc   MORE 2 Jul 1862

STEELE, Eyre Massey of Kyle, Queens Co. IRE 29 Aug at his home, 228 Biddle.   MORE 30 Aug 1864
   Interred Bellefontaine.

STEELE, Kittie "at the house of Moll Slattery" of an overdose of morphine, ae 18.   MORE 26 Nov 1864
   "Quite pretty and very attractive."

STEELE, Mrs. Susan J. in Monroe Co. 17 Aug in her 44th year.   PALS 28 Aug 1863

STEELE, William ae 25 accidentally shot by his brother George (Morgan betw 12-13).   MORE 22 Mar 1861
   Interred Bellefontaine.

STEEN, Mary E. wife of Col. Enoch 19 Feb in her 26th year, of consumption. Left   MORE 20 Feb 1862
   2 young daughters. Funeral from Immaculate Conception Church.

STEENBERGER, Col. John Beal 10 Oct ae 59. Funeral from Smithers, 113 Chestnut. MORE 11 & 12 Oct 1862

STEIGERS, F.J. of 128 Olive St. 22 Mar of heart disease ae 54.   MORE 23 Mar 1863

STEIN, Henry W. drowned in the river opposite Bremen ae 11. Parents lived at   MORE 13 Jul 1862
   1137 Bellefontaine Rd.

STEINHAUER, Sarah Wells ae 5y 4m on 10 Oct and Jemima ae 3y 6m on 15 Oct, daughters   MORE 18 Oct 1861
   of Henry F. and Jemima. Diphtheria. Nashville pc

STEINMETZ, Aaron M., recently wounded at Glasgow, 18 Oct in his 17th year and his   MORE 18 Nov 1864
   brother Capt. Samuel W. in his 22d year. Presbyterians.

STEMBEL, Ferdinand, 159 S. 2nd, suddenly ae 60, of old age, intemperance, debility.   MORE 11 Feb 1862
   "He made his living exhibiting a miniature silver mine in a box, complete
   with workers."

STENER, Joseph fell from the RR bridge at Sulphur Springs 21 Nov ae 20y 9m 1d. Notice MORE 24 Nov 1864
   by his mother Josephine, 24 S. 14th, mentions brothers and sisters.

STENSTRA, ___ killed in Chariton Co. in retaliation.   MORE 10 Jan 1865

STEPHANI, Marie Josephine consort of Charles A. 8 Nov at Carondelet.   MORE 12 Nov 1865

STEPHENS, ___ a guerilla killed on the Big Perry near McCourtney's Mill in the   MORE 20 Jan 1865
   general area of Waynesville. McCourtney and Anthony also killed.

STEPHENS, Mrs. F.S., wife of James H., 18 May.   WEST 21 and 28 May 1864

STEPHENS, James murdered near Fulton for his money; lived near Jackson's Mill in   MORE 9 Aug 1864
   eastern part of Callaway Co. (FULT 5 Aug) (PALS 12 Aug says died 5 Aug.)

STEPHENS, John Emery son of John and Adeline, living near Normandy P.O., 24 May   MORE 25 May 1861
   ae 8y & nearly 8m. Funeral from St. Ann's Church to Mrs. Kienlen's home.

STEPHENS, Joseph 22 Sep in Monroe Co. in his 86th year, old and respected; once   COWS 4 Oct 1861
   represented the county in the Legislature.

STEPHENS, Dr. Locke W. in Callaway Co. 9 Jun in his 50th year. Baptist.   COWS 20 Jun 1862

STEPHENS, Elder Thomas P. in Callaway Co. 2 Apr.   COWS 14 Apr 1865

STEPHENSON, Margaret eldest daughter of the late Judge William 12 Jul ae 64y 6m.   LAJ 24 Jul 1862

STERLING, Philo Calhoun son of E.J. and S.E. 10 May ae 3y 5m.   MORE 12 May 1861

STERRETT, Cora daughter of Mrs. Eliza J. 29 Nov in Oregon (Holt Co.) of typhoid   HOLS 1 Dec 1865
   ae 11.   SJH 3 "

STEVENS, C. Allen (of Morgan, Stevens & Co.) 3 Sep at Rockford near Fort Scott KS,   MORE 7 Sep 1865
   traveling for his health; family was with him when he died.

STEVENS, Miss Dora, former music teacher in Jefferson City, at Janesville WI 3 Aug.   JEST 18 Aug 1865

STEVENS, John H. 23 Feb ae 44y 5d. Mason. Funeral at Christ Church. NY & IA pc   MORE 25 Feb 1864

STEVENS, Kate Ellen daughter of Edward and Mary 1 Jul ae 3y 9m.   MORE 1 Jul 1862

STEVENS, Love youngest daughter of Robert and Anne R. (nw corner Salisbury-9th)   MORE 26 Jan 1864
   25 Jan in her 11th year. Interred Calvary. NY & Richmond pc

STEVENS, William H. 6 Jan ae 28. Born in Kaskaskia, left mother, 2 sisters. IOOF.   MORE 12 Jan 1862

STEVENSON, Hallie Dunlap youngest child of Gen. John and H., 313 Chestnut, 4 Jul   MORE 5 Jul 1863
   ae 3y 8m.

STEVENSON, James R., Chariton Co.: public administrator took over his estate.   CECB 24 Jul 1862

STEWART, Alexander in Columbia 26 Oct ae ca 41.   COWS 30 Oct 1863

STEWART, Charles W. in Jefferson City 12 Aug. Born King George Co. VA 1 May 1809,   MORE 19 Aug 1863
    to MO ca 1836. Heart disease and typhoid pneumonia. Methodist South,
    Mason, left wife and children. Baltimore pc

STEWART, Harvey youngest son of Chambers and Eliza of Danville 30 Dec ae 3y 6m.   MORE 8 Jan 1864

STEWART, James found dead in bed 19 Jul at his home, 16th-Chouteau, in his 59th   MORE 20 &
    year. Heart disease. Wife mentioned.   21 Jul 1861

STEWART, John M. of disease of the bowels and lungs; a druggist, ae 36. Left "friends." HAM 23 Apr '61

STEWART, Dr. Judson G. hanged himself on a tree near Rose Hill, Cass Co.; had been   CAWN 9 Mar 1861
    acquitted of the murder of Miles Cary in Johnson Co.; was actually
    Dr. Jeamison the Kansas outlaw. (Marshall Democrat)

STEWART, Miss Margaret 4 Nov in her 25th year, on 17th betw Biddle-O'Fallon.   MORE 6 Nov 1862
    Interred Wesleyan. Alton pc

STEWART, Mary Ann Bertram wife of William P., Morgan above 22nd, 1 Mar ae 47y 20d.   MORE 2 Mar 1865

STEWART, W., former deputy sheriff, killed near Waynesville some days ago by   MORE 21 Aug 1865
    Miller Co. militia under Col. Babcocke.

STEWART, William P.B. of Lewis Co. in Gratiot Prison, of enteritis, 6 Nov.   MORE 9 Nov 1862

STICKER, Margaret, inquest: fell off porch at 6th & Green. Widow, husband a soldier   MORE 5 Sep 1865
    killed at Atlanta, she later became addicted to drink. Ca 40, left a
    daughter ae ca 11.

STIEFANS, Andreas (later shown as Andrew Stevens) 18 Apr at Sisters Hospital of   MORE 20 Apr 1863
    consumption ae 27.

STILLWELL, Samuel B. only son of Enoch and Margaret 25 May ae 3y 9m, at 62 Myrtle.   MORE 26 May 1863

STINDE, Adelia Elizabeth only daughter of C.R. and Augusta, at Clark-Naomi,   MORE 7 Feb 1863
    3 years less 22d.

STOCK, Dominique Saturday ae 46.   MORE 17 Apr 1861

STOCK, Mary widow of John in Boone Co. 15 Apr ae 81. Fayette MO & Lexington KY pc COWS 1 & 8 May 1863
    (8 May shows age as 84)

STODLER, Henry a boy run over by Franklin Ave. street car betw Pratte-Beaumont.   MORE 16 Apr 1862

STOEBER, Miss Lucinka drowned in a well, ae 20. Parents live on Buel betw Barton-   MORE 3 Feb 1863
    Martha. Verdict, accidental.

STOEWENER, Joseph son of Ferdinand and Carolina near Soulard's Market 6 May ae 19y6m15d.   " 7 May 1863

STOKES, Sarah Julia daughter of T.E. 28 Dec ae ca 3.   LAJ 7 Jan 1861

STOLL, Laura M. eldest daughter of Rebecca and the late Peter H. 24 Dec ae 18y 9m.   MORE 25 Dec 1862
    Short illness. Funeral at St. John's, 6th-Poplar.

STOLLE, Elizabeth Pols (Puls?) wife of Caspar 12 Dec ae 38y 6m. St. Joseph's Church,   MORE 13 Dec 1863
    interred Calvary.

STONE, Ida May only daughter of W.H. and M.A. 26 Oct ae 6y 6m, Chambers betw 11-12.   MORE 27 Oct 1864
    Interred Bellefontaine.

STONE, M.H.N. of Zanesville OH at Sisters of Charity 21 Oct ae (53?).   MORE 23 Oct 1865

STONE, Oliver C. 5 Nov of typhoid ae 26. Peoria pc   MORE 6 Nov 1864

STONEBREAKER, George shot near Cape au Gris, Lincoln Co., by John Mathews over a   MORE 14 Apr 1865
    remark made by James Mathews, brother of John.

STONEMAN, J.H. in Newton Co. 12 Feb ae 19.   MORE 28 May 1861

STONEY, George, an old miner, in Granby, Newton Co. 3 Mar ae 69.   MORE 8 Mar 1862

STORY, Mrs. Catharine 2 Jun in her 19th year at 11th-Market.   MORE 3 Jun 1862

STORY, David at his home in Benton Co. 28 Feb in his 47th year.   MORE 9 Mar 1862

STOTTEMEYER, Charlie son of Ben F. and Mary E. 21 Mar ae 4 and his sister Bettie,   MORE 21 Apr 1864
STOTTLEMEYER their only daughter, 19 Apr ae ly 4m22d. Lived on Wash betw 19-20.
    Louisville, Baltimore, Hagerstown MD pc

STOUT, Delia wife of B.F. 2 Mar of consumption ae 37.   MORE 3 Mar 1861
    B.F. of St. Louis in Chicago 14 Jul. A banker. Funeral from the home   "   17 Jul 1861
    of D. Preston, 6-Myrtle. Interred Bellefontaine.

STOUTMORE, Amanda wife of Josiah of Clinton Co. and daughter of David Lincoln   LIT 1 Sep 1865
    21 Aug ae 43; also her daughter Josie 13 Aug ae 2.

STOWERS, Mrs. Elvira E. widow of David L. at her father's home 22 Jul in her 34th y.   PALS 7 Aug 1863
    Left husband, 2 little girls.   Cincinnati pc

STRACHAN, Alexander J. only son of the late William, this morning ae 23. Funeral from 2nd Presbyterian.	MORE 20 Jan 1864
STRAIN, Samuel of Pulaski Co., arrested 2 Sep, in Gratiot Prison of intermittent fever.	MORE 18 & 20 Nov 1862
STRATTON, Mr. ___ of Howard Co. lost his wife and 2 children of spotted fever in less than 2 weeks. (Fayette Advertiser)	LIT 1 May 1863
STRATTON, ___ killed "lately" in Chariton Co.	MORE 10 Jan 1865
STRAWBEL, John, inquest: brain congestion. Laborer, boarded, "little known of him."	MORE 27 Sep 1863
STREET, Robbie K. eldest son of Mary A. and the late James 22 Sep ae 11y 9m 18d. Interred Bellefontaine. Baltimore, Pittsburgh & Louisville pc	MORE 23 Sep 1863
STREET, Col. William A., formerly of Franklin Co. VA, 22 Mar at Planters' House in his 47th year.	MORE 23 Mar 1863
STRICKLAND, ___ "little son of P.G." living 5 or 6 miles from town, only child, ran into a kettle of boiling water while playing with his wagon.	SPRIP 19 Oct 1865
STRICTLER, E.C. consort of Mark in Forest City, Holt Co., 15 Oct. Left 3 small children.	SJH 18 Oct '63
STRINGLEY, Mrs. R.G., former resident of Andrew Co.; family removed to Winterset IA. Gun in wagon accidentally discharged, killing her "a few weeks since."	" 23 Dec 1864
STROEMER, John H., Chariton Co.: letters of administration to Wm. Stroemer 19 Jan.	CECB 12 Feb 1863
STROTHER, C.G. late surgeon 31 MO Vols at Wood's Hotel, Warrenton, 12 Apr.	MORE 20 Apr 1864
STROTHER, Mrs. Elizabeth W. of Galena, mother-in-law of John C. Gairns of St. Louis, 11 Oct in her 66th year.	MORE 13 Oct 1862
STROUP, John of Jefferson Co. thrown from a horse, ae 51. Left large family.	MORE 25 Nov 1862
STUMPF, Mrs. ___ at the home of her son-in-law John F. Tolle, 11th betw Howard-Brooklyn, 18 Oct in her 69th year.	MORE 19 Oct 1863
STUMPF, Herman, a German shoemaker, drowned Friday night in the Mississippi. Suicide, "long partially insane." Ca 40, left wife, large family. His wife had previously prevented his suicide.	MORE 21 Dec 1862
STUMPH, George son of Charles and Anna, ca 6, drowned in Mill Creek when the bank gave way.	MORE 4 May 1862
STURDER, John drowned in a pond on Gravois Road near Jefferson. Left wife and 3 children in "great indigence."	MORE 15 Apr 1863
STURDY, John a policeman of injuries received when he was beaten by ruffians 29 Mar. Lived on 4th near Cerre, ca 33, left wife and 3 children.	MORE 11 Apr 1863
SUBLETTE, Esther Frances only surviving child of the late Solomon and Frances 16 May ae 7y 8m.	MORE 18 May 1861
SUITE, Benjamin T. son of Jesse in Hannibal Saturday of measles and pneumonia. In Capt. Gentry's state militia, ae 27y 4m.	PALS 7 Apr 1865
SULLINGS, Henry and party of six all killed by Indians near 32 Mile Creek, all citizens of St. Joseph. (Wire from Ft. Kearney, subsequent letter.)	SJH 12 Aug 1864
SULLINS, John C. of rheumatism and typhoid 3 Dec in his 59th year. Left wife and 6 children.	COWS 22 Dec 1865
SULLIVAN, Ann wife of Timothy Friday ae 37. St. Michael's Church, interred Rock Spring.	MORE 27 Aug 1865
SULLIVAN, Catherine ae 12 suddenly after complaining of a violent headache. Her mother lived on Wash betw 22-23.	MORE 28 Oct 1864
SULLIVAN, Miss Elizabeth B. daughter of Daniel and Susan at their home on Florissant Plank Road near Ferguson Station, N. MO RR. Funeral from Bellefontaine Church. Louisville, Vincennes, & Quincy pc	MORE 27 Jul 1863
SULLIVAN, Giles D., former soldier 7th MO, found dead in bed; congestion of the lungs caused by heat.	MORE 1 Jul 1864
SULLIVAN, John D. brother of C.D. of St. Louis in Dubuque 1 Apr ae 52.	MORE 4 Apr 1865
SULLIVAN, Margaret, found dead in a waste house at the rear of John Otolini's fruit shop (w side of 6th betw Biddle-O'Fallon). Some indication of violence - he had driven her out of the store earlier - but verdict was apoplexy due to intemperance.	MORE 14 Jul 1863
SULLIVAN, Patrick found floating opposite Quarantine Island, ae ca 26.	MORE 24 Nov 1862
SULLIVAN, Patrick (Franklin betw 23-24) ae 25.	MORE 6 Apr 1864

SULLIVAN, Mrs. Susan at her home near Ferguson's Station 9 Nov. ae 79y 9m. Funeral from ?Tulee? Church. (Possibly Fee Fee Baptist?)	MORE 10 Nov 1864
SULLIVAN, Wat, wagoner and cartman, drowned with his team in Glasgow's Pond.	MORE 25 Apr 1863
SULLIVAN, William 16 Aug ae 19y 8m 5d at his parents' home, Cerre betw 5-6.	MORE 16 Aug 1865
SUMMER, S.P., citizen of Randolph Co., 28 Dec of pneumonia. (Undertakers' list)	MORE 2 Jan 1865
SUMMERS, Annabell, youngest daughter of William, of hemorrhage of the lungs.	MORE 1 Mar 1863
SUMMERS, Elizabeth wife of Maj. Jesse at the home of her son-in-law Dr. A.M. Richardson, in Parkville, of "affection of the heart" ae ca 64.	COWS 19 Apr 1861
SUMMERS, John killed near the Pacific RR Machine Shop Friday last during the storm.	MORE 27 Sep 1864
SUMMERS, Stephen F., 225 Chestnut, 28 Feb ae 49.	MORE 3 Mar 1862
SUMMONS, Benjamin F. 3rd MO CSA, captured in Vicksburg 4 Jul, in the prison hospital of remittent fever.	MORE 25 Sep 1863
SUMNER, John S., assistant cook on the Enterprise, fell overboard and drowned at the mouth of the White River.	MORE 21 May 1865
SUTTER, Christina Fischer wife of Michael, 63 S. Levee, ae 55y 5m 28d.	MORE 24 Feb 1864
SUTTER, Michael (Levee betw Almond-Poplar) 16 Sep ae 52. Interred Old Picker.	" 17 Sep 1864
SUTTLES, Mrs. Christina 5 Jan ae 78 at the home of her granddaughter Mrs. Nancy G. Hall, Jackson Co.	MORE 27 Jan 1861
SUTTON, Adaline H. wife of A.J. and daughter of James and Matilda Moran 13 June in her 30th year. Born in Madison Co. KY.	LIT 20 Jun 1862
SUTTON, Mary relict of Joseph 16 Jan ae 60. Funeral from the home of her son-in-law William McNeal, 133 N. 12th.	MORE 17 Jan 1861
SUTTON, Mary A. wife of William T. of Boone Co. at Sulphur Springs, Howard Co. in her 27th year. Warrensburg pc	COWS 2 Oct 1863
SVACHAMMER, William, prisoner of war, 8 Oct of consumption. (Undertakers' list)	MORE 12 Oct 1862
SWAIN, Robert at 11 Orange St. 8 Mar in his 73rd year. Funeral St. Xavier, NY pc.	MORE 11 Mar 1865
SWANSON, Charles 6 Oct "worthy citizen, parent"; a Mason. CA Lodge 183 AF & A.	CALM 14 Oct 1865
SWARTZ, James H., 319 Franklin, 23 Nov ae 44. Formerly of Martinsburg WV. Died of dysentery. Interred Calvary.	MORE 26 Nov 1864
SWEATNAM, Addie daughter of T.T. 17 Apr ae ca 10.	LIT 1 May 1863
SWEENY, John, inquest: Irish ae 55, lung congestion. No family. Broadway nr Howard.	MORE 4 Sep 1863
SWEET, Mrs. Galusha B. 15 Mar ae 34.	MORE 18 Mar 1863
SWEET, Mary Jane wife of H.R. of Franklin Co. 25 Mar in her 35th yr, of consumption.	MORE 6 Apr 1864
SWETNAM, John in Howard Co. 6 Jul ae 65.	COWS 22 Jul 1864
SWIKHART, John (15th betw Wash-Carr) killed in the Camp Jackson affair.	MORE 14 May 1861
SWITZELAN, Jerry, a well-known engineer on the river, killed in the Camp Jackson affair.	" "
SWITZER, A.G. on 26 May ae 52. Came to St. Louis in 1828, owned one of its oldest merchant houses. Lingering illness. Interred Bellefontaine.	MORE 27 & 29 May 1864
SWITZER, Joseph (also referred to as Michael in inquest notice), found floating. Last Tuesday had been unloading the Leonard at the levee, was intoxicated. Lay down, not found later. Left wife, 4 children, 6th betw Cass-O'Fallon.	MORE 8 Sep 1865
SWITZER, William N. Jr., son of William N. and Mary J., 31 N 6th, 1 Jun ae 5y 3m 25d.	MORE 2 Jun '64
SWITZLER, Harriet wife of Clark P. at Warsaw 5 Feb.	COWS 11 Mar 1864
SWITZER? Clark P. at Parker House in Sedalia, many years in business in Warsaw, ae 48. (MORE 29 Jun & 3 Jul gives name as Switzer; native of Franklin, Howard Co.)	" 1 Jul 1864
SWITZLER, Newton eldest brother of the editor of the Missouri Statesman 29 Mar at Huntsville in his 40th year, of consumption.	MORE 7 Apr 1861
TABOR, Mrs. C.J. consort of Seamon(?) in St. Joseph 22 Aug in her 33rd year.	SJH 24 Aug 1865
TAFT, Clark B. late of NY at the home of his brother S.F., of typhoid, 21 Jan ae 22.	HAM 27 Jan 1861
TAFT, Mary daughter of Dr. H.S. and J.C. 16 Jan ae 13m 17d.	HAM 17 Jan 1861
TAFT, ___ little son of Dr. ae 3 or 4 drowned yesterday near Hixon's old ice house. (Notice says Howard Dickinson, son of Dr. H.S. and Jane C., ae 3y 10m.)	HAM 22 Aug 1861
TALBOT, Mrs. Joseph 5 Aug ae 30, Broadway at Ferry. NY & Philadelphia pc	MORE 6 Aug 1863

TALLIS, Charles Washington son of Thomas, Randolph near 14th, of the accidental discharge of a gun. (MORE ae 14, SLMD ae 10y 6d) 27 Dec.	MORE 28 Dec 1861 SLMD 31 "
TANNER, Edward shot by Thomas Reilly on or about 5 Aug.	MORE 16 Aug 1865
TANNER, Simon killed in a mill explosion 5 miles west of Knoxville. (RICON)	RANC 24 Jan 1861
TARRANTS, H.K., Co C 43rd MO Vols., killed at Glasgow.	GAL 17 Nov 1864
TARRANTS, Ophelia 11 Apr near Cheltenham ae 7y 10m. Int. Bellefontaine.	MORE 14 Apr 1863
TARUM, Elizabeth, "of laudanum and whiskey." Ae 15, married last Sep, died at her parents' home, alley betw 6-7-Carr-Biddle. Husband in the army, at Corinth. Supposedly, she overdosed.	MORE 28 Aug 1862
TATE, Mrs. Allen in Union Twp., Lewis Co., 27 Sep of cancer of the breast.	CANP 29 Sep 1864
TATUM, David son of the late David and Sophie 27 Oct at Pittmans Ferry ae 19y 9m.	MORE 7 Dec 1862
TAYLOR, Alexander L. in Beaver Co. PA 7 Jun in his 27th year. Funeral from the home of his parents, Clark betw 20-21.	MORE 12 Jun 1863
TAYLOR, Alex M., tribute by Clarence Lodge I.O.G.T. (Good Templars)	MORE 21 Nov 1861
TAYLOR, Ann Eliza wife of Levi 8 Aug at Locust-Ewing. Left 2 children.	MORE 9 Aug 1862
TAYLOR, Charles Hunt son of William C. and Mary L. 3 Aug of diphtheria ae 16.	MORE 7 Aug 1864
TAYLOR, Edward J. 14 Feb ae 25.	MORE 16 Fb 1863
TAYLOR, John "respectable and worthy citizen of Lincoln Co." about 3 miles west of New Hope, shot himself; had been ill. Left wife and children.	LAJ 30 May 1861
TAYLOR, Capt. John in Caledonia, Washington Co. 11 Jun in his 78th year. Native of VA, in War of 1812 and BlackHawk War; in Caledonia 20 years.	MORE 20 Jun 1862
TAYLOR, Joseph P. of congestive chills in his 21st year. Funeral from the home of his uncle, 266 Biddle. Interred Wesleyan.	MORE 31 Mar 1863
TAYLOR, Laura Belle daughter of J.F. and Mary 11 Oct ae 6y 1m 17d. CA pc	MORE 12 Oct 1864
TAYLOR, Mrs. Mary widow of Capt. George 3 Nov ae 54.	MORE 4 Nov 1863
TAYLOR, Peter show in Tuscumbia by ___ Morrison, Saturday last. (CAWN) (CAWN 29 Apr says Morrison was killed by militia)	SEDA 18 Feb 1865
TAYLOR, Rachel wife of George W. in Huntsville 29 Apr, of a long illness. Left 2 children, father, brother, sister.	RANC 2 May 1861
TAYLOR, Susan H. 31 Aug ae 17y 11m. Family home at Levee & Lewis.	SJH 1 Sep 1865
TAYLOR, Mrs. Susannah 24 Dec in her 65th year at the home of her daughter, Mrs. Ann Heely, 137 7th St. Manchester ENG pc	MORE 25 Dec 1863
TAYLOR, Theodore, ae 43, after a long illness. Native of VA, long time resident of St. Louis. Lived on Morgan near 22nd. Hannibal pc	MORE 14 Nov 1865
TAYLOR, William C. of Shaler's Command, captured in Marion Co. 13 Dec, in Gratiot Prison of chronic diarrhoea.	MORE 19 Apr 1863
TAYON, Marie Louise 2 Jun ae 72. Funeral from her daughter's home, Madison betw Broadway-9th.	MORE 4 Jun 1861
TEAHON, John T., native of Hamilton, Canada West, 19 Dec of typhoid ae 24. Funeral from the home of his uncle, M.J. Henley, 378 Morgan.	MORE 21 Dec 1862
TEASDALE, Mrs. Mary 4 Apr ae 61; of Kendall, Westmoreland Co. ENG. Funeral from the home of her son, 18th & Carr. Interred Bellefontaine.	MORE 5 Apr 1863
TEERNON, Mrs. Laura A. 19 Dec at the home of C. Stephens ae 31y 7m. Cincinnati & Louisville pc	MORE 22 Dec 1864
TEMME, Ernest, of 16th & Bremen, killed by a fall from a tree.	MORE 22 Sep 1863
TEMPLETON, Mrs. Susan 18 Feb of consumption. Left "a large family of daughters."	LAJ 20 Feb 1862
TERRIL, Elizabeth wife of John near Liberty 15 Aug ae ca 65.	LIT 19 Aug 1864
TERRY, Hannah L. wife of Lucius H. and daughter of Dr. Stephen W. Adreon of St. Louis 26 Jun ae 28y 9m. Baltimore & Hartford CT pc	SLMD 2 Jul 1861
THANNBERGER, Arthur only son of Louis and Eliza 2 Dec ae 24y 6m 2d, of nervous fever. Lived a #7 S. 2nd.	MORE 4 Dec 1864
THATCH, Henry, ae ca 10 or 11, run over by a street car while hitching rides. Only son of Thomas M., had been living with his grandmother. Funeral from the home of W. James on High St.	MORE 18 & 19 Jan 1861
THAYER, Ann Eliza wife of Capt. B, suicide by arsenic; had given a dose to her (cont.)	MORE 28 & 30 Apr 1861

THAYER, Ann Eliza, cont. -- 13-year-old daughter Delia, who survived. Died 26 Apr ae 33, lived at 201 Washington. Had married Thayer ca 5 yrs ago. Boonville pc	MORE 28 & 29 Apr 1861
THIXTON, Peter killed by guerillas in Moniteau Co. (CAWN)	MORE 24 Jul 1864
THOM, Rev. C.C., pastor of the Pine St. Presbyterian Church, 28 Nov ae 35. Philadelphia & Columbus OH pc	MORE 29 Nov 1865
THOMAS, ____, wife of a carpenter, died of smallpox, he also has it. (Story about neglect of quarantine.)	MORE 7 Jan 1865
THOMAS, Eugene Ryan son of George W. and Kate 20 Dec ae 3y 10m 6d. SE cor 16-Pine.	MORE 23 Dec 1862
THOMAS, Isabel wife of A.C. formerly of Columbia in Mexico 17 Feb in her 47th y.	COWS 3 Mar 1865
THOMAS, Jane Julia wife of B.F. in St. Louis Co. 12 Aug in her 38th year. Funeral from St. Xavier.	MORE 13 Aug 1862
THOMAS, James murdered on the train at Centralia by Anderson's men, en route home from Atlanta. (Old 25th MO Vols, now 1st MO Engineers.)	SJH 2 Oct 1864
THOMAS, Dr. John H. in St. Louis 23 Jul of bilious diarrhoea. Born 10 May 1830, of large and respected family. Buried Presbyterian Cem., Caledonia. Mason.	MORE 19 Aug 1863
THOMAS, John M. of Lincoln Co., Co F 2nd MO CSA, killed either at the battle of Champion Hills, Big Black Bridge, or the siege of Vicksburg.	MORE 19 Sep 1863
THOMAS, John W. "well known and worthy" near Fulton 6 Nov.	FULT 10 Nov 1865
THOMAS, Joseph fell overboard the Hillman (in the dock for repairs). Drunk, ae 23. Employed by Sectional Dock Co. Left young wife.	MORE 18 Oct 1863
THOMAS, Lillian H. daughter of George and Polly Ann 5 Dec ae 7.	JCPT 13 Dec 1865
THOMAS, Mary Viola daughter of John L. and Sarah E. at Hillsboro 28 Dec of diphtheria ae 5y 1m 16d.	MORE 6 Jan 1864
THOMAS, Melissa wife of Elijah A. of Scotland Co. near Mt. Sterling IA of apoplexy ae 45.	MORE 8 Jan 1861
THOMAS, Rubin G. 29 Jul at the home of his father Dr. M., in Iron Co., ae 13y 1m 22d.	MORE 25 Aug 1861
THOMAS, Thomas of Franklin Co. at the home of his brother-in-law in St. Louis 11 Nov ae 67.	MORE 18 Nov 1864
THOMASON, Margaret wife of William M. near Liberty 13 Mar in her 34th year.	LIT 18 Mar KCJC 19 Mar'64
THOMPSON, Amelia Nye wife of Macklot 6 Apr ae 22y 6m. Funeral from St. George's Church. New Bedford MA & Baltimore pc	MORE 8 Apr 1862
THOMPSON, Sgt. Claib murdered at Centralia by Anderson's bushwhackers en route home from Atlanta. (Old 25th MO Vols., now called 1st MO Engineers.)	SJH 2 Oct 1864
THOMPSON, Catherine wife of Nelson of Kansas City in Louisville KY 30 Mar ae 48.	KCJC 25 May 1864
THOMPSON, Eleanor M. wife of J.C. of Arrow Rock in St. Louis 28 Jan in her 35th year. Methodist. Washington DC pc	MORE 2 Feb 1865
THOMPSON, Elias 26 Feb 4 miles west of Canton. Born in VA 1 Feb 1791, to MO 1837.	CANP 2 Mar 1865
THOMPSON, Elizabeth relict of William and mother of Calvin 4 Feb ae 67. Born OH, to MO with her husband 20 or 30 years ago, among the first settlers on Bozier Prairie. Methodist.	CANP 9 Mar 1865
THOMPSON, Fanny Clement wife of J.M. of St. Louis at the home of her brother, William H. Clement, in Morrow (near Cincinnati), 23 Dec(?).	MORE 25 Dec 1864
THOMPSON, Col. J.P. in his 76th year. Funeral from home of Mrs. Beverly Allen, Bellefontaine Rd.	MORE 12 Dec 1862
THOMPSON, John formerly of Baltimore 16 Sep ae (65?)y 6m 28d. Lived 7th betw Park-Barry.	MORE 17 Sep 1864
THOMPSON, John Andrews son of A.B.M. and Rebecca 9 Feb ae 2y 3m 4d. Lived on 21st north of Clark. Interred Bellefontaine.	MORE 10 Feb 1861
THOMPSON, John E., 359 Broadway, 11 Mar ae 35. Pittsburgh pc	MORE 12 Mar 1865
THOMPSON, Dr. John W. in Huntsville Thursday of consumption, formerly of Callaway Co., in his 34th year. Brother of James B., editor of the Huntsville Citizen.	COWS 15 Dec 1865
THOMPSON, Dr. John Wardale 9 Feb at his home in DeSoto, of erysipelas, in his 49th y.	MORE 25 Feb 1865
THOMPSON, John William oldest son of Harrison S. of Mississippi Co. at Central College, Fayette, 9 Feb. Interred on family farm, Dog Tooth Bend.	CHAC 22 Feb 1861
THOMPSON, Joseph H., a merchant, killed in a mill explosion 5 miles west of Knoxville. (RICON) Mason, left wife and children.	RANC 24 Jan 1861 LIT 8 "

THOMPSON, Julia A. Hand wife of Hugh M. at Cape May Court House, NJ 17 Aug ae 42.	MORE 30 Aug 1864
THOMPSON, Miss Mary D. 30 Dec in Rockport, of diphtheria, at the home of F.M. Thompson. Ae 24y 3d.	SJH 9 Jan 1864
THOMPSON, Missouri wife of Dr., of St. Francois Co., 11 Feb. Left baby girl.	MORE 28 Feb 1865
THOMPSON, Notley W. son of Thomas E. found dead near the college at Palmyra. Apoplexy. Member Sons of Temperance.	HAM 26 Feb & 7 Mar 1861
THOMPSON, P.L. of 2nd MO Rebel Cav., arrested 23 Oct (in Greene's Command) died 16 Nov of pneumonia.	MORE 19 & 24 Nov 1862
THOMPSON, Robert C., son of the late R.C., at Vicksburg.	LIT 24 Jul 1863
THOMPSON, Theodore 3 Feb, chronic diarrhoea and pneumonia. (Undertakers' list)	MORE 8 Feb 1863
THOMPSON, William, President of William Jewell College, died 13 Apr in Sydney IA. Tribute from the General Assn. of Baptists of MO.	LIT 29 Sep 1865
THOMSON, Alexander at Memphis, late of Lawless & Thomson boilermakers.	MORE 6 Mar or 6 May 1864
THOMSON, Emma wife of Almon 9 Apr, 12th near Christy. Lingering illness.	MORE 10 & 13 Apr 1865
THOMSON, John, brother of Dr. H.B. Thomson of Saline Co., in Florence Italy in Dec 1859. (also see Janet Sharpe)	MORE 14 Feb 1861
THOMSON, Margaret Foote wife of William Holmes and eldest daughter of Thomas H. and Susan Ross Larkin 15 Apr ae 20y 10m 18d.	MORE 16 Apr 1863
THORNBURGH, Elizabeth S. wife of J.W. 4 Jan in her 41st year, at 177 Olive. Wheeling pc	MORE 5 Jan 1862
THORNTON, Anna wife of Charles H. of Memphis TN and daughter of Col. J.H. Howard of St. Joseph, 8 Jul. Funeral 6th St. Presbyterian, St. Joseph.	SJH 10 Jul 1864 MORE 13 "
THORNTON, Elizabeth Hammond wife of John 22 Nov ae 38y 7m, at 8th-Gratiot. Brooklyn NY pc	MORE 23 Nov 1864
THORP, Clara only daughter of the late George H. and Julia S., of burns, 29 Jan.	MORE 30 Jan 1863
THORP, Elder G.B. brother of Judge Joseph of Clay Co. at his home in Holt Co. after a short illness, ae ca 51.	LIT 21 Apr 1865
THORP, Molley M. daughter of Joseph and Nancy 27 Jun ae 15y 8m 6d, after a short illness.	LIT 3 Jul 1863
THORPE, Dr. Alonzo V. 15 Feb ae ca 35. Resident of California MO 9 years. Member IOOF. Husband, father.	CAWN 20 Feb & 5 Mar 1864
THORPE, George H. 6 Apr of lung congestion ae 38y 10m 6d.	MORE 20 Apr 1862
THORPE, James fell into the river at the foot of Mulberry St. and drowned. (Later spelled Thorp, "a youth," drowned in the Meramec?)	MORE 24 Jul & 4 Aug 1861
THORPE, Permelia J. daughter of Francis P. 6 Jul ae 18.	LEXUN 8 Jul 1865
THORPE, Thomas J. of Oregon Co. executed 1 May at Gratiot Prison, charged with being a guerilla, murdering Obediah Leavitt in Shannon Co. Born near Boonville 30 Sep 1835, enlisted in Confederate army Jul 1861, sent to Shannon Co., surrendered to Federals, sent home to Oregon Co, where his wife and 2 children live. (Wife's name Sarah.) Had 2 brothers and 4 sisters in MO, mother in TX. Catholic.	MORE 2 May 1865
THOROUGHMAN, John ae 74y 4m at the home of his son-in-law George W. Morrison, 3 miles west of Savannah, 18 Nov. Veteran War of 1812 and Black Hawk War.	SJH 28 Nov 1865
THRAILKILL, Juliann daughter of W.L. and Manerva J. in Laclede Co. 2 Nov ae 5y 10m.	MORE 11 Nov 1863
THRELKELD, Cynthia relict of John of Fleming Co. KY and mother of B.W. Alexander in Mexico MO 24 Nov in her 78th year.	MORE 27 Nov 1861
THROCKMORTON, William of Platte Co., a rebel, killed Friday by Maj. Pace's Command. Enrolled 3 years, probably home on furlough.	SJH 1 Nov 1864
THURMON, John T. 18 Oct at his home in Franklin Co. ae 59y 10m 25d. Born in Pulaski Co. KY.	MORE 1 Nov 1863
THURMOND, Oscar F. in Concord, Callaway Co. 17 May in his 28th year.	FULT 27 May 1864
THURSTON, William J. of Boone Co. 11 Oct ae 28.	COWS 18 Oct 1861
TIDWELL, A.F. private in Chalmers' Reg. in Gratiot Prison of chronic diarrhoea.	MORE 16 Aug 1863
TIEMAN, Mrs. ___ fell into a cistern and drowned; lived on Monroe betw 13-14. Was getting wash water when wall caved in. Husband an invalid, belonged to 5th MO Reserve Corps, missed her after a time and summoned help to look for her. She was about 30, left 3 children.	MORE 24 Dec 1862

TIEMEYER, William drowned while bathing in a pond near Franklin and Grand. One of   MORE 12 Jun 1864
    Col. Coff's men, ae 21, unmarried. Father on 18th betw Franklin-Wash.

TIFFANY, P. Dexter, suicide; cut his throat with a razor. Ae ca 45, had been   MORE 15 Feb 1861
    subject to insane fits. Wife (daughter of Matthew Carr) and
    2 children presently in NY.

TIGH, John "inebriate" fell dead in alley -- "heart disease from intemperate   MORE 18 Sep 1861
    habits." Ae 37, native of Tuam, Co. Galway IRE.

TILFORD, John W. 29 Sep in his 68th year at the home of his son-in-law, 178 Pine.   MORE 3 Oct 1863
    NY & Philadelphia pc

TILLARD, Mrs. Titus in Canton 26 Jan.   CANP 29 Jan 1863

TILLERY, Mildred Ann daughter of Noah and Mary E. 30 May in her 9th year.   LIT 5 Jun 1863

TILLERY, Woodson M. 13 Nov ae 21.   LIT 6 Dec 1861

TILLMAN, Charles 14 Jun in his 59th year, at Decatur & Park. Funeral St. Vincent's.   MORE 16 Jun 1865

TILLMAN, Moses T., 3rd MO, captured in Wright Co. 26 Jan, in Gratiot Prison   MORE 25 Feb 1863
    of pneumonia.

TILLSON, Charles H. of St. Louis 25 Nov ae 42, in St. Paul.   MORE 29 Nov 1865

TILSON) L.D. of Poindexter's Band, captured in Randolph Co. 4 Oct, in Gratiot Pr.   MORE 10 Dec 1862
TILLISON) S.D., of typhoid, 8 Dec. (Undertakers' list)   "   15   "

TIMMER, Lorrence in Texas Settlement 21 Jul of thoracic dropsy.   CHAC 24 Jul 1863

TIMMERMAN, Frederick F. 26 Oct ae 46. (This name had appeared as Zimmerman   MORE 28 Oct 1863
    Funeral 9th-Market.   in MORE 27 Oct)

TIMMS, Minnie daughter of J.H. and Patsy 10 Jul ae 16y 2m 27d. Born in   LIT 15 Jul 1864
    Wood Co. VA. Baptist.

TINCHER, Mary Mackenzie 30 Sep ae 21y 10d. Cincinnati & Memphis pc   MORE 3 Oct 1864

TINCHER, Dr. Cortes, late of Osceola (St. Clair Co. MO) in Lamar Co. TX about 1 Apr.   MORE 25 Aug 1863
    Formerly of Audrain Co. Died of scrofula, ae 26.

TINCHER, Mrs. Susan in Platte City 18 Mar ae 25.   WEST 24 Mar 1865

TINDALL, John A. 10th MO Cav CSA in Gratiot Prison of lung inflammation.   MORE 21 Jan 1864

TINSLEY, Thomas of Clay Co., near Smithville, shot near Union Mills in Buchanan Co.   SJH 5 Apr 1865
    Monday; regarded as a rebel sympathizer.

TISON, Hypolite at his farm near Manchester 27 Feb ae 51. New Orleans pc   MORE 2 Mar 1861
    (SLMD 5 Mar says ae 54, native of St. Louis Co.)

TOBIN, Alfred "old and worthy citizen" at Bloomington 7 Apr of consumption.   MAG 16 Apr 1862

TOBIN, Mary Alice daughter of Robert and Alice, 412 Morgan, of whooping cough.   MORE 9 Sep 1863
    Interred Rock Spring.
    Alice wife of Robert 18 Jun ae 28, at 412 Morgan.   MORE 19 Jun 1865

TOBIN, Miss Maria F. daughter of Francis and Mary 18 Jul at 82 Morgan.   MORE 19 &
    Funeral St. Xavier, interred Calvary.   21 Jul 1865

TOBIN, William, corner 11th and Market, 27 Aug ae 32. Interred Calvary.   MORE 28 Aug 1863

TOD, George M., native of Scotland and late resident of Kansas City, in   KCJC 20 Mar 1864
    Syracuse MO of apoplexy ae 56.

TODD, Charles M. in Marshall 14 May ae ca 65, native of KY; editor of the   COWS 29 May 1863
    Boonville Observer for many years.

TODD, Elizabeth Parr relict of Hon. David 2 Dec in her 76th year.   COWS 9 Dec 1864

TODD, George, "notorious bushwhacker," killed near Harrisonville.   LIT 17 Jul 1863
    (Later: "infamous guerilla," killed by Maj. Smith of 2nd Colorado,   "   4 Nov
    buried at Mrs. Burns' house in Independence. From KCJC)

TODD, George M. same as TOD, George M.   MORE 16 Mar 1864

TODD, Laura youngest daughter of Edmund and Eliza in New Harmony 11 Jul ae ca 2.   LAJ 25 Jul 1861

TODD, Sallie wife of Robert L. of (and in) Columbia 9 Jul, of sporadic cholera.   COWS 17 Jul 1863
    Born Lexington KY, daughter of Dr. Nathan Hall. Presbyterian. Ae 34.   MORE 12 & 22 "
    Married in 1850, 4 surviving children.
    Robert Levi youngest child of R.L. and Sallie Hall, b 2 Nov 1860, died 17 Mar.   COWS 21 Mar 1862

TODD, Sarah Douglass, corner Market and Targee, ae 77. Interred Bellefontaine.   MORE 19 May 1865

TOGNOLA, Pietro, 105 S. Main, 12 May ae 34 of consumption. Born in Italy.   MORE 13 May 1865

TOLIN, Porterfield son of Washington and Harriet 7 Jul in Buchanan Co. ae 19y 8m 29.   SJH 9 Jul 1865

TOLIN, John Potterfield son of Hugh and Mary Jane 24 Oct ae 10y 7m 14d. — SJH 26 Oct 1865

TOLSON, Rebecca wife of John in Howard Co. 6 Sep. — COWS 17 Oct 1862

TOLSON, Sallie wife of B.F. in Howard Co., 4 miles east of Fayette, 11 Sep ae 30y 3m 14d. And her infant Sallie on 4 Oct. — COWS 9 Oct 1863 " 16 "

TOMLINSON, James Henry yesterday at Sisters Hospital ae 27. Lived on 14th St. near the Pacific RR. — MORE 2 Dec 1863

TOMLINSON, Mrs. Jane in her 57th year. Funeral from the home of her daughter, Mrs. Mary Weaver, 14th-Wash. — MORE 16 Jul 1865

TOMPKINS, Mary W. wife of Dr. J. and daughter of F.W. and Caroline Cleveay in Canton 1 Nov ae 29y 9m 11d. Maysville KY pc — CANP 2 Nov 1865

TONEY, Joab Sr. 29 Aug ae 68, "sudden and painful illness." Lived in Toney's Addition. Interred Bellefontaine. — MORE 31 Aug 1862

TONG, Hirman N., formerly of Ironton, 5 Jan of chronic diarrhoea ae 47. — MORE 7 Jan 1865

TONGE, Richard, Friday of consumption ae 39y 5m 28d. Funeral from St. John's. Washington DC pc — MORE 16 Nov 1862

TOOKE, Mary wife of James H. in her 22nd year. "Mother." — MORE 7 Feb 1865

TOOLY, John W. near St. Louis 7 Aug ae 48. "Commenced life as a poor boy, and came west." Catholic last rites. Louisville pc — MORE 8, 9, & 11 Aug 1863

TOPHOFF, Mons., long-time ballet manager at the Varieties Theatre, Thursday of inflammation of the bowels. — MORE 29 Sep 1865

TOTTEN, Mrs. Rachel wife of the late Samuel of Smith Co. VA near Crittenden, Daviess Co., 28 Jul in her 98th year. IN pc — GAL 7 Sep 1865

TOWER, Rufus Chapin only child of R.E. and U.J. 3 Jul of dysentery. — MORE 7 Jul 1864

TOWERS, Mrs. Ann B. 24 Nov in her 65th year at the home of her son-in-law, 691 Morgan. Interred Wesleyan. — MORE 26 Nov 1863

TOWNSEND, Euratus at his home in Carondelet Friday in his 45th year. (SLMD same date says he died Tuesday, gives middle initial M.) — MORE 13 Aug 1864

TOY, John C. fell from a train between Washington and Hermann MO; body returned to St. Louis. "Son, brother" ae 24y 4m. (Name originally given as Foy.) — MORE 30 Nov 1 & 6 Dec 1863

TRACY, Charles W. "one of the most promising young men in Randolph Co." 30 Aug in Huntsville ae 20y 7m 24d. — COWS 9 Sep 1864

TRACY, Capt. Edward H., clerk of the Land Court, thrown from a yacht, drowned. Lived on Pine betw 15-16, ae ca 35, left wife and 6 children. — MORE 21 Jun 1861

TRACY, Edward J. son of Charles F. and Sophia, ae 18. — MORE 2 Jul 1861

TRACY, Keren, Irish, killed when Col. Kallman's Regiment fired on civilians. Lived on Gay betw 15-16. — MORE 18 Jun 1861

TRACY, Marietta daughter of Lewis at the home of J.M. Tracy in Elmwood KS 1 Jan of diphtheria in her 17th year. Interred Mt. Mora Cemetery, St. Joe. Harry son of John M. near Elmwood KS of diphtheria ae 3y 2m. — SJRL 5 Jan 1861 " 19 "

TRACY, Thomas son of B.N. and F.J. in Huntsville 28 Mar of pneumonia ae ca 15. — COWS 7 Apr 1865

TRAINER, Philip 29 Apr at Sisters Hospital ae 35. — MORE 30 Apr 1865

TRENCHAN, Louis a Frenchman, living at the foot of O'Fallon, yesterday of sunstroke "a steady, industrious man." Left wife, 5 children. — MORE 2 Sep 1863

TRENHOWER, William, residence unknown, killed in the Camp Jackson affair. — MORE 14 May 1861

TREVILLA, Thomas Wilkins 13 Nov at the home of his mother on 6th St. Born in Kent Co. MD 24 Nov 1833, lived there till ae 17. Left mother, sister. Interred "burial ground near Squire Cassell's." — SJH 14 Nov 1863

TRIBBLE, ____ small daughter of John and Lucretia of Platte City drowned in a 125-foot well. — SJH 28 Nov 1863

TRIBLY, George, suicide: tied bricks to himself and jumped into the river. Left son about 16. "Addicted to hard drink." — MORE 10 Dec 1862

TRIMBLE, Margaret widow of John at the home of her daughter Mrs. Trewitt near Millersburg 24 Feb ae 72. Member of the Christian Church. — FULT 29 Mar 1861

TRIP, Dr. Talman of Greenton Valley killed near Independence by 4 men. — LEXUN 8 Oct 1864

TRIPLETT, Capt. John M. in Manchester, St. Louis Co. 29 Oct at the home of Col. Stevenson, ae ca 35. Recently returned from Montana. Maysville KY pc — MORE 31 Oct & 1 Nov 1865

TRIPLETT, Mrs. Leonard; dress caught in a machine at Hanley & Metcalf's Mill. Ae ca 24, left a child about 8 months old.	PALS 2 Sep 1864
TRORLICHT, Mrs. Maria A. 28 Oct ae 27, at 185 N. 6th. Cincinnati pc	MORE 30 Oct 1865
TROTTER, Caroline M. youngest daughter of George W. and Nancy in Canton Twp. 2 Feb of inflammation of the spine, ae 8y 6m 24d.	CANP 11 Feb 1864
TROUP, Mary Alice daughter of Robert and Lucy Jane, Monroe Co., ae 4y 1m 4d.	MORE 22 Mar 1864
TROUT, Gustavus ae 19 murdered by a gang in St. Charles Co.	MORE 11 Sep 1864
TROWER, George shot at Ashley, Pike Co., after a guerilla raid; they had told him they were from his brother's company.	MORE 6 Sep 1862
TRUETT, K.J. in Hannibal 11 Mar ae 28.	HAM 13 Mar 1862
TUCKER, Frank arrested last week and tried in Perryville, proved dishonest and dangerous, was turned over to US troops, who shot him (with __ Winsett).	PERU 24 Jun 1864
TUCKER, Harriet Ann daughter of Benjamin H.H. and Martha Ann in Lewis Co. 14 Feb of scarlet fever ae 4y 11m 6d.	HAM 27 Mar 1862
TUCKER, James, Gratiot betw 9-10, Friday morning ae 40.	MORE 8 Feb 1862
TUCKER, Obediah stabbed by William A. Johnson at a sale at the home of the late James Cornelius, Johnson Twp., Scotland Co. Tucker's son had assailed Johnson; they were all from Clark Co.	CANP 30 Jul 1863
TUCKER, William Robert 11 Feb at his father's home, 32 Biddle, ae 20y 2m.	MORE 12 Feb 1863
TUCKER, family of Wm., his father, in Boston 22 Feb ae 73. Charles L. Charles Wm., his son, drowned 13 Jun 1861, ae 10.	MORE 27 Feb 1862
TUCKER, Zerelda wife of Benjamin and daughter of Levi Bennett of Boone Co. 23 May in Cooper Co. ae 26y 17d.	COWS 19 Jun 1863
TUEMLER, Charles Ferdinand eldest son of Charles F. and Sarah S. 4 Nov of brain congestion ae 5y 24d.	MORE 5 Nov 1861
TULL, John at Carrollton MO 27 Jul in his 80th year. Native of Delaware, early to KY, to MO 1835. Left large family. Member of the Christian Church.	MORE 3 Sep 1862
TULLY, Catherine Presly consort of Dr. D.O. at Lexington 24 Sep. Left husband and children.	MORE 18 Oct 1863
TUNIS, Miss Mattie Ann 25 Dec at the home of her mother, N. Tunis, 2nd St. betw Mullanphy and Florida, of consumption ae 22y 2m 25d.	MORE 27 Dec 1863
TUNNELL, John B. son of Southey W. and Zerilda E., 2 miles from Weston, ae 9y 4m 13d. New Albany IN, Shawneetown & Springfield IL pc	WEST 2 Apr 1864
TUNSTALL, Lieut. Thomas F. 12 Dec at Meridian MS, in Confederate service. Typhoid pneumonia. Louisville & Cincinnati pc	MORE 14 Jan 1864
TUPPER, L.B., M.D., native of Baltimore, several years a practicing physician in St. Louis, 27 May at 593 Broadway.	MORE 28 May 1865
TURNBULL, Carro Virginia Chopion at the home of her parents, 73 N. 5th St., 22 Dec ae 16y 6m 13d. NY, Philadelphia, southern states pc	MORE 23 Dec 1864
TURNBULL, Mrs. Nancy, inquest; died suddenly in Carondelet of lung congestion.	MORE 2 Mar 1864
TURNER, Charles Edward only son of Capt. William and Eliza J. 3 Oct when he was thrown from a buggy. Father's residence, 12th betw Morgan-Christy. Ae 25.	MORE 5 Oct 1861
Eliza Jane wife of William of St. Louis in Fayette Co. KY ae (60?). Funeral from Christian Church. Interred Bellefontaine.	MORE 24 Feb 1865
TURNER, Elizabeth 23 Feb at her home in Carondelet.	MORE 25 Feb 1865
TURNER, Gabriel, citizen of Columbia, taken from Mexico MO jail to the train for Macon, shot trying to escape, died the next day.	MORE 14 Oct 1864 COWS 21 "
TURNER, George W., native of Calhoun Co. IL, in St. Louis 25 Dec ae 27.	MORE 28 Dec 1861
TURNER, Henry fatally shot by Joel Morris, both of Rocheport, in a dispute over a note Morris' father-in-law had held against Turner. (The father-in-law had died "sometime since.")	COWS 4 Dec 1863
TURNER, J.P., prisoner of war, 1 Feb of variola confluens. (Undertaker's list)	MORE 15 Feb 1863
TURNER, James at Sisters Hospital. Member of the Iron Moulders International Union.	MORE 22 Nov 1863
TURNER, John 14 Dec of typhoid ae 64y 4m 2d. Funeral 1st Colored Baptist Church.	MORE 18 Dec 1864
TURNER, John shot trying to escape; was supposed murderer of Maj. Wilson, and was arrested near his home in Taos (Buchanan Co.).(St. Joseph News 29 May)	MORE 1 Jun 1864

TURNER, Neomi Jefferson wife of Gerrard R. near Fayette 17 Apr ae 39y 1m 16d.	COWS 8 May 1863
TURNER, Rebecca F. wife of James H. 23 Aug ae 23y 10d. Funeral from the home of her father, Capt. Patterson, 124 Pine.	MORE 24 Aug 1861
TURNER, Samuel D. formerly of St. Louis at Sacramento City CA 7 Sep ae 69. Salem MA & NJ pc	MORE 18 Oct 1863
TURNER, Willie Lee son of James H. and Sallie C. 8 Mar ae 2y 11m 4d.	COWS 20 Mar 1863
TURNEY, Capt. J.W. of Clinton Co. "fell in a skirmish near Plattsburg." Left parents, brothers and sisters.	SJH 28 Jul 1864
TURNHAM, Henry C. son of Henry C. and Louisa 5 Dec ae 5y 6m 27d.	LIT 22 Dec 1865
TURNHAM, Joel, late of Clay Co., in Milan TX about July 1862, ae ca 79.	MORE 14 Jun 1863
TURPIN, Capt. Charles M. of the Confederate Army in Hartsville MO 8 Jan ae 24. Formerly of Bedford Co. VA, resident of MO several years.	MORE 4 Apr 1863
TUTT, Davis killed on the street "week before last." William Haycock tried but found not guilty.	SPRIP 10 Aug 1865
TUTT, Felix W. at Versailles 10 Feb ae 33.	MORE 15 Feb 1865
TUTT, James A. at Calhoun, Henry Co. 5 Dec ae 42y 4m 20d, of consumption. Left wife and daughter. "Distinguished citizen," member of the Legislature in 1860. Richmond VA pc. (SJH 18 Dec says he was a native of VA)	MORE 11 Dec 1863
Margaret Ellen youngest daughter of James A. and Martha E. of Calhoun, Henry Co. (27 Aug?) ae 11y ?m 2d. Louisville & Richmond VA pc	MORE 2 Sep 1862
TUTT, Mrs. Sallie Rollins 19 Aug ae 26 at Cleveland, OH, wife of Thomas E. of St. Louis; daughter and last surviving member of the family of the late Dr. James H. Bennett of Columbia, MO. "Wife and sister."	MORE 26 Aug 1864
TUTTLE, Annie only child of W.P. and Nannie in Boone Co., at Providence, ae 2y 2m.	COWS 10 Oct 1862
TYLER, ___ accidentally shot himself while hunting on Contrary Lake Monday, left wife and 1 child.	SJH 11 Nov 1865
TYLER, James, funeral notice: from the home, 2nd St. north of Michael. "Shot by a soldier while quietly walking." Left a large family.	SJH 21 Dec 1864
TYLER, James M. 8 Sep ae 43. Funeral from Sisters Hospital. Interred Bellefontaine. Cincinnati pc	MORE 9 Sep 1863
TYRE, James of Osage Co. killed by ___ Mitchell, a constable. Tyre was "old and highly esteemed." Some complaint had been lodged against him by some Irishmen; the constable had gone to his home, and a fracas ensued.	ROLEX 11 Mar 1861
TYREE, Benjamin of Forrest's Command, captured in Lawrence Co. 10 Jan, in Gratiot Prison of pneumonia.	MORE 21 Feb 1863
UBSDELL, John A. Sr. of St. Louis at Southampton ENG 2 Jan in his 64th year; of the firm of Ubsdell, Barr, Duncan & Co.	MORE 26 Jan 1865
ULLERY, Dodrid H., youngest son of Samuel and Levina E., 22 May ae 5y 4m. Samuel 28 May of varioloid ae 58. Dayton pc	MORE 3 Jun 1864 "
ULRICI, Bertha Estelle only child of Richard W. and Estelle Paul 6 Jul of diphtheria ae 4y 10m 21d. The family had lost an infant shortly before.	MORE 7 Jul 1864
ULRICI, Georgetta Jacqueline wife of Rudolph and daughter of the late Peter Ham of Winchester VA, suddenly of heart disease 26 Apr in her 35th year -- later 34y 33d. Interred Bellefontaine.	MORE 28 & 29 Apr 1864
ULRICI, Reinhard 2 Sep in his 40th year of congestion of the liver. Lived at 2nd Carondelet-Park. Interred Calvary.	MORE 3 Sep 1864
UNDERHILL, Mary H. wife of Edward 24 Dec ae 49, at 70 S. 5th. "Interred in the east." NY pc	MORE 27 Dec 1861
UNDERWOOD, J.W., a Confederate soldier from St. Louis, at Port Gibson.	MORE 28 May 1863
UNDERWOOD, John, Brooklyn near 12th St., killed in the Camp Jackson affair.	MORE 18 May 1861
UNDERWOOD, Kate wife of Robert G. and niece of Austin Piggett 13 Oct ae 30. Funeral from the Cathedral, interred Calvary.	MORE 14 Oct 1861
UPDIKE, Maggie wife of G.W. 4 Jun ae 25y 2m. Interred Peoria. "Daughter, sister."	MORE 5 Jun 1865
UPTON, James 1 Nov in Gratiot Prison of pneumonia.	MORE 9 Nov 1862
URQUHART, Fanny Foster daughter of George and Margaret 17 May ae 2y 9m 25d, of diphtheria. NY pc	MORE 20 May 1862
UTZ, James M., native of St. Louis Co. near Bridgeton, hanged at Gratiot Prison as a spy.	MORE 28 Dec 1864

UZZLE, Bennett at his home in Audrain Co. 12 Jan ae (65?)y 5m 6d.   SJH 13 Jan 1864

VALANDINGHAM, James living near Columbia 21 Mar in his 70th year. Native of   COWS 3 Apr 1863
    Bourbon Co. KY, had lived 37 years in Boone Co. on the farm where
    he died.

VALENTINE, Peyton S., one of the oldest citizens of Clay Co., 5 Jan in his
                                                          (80th?) year.   LIT 13 Jan 1865

VALLANDINGHAM, W.M., citizen of Boone Co., 7 Jan of brain inflammation.
                                                    (Undertakers' list)   MORE 15 Jan 1865

VALLANDINGHAM, Amanda in Boone Co. 2 Jan of scarlet fever ae ca 17.   COWS 8 Jan 1864

VANAUSDAL, Cornelius 22 May in his 69th year. Born in Greenbriar Co. VA 10 Mar 1793. COWS 13 Jun 1862
    Veteran War of 1812. To MO 1828, in St. Louis Co. until 1851, then   MORE 15 "
    removed to Boone Co.

VANCE, Emily consort of C.C. in DeKalb Co. 30 Jan in her 27th year.   LIT 21 Feb 1862

VANCE, Mary Jane consort of N.M. and daughter of William and Peace Hughes, in   MORE 11 Jun 1862
    Plattsburg 18 May. Born in Nicholas Co. KY 12 Mar 1821; to MO 1830;
    married 26 Apr 1840; joined the Methodist Church South in 1845.
    Survived by 4 children, predeceased by 3 others.

VANDENBURGH, Samuel, carpenter on the Welcome, suddenly Saturday of inflammation   MORE 19 Jul 1864
    of the lungs. Married, lived in Florissant, ae 35.

VANDERBURG, Mrs. ____ ae ca 60, corner of 7th and Chestnut, suddenly while   MORE 19 Sep 1863
    returning from market. (May be PANDERBURGT, which see.)

VANDERSPLICE, Andrew, doorkeeper of the pit at the St. Louis Theatre, knocked   MORE 20 Jun &
VANDERSLICE   overboard from the ferry (he was watching a fight) by John   3 Jul 1865
    Trendley. Left wife and 2 children, 2nd betw Florissant-Mullanphy.
    Body recovered 2 Jul. Interred Bellefontaine.

VAN DEVENTER, Peter E. (?) at New Brunswick NJ 14 Feb ae 47, many years a resident   MORE 15 Feb 1863
    of St. Louis.

VANDUSEN, John 9 Jul ae 48 (or 43), 12th St. betw Cass-O'Fallon.   MORE 10 Jul 1863

VAN HORN, Martha wife of Ishmael near Columbia 3 Mar in her 36th year.   COWS 7 Mar 1862
    (later: in her 36th year.)   "   5 Jun "

        William A. son of Ishmael, 22 Sep.   COWS 2 Oct 1863

VAN HORNE, Ishmael, "old and highly respected" in Boone Co. 4 Dec ae 63.   COWS 8 Dec 1865

VAN HOY, Col. John M. in Georgetown MO 29 Mar of a lingering illness (typhus).   MORE 6 Apr 1862
    In his 56th year. Born in Forsyth Co. NC, to Henry Co. MO in 1840.
    Left wife and 12 children.

VAN LANDINGHAM, James in Boone Co. 30 Aug ae 39.   COWS 1 Sep 1865

VAN LANDINGHAM, Mathenis J. 18 Oct of typhoid ae ca 47.   COWS 20 Oct 1865

VAN LEUVEN, Fanny A.D. wife of John 2 Jul ae 61y 3m, in Tarkio Twp., Atchison Co.   HOLS 21 Jul 1865

VANNOY, Mrs. N. on Sunday last.   CAWN 9 Feb 1861

VAN NUISE, Eliza daughter of James and Emily 11 Nov of consumption ae 20y 7m,   MORE 21 Nov 1864
    at 96 Myrtle.

VAN RENSSELAER, Philip late of Albany NY 8 May ae 64. Funeral from the home of   MORE 9 May 1862
    his son-in-law S.H. Gardner, 40 S. 16th.

VAN WAGONER, Ella Cohen daughter of G.S. and Adeline H. 18 Mar ae 4y 1m 6d, at   MORE 19 Mar 1863
    21 N. 8th.

VARBLE, Jacob 23 Feb ae ca 32.   LIT 7 Mar 1862

VARRELL, Sarah daughter of Solomon and Amanda 25 Apr of congestion of the brain   MORE 26 Apr 1862
    ae 4y 10d.

VASQUES, Joseph (Bernard betw Pratte-Emily) 17 Aug in his 32d year.   MORE 19 Aug 1865

VAUGHAN, Tillman, an old citizen, Wednesday night last.   FULT 1 Apr 1864

VAUGHN, Capt. George of Osceola, St. Clair Co., at Stockton 12 Jul ae 24y 6m.   MORE 7 Sep 1863
    Washington DC pc

VAUGHN, Mrs. Laura L., late of Pike Co. MO, at Woodlawn, Ballard Co. KY 9 Jul.   MORE 10 Aug 1863
    Born in Pike Co., married first to the late Peter Carr. Wrote poems, some
    of which had been published in MORE.

VAUGHN, Mrs. Nancy J., citizen of Jackson Co., 17 Mar of brain congestion.   MORE 19 Mar 1865
                                            (Undertakers' list)

VAUGHN, Wesley son of John and Ruth at Shelley's Ridge 8 Jul, of brain congestion, ae 18.   CHAC 25 Jul 1862

VAULT, Daniel 2nd MO Cav in the Prison Hospital. (Rebel Cavalry)   MORE 24 Apr 1863

VEALL, George hanged near Keytesville. (Brunswicker 18 Jun)   MORE 24 Jun 1864

VEDDER, Henry H., a Federal soldier living with J.H. Gladden, shot his wife Nancy and himself. Left children, Rosa Jane and Alonso.   FULT 27 May 1864

VENABLE, James, a citizen, died as a result of a guerilla raid at Elmore's Store, in Ashley (Pike Co.).   MORE 6 Sep 1862

VERMILION, Matilda wife of R.L. 27 May ae ca 19.   LIT 31 May 1861

VERMILLION, William a rebel soldier from Monroe Co. accidentally shot himself at the home of Henry Graves, Ralls Co., Saturday evening.   HAM 29 Aug 1861

VEST, Taylor, citizen of Randolph Co., 17? Jan of typhoid pneumonia. (Undertakers' list)   MORE 22 Jan 1865

VESTAL, David, a bushwhacker, killed between Arnoldsville and Agency Ford, Buchanan Co.   SJH 9 Jul 1863

VIA, Margaret wife of Pleasant V. in Boone Co. 29 Mar in her 77th year.   COWS 1 Apr 1864

VINEYARD, John T. at his home in Tipton Tuesday last, "highly respected." Left wife Louisa, no children mentioned.   CAWN 19 & 26 Jan 1861

VINEYARD, "Uncle Billy" an old man living in Bellevue Twp., Washington Co., "shot and mortally wounded."   MORE 13 Aug 1861

VINTON, Emily Virginia daughter of Col. Sam S. and Camilla Frances 12 Dec when her clothing caught fire. Ae 4y 2m 27d.   SPRIP 28 Dec 1865

VITALIS, Dr. Louis of apoplexy 15 Aug ae 75. Lived on Chouteau betw 12-13. Father-in-law of Socrates Newmark.   MORE 17 Aug 1861

VOEPEL, Daniel ae 25 on 20 Oct. Funeral from the home of his father, N., Franklin betw 21-22.   MORE 21 Oct 1865

VOGEL, John G., 7th & Barry, of consumption ae 26. Interred Picot's Cemetery.   MORE 29 Jan 1861

VOGT, Linna "an interesting little girl ae 4" drowned in a pond at 15th-Cass.   MORE 15 Aug 1861

VOLKNER, John ae 17, "a drunkard, son of a drunken mother," drank a half-gallon of whiskey and expired.   MORE 17 Oct 1861

VONDERBEIT, Jacob, a drayman, working in the vault of Koch, Chow & Co., killed when the sidewalk above (the vault extended below it) caved in on him. His wife and 3 children survive, near Willow Grove House, lower part of city.   SJH 13 Jun 1865

VOULLAIRE, Mrs. Letitia 22 May ae 48y ?m 20d. Funeral from the home of her son-in-law Alfred Peterson, on Clark betw 22-23.   MORE 23 May 1863

WADE, Mrs. Ann formerly of Philadelphia but a resident of St. Louis 26 years, on 11 Jun. Funeral from home of her son-in-law Charles Hodgman, 232 Pine.   MORE 12 Jul 1862

WADE, Bartley, deckhand on the Lebanon, drowned en route from Cincinnati. He was bringing his children, 2 girls and a boy, to live with their uncle in St. Louis, Thomas Bartley.   MORE 6 Jun 1862

WADE, Joab 19 Aug ae 29.   LIT 28 Aug 1863

WADE, John M. of Ralls Co. shot at Palmyra by Gen. Merrill in retaliation for the abduction and murder of an old man named Allmstedt at the time of Porter's Raid into Palmyra. Others also shot. (Palmyra Courier)   CAWN 1 Nov 1862

WADE, Mary Hodgman eldest daughter of Jane and the late William near Jacksonville IL 16 Jan as 4y 1m. Funeral from the home of Charles Hodgman, 232 Pine. Interred Bellefontaine. (Family had lost a younger child few weeks before.)   MORE 20 Jan 1864

WADE, Laura Bell 11 Jun of liver disease ae 15y 4m, daughter of Mrs. Jane Parris of St. Louis Co.   MORE 14 Jun 1863

WADE, Col. William, many years a resident of St. Louis, native of MD, in the bombardment at Grand Gulf MS 29 Apr. (A Confederate soldier.)   MORE 28 & 31 May 1863

WADMORE, David B. at his home in Clark Co. 4 Aug ae 49.   CANP 6 Aug 1863

WAGES, Shad R. 1 May in his 49th year, "old, well-known citizen." Presbyterian.   SJH 2 May 1865

WAGNER, Emma daughter of Wendel and the late Mary, 141 N. 3rd St., ae 2y 11m, on 4 Apr. Interred Bellefontaine.   MORE 6 Apr 1861

WAGNER, Philip, inquest: a carpenter living on Clark Ave., died of sunstroke. Left wife and 5 children.   MORE 1 Jul 1864

WAINWRIGHT, Adella wife of G.W. 8 Aug ae 19y 6m 7d, at 9th-Marion.   MORE 9 Aug 1861

WALDEN, Robert M., arrested in Barry Co. 5 Oct, of Hunter's Rebel Regiment; died   MORE 10 Nov 1863
        in the prison hospital of laudanum poisoning.

WALDOCKER, Jacob, a mattress-maker, "from the effects of heat and whiskey."   MORE 5 Aug 1861

WALKER, ___ a well-known citizen of Ray Co. killed at Richmond by James Green -   SJH 9 Aug 1864
        "a private grudge."

WALKER, Orderly Sgt. Albert G. of Co. H 43rd MO Vols, killed at Glasgow.   GAL 17 Nov 1864

WALKER, Andrew, inquest: ae ca 40, intoxicated, fell into the sewer at the foot of   MORE 17 Mar 1864
        Carroll St. where it flows into the river and drowned in a puddle -- may
        have struck his head. Left a wife.

WALKER, ___ hanged in Chariton Co. by Trueman, serving under Rosecrans.   MORE 10 Jan 1865

WALKER, Anthony H. only child of H.R. in Cooper Co. 11 Sep, left young wife and   COWS 13 Oct 1865
        infant boy, aged grandmother and father. Son-in-law of Emily Branham   MORE 24 Sep "
        of Columbia. Interred at Pleasant Green with his mother and sister.

WALKER, Eliza H. consort of John of Howard Co. 23 Apr, only daughter of Gerrard   MORE 3 May 1864
        / (see Mrs. John, below)   and Ann Robinson.

WALKER, James B. 3 Oct ae 64 at the home of his son-in-law R.R. Stone, Richmond KY.   COWS 25 Oct 1861

WALKER, Jane wife of C.P. and youngest daughter of John and Sarah McMinn of   ROLEX 10 May 1862
        Maries Co. in Rolla 28 Apr ae 22. (also see Isabella BUCK)

WALKER, Miss Jane daughter of the late Nathaniel and Margaret of Saline Co.   MORE 19 Feb 1865
        17 Feb of pneumonia.

WALKER, John 10 April at Jefferson Barracks in his 29th year. Lingering illness.   MORE 12 Apr 1864

WALKER, Mrs. John -- same as Eliza, above, but adds that her parents, now   SJH 17 May 1864
        nearly 80, survived 12 children.

WALKER, Dr. Joseph a wealthy citizen of Platte Co. killed Sunday near his home at   SJH 31 Aug 1864
        Platte City. A southern sympathizer, had been banished to Chicago but
        returned. Many years a surgeon in the U.S. Army. Son mentioned.

WALKER, Mrs. Mary wife of the late Benjamin, paymaster U.S. Army, 10 Mar. Funeral   MORE 11 Mar 1864
        from Presbyterian Church 11-Pine, interred Jefferson Barracks.

WALKER, Mary Jane only daughter of George A. of Woodbridge CA in St. Louis 16 May   MORE 17 May 1865
        at the home of S.S. Boyce, ae 8y 8m 10d. Interred Farmington.

WALKER, Neal 25 Aug in his 69th year, resident of St. Louis (43? 48?) years.   MORE 26 Aug 1862
        Funeral from his home, Bremen-16th, to Presbyterian Cemetery. Vandalia IL pc

WALKER, Samuel in Moniteau Co. 16 Jun ae 75y 7m 16d.   CALM 22 Jul 1865

WALKER, Warren at his home near Wentzville 17 Feb ae 68y and a few weeks.   MORE 6 Mar 1863

WALLACE, Minnie daughter of W.A. and F.J. in Howard Co. 28 Dec of congestion of   COWS 10 Jan 1862
        the brain, ae 3y 9½m.

WALLACE, Loren C. wife of William and daughter of Mrs. Mary Sedgwick 10 Feb in   MORE 11 Feb 1863
        her 23rd year at their home, corner 9th-Spring.

WALLACE, Sophia wife of H.L. of St. Louis last Tuesday of pulmonary disease.   COWS 5 Sep 1862

WALLACE, William G. citizen of Carroll Co. 26 Apr of typhoid. (Undertakers' list)   MORE 1 May 1865

WALLAN, Mrs. Celeste wife of William in her 39th year, after a lingering illness.   MORE 23 Jul 1865

WALSH, Andrew 10 Jul ae 27, on 2nd St. betw Mound-Howard.   MORE 11 Jul 1863

WALSH, Mrs. Ellen ae 52y at the home of her son-in-law Matthew Brady. Had lived   MORE 2 Dec 1863
        at 443 N. Main. Native of the Parish of Mullinavat, Co. Kilkenny IRE.

WALSH, James 4 Dec in his 56th year at 13th-Poplar. Interred Bellefontaine.   MORE 5 Dec 1861
        Baltimore & Louisville pc

WALSH, John, a soldier coming from Vicksburg and thought to have relatives in   MORE 20 Jul 1863
        St. Louis, fell from the Minnehaha and drowned.

WALSH, Laura Busby consort of Martin F. 22 Jan. Funeral from Clark betw 21-22.   MORE 24 Jan 1865

WALSH, Margaret relict of Patrick 24 May in her 74th year. Funeral from the home   MORE 26 May 1863
        of her son Edmund P., Clark betw 22-23, to the Cathedral, int. Calvary.

WALSH, Peter W. 21 Jan in his 62nd year. Funeral from the Cathedral.   MORE 22 Jan 1861

WALSH, Richard 7 Sep ae 49 at his home, 8th betw Biddle-O'Fallon. Interred Calvary.   SLMD 8 Sep 1864
        St. Paul pc (MORE, same date, shows age as 40.)

WALSH, Thomas brother of Rev. William of St. Louis in Dubuque 9 Mar ae 38. Funeral   MORE 12 Mar 1865
        St. Bridget's, interred Calvary.

WALSH, William 12 Feb ae 72. Funeral from St. Michael's Church.	MORE 14 Feb 1862
WALSH, Sgt. William of Co. F, 5th Reg Mo Vols CSA, killed at Corinth MS; he had written poetry published in local papers signed Wilhelm. (Slurring remark about Gen. Van Dorn's leadership included.)	MORE 1 Feb 1863
WALTER, Annie, inquest: found dead in a house on Waddingham Alley betw Cherry, Carr, Main, 2nd, age ca 30. Lung congestion, exposure, and want.	MORE 1 Feb 1863
WALTER, William sentenced to be hanged 31 Oct for the murder of a soldier at the new House of Refuge Hospital January last.	MORE 19 Sep 1862
WALTMAN, Bruno, a German ae ca 47, killed in a fall downstairs at 71 S. 7th.	MORE 29 Jul 1862
WALTMAN, James son of A.C. of LaGrange drowned in the Mississippi Tuesday last ae 11.	PALS 29 May 1863
John ae ca 14 blown into the river by the concussion of an explosion at J. H. Talbot's Pork House. (CANP) (Same boy?)	PALS 6 Jun 1863
WALTON, Ann widow of Joseph 30 Oct in her 81st year.	MORE 3 Nov 1862
WALTON, Isabella consort of the late James in Central Twp. ae 73. Interred Fee Fee.	MORE 28 Jul 1864
WALTON, Rebecca widow of Judge, living on St. Charles Rock Road, 21 Jun ae 76.	MORE 23 Jun 1863
WALTON, Tom B. son of George and Mary Ann 2 Feb ae 12; fell from a railroad car. Cincinnati & Louisville pc	MORE 4 Feb 1862
WALTZ, Henry 3 Mar in his 55th year, at 5th-Spruce.	MORE 4 Mar 1863
WARD, Amy wife of Joab at their home near Ridgeville, Randolph Co. 27 Aug ae 67. Resident of the county nearly 45 years, married nearly 51 years.	SLMD 6 Sep 1864
WARD, James severely beaten on the head with a Catawba bottle in the hands of a woman named Chicago Joe, alias Johanna Donovan, Tuesday night in a low drinking establishment on Almond St., died of contusions of the brain.	MORE 29 May 1864
WARD, John M., 3rd Mo Cav, in the Prison Hospital of lung inflammation.	MORE 3 May 1863
WARE, Edward, a colored man, shot by Albert Snowden, also colored, a fireman on the Lady Gay. They had been on bad terms.	MORE 27 Nov 1865
WARFIELD, Sarah Elizabeth 6 Dec of diphtheria ae 2y 6m and her sister Martha Isabel 8 Dec ae 4y 6m, same disease, youngest daughter os Daniel of St. Louis Co. Baltimore & Lexington KY pc	MORE 12 Jan 1862
WARRANCE, Mrs. Marian 22 Jul at the home of her father-in-law William Warrance at Mt. Pleasant MO ae 53. Philadelphia pc	MORE 25 Jul 1863
WARREN, George W. of 1st MO, captured in Texas Co. 20 Jan, in Gratiot Prison of erysipelas.	MORE 25 Feb 1863
WARREN, James in New Orleans 22 Sep ae 50, many years a merchant in St. Louis. Moved to NO some years ago. Born Mercer Co. KY, lived in Rodney MS some years, where he married Emily Snodgrass who died early leaving an infant daughter, now the wife of Dr. Isaac S. Warren of St. Louis.	MORE 6 Oct 1863
WARREN, John of St. Louis in Memphis 2 Sep ae 39. Funeral from his father's home, 180 S. 5th.	MORE 18 Sep 1863
WARREN, Josephine youngest child of Samuel D. and M. Josephine of St. Louis in Frederick IL 3 Jan in her 5th year.	MORE 14 Jan 1864
WARREN, Mary wife of Peter 29 Apr ae 66, after a lingering illness, at 182 S. 5th. Interred Calvary. Paterson NJ & NY pc	MORE 30 Apr 1865
WARREN, Newell Hall son of Robert and Timothia A. 28 Apr at Gray's Summit ae 2.	MORE 29 Apr 1862
WARREN, William 23 Sep in his 80th year. Came from Lincoln Co. KY nearly 40 years ago, settled in this county. Member Church of Christ.	COWS 17 Oct 1862
WASH, Peggy servant of the late Capt. Marlin Wash at the home of Giles Bradford in Central Twp., St. Louis Co., 12 Mar ae 111.	MORE 15 Mar 1864
WASH, Anna Warder daughter of R.E. and Sarah B. at the home of her grandmother in Johnson Co. 2 Mar of diphtheria ae 4y 10m 26d.	MORE 19 Mar 1864
WASH, Martin 14 Mar in his 85th year at his home in St. Louis Co., 8 miles out on St. Charles Road.	MORE 16 Mar 1862
WASH, Capt. Thomas at his home in Johnson Co. MO 21 Jan in his 73rd year. Native of Louisa Co. VA, to MO with his family in 1833, settled on the present site of Kirkwood. Sold part of his farm for the town in 1852, sold the remainder in 1856 and moved to Johnson Co. Member of the General Assembly from St. Louis in 184?(2?). Leaves feeble wife, 3 sons, 4 daughters, many grandchildren. (Obituary from his son, T.R.A. Wash, in Allenton.)	MORE 30 Jan 1864

WASHINGTON, Jim, a negro shot by soldiers for giving aid to bushwhackers, died Wednesday.	COWS 3 Jun 1864
WASSON, Thomas D. of St. Louis at Lawrence KS 29 Aug ae 56. Funeral from the ne corner 11-Cass. Interred Bellefontaine. NY & MA pc	MORE 1 & 3 Sep 1865
WATERBURY, Lida at Oakland MO at the home of J. Farr, 15 Apr ae 7y 11m 12d. Cincinnati & NY pc	SLMD 30 Apr 1861
WATERHOUSE, Michael of Co B 8th MO at Big Shanty GA 23 Jun.	MORE 6 Jul 1864
WATERS, Alverda Jeannie only daughter of the late John S. 23 Feb ae 5y 10m. Funeral from her mother's home, St. Charles betw 6-7. Interred Calvary. Baltimore pc	MORE 24 Feb 1865
WATERS, Benjamin of Franklin Co. at the home of Joseph Locke, corner Sidney-5th, in his 53rd year. Remains to Pacific RR Depot (presumably to return to Franklin Co., but not stated.) Pittsburgh pc	MORE 12 Jun 1864
WATERS, George A. shot at his home in northeast Pike Co. 13 Aug. Suspect fled.	MORE 29 Aug 1865
WATERS, John killed in the Camp Jackson affair.	MORE 14 May 1861
WATERS, John S. of St. Louis at Denver City, K.T. ae (36? 38?) Baltimore & Philadelphia pc	MORE 18 Jul 1861
WATERS, Kate Adelia daughter of William H. and Sarah G., 297 Chestnut, Saturday ae 6.	MORE 23 Mar 1862
WATERS, Legrand killed in the explosion at the Farber Flouring Mill in Louisiana, MO. (LAJ)	MORE 7 Sep 1863
WATERS, Robert C. at his home in Perry Co. 9 Aug in his 45th year.	MORE 18 Aug 1865
WATHEN, Ignatius B. at Cape Girardeau 22 Sep in his 57th year, had come to MO from KY as a young man. Catholic. Left widow and children.	MORE 2 Oct 1865
WATKINS, Charles A., tribute by Richmond Masons. Died suddenly, left aged mother, wife, and children.	RICON 21 Apr 1864
WATKINS, Philip at House Springs, Jefferson Co. (13 or 15) Mar ae 58y 6m 11d, of pneumonia. "Father." Baptist. Lynchburg pc	MORE 21 Mar 1861 SLMD 28 "
WATSCHKO, Edward, inquest: accidentally shot himself while hunting on Arsenal Island. Bohemian.	MORE 11 Dec 1865
WATSON, Albert son of Lysander and Orleans ?? Nov of diphtheria ae 7y 6m 20d.	COWS 29 Nov 1861
WATSON, Andrew ae 67 at his home 5 miles east of St. Joseph, of dropsy, 11 Jul. Pittsburgh pc	SJH 15 Jul 1863
WATSON, Mrs. Catherine 26 Mar in Bloomington ae 71y 2m 12d.	LIT 11 Apr 1862
WATSON, Frances relict of Ringrose D. 26 Feb in her 74th year. Funeral from Fruit Hill Farm to St. Martin's Church, Central Twp.	MORE 27 Feb 1862
WATSON, Lamiol, inquest: a negro, found dead in a house near the corner of 10th & Biddle, ca 30. A steamboat man, no relatives in St. Louis. Debility.	MORE 1 Feb 1863
WATSON, Richard, a hackman, 5 Jan at City Hospital. His friends were unaware of his death and he was buried on quarantine island. When they heard of it, they had the coffin disinterred and were holding a wake when someone opened the coffin and it wasn't Richard. (It's not clear whether they ever did find him!) He left a wife and 2 children.	MORE 12 Jan 1864
WATSON, Sarah wife of William B. 7 Mar ae 45y 8m. Mt. Vernon IL & Memphis pc	MORE 8 Mar 1862
WATSON, Sarah G. wife of Thomas 31 Aug in her 74th year.	MORE 3 Sep 1863
WATTS, Mrs. Julia A. consort of Washington 7 Jun in her 49th year. Daughter of James Smith, partly raised in Pike Co. Member of the Buffalo Cumberland Presbyterian church.	LAJ 25 Jun 1864
WATTS, Lafayette J., arrested in Grundy Co. 8 Aug, in Gratiot Prison of diphtheria.	MORE 15-19 Nov'62
WATTS, Leonice wife of W.W.W. near Clarksville 17 Apr in her 51st year.	MORE 7 May 1863
WATTS, Mary daughter of Dr. James in Fayette 6 Aug in her 19th year.	COWS 25 Aug 1865
WATTS, Mrs. Mary H. at the home of her son near Savannah 23 Sep ae (69?). Had been ill 11 months.	SJH 26 Sep 1863
WATTS, William H. at his father's home near Clarksville, Pike Co. 28 Mar ae 24.	MORE 9 Apr 1865
WAYNE, Lucy step-daughter of Elder P.H. Steenberger, of flux, 29 Jun near Fulton ae 18.	COWS 18 Aug 1865
WEAVER, Daniel, 17 Sep. (No other data.)	MORE 18 Sep 1862

WEAVER, Miss Sabina Monday morning last ae ca 60.	PALS 10 Nov 1865
WEBB, Ruth Ann Williamson consort of T.H., of consumption, 22 Jan. Native of St. Louis, ae 24, had been in New Orleans last 16 years.	MORE 10 Feb 1863
WEBB, Mrs. Mary E. wife of Bird S., in Monroe Co., 7 Nov in her 69th year.	MORE 18 Nov 1863
WEBBER, John O. eldest son of John of Phelps Co. 4 Jan of brain illness, ae 19.	ROLEX 7 Jan 1861
WEBER, Mrs. Barbra (sic) 11 Oct ae 50.	WEST 21 Oct 1864
WEBER, Mrs. Louise F.C. wife of Ely, 277 Carr St., 29 Aug in her 36th year. Interred Bellefontaine. NY City pc	MORE 30 Aug 1862
WEBSTER, Mrs. Elizabeth in Fulton 7 Dec in her 63rd year. Native of VA, in MO since 1845 - came with son-in-law P.A. Heitz. Baptist, 1 child.	PALS 15 Dec 1865
WEBSTER, Laura wife of Francis 24 Feb ae 46. Funeral from St. Paul's Episcopal.	MORE 26 Feb 1862
WECKBACK, Adam, formerly in the Prov. General's office, died of injuries received when he was knocked down and robbed a few days ago.	MORE 16 Nov 1865
WEEDEN, John B. of Co H, 35th MO Vols, 19 Sep of smallpox at Helena AR.	MORE 18 Nov 1863
WEEKS, John, captured in Ripley Co., in the prison hospital of erysipelas 25 Dec.	MORE 7 Feb 1864
WEGMAN, Philomena daughter of Peter 31 Oct ae 3. Family lived on 2nd Carondelet betw Geyer-Lafayette.	MORE 3 Nov 1861
WEIGLE, Egenas 16 Jul ae 41. Lived at (556?) Broadway.	MORE 17 Jul 1865
WEINEGER, Margaret, inquest: ae 5-1/2, cause of death not given. An old man, Charles Tolle ae 65, had been accused of raping her but the court discharged him ruling it an extortion attempt on the part of her relatives, as Tolle was well-to-do.	MORE 10 Apr 1865
WEINERT, Mary wife of Louis M. 3 Mar of dropsy, at 244 Chestnut. "Long, painful."	MORE 4 Mar 1865
WEIS, John, body found in the river at Carondelet. Ae 45, 5'7", sandy hair, no whiskers. Left family on DeKalb betw Lesperance-Picott.	MORE 3 May 1863
WEISSENFELS, Henry of consumption 21 Sep. Funeral from Central Church. NY, NJ, & Owensboro KY pc	MORE 22 Sep 1864
WELCH, Ann murdered by her husband Patrick. He beat her with a poker. They had married the previous Apr, and she was pregnant.	MORE 17 Mar 1861
WELCH, Mrs. Ann run over by a railroad train near her home in Carondelet; she was apparently trying to go between the cars, and the train started up.	MORE 30 Aug 1863
WELCH, Jacob 14 May of bronchitis ae 33, at 110 S. 3rd. Chicago & Allegheny City pc	MORE 15 May 1862
WELCH, Martin, inquest: steamboat man, run over by omnibus while sleeping on the levee. Friends had moved him once. Previously known in St. Louis, had lived in New Orleans since the rebellion, left widow and children there. Was about 40, boarded with Patrick Gannon at 59 N Levee.	MORE 13 Aug 1863
WELCH, Mrs. Sarah 23 May in Warren Co. ae 77, wife of the Rev. James E. and mother of Aikman Welch, attorney general of MO.	MORE 1 Jun 1864
WELCKER, Amelia wife of the late Capt. Frederick 21 Jul ae 55. Funeral from the home of her son-in-law, Maj. Henry J. Sterling, ne cor 14-Clark. (Stierling)	MORE 22 Jul 1865
WELDON, Mrs. Mary Jane at the home of her brother G.T. Moore in Canton Twp. 19 Jul ae ca 47.	CANP 27 Jul 1865
WELKER, Capt. John of Co B, 26th MO, killed at the battle of Champion Hills, body Connected with St. Louis police. Funeral Holy Trinity, int. Calvary. Born in Greenup Co. KY 1831, joined army at 18, served in the Mexican War. Resident of St. Louis 13 years, left wife and 2 children.	MORE 6, 7, & 8 Nov ??
WELLINGTON, Darius old and respected citizen in Memphis Monday last. Member of the 21st MO, returned from the south, "one of the oldest Masons in Scotland Co."	CANP 3 Sep 1863
WELLMAN, Col. Harvey at his home in Ralls Co. 1 Nov, ill 4 weeks. Member of the Methodist Church about 21 years.	HAM 21 Nov 1861
Harriet M. relict of Col. Harvey in Saverton, Ralls Co., 17 Nov ae 65y 10m.	COWS 8 Dec 1865
WELLS, Addison L. of Porter's Band, captured in Boone Co. 1 Oct, 22 Jan of typhoid, in prison. (also 26 Jan, undertakers' list)	MORE 23 Jan 1863
WELLS, Albert son of Erastus and Isabella B. 22 Nov ae 5y 4m, Olive betw 15-16.	MORE 23 Nov 1863
WELLS, Judge Carty, many years Judge of the Circuit Court, in Troy, Lincoln Co.	CAWN 19 Jan 1861

WELLS, Crawford E. son of Alanson and Lucinda in Clark Co. 17 Jun of scarlet fever   CANP 9 Jul 1863
    and dropsy, ae 3y 3m 21d.

WELLS, Mrs. E.J. wife of L.M. near Ashley, Pike Co., 3 Dec of cancer. Daughter of   MORE 9 Dec 1865
    Col. John Thorniby of Marietta, Washington Co. OH. Wheeling & Marietta pc

WELLS, Samuel 17 Feb in his 76th year.   MORE 21 Feb 1864

WELLS, Virginia Artemesia daughter of Charles and Virginia of Osage City MO   MORE 4 Dec 1861
    30 Nov ae 3y 10m 14d.

WELLS, William B. at his father's home near Clarksville, Pike Co., 28 Mar.   MORE 3 Apr 1865

WELSCH, Michael killed in an affray on the levee when William Clark, mate of   MORE 9 May 1865
    Brilliant, fired into a crowd of workers.

WELSH, James, a young boy, pinned under an outbuilding blown over by a high wind,   MORE 10 Aug 1861
    at Summit and Clark, "only son of a respectable family in the neighborhood."

WELSH, Mary suddenly of brain congestion ae 23, at 115 O'Fallon. Left husband.   MORE 29 Nov 1862

WELSH, Mike, roustabout on the Belle of Memphis and a resident of St. Louis,   MORE 13 Sep 1862
    accidentally killed by his partner.

WELSH, Patrick, employee of the Hannibal & St. Joseph RR, killed Wednesday night   WARS 13 Oct 1865
    near Carbon, west of Macon -- how he got on the track was not known.

WELSH, Peter Joseph 11 Sep ae 35. Funeral from the home of Simon Horane, 32 Orange,   MORE 12 Sep 1863
    to Calvary Cemetery. Boston Pilot pc

WENDELL, Mrs. Margaretha Elizabetha 15 Oct ae 57y 9m, Geyer betw 9-10. Sister of   MORE 16 Oct 1863
    George H. Fichtenkam.

WENDOVER, Susan wife of J.R. of St. Louis aboard a steamboat betw Cleveland and   MORE 10 &
    Buffalo 9 Jun; daughter of Peter Luyster, Astoria, Long Island.   17 Jun 1864
    Interred Staten Island.

WENTWORTH, Mattie E. youngest daughter of Stephen G. and Eliza J., 3 Jan.   LEXUN 10 Jan 1863

WERDEMANN, Hermann killed by bushwhackers about 14 Apr near Cole Camp, his pockets   COWS 10 Apr 1863
    rifled of $50. Left wife, 5 children, brother in Columbia.

WESLEY, William youngest son of John, one of the oldest residents of St. Louis.   MORE 18 &
    Born 1 Mar 1843, died 1 Feb 1863. Funeral from St. Xavier's, 26 Feb.   25 Feb 1863

WESSELLS, William 27 Dec of consumption in his 44th year. NY & NJ pc   MORE 28 Dec 1863

WEST, Capt. Charles B., CSA, in Texas Co. at the home of Mrs. Smith when he was   MORE 3 Apr 1863
    thrown from a horse (23 Feb). In his 23rd year.

WEST, Horace B., an old St. Louis pilot, 27 Sep in IL ae 39.   MORE 6 Oct 1865

WEST, Sally relict of Bransford in Boone Co. 28 Oct ae 62y 4m 15d. Richmond KY pc   COWS 1 Nov 1861

WEST, Mrs. Samantha H., funeral notice: from the home of George H. Reader,   MORE 7 May 1862
    Montgomery betw 9-10.

WEST, Dr. William 8 Jan in Pevely of erysipelas in his 53rd year, "one of our   MORE 12 Jan 1865
    oldest, much esteemed and useful citizens."

WEST, William Edwin son of John and Elizabeth in Fulton 23 Jul ae 11y 7m.   MORE 10 Aug 1863

WEST, Willis A. son of John W. of Victoria, Daviess Co., returning from Nashville   MORE 18 Oct 1864
    where he had been in government employ, prostrated by sickness, died
    4 Oct of flux ae 23. GAL 24 Nov 1864: died St. Charles 15 Oct, Masonic
    tribute thanks St. Charles Masons for their kindness to a young brother in
    his last illness.

WESTCOTT, Linneaus, 2nd son of R.H. of St. Louis, 18 Jun at Petersburg VA.   MORE 19 Jul 1864
    With the 6th Reg. WI Vols.

WESTERBURG, Capt. C.G.E. Napoleon, 21 May of consumption ae 23y 20d. Funeral   MORE 22 May 1863
    from the home of his father-in-law Jacob Blattmer, St. Ange-LaSalle.

WESTERMAN, Henry, a German teamster, of apoplexy ae 38. Native of Prussia, in the   MORE 3 May 1861
    US 5 years. Left wife and 1 child.

WESTON, D.G. in Bolivar, Polk Co., 6 Feb of pneumonia ae 26.   MORE 20 Feb 1863

WESTWOOD, Martha wife of Joseph and daughter of James and Elizabeth Clark -- of   MORE 18 Jun 1863
    Bradford, Yorkshire, ENG -- in St. Charles.

WETHERELL, Mrs. Sarah C. on 6 Dec ae 65. Funeral from the home of her son-in-law   MORE 9 Dec 1865
    George H. Wiley, 299 Pine.

WETTERMAN, Augustus, an unmarried German ae ca 35, threw himself into a privy   MORE 4 Oct 1865
    vault, was rescued, threw himself in again and died. "Not long in
    St. Louis."

WEUGHAUS, William, a locksmith at Clay and Spring, found dead in his chair of apoplexy. German, left 3 children; wife had died ca 4 months before.   MORE 22 Mar 1861

WHALEY, Cornelius, inquest; fell backward from a seat at the circus Tuesday; was sitting in the upper level and forgot there was no back to the seat. Ae ca 26, served 4 years in the Army, Co F, 6th MO.   MORE 15 Sep 1865

WHALEY, Harriet consort of Benedict 13 Apr ae 57y 10m 13d.   FULT 2 Sep 1864

WHEALON, Mary wife of John 4 Apr ae 26. Funeral from 11th-Market, interred Calvary.   MORE 5 Apr 1861

WHEELBARGER, Henry, Chariton Co.: public administrator took over his estate.   CECB 2 Jul 1863

WHEELER, Bettie daughter of William L. of Portland MO at Christian College, Columbia ae 16y 1m 3d.   COWS 13 & 20 Oct 1865

WHEELER, Daniel W. 18 Sep ae 36. Lived on 15th betw Clark-Walnut. New Haven CT, NY, Nashville & Charleston pc   MORE 19 Sep 1865

WHEELER, Electa wife of Coleman at Mrs. Bartling's Hotel, 12th-Olive, 10 Jan.   MORE 11 Jan 1861

WHEELER, George J., #7 13th St., 18 Mar ae 21y 4m.   MORE 19 Mar 1862

WHEELER, Dr. Griswold W. of Perryville in St. Louis 6 Jun ae 57. Boston & St. Paul pc   MORE 9 Jun 1865

WHEELER, Margaret wife of John 23 May in her 46th year, 7th betw Franklin-Wash. Died of hydrophobia; her husband kept a livery stable and she was bitten by a little dog there. Husband was a brother of Fr. Wheeler. Int. Calvary.   MORE 24 & 25 May 1865

WHEELER, William O. 28 Apr in his 42d year at 6th-Chouteau. Funeral from Church of Annunciation. Cincinnati & New Orleans pc   MORE 29 & 30 Apr 1861

WHELAN, James 3 Jul at 120 Christy. Interred Calvary.   MORE 4 Jul 1864

WHELIN, J.P. in Gratiot Prison of rubeola 5 Dec.   MORE 7 Dec 1862

WHELON, Francis, a quarryman, died of wounds received in the Camp Jackson affair. Left wife, 2 children on 14th St. Ae 46. Had been living in the country and had come to St. Louis only a few days before.   MORE 14 May 1861

WHERRITT, Barton in Cass Co. 9 Aug ae 66, "long and painful disease of the liver."   MORE 25 Aug 1864

WHERRY, Dr. Macky M. in Florissant 26 Jun in his 61st year. Born in St. Charles Co. MO 17 Nov 1803, 2nd son of Macky and Louise Camp. Studied medicine in KY, married in the south; wife died a few years ago. After his elder brother Joseph A. died he moved to St. Louis Co., removed 1843, moved to Florissant 1853. Left a widow (second wife?), 2 daughters, 3 nephews "like sons to him." Interred Bellefontaine.   MORE 27 Jun & 2 Jul 1864

WHITAKER, Jonathon P. at Benton Barracks Hospital 7 Oct of chronic diarrhoea. Member 26th MO Inf. Vols, formerly asst. foreman MORE printing.   MORE 12 Oct 1863

WHITCOMB, Otis and his entire family said to have died in Waldo MO - father, mother, 4 children. The two little boys had been nursing sick twin calves, which died, and caught the disease which then spread through the family. (Belfast MO Age)   CANP 8 Sep 1864

WHITE, A.W. in Crawford Co. 4 Nov 1864 ae 51. Born in Pulaski Co. TN, to MO 1838.   MORE 25 Jan 1865

WHITE, Allen in Boone Co. 19 Dec of typhoid pneumonia ae (68?).   COWS 22 Dec 1865

WHITE, Annie daughter of J. Stockton and Emme S. 16 Aug ae 12.   MORE 18 Aug 1862

WHITE, Ben F., Orderly Sgt. from St. Louis, in Gen. John Bowen's Brigade, killed at Shiloh.   MORE 4 May 1862

WHITE, C.P. of Mississippi Co. in Gratiot Prison 5 Nov of pneumonia.   MORE 9 Nov 1862

WHITE, Constantia consort of Thomas of Liverpool ENG, resident of Gratiot St., yesterday in her 43rd year.   MORE 16 Aug 1864

WHITE, Euphemie Heline Chauvin consort of E.C. 9 Nov at their home, 243 Washington. Funeral from St. Xavier's. Interred Calvary.   MORE 10 Nov 1864

WHITE, Isham "many years a citizen" Saturday ae 54y 9m 15d.   PALS 15 Apr 1864

WHITE, Mrs. Jennie L. in Dover, Lafayette Co., 28 Jan ae 19y 3m. "Wife and only child" but name of husband and parents not shown.   MORE 25 Feb 1864

WHITE, Col John Preston in St. Charles Co. 4 Apr while hunting when his gun accidentally discharged, striking him in the arm; he died a few days later. (St. Charles Reveille 6 Apr) Born in Hanover Co. VA 11 Jul 1796.   MORE 5 & 9 & 15 Apr 1864

WHITE, Juliet P. wife of William H. in Mexico, Audrain Co. 13 Jun ae (55?).   MORE 19 Jun 1864

WHITE, Lizzie, inquest: native of TN, brother in the army, ae ca 20. Found dead in Col. John O'Fallon's sheep barn, of intemperance and exposure.   MORE 20 Jan 1865

WHITE, O.P. of Mississippi Co. in Gratiot Prison (5 Nov -- probably date he was captured, not death date).	MORE 11 Feb 1863
WHITE, Cornelia daughter of William H. 17 Mar of scarlatina, at 699 Morgan, ae 3.	MORE 18 Mar 1862
WHITE, Evalina daughter of John W. and Betty 12 Apr ae 7.	LEXUN 22 Apr 1865
WHITE, James in Hannibal 28 Apr ae 73.	HAM 2 May 1861
WHITE, Capt. John L. 23 Jul in Schuyler Co. of heart disease, ae 45y 7m 20d. Formerly of NC, where he leaves many friends.	HAM 8 Aug 1861
WHITE, John W. at Roanoke 21 Sep in his 50th year, of a protracted illness.	MORE 26 Sep 1861
WHITE, Mary Catherine wife of A.D. 17 Mar ae 17y 7m 3d.	COWS 21 Mar 1862
WHITE, Pollie F. youngest daughter of J. Stockton and Ennie, 4 Mar ae 6. Lived ne corner 6th-Gratiot.	MORE 5 Mar 1862
WHITE, William of Bledsoe's Battery captured in Springfield 8 Jan, in Gratiot Prison of lung inflammation.	MORE 29 Apr 1863
WHITEHILL, Ingham Wood 2nd son of William B. and Ann E. of encephalitis ae 25y 2m. Lived on 6th St. Lancaster PA pc	MORE 1 Oct 1862
WHITELEY, George M. son of Lieut. Col. H.K., formerly of St. Louis, 19 Apr in Brooklyn NY in his 24th year.	MORE 30 Apr 1864
WHITENECK, Henry, living 2 miles south of Mirabile, shot by bushwhackers. Wife and daughter mentioned.	CAB 19 Aug 1864
WHITESIDE, Eliza wife of John, Olive-18th, 5 Aug ae 41.	MORE 7 Aug 1864
WHITESIDE, Sarah Elizabeth wife of C.H. and daughter of the late Andrew Kayser of Fulton in Orange Co. TX 4 Nov 1863, of consumption, in her 22nd year. Left husband and 1 daughter.	FULT 13 May 1864 MORE 17 "
WHITESIDES, David of Lincoln Co., a guerilla, died of wounds received at Ashley, Pike Co.	MORE 6 Sep 1862
WHITFIELD, George W. ae 36 in Pettis Co. 3 Jul.	MORE 12 Jul 1865
WHITFORD, Thomas W. eldest son of A.S. and Louisa A. suddenly 7 Apr, ae 15. Cincinnati & Covington KY pc	MORE 8 Apr 1865
WHITING, William J. in St. Joseph 30 Jun ae 26. Funeral from the Baptist Church.	SJH 1 Jul 1864
WHITLEDGE, Lewis M. 11 Oct at Clarksville of typhoid, in his 24th year.	MORE 15 Oct 1862
WHITLOCK, Columbus killed near Smithfield (Clay or Platte Co.) by bushwhackers when he went to get a doctor for his mother. Had married Angeline J. Cox the day before, also left 3 small children by a previous marriage. Interred Mrs. Rollins' burial ground. (Unidentified newspaper)	MORE 25 Aug 1864
WHITMAN, Thomas L. 14 Mar of consumption in his 31st year, at 268 Franklin. Boston & NY pc	MORE 15 Mar 1865
WHITMORE, Charles, a merchant in St. Louis for 18 years, suddenly 4 Jul ae 62. Funeral Church of the Messiah, interred Bellefontaine. Tribute from Armory "Old Guard" refers to family and friends.	MORE 6, 11, 12 Jul 1863
WHITMORE, Emily G. widow of Charles 4 Mar ae 46, nw cor 12-Randolph.	MORE 5 Mar 1865
WHITNEY, Robert S. of apoplexy 25 Apr ae 39, formerly of MA but many years a resident of St. Louis. Funeral from Congregational Church.	MORE 27 Apr 1864
WHITSON, Isaac killed by bushwhackers. Family and brother James mentioned. (Lebanon Union)	SEDA 3 Sep 1864
WHITTAKER, Harvey L. son of Jonathan and Sarah drowned when he was pushed into the river in a fight. Ae ca 10, lived at 211 N. 9th.	MORE 5 & 6 Oct 1862
WHITTLESEY, Bessie Groome eldest daughter of Charles C. and Annie G. of St. Louis at Philadelphia 18 Oct.	MORE 20 Oct 1862
WHITTON, Mollie wife of John 10 Oct ae 20.	WEST 21 Oct 1864
WHRI (sic), Martin, a boy, accidentally drowned Saturday in a quarry pond betw Sidney-Barton-Carondelet-7th; parents lived at Lafayette-Jackson.	MORE 29 May 1864
WHYTE, Catherine wife of Richard, Gamble betw Pratte-Emily, 29 Mar ae 51. Funeral St. Malachy's. NY & Ballinsloe IRE pc	MORE 30 Mar 1864
WICKS, Mrs. Elizabeth J. wife of F.C. in Monroe Co. 16 Oct of dropsy of the heart. Left husband and 4 small children. Cumberland Presbyterian more than 20 years.	LAJ 7 Nov 1863
WIDBIN, James of 108 Washington Ave. 15 Sep ae 39.	MORE 16 Sep 1865

WIEGMAN, Henry son of Frank, 16th betw O'Fallon-Cass, thrown from a cart and run over, ae ca 13.	MORE 18 Feb 1863
WIGGINS, Edward C. 6 Apr in his 41st year. Funeral from the home of his brother Samuel B., 111 Walnut. Interred Bellefontaine.	MORE 8 Apr 1862
WIGGINS, Maj. Peter 24 Jun ae 73y 5m 11d. Harrodsburg & Lexington KY pc	MORE 26 Jun 1864
WILCOX, Dr. G.B. of Rocheport 19 Feb in his 69th year. Born 20 Jan 1794 in Shelby Co. KY, veteran of the War of 1812, emigrated 1817, joined the Methodist Church in 1843.	?MORE 28 Feb 1862 COWS "
WILCOX, Ida May only child of George A. and Mary 3 Mar at 16th-Cass, ae 2y 9m.	MORE 4 Mar 1863
WILD, Martin stabbed at Chester Landing on the Missouri side by Henry Manning last Thursday, died Sunday. Quarrel about a stean (steer?) which had been trespassing on Manning's property; he was found guilty of manslaughter.	PERU 21 & 28 Nov 1862
WILES, Ben F., an old resident, funeral yesterday. A Mason.	MORE 1 Feb 1865
WILES, George W. at Fulton 13 Sep, formerly of Howard Co., ae ca 49.	MORE 1 Oct 1865
WILEY, Kate wife of Woodville 16 Mar in her 35th year. Funeral from the 8th St. Methodist Church, interred Bellefontaine.	MORE 18 Mar 1865
WILEY, Margaret mother of George W. of St. Louis in Shannondale, Ralls Co. at the home of Mrs. William P. Samuel, 14 Sep. TX pc	MORE 20 Sep 1861 HAM 26 "
WILGUS, Asa born in NJ 1799, died at Planters' House ae 65y 8m 18d. Moved first to Lexington KY, was apprenticed to a painter; married Parma Reed, daughter of Capt. Jacob who navigated the first steamboat to St. Louis. Funeral from Christ Church.	MORE 23 Mar 1865
WILHITE, Joel and old citizen of Boone Co. 26 Jul ae 74.	COWS 18 Sep 1863
WILHITE, Sally wife of Henry of flux, near Barry in Clay Co., during the past week. Four others died of the same ailment.	SJH 11 Aug 1864
WILKENSON, William shot near Smithland, Clay Co. Considered a rebel sympathizer. (St. Joseph Union)	MORE 27 Mar 1865
WILKERSON, Charles, Chariton Co.; final settlement by Frances Wilkerson.	CECB 28 Aug 1862
WILKERSON, William Skelton at his home near Plattsburg 9 Mar ae 53.	LIT 3 Apr 1863
WILKIE, ____ wounded by Phillips who was repairing a gun at the time. Wilkie was a bushwhacker. (See C.M.W. Phillips)	MORE 1 Jun 1864
WILKINSON, Mrs. Cornelia B. wife of Charles B. Sr., editor of the St. Joseph Herald, 2 Dec ae 37y 8m 12 d, after a lingering illness.	SJH 3 Dec 1865
WILKINSON, Eva daughter of R.J. and Julia Ann, Clark-15th, of diphtheria ae 8y 4m. Appoline daughter of R.J. and Julia Ann of diphtheria ae 5y 11m.	MORE 12 May 1862 " 23 "
WILKINSON, Margaret 4 Nov ae 74. Funeral from her home, 228 S. 7th to St. John's Church. Interred Calvary.	MORE 7 Nov 1864
WILKINSON, Mrs. Sarah A. 7 May at the home of W.L. Harper ae 70. Funeral from St. George's Church. New Orleans pc	MORE 8 May 1865
WILKINSON, Walter B. in Perry Co. 31 Oct in his 50th year. Had held various political offices, took the census in 1860.	MORE 16 Nov 1863
WILLARD, Mrs. E.A. wife of C.W. 7 Jun in her 34th year, at 47 Christy. Int. Wesleyan.	MORE 9 Jun 1864
WILLARD, Mary Eliza wife of William at Dillon 29 May ae 26.	ROLEX 10 Jun 1861
WILLCOX, Wallace C., Jr. youngest son of Wallace C. and Sarah J. 5 Feb on Olive near Garrison, ae 3y and nearly 8m.	SLMD 6 Feb 1861
WILLHITE, Sally wife of Maj. Stephen 8 May ae 63y 6m. Joined the Baptist Church in KY in 1818, came to Boone Co. MO in 1819.	COWS 22 May 1863
WILLIAMS, Alonzo, ae 7, drowned in a pond on Jefferson betw Wymer-Cherokee.	MORE 14 Jul 1864
WILLIAMS, Amanda Margaret daughter of J.D. and Eliza 23 Jan of scrofula ae 5y 3m 23d.	COWS 29 Jan 1864
WILLIAMS, Anna E. daughter of N.H. and Sarah 29 Jan in S. Hannibal ae 4m.	HAM 29 Jan 1861
WILLIAMS, Asa 12 Jun at the home of Ambrose Hill, of rheumatism and other diseases he'd had for 6 or 8 years, ae 39y 4m 8d.	FULT 17 Jun 1864
WILLIAMS, Barney in Howard Co. 8 Sep at the home of R.J. Payne, ae 75. COWS 29 Sep &	MORE 1 Oct 1865
WILLIAMS, Frances - "Black Fan" - suicide after her loved deserted her, Almond-3-4.	MORE 23 Jul 1864
WILLIAMS, Francis near Fayette 30 May ae ca 60. Father of Lieut. Col. J.F. of Col. Guitar's Reg.	COWS 6 Jun 1862

WILLIAMS, J. Sam, ae ca 28, on 18 Nov from the effect of a blow on the head received in an accident in IL.	COWS 1 Dec 1865
WILLIAMS, James Q. at the home of J.L. Sheaffer in his 23rd year.	MORE 16 Jan 1862
WILLIAMS, Jerusha wife of Franklin T. at Trenton 3 Aug in her (25th?) year.	MORE 15 Sep 1865
WILLIAMS, John, held in jail for petty larceny, died.	MORE 11 Nov 1865
WILLIAMS, John H., formerly of Boonville, 8 Jul at Bridgeport IL ae 53.	MORE 9 Aug 1864
WILLIAMS, Lucy A. wife of Dr. Orsino and daughter of William F. and Elizabeth Miller at Versailles 13 Aug of a protracted illness. Wife, mother, born in Buckingham Co. VA, member Methodist Church South.	MORE 23 Aug 1864
WILLIAMS, Margaret, an Indian woman, came into town, asked permission to sleep at a colored woman's house and was allowed to do so, but died. Verdict, exposure and intemperance. Had 2 children, whereabouts not known.	MORE 9 Oct 1863
WILLIAMS, Mary Hannah wife of Henry T. in her 26th year. Funeral from the home of Mrs. Covert, 71 Centre, to Bellefontaine.	MORE 6 Jun 1861
WILLIAMS, Polly wife of James 24 Oct in her 77th year. Baptist, to Marion Co. 1824.	PALS 6 Nov 1863
WILLIAMS, Robert, cutting house logs for Manoah Goodman at Clarksville, killed by a falling limb ca 12 May.	LAJ 23 May 1861
WILLIAMS, Robert, a policeman on the force about 6 years, Thursday of consumption. Native of IRE, ae 45; left wife, 3 children. Interred Calvary.	MORE 19 Nov 1864
WILLIAMS, Maj. Thomas E. at his home in Louisiana 25 Aug in his 41st year, of flux. "Good citizen, businessman." Member IOOF. Left wife.	LAJ 27 Aug 1864
WILLIAMS, William J. of Co H 43rd MO Vols killed at Glasgow.	GAL 17 Nov 1864
WILLIAMSON, Coronne S. ae 16y 4m. Funeral from parents' home, 201 N. 14th.	MORE 4 Jan 1865
WILLIAMSON, Daniel killed by bushwhackers near Lexington. (LEXUN 20 Aug)	MORE 25 Aug 1864
WILLIAMSON, George Esq. "Judge" 4 Sep ae 67. (Paris Mercury)	MORE 16 Sep 1863
WILLIAMSON, Hiram Jr. (son of Hiram who has had 7 sons in service, 2 died, one discharged for disability, 4 still in) "a few days ago."	CAB 18 Nov 1864
WILLIAMSON, Thomas F. in Louisiana 30 Dec of consumption ae 30y 10d. Formerly of Davis Co. IA. Left wife, 3 children. (MORE 20 Jan gives age as 24, date of death 4 Jan "near Elder Johnson's in Pike Co.")	LAJ 16 Jan 1862
WILLIAMSON, William of Reeves Command, captured in Ripley Co. 25 Dec, in the prison hospital of measles.	MORE 4 Feb 1864
WILLING, Sallie Stoughton wife of George W. Sr. 12 Dec of lung disease at Market & Summit, ae 61.	MORE 14 Dec 1863
WILLIS, Annie at her home in Fayette some days ago, "estimable young lady." (RANC)	MEMP 14 Oct 1865
WILLIS, Maj. Henry near Philadelphia Tuesday last, a Mason. (PALS 25 Sep)	MAG 1 Oct 1863
WILLIS, John E. formerly of Boone Co. in southwest MO recently in a skirmish with some enrolled militia. Two or three other rebels also killed.	COWS 1 May 1863
WILLIS, Mary K. killed in an affray at Springfield by A.J. Rice. She had come from Arkansas in the late winter, having lost two sons to bushwhackers. (Springfield Missourian)	MAG 11 Jun 1862
WILLIS, Willie son of Joseph and Sarah J. of Richmond 17 Oct ae 7.	RICON 11 Nov 1865
WILLOUGHBY, Elizabeth P. wife of W.J. 18 Oct ae 21y 11m 1d.	WEST 21 Oct 1864
WILLS, Elizabeth mother of J.W. of St. Louis in Richmond VA 29 Mar in her 84th y.	MORE 13 May 1862
Edward Carrington 2nd son of J.W. and Eliza H., 18 Aug ae 3y 4m.	MORE 19 Aug 1863
WILMOT, Mary daughter of John D. 7 Jul ae 5.	LEXUN 8 Jul 1865
WILMOT, N.N. 2 Sep at 319 Franklin in his 63rd year. Boston pc	MORE 3 & 4 Sep 1865
WILSEY, Anna wife of C.C. 8 Jan ae 25. Interred Calvary.	MORE 10 Jan 1861
WILSON, ___ an old man of 60 beaten by his wife and her female companion, ___ Cobb. Wife tried and sentenced; they lived in Oregon MO.	HOLS 25 Aug 1865
WILSON, Ann C. 31 Jul in her 56th year. Funeral from the home of her nephew William W. Sanford, 75 Spruce. Brooklyn NY pc	MORE 1 Aug 1863
WILSON, Charles H., resident of Cass Ave., died of a beating by soldiers at Fort No. 6 about 14 July - died 24 Jul. Arrests made.	MORE 11 Aug 1863
WILSON, Charles Henry 5 Jan ae 29; funeral 101 Pine. Boonville MO & Paris KY pc	MORE 6 Jan 1865

WILSON, David, who had been arrested with his brother James for robbery in Central Twp., attempted escape but was shot and killed by Dep. Constable Grosby.	MORE 22 Sep 1865
WILSON, Egbert Freeland 24 Jan in his 17th year, eldest son of Frances B. and the late Robert J., of Fayette Co. KY, at the home of his uncle, of typhoid.	MORE 26 Jan 1863
WILSON, Mrs. Elizabeth P. 29 Dec in her 53rd year of tubercular infection of the lung. Native of ENG, lived on Wright betw 9-10.	MORE 29 Dec 1864
WILSON, Ella D. 31 Dec ae 17y 10m. Funeral from her mother's home, Morgan betw 14-15. Left brother and sister. Interred Bellefontaine.	MORE 1 Jan 1861
WILSON, Fanny (alias Hopmayer), waitress in Michael Sutter's beer saloon, suicide by laudanum.	MORE 10 May 1863
WILSON, George an old citizen and well-known early resident died at the City Hospital ae 56, was buried in the Quarantine section of the City cemetery. Native of NY.	MORE 8 Apr 1865
WILSON, George R. "good citizen and honest man" in Rocheport 12 Mar ae 50. Born in Frederick Co. VA, to MO 1840. Mason, member of the Sons of Temperance. Louisville pc	COWS 12 Mar & 25 Apr 1862
WILSON, Mrs. Hannah Harris relict of Robert Theodore of Eastern Shore MD, later of Philadelphia and St. Louis. Born in Providence RI 1 Oct 1794, late resident of Francis St., St. Louis. Palmyra pc	MORE 26 Nov 1862
WILSON, J.F., Masonic tribute - "son and brother."	SJH 28 Jun 1865
WILSON, James, citizen prisoner from Wayne Co., arrested 2 Feb, of inflammation of the lungs and erysipelas, in Gratiot Prison.	MORE 10 Mar 1864
WILSON, Jennie, an Irishwoman living at 337 S. 2nd, intemperance, ae 23.	MORE 12 Jul 1862
WILSON, Malvina D. 9 Dec ae 14 at the home of John J. Stevenson.	RICON 16 Dec 1865
WILSON, Margaret Elizabeth wife of Thomas J., late of Parkville, at Quindaro KS 5 Oct leaving a husband and 9-m-old son. Buried in the family burying ground inside Parkville Cemetery.	WEST 21 Oct 1864
WILSON, Mrs. Margarette 23 Dec ae 72. Funeral from Asbury Chapel.	MORE 24 Dec 1861
WILSON, Mrs. Mary at the home of her daughter-in-law in Rocheport 12 Jan of pleuro-pneumonia ae 83y 3m 12d. Louisville, Henderson CT, St. Louis pc	COWS 22 Jan 1864
WILSON, Mrs. Matilda of 56 Mound St. found dead, probably from effects of heat.	MORE 5 Aug 1861
WILSON, Lieut. N.W. in Osage Co. 28 Jul.	COWS 4 Sep 1863
WILSON, Richard killed by guerillas in Carroll Co. (Carrollton Democrat)	MORE 21 Jul 1864
WILSON, Robert at his home in Jackson Twp., Buchanan Co., 12 Nov. Among the earliest residents of Platte Co., having come from Ohio more than 20 years ago. Died of pneumonia. His only son recently killed by guerillas.	SJH 15 Nov 1864
WILSON, Samuel K. 14 Aug ae 46, at #9 Madison. Baltimore pc	MORE 16 Aug 1864
WILSON, Susan Mary widow of William M., formerly of Woodford Co. KY, 23 Nov ae 51y 1m 12d. "Mother, sister, aunt."	LIT 4 Dec 1863
WILSON, Theodocia wife of W.R. in the flux epidemic.	FULT 2 Sep 1864
WIMER, John, a Confederate soldier, died in the battle of Hartsville. Had been identified with St. Louis nearly 30 years - supt. of the waterworks, alderman, constable, mayor, postmaster, sheriff, etc. Born Albemarle Co. VA in 1811-12, to St. Louis with his father's family in 1828. His father died about 15 years ago, his mother about 4 years ago at very advanced age. Three brothers and 3 sisters also came; all but one, Mrs. Ward, have died. Married Abigail T. Wise, native of Mason Co. KY; survived by wife and 2 sons. Presbyterian, interred Bellefontaine. (However, when his body was returned he was buried in Wesleyan because of fear of problems -- see Emmet McDonald.)	MORE 6 Feb 1863
WINENBROCK, Emma Marquetis daughter of Ernst and Charlotte 12 Mar ae 21y 7m. Lived at Pratte & Market.	MORE 13 Mar 1864
WING, Emeline R. wife of Andrew H. at 137 N. 5th on 7 Sep ae 50.	MORE 8 Sep 1864
Kate Frances youngest daughter of Andrew H. and Emeline 25 Sep ae (13? 18?)y 9m. Hartford CT pc	MORE 26 Sep 1862
WINGO, Mary Frances wife of J.G. in Washington Co. 4 Jan ae 43, daughter of the late Ambrose Panell.	MORE 8 Jan 1865
WINN, Alonzo, of Poindexter's Band, captured in Howard Co. 20 Sep, in Gratiot Prison of pneumonia.	MORE 13 Feb 1863

WINN, Mrs. Emily in this city 10 Jun ae 66, relict of George of Clarksville TN.	WEST 17 Jun 1864
WINNING, Edward at his home in Saline Co. 9 Jun, "afflicted many years." Born in Berkeley Co. VA 9 Jan 1794; joined the Old Side Presbyterian Church at ae 32. His father died when he was about 16. At 26 he married Catherine Grantham, who survives. Veteran War of 1812. Was Justice of the Peace and Overseer of the Poor in VA. Came to MO in 1841.	MORE 1 Jul 1861
WINSETT, ____ arrested last week and tried in Perryville proved dangerous and dishonest, was turned over to US troops, who shot him. (Frank Tucker also shot.)	PERU 24 Jun 1864
WINSHIP, Charles at Sisters' Hospital 7 Jul ae ca 24. Funeral from 55 N. 5th St. Interred Bellefontaine.	MORE 8 Jul 1863
WINSOR, WINSER, Mrs. Mary 5 Oct in her 75th year. At the home of her son Edward in Lexington. Cincinnati & Baltimore pc	LEXUN 8 Oct 1864 MORE 15 "
WINSOR, Mary Jane wife of Arnold and daughter of William R. and Jane Walton, of pneumonia, 7 Nov in her 27th year.	LEXUN 28 Nov 1863 MORE 18 "
WINSTON, Mrs. Matilda in Canton 2 Oct.	CANP 5 Oct 1865
WINTER, Victor son of C. and Mary in Lexington Thursday ae 3.	MORE 27 Jan 1861
WIRT, Adam in Boone Co. 30 Mar ae 75y 18d.	COWS 15 Apr 1864
WISE, Agnes C. wife of David in St. Louis Co. 1 Sep ae 34.	MORE 3 Sep 1865
WISE, Godfrey A., 7th betw Hickory-Rutger; member Iron Moulders Union.	MORE 13 Dec 1863
WISE, Leon son of Louis and Eva, 6th near Chouteau, 8 Feb of diphtheria ae 3y 6m.	MORE 9 Feb 1863
WISE, Noah killed in Jefferson Co. by 47th MO Vols under Col. Fletcher.	MORE 17 Oct 1864
WISE, Mrs. Phebe Ann, ae 70, at the home of F.A. Wise in Central Twp., St. Louis Co., on 13 Apr. PA pc	MORE 15 Apr 1863
WISELY, Henry T. in Callaway Co. 28 Mar in his 38th year. Left wife, 5 children, and his father.	MORE 9 Apr 1864
WISEMAN, Mary C. wife of James Sr. in her 78th year, near Ashland, 15 Aug.	COWS 18 Sep 1863
WISHON, Bennett, shot at Savannah "a couple of weeks ago" by Reed Murphy, died 14 Jul "after 12 days excruciating torment occasioned by a pistol shot in the chest" ae 27. Buried with military honors. Murphy in jail.	SJH 15 & 16 Jul 1864
WITHERS, Elisha T. 25 Jul ae 29.	COWS 4 Aug 1865
WITHERS, Enoch D. 25 Feb of consumption in his 49th year. Madison IN pc	MORE 26 Feb 1862
WITHERSPOON, F.A., tribute by Pleasant Grove Lodge #142, AF & AM, Otterville.	MORE 13 May 1863
WITHINTON, Thomas 5 Nov ae 70y 8m. Funeral from the home of his son George, in St. Ferdinand Twp., to Florissant.	MORE 6 Nov 1863
WITHROW, Capt. Mordecai, native of MO, 6 Apr in his 30th year.	MORE 8 Apr 1862
WITT, Helen daughter of the late Rufus 7 Jun ae 7.	MORE 13 Jun 1863
WITT, Judge Nelson at his home in the south part of Buchanan Co., on 13 Aug. An old resident, in the neighborhood 25 years.	SJH 16 Aug 1863
WITTEKEIM, Henry fell from the 2nd story of Henry Brant's home on Mallinckrodt betw 4th & 11th (sic) and was killed. Native of GER, ae ca 45, in the US about 10 years, unmarried.	MORE 13 Jul 1865
WOLF, Amanda wife of Judge H.J. and daughter of James and Melina Leachman, ae 25, on 30 Jul. Mentions sister, obit sounds as though her parents were deceased. "Just in the prime of womanhood."	WEST 4 & 18 Aug 1865
WOLFE, Basmatha A. wife of Thomas M. at their home on Manchester Rd. 11 Sep ae 33y 9m 6d. Warren, Trimble Co. OH, Pittsburgh & Philadelphia pc	MORE 12 Sep 1865
WOLFF, Abraham ae 71 of typhoid pneumonia. Friends of his family and of his sons invited to the funeral, 1st Methodist Church. (George C. and Marcus A./)	MORE 23 Nov 1865
WOLFLIN, Nicholas eldest son of N. and Mary A. in Canton 11 Oct ae 9y 9m.	CANP 13 Oct 1864
WOLFF, Henrietta, sister of John, Bellefontaine Rd., 13 Dec. Int. Calvary.	MORE 15 Dec 1864
WOLFF, Michael, employed at Schnell's Brewery, fell into a vat of boiling beer.	MORE 28 Feb 1861
WOLFSTEIN, Isaac, formerly of Palmyra, fell off the Pike at Hannibal.	PALS 10 Mar 1865
WOMACK, Annie at the home of her brother-in-law 4 Feb in her 57th year. Born in Bedford Co. VA. Baptist.	FULT 1 Mar 1861
WOOD, Charles H. 16 Jan ae 42. Funeral from the home of Charles Penine, __2? Olive.	MORE 19 Jan 1865

WOOD, Fannie in Chapel Hill, Lafayette Co. ae 18. Obituary by cousins, Lizzie and Jennie.   MORE 21 May 1863

WOOD, James Alexander in Callaway Co. 5 May at the home of his father-in-law, John Gibony, ae 38.   COWS 26 May 1865

WOOD, Phineas, a rebel, son of Kemp of Clay Co., killed Friday by Maj. Pace's Command. Had been enrolled 3 years, probably home on furlough.   SJH 1 Nov 1864

WOOD, Thomas, an old settler more than 30 years, 4 Jan ae 58.   LIT 11 Jan 1861

WOODEN, William J. citizen of Carroll Co. in Gratiot Prison of laryngitis.   MORE 22 Mar 1864

WOODS, Andrew at the home of his brother Robert K. in St. Louis Co., 7 Jun in his 29th year. Funeral 2nd Presbyterian Church. Nashville pc   MORE 9 Jun 1864

WOODS, Archibald, ca 56, of flux during the past week near Barry, Clay Co.; four others died of the same disease.   SJH 11 Aug 1864

WOODS, Dunbar 27 Feb at 44 N. 7th, ae 49y 1m 21d.   MORE 28 Feb 1861

WOODS, E.P., a Confederate soldier from St. Louis, at Port Gibson.   MORE 28 May 1863

WOODS, Edward Peter son of C.P. 27 Mar of croup ae 3y 8m 18d. Interred Calvary.   MORE 28 Mar 1861

WOODS, Ellen Neel oldest child of Luther T. and Mary Eliza, 15th-Spruce, 23 Apr ae 3y 7m.   MORE 27 Apr 1861

WOODS, Jay only son of J.B. 21 Sep of flux ae ca 10.   LAJ 24 Sep 1864

WOODSON, Miller S. only son of Judge Silas 22 Jun of consumption ae 21y 1m 7d.   SJH 24 Jun 1865
Olivia wife of Judge Silas 26 Oct ae (35?)y 11m.   SJH 27 Oct 1865

WOODWARD, James, 1st MO Cav, captured at Vicksburg, in Gratiot Prison hospital.   MORE 22 Sep 1863

WOODWARD, Joseph W. son of Corydon R. and Christina M. drowned Saturday at the foot of Jefferson. Lived on 11th betw Warren-Montgomery.   MORE 6 Oct 1862

WOODWORTH, Richard, native of KY, Sunday of brain congestion in his 31st year. Lived on 15th betw O'Fallon-Cass. Quincy, KY, & Cincinnati pc   MORE 26 Aug 1863

WOODWORTH, William Lyman at Lebanon IL 13 Mar? ae 13y 7m 6d. Grandson of Mrs. Sarah Wetherell. Interred Bellefontaine.   MORE 15 Feb 1864 ? (Mar?)

WOOLDRIDGE, Powhatan at his home in Georgetown MO 20 Mar of pneumonia, in his 73rd year. Born in Woodford Co. KY.   MORE 1 Apr 1862

WOOLFOLK, Carrie L. 23 Feb ae 25y 3m at the home of her brother-in-law W.H. Block. Interred Troy, MO.   MORE 24 Mar 1865

WOOLFOLK, Charles T. 28 Jul in Henry Co. of brain disease ae 58. Many years resident of Boone Co. A Baptist. Fulton MO & Hopkinsville KY pc.   COWS 29 Aug 1862
Catherine daughter of the late Charles T. and P.A. in Henry Co. 29 Dec of pneumonia ae ca 20.   COWS 16 Jan 1863

WOOLFOLK, Dr. George 8 Mar at the home of Dr. John T. Hodgen, 4th-Walnut.   MORE 9 Mar 1862

WOOLLAM, Joseph Grundy 17 Feb ae 56 at his home on Bear Creek, Montgomery Co.   MORE 21 Feb 1863

WORLEY, Mrs. Peter 18 Jul in Canton.   CANP 27 Jul 1865

WORLINE, Justice Rudolph of the 7th Ward suddenly Friday. Had been ill.   MORE 23 May 1863

WORSHAM, ___ of Pike Co. killed at Elmore's Store, Ashley; result of guerilla raid.   MORE 6 Sep 1862

WORSLEY, Richard killed in a coal pit accident at Gravois Coal Mines, 6 miles from St. Louis. Unmarried, left father and sister living at Gravois.   MORE 4 Nov 1863

WORTHINGTON, Col. William of Iowa 5th and his son Rev. J.T. of Louisiana MO killed by own pickets, by mistake, last Thursday. Interred Keokuk.   LAJ 29 May 1862

WORTMAN, Mrs. Sarrah E., wife of Frank M., 2 Mar in Hannibal ae 27.   HAM 13 Mar 1862

WREN, Mary Ann "grown daughter" of David of Cedar Twp, Boone Co., lost her arm in a sugar mill accident and subsequently died.   LAJ 17 Oct 1861

WRIGHT, ___ "noted guerilla" killed in Lafayette Co. by Capt. Clayton Tiffin's Ray Co. EMM.   MORE 3 Feb 1865

WRIGHT, Annie Cheever daughter of S.A. and D.T. 23 Sep, on Spring Ave., ae 7y 11m.   MORE 24 Sep 1864

WRIGHT, Sarah L. wife of Dr. C.M. and daughter of George N. Stevens of St. Louis in Cincinnati 21 Sep of puerpueral convulsions.   MORE 25 Sep 1865

WRIGHT, Erie Jr. killed at Camp Jackson 10 May ae 37y 1m 23d. Lived on Bernard near Pratte. Interred Bellefontaine.   MORE 12 May 1861

WRIGHT, J.P. a bushwhacker executed (shot) at Warrensburg 2 Jun.   WARS 17 Jun 1865

WRIGHT, John 24 Sep ae 35. Missionary Baptist. Left 4 children.   WEST 13 Oct 1865

WRIGHT, Judge Lewis F. and four of his sons taken from their home and murdered on the road between Rolla and Houston last Tuesday by militia under Col. Babcoke of Miller Co. Two sons had been in the rebel army. A 5th son was left at home with his stepmother.	LIT 1 Sep 1865 MORE 21 Aug "
WRIGHT, Mrs. Nancy "first white female born in Harrodsburg KY" 26 Mar ae 77y 5m.	COWS 5 Apr 1861
WRIGHT, Mrs. Nancy 7 Mar ae 65y 1m 3d. Funeral from the home of L.W. Mitchell, 9th betw Salisbury-Mallinckrodt.	MORE 9 Mar 1864
WRIGHT, Mrs. Rachel Ann wife of John, 6 Nov. 1864. Missionary Baptist.	WEST 14 Apr 1865
WRIGHT, Mrs. Sarah in Boone Co. 22 Feb in her 80th year.	COWS 3 Mar 1865
WRIGHT, Sarah G. wife of Maj. Uriel near St. Louis 2 Nov ae 56. Funeral from the Methodist Church at 8th-Washington.	HAM 7 Nov 1861 MORE 3 "
WRIGHT, T. Barber youngest child of Henry C. and Frances M. 23 Jan at Wright City of scarlet fever in his 14th year.	MORE 24 Jan 1864
WRIGHT, Thomas at the home of Dr. L.B. Brown in Boone Co. 2 Feb.	COWS 11 Mar 1864
WRIGHT, Virginia wife of James and daughter of George Sheley in Weston 17 Dec.	SJH 13 Jan 1864
WRIGHT, William, member of Fremont's Body Guard, at Springfield 25 Oct in 20th y.	SLMD 19 Nov 1861
WUELKER, Augusta wife of Louis 10 Apr ae 35, ill two years. Lived at 363 Market. Interred Calvary.	MORE 12 Apr 1865
WUNSCH, ___ little son of Elmer, ae 7, drowned Saturday at the foot of Miller St.	MORE 14 Jun 1864
WURSTDORF, Frederick W., inquest: lived in cellar at 61 S. 7th, found dead of debility, intemperance, exposure.	MORE 4 Oct 1862
WURZ, Antonette Dorothea, 244 Broadway, 6 Dec ae 84y 2m.	MORE 7 Dec 1864
WYATT, John J. in Central Twp. 17 Apr ae 28.	MORE 19 Apr 1861
WYATT, Margaret widow of Isaac, many years a resident of St. Louis, 26 Feb at Sharpsburg, Marion Co. ae 66.	MORE 1 Mar 1863
WYATT, Miss Sarah J. at the home of her mother on 2nd St. of consumption, in 18th y.	SJH 16 Apr 1864
WYCHE, William of Dennison's Cav. 7 Feb of diarrhoea. (Undertakers' list)	MORE 15 Feb 1863
WYKER, John, a tailor, formerly of PA, suddenly of convulsions and hemorrhage of the lungs. Lived at 5th-Edmond.	SJH 30 Jan 1864
WYMAN, Ella oldest daughter of Edward, 16th-Pine, 4 Mar in her 20th year.	MORE 5 Mar 1863
WYMAN, Susan F. consort of Col. Nehemiah, formerly of Charlestown MA, suddenly at Hillsboro IL 14 Nov in her 76th year. Funeral from the home of her son Edward, 16th-Pine.	MORE 16 Nov 1864
WYRICK, Mrs. Catherine Dickson Williams 11 Aug ae 30, wife of M.L., at Marshfield MO. Late of Greenville TN. Culpeper VA, Nashville, & Greenville TN pc	MORE 26 Aug 1862
YANCEY, Dr. Edward 15 Dec near Providence, Boone Co., ae 35.	COWS 22 Dec 1865
YANDLE, William, citizen of Taney Co., 14 Jan of pneumonia. (Undertakers' list)	MORE 19 Jan 1863
YATES, Charles, prisoner of war, 10 Sep. (Undertakers' list)	MORE 14 Sep 1862
YATES, Joseph H. 2 Nov of consumption ae 27. Funeral from home of Herbert Bell, 181 Clark.	MORE 4 Nov 1865
YEAGER, John B. in Randolph Co. 13 Sep of consumption ae ca 40. Left wife and several small children.	MORE 18 Sep 1864
YEAGER, Thomas, a citizen of Ralls Co., killed on the rebel side at the Battle of Pea Ridge AR. Has a brother in CA, a Union man. Member of Wilson's Company, Birge's Regiment.	HAM 1 May 1862
YEATS, Miss Ellen T. at Kirkwood 4 Feb ae 24y 19d.	MORE 5 Mar 1864
YEATS, Joseph W. eldest son of the late Thomas D. at Kirkwood 22 Sep of hemorrhage of the lungs, ae 34. Funeral from Des Peres Presbyterian Church.	MORE 23 Sep 1862
YEOMAN, George, formerly of St. Louis, at Sacramento CA 16 Sep.	SLMD 22 Oct 1861
YORK, William, living with his father at the head of Little Piney, accidentally shot himself 14 Nov, ae 21 or 22. (ROLEX)	SJH 26 Nov 1863
YOSTI, Lizzie wif of Thomas J. near Bridgeton 11 Jan ae 28.	MORE 13 Jan 1864
YOUNG, ___ murdered in Audrain Co. by bushwhacker Jim Jackson and 5 others; left wife and several children. (Mexico Beacon)	MORE 27 Feb 1865
YOUNG, ___ a Union man killed by Todd's men in Chariton Co. (William in Co. History)	MORE 10 Jan 1865

YOUNG, Alice daughter of A.C. and S.J. in Morgan Co. ae 2 at the home of (? paper   CAWN 9 Feb 1861
        hard to read - John C. Morgan?).

YOUNG, Mrs. Anne ae 49, mother of John M., a Justice of the Peace, and Samuel H.,   MORE 9 &
        Recorder, found murdered under a bridge at Mullanphy-17th. May have been a   10 Feb 1861
        case of mistaken identity. Story went on for days. She lived with John M.
        at 12th-Christy.

YOUNG, D.W. of Boone Co. in Alton Prison in December.   COWS 9 Jan 1863

YOUNG, Maj. Edward in Boone Co. 9 Sep ae 92y 6m 24d. St. Louis & Winchester KY pc   COWS 23 Sep 1864

YOUNG, Emma C. oldest child of William G. and Ann S., Spruce betw 21-22, 15 Mar of
        scarlet fever ae 8y 2m 6d. Belleville, Bloomfield & Chester IL pc   MORE 17 Mar 1864

YOUNG, Mary Catherine daughter of William and E.J., 118 Mound, 4 Dec of brain   MORE 6 Dec 1863
        fever ae 5y 7m 4d.

YOUNG, Col. Merit L. of Price's Army, resident of Weston, ae 39, near Westport   MORE 1 Nov 1864
        23 Oct. Joined the Confederates Aug 1861, Marmaduke's Command. Born in   LIT 4 "
        Shelby Co. KY, to MO when quite young. Left wife, 1 child.

YOUNG, Col. Samuel "at one time a prominent politician in MO" in Leavenworth City   LIT 13 Nov 1863
        in destitute circumstances. Family in Columbia.

YOUNG, Rev. William H. 18 Apr in Wolf Island Twp. Born in England, a Baptist; was   CHAC 24 Apr 1863
        preaching in Columbus KY as early as 1848.

YOUNGMAN, John, Howard-13th, Sunday ae 42. Funeral from St. Liborious Church.   MORE 28 Mar 1864

YOUTSAY   Esther wife of George in Gallatin 6 Oct. Born in Addison Co. VT   GAL 23 Oct 1864
(YOUTSEY) 4 Mar 1801?, to Clinton Co. NY with parents in 181?, married Dr. Greene
        1830; next year to MI; joined Missionary Baptists in 1832, husband died
        the same year. Moved with her father Mr. (Pearl?) to IN and in 1838
        married George Youtsey. (Dates very blurred.)

ZALLEE, Louis and Charles, sons of John C. and Delima, 30 Mar.   MORE 31 Mar 1862
        Pelage, oldest daughter of Rose D. and John C. 7 Jul ae 7y 4m.   " 8 & 9
        Lived at 186 Pine. Funeral College Church, interred Calvary. (9 Jul gives   Jul 1863
        cause as hemorrhage of the bowels and age as 9y 4m.)

ZAMOUDE, Mrs. Pelagie 2 Mar ae 92. Funeral from the home of Charles Roderman,   MORE 3 Mar 1863
        8 miles out on Market St.

ZERLEIN, Henry of dropsy of the heart ae ca 20. An amateur chemist, made inks, etc.;   MORE 12 Oct 1864
        lived on Cedar St.

ZIEGLER, Barbara 4 Oct at Ste. Genevieve ae 65.   MORE 14 Oct 1862

ZIEGLER, Francis Joseph at his home in Cape Girardeau 28 Apr of congestive chills   PERU 5 Jun 1863
        in his 63rd year. St. Charles & Dubuque pc. (MORE says died 27 Apr in   MORE 11 "
        66th year; born Baden, emigrated with brothers Mathew and Sebastien in
        1817, settled in MO 1818, left wife and 7 children.)

ZIEGLER, John at Valle Mines 26 Sep of congestive chill. Born in Ste. Genevieve,   MORE 3 Oct 1865
        oldest of a large family - 4 brothers, 1 sister. Father Michael raised
        tobacco, died suddenly when John was not yet 20, he continued his father's
        business and raised the younger children. Married a member of an old
        Ste. Genevieve family but left no children.

ZIEGLER, Sebastian, "old and highly esteemed" in Ste. Genevieve 20 Jul.   MORE 24 Jul 1861

ZIEGLER, Mrs. Theresia, native of Baden, 31 Jan of phthisis ae 68y 3m.
                                        Ste. Genevieve pc   MORE 6 Feb 1865

ZIMMERMAN, see Frederick TIMMERMAN

ZIMMERMAN, George W. at his home near New Hope, Lincoln Co. 27 Dec 1862 in his   MORE 6 Apr 1863
        69th year. (LAJ says late a meber of MO State Convention from the   LAJ 25 "
        2nd Senatorial District - vacancy to be filled.)

ZOECHLER, J. George, 2nd betw Convent-Sycamore, 7 Feb ae 40y 8m.   MORE 8 Feb 1865

ZUMBALEW, Henry, 244 Broadway, 2 Dec ae 43y 6m. Interred Calvary.   MORE 3 Dec 1864

/-/

CROSS-REFERENCES

Additional surnames -- relatives and in-laws -- found in some notices, which may provide helpful clues.

ALEXANDER - Cynthia Threlkeld
                John Glime
ALLEN - Maggie and Lizza Scott
ALLIN - John Conner
AMOS - Col. C. Gleim
AUSTIN - Joseph Leighton, Sr.
BAGBY - S.B. Dickinson
BARNARD - Mrs. Amie D. Robeson
BARRETT - Henry Hooven
BARTHALOW - Mrs. Mary B. Browne
BARTLEY - Bartley Wade
BARTLETT - David Green
BAYES - Paul Longtain
BERGIN - Edward Heenan
BEATTIE - Rosa Gaines
BILBROUGH - Samuel Rimmer
BIRCH - Capt. Christopher Morrow
BLANK - Jane Farmer
BLOCK - Carrie L. Woolfolk
BOERINGER - August Mellinger
              Edward Mellinger
BOOTH - William B. Ferry
BOYCE - John O'Brien
BOYES - Paul Longtain
BOYLES - R. Louisa Atkeson
BRADLEY - Patrick McCreanor
BRADY - Mrs. Ellen Walsh
BRANHAM - Anthony W. Walker
BRASHER - David B. Lamberson
BROADWELL - Lizzie Doubleby
BROWDER - George W. Kelly
BROWN - William B. Gilbert
BUCKLEY - Mrs. Ellen Lynch
BUDD - Mrs. Hannah Patterson
BURGESS - Sarah L. Spencer
BURNES - ___ Henry
BYRNE - Francis Byrne Haydel
CADY - Catherine Darby
CAFFRAY - Louisa A. Ivory
CALHOUN - Lavinia E. Bell
             Eleanor Small
CARR - Mrs. Laura L. Vaughn
CARTER - Eddie Boughan
CASON - Perry Earickson
CHADBOURNE - Mrs. Tabitha Robinson
CHEW - William E. Forbes
CLAIBORNE - Mrs. Tabitha Robinson

CLARK - George F. Muldrow
COLBURN - Martha Hawken
COFFMAN - James W. Smith
CONWAY, Mrs. ___ Murphy
CORDANAU - Catherine Reynolds
CORKINS - May McKenzie
COTTING - Elizabeth Jameson
COULES - Charles Joseph Neaf
CUTTING - Alex R. Jameson
DAVIS - Mrs. Eleanor P. Baker
          Mrs. Susan Bell
DAY - Mrs. A.J. Aull
DEAN - Emmet McDonald
DEAVER - David W. Graham
DENNISON - Hiram Brown
DEVIN - Mrs. Lucy Beck
DIX - William Longwell
DRAKE - James Kelly
DUGAN - Mrs. Elizabeth Fullerton
DUNCAN - Singleton Sheley
DUNHAM - Mrs. Mary Jane Akins
DUROW - James Ferguson
EDWARDS - Annie Calloway
EMMONS - Pilagu Chauvin
ENGLISH - Timothy Kelleher
ESTES - Mrs. America Lincoln
FALLON - Arsinoe Martin
FARMER - Emelia Grumley
FILLEY - Mrs. Mary Farmington
FINLEY - Andrew Mitchell
FITZPATRICK - Peter Byrne
FLEMING - Mrs. Joyce Rennicks
FOGG - Mary Brooks
FORNSBY - Thomas F. Pim
FRASER - Mary R. Boyce
FRAZER - Mrs. Elizabeth Roberts
GAIRNS - Mrs. Elizabeth Strother
GALBRAITH - Ann Barron
GANNON - Patrick Killoran
GARDNER - Mrs. Lucy Beck
           Philip Van Rensselaer
GARVIN - William Cody
GERHART - Francis Flandrein
GHIO - Lucinda Garth
GIBONY - James Alex'r Wood
GOLDING - Mrs. Deborah Derieux

GRAY - Jerome H. Bacon
GREEN - Hiram Rich
GRESHAM - John Regan
GUNN - Morris Shaw
HAGEN - Joseph Boyle
HALL - Jessie E. Miller
        Mrs. V. J. Mitchell
        Mrs. Christina Suttles
HAMILTON - John Alfred Harris
HARPER - Hannah Hardin
HARRIS - Rosa Johnson
HARRISON - Cecelia Brennan
HASKINS - George Scamell
HAUK - Capt. S. Y. Conner
HEELY - Mrs. Susannah Taylor
HEITZ - Mrs. Elizabeth Webster
HENLEY - John T. Teahon
HENRY - Christopher Dean
HEQUEMBURG - Ezekiel Pratt
HERN - Leanah Patton
HINEMAN - Willie Smith
HODGMAN - Mrs. Ann Wade
HOOD - Sallie Speed
HOPKINS - Thomas Hobbs
HORRES - Miss Rosa Johnson
HOWE - John Brickey
HUNTER - Col. William Myers
HURCK - Luke Fleming
HURT - Horatio Philpot
KASPAR - Adelbert Cusna
KELLOGG - Rev. James Kimball
KING - Mrs. Mabel K. Gates
KLUNK - Mrs. Maria Magchan
KNAPP - William L. Major
LANE - Almira Price
LAWS - Lizzie Doubleby
LEDUC - John Eyma
LEWIS - Mrs. Jedidah Banks
LINCOLN - Mrs. Fanny Gatewood
LOVE - G.G. Presbury Sr.
LYNCH - William J. Conran
McCABE - Frances Farish
          Paul Farish
McCLEERY - Wm. James Sleater
McCLINTOCK - Elenor Northcutt
McCORMICK - Jane Jackson
McCOY - William A. Gibson

McCOY - Mrs. Ellen Lattin
McCUNE - Mrs. Ruth Glasby
McDERMOTT - John Eyma
McDOWELL - Mrs. Abigail Brown
          Artemus Hitchcock
McFAUL - Gregory Byrne
McGRATH - Catherine Owens
McGUIRE - Mrs. Mary P. Cook
McKENZIE - Mrs. Angeline Porter
McKEON - William A. Sharkey
++ McNEAL - Mary Sutton ++
McWEENEY - Margaret Beirne
MANION - James O. Harris
MARTIN - Robt. Elam Farmer
MARVIN - Mrs. Sylvia Sherman
MASEY - Mrs. Lucy Beck
MATTHEWS - Mack Gorman
MEARS - Mrs. Victoria Baxter
MEHAFFY - Lt. Joseph Pennock
MONAHAN - Catherine Collins
MONROE - Thomas I. Randall
MOONAN - Mrs. ___ Ryan
MOORE - Mrs. Ruth Elliott
       Rachel R. Handy
MORRISON - John Thoroughman
MURPHY - Francis Mooney
NANSON - Mrs. Jane Cornelius
NELSON - Dr. Charles Rossiter
NESBITT - Mrs. Margaret Robnett
NEWKIRK - Asenath Asher
NEWMAN - Lucretia Hedenburg
NICHOLS - Mary S. Boles
NEWMARK - Dr. Louis Vitalis
NICHOLSON - Mrs. A. McCaig
OLIPHANT - Mrs. Elizabeth Harding
OWEN - James A. Ingram
++ McSHERRY - Mrs. Margaret Henry ++
PARKER - Edward Bates Block
PARRIS - Laura Bell Wade
PETERSON - Letitia Voullaire
POMROY - Jeremiah Healy Sr.
PORTER - Rebecca Alabagh
       Margaret Breckenridge
RANNEY - Jane Shackelford
READ - Mrs. Mary Pointer
RILEY - Bridget Jennings
RINGO - Lizzie G. Nuckols
RIPPEY - Mrs. Mary Marks
ROGERS - Mrs. Jane McKee

ROSECAN - Mary M. Morehiser
ROSS - Arthur Holmes
ROZIER - Mrs. Mary Seaman
RUFF - Maj. John Daugherty
RUSSELL - John Duke
SALLSMAN - Mary Hanlan
SANFORD - Ann C. Wilson
SASS - Mrs. F. A. Hamilton
SAWYER - H. C. Scribner
SCHIELE - Elleck Shulman
SCOTT - Margaret A. Newman
SHEPPARD - William Crabtree
SIBERT - Ernest Fink
SIMPSON - Capt. Abner Howes
SMITH - Mary McDougal
       William Ryan
SMITHERS - Matilda Gibbons
SPECK - Eliza C. Newsham
SPENCER - John H. Clark
STEENBERGER - Lucy Wayne
STIERLING - Amelia Welcker
STILES - Joseph Arrington
STILLWELL - Mrs. ___ Holeman
STOEWENER - Mary Schneeberger
STONE - James B. Walker
TERRILL - Hudson M. Cave
THOMPSON - Rebecca Barnhurst
       Mary Ella Bright
THOMSON - Janet Sharpe
TISEMAN - Mrs. Franciska Scharwitz
TOLLE - Mrs. ___ Stumpf
TREWITT - Margaret Trimble
VAN NOSTRAND - Lorinda Avery
VERSBETZ - Adelbert Cusna
VIEN - Charles Leguerrier Sr.
WATERS - Sarah Glossop
WATSON - Matilda Pemberton
WEAVER - Mrs. Jane Tomlinson
WETHERELL - William Lyman Woodworth
WHITEHILL - Clara Jordan
WILEY - Mrs. Sarah C. Wetherell
WHITELY - Alex G. Anderson
WILLIAMS - Mrs. Jane Page
WOOD - Mary Ann Kelly
WOODS - Ida Emogene Beamer
WRIGHT - Johanna Bennett

ADDENDA FROM RALLS COUNTY RECORD AND HOWARD COUNTY UNION

A few issues of these newspapers, from the last half of 1865, were unavailable until the rest of the book was completed. We include these items with the thought that any one of them might help someone. A number of items appearing in both papers are in the main portion of the book, having been picked up by a neighboring newspaper. The Record was published in New London; the Union in Glasgow.

RALLS COUNTY RECORD

BOYCE, Mrs. Elizabeth, wife of Judge Richard Boyce in this county 27 Oct, ae ca 70.   2 Nov 1865

DICKERSON, family of W.H. who moved from Macon Co. MO to Nebraska in March: Daughter Mattie died 25 June ae 17; Mr. Dickerson 20 July; Mrs. Dickerson 25 July; and their son Willie, ae 12, on 29 July; all of typhoid.   7 Sep 1865

GALLAHER, Rev. Allen G. at his home in Ralls Co. 12 Nov, of paralysis, ae 67y 19d.   14 Dec 1865

HELMS, Sarah consort of Peter C. at their home in this county 2 Aug ae 35y 10m; and on 16 Sep their youngest daughter, Maggie, ae 7m 8d.   21 Sep 1865

LONG, Rufus son of Forman, at the home of Capt. A. McPike, of typhoid, 20 Oct ae 21y.   26 Oct 1865

LITTLE, Joseph ae 21 at his father's home in New London 28 Nov of typhoid. Burlington IA pc   7 Dec 1865

PEAKE, Dr. William H. at his home in New London 30 Jul ae ca 50. "Friend of childhood, friend of mature years, child of persecution."   24 Aug 1865

TRIPLETTE, G.M., ex-mayor of LaGrange MO, killed in a saloon fight with a man named Simms.   21 Sep 1865

YOUNG, Winfield B. at the home of his mother, Mrs. T___ Young, in New London ae 15y 10?m 6d, on 12? Oct. (Faded)   19 Oct 1865

HOWARD COUNTY UNION

BECKER, Jacob, formerly of Fayette, 6 Sep of typhoid ae ca 45.   7 Sep 1865

BROOKS, Catherine wife of James, of Glasgow, 17 Sep.   21 Sep 1865

DUGGINS, John 22 Jul in his 69th year.   24 Aug 1865

MOORE, Mrs. C.G. wife of Robertson, formerly of Chariton Co., on 10 Aug.   24 Aug 1865

/ - /

www.ingramcontent.com/pod-product-compliance
Lightning Source LLC
Chambersburg PA
CBHW020650300426
44112CB00007B/319